THE
SECRET HISTORY
OF THE WEST

Copyright © 2005 O Books
O Books is an imprint of The Bothy, John Hunt Publishing Ltd.,
Deershot Lodge, Park Lane, Ropley, Hants, SO24 0BE, UK
office@johnhunt-publishing.com
www.O-books.net

Distribution in:
UK
Orca Book Services
orders@orcabookservices.co.uk
Tel: 01202 665432 Fax: 01202 666219 Int. code (44)

USA and Canada
NBN
custserv@nbnbooks.com
Tel: 1 800 462 6420 Fax: 1 800 338 4550

Australia
Brumby Books
sales@brumbybooks.com
Tel: 61 3 9761 5535 Fax: 61 3 9761 7095

New Zealand
Peaceful Living
books@peaceful-living.co.nz
Tel: 64 7 57 18105 Fax: 64 7 57 18513

Singapore
STP
davidbuckland@tlp.com.sg
Tel: 65 6276 Fax: 65 6276 7119

South Africa
Alternative Books
altbook@global.co.za
Tel: 27 011 792 7730 Fax: 27 011 972 7787

Text: © Nicholas Hagger

Design: BookDesign™, London, UK

ISBN 1 905047 04 5

A CIP catalogue record for this book is available from the
British Library.

Printed in the USA by Maple-Vail Manufacturing Group

NICHOLAS HAGGER

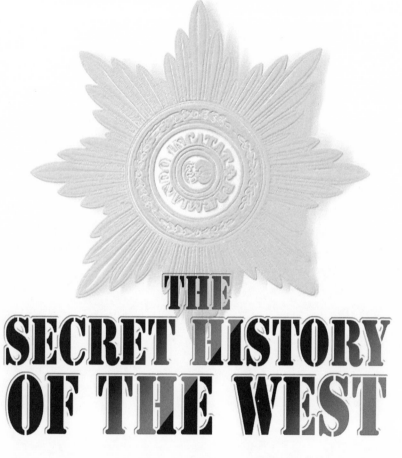

THE SECRET HISTORY OF THE WEST

THE INFLUENCE OF SECRET ORGANIZATIONS ON WESTERN
HISTORY FROM THE RENAISSANCE TO THE 20TH CENTURY

BOOKS

WINCHESTER UK
NEW YORK USA

Vast and innumerable are the sources of secret history which, during the last half-century, have accumulated in masses....It was fated that England should be the theatre of the first of a series of Revolutions which is not yet finished.
Isaac D'Israeli, *Life of Charles the First*, vol 2, 1828/1851

The fire is in the minds of men, not in the roofs of buildings.
Dostoevsky, *The Possessed*

Revolutions have never lightened the burden of tyranny; they have only shifted it to another shoulder.
George Bernard Shaw, 1903

I have suggested that the cultural health of Europe, including the cultural health of its component parts, is incompatible with extreme forms of both nationalism and internationalism.
T. S. Eliot, "The Man of Letters and the Future of Europe", 1944

Those who do not learn from history are doomed to repeat it.
George Santayana

The revolutionary spirit tries to assure man his crown in the realm of time, and, rejecting God, it chooses history with an apparently inevitable logic.
Albert Camus, *The Rebel*

ACKNOWLEDGMENTS

I am indebted to Michael Mann for suggesting the idea of this book, and to Charles Beauclerk with whom I discussed most of the revolutions. He read the text and made valuable suggestions. I am grateful to John Baldock, who read the text and made observations. Once again I am indebted to John Hunt, who immediately grasped how this book connects with *The Syndicate* and how it should be projected, and whose wise advice I acknowledge.

CONTENTS

PART TWO: TOWARDS A UNIVERSAL REPUBLIC

APPENDICES

A. The Hidden Hand in Western History

B. The Hidden Hand: The Kabbalistic Roots of Revolution

C. Venetian Foreign Policy and Rosicrucian Freemasonry

PREFACE

This is the first major study of the influence of secret organizations on Western history – through its main revolutions. It explains the revolutions in terms of secret societies, situations and influences that have hitherto been unexpressed, hidden, "secret". It relates revolutions to the activities of factions within Freemasonry and of families such as the Rothschilds, and therefore narrates "a secret history of the West." In drawing together much new material this study is ground-breaking. It prepares the way for the book's companion volume, *The Syndicate: The Story of the Coming World Government* (published in October 2004), which carries the story forward from 1900 to our own day.

In the course of charting the activities of the secret organizations, the book offers a chronological narrative of all the revolutions from the Renaissance (which began in 1453) to the Russian Revolution. It covers the exploits of all the legendary revolutionaries such as Robespierre and Lenin. It shows how Utopian visions of ideal societies end in massacres and guillotinings, and is therefore something of a cautionary tale. I present each revolution in terms of a completely new and original four-part revolutionary dynamic. An idealist has an occult vision, which others state in intellectual terms. This becomes corrupted by a political regime, and results in physical suppression (such as Stalin's purge). The Summary at the end of each of chapter includes tables summarising this dynamic as it applies to each revolution.

The book sees all the secretly-inspired revolutions as waves within a tide of world revolution that has reached high-water mark in the world government which is being established in our own time. It will therefore help you understand the roots of the New World Order Revolution, which I have dealt with separately in *The Syndicate*.

A Western man of letters focuses on the cultural map of Europe and the way events such as revolutions have affected the health of European culture. For me there has been a personal fascination in considering this material, for poets from Sidney to Yeats, playwrights from Marlowe to Shaw and writers from Ficino to Dostoevsky have written works coloured by secret organizations. In particular, in my capacity as an epic poet (of *Overlord*, which draws on secret history) I have been very interested in the way Milton based Satan on Cromwell, whom he knew, and wrote admiringly of revolution, as did Blake and Wordsworth. Many writers have performed the will of secret organizations as devotedly as revolutionary activists, and it has been a joy to fix their attitudes within the secret history of the West so that their true worth can be assessed and our grasp of the crisis facing European culture can be advanced. While such poets, playwrights and writers can be understood in terms of their dealings with secret organizations, the healthiest European culture is to be found in those poets, playwrights and writers who have stood apart from, and resisted, the Freemasonic hidden hand.

Nicholas Hagger
March 2005

INTRODUCTION

550 YEARS OF REVOLUTIONS

This book tells the story of how the world revolution grew out of the last 550 years. It is the first book to examine the roots of world revolution and tells the submerged history of the events that shaped our time, the history that does not appear in the history books or newspapers. What kind of New World Order will the North American and European civilizations turn to? If we are to understand the world revolutionary movement in our time, it is vital to obtain an in-depth view of the New World Order as a process shaped by and growing out of the impact of successive revolutions.

How far back should we go in search of the revolutions that have culminated in the New World Order Revolution? Working backwards, the Russian Revolution is causally linked to the New World Order Revolution, and so is the Imperialist Revolution of the 19th century. Both grew out of the climate created by the American and French Revolutions. The climate that created these revolutions could not have happened without the three earlier Protestant revolutions: the Reformation, Puritan and Glorious Revolutions.

We are focusing on the period from the Reformation to the present. After the long stability of the Church-dominated Middle Ages, when there were heresies, crusades, dynastic families and struggles for power, revolutions crowd in. The Renaissance was a revolution whose beginning can be dated to 1453. In 1485 Henry Tudor carried out something of a revolution in England. In 1494 the Medici were overthrown and fled from Florence and Savonarola set up a brief democratic republic. His sermons against Papal corruption inspired the Reformation, which began with Luther, spread in the 1530s to England, where Thomas Cromwell brought about a social revolution, and to France through Calvin, and split Christendom. The Reformation has to be seen as a revolution to be fully understood, and a hidden hand was at work behind it. The Counter-Reformation of the 1550s further opened the Catholic-Protestant divide. The Cecilian revolution in government in England during the reign of Elizabeth I created a new imperialist outlook, while the subsequent Puritan Revolution dominated the 17th century. The Restoration was a counter-revolution against the Puritans. Then the Glorious Revolution took place: the Catholic James II was driven from the throne and England finally became Protestant, again widening the division in Christendom. Again, a secret organization was at work in the background.

In the 18th century the American Revolution stunned England. This led almost immediately to the French Revolution and the so-called Age of Reason. Secret organizations were at work behind both these revolutions. Out of revolutionism grew Romanticism (itself a revolution), while the new religion of Reason spawned the Industrial Revolution that drove the (second) British and German Empires. Against this background there were so-called revolutions in Europe in 1830, 1848 and 1871. In Russia there was much revolutionary activity in the second half of the 19th century, which culminated in the 1917 Revolution and the advent of Stalin. Secret Organizations were at work. The 20th century has seen moves towards a world revolution.

For 550 years secret-organization-influenced revolution has succeeded revolution in earthquake after earthquake and tidal wave after tidal wave. All these revolutions began with an occult idea, though they are perceived in the media as being merely political. In all of them the idealism that was stimulated in the early days was corrupted in practice.

What is the meaning of the most recent events in the world revolution that is happening now? To understand this we need to go back into the past and take a look at the main revolutions of the last 550 years, to see if a pattern will emerge that is also behind the most recent events.

Our method will be to start 550 years ago and build up a progressive picture of the influence of a secret organization on each revolution, one by one, which will enable us to understand the present time. As we move from revolution to revolution we will look at each of the four stages of our revolutionary dynamic, which is an entirely new concept. (For a fuller explanation see Appendices A, Appendix 2.) We will necessarily proceed chronologically, selecting those events that are necessary for the revolutionary dynamic to be revealed, but also those events that will give a picture of the revolution and a feel for its meaning. This may involve some detail. Some detail is essential, for what is missing in our understanding of these revolutions is their meaning. The events have not been lost; they have been left behind by the tide of history like a crabshell, seaweed or pebbles on a beach, but the tide of meaning has receded. To understand the present world revolution we have to rediscover the lost knowledge that threw up the events of past revolutions, and this can only be done by reinterpreting salient details in relation to that lost knowledge, in a new way. Having recaptured the revolutionary dynamic of a revolution through its main events and their lost meaning, we will then stand back and ponder and reflect and reconnect ourselves to our main theme.

This method will bring out the influence of secret organizations on the revolutionary dynamic of each revolution, and will also show how secret organizations have used revolution as a driving-force of modern history in the West to achieve a "better" society, how revolutionary Utopias have an unfortunate propensity to end in massacres, and how all revolutions are part of a single world revolutionary movement committed to the creation of one world government.

In all these revolutions, change seems at first to have come from within the nations themselves. Without exception, however, they were all generated from without, by secret organizations located outside the nation's frontiers. Without exception, all these revolutions have been intrigued and funded from abroad. Do certain intriguers and funders recur? Is there a pattern? Who are the secret organizations that have conceived and orchestrated the revolutions of the past? Did all the revolutions we have looked at since 1776 – indeed, since 1453 – have a common source of inspiration? Some of our conclusions will be startling, and readers are requested to delay making up their minds until they have assimilated the *whole* picture, all the evidence (both corroborative and circumstantial) that will be laid out for their examination, and not to form too speedy an opinion.

In all our revolutions we shall see how an occult (literally "hidden from view" from the Church and so "heretical") vision degenerates as it is interpreted into physical reality. Again and again we will encounter, side by side, a noble view of man and the weaponry of systematic execution, for example the guillotine. It seems that an idealistic vision which is Utopian and against a particular social class contains within it a dark, murderous will that achieves its ends by killing and is inspired by the shadow side of the human psyche. As we shall see, the Utopian vision and the massacring are both conveyed by the secret organizations that inspired the revolutions.

The roots of the New World Order can be found in the dismantling of the old Catholic Europe, and it is to the Reformation and its effect on the Elizabethan world that we must first look, a revolution that influenced Utopians for the next 550 years.

PART ONE

THE PROTESTANT
REVOLUTION

CHAPTER ONE

THE REFORMATION REVOLUTION

> The Merovingians had a "Secret Doctrine" (also called the "Great Plan"), which in part called for the creation of a Universal Throne in Europe....The holder of the Universal Throne must...possess the Spear of Destiny; ...also be the Holy Roman Emperor; and...hold the title, "King of Jerusalem"....The Plan began...after the Priory of Sion officially separated from the Templars in 1188.... The Merovingians planned to diminish the influence of the Church through...a clandestine tradition...that found expression in Hermetic and esoteric thought, such as in Rosicrucian and Freemasonic secret societies.
>
> John Daniel, *Scarlet and the Beast*

Taken as a whole, the Reformation, which lasted from 1453 to 1603, though a religious movement rather than a political or social movement, amounts to a revolution against the Papacy to reform the Church. It sought to transform all Europeans into Protestants, who would disregard the corrupt Church.

To understand the Reformation fully we need to trace its origin back to the Cathars, who opposed the Papacy from their strongholds in southern France and who were crushed and suppressed by Papal forces in the 13th century, and to Mani, the founder of Manichaeism in the 3rd century AD, who was influenced by Kabbalism and inspired their vision.

THE CATHAR REVOLUTION

The Cathar rebellion against the Catholic Church looked back to dualistic Manichaeism.[1] Dualism sees and describes the Universe and creation in terms of a conflict of opposites: Light and Darkness, the forces of Light and the forces of Darkness, good and evil. The heretical Iranian dualism of the 3rd century AD, Zoroastrianism, taught that Darkness was a Demiurge who was responsible for material creation, including man. He had his own Angels of Darkness, demons who could be invoked and placated by following the laws of Ahriman, the Iranian god of Darkness, or magic, to which the Zoroastrian Magi gave their name. Darkness was co-creator, and so there were now two creators and the unity of spiritual knowledge was shattered and evil glamorized. Into this dualist world (as he saw it) came the Manichaean leader, Mani, "the Illuminator," "Apostle of Light," to teach ascetic rules to the Elect, who would combat Darkness.

Mani

Mani was brought up among the Jewish-Christian Baptistai or Elkhasaites, a Gnostic-influenced sect his father joined after hearing a voice in the Temple at Ctesiphon (the Iranian Parthian winter capital which is now in Iraq). The sect taught Mani about Jesus and the Gnostics Marcion and Bardesanes (see Appendices B, Appendix 4), both of whom ascribed the creation of the Universe to a Demiurge.

Mani's dualism featured Darkness attacking – aggressing against – the Light. The good principle lived with five emanations ("beings of Light") in the place of Light, and the evil principle (the King of Darkness, the Demiurge) lived in five worlds of Darkness, an echo of the 10 sephiroth of the Kabbalah. Mani's Primal Man also echoes the Kabbalah's archetypal first being, Adam Kadmon. In 240 at the age of

24 Mani, the Apostle of Light, the Illuminator, experienced illumination and was called to rescue soul from Darkness and lead it to the Light. Like Christ, the Light of the World, he was executed – flayed to death and decapitated – following a passion lasting 26 days before the Zoroastrian Magi, a reliving of the trials of Jesus, whom Mani declared to be mortal. (Like Basilides he maintained that Jesus did not die on the cross; the crucified man who died was a substitute.)

Mani issued ascetic rules for the Elect, a monastic élite who influenced Christian monasticism. Through their meditations, they became part of the Kingdom of Light on earth and went to the "Paradise of Light," being ferried to the moon by a "Ship of Light," then being raised to the sun on the rotating wheel of the zodiac like a gigantic fairground wheel. Thence the dead went to the World of Light. The Manichaean promise was that in the end the power of Darkness would be destroyed and Light would be safe.

Cathar Purity

Mani's Kabbalistic insistence on dualism, the monastic Elect, the sun and living close to the Light reached the south of France and was kept alive in Languedoc in the Jewish Kabbalistic schools of Lunel and Narbonne in what used to be the Jewish principality of Septimania (see Appendices B, Appendix 6). They passed it on to the Cathars,[2] who were flourishing by c.1140. By then they had their own language (*langue d'Oc*) and they were an organized church with a hierarchy, a liturgy, and their own doctrines that looked back to Kabbalist-influenced Manichaean dualism and held that the material world was created by a Demiurge and therefore intrinsically evil. There was a Cathar view that this Demiurge was the God of Israel. To distance themselves from the Catholic orthodoxy of the day, most Cathars identified this Demiurge with Satan or Lucifer. They saw man as an alien in an evil world, and they wished to return to the world of Light from which they were separated. They withdrew from the world to the tops of mountains and built strongholds up near the light. Climbing to the fortress of their capital Montségur, which is 1,207 metres high, one cannot fail to be struck by how near the sun one is; all the surrounding

Pyrenean peaks seem lower down and there are huge drops to the world below.

There were many Cathar strongholds in Languedoc: Minerve, Termes, Puivert, Cabaret, Foix, Peyrepertuse, Puilaurens, Quéribus and Arques to name a few. Here the Cathars lived in huts ranged round the fortresses with their families in extreme asceticism – meat and sex (except for procreating their race) were prohibited – and communed with the Light. Their priests were called *Parfaits* ("Perfects," Perfect Ones). They were escorted along the roads of southern France by the defenders of Montségur.

The only rite the believers were permitted by the Parfaits was the mystic feast at which some sort of a Grail cup was used. This feast, called the *manisola,* was both an initiation ceremony and a Mass or communion. In the ruined Montségur stronghold it is possible to see two solar windows with arrow slits, one facing east, one west. On midsummer's day, on the summer solstice (June 21), the sun shines through one and out of the other. It seems that something like the Grail cup stood between the two windows and was bathed in sunlight which still lights the whole chamber and which symbolized the Light. After the *manisola* they kissed each other – passed a kiss from one to another round the congregation and received a "pure" laying on of hands ("the consolamentum"). This sacrament made the believer a "Bon Homme" (good man), and the right to have the sacrament was granted to a believer on his deathbed. *Manisola* suggests "Mani" and "solar," and the ceremony undoubtedly had its roots in Mani's Manichaean view of the sun as a half-way house to the world of Light.

The Cathars regarded Jesus as an angel and denied the Incarnation. To them, the God of Israel was false, a Demiurge who tainted the design of the true God, who was the Father of Light. They criticized the corruption of the Catholic Church, and referred to Montségur as "Mount Tabor," which was the scene of Christ's Transfiguration by Light (*Matthew* 17, 1-3). The Cathar doctrines consequently challenged Orthodox Catholicism and the political institutions of French Christendom, and Church and State united to attack them. Two

Parfaits had rebuilt Montségur between 1204 and 1209 on the orders of Raymond de Péreille, co-lord of Lavelanet, who responded to a request from the Cathar hierarchy. A decision to step up the fortification of Montségur was taken at the Cathar synod of 1206, which was held in Mirepoix, the town of Pierre-Roger de Mirepoix. He was known to the Catholic Church as a fervent heretic who gave intellectual expression to the Cathar Revolution, and this decision sealed the Cathars' fate.

Pope Innocent III (1198-1216) tried to compel Raymond VI, Count of Toulouse, to join forces with him to suppress the Cathars. Raymond was not keen, and in 1208 the papal legatee was murdered. Raymond was implicated, and as a result he was excommunicated. A crusade was called against the heretics, known to history as the Albigensian Crusade. A group of 6,000 barons or knights, "Soldiers of God," and their followers assembled in Lyons in northern France under the leadership of the Abbot of Cîteaux, and marched south and took Béziers. The footsoldiers who assisted the knights and served as valets or equerries entered the town and pillaged it. Annoyed that the French barons wanted their share of the booty, they set fire to the timber buildings and the whole town was soon ablaze. The population was part-Cathar and part-Catholic, and when asked how the footsoldiers could tell who was Cathar and who was Catholic, the leader of the Crusade, Pope Arnaud Amaury, Abbot of Cîteaux, is reported to have said, "Kill them all; the Lord will recognize his own." The terrified people of Béziers sought sanctuary in the church of St Mary Magdalene and the Cathedral of Saint-Nazaire. They huddled inside, but the Crusaders set fire to both buildings. They slaughtered the entire population: 20,000 people.

The Crusaders then marched to Carcassonne and besieged the medieval Cité and cut off its water supply. Carcassonne surrendered within two weeks, and all citizens were allowed to leave, "bearing only their sins." Simon de Montfort took up residence in the Castle, the Château Comtal. He ran the Crusade from the Castle courtyard. The Crusaders prayed at the basilica of Saint-Nazaire, Carcassonne. They assembled in the square outside and set off for Montségur, which they nicknamed "the Vatican of Heresy"; "the Dragon's Head"; and "Satan's Synagogue."[3] Not Satan's church, but Satan's *synagogue*. This suggests that the Crusaders believed there was a strong Jewish/Kabbalistic involvement among the Cathars.

The Crusaders could not take Montségur, and the Crusade dragged on until 1215, when Toulouse fell and Simon de Montfort proclaimed himself Count of Toulouse. There were pyres and massacres as Cathars were relentlessly pursued. Then in 1218 Simon was killed during the siege of Toulouse. (The siege stone recording that siege together with Simon's tombstone are now in the basilica of Saint-Nazaire, Carcassonne.)

For more than twenty years the persecution of the Cathars continued. In 1232 the head of the Cathar church Guilhabert de Castres, who also gave intellectual expression to the Cathar Revolution, asked Raymond de Péreille if he could establish "the head and seat" of the Cathar church in Montségur. Raymond agreed, although he must have known he was taking a huge risk. Pierre-Roger de Mirepoix established a garrison of 50 knights and squires there. The hardpressed Cathar clergy now looked on Montségur as their centre.

Eventually Pope Louis IX called for the final suppression of the heresy and ordered Raymond VII, Count of Toulouse, to defend the Catholic faith and wipe out the "nest of heretics." Raymond appeared to accept and marched his troops to Montségur. After a token siege he left. He was in collusion with the heretics and was actually planning a Cathar uprising. He gave political expression to the Cathar Revolution at this time. In May 1242 Montségur soldiers murdered two Inquisitors at Avignonet. Raymond VII was blamed. In 1243 the Council of Béziers decided that "the head of the dragon" (a reference to Satan) had to be "cut off." The new action was led by Hugues des Arcis and the Archbishop of Narbonne. In May 1243 the Crusaders took up position at the foot of the pog ("peak" in Occitan). No progress was made until shortly before Christmas 1243 when a troop of Basques scaled the rock face at night to capture Tower Rock. It may have been at this time that a Parfait, Pierre Bonnet, and a believer, Mathieu, escaped with the treasure of the Cathar church, which they hid in a cave in the Sabarthès. The Crusaders were now able to bombard the barbican and castle. The position of the Cathars grew quickly worse. At the start of the siege there were 160 believers and 180 Parfaits, but the numbers were dwindling. In March the Cathars' leader Pierre-Roger de Mirepoix asked for a 15-day truce to negotiate. The Cathars were ordered to renounce their faith, but refused. The day before the final surrender was due four Parfaits escaped with funds and, rumour has it, treasure: perhaps the Grail. They lodged this at Usson castle and then disappeared.

On March 16 the Crusaders took the stronghold. A mass pyre was built in a field beneath the spur. This fire was a symbol of the fires of Hell to which the Crusaders believed the Cathars would be going, and it was a way of making sure that none of the "dark" energies that had lived in their bodies survived. Two hundred Cathars descended and were burned. They joined hands, voluntarily climbed ladders and leapt joyfully in pairs into the flames of the pyre, sure that by retaining their faith they would enter the world of Light. The heretical Cathar challenge to Catholicism was over.

The Cathar treasure may well have passed to another heretical sect, the Templars or the "Poor Knights of Christ and the Temple of Solomon" to give them their full name, who were founded in 1118. After they were suppressed many surviving Cathars joined the Templars and in due course their descendants became Templar Masons.

The Grail

As news of the fall of Montségur spread, interest grew in the Grail literature of the region.[4] Wolfram von Eschenbach, the author of *Parzival* (1207), may have been a Cathar. He seems to have based his Muntsalvache or Montsalvat – the mountain of Salvation or Paradise on which the Grail chapel or temple stood – on the Cathar stronghold at Montségur. Dante's *Commedia* was on the fringe of the early French-Spanish Renaissance. An exile himself, having had his own differences with the Pope, Dante was on the side of the Cathars, and Mount Paradise in his *Paradiso* (c1318-21) seems to have been based on

Montségur.

Chrétien de Troyes introduced the mysterious "Graal" (a silver cup covered with precious stones) in *Perceval* or *Le Conte du Graal* (c1190), and Robert de Boron in *Joseph d'Aramathie* or the *Roman de L'estoire dou Saint Graal* (c1200-1210) linked the "Graal" with the cup used by Christ at the Last Supper. Both these had a Christian context, as had two prose versions of Robert's poem, one in German, and one in Old French – the *Quest del Saint Graal* (c1220). Wolfram's *Parzival*, however, contains eastern elements: the "Graal" becomes a precious stone fallen from Heaven, which suggests the emerald that fell from Lucifer's crown.

Wolfram apparently obtained his material from a source in Toledo, a Jewish astronomer called Flegetanis whose Arabic manuscript was reputedly given to Wolfram by a singer (troubadour) called Koyt. The Sefardic Jewish Flegetanis presumably had links with the Moors or Saracens in Spain and with the Middle East where Jerusalem had just fallen, and the idea that the Grail was a precious stone fallen from Lucifer's crown seems to have come from the false Kabbalah (see Appendices B, Appendix 2).

The legend claims that Satan originally owned the stone. During his fall from Heaven as Satanail, God's eldest son Lucifer, he lost an emerald from his diadem. This was apparently found and brought to a famous stonecutter, who made a beautiful vase of jasper or lapis and mounted the emerald in it. It was called the Emerald Cup.[5] This became the Cup of God, Abraham and Jesus, the Holy Grail, and symbolized the power of God and his second son Jesus over the power of Darkness. In due course the cup fell into the hands of Visigoths when Alaric sacked Rome, and when they made Narbonne their capital they hid it in a cave near Montségur. Cathars found it, the legend goes, and used it in their *manisola* ceremony. It stood between the two arrow-slit windows. It was removed just before Montségur surrendered to the Crusaders in 1244, some say by a lady Cathar called Esclarmonde de Foix. (Later on the Grail cup may have been found by Father Saunière, priest of nearby Rennes-le-Château. Knowing that Satan still claimed it,

Saunière placed a statue of Asmodeus inside the doorway of his church. In mythology, Asmodeus was guardian of hidden treasure in which Lucifer has an interest.)[6]

The Christian story, then, retells legends in which chivalrous knights search for the cup of Christ's Last Supper which glows, and which may have been part of the treasure that was brought from the sack of Rome or from the sack of Jerusalem. The false Kabbalah, on the other hand, has Lucifer's cup at the centre of the Grail story.

If the Cathars at Montségur were Jews as the Crusaders' nickname "Satan's Synagogue" suggests, then there is a strong Jewish-Kabbalist link between the Luciferian Grail legend, the synagogue at Montségur which has the five-pointed shape of a pentagon, and the Cathars.

Laurence Gardner in *Bloodline of the Holy Grail* states that the Cathars were known to be "adepts of the occult symbolism of the Cabbala."[7] They were certainly very tolerant of Jewish culture, and seem to have been originally Jewish rather than infiltrated by Jews and egged on to subvert Christianity. The strict observances of the Pure Ones recall the practices of Strict Observance Jews. There is a strong link between the old Jewish kingdom of Septimania (see Appendices B, Appendix 6) and what happened at Montségur.

What is certain is that following the Albigensian Crusade against what may have been a Jewish stronghold ("Satan's Synagogue"), the persecution of the Jews in Europe increased. In 1290 Edward I expelled all Jews from England, and in 1306 the Jews were finally expelled from France.

Early "Heretics": Wycliffe and Hus

The Reformation that triggered modern revolutionary history grew out of doubts concerning the Catholic Church's interpretation of the Judaeo-Christian tradition. Some of these doubts had surfaced in the Cathar vision of the 12th and 13th centuries and had caused the Albigensian Crusade against the Cathars and the suppression of the Templars. Both the Cathars and Templars challenged the Church with their occult vision and helped precipitate the Reformation. Reforms of the Church had been called for in the 12th and 13th centuries by the reforming Dominicans and Franciscans.

In the 1370s the occult – literally "hidden from view, concealed, kept secret" in the sense of "hidden from the orthodoxy, the established Church, and heretical" – interpreter of the Reformation Revolution was the English theologian John Wycliffe.[8] Wycliffe's "Lollard" reform movement held that the Church should not possess property and that the sacraments were less important than personal faith. The Lollards sent poor preachers round England calling for reform and denying the doctrines of the Church. William Langland's *Piers Plowman* catches the early Protestant outlook of a poor man for whom popes, cardinals, bishops, clergy, monks and friars were irrelevant. Wycliffe was supported by the English King, Edward III and his son John of Gaunt, but his revolutionary movement (pronounced heretical by the Church) influenced another occult interpreter of the Reformation Revolution Jan Hus, a Bohemian professor who taught many of Wycliffe's doctrines at the University of Prague. Hus attacked the Church for its worldliness, denied the supremacy of the Pope and urged that sinful clergy should be excluded from being practising priests. He did not have Wycliffe's support in high places and the Pope excommunicated him as a heretic. The Church moved against heresies across Europe, and in England for the first time heresy was made punishable by burning in 1401.

The Holy Roman Emperor Sigismund gave Hus safe conduct to address the Council of Constance to settle the Great Schism in 1410. The Emperor then withdrew the safe conduct, arguing that promises made to heretics were not valid, and allowed Hus to be burned as a heretic. The Bohemians were outraged and when shortly afterwards Sigismund was elected king of Bohemia (in place of Wenceslas IV, who had died), many refused to recognize him. The Pope called for a crusade against the Hussites, who invaded Germany, but they could not be subdued. The extremist Hussites called themselves Taborites. (The Cathars called Montségur Mount Tabor.) They were never suppressed, and eventually formed the Bohemian or Moravian Brethren.

THE RENAISSANCE REVOLUTION

In a sense the Renaissance began with the fall of Constantinople to the Moslems in May 1453 after a siege lasting two months. The last Emperor of Byzantium was last seen in the thick of the fighting. With Constantinople fell the Byzantine Empire (c330-1453) and eastern Christendom – to an Ottoman Empire led by a 21-year-old, Sultan Mehmet. Greek survivors were to form a self-governing community within the Sultan's Empire. Byzantines fled northwards to Orthodox Russia, but as the rape and pillage subsided horror spread through Christendom. After all the Crusades, the Moslems had taken over. Nothing was safe. Greek scholars took the most precious manuscripts from the looted libraries and migrated to Italy, the home of western Christendom. As Italian scholars studied the classical texts of Greece and Rome, which had been locked in libraries throughout the medieval period unread, and searched the monasteries for more works of classical learning, they renewed contact with the ancient world. With the spread of printing, these classical masterpieces were reproduced and sold, and became the treasured possessions of European civilization. Descendants of the barbarians who had sacked Rome, these Italians were fascinated by Graeco-Roman man who was at the source of Western civilization and a new spirit of intellectual inquiry transformed art, music, literature, science and religion.

The Italian Humanist Renaissance,[9] the first intellectual expression of the Reformation, was a revolution of rapid intellectual, social and economic changes of outlook against the medieval ethos. It was a revolution in consciousness that viewed man as heroic and god-like. It revealed itself in social attitudes and the arts, and like the Industrial Revolution reflected itself in social and economic change that transformed the towns of the 15th century. With it came a new interest in man, a new urban consciousness that spread across Europe. It began in Florence at the court of the Medici, the great Florentine banking family which supplied generations of enlightened despots who ruled in splendour, and to the great benefit of the arts.

The Medici and Ficino

The first of them was Cosimo de' Medici, whose return to Florence in 1434 began the Medici principate. He had wanted to leave for the Holy Land to search for Greek manuscripts in 1418, but had been set to work in the Medici bank as the Papacy's banker. In the 1430s he built the Palazzo Medici, San Marco and other fine Renaissance buildings, and later acted patron to Ghiberti, Donatello and Fra Angelico.

Italian interest in Plato had been fired by the visit of Gemistos Plethon, the Byzantine philosopher and humanist scholar, in May 1439, when the Byzantine Emperor's delegation to bring the Orthodox and Catholic faiths closer together was received in Florence by Cosimo de' Medici. Gemistos spoke "On the Difference between Aristotle and Plato" and gave the Italian humanists a new interest in Plato. Gemistos (acting in his capacity as Platonist rather than Orthodox cleric) suggested to Cosimo (who was now 50) that all Plato's works should be translated and he inspired Cosimo to found the Platonic Academy of Florence. Cosimo committed the project to the care of his doctor's son Marsilio Ficino, who (as occult revolutionary originator) translated all Plato's works into Latin and revived Plato's Academy which had run from 385 BC to AD 529.

From 1462 the new Academy was based at the villa at Careggi which Cosimo had given Ficino that year. Ficino also translated the *Corpus Hermeticum* (a body of Kabbalistic-Gnostic documents dating from the 1st-3rd century AD which had been discovered by one of Cosimo's agents), a work which was to have enormous influence on his subsequent thought. Arguably Ficino's Kabbalism and Gnosticism made him readily accept Plato's Forms. Cosimo revived the teaching of Greek and inspired interest in humanism. He died at Careggi, and was succeeded by Piero, who was in turn succeeded in 1469 by Lorenzo the Magnificent.

As a boy, Lorenzo had played chess with Cosimo, who allowed him to sit in on philosophical discussions. Lorenzo lived close to nature – for example, the grape harvests at Careggi – as his verses attest. Under him Ficino continued to run the Academy. Ficino became a priest in 1473 and, like Clement of Alexandria, united Christian, Platonic and Kabbalistic Hermetic teachings. (The spiritual and the occult were mixed in 1470s Florence, giving a Humanist shade of grey). He later wrote a study of the immortality of the soul (*Theologica Platonica*, 1482), taking from Plato, Plotinus and the Hermetic writings the concept that part of the individual soul is immortal and divine.

The divinity of the soul was the basis for the "dignity of man," which the Renaissance writers and artists sought to express in a number of ways. Ficino found the dignity of man best expressed in Lorenzo the Magnificent, who could switch abruptly from war and affairs of State to philosophy, scholarship, poetry, music and art, in each of which he excelled. His authority arose naturally from his nature and not his position. He absorbed Ficino's Humanist ideas in the 1460s and introduced them into the running of the Florentine State when he came to power in 1469.

Ficino's influence on the courts of the Italian Medici despots was great, and under Lorenzo the Magnificent, the greatest Renaissance prince of the day – an effective ruler of the Florentine city state as well as a poet – there was an Italian artistic Renaissance. Ficino gathered round him at the Academy perhaps the most brilliant group of men ever to have assembled in modern Europe: Lorenzo the Magnificent, Alberti, Poliziario, Landino and Pico della Mirandola. The great Renaissance artists were directly inspired by Ficino: Botticelli (Grand Master of the Priory of Sion, see Appendices B, Appendix 7, from 1483-1510), Michelangelo, Raphael, Titian and Dürer. Ficino's Neoplatonism influenced Botticelli in 1478, when he was painting the *Birth of Venus* and *Primavera*, in which the creative principle of spring is shown as the earth goddess Venus, an embodiment of Plato's divine reality.

The idea of this embodiment was passed on to Leonardo da Vinci, who succeeded Botticelli as Grand Master of the Priory of Sion in 1510. He must have been involved with the Priory of Sion before this date in order to have become Botticelli's successor, and his Mona Lisa, begun in 1503 and carried with him and endlessly worked on until his death in 1519, was his equivalent of the Ficino-esque spiritual (or perhaps occult) Beauty which Botticelli had shown as Venus. Leonardo's version was an earth goddess who was also spiritual (or perhaps occult) Venus – hence her enigmatic smile.

The secret knowledge of spiritual/occult Beauty, and of scientific advances, would have been transmitted to him through the Priory. This throws new light on Leonardo's scientific drawings of mechanical and engineering innovations – for example, a prototype hang-glider, diver's suit and tank. As a member of the Priory he would have had access to the innovatory thinking of fellow members, and is likely to have acted as the Priory's illustrator. The story of Leonardo is not, therefore, of a solitary genius imagining inventions which were not to be implemented until the 20th century, but of a mouthpiece and illustrator for a secret group which would later make available material that would help Fludd, Andreae, Boyle and Newton, who were all subsequent Grand Masters of the Priory.

The whole intellectual life of 15th-century Florence was under Ficino's influence: he wrote letters to eminent men throughout Europe – Colet (Dean of St Paul's, England), de Ganay (Chancellor of the Parliament in France), the German humanist Reuchlin, King Matthias of Hungary – and awoke Europe to the full significance of the Platonic tradition.

Pico

Ficino's follower Pico della Mirandola, the Christian Kabbalist and author of the Renaissance humanist manifesto *Oratio de Hominis Dignitate*, developed the idea of the Mage, the ideal man (often portrayed as Christ) who mastered "Magia and Cabala" (Kabbalah) while practising Christianity. Preaching a Christian Kabbalism that amounted to a universal religion and doing scientific work that anticipated the 17th-century Puritan scientific revolution which culminated in the Royal Society, Boyle and Newton, Pico saw Jesus as a Mage who continued the tradition of the Kabbalah. At the heart of the humanist Renaissance was the new conception (drawn from studies of classical texts) of Jesus as a mystic versed both in Magia and Kabbalah. To humanists Jesus was a man in their own image, albeit one with magical powers.

Tudor Rose and Sion

Across Europe in the 15th century a new social revolution was spreading. In all European countries, feudalism was being destroyed, mercantilism was increasing and the landed nobility was under attack from the new bureaucratic élite. The nation-state was evolving, and nowhere more dramatically than in England where, following the Wars of the Roses, the House of Lancaster defeated the House of York in the battle of Bosworth in 1485, and the new Tudor dynasty of Henry VII came to power with its emblem of the Tudor rose: a mixture of white York and red Lancaster to symbolize national unification after the national division of civil war.

The Grand Master of the Priory of Sion Jean de Gisors founded the Order of the True Red Cross (Rose-Croix) before 1220.[10] Its rose seems to have been the embryo of Rosicrucianism, which did not officially emerge until the publication of the first Rosicrucian texts of 1614-16 – texts that combined the "Magia, Cabala and Alchymia" of the Renaissance Hermetic-Kabbalist tradition formulated by Ficino and Pico – but is widely thought to have begun earlier, perhaps with Gisors' Sionist Rose-Croix. Was the Tudor rose a symbol of Renaissance Sion's support for the Tudor dynasty after the suppression of the Templars? Had the Templar gold (see Appendices B, Appendix 7) arrived in England to be guarded by Sion, and had Sion's man won the battle of Bosworth to rule as a Sionist figurehead? Was Sion therefore behind the new Tudor mercantile outlook?

Henry Tudor, who had only the barest right to the throne, embraced the Lancastrian cause, invaded England with a French army, defeated and killed Richard III and won the English throne by conquest like the Italian soldier-adventurers. He legitimized his reign by marrying Elizabeth Woodville, daughter of the Yorkist Edward IV and so heiress of the House of York. To answer the question of the Tudor Rose a link has to be established between Henry Tudor and one of the contemporary Grand Masters of the Priory of Sion listed in the *Dossiers Secrets,* secret records of the Priory of Sion allegedly discovered by Father Saunière inside a hollow 8th-century altar support at Rennes-le-

Château (see Appendices B, Appendix 7)[11]: René d'Anjou (1418-80); René's daughter Iolande de Bar (1480-3); and Sandro Filipepi, alias the painter Botticelli (1483-1510). René d'Anjou's daughter Marguerite d'Anjou married the last Lancastrian king before the Wars of the Roses, Henry VI of England, in 1445, and played a prominent part in the Wars of the Roses which began in 1455. It was Marguerite's sister Iolande who became Grand Master of the Priory of Sion in 1480, and who could have organized behind the scenes, at the end of her life, the French army that would bring Henry Tudor to power. If this is so, the Priory of Sion was behind the Tudor revolution which brought a new dynasty to the English throne and new Renaissance ideas pouring into England.

SAVONAROLA'S REVOLUTION

The princes who ruled the Italian cities were soldier-adventurers who hired mercenary armies and won and maintained their position by force. In Milan the Visconti and Francesco Sforza, and in Rome Cesare Borgia were such *condottieri*. All were patrons of the arts, which had become more naturalistic, and Giotto, Titian, Leonardo da Vinci (Grand Master of the Priory of Sion after Botticelli), Santi and Michelangelo all reflected the new religious outlook. Against the background of a more secular society and worldly cities in which ambition and the pursuit of earthly wealth were seen as virtues, all caught the humanist impulse that humanity mattered more than God. But despite the fact that human beings had shifted to the foreground God was still very much omnipresent.

The Popes had become like Renaissance princes. The early humanist Popes Nicholas V and Pius II collected manuscripts and patronized the new learning and classical revival. Sixtus IV, Alexander IV and Julius II were typical Italian despots, as well as patrons of the arts and builders of fine buildings. They all needed money both for the maintenance of the Curia and for their aesthetic activities, which were sustained by the sale of indulgences. Indulgences pardoned sins and alleviated pain in Purgatory, and – most importantly – helped fill the Church's coffers. The Popes themselves were lax in matters of morality – they had mistresses and some put erotic paintings on the walls of their bedrooms – and no Pope attempted the long overdue reform of the Church, which seemed increasingly corrupt to those Italian Christians who clamoured for reform.

The rise of Savonarola,[12] who articulated anti-Papal feeling but was against the laxness of the Renaissance, must be seen against the Inquisition of 1492, a pivotal year in the birth of modern revolutionary history when Tomás de Torquemada, Grand Inquisitor or Inquisitor General until he died in 1498, expelled the Jews from Spain. He established the Spanish Inquisition everywhere in Spain by around 1480 following the inspiration of Cardinal Mendoza, and appointed Inquisitors throughout Spain to conduct tribunals as an instrument of royal policy (see Appendices B, Appendix 8).

The Dominicans largely staffed the Inquisition and devoted themselves to learning. The Franciscans also pursued learning and no longer helped the poor. Both had grown rich, and both sold indulgences for the Pope. By the end of the 15th century the Dominicans and Franciscans, who came into existence to preach religious truths and help the poor, were themselves in need of reform.

From around 1490 a reforming Dominican friar and fiery preacher, Girolamo Savonarola, condemned the corruption of the Church, and urged reform: it should be scourged and then renewed. He had arrived at the Convent of San Marco in Florence in 1482. He left Florence in 1487 to work in Bologna, and was then sent to preach in different cities until Lorenzo de' Medici sought his return in 1490. It was at this time that he condemned the corruption of Lorenzo's government in his sermons.

Savonarola wore coarse cloth, ate little and did not drink. A small ugly man with a hooked nose and a harsh voice, he declaimed sermons of great power. San Marco was soon full to overflowing and to accommodate everyone he had to preach in the Cathedral. He fulminated about the Florentines' wickedness, their dissolute carnivals, their gambling, their fine clothes, their scent and powder and the sensual pleasures that would prevent them from reaching the Kingdom of God. He attacked the Renaissance – the pagan works of Aristotle and Plato who were now in Hell, he claimed – and called on Florence to repent while there was still time. His sermons greatly impressed Michelangelo, terrified Botticelli and made Pico della Mirandola's hair stand on end.

Lorenzo died in 1492 at the Villa Careggi, the Medici's summer palace. Pico brought Savonarola to his bedroom there. The humanist Lorenzo asked to be read the Passion of Christ and followed the reading until his death. He asked Savonarola for Absolution. Although there is a tradition that Savonarola refused to give it, the consensus is that he obliged and that Lorenzo died a Christian. He was succeeded by the young Piero, who did not know how to control the puritanical preacher.

Savonarola brought about a brief revolution in Florence following the invasion of Charles VIII, King of France, whom he considered an instrument of God sent to shock Florence into obedience, and whose coming Savonarola had predicted in 1492. The Medici were overthrown, the nobles were driven out, and from 1494 till 1498 Savonarola was in sole command of Florence. He set up a democratic republic and purified the city. His outlook recalls the Kabbalism of the Cathars, the "Pures," and the Kabbalism of Ficino which had imbued the Medici court. He was no doubt influenced by Pico's Christian Kabbalism. His was a puritanical rule that anticipated Cromwell's: he had founded a City of God in Florence, a well organized Christian republic that could initiate the reform of Italy and the Church – his twin aims. It seemed to many that Paradise had arrived in Florence.

Now, crucifix in hand, Savonarola called on the government to support him. He enjoined the citizens of Florence to put off their fine clothes and ornaments, sell their jewels and give the money to the poor. Silver candlesticks and illuminated books were to be removed from monasteries. He called on children to march through the streets and search houses for objects of vanity and luxury, and exhorted their parents to abandon vice and choose virtue. The people of Florence obeyed. Courtesans stayed indoors, fashions quietened and gaming-tables were not to be seen.

It was too much for his detractors, who founded a Florentine party, the *arrabbiati,* to oppose him. They allied with the Duke of Milan and the Pope, who had joined the Holy League against Charles VIII of France. (Florence had rejected the League.) Pope Alexander VI praised Savonarola and called him to Rome so he could hear his prophecies in person. Savonarola realized the meeting was a trap and said he was too ill to travel. The Pope sent a second letter, now criticizing Savonarola, who wrote back respectfully, pointing out eighteen mistakes in the Pope's document. In October 1495 the Pope wrote again, forbidding him to preach and admitting that the Holy League had called for this ban. Florentine ambassadors called for a revocation of the ban, and although the Pope verbally, unofficially, agreed to a revocation, he would not formalize his agreement. Savonarola now gave more sermons in which he attacked the Roman Court and referred to Alexander VI's scandalous private life. The Pope was offended and asked a college of theologians to study what Savonarola had said. When they found in Savonarola's favour, the Pope offered to make him a Cardinal, but he declined.

Pressed by the League and the *arrabbiati,* the Pope placed the congregation of San Marco under anathema. If Savonarola obeyed he would lose his authority; if he disobeyed he would be excommunicated. He did not disobey but just carried on preaching, and no one enforced the Pope's wishes.

In Lent 1497 his sermons were on *Ezekiel* and he ordered the notorious "bonfire of the vanities": all personal ornaments, scent bottles, wigs, rouge, mirrors, necklaces, gaming-tables and pictures of beautiful women were to be burned in the Piazza della Signoria at the foot of a scaffold. Books by Boccaccio and sensual paintings were thrown on the flames. Savonarola declared it a capital offence not to burn such things. It was through such methods that he implemented the City of God on which he preached so passionately.

The *arrabbiati* now became the government, and they stopped Savonarola preaching by inciting riots against him. They obtained a bull of excommunication, which however contained errors that made it null and void. The Pope disowned it, but made withdrawal of the censure conditional on Florence's membership of the Holy League. Savonarola studied and prayed, and preached again in Lent 1498. He appealed to a Church council but they burned his letters.

Then one of his followers, Fra Domenico da Pescia, made a mistake. He responded to a Franciscan who challenged anyone who maintained that Savonarola's excommunication was invalid to ordeal by fire. Domenico and the Franciscan were to take part in the ordeal by fire, and the loser would be the first to withdraw. Everyone in Florence wanted the ordeal to take place. The Franciscan did not appear. It was now said that Savonarola had not been vindicated by the Franciscan's default, and that he could only be vindicated by Domenico's miraculously surviving the flames.

The next day the *arrabbiati* led the mob to San Marco and beat back the defenders and seized Savonarola and Fra Domenico and another follower, Fra Silvesto. Savonarola was examined by his enemies and tortured. There was an ecclesiastical trial, and with his two companions he was hanged and burned with Papal approval in the Piazza della Signoria.

A triple gallows stood in the centre of the Piazza. A ladder led up to its three arms which met in a communal shoulder. Before mounting the scaffold Savonarola received the Pope's absolution and indulgence. They were hanged in order, Savonarola last. In turn they climbed the ladder. There was not much of a drop and it took them all a long time to die. Then a fire was lit on the platform below and the bodies were cut down and fell into it. Their ashes were scattered in the river Arno so no trace of them would survive.

THE PROTESTANT REVOLUTION

Luther

On the eve of All Souls' Day, October 31, 1517, an obscure 33-year-old German monk, clutching a sheaf of papers and holding a hammer, strode across the church square and banged a series of documents onto the north door of the Castle church at Wittenberg – documents which challenged the Papacy.[13] The blows of Martin Luther's hammer began the Reformation and have reverberated through history ever since.

The church door was used as a noticeboard. The sheaf contained 95 theses that announced a fresh approach to Christianity. Written in moderate, academic language they proposed among other things a discussion on the theology of indulgences. Nevertheless news quickly spread throughout Europe that the authority of the Catholic Church had been poignantly challenged.

The Reformation Revolution was primarily expressed by Luther, who articulated the cries to reform the Church which had been heard for 300 years since the time of the Cathars, and gave them political currency among the protesting German princes.

Luther was born in Eisleben, in German Saxony, in 1483, the son of a miner who wanted him to become a lawyer. He attended the University of Erfurt, becoming a BA and MA, and then became an Augustinian monk and was ordained priest. He taught at the University of Wittenberg from 1508 to 1546, where he obtained his doctorate in theology in 1512 and was appointed Professor of Biblical Theology. In 1514 he became preacher in the parish church.

Towards the end of the 15th century the Italian Renaissance spread beyond the Alps following the invasion of Italy by Charles VIII, who took examples of Italy's cultural achievements back to France and sought to have them imitated. In Germany, France and England there was a revival of classical learning: the Greek and Latin classics had more influence on new literary work, and there was a more rigorous approach to the study of the Bible. Scholars like the German Reuchlin (a scholar

Martin Luther

of Hebrew as well as Greek), and the Frenchman d'Etaples found discrepancies in the existing Latin texts of the Bible – and their works were banned. The Dutch Desiderius Erasmus produced a Latin New Testament and translated many Greek classics.

By the start of the 16th century the system of indulgences had fallen into abuse. Originally they were merciful pardons that released a sinner from penance imposed by a priest, but the original practice had become corrupted and indulgences had become guarantees in exchange for money that there would be no punishment in Purgatory. The Church taught that if the dying were forgiven and blessed by a priest, they would enter Heaven (the key to Heaven's gates being held by the Church). But before they reached Heaven the dead had to be cleansed from their sins by a painful stay in Purgatory. Even Dante believed this.

Only the Pope had the authority to shut the gates of Hell and open the door to Paradise. The stay in Purgatory could last hundreds of years – the relics in the Castle church in Wittenberg were reckoned to have saved pilgrims from 1,902,202 years and 270 days in Purgatory[14] – and indulgences shortened the time spent in Purgatory.

In every market-place in Europe, under a banner symbolizing the Pope's authority, clergymen and bankers' agents sold indulgences that absolved the purchasers from their sins and shortened their time in Purgatory. It might cost a month's, or even a year's wages depending on the weight of their sins, but they could literally buy their way out of Purgatory after living a morally loose life. Luther challenged the Pope's authority, believing that indulgences turned men's minds from Christ and God's forgiveness. They could live as they pleased and then buy remission from Purgatory.

Luther held that faith in God gave remission from Purgatory; there was no need to buy an indulgence. In other words Luther replaced the authority of the Pope with the word of God in the Bible. All across Europe people immediately understood that Luther had questioned the authority of the Church and the everyday practice of Christianity in the market-place. All across Europe questions were asked. Pope or Bible? Indulgences or faith? Buying a guarantee from Purgatory or praying to God?

Since the sale of indulgences now bought guaranteed places in heaven, no matter how wicked the purchasers had been, many in Europe began to doubt whether such a corrupt Church could be effective as an intermediary between humanity and God. There were rumblings that a separate Church should be set up. Pope Julius II increased the sale of indulgences to pay for the tomb Michelangelo was to sculpt for him. When a new seller of indulgences arrived in Germany in 1517 and good Christians flocked to him Martin Luther nailed his 95 theses to the door of Wittenberg church. One of them said, "Indulgences confer absolutely no good on souls as regards salvation or holiness." Men could be saved by the mercy of God, and therefore by faith. Faith alone was necessary for salvation. Salvation was a matter between the individual and God alone and did not involve the Church: "every man his own priest." The Bible, and not the Church, was the sole authority over men.

Luther's 95 theses were addressed to Albert, Archbishop of Mainz as a protest against the sale of indulgences. The Archbishop forwarded the documents to the Pope in Rome. In a papal bull Luther was ordered to retract within two months or be excommunicated. Luther retaliated by burning the papal bull on a bonfire together with books of canon law. Eventually he was excommunicated by the Pope in 1520 and outlawed by the Holy Roman Emperor Charles V at Worms in 1521.

Luther was now outside the protection of Pope and Emperor, and very vulnerable. The Elector Frederick, who resented Catholicism's rake-off on the sale of indulgences – he owned the 17,433 relics in the Castle church – carried out a pretended kidnapping of Luther and hid him in the castle of Wartburg for a while, protecting him by a form of imprisonment. In due course Luther shut down his monastic house of Augustinian canons, married off the local nuns and in 1525 made the last one, Katherina von Bura, his wife. From now on Protestant clergymen would not be separated from the sinful life of the world, including marriage.

Luther's act brought in the Protestant Reformation for his statement of the personal relationship between man and God made it possible for a new Lutheran Church to separate from the old Catholic Church. The 95 theses were a sensation, and Luther had to answer to his ecclesiastical superiors and eventually the Holy Roman Emperor, Charles V, who summoned him to a Diet. The German princes protested at the Emperor's opposition to the new reformed religion, and used the issue as a pretext to free themselves from the rights the Pope held over German clergy and set up their own churches. Luther was under the protection of Frederick the Wise of Saxony, who gave him safe conduct to the imperial diet. The Emperor honoured his word (in contrast to his predecessor Sigismund, who failed to honour the safe conduct for Hus). The German princes thought there was merit in Luther's position, as they could now appoint bishops and keep the revenues that had formerly gone to the Papacy.

Luther's theology had much in common with Gnosticism. In contrast to Calvin, Luther considered the world incorrigible and best left to the Devil (or Demiurge); in this his thinking was essentially dualistic. His theory of predestination (which was different from Calvin's) led him to believe in an élite ("the Elect"), leaving the great mass of humanity beyond the pale of salvation, while the episcopal structure of the Catholic Church was replaced in his thinking by a "priesthood of all believers." Compare the Cathar distinction between the Parfaits (or priests) and believers. To believe, Luther's believer only required faith.

The seal of Luther. Like the Rosicrucian emblem,
it is based on a rose-and-cross motif.

Luther wrote in the margin of his Bible, "Live by *Fides Sola*" (faith alone).[15] It seems that Luther's "justification by faith alone" was influenced by the Kabbalah's faith in the Ineffable Name of God. Descendants of the Jewish Kabbalists who were behind the Cathars had links with Luther and Calvin, and there is some evidence that they exerted a Kabbalist influence on both of them. See Luther's seal (above), which was based on the Rosicrucian rose-and-cross motif. It seems that Kabbalists encouraged Luther to nail his 95 theses on the church door, perhaps as part of a deliberate plan to split Christendom. Certainly Luther was influenced by Jewish legends concerning Jesus which were found in the *Talmud* and *Midrash* in the Middle Ages and in the *Toledot Yeshu* (*Life of Jesus*) which originated before the Middle Ages.

This Jewish Kabbalist view of Jesus, written by a Rabbi initiated into the mysteries of the Kabbalah, has Jesus as Jeschu, the illegitimate son of a Bethlehem hairdresser (Miriam) who was initiated into the secret doctrines of the Egyptian priesthood as a boy, and on his return to Palestine practised magic and showed curiosity about the Tetragrammaton or Schem Hamphorash, the Ineffable Name of God. According to the *Toledot Yeshu* Jesus read the Name in the Holy of Holies. He was hauled before the Sanhedrin and killed to suppress his knowledge. This book was translated by Raymond Martin towards the end of the 13th century and was summarized by Luther in German in *Schem Hamphorash* – evidence that Luther had opened himself to Kabbalism,[16] in which only faith in the Ineffable Name saves.

Luther did not think of himself as a revolutionary. He saw the Papacy as a foreign institution that had no place in Germany, and he supported the German princes who rebelled and set up their own churches and opposed those peasants who tried to use the religious turmoil to overthrow them. He quarrelled with Zwingli, who began the Reformation in Zurich in 1518, and with Erasmus, whose thinking about the Church had inspired Luther's position, though Erasmus himself had remained a Catholic. Erasmus was against violence and extremism, and opposed the Catholic Church in as far as it appealed to ignorance and superstition. (The Inquisition considered Erasmusism as much of a heresy as Lutheranism.) Nevertheless Erasmus viewed Luther as authoritarian, and did not like his belittling of the human will.

Calvin

Against a background of massacres of Anabaptists[17] in the 1520s, in the 1530s John Calvin was suddenly converted to Protestantism in Paris. Calvin, who was born at Noyon in French Picardy in 1509, was of a Jewish family (Cauin, possibly a French attempt to spell Cohen).[18] He wrote, "All who were looking for a purer doctrine began to come to learn from me." In 1534 he left Paris and settled in Switzerland, where he wrote *Institutes of Christian Religion* (1536). He led the reformed Protestantism movement in Geneva, which spread to France as the Huguenots and eventually to Scotland as Presbyterianism under John Knox.

Calvin's predestination was unlike Luther's, for he held that each man is predestined from before birth to salvation or damnation, and the human will is powerless to change this destiny, no matter how much Lutheran faith it has. Godly behaviour on earth demonstrated that a person was of the Elect (a Cathar belief), just as ungodly behaviour demonstrated that a person was damned. The ungodly had no right to interfere with the godly, who supervised the morals of the community.

It followed, therefore, that if a State was ruled by an ungodly tyrant, a Calvinist should resist and attempt a revolution. The diarist John Evelyn (on January 30, 1685) associated Calvin with "those pretended Reformists, who in divers of their Writings have favour'd the Killing of Kings, whom they found not complying with their discipline; among these...he reckoned *Calvine* (who) implicitly verges that way." In the Netherlands, Calvinists in revolt against the Habsburg ruler Philip II of Spain regarded themselves as in just revolt against an ungodly tyrant. In due course Calvin was succeeded by Theodore Beza, who related his philosophy of predestination to God and Providence rather than to Christ's salvation or damnation. French Calvinism, "a purer doctrine" for the Elect, has echoes of Kabbalistic Catharism, a doctrine for the Pure Ones of the Elect.

There is evidence that Calvin, who "deemed the Sabbath to have been a Jewish ordinance, limited to the sacred people" (Isaac D'Israeli),[19] organized a great number of revolutionary orators in Geneva and sent them into England and Scotland. In both England and Scotland these orators preached a religion that required a rigid observance of the Sabbath, and, D'Israeli states, the nation was divided into "Sabbatarians and Sabbath-breakers." This link between "a purer doctrine" and strict-observance Jews can be found a century later in the rise of Puritanism.

It is interesting to note that in 1630 in a letter to Archbishop Abbott, Matthew Brook, the master of Trinity College, Cambridge, wrote: "This doctrine of pre-destination is the root of puritanism, and puritanism is the root of all rebellions...and of all schism and sauciness in the country."[20]

ANTI-PAPAL POLITICAL RULE

Henry VIII and Thomas Cromwell

Political expression was given to the Reformation Revolution in England by Henry VIII.[21] He argued against Luther's theses in 1521 and the Pope awarded him the title "Defender of the Faith" (which the English monarch still curiously retains). He sided with Luther, however, when he sought to annul his marriage to Catherine of Aragon, the aunt of Charles V (King of Spain and Holy Roman Emperor), who urged the Pope to refuse permission.

Thomas Cromwell came forward with a clear (and clever) idea of how to achieve Henry's purpose of assuming supreme power outside the Pope's control. Cromwell proposed to destroy Rome's power in England and replace it by royal supremacy, which would allow the annulment to take place. Cromwell was behind the first attack on the Papacy (in 1532) and Henry's opposition – like that of the German princes – to bishops paying their first year's revenue to Rome. In 1533 he prevented appeals to Rome in certain legal cases.

Henry broke with the Pope. The day the Pope's ultimatum expired, Good Friday 1533, was caught by Holbein in his painting *The Ambassadors*, which depicts two French ambassadors standing in Westminster Abbey with troubled eyes and a look of doubt and foreboding – effectively on the day the Church of England was born. Henry divorced Catherine, married Anne Boleyn and (re)created the Church of England. He still regarded himself as a Catholic, albeit one who had repudiated Papal leadership of the Church in England and assumed it himself.

Thomas Cromwell now had complete control of the government, though he was always careful to claim he was acting on the King's authority. In 1534 he secured the passing of the Act of Supremacy which made Henry VIII supreme head of the Church of England. Cromwell was then appointed the King's Vicar General with powers to visit and reform all monastic institutions.

Henry was not sure what to do. Cardinal Wolsey had shown the way by dissolving certain priories and monasteries so that he could build his two educational institutions: Cardinal's College, Oxford, which became Christ Church; and Cardinal's College, Ipswich, which was to have been the biggest school in the country, rivalling Eton and Winchester and preparing pupils for Oxford. He opened this school in 1528. (Henry confiscated it after Wolsey fell in 1529 and closed it.)

There is no overt evidence connecting Thomas Cromwell with Kabbalism, and we can only speculate circumstantially. Thomas Cromwell was born in Putney, London c1485 and went abroad at an early age. He resided in the Low Countries and visited Italy, and was involved with the Merchant Adventurers, English merchants who traded with the Spanish Netherlands, principally in finished cloth (an export from England's wool trade). It is quite possible that in the Netherlands he met exiled Sefardic Jews who had been expelled from Spain in 1492, and that they encouraged his opposition to the Catholic Church of the Inquisition, their persecutor.

More

Into the problem of Henry's divorce came Sir Thomas More, who was an amazing man. He had a good education at the City's best school and in the household of the Archbishop of Canterbury, and studied at Oxford and Lincoln's Inn. He then spent four years residing in a Carthusian monastery near Lincoln's Inn and lived the life of a monk while practising as a lawyer and barrister. In 1504-5 he took a wife, who made demands on his time. Erasmus lived at his house for 20 years. More rose early, prayed, fasted and wore a hair shirt to be close to God, and despite his active life still had time for his Humanist pursuits. When his wife died in 1511, perhaps in childbirth, he remarried within weeks and turned his home into a school where girls were given a classical and Christian education by tutors.

A many-sided Renaissance man, Sir Thomas More wrote of a Utopia where men could live as free human beings, and translated the Christian Kabbalist Pico della Mirandola. His *Utopia* was begun in Flanders. In May 1515 he was part of a delegation to Bruges to revise an Anglo-Flemish trade treaty, and he wrote the book for other

Christian Humanists. Influenced by his discussions with Erasmus, its subtitle was (in English) "Concerning the highest state of the republic and the new island Utopia." It describes a city-state governed by reason that contrasts with the unreasonable greed of Christian Europe. Utopia is communist; the traveller Raphael Hythloday claims that an early form of communism (regarding "the whole island...as...one family or household" in a "commonwealth of public weal") is the only cure for egoistic greed in private and public life. More described Utopia's prison-system, education, religious tolerance, marriage laws (including divorce), practice of euthanasia and women's rights, and it seems as though Wolsey, the Lord Chancellor, was in sympathy with some of his ideas. Looking back to Plato's *Republic*, More founded the genre in English Literature that was to inspire the composition of Bacon's *The New Atlantis* and Swift's *Gulliver's Travels*.

More campaigned for theology to be reconnected with Greek studies, an idea that formed part of Erasmus's religious and cultural proposals. Erasmus described More as the perfect European Humanist. In 1523 More defended Henry VIII against Luther, and was appointed Speaker of the House of Commons and Chancellor of the duchy of Lancaster. From 1528 to 1533 his job was to read all heresies and refute them, and it was during this period that he wrote *A Dyaloge Concerning Herecies*. In 1529 he replaced Wolsey as Chancellor.

More, a Counter-Reformation man who wanted the Reformation Revolution checked and the Catholic Church's authority restored, was now caught up in the King's wish to divorce his wife. In 1531 and again in 1532 he tried to resign as the clergy moved towards acknowledging Henry VIII as head of the Church. When he refused to attend the coronation of Anne Boleyn, the accusations against him began to mount.

In 1534 he was imprisoned in the Tower, which suited his life of prayer, and in 1535 he was tried before Richard Rich, the Solicitor-General, who claimed that More had denied Henry VIII's title as supreme head of the Church of England. More spoke: "No temporal man may be head of the spirituality [realm of the spirit]." He was sentenced to beheading and on the scaffold put on his own blindfold. Erasmus described him as "*omnium horarum homo*" (translated by Robert Bolt as "A Man for All Seasons" in the title of his play) and wrote that his "soul was more pure than any snow" and that his "genius was such that England never had and never again will have its like."

Thomas Cromwell now applied Wolsey's tactics across the nation. Between 1536 and 1540 he secured the surrender of the greater monasteries by pressure and persuasion. By 1540 all monasteries were closed and Henry sequestrated their wealth. He saw himself as taking it from the Pope, and the Catholics were appalled.

Cromwell was now the King's deputy as head of the Church, and was associated with reform, and Reformation. He favoured an alliance with Lutherans and tried to force through an alliance with the German princes by compelling Henry to marry Ann of Cleeves. Henry hated his fourth wife, and by 1540 the alliance with the German princes was no longer necessary. The King decided Cromwell was a heretic and he was beheaded without trial in July.

By expelling the Papacy, Thomas Cromwell had made England into a sovereign national State that was independent of Rome. He had brought about an administrative revolution which strengthened the royal administrator, but which would have dangerous consequences a hundred years later when the Puritans challenged the spiritual authority of the King.

CONSOLIDATION: DEFEAT OF THE PAPISTS, THE IMPERIAL REVOLUTION

Counter-Reformation

The physical consolidation of the Reformation Revolution took place against the background of the Spanish Counter-Reformation.[22] At first the Catholic Church did little to counteract the spread of the Reformation. Pope Leo X, a Medici, who seems to have had little idea that the Church needed reforming, banned Luther's works in Germany and excommunicated him.

Michelangelo was typical of the Catholics, who remained loyal to the Pope. He had supported the Papacy against Savonarola and the Medici, and while working on Julius II's tomb was loyal to his sponsor and not to Luther who opposed Julius's fund-raising for the project. Before working on the Last Judgment fresco in the Vatican's Sistine Chapel (1531-1541), he had been inspired by the medieval hymn "Dies Irae" and the works of Dante – he loved Dante and wrote in one of his poems, "Would that I were he!" – and in his painting he tried to catch the spiritual pride of the Renaissance and Reformation giants, representing them as overreachers who were reaching too high in relation to their position under God:

> "Giants they are of such a height
> That each it seems doth take delight
> In mounting to the sun to be blinded by its light",

and

> "A giant there is of such a height
> That here below his eyes do see us not...."[23]

In other words, Michelangelo was critical of the Renaissance humanists and Reformation giants.

It was not until Charles V of Spain put pressure on the Papacy to compromise with the Protestants that the Catholic Church began to move to defuse the Reformation. Pope Paul III agreed to call a Council, which was held at Trent on and off from 1545 to 1563.

As a result of the Council of Trent, the reformers ousted the Renaissance Papacy and its worldly attitudes and policies and took the initiative. They found it impossible to compromise with the Protestants who espoused justification by faith, but the desecularization of the Church held off criticism and checked the spread of Protestantism in

Europe. They decided that Catholic doctrine should be stated more clearly, and that all Catholics should be instructed in the catechism; there was also to be an Index of Forbidden Books. An Inquisition had been established in 1542 to combat heresy, and there would now be a strengthening of the Inquisition. New religious orders were founded, such as the Theatines, Capuchins, Ursulines and Jesuits.

The countries that had been lost to the Catholic Church had to be won back: notably South Germany, England, parts of the Low Countries, Poland and Hungary. The Church gave this work to the Society of Jesus, which had been founded in 1534 by St Ignatius of Loyola (1491-1556), who had organized it on a military model. Loyola was a former Spanish soldier who had turned to Christianity while recovering from being hit by a cannonball, and who had had a spiritual vision in 1522 while sitting by the river Cardoner at Manresa.[24] It was this militant drive that led the Protestants to call it "the Counter-Reformation." The Jesuits took a vow of obedience to their General, who in turn took a vow of loyalty to the Pope. They went into the lapsed countries and targeted influential people, finding success in South Germany, the Low Countries, Poland and Hungary, but not in England, where they were considered guilty of treason. St Francis Xavier, Ignatius's roommate in Paris c1529, took the Jesuit cause to India, Malaya and Japan and established the Jesuits as world-wide missionaries.

Meanwhile Charles V attacked the German princes in 1546, and there was war until the Religious Peace of Augsburg in 1555, which allowed the German princes to retain the Protestant religion. In England, when the Catholic Mary died in 1558 her widower Philip of Spain sought to impose the Counter-Reformation throughout the reign of Elizabeth I until the Spanish Armada was defeated in 1588. In due course the Catholic Habsburgs fought the Thirty Years War to win back Bohemia and Poland for the Counter-Reformation, but were eventually defeated in 1648.

The Counter-Reformation found expression through the Carmelite Order, which St Teresa of Avila reformed in 1562 after a series of visions in 1555. In 1568 she met a young Carmelite priest St John of the Cross, who later became her confessor and initiated Carmelite Reform for men. St Francis de Sales later continued this Carmelite work.

Sir Walter Raleigh, writing in the Introduction to his *History of the World*, accused the Jesuits of fomenting world revolution through their reconversion and missionary activities. There has often been speculation regarding a connection between the Jews and the Jesuits. It is known that in 1714 the Jesuits used the mysteries of the Kabbalist Rose-Croix.[25] Were they a Rosicrucian organization created to widen the split in Christendom? Were Jewish Kabbalists as committed to infiltrating the Catholic Jesuits as they were the Protestants? It is interesting that Adam Weishaupt was brought up by the Jesuits and modelled the Illuminati on the Jesuit organizational structure. It has been suggested – fancifully – that the Jesuits were the secret inspirers of the Illuminati.

The Jesuits certainly widened the Catholic/Protestant schism. They influenced the reforming Protestants and the Catholic counter-reformers, both sides of Christendom's split, and secretly sought to widen the gulf. In his play *The Jew of Malta*, Marlowe described this sort of double-crossing through the character of the Jew himself, Barabas:

"And after that was I an engineer,
And in the wars 'twixt France and Germany,
Under pretence of helping Charles the fifth,
Slew friend and enemy with my stratagems." (II,iii,190-3)

Elizabeth I

In England the Reformation Revolution led to a new imperialism as England sought to defeat Spain. Henry VIII had been succeeded by his sickly 10-year-old son Edward VI, and when Edward died by his eldest daughter Mary (daughter of Catherine of Aragon), who restored Catholicism. Mary was married to Philip II of Spain (inheritor of Charles V's western possessions) and she brought the Counter-Reformation to England for five bloody years (1553-8). She was succeeded by Henry VIII's younger daughter, the Protestant Elizabeth I (1558-1603),[26] the daughter of Anne Boleyn, whose marriage to Henry VIII was deemed illegal by the Pope. Elizabeth advanced the country and gave it a sense of national identity. Though her hand was sought by many foreign rulers, including Philip of Spain himself, she refused them all (no doubt aware of how unpopular her half-sister Mary's marriage to Philip had been). She would not marry any of her subjects but ruled by manipulating her suitors and favourites, outwardly a spinster – a "virgin queen" – and avoided war so as not to be compelled to call a Parliament that might impose conditions. In particular and in view of growing Calvinist influence she did not want Parliament to question the Church Settlement of 1559, which had instituted the Catholic Anglican ritual.

Following her father's death in 1547 (when she was 14) her guardian was the dowager queen Catharine Parr, who married the Lord High Admiral, Thomas Seymour. His older brother the Duke of Somerset was protector of the realm while Edward VI was a minor, and Thomas now schemed against him and in January 1549 was arrested for treason and accused of plotting to marry the 16-year-old Elizabeth to rule the kingdom. Hearings found that he had several times been seen to flirt with Elizabeth and act in an overfamiliar way. Thomas Seymour was beheaded.

Cecil

It is possible that when she was sixteen Elizabeth had a child by Thomas Seymour, and that William Cecil solved the problem and kept the episode secret. Whether this speculation is true or not and whether or not he had some hold over her, the fact is that when Elizabeth came to the throne in 1558 she appointed William Cecil as her principal Secretary of State on the morning of her accession, and he served her for 40 years (after 1571 as Lord Treasurer) as her most trusted adviser. He was the most powerful man in her government – even Walsingham, the spymaster, was under him – and later took the title Lord Burghley.

Cecil's contribution to the Reformation as a revolution was vast. Alan Gordon Smith observed in *William Cecil, the Power behind*

Elizabeth that the Reformation was a social, economic, moral and religious revolution as far-reaching in its repercussions as the French and Russian revolutions. Its triumph in England was principally the work of Cecil, who imposed the great change on a reluctant people and in the course of a generation converted the nation to the new religion, which was a mixture of nationalism and individualism that brought modern England into being.[27]

The Cecilian revolution in government (1558-98) built on the reforms of Thomas Cromwell. William Cecil organized a new centralized government and bureaucratic nobility which came to be known as "regnum Cecilianum." The Church of England, which on a mystic plane was rooted in Celtic Christianity and the undefiled message of Jesus, was established as a political settlement. Foundations were laid for the British Empire with voyages of discovery and the attempted colonization of America. As a result England's naval power was greatly increased – Elizabeth maintained a fleet that could be supplemented by vessels from the merchant fleet – and England was able to defeat the Spanish Armada of 1588. This Spanish fleet came to take England for the Catholic Philip II of Spain, Mary's widower, who had paid heed to Pope Pius V's excommunication of Elizabeth in 1570 and Pope Gregory XIII's proclamation in 1580 that it would be no sin to rid the world of such a miserable heretic as the Queen of England.

Central to Cecil's revolution in government was Elizabeth's own charismatic personal appeal. Without a standing army, efficient police force or effective bureaucracy, Elizabeth had to raise taxes from a reluctant Parliament to govern, and she did this by using her charm and eloquence, as when she addressed the soldiers at Tilbury on the eve of the Armada. Her tactic was to encourage a cult of love in which she was seen as Diana, goddess of the moon, Astraea, goddess of justice, and Gloriana, queen of the fairies – Spenser's Fairie Queene. Thus she expressed her diplomatic goals in the language of love.

Out of Elizabeth's reign grew a new secular imperialism, which Shakespeare objected to in his plays. *Hamlet* and *Troilus and Cressida* denounce Cecil/Burghley in the guise of Polonius and Pandarus.

Correspondingly, Shakespeare exalted the concepts of sovereignty and chivalry, for example in *Richard II* (Gaunt's speech about "this scept'red isle") and in *Henry V*, with its appeal to patriotism before Agincourt. Shakespeare was opposed to the new mercantile ethos espoused by Lord Burghley, and it is partly because he was so antipathetic to Burghley that some believe that "Shake-speare" (which they claim, was a *nom-de-plume* first used in 1593) was not Shakspere of Stratford (the spelling in the Parish Register) – the son of illiterate parents who never travelled outside England or taught his children to read or left a book when he died – but Edward de Vere, the 17th Earl of Oxford. Oxford had married Lord Burghley's daughter Ann Cecil (Ophelia in *Hamlet*) and fallen out with his father-in-law after she became pregnant while he was living in Venice and travelling in Italy (Verona, Padua, Mantua etc) in 1575/6. It must be emphasized that many more believe, with good reason that Shakespeare of Stratford wrote Shakespeare's works.

Dee

Behind the new Cecilian imperialism, which was continued by Lord Burghley's son Robert Cecil (later Lord Salisbury) who invited James I to succeed Elizabeth, was the Welshman John Dee. An alchemist, astrologer and mathematician who lectured in Europe before becoming astrologer to Mary, he was imprisoned for being a magician but was released to practise astrology and plot horoscopes in Elizabeth's court. (He also gave the Queen lessons on the interpretation of his writings.) He was an imperialist – it was Dee who had coined the term "British Empire" in 1568 – who wanted England to become a world maritime power. Dee gave advice to navigators about to explore the New World, and in 1577 he wrote a *Treatise on Naval Defence* which was a blueprint for an imperial fleet that would rule the waves and protect British interests worldwide.[28]

Dee was central to Elizabeth's court as well as the Queen's teacher. He was a scholar-magician like Pico della Mirandola. His roots were in Ficino's occult Neoplatonism, and he boldly affirmed the power of Kabbalism: "no science gives greater proof of the divinity of Christ than magic or the Kabbalah." From 1583 to 1589 he toured Poland and

Bohemia, displaying his magic to many of the European princes, and he was associated with Giordano Bruno, the Hermetic Magus, who visited Dee in England in 1583. The Renaissance (through Pico) had thrown up the figure of the Magus, the intellectual who practised magic arts, the "Magia and Cabala," and who came to be seen as the ideal man. Between them Bruno and Dee stood for an occult Neoplatonism that was steeped in magical Kabbalism.

Shakespeare seems to have based Prospero on Dee. It seems that in Shakespeare's mind it was Dee who conjured Ariel, caused the shipwreck by his magic, and promised to burn his books at the end of the play. Bruno was burned at the stake for his "pantheistic" beliefs in 1600, but Dee survived, and became warden of Manchester College in 1595.

Sidney and Raleigh's Circle

The growing Catholic-Puritan conflict in Elizabethan England led many – such as Sidney, Raleigh and his Durham House Circle of Northumberland, Hariot, Hues, Warner, Cavendish and White – to interest themselves in the work of Bruno and Dee and other occult sources, including the Priory of Sion.

Sir Philip Sidney, the flower of Elizabethan youth, who had quarrelled with the 17th Earl of Oxford, seems to have been lampooned as Sir Andrew Aguecheek and died in battle in Holland in 1586, was a pupil of John Dee. He wrote *Arcadia* at Wilton in 1582, the year he was visited by the Grand Master of the Priory of Sion (1575-1595), Louis de Nevers, a Gonzaga of Mantua who knew Bruno and was involved in Hermetic societies. (The purpose of his visit to England was to spend time with Sidney and John Dee.)[29] Nevers would have brought with him the tradition of René d'Anjou, a former Grand Master of Sion, who had painted *La Fontaine de Fortune* (1457) with its legend that the "sorcerer Virgil" brought forth a spring in Arcadia. (This spring was Alpheus in Western culture, Alph in Coleridge.)

The concept of Arcadia, so resonant in 1582, is mysteriously linked to the papers discovered by Abbé Saunière at Rennes-le-Château. In 1781, the story goes, the Abbé Antoine Bigou, parish priest for seven years at Rennes-le-Château, was told a secret and given documents by Lady Blanchefort, a descendant of Bertrand de Blanchefort, who knew she was dying. The secret may have been that Jesus survived crucifixion and married Mary Magdalene, had children (from whom the Merovingians claim descent) and retired to France, and died at Rennes-le-Château. The Abbé was terrified by what he had learned, and as France turned revolutionary in 1789 he hid the documents in the Carolingian pillar that held up the altar in the church of St Mary Magdalene, hoping to preserve the secret for future generations. These were the documents Abbé Saunière claimed to have found, which listed the Templar and Sion Grand Masters. In 1791 Bigou laid a large gravestone flat on the tomb of the Marquise de Blanchefort. On it was engraved a Greek inscription which said: *"Et in Arcadia Ego."* This flagstone had been removed from the tomb of Arquez, a very old tomb (razed in 1988 by its new owner) that bears a striking resemblance to the tomb in Nicolas Poussin's painting *Les Bergers d'Arcadie* (c1640-2), which also bore the cryptic inscription *"Et in Arcadia Ego."* The occult symbolism of Arcadia first found its way into Western art in Guercino's painting *Et in Arcadia Ego* (c1618) and again in Poussin's work of the same name, where figures are reading the inscription on a tomb (1629-39). By now Arcadia clearly had a significance beyond that of the pastoral Eden in classical Greece. It was a pun on Arques: Arques-adia.

Why was de Nevers, possessor of the Arcadian tradition since 1457, sitting with Sidney while he was writing *Arcadia* in 1582? Did Sidney have Templar-Sion links? We have seen that Sion began the Rose-Croix in the 13th century, and Rosicrucianism made a cult of the tomb of Christian Rosycross (i.e. Rosenkreutz). Christian Rosycross may have been a cryptic alias for the post-crucified Jesus, suggesting that Christ survived crucifixion and was eventually buried in a tomb (empty when opened in the 1920s) in Arques, six miles from Rennes and three miles from Blanchefort in French Arques-adia/Arcadia. Arcadia clearly had an early Rosicrucian significance (Arques-adia).[30] Did Sidney know that the Templar headquarters were at Rennes-le-Château? He was certainly drawing on de Nevers' Hermetic knowledge and acquaintance with

Bruno.

Sir Walter Raleigh also knew John Dee and invited him and the mathematician Hariot to his study at the top of Sherborne Castle. (This is at the very top of the house, in an area closed to the public.)[31] Tales of Raleigh's involvement with Dee's occult spread throughout Dorset. His Durham House in London was also a meeting-place where those who had despaired of Christianity following the Reformation and the growth of Calvinist Puritanism, pursued a Kabbalistic alternative, no doubt unaware that those who sought to destroy Christianity through schism were the very people who were promoting the new Kabbalistic magic of Dee and Bruno.

Raleigh's globalist *The History of the World*, written in the Tower of London and published in 1614, came to be "the backbone of anti-authoritarian thought" and the revolutionary "*Das Kapital* of the 17th century."[32] Raleigh opposed James I, his imprisoner, and argued that it was legitimate to dethrone a king who does not have the support of his people. Oliver Cromwell read the book and recommended it to his son. John Milton's debt to it was "incalculable."[33] Marvell and Lilburne praised it. Raleigh's questioning of the divine right of kings in this work provided a distant clarion call for the revolutions of the 17th and 18th centuries.

Columbus and Voyagers

Protestant Europe became expansionist and imperialistic as it consolidated the Reformation Revolution, and looked towards the New World. The European colonization of North America was part of a wider European expansion throughout the globe.[34] It had been led by Portuguese voyages to West Africa (1418), South Africa (1487), the Cape of Good Hope (which enabled explorers to go round Africa and up the east coast like Vasco da Gama in 1497) and to Brazil (1500). The Spanish closed the gap with the Portuguese after Columbus reached America, with voyages to the Caribbean, New Spain and Peru.

In 1492, against the background of the Inquisition the Genoese sailor Christopher Columbus, with three ships and the backing of Ferdinand and Isabella of Spain, discovered America. A pirate in the service of René d'Anjou in the 1470s, he believed he was divinely chosen for such a voyage and had read the French Cardinal Pierre d'Ailly's *Imago Mundi* (*Image of the World*) in 1483, which had convinced him that the earth is round and that the East Indies could be reached by sailing west. This work was regarded as heretical by the Church. Following prophecies in *Isaiah* 11,10-12 and the apocryphal *Second Book of Esdras* 3,18, which further confirmed that the earth is round, he tried to reach India from the west. After a voyage of 33 days he landed in October in the island of Guanahami near the Strait of Florida and thought he had reached the Far East. He went on to Cuba and took possession of Santa Domingo (Hispaniola) and then returned to Spain where he was received in triumph in March 1493, without realizing he had discovered a new world. After two more voyages (to the West Indies and South America) he died forgotten in 1506.

However, new explorers returned to Venezuela and the Amazon and recognized that these lands were different from Asia. In 1497 an Italian in English service, John Cabot, discovered Cape Breton Island in North America. In 1507 the Florentine Amerigo Vespucci, another Italian in Spanish service, voyaged to Brazil and recognized the new discoveries as a separate continent. It is from him that America takes its name. Soon afterwards a Portuguese in Spanish service, Ferdinand Magellan, sailed round the world, leaving Seville in 1519. He was killed in the Philippine Islands, which he claimed for Spain, but one of his ships returned in 1522. The French had gone to Newfoundland (1534) and had attempted to found colonies in Florida and Brazil. The Renaissance's view of the world was now changing to include America, and new possibilities of exploration westwards were opening up.

English voyages

The English had lagged behind the Portuguese and Spanish efforts. Although they had sailed to North America (1497, John Cabot), they relied on private trading companies interested in commercial rather than territorial expansion, notably the Muscovy Company (1554). The Reformation Revolution stirred English imperialism and inspired voyages to the New World that were very daring in their day as it was still thought that mariners might plunge over the edge of the world as over a waterfall. They are comparable to the voyages to the moon of astronauts in our own time.

Martin Frobisher made three voyages in search of the North West Passage to the Far East (1576-78), in one of which Edward de Vere (17th Earl of Oxford) was an investor and lost £3,000 to Michael Lok (perhaps later lampooned as Shylock). Sir Francis Drake sailed round the world in 1577, plundering South America on his way, and in 1578 Sir Humphrey Gilbert attempted to found colonies in North America and Newfoundland, but without much success. (He was drowned off the Azores in September 1583.)

Gilbert's half-brother Sir Walter Raleigh then founded a colony (1584-6) of over 100 souls at Roanoke Island, North Carolina, which disappeared when it was apparently overrun by Indians, who absorbed the survivors. (There are still tales of blue-eyed Indians in that part of America.) The Roanoke colony included Virginia Dare, the first girl to be born in the New World, who may have been Shakespeare's model for Miranda in *The Tempest*. Shakespeare may also have regarded Prospero as being on Raleigh's expedition.

Bartholomew Gosnold and Empire in the New World

Following the failures of Frobisher, Gilbert and Raleigh, a young man trained by the Earl of Essex, Bartholomew Gosnold, made two attempts at colonizing North America, both of which were visionary – he envisaged the founding of a new English-speaking civilization – rather than purely mercantile. The first attempt in 1602 – thought to have been planned at Otley Hall, Suffolk, where his uncle was Essex's secretary, and funded by his closest Cambridge friend (and Shakespeare's patron) the Earl of Southampton – ended in failure after 12 weeks at Cuttyhunk, near Martha's Vineyard, which Gosnold named after his infant daughter. Gosnold returned and seems to have told Shakespeare about finding Indians there, for Shakespeare's *Tempest* is based on the geography of Martha's Vineyard.[35]

The second attempt, also thought to have been planned at Otley Hall, which acted as a recruiting base, was successful. It took three years to organize, and with Gosnold as "prime mover" 105 English colonists settled the Jamestown Fort in 1607. Some 40 of these first settlers came from villages round Otley. Bartholomew Gosnold died inside the Jamestown Fort and John Smith later took over the running of the colony which Gosnold had planned and organized. John Smith's statue, not Gosnold's now stands over the recently discovered Jamestown Fort. The Jamestown Settlement was the first non-Spanish, non-Indian, English-speaking colony to survive.

This was 13 years before the sailing of the *Mayflower* from Plymouth, and the founder of the surviving Jamestown Settlement should be regarded as the founder of modern English-speaking America. That person is arguably Bartholomew Gosnold.

Gosnold had promised the settlers 500 acres of land, which they could not have hoped to own in England with its fixed, hierarchical, landed class-system. Gosnold exported to Virginia the Elizabethan landed way of life which was still alive round Richmond before the American Civil War, and whose passing is still lamented in the nostalgic South. Gosnold also exported the Christian vision to America, and this was eventually embodied in the first Jamestown church.

Gosnold was a cousin twice over of Francis Bacon, and his American colony anticipated Bacon's own *New Atlantis* (1624), which was written in the tradition of Sir Thomas More's *Utopia* and drew on the founding of America. Had Bacon not prosecuted the Earl of Essex and secured the death penalty following Essex's rebellion in 1601, thereby alienating the pro-Essex Gosnolds, it is possible that Bacon would have been one of those behind the 1607 voyage and would have given funding support of the kind given by Sir Thomas Smythe, a relative of Gosnold's wife, who had become the richest merchant of his day and chartered the three ships in late 1606. Gosnold persuaded several of his relatives to be involved in the voyage, and when Bacon became MP for Ipswich in 1597 – he was readopted in 1601 and 1610[36] – just seven miles from Otley Hall, he was very close to the seat of the Gosnolds. It was certainly through Bacon that America became the focus of the Rosicrucian ambition for a New Atlantis.

SUMMARY: THE REVOLUTIONARY DYNAMIC OF THE REFORMATION

For the revolutionary dynamic and the way the occult vision is interpreted and intellectualized, see Appendices A, Appendix 1 and Appendix 2. The Kabbalistic Cathars first enshrined the Reformation's occult vision and passed it on to its occult interpreters Wycliffe and Hus. Its occult revolutionary originator was Ficino, who interpreted the vision in terms of his hidden Neo-Platonism. The thoughtful intellectual who gave the occult vision a new slant was the Christian Kabbalist Pico della Mirandola, who met Ficino in Florence. Both Ficino himself and Pico had also given intellectual expression to the anti-Papal feeling. The semi-political intellectual interpreters were first Savonarola, who ruled Florence for four years, and then Luther, who was influenced by Christian Kabbalism and led the German princes. The first part of the revolutionary dynamic of the Reformation Revolution can be defined as follows:

Heretical occult vision	Heretical occult interpreters	Occult revolutionary originator	Thoughtful intellectual interpreter	Semi-political intellectual interpreters
Kabbalistic Cathars	Wycliffe/Hus	Ficino	Pico della Mirandola	Savonarola/ Luther

The Reformation Revolution found its intellectual expression in Ficino, Pico, Savonarola, Luther and Calvin. Its political expression was embodied by Henry VIII and Thomas Cromwell's dissolution of the monasteries. Its physical expression can be found in Germany through the German princes who accepted Lutheranism and banded together into the Schmalkaldic League in 1531 to defend the new churches; and in the war that erupted between the Protestants and Spain: between the German princes and Charles V until the Religious Peace of Augsburg of 1555, and between England and Philip II throughout the reign of

Elizabeth I, who countered Spanish imperialism by founding the First British Empire.

Frederick the Great said of the Reformation Revolution: "A revolution so great and so singular, which changed almost the entire System of Europe, deserves to be examined with philosophical eyes."[37] Looking "with philosophical eyes" enables us to summarize the revolutionary dynamic of the Reformation Revolution as follows:

Heretical occult inspiration	Intellectual expression	Political expression	Physical consolidation
Kabbalistic Cathars/ Wycliffe/Hus	Ficino/Pico della Mirandola/ Savonarola/ Luther/Calvin	Henry VIII/ Thomas Cromwell/ German princes/ destruction of the monasteries	Defeat of Spanish Counter-Reformation: war of German princes and England against Spain/First British Empire in the New World

The incubatory phase of the Reformation Revolution can be found among the Cathari ("Pure Ones") of Languedoc. It can be argued that the Cathar movement was a religion rather than a revolution. To many, the Cathars wanted to live apart from the world, not transform its social institutions. Nevertheless, the movement had a heretical occult vision (a vision deemed heretical by the religious orthodoxy of the day – Mani's) and an intellectual expression (Pierre-Roger de Mirepoix and Guilhabert de Castres). It had political expression: Raymonds VI and VII (Counts of Toulouse), who also presided over the physical phase that saw attacks on representatives of the Catholic Church. Mirepoix was the military leader of the Montségur Cathars for much of the first half of the 13th century. In a sense the movement did seek to transform the whole of society – into protesting Cathars – and though Cathar armies never threatened Paris, the movement did lead to two civil wars (the Albigensian Crusade and the final siege of Montségur), recruitment for which involved Paris. In attacking the religious orthodoxy of their time, the Cathars were the precursors of the Puritans, who carried through their revolution by murdering the English King rather than a papal legatee and two Inquisitors. The Puritans had a successful revolution, and there is a case for regarding the Cathar movement as an unsuccessful revolution that attempted to create a non-Papal society of Parfaits and believers. There is equally a case for regarding them as seceding from society in their desire to be left alone.

The revolutionary dynamic of the unsuccessful Cathar revolution can be stated as follows:

Heretical occult inspirer	Intellectual expression	Political expression	Physical consolidation
Mani	Pierre-Roger de Mirepoix/ Guilhabert de Castres	Raymonds VI and VII	Cathar attacks on the Catholic Church

The Renaissance found its heretical occult vision in Plato and other classical works. Its heretical occult interpreters were Gemistos Plethon (acting in his capacity as Platonist rather than Orthodox cleric) and Cosimo de' Medici, who acted as patron to both after he succeeded as sole ruler of Florence in 1434. The wealthiest man of his time, until 1455 he avoided the political limelight and gathered round him artists and humanists to whom he acted as patron. The occult revolutionary originator was Ficino, who revived Plato's Academy. The intellectual interpreter was Pico della Mirandola, who introduced the concept of the Mage. The semi-political intellectual interpreter who later became political was Lorenzo de' Medici, the Magnificent, who absorbed Ficino's Humanist ideas in the 1460s and introduced them into the running of the Florentine State when he came to power in 1469. The early revolutionary dynamic of the Renaissance Revolution is as follows:

| Heretical | Heretical occult | Occult | Intellectual | Semi- |

occult vision	interpreter	revolutionary originator	interpreter	political intellectual interpreter
Plato/ Kabbalists	Gemistos Plethon/ Cosimo de' Medici	Ficino	Pico della Mirandola	Lorenzo de' Medici, the Magnificent

The political expression of the Renaissance Revolution was in the Medici, particularly Lorenzo the Magnificent [and Cosimo], in Charles VIII, and in the Renaissance Popes. Its physical expression was exemplified by the replacement of Christianity by the occult in the figure of the Mage (for example, Pico) and in Ficino-inspired artists such as Botticelli who reflected the new Humanism in their art by focusing on the naked or scantily-clad human body (such as Venus's) and swept away the halo and contemplative concerns of medieval painting. The full revolutionary dynamic was:

Heretical occult inspirer	Intellectual expression	Political expression	Physical consolidation
Plato/ Gemistos	Ficino/Pico della Mirandola	Lorenzo de' Medici [and Cosimo]/Charles VIII/ Renaissance Popes	Occult replacing Christianity in the Mage/Botticelli et al

Savonarola's City of God was the result of a revolution against the Medici and an attempted revolution against the Papacy. His occult vision went back to earlier Kabbalists, and drew on the Cathar revolution. Savonarola gave both intellectual and semi-political expression to the Reformation Revolution. He also gave intellectual and political expression to his Revolution, but was killed by the *arrabbiati* before there could be a brutal physical stage. The revolutionary dynamic of Savonarola's Revolution looks as follows:

Heretical occult	Intellectual	Political	Physical

inspiration	expression	expression	consolidation
Kabbalists	Savonarola (sermons in San Marco)	Republic of Florence (after 1494)	City of God/ bonfire of the vanities

The climax of the Imperial Revolution of the First British Empire in the New World was the 1607 founding of Jamestown, the first English-speaking colony to survive. Its "heretical occult vision" (the intuitive inner vision of the world denounced as heretical by the religious orthodoxy of the day, the Church, which regarded the earth as flat) can be found in the heretical French Cardinal Pierre d'Ailly's conviction that the earth is round and his pioneering discovery of the New World. The heretical occult interpreters were Christopher Columbus, who adopted the view that the earth is round, came into conflict with the Church (Bishop Talavera of Avila, Queen Isabella's confessor, who reported unfavourably on his proposed voyage) and staked his life on putting it to the test; and Amerigo Vespucci, who identified America as a new continent. The occult revolutionary originator who gave the vision a new slant was John Dee, the first to coin the phrase "British Empire." In Paris in 1550, when he was 23, Dee had met Gulielmus Postellus, a Kabbalist who dreamed of establishing a world religion and government, an ideal Dee shared. He claimed that Elizabeth I derived from the conquests of King Arthur a title to numerous foreign lands, including Greenland, Iceland, Friesland, the northern islands towards Russia and the North Pole, and he believed that the New World was appointed by divine Providence for the British, an outlook that encouraged Elizabethan expansion to take place.[38] The thoughtful intellectual interpreter of Dee's occult vision was Sir Walter Raleigh, who organized several voyages (and later produced a *History of the World*). The semi-political intellectual interpreter who later became political was Bartholomew Gosnold, who pioneered the southern route to the New World when settling Cuttyhunk in 1602 and then organized the founding of the Jamestown settlement in 1607. He was the power in the Jamestown Fort until his death and military funeral there in August 1607. The early revolutionary dynamic of the Imperial Revolution of the First British Empire was as follows:

Heretical occult vision	Heretical occult interpreters	Occult revolutionary originator	Thoughtful intellectual interpreter	Semi-political intellectual interpreter
D'Ailly (earth round)	Postellus (Kabbalist), Columbus (earth round), Vespucci (new continent)	John Dee	Raleigh	Bartholomew Gosnold

The intellectual expression of the Imperial Revolution of the First British Empire encompasses the voyages of Frobisher, Gilbert and Raleigh and the spreading of the imperial idea through the Durham Circle. The political expression can be found in Elizabeth I's attempts to found the First British Empire under Lord Burleigh and the geographer Hakluyt. The consolidation of the Revolution can be found in Bartholomew Gosnold's settlement of Jamestown under Sir Robert Cecil, and John Smith's later work which made Jamestown safe from the Indians. The full revolutionary dynamic of the Imperial Revolution of the First British Empire was as follows:

Heretical occult inspiration	Intellectual expression	Political expression	Physical consolidation
D'Ailly/ Postellus/ Columbus/ Vespucci	Dee/Raleigh and Durham Circle/Bacon	Elizabeth I's attempts to found the First British Empire through voyages and Hakluyt's geography	Jamestown settlement of Bartholomew Gosnold/John Smith

Taking stock of the ideas behind the Reformation Revolution as a whole, we can state the revolutionary dynamic of the ideas behind the

Reformation Revolution as follows:

Heretical occult inspiration	Intellectual expression	Political expression	Physical expression
Kabbalistic Catharism (rebellion against Pope/Catholic Church)	Renaissance Humanism	Protestantism	Defeat of Papists, empire in the New World: war against Catholic nations

By 1610 the Reformation had split a unified Christendom into warring sects, which sent the intellectuals off into occult Neoplatonism and Rosicrucianism. Out of the Reformation had come a new force: Puritanism, whose Calvinism had been adopted in Scotland by the new English King, James I. In relation to the hard line of Elizabeth I, James was more lenient towards the Puritans, and both they and the Hermetic tradition grew in influence under him.

CHAPTER TWO

THE PURITAN REVOLUTION

Oliver Cromwell was a Socinian, and...introduced Freemasonry into England. Certainly, Cromwell's sympathies were not for the Church favoured by the monarch he supplanted, and were much with the Independents. If he was a Socinian we can easily understand how the secret society of Vicenza could have attractions for one of his anti-Catholic and ambitious sentiments. He gave its members in England...the title of Freemasons, and invented the allegory of the Temple of Solomon....This Temple, destroyed by Christ for the Christian order, was to be restored by Freemasonry after Christ and the Christian order should be obliterated by conspiracy and revolution.

Dillon, *Grand Orient Freemasonry Unmasked*

The central event of the Puritan Revolution was the beheading of Charles I, who was widely perceived as being sympathetic towards Roman Catholicism. That was the moment power transferred to the regicides and the transformation of English society could properly begin.

The origins of the Puritan Revolution can be found in the anti-Papal feeling of the Reformation, which shaped the rise of Puritanism and its yearning for the English to appear as neo-Israelites. This feeling was reinforced by a new development in a kingdom surrounded by German states, and swelled by the arrival in England of refugees from central Europe's wars of religion.

THE ENGLISH ISRAELITES

The Puritans positively desired to become British Israelites[1] and to wear Jewish-style clothes (long black cloaks and hats). At the time they were seen in negative terms, as refusers of the dress and paraphernalia of the high Church of England, as recusants. In fact, Puritanism began as a late 16th-century Reformation movement in the Kabbalistic/Cathar tradition to "purify" the Church of England of the residual Catholic Popery that had been left behind by Elizabeth I's Settlement. Its origins can be traced to the Dutch Familists (or Family of God) of the Hermetic Hendrik Niclaes, who united Christians and Jews within one sect, and to the Kabbalist-influenced Bible translator William Tyndale (died 1536), the "Apostle of England," who believed that like Israel England had a covenant with God and that the British were neo-Israelites (see Appendices B, Appendix 10). (Cranmer's *Book of Common Prayer* is imbued with feeling for the special destiny of the British people.)

Tyndale

Tyndale lived in hiding during the last twelve years of his life on the Continent, at the end in Antwerp; hence his influence on Niclaes. He was regarded as a great heretic. At Cambridge he had been influenced by Erasmus's Latin translation of the New Testament, and later as a schoolmaster and chaplain to a wealthy Cotswold landowner at Little Sodbury he followed Luther's challenge to the Church with great interest and preached to the neighbouring villages. In 1523, a year after Luther's translation of the New Testament into German, he went to London and became chaplain in the house of a wealthy draper, who helped him visit Hamburg, Germany. Luther had been declared a heretic in England and his books had been burnt at St Paul's Cross. Tyndale went straight to Luther in Wittenberg with another Englishman, Roye, and translated his New Testament into English. Printing began in Cologne. News of the translation leaked when a printer boasted to a priest named Dobneck that England would soon be Lutheran in spite of the King and Cardinal. Printing of the translation was completed, and a report was sent to Henry VIII and Wolsey. The two Englishmen escaped by boat up river to Worms, and copies of the unfinished quarto edition of 1525 were sent to England. Another octavo edition was printed at Worms.

Unauthorized translations of the Bible were subject to punishment, and, unable to return to England, Tyndale went to Marburg and published two polemical and provocative works. Sir Thomas More refuted them, and Tyndale wrote a reply. He then translated the Old Testament, and it was at this time that he was struck by the parallels between the Israelites and the British. Thomas Cromwell tried to persuade him to return to England, offering a safe-conduct. Tyndale refused and Henry VIII angrily denounced him as an "arch-heretic." In the Prologue to his Book of Jonah, Tyndale called on the English to repent, just as Jonah had called on the Ninevites to repent.

In 1535 More was beheaded and the atmosphere in England changed following Henry VIII's marriage to Anne Boleyn. Four reprints of Tyndale's idiomatic translation of the New Testament into English were sent to England. He was now living in Antwerp, and a false friend, Henry Philips, invited him to dinner and had him arrested by officers from Brussels. He was burned at the stake 135 days later in October 1536. His last words (according to Foxe) were, "Lord, open the King of England's eyes." Seven years later an English Bible was in every parish church in England. Then Tyndale was a hero among the Family of God.[2]

Niclaes

James I believed that Hendrik Niclaes's Family of God was the source of Puritanism. Niclaes was a Dutch merchant who operated in Emden, East Friesland between 1540 and 1560. He welcomed all religious believers into his universalist family – all "lovers of truth, of what nation and religion soever they be, Christian, Jews, Mahomites, or Turks, and heathen" – but all were within the body of Christ. He had taken over the Hermeticist doctrine and believed that every member of his Family of Love became a Son of God. Niclaes's largest following was in England, where Elizabeth I banned the Familists in 1580.

The Rise of Puritanism

The brief reign of the boy-king, Edward VI, which ended with his death in 1553, was spectacular for its iconoclasm. The Protestant Reformers sought to destroy the holy statues and pictures of a thousand years of devotional life, and Edward was spoken of in terms of another boy-king, Josiah of Judah, who purged his land of idols. Henry VIII had seen himself as both David and Solomon; his son also looked to Israel and Judah, and besides seeing himself as Josiah the idol-smasher and Hezekiah (who was saved from besieging Assyrian armies by divine intervention), saw himself as Solomon, the Temple-builder of godly religion.[3]

Elizabeth's Settlement of 1559 allowed Protestant clergy to wear what they chose when leading worship. Many preachers did away with formal clothes and anything that smacked of the Catholic Mass. In 1564 Elizabeth ordered the Archbishop of Canterbury, Matthew Parker, to enforce uniformity in the liturgy, and reluctantly he stipulated a formal dress code. Those who refused to wear it were scornfully described as "Puritans" or "precisians" for refusing to submit to the supremacy of the Queen.

In the 1570s the Puritan Thomas Cartwright turned against the "Popery" of the bishops and proposed Presbyterianism (government by local councils of clergy and laity); in this he was strenuously opposed by John Whitgift, who defended bishops. Indeed, most Puritans supported bishops in some form, but a group of Separatists broke away from the Church of England parish system; they set up new congregations covenanted with God and put Puritan thinking about services into practice.

The Puritan leaders did not become Separatists but set up

"presbyterianism in episcopacy." They held public meetings (called "prophesyings") of clergy and laity to teach the Bible. In 1576 the Queen ordered the new Archbishop of Canterbury to suppress these meetings as they had become cause for action and represented a political threat. Archbishop Grindal refused. The Queen suspended his right to act. Meetings continued. When Grindal died in 1583 his successor Archbishop Whitgift closed the meetings and prosecuted the leading Puritans.

Moderate Puritanism was now finished, and with no prospect of forcing a reform of the Church under Elizabeth, Puritans dispersed into groups and turned to preaching and pamphleteering. Some practised non-separatist congregationalism. Others openly subverted the Church of England.

In the 1590s Puritanism was not a theological movement. It had no original ideas in theology or divinity; indeed, it borrowed ideas from Zwingli and Calvin. What distinguished it from other branches of Protestantism was its moral consciousness, its high respect for the individual conscience, its opposition to all forms of selfishness (including greed) and its championship of the clergy. Puritans took the Bible literally and aimed for simplicity and plainness in all things.

Shakespeare caught the Puritan spirit in Malvolio, who was opposed to the Merrie Englander Sir Toby Belch. Since Tyndale the Puritan spirit had been closely identified with Israel, and very early on Shakespeare made a link we shall be hearing more of, between Puritanism and orthodox Judaism. His Shylock in *The Merchant of Venice* is a Puritan Jew who is out of touch with the true spirit of the Kabbalah (grace, mercy and beauty for all mankind, including Christians) and who adheres to the letter of the law (as he would have been instructed to do by the *Talmud* and Kabbalistic *Zohar*) to the exclusion of justice.

The Templars (see Appendices B, Appendix 7) controlled the Stuart dynasty in Scotland, and it was as a Templar that King James I came to London in 1603. James perpetuated the idea that England was Israel. He said that the Lord had made him "King over Israel," and on his way to London to be crowned declared that he was going to the Promised Land. James practised religious tolerance and so fell foul of the uncompromising Puritans, who had at first been pleased to have a Calvinist king. The Gunpowder Plot (1605) was a Puritan ruse devised by Robert Cecil to whip up anti-Catholic feeling and create the impression that the Church of England was too lenient on Catholicism and its treasonous dealings.[4]

The English middle classes hated the ruling class for its moral turpitude. The English lady Mrs Lucy Hutchinson gives us a feeling for the general disgust in her *Memoirs*: "The court of the King (James I) was a nursery of lust and intemperance....The nobility of the land was utterly debased....Every great house in the country soon became a sty of uncleanness."[5] When such feelings and attitudes and tensions were on everyone's tongue, then a revolution was gathering. Even before Charles I came to the throne, there were proclamations against "seditious and Puritan books" and "libels and dangerous writings" which criticized the ruling class.

Bacon

The English Revolution formed itself round the Utopian millennial conception of Francis Bacon, who interpreted Tyndale's vision. He believed that God's chosen people were no longer the Israelites but the English, and that the Temple of Solomon should be rebuilt by English Israelites.[6] This view of Bacon's linked with Tyndale's identifying of the English as latter-day Israelites, the Priory of Sion's – and the Templars' – focus on the Temple of Solomon in Jerusalem, and Sion's championing of David's throne in Jerusalem, which was held by the Merovingian Kings of Jerusalem. Besides being the occult interpreter of Tyndale, Bacon has long been thought to have inspired the creation of Rosicrucianism, which arrived quite suddenly on the European scene. The Puritan Revolution, (as distinct from Puritanism) began with the Rosicrucians, whose first appearance seemed dramatic.

THE ROSICRUCIAN REVOLUTION

There are claims that the origins of Rosicrucianism,[7] which we shall see can be regarded as an attempted and unsuccessful revolution, are to be found in Hermeticism, and that it was first founded in the 15th century BC by Thothmes III – the name meaning "born of Thoth" – the ibis-headed god of wisdom who was equivalent to Hermes, and that the three Magi who were present at Jesus's birth were initiates of the Order. Charlemagne may have founded a Rosicrucian lodge in Toulouse in the 9th century. As we saw on p38, the Priory of Sion's Grand Master Jean de Gisors is credited with founding the Rose-Croix by taking a red cross as his emblem before 1220 (see Appendices B, Appendix 7). It is thus possible that as has been claimed past Grand Masters of the Rosicrucian Order include Raymond VI, Count of Toulouse, which adds a new dimension to his conflict with the Church on behalf of the Cathars; Dante; Cornelius Agrippa, who wrote about the Templars; Paracelsus (a Swiss alchemist who died in 1541 and is sometimes regarded as the real founder of Rosicrucianism); John Dee; Bruno; and Bacon.

Bacon's Rosi Crosse Society

There are also claims that Bacon founded Rosicrucianism shortly after he founded Freemasonry. In 1579, when he was eighteen and there was as yet no lodge of Freemasons in England, Bacon saw the need for his studies to be secret and to have "sworn brothers-in-arms." There are hints (sometimes jests) in Gabriel Harvey's correspondence with Bacon at the latter's Freemasonry.

The Two Pillars of Freemasonry.
From Whitney's Choice of Emblems,

In 1586 Bacon published Whitney's *Choice of Emblems*, and on page 53 stand the Two Pillars of Masonry with a "SoW" (Sun or Son of Wisdom) pointing at a favourite motto of Bacon's that hangs between the pillars, "*Plus Ultra*": "There is more beyond." At a very early age Bacon had been head of the Order of the Knights of the Helmet, which promoted the advancement of learning. Learning was symbolized by the goddess known variously as Minerva, Pallas, Pallas Athena, Athena and Athene, who wore a helmet (which bestowed invisibility), carried a spear and had a serpent at her feet. To signify their vow of invisibility the Knights each had to kiss the helmet. By 1586, when he was 25, the Order of the Knights of the Helmet had spawned Bacon's English Order, Fra Rosi Crosse Society, which became a degree in the Knights of the Helmet. Judging from his *New Atlantis*, Bacon had plans to create other orders besides these two, notably the Sons of Solomon or Society of Solomon's House.[8]

Alfred Dodd in *Francis Bacon's Personal Life-Story* describes how Bacon's Rosi-Crosse Society came out of the new Freemasonry he was creating. While on the Continent – he went to France in 1576-9 as a member of the English Ambassador's suite – Bacon outlined the Freemasonic movement and what is now known as the Rosicrucian Fraternity. He and a few Continental thinkers inaugurated this movement. It was a reorganization of the old Knights Templar Order, whose nine-degree ceremonial it took over. The new "Rosicrucian College" was to be established as an inner rite to the Freemasonic Brotherhood he planned to establish in England. No one could become a member of a Continental Rosicrucian College unless he was first a Master Mason.

On his second visit to the Continent some time between 1580 and 1582, he was able to report progress. Freemasonry was now established in England and the Lodge System could be transplanted to France and Germany. Bacon now wrote a series of pamphlets to spread the tenets and principles of Rosicrucianism and Freemasonry, two Orders that shared the same ideal. These explained that ethics had taken the place of creeds; philanthropic acts of goodness the place of credulous belief;

straight conduct the place of hypocrisy and deceit; and brotherly love the place of the hatred that was dividing the Church. On this view, he took with him to the Continent the first of the Rosicrucian Manifestos. Before long it was secretly circulated in England and on the Continent. More Manifestos appeared. Eventually the Manifestos were published anonymously in Germany. The Rosicrucian Manifestos were founded on Bacon's principles which he called *"Philanthropia."*[9]

Frederick V, Elizabeth Stuart and the Palatinate

The Rosicrucians were invisible, operating secretly and under cover, until 1613 when the new young ruler of the Palatinate married into the English royal family.

The Marriage of the Elector Palatine and the Princess Elizabeth

The anonymous Rosicrucians swiftly gathered round Frederick V, Elector Palatine of the Rhine,[10] a Calvinist and nephew of the French Protestant leader Henri de la Tour d'Auvergne, who had links with the Priory of Sion. On February 14, 1613 Frederick (who had succeeded his father in 1610 as a 14-year-old boy) married the daughter of James I of England, Elizabeth Stuart in the Royal Chapel at Whitehall, London. Wedding prints showed sun-like rays from the Divine Name in Hebrew (the Tetragrammaton) falling round Frederick and Elizabeth. There were performances of Shakespeare's *Othello* and *The Tempest* to celebrate the wedding. The Earl of Southampton, Shakespeare's patron, was probably present. According to Chamberlain, Sir Francis Bacon was the chief contriver of the masque of Gray's Inn, *The Marriage of the Thames and the Rhine.* In June Elizabeth travelled to Heidelberg in the Palatinate, a land-locked country surrounded by the Spanish Netherlands, Lorraine, Württemberg and the various German states, south-west of modern Frankfurt.

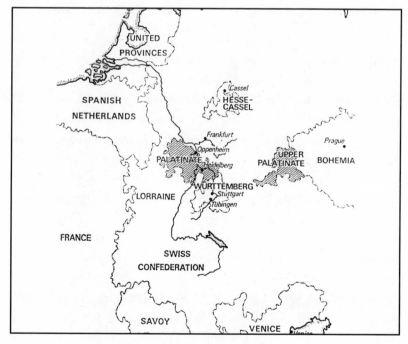

Map showing the position of the Palatinate in the early seventeenth century

It seems that she was escorted by the Earl of Southampton, and soon afterwards built a replica of the Globe theatre in her wing of Heidelberg castle. (It can be visited today; it is possible to walk round the top and look down, though the inside of the "well" is now ruined.)

Frederick V, King of Bohemia

Elizabeth, Queen of Bohemia

Both bride and groom were 17, and the marriage had ancestral links to Marie de Guise whose two marriages brought together the Houses of Lorraine and Stuart. Elizabeth knew Bacon in England and was an avid reader of his works, so it was only natural that he should have composed one of the entertainments for her wedding. Of this marriage, Frances Yates wrote that a culture was forming in the Palatinate which came out of the Renaissance but with more recent trends added, "a culture which may be defined by the adjective 'Rosicrucian'." The movement round Frederick, Elector Palatine was an attempt to give politico-religious expression to the ideal of Hermetic reform. There was now a Rosicrucian state with a court at Heidelberg.[11]

Andreae

In 1614 two books appeared which caused a sensation in Europe: *Fama Fraternitatis* and *Confessio*, both attributed to Johann Valentin Andreae (or Andrea, or even Andreas). These two books were the first so-called "Rosicrucian Manifestos," and they described the travels of the German Christian Rosenkreutz who, it was claimed, was born in 1378 and died in 1484 at the age of 106, having studied the Kabbalah in the east. In 1616 a third Rosicrucian Manifesto appeared, *The Chemical Wedding of Christian Rosenkreutz*, which was steeped in Hermetic ideas and eventually proved an inspiration for Goethe's *Faust*. (Published anonymously, its authorship was later acknowledged by Andreae.)

Andreae was born in Württemberg, the Lutheran state that adjoined the Palatinate. His grandfather was a well-known Lutheran theologian, who was dubbed "the Luther of Württemberg." Andreae himself became a Lutheran pastor, but maintained his interest in Calvinism. In 1601, at the age of 15, his mother took him to Tübingen so that he could study at the university of Württemberg. As a student he wrote two comedies and an early version of *Chemical Wedding*, which was rewritten before 1616 to include

Johann Valentin Andreae

references to Heidelberg and Frederick V, King of the Palatinate. Frederick I, the Duke of Württemberg, was an Anglophile who had visited England several times. John Dee had been in Bohemia in the 1580s, and his Kabbalistic influence may have reached Andreae through the Duke of Württemberg's court or those around the Elector Palatine. As early as 1610 Andreae travelled across Europe and was rumoured to be a member of a secret society linked with Hermeticism. (This may have been the Priory of Sion.)

The Rosicrucian Manifestos seem to have emanated from movements round Frederick. The *Chemical Wedding of Christian Rosenkreutz* of 1616 contains references to the Elector Palatine and his court at Heidelberg, to the first two Rosicrucian Manifestos and to Frederick's wedding. In fact, Andreae's rewritten version of his *Chemical Wedding* contains details that model the Royal Wedding to which Rosenkreutz is invited on the wedding of Frederick V and Elizabeth, and the castle in the *Chemical Wedding* on the Heidelberg castle whose gardens (which contained mazes) were full of the works of Salomon de Caus (lions and lion fountains). Frederick had made gardens for his wife by cutting terraces in the steep cliffs below the castle, planting orange and mulberry trees and creating waterfalls. Hopes were pinned on Frederick that he would initiate the reform which the *Fama* and *Confessio* heralded, and there was a brief Hermetic golden age inspired by the Rosicrucian movement.

Fludd

The English physician Robert Fludd, the son of the paymaster to Elizabeth I's forces in France and the Low Countries, an Oxford graduate who had travelled in Europe and was steeped in Hermetic philosophy, was involved in the first appearance in the public arena in 1614 of the Order of the Rose-Croix. In 1617 he wrote a treatise in defence of the Rose-Croix *Tractatus Apologeticus*, and it was clear he had derived many of his ideas from the Jewish Kabbalah. He was the author of *Philosophia Mosaica* (*The Philosophy of Moses*), the title of which suggests a strong Kabbalistic interest. He may have been influenced by the Familists. He taught that Heaven can be attained on earth: "The Rosicrucians call one another brethren because they are 'Sons of God'." Fludd was now identified as the main interpreter of Rosicrucianism in England, where the new philosophy was less well known than on the Continent. He declared his support for Rosicrucianism by announcing that the "highest good" was "the Magia, Cabala and Alchymia of the Brothers of the Rosy Cross."

The Palatinate, a Rosicrucian kingdom that inspired the Invisible College and emphasized invisibility as a Rosicrucian way of life, was in fact responsible for publishing the major Rosicrucian works. Robert Fludd's *magnum opus* was published in the Palatinate by Johann Theodore De Bry at Oppenheim during the reign of Frederick V. The three volumes of *Utriusque Cosmi Historia* or *History of the Macrocosm and the Microcosm* came out in rapid succession in 1617, 1618, and 1619, during Frederick's reign, with the first volume dedicated to James I. The three vast books came out so rapidly that it was clear that there was a policy to publish quickly all material that might be helpful to the Palatinate's Rosicrucian movement. Fludd's mission was to bring Renaissance philosophy up to date – the Renaissance "Magia and Cabala," Ficino's Hermetic texts, Pico della Mirandola, Paracelsist alchemy and Dee, a tradition from which much of his material was taken. Furthermore his plan for the reform of the sciences, stated in the three volumes, recalled Bacon's *The Advancement of Learning*.

We can only guess at the frequency of Fludd's visits to the Palatinate. De Bry's father had many connections in England, and there were frequent messengers between London and the Palatinate as James I kept in touch with his daughter Elizabeth Stuart. These messengers provided a postal service for Fludd and De Bry to keep in touch. The fact that Fludd was so close to Janus Gruter, librarian at the Palatinate library at Heidelberg (and a close personal friend of Andreae), suggests that Fludd (and indeed Andreae) made visits to Heidelberg to see his publisher and visit the library.

A friend of Robert Fludd's, the German alchemist Michael Maier, who often visited England, wrote a treatise in defence of the Rose-Croix – *Apologia Compendiaria Fraternitatem de Rosea Croce* (1616, Brief Apology for the Fraternity of the Rosy Cross). His *Atalanta Fugiens* was published by De Bry in the Palatinate in 1618. Like the English Fludd, Maier, a Lutheran Bohemian from Prague, was a Paracelsian physician; he had been physician to Rudolf II in the Palatinate and was made a Count. He was also the Rosicrucian secretary, and actually ran the Order in the Palatinate.

Fludd must have met Andreae during his visits to their mutual friend Gruter in Heidelberg. Fludd was Grand Master of the Priory of

Sion from 1595 to 1637, after which Andreae succeeded him. They must have known each other for Andreae to succeed him. Both men found positions.

In 1602 Fludd became tutor to Charles, Duke of Guise, who in 1610 married Henriette-Catherine de Joyeuse whose possessions included Couiza near Rennes-le-Château, and Arques, the site of the tomb in Poussin's painting, both of which she eventually sold to the crown. In 1614 Andreae was ordained Deacon of a small town near Stuttgart and lived there until 1640, when he was appointed preacher, then chaplain, to the Duke of Brunswick. These positions gave the two men opportunities to meet on the Continent.

The accession of the Templar James I in 1603 had shocked the Order of the Priory of Sion, which had controlled English monarchs since Henry II. It had brought an end to a line of Sionist Tudors who wore the rose of Sion's Rose-Croix (which had allegedly been founded by de Gisors in 1220), and it meant they had lost the patch that had been theirs for 400 years.[12] The Grand Master during the time of this loss was of course Fludd, and it is likely that the Rosicrucian state surrounding James I's daughter Elizabeth was an attempt to win England back, the hope being that somehow, one day, Elizabeth would succeed her father to the English throne – and Frederick V would be her Sionist-Rosicrucian consort. That thought must have occurred to Bacon and the Earl of Southampton at the time of the wedding of Elizabeth Stuart, and may have been entangled in the appearance of the Rose-Croix in England in 1614, a year after the wedding.

Fludd was thought to have been helped in founding the Rose-Croix Order in England by Francis Bacon.[13] To what extent was Fludd managing the move of the Rose-Croix into the public arena on Bacon's behalf? As we have seen, it seems that Bacon had already founded a Rosi Crosse Society before Fludd started the Order or Fraternity of the Rose Cross in England. Paoli Rossi has shown that Bacon's work came out of the Hermetic tradition which in his time was embodied by Fludd, Grand Master of the Priory of Sion, and was according to the *Encyclopaedia of Freemasonry* "the immediate father of Freemasonry."[14]

Yates writes of the parallelism between the Rosicrucian and Baconian movements.[15]

Dodd credits Bacon with the founding of post-1614 Rosicrucianism, and indeed the writing of the Rosicrucian Manifestos. Many books have commented that both the Manifestos and the writings of Robert Fludd are Baconian. (Frances Yates, however, sees the hand of John Dee in the Manifestos.) Yates in *The Rosicrucian Enlightenment* states that until Bacon's *The Advancement of Learning* (1605) there is no evidence as to what Bacon himself may have thought about the Rosicrucian Manifestos.[16] All we can safely say is that there was undoubtedly a Rosicrucian movement between 1614 and 1617 which was associated with Bacon, who in his youth had studied Hermetic, Gnostic and Neoplatonist philosophy as well as the Kabbalah.

According to Manly P. Hall,[17] in *The Secret Teachings of All Ages*, the original programme of the Rosicrucian Fraternity was revolutionary and had three aims: (1) the abolition of all monarchical forms of government and their substitution by "the rulership of the philosophic elect"; (2) the reformation of science, philosophy, and ethics; and (3) the discovery of the Universal Medicine, or panacea, for all forms of disease.

These three aims were pursued in secrecy as the Rosicrucian organization was liable to be suppressed by dogmatic Christianity. The anti-monarchic aim of Rosicrucianism did not become generally known to Rosicrucians until after 1620, as we shall see; before then it was possible to be a monarchist *and* a Rosicrucian (as was probably true of Shakespeare). The second aim was Baconian, and covers the advancement of learning and the *great instauration* (the reorganization of the sciences to restore man to the mastery over nature that he lost with the Fall). The third aim involved alchemy and the search for the philosopher's stone, a universal panacea that would make possible eternal youth.

The Collapse of the Rosicrucian State

Frederick V's entanglement with Bohemia was his undoing. The

Bohemians had deposed Ferdinand II, an unpopular King who was bent on abrogating their political and religious liberties. In sympathy with the Counter-Reformation, Ferdinand reversed his predecessor's policy of tolerance and began to suppress the Bohemian churches. In Prague, where the rebels defied the Habsburg sovereign and declared that the crown of Bohemia was elective, two Catholic leaders were thrown out of a window. Following Rosicrucian exploitation of Ferdinand's intransigence, the Protestant Frederick was offered the crown of Bohemia in 1619. (Bohemia had been toured by the Protestant John Dee in the 1580s.) In September 1619 Frederick accepted the Bohemian crown and journeyed to Prague. Hussite clergy conducted the coronation of Frederick and Elizabeth in Prague cathedral. The Queen of Bohemia was now English.

A Catholic educated by Jesuits, Ferdinand had resisted. The decree that deposed him was dated August 16, 1619, and he was chosen Emperor of Germany on August 18. He was backed by the mighty Habsburg powers and had cast his vote as king of Bohemia in the imperial election. Of the seven Electors, three were Catholic and three Protestant. With his casting vote going to himself, he was regarded as Emperor by all Catholics, but not by the Protestants and Bohemians. So began the destructive Thirty Years War in Germany (1618-48) between Catholics and Protestants, which further split Christendom.

Frederick only survived two years as King of Bohemia. Ferdinand II turned on his former kingdom and with the aid of the Duke of Bavaria defeated Frederick at the battle of the White Mountain outside Prague in November 1620. Bohemia was incorporated into the Habsburg lands, while Spanish Catholic forces under General Spinola arrived in the Palatinate. Heidelberg was filled with Catholic troops, and there were executions and purges.

King James I chose to desert his daughter Elizabeth rather than incur Habsburg anger, for he was hoping to obtain a large dowry through a Spanish marriage for the Prince of Wales. His aim was to avoid war with the Habsburg powers – his greatest fear – by balancing the marriage of his daughter to a German Protestant prince with the marriage of his son to a Spanish Catholic princess.

We can see it from James's point of view. His son-in-law was trying to involve him in an anti-Habsburg crusade he opposed and a Rosicrucian philosophy he was uncomfortable with. James was a Templar; Frederick – like Fludd – was Sionist-Rosicrucian. (Fludd had dedicated the first volume of *History of the Macrocosm and the Microcosm* (1617) to the King on the assumption that James would be interested in a book published in his son-in-law's kingdom. Fludd was one of the scholars who translated the King James Bible. As Grand Master of Sion his role in the translation may explain why "Zion" appears with the French spelling of "Sion.") The King, who found the whole situation embarrassing and distasteful, wanted to distance himself from Sionist Rosicrucianism. What had happened amounted to a disastrous attempt by Rosicrucians to seize the Bohemian crown and expand the Rosicrucian cause overtly and visibly. Now Rosicrucianism would have to be expanded by stealth.

James had, however, asked the Dutch to defend his daughter's rights and consented to allow Count Dohna to raise a body of volunteers in England to defend the Palatinate. Count Dohna offered the command to Sir Horace Vere (Edward de Vere's cousin, arguably Horatio in *Hamlet*), who since his brother Francis's death was the ablest English soldier. Vere took his leave of the King in July 1620. He had a tiny force of some 2,000 men which the German princes supplemented with 4,000 horse and 6,000 foot. Spinola by contrast had 24,000 men, and Vere was hugely outnumbered at the battle of the White Mountain. After the Protestant defeat James would not allow his daughter to come back to England for fear of offending the Habsburgs. A portrait of James painted about this time shows him sitting beneath a decorative rose, which may suggest his support for his Rosicrucian daughter as well as his continuation of the Tudor tradition.

All through 1621 the English protected the last three Palatinate strongholds, but they were fighting a losing battle. In June 1622 Frederick left Manheim, never to return. Vere was besieged at Manheim and eventually returned to England in January 1624, when he was received by King James, who was so grateful that he forgot to cover his bare head when greeting him.

Frederick and Elizabeth were driven into exile in Holland, and arrived at The Hague in 1622. From there the Rosicrucian couple looked with anger across the sea towards England, where Elizabeth's father would only send financial help. Bacon had disagreed with James's policy and had urged support for Frederick, but he was cautious, having seen how the King had shunned Dee (whereas Elizabeth had asked him to explain his *Monas Hieroglyphica* to her).

To what extent was Andreae attempting a Rosicrucian revolution in the Palatinate? Did Andreae intend to create a Rosicrucian monarchy that could one day replace the Templar James I with his Sionist Rosicrucian daughter Elizabeth? Quite possibly. Arguably Bacon's idea, Rosicrucianism was given intellectual expression by Andreae himself, Fludd and Maier, and political expression by Frederick V. The Rosicrucian state collapsed before physical consolidation could take place, making the revolution (if it was intended to be a revolution) abortive. We cannot fully answer the question about Andreae's intentions without knowing the extent of Bacon's involvement, but the three Manifestos for which Andreae took public credit clearly created a suddenly transformed climate that can be regarded as a revolution.

The Rosicrucians Go Underground

The expulsion of Frederick led some to predict that 1620 would prove to be the end of the Rosicrucian movement. In fact the Rosicrucians went underground, readopting their vow of invisibility. In 1623 in Paris, the Brothers of the Rose Cross announced on a placard: "We, being deputies of the principal College of the Brothers of the Rose Cross, are making a visible and invisible stay in this city through the Grace of the Most High, towards whom turn the hearts of the Just. We show and teach without books or marks how to speak all languages of the countries where we wish to be, and draw men from error and death." An anonymous work published in 1623, titled *Horrible Pacts made between the Devil and the Pretended Invisible Ones* said: "We deputies of the College of the Rose Cross, give notice to all those who wish to enter our Society and Congregation, that we will teach them the most perfect knowledge of the Most High, in the name of whom we are today holding an assembly, and we will make them from visible, invisible, and from invisible, visible."[18]

The Invisible Colleges had now announced themselves as such. It seems that many of the Brothers were readers of the false magical, Hermetic Kabbalah, for increasingly devil-worship and witchcraft came to be associated with the Invisible Ones by their detractors. Michael Maier was still the secretary in 1623, but by now there were said to be 36 Invisible Ones, and inn-keepers hung roses in their taverns to indicate that anything said there should be kept secret.

In 1623 the suppression of Bohemia and the Palatinate was complete, and, against the background of the Thirty Years War, the Catholic Counter-Reformation and Habsburg power, a campaign began in France to suppress Rosicrucian publications, manifestos, placards – everything. Displaced Europeans fleeing the Catholic Inquisition began to flow from Europe to England (the native country of Elizabeth Stuart, ex-Queen of the Palatinate).

Also against this background of the Thirty Years War between Catholic Spain and the German princes/Palatinate, the publication of the *First Folio of Shakespeare's Works* took place in 1623. It was sponsored by a son-in-law of the 17th Earl of Oxford, the Earl of Montgomery, and his brother, the Earl of Pembroke (who had been engaged to another of Oxford's daughters). They were backed by a group of Protestant nobles including the Earl of Southampton (Shakespeare's patron). This group opposed James I's proposal that his heir Prince Charles should marry the Infanta, daughter of Philip III of Spain. They were probably in touch with James's recently deposed daughter Elizabeth Stuart, who Rosicrucians hoped would succeed James. The *First Folio* provides an astonishing defence of English sovereignty, championing English kingship (for instance through Hamlet who is opposed by the imperialist "cutpurse of the empire," William Cecil/Polonius), and it seems that the publication may have been linked to the exile of Frederick V and Elizabeth in The Hague. Sir Horace Vere, who had led James I's force to the Palatinate and was in charge of the Palatinate forces at Manheim before Frederick left the town, presumably discussed Shakespeare's works with Frederick. Two of Shakespeare's plays had been performed at Frederick's wedding, and as we have seen his wife had built a replica of the Globe theatre in Heidelberg castle. Shakespeare's plays were performed there, and it is not impossible that the Earl of Southampton brought manuscripts of the plays for the actors to study in 1613, and lodged them in the castle library, where they may have remained until Frederick was driven into exile. (A hunt for Shakespeare's missing manuscripts should begin in castle archives around Heidelberg and The Hague, where Elizabeth Stuart lived in exile.) Sir Horace may even have informed him that Shakespeare was an early pro-monarchist Rosicrucian who had been linked with Bacon's Rosi Crosse Society and who was in fact his relative Edward de Vere, the 17th Earl of Oxford. (It is thought by some that Horace – or Horatio – Vere was the model for Horatio in *Hamlet*, who is urged by the hero in the final scene to "report [his] cause aright to the unsatisfied.")

Frederick and Elizabeth wanted to urge James not to ally with their enemy, Spain. Publication of the *First Folio* would send a clear message to James that he should take note of the line of English kings dealt with in the plays, and that English kings had always been nationalistic and should continue to assert their independence and sovereignty in the face of Spain. The Earl of Southampton may have acted as a go-between (as Sir Horace Vere was still fighting in Germany). (We have seen that the Earl of Southampton was probably present at the royal wedding of Frederick and Elizabeth in 1613; Prince Henry, Elizabeth's brother, wished him to escort Elizabeth to Heidelberg – she arrived on June 6 to be greeted by Frederick's mother and sister – and he is known to have been on the Continent at this time.)[19] Frederick hoped to recover his thrones, and was clearly a pro-monarchist Rosicrucian rather than a republican (having had two crowns himself). It was only later that Rosicrucianism became associated with republican opposition to monarchy.

Bacon's Rosicrucian Invisibility

Bacon was appointed Lord Chancellor in 1618 but fell from power in 1621 amidst accusations of bribery. After spending time in the Tower he passed the last five years of his life writing frantically. He lamented the passing of the lost Rosicrucian paradise of the Palatinate, which he described in his *The New Atlantis* (1624). The Palatinate, having been the most prosperous country in Germany before Frederick accepted the Bohemian crown, was now devastated by successive armies. The name Salomon, which appears in *The New Atlantis* ("the House of Salomon"), is linked to the Palatinate, for it was the name of the designer of the gardens at Heidelberg castle. Bacon was looking back on the Palatinate with nostalgia and set its Rosicrucian ideal in America, the first lasting settlement in which his cousin Bartholomew Gosnold had founded. Quite simply, New Atlantis = Palatinate + Gosnold's Jamestown Settlement. At the same time, the utopia at Bensalem, or "son of (Jeru)Salem," also suggests what England could become.

In *The New Atlantis* there is plenty of evidence that Bacon knew the Rosenkreutz story. A New Atlantis official hands the travellers a scroll "signed with a stamp of cherubim's wings, not spread, but hanging downwards, and by them a cross" (*The New Atlantis*). The Rosicrucian *Fama* was sealed at the end "Under the shadow of Jehovah's wings." The travellers in Bensalem offer payment to those who have cared for the sick, but this is declined. The Rosicrucian brothers always healed free of charge. An official at the Strangers' House in Bensalem wears a white turban "with a small red cross on top." This is a Rosicrucian emblem. Every twelve years three of the officials at Salomon's House go on a mission to the outside world, adopting the clothes and customs of the country they visit, to seek "for God's first creation, which was light." Yates observes that though the Rose Cross is not mentioned in *The New Atlantis*, "New Atlantis was governed by R. C. (Rosicrucian) Brothers, invisibly travelling as merchants of light."[20] The travellers, in other words, have reached a Rosicrucian utopia or paradise.

It has been suggested that as Bacon seems to have had such a hand in writing the Rosicrucian Manifestos, which were based on his principles, perhaps Andreae never lived and was a cover-name – or *nom-de-plume* – for Bacon. The evidence for such a view is in Robert Burton's *The Anatomy of Melancholy*, which first appeared in 1621 under the name Democritus Junior. Burton was close to Bacon. In this work a reference states that the founder of the Fraternity of R. C. (Rosi Crosse) was still alive (in 1621), and there is a short footnote, described by Manly Hall as being "of stupendous import": "Joh. Valent. Andreas, Lord Verulam." Bacon was Lord Verulam (St Albans), and the punctuation in this footnote suggests that Andreae was another name for Bacon.[21] In other words, it is conceivable that Andreae and Bacon were one and the same individual.

It has been suggested that Andreae permitted his name to be used as a pseudonym by Bacon, and that perhaps Bacon did not die in the Earl of Arundel's house near Highgate on April 9, 1626, but slipped off to the Continent at the age of 65 and assumed the identity of the German pastor Andreae, who was Grand Master of the Priory of Sion from 1637 to 1654, when Bacon would have been 93. In this case in 1640 it was Bacon – not Andreae – who became preacher and then chaplain to the Duke of Brunswick (who must have been in on the plot) and it was Bacon who taught Comenius, who became a Baconian. There is however no clinching evidence for this speculation. (It is interesting to note that Robert Fludd was descended on his mother's side from the ancient Somerset family of Andros. By making a feminine adjective from "Andros," one arrives at "Andrea." It is thus possible that Fludd, not Bacon, was Andreae.)

The likelihood is that Bacon's Rosicrucianism and Freemasonry were located at a particular building in London. If Bacon, who was known as the Solomon of his age, was the architect of Freemasonry, which focused on the rebuilding of the Temple of Solomon, then his first Lodge of Masons must have met in London and not Jerusalem. Masonic lore (for example, Mackey's *Revised Encyclopaedia of Freemasonry*, 1950 edition, p601) states that all early Masonic documents came "from the Lodge of the Holy Saint John of Jerusalem." *Of* Jerusalem, not *at* Jerusalem. Bacon's "Lodge of the Holy St John of

Jerusalem" (or Knights of the Helmet or Acception Masons) seems to have been located in London, in a building known as the Priory of St John of Jerusalem in Clerkenwell, which had a St John's Gate south entrance gatehouse. This had ceased to be a priory following Thomas Cromwell's dissolution, and was the seat of the Revels Office from at least 1571-1610.[22] John Lyly (the 17th Earl of Oxford's secretary in the 1580s) was in charge, and according to R. Warwick Bond's *The Complete Works of John Lyly*[23] his chief duty was to coach the actors for plays to be performed before the Queen. Rehearsals may have been held in the Great Hall of the Revels Office at the dissolved Priory. From October 1591 to 1599, the Priory was closed to the actors, probably for religious reasons. Referring to religious conflict on stage incurred official wrath on other theatres in 1589.[24]

Bacon knew both the Priory and Lyly well, and may have assisted Lyly in coaching the players, while Lyly may have acted as one of the first Masonic coaches. It seems that Bacon's early Lodge Masons met at the Priory before or soon after 1586 and were thrown out of the Priory some time before October 4, 1591 as the Queen was alarmed at the secret meetings of Bacon's Freemasonry. It is interesting that the date nearly coincides with his meeting (in July 1591) with the young Earl of Essex, the Queen's favourite who was still in disgrace with Elizabeth for marrying Sir Philip Sidney's widow without her permission. Essex became Bacon's patron from 1591 until 1601, when Bacon denounced Essex as a traitor and spearheaded the prosecution which led to his execution. Bacon seems to have returned to the Priory during the Rosicrucian years. From 1616 to 1625 he leased Islington's Canonbury Tower, and in Bacon's day there was an underground passage from the Tower in Islington to the gate of the Priory.[25]

The Priory seems to have been the focus for the invisibility Bacon demanded of all his followers. Along with all members of the Order of the Knights of the Helmet, Bacon had made a pledge to assume complete invisibility in promoting the advancement of learning, and therefore in his writing. He evidently found this hard to keep, and in 1597 he openly published the first of his essays under his own name.

This was during the time when the Order of the Knights of the Helmet and Goddess of Wisdom was turning away from Athena to the Freemasonic Grand Architect of the Universe, the God of Supreme Wisdom, who was celebrated in the Order of Acception Masonry, which did not require complete invisibility.[26] The design of Freemasonry was not completed until the publication of *The New Atlantis*, which provided its philosophical foundations. (This emerged from Sion's Rose-Croix, via Bacon's own Rosi Crosse Society and the preparations of Fludd.)

The invisibility assumed by Bacon's Knights of the Helmet, which Bacon observed until 1597, may have been responsible for Shakespeare's anonymity. If "Shake-speare" is a pseudonym, then perhaps Shakespeare was a member of the Rosi Crosse Society – hence his knowledge of Dee/Prospero – and took the idea of the spear from statues of Pallas Athena. The gold tip of the spear of her statue on the Acropolis in Athens was seen glinting in the sun far out to sea, reassuring Greek shipping that Athena guarded the waves (like Britannia who also wore a helmet and held the equivalent of a spear). If this is so, it is worth observing that the praise the 17th Earl of Oxford received from Gabriel Harvey in the presence of the Queen at Audley End, "Thy countenance shakes spears," possibly refers to Pallas Athena's spear known to the Knights of the Helmet and which Harvey knew about from his correspondence with Bacon. Oxford moved to Hackney, not far from the Priory and his relative Bacon, in 1593 and spent the last eleven years of his life there, perhaps continuing to meet ex-Knights of the Helmet and feeling himself bound by a pledge of invisibility that Bacon himself neglected. That pledge of invisibility would shortly have strong Rosicrucian connections.

Both Bacon and Shakespeare may have undergone the Rosicrucian "philosophic death." Manly Hall relates that the Rosicrucian supreme council was composed of a certain number of individuals who had died what is known as the "philosophic death." When an initiate entered the Order, he conveniently "died" in mysterious circumstances. In reality he changed his name and address, and a coffin filled with rocks or someone else's body was buried in his place. It is believed that this happened in the case of Bacon, who renounced all personal credit and permitted others to be regarded as the authors of documents he wrote or inspired.[27].

Bacon's brothers of New Atlantis and their great college were "unseen" to the outside world. The Rosicrucian Grand Master Michael Maier wrote in *Themis Aurea* that a resolution was passed at a meeting held in 1617 in which it was agreed that the Brotherhood of the Rose-Croix must maintain total secrecy for a hundred years (i.e. until 1717, the year Freemasonry was officially instituted). On October 31, 1617 the Convention of Seven at Magdeburg agreed to refer to its members during the coming hundred years as "The Invisibles." It renewed its oath to destroy the Christian Church and decreed that in 1717 it would transform the Rose-Croix into an association which could openly broadcast its propaganda.[28]

By now Rosicrucian and clandestine Freemasonry were intertwined, and yet both invisible. As De Quincey said, "Freemasonry is neither more nor less than Rosicrucianism as modified by those who transplanted it into England." Through Fludd and Andreae/Bacon Rosicrucianism and Freemasonry would have a huge influence in shaping the political direction of Puritanism.

Enough has been said to show that Invisible Rosicrucianism – "the Invisible Rosicrucian brotherhood" – flowed from the Palatinate of 1619 underground to those around Bacon's *The New Atlantis*, whence it would pass to the English Royal Society of 1660. The Invisibles had pledged to be invisible in their works during their lifetime, and to die quietly and be buried unostentatiously, without pomp. Either there was no gravestone, or the inscription was ambiguous. It now seems that the tomb at Arques and the burgers of Arcadia/Arques-adia peering at an inscription conveyed a Rosicrucian invisibility; the burgers were Rosicrucians, and the tomb and inscription represented the tomb of Christian Rosenkreutz, on which there was ambiguous lettering (*Et in Arcadia Ego*) which became the epitaph of an Invisible.

Arcadia then seems to have been a reference to the Palatinate as well as to France, and the lost Rosicrucian paradise there. The tomb suggests Rosicrucian invisibility in death. Across Europe, the Invisible Rosicrucians masked their activities by labelling their groups Christian Unions or societies, a network of secret societies operating under a Christian label. Many of the Rosicrucian exiles in England would likewise call themselves Puritans and throw in their lot with the Puritan Revolution.

In *The Occult Philosophy in the Elizabethan Age*, Frances Yates describes how Andreae's failed Rosicrucian revolution in the Palatinate passed into the Puritan revolution: "The Rosicrucian movement had failed on the continent. Refugees from that failure poured into Puritan England as the refuge from Antichrist. And the Puritan revolution took over some of the aspects of the projected Rosicrucian revolution. This is why there was a 'Puritan occultism,' why an English translation of the Rosicrucian Manifestos was published in Cromwellian England, and why the philosophy of John Dee was cultivated by earnest Parliamentarians."[29]

HARTLIB'S INVISIBLE ROSICRUCIAN SOCIETY

Many of the displaced Europeans arriving in England as refugees from religious armies in Germany were Andreae's personal associates: Samuel Hartlib (Andreae's friend) from occupied Prussia; John Amos Komensky or Comenius (with whom Andreae continued to correspond), a Moravian; Theodore Haak, a personal friend of Elizabeth Stuart; and Dr John Wilkins, Frederick V's chaplain. Having arrived in England, they were drawn into Masonic circles and guilds prepared by Fludd, which were now intermeshed with the Rose-Croix. All these Rosicrucians became Puritans. They met Robert Moray who was inducted into a lodge in 1641, as well as Elias Ashmole (a Mason from 1646) and the young Robert Boyle.

Hartlib and Andreae

Samuel Hartlib was the link between Andreae and Oliver Cromwell, and gave intellectual expression to Andreae's occult vision. He came from Elbing in Polish Prussia, and was at Cambridge when Milton was an undergraduate (1625-6), in the last year of Bacon's life. There is no evidence that Milton and Hartlib met then, but Hartlib knew everybody,[30] including Thomas Young, Joseph Mede, the Scottish educational reformer John Dury and Lady Ranelagh, whose aunt (sister of Edward King, Milton's Lycidas) Dury married.

After Cambridge Hartlib returned to Elbing and was at the centre of a mystic and philanthropic society. It was an "Antilia"; in other words, a model of Christian society based on Andreae's writings which combined piety and science. This "reformed" society was a preparation for a universal reformation. So Hartlib knew of Andreae's writings in 1627-8, and his focus on the new science combined ideas from Bacon and Andreae.

Andreae saw his Christian Unions forming a Rosicrucian "*societas Christiana,*" such as is described in two works he wrote in 1619 and 1620, *A Modell of a Christian Society* and *The Right Hand of Christian Love Offered.* These were thought to be lost, but copies turned up in Hartlib's papers.[31] John Hall translated them from the Latin in 1647 and addressed Hartlib: "Yourself (who were acquainted with some members of this Society in Germany) can witnesse tis more then an Idaea; and tis a great deal of pitty both that warre discontinued it when it was first instituted: and that it is not again revived." According to the *Modell:* "The Head of the Society is a German Prince, a man most illustrious for his piety, learning and integrity, who hath under him twelve Colleagues, his privy Counsellors, everyone eminent for some gift of God."

In 1642 Andreae wrote to the Duke of Brunswick, whose chaplain he had become, and hinted that he (the Duke of Brunswick) was the Prince. In his letter Andreae said that the place where the *Societas* started must soon become a seat of war because the group had already been broken up in the war of religion (i.e. the Thirty Years War). The book about the *Societas* had been burnt, and the members dispersed.[32]

The *Modell* says that nothing approaches nearer to God than unity, and that the avoidance of dissension between men is vital, which is why men gather into societies. The 12 colleagues of the German Prince represented different branches of study: religion, virtue, learning, divinity, censorship, philosophy, politics, history, economics, medicine, mathematics and philology. There was a strong scientific culture in Andreae's *Societas*. It was based on mathematics and emphasized technology and utility. An examination of the *Fama* indicates that the subjects of these 12 specialists are not unlike the subjects offered to the Rosicrucian Brothers in that work. Andreae enlarged on these themes in his *Christianopolis* (1619).

Between 1619 and 1620, then, Andreae had recommended science-led societies, the first of which he imagined under the leadership of the Duke of Brunswick. (A very early example arose in Elbing under Hartlib.) The Thirty Years War put an end to societies in Germany, though Andreae tried to restart the Rosicrucian *Societas* in Nuremberg in 1628. But, and this is the point, the *Societas* was continued in England by one of its chief enthusiasts, the Rosicrucian Hartlib, whose importance to Andreae can be grasped by recalling that he alone preserved Andreae's 1619 and 1620 works.

The countryside of Polish Prussia, Calvinist since the 16th century, was now fought over by mercenary armies, and the Catholics moved in and conquered Elbing. In 1628 Hartlib returned to England as a refugee, and collaborated with John Dury, who had met him at Elbing. They shared ideas on the need for all Protestant churches to be united, for universal education, for school reforms and teacher training. Hartlib started a school for refugees from Poland, Bohemia and the Palatinate in Chichester, then returned to London to organize philanthropic, educational and scientific projects that were linked with Invisible religious zeal.

Hartlib's Invisible Rosicrucian Group

As a close friend and correspondent of Andreae's, Hartlib was at the centre of a reforming group in the 1630s which produced many tracts and treatises. To be reformist in the 1630s was to oppose the King, and while discussing educational reform and universal education Hartlib was in fact talking of a new society. In this connection he was very closely associated with John Pym, the revolutionary leader of the opposition who "denied the very existence of sovereignty"[33] and gave political expression to the Puritan revolution, which would replace the existing society by revolutionary means. From 1621 to his death in 1643 Pym sat in every Parliament, and from 1629 he brought together the men who would lead the Parliamentary opposition to the King in the 1640s. Charles Webster describes in his exhaustive study of the period how, though without funds for himself, Hartlib tried to help others. Pym persuaded Hartlib to supply foreign intelligence and to provide technical advice that would prevent flooding in coalmines at Coventry. Pym corresponded from Fawsley in Northamptonshire and distributed Hartlib's news to other Puritan politicians from there. Pym made small payments to Hartlib, expected to be asked to help his public-spirited protégés, and took an active interest in promoting the visit of Comenius to England. Their correspondence shows that there was a warm relationship between Pym and Hartlib. Dury was probably right in describing Hartlib as "Mr Pym's intimate and familiar acquaintance."[34]

During the 1630s the chief patron of Hartlib's Invisible Rosicrucian group – and of Dury – was, according to Hugh Trevor-Roper,[35] Elizabeth Stuart, Queen of Bohemia, the royal figurehead of opposition. As Frederick V's widow, Elizabeth received refugees from the Palatinate and Bohemia and elsewhere in war-riven Europe, and recycled some of the funding she received from the English Parliament and Dutch government to Hartlib – perhaps at Andreae's request. So Hartlib's Andreaen *Societas* in London was funded by Elizabeth Stuart, and in return Hartlib took an interest in the restoration of Elizabeth's son Charles Louis to the Palatinate. In 1637 Charles Louis enrolled Hartlib as a minister of the Elector Palatine by a patent because of his service to exiles from the (Rosicrucian) Palatinate and his reputation among "great ones."[36] John Dury was also in touch with Elizabeth of

Bohemia and he too took an interest in the restoration of Charles Louis.

Hartlib's group came into its own in the early 1640s when it widened and became more influential. Hartlib's friend Comenius, who was also funded by Elizabeth of Bohemia, had studied at the University of Heidelberg in the Palatinate and had come under the influence of Millennialists who believed that men could achieve salvation on earth. He had read Bacon's works with enthusiasm and believed that the millennium could be attained with the aid of science. In Heidelberg he had met George Hartlib, Samuel's brother, and he may also have met Andreae there. In any event, matriculating twelve days after the arrival of Elizabeth Stuart in June 1613, he would have known about the Rosicrucian Manifestos. When the Spanish closed in on Heidelberg in 1618 he fled to Poland. Hartlib had sent him treatises supporting his reforming views and had translated many of Comenius's works including *Pansophiae prodromus* (*pansophia* representing universal knowledge).

With the blessing of Parliament Hartlib invited both Comenius and Dury to England in 1641. He gave Comenius his brief: to set up a college of social reform, to change society by education. This was to become the Invisible College, and in due course the Royal Society. The arrival of Comenius increased the influence of Hartlib's group, which included John Hall, Sir Cheney Culpeper – both of whom approached Milton through Hartlib – the absentee abroad Robert Boyle (Lady Ranelagh's brother), the mathematician John Pell, Benjamin Worsley, John Sadler, Henry Oldenburg and the Rosicrucian from the Palatinate Theodore Haak.

In 1641 Hartlib published *A Description of the Famous Kingdome of Macaria*, an outline of a Utopia based on his Antilia (his Andreaen society), which was now called Macaria. It was based on the fictions of Sir Thomas More and Bacon, and on the philosophy of Bacon and Comenius, and was addressed to the Long Parliament. It describes a Rosicrucian dreamland in which happiness reigns as in Paradise before the Fall. Hartlib was confident that this Parliament would "lay the corner Stone of the world's happinesse before the final recesse thereof."

It was a thrilling time for suddenly England seemed to be the land chosen by Jehovah, and dreams of a Utopian commonwealth looked capable of becoming a reality. Comenius and Dury were mentioned in Parliament as being philosophers who could help bring in future reforms. Comenius, whose earliest teacher may have been Andreae, believed Parliament had given him a mandate to build Bacon's New Atlantis in England.

Also in 1641 Dury published a work prophesying the advancement of learning, Protestant unity and the restoration of the Queen of Bohemia's son to the Palatinate. The hope was that England would escape the bloody civil war that had engulfed Germany, and the movement round Frederick V could happen all over again round his son. In 1641 England, the clock could be put back to the Palatinate of 1617.

In the same year Comenius wrote *The Way of Light*, which was full of hope for the future. He envisaged a time of universal enlightenment in which all would possess "an Art of Arts, a Science of Sciences, a Wisdom of Wisdom, a Light of Light." The "universal books" would make it possible for all mankind to learn and join in the advancement of learning. He also advocated a College, or a sacred society, devoted to the common welfare of mankind and held together by laws and rules. This was the college he had been called to England to found. In Comenius, Bacon's merchants of light became Rosicrucian Brothers.

Hartlib, Dury and Comenius, refugees in England to propagate universal reformation, advancement of learning and Utopian ideals, all tapped into the revival of Baconianism which was flourishing in the 1640s. In Hartlib's group, German Rosicrucians and English Baconians came together in a new attempt to introduce the advancement of learning. Frances Yates describes how Hartlib, Dury and Comenius brought the reformation movement to Parliamentarian England, which had returned to the old Elizabethan role of champion of Protestant Europe. Rosicrucian hopes had been raised by the Elector Palatine's marriage to an English princess, and now those hopes had failed Hartlib's group looked to an England restored to its Elizabethan role.[37]

Though Andreae and followers such as Comenius ceased to use the discredited term "Rosicrucian" during the Civil War, they still clung to their Utopian ideal of an enlightened philanthropic society in touch with occult agencies. Reforming Utopianism as proclaimed by Andreae's Christian societies was a great subterranean force of the Civil War years.[38]

However, the hopes of 1641 collapsed and realizing that civil war loomed in 1642, Comenius left England to work in Sweden and Dury left to work at The Hague with Elizabeth of Bohemia. Hartlib stayed in England and continued to plan a *Societas* – a Macarian society – which might be a model for the future. He now operated under the label "Puritan."

Hartlib and Milton

Hartlib first mentioned Milton in 1643 as a "great traveller,…full of projects and inventions." (Milton had had the idea for an epic poem during his Italian travels in 1638-9, but would not write it until the 1660s.) Milton was now a member of Hartlib's group, and sometimes hosted meetings at his house in London's Petty France. The poet seems to have had links with the Hermetic tradition through his neighbour in Buckinghamshire, Robert Fludd. He possessed a copy of the Hermetic writings, referred to "thrice-great Hermes" (Hermes Trismegistos, their 3rd-century-AD author) in an undergraduate poem and to John Dee twice. The daemons in "Il Pensoroso" and attendant spirit in "Comus" may be Hermetic, like the "spiritual creatures" who "walk the earth unseen" in *Paradise Lost* (4, 677-8). The names of some of Milton's angels came from Fludd, and it was Fludd who gave Satan the name of Lucifer before the Fall – which Milton followed. Like Fludd Milton used mathematical arguments against the Trinity and speculated as to whether light was created or eternal.

From these and many more instances we may conclude that Hartlib's group had an effect on Milton. If Milton was not already a Rosicrucian in 1643, then Hartlib Rosicrucianized him, for it is almost certain that Hartlib was politicizing and revolutionizing the members of his group. In 1644 he persuaded Milton to write his pamphlet *Of*

Education, which the poet dedicated to him.

There were many groups at this time – the Antinomians, the Socinians, the Ranters, the Diggers and the early Quakers – and all stressed the perfectibility of man on earth and the possibility of all men being Sons of God and therefore brothers. Milton is typical of this belief in perfectibility. He saw the Son as a perfect man. The Hermetic texts taught how man could serve the divine in himself, and through gnosis become like a god. Servetus shared this Hermeticist view, and like Servetus and his radical contemporaries, Milton derived the Sonship of all Christians through Fludd's Hermetic text more than through the Hermetic Familist tradition which echoed anti-Trinitarian Unitarianism and the Bible.[39] In *Paradise Lost* God the Father addresses first Christ and then the angels:

"Then thou thy regal sceptre shalt lay by,
For regal sceptre then no more shall need,
God shall be all in all. But all ye Gods...."

(3.339-41)

When men become gods, the monarchy of God will cease to be important. We will not need power or obedience when we are gods. Winstanley anointed believers and told them they had become Christs. Milton referred to the Lord's "anointed." To Milton man could be perfect on earth because there is unity based on sons in the Son. In his view, the Church and State would wither away.

Just as the Thirty Years War set back Rosicrucian hopes, so the English Civil War set back neo-Baconian/neo-Rosicrucian hopes. But now Hartlib was preparing a programme that would be implemented following the success of the revolution. He was anticipating the Protectorate. Dee's influence has been seen in Hartlib, but fundamentally Hartlib was giving intellectual expression to Andreae's occult vision which was a reinterpretation of Bacon's. If Andreae was the Marx of the Puritan revolution, Hartlib was the Trotsky.

THE RISE OF OLIVER CROMWELL

The rise of Oliver Cromwell,[40] implementer of the political and physical aspects of the Puritan revolution, was dramatic. He was born of Protestant parents in Huntingdon, near Cambridge, England in 1599. His father was an MP in Queen Elizabeth's Parliaments. He was descended from Thomas Cromwell, who dissolved the monasteries in the 1530s and gave Hinchingbrooke, a mansion in Huntingdon, eastern England, that had served as a nunnery, to his great grandfather. There King James visited his uncle Sir Oliver Cromwell on his progress to ascend the throne in 1603. It is said that Cromwell, aged four, bloodied the nose of the two-year-old Prince Charles Stuart (the future King Charles I).

The story that Oliver was of Jewish descent might have had its origin in Sir Oliver's second wife, Anne Hooftman, who was the Dutch widow of the Catholic Genoese Sir Horatio Palavacino (died 1600). In 1578 a loan Palavacino made to Dutch rebels to fight Spain was underwritten by Elizabeth I. Two step-children of Palavacino's first marriage married two of Anne Hooftman's own Cromwell children. It is not certain that the Palavacinos were Jews as they were practising Catholics, but it was rumoured that they were Marranos (Jews forced to become Roman Catholics).

Oliver Cromwell

Oliver was educated at Huntingdon grammar school and spent a year at Sidney Sussex College, Cambridge. Both his schoolmaster at school and his Master at Cambridge were (Kabbalistic) Calvinists; they taught Cromwell that God guided the Elect onto paths of righteousness. After he had been at Cambridge a year his father died and he was left to look after his widowed mother and sisters. This was in 1617, at a time when he was living a debauched life in the ale-houses of Huntingdon. To get him into more salubrious company his mother sent him to study at Lincoln's Inn, and in 1620 he married a London merchant's daughter Elizabeth, by whom he had nine children.

They lived in the freehold house in Huntingdon in which he had been born. In his twenties Cromwell became a Unitarian, and moved away from Calvinism into the deist outlook of Unitarianism which resembled Freemasonry and looked back to the Old Testament. It emphasized God (the "Lord") rather than Christ and it held that God is one person and not a Trinity.

According to Dillon, Unitarianism and Freemasonry were both elaborated by Faustus Socinus, the nephew of Laelius Socinus, who arrived in Venice when 21 and attended a conference of heretics at Vicenza in 1547, when the destruction of Christianity was resolved upon. The Republic of Venice seized and then strangled two of the main heretics, but Laelius escaped. Faustus inherited his uncle's anti-Trinitarianism, eventually settled in Poland, was influential in the founding of Unitarianism and founded the Socinian sect which affirms that Christ did not have a divine nature.

The Socinian aim was to destroy the Church, according to Dillon, and to raise another temple into which any enemy of orthodoxy (i.e. the Catholic Church of Rome) might enter freely, where all heterodox believers might be brothers – United Brethren, Polish Brothers, Moravian Brothers, Brother Masons, and finally Freemasons. Socinian disbelief in the divinity of Christ was fundamental to Freemasonry.

Dillon quotes Abbé Lefranc as believing that Cromwell was a Socinian, founded Freemasonry and invented the allegory of the deistic Temple of Solomon in which all creeds could worship. This Temple, which was destroyed by Christ (who overturned the tables in the Temple courtyard), was to be restored by Freemasonry after Christianity was obliterated.

Whether Cromwell was aware of such considerations at the time he became a Unitarian we do not know. In 1627 Hinchingbrooke was sold; the following year Cromwell was elected MP for Huntingdon. He was known as a fiery, uncouth Puritan who made Calvinist attacks on Bishops. (He spoke in Puritan terms as one would expect of a member of the heavily Puritan Independent Party.) Until the dissolution of Parliament in 1629 he had deep psychological problems – perhaps connected with his move from Calvinism to Unitarianism – but in that year at the age of almost thirty, he experienced a conversion. Later (in 1638) he described it to his cousin Mrs St John: "Oh, I lived in and loved darkness, and hated light; I was a chief, the chief of sinners....My soul is with the Congregation of the First-born....He giveth me to see light in His light."

It is from this point, in 1629, that he seems to have thought of himself as a Congregationalist. Many years later a friend who knew Cromwell at this time wrote: "Religion was thus 'laid into his soul with the hammer and fire'; it did not 'come in only by light into his understanding.'"[41]

After his conversion he felt he was one of God's Chosen – one of the few, the Elect – and he was now open to "the sudden providences in things." He felt he was a blind instrument in the hands of a higher power, that historical events were determined by God's will – "God's revolutions" – and that it was his task to discover the hidden purpose behind events, or "what the mind of God is in all the chain of Providence."

In 1631 the freehold house in Huntingdon was sold and Cromwell became a tenant of a farm in St Ives, five miles away. He was a country gentleman for most of the 1630s. There were bad harvests in 1631 and 1632, when he considered emigrating to America. When he did eventually make an attempt to emigrate, he was drawn by the Puritan New World across the seas.

The story is that in 1638 he embarked on a ship that was on the Thames ready to sail, accompanied by his relatives Arthur Haselrig and John Hampden. (Hampden had been sent to prison in 1637 for refusing to pay his 20-shilling Ship Tax. Both men would become opposition Parliamentary leaders.) They were due to sail with the New Providence Company, but at the last minute the Council of State refused to grant permission for them to leave and the three men had to return down the gangplank. Cromwell always felt that the Council's refusal to let him go was Providential. Ten years later the Council must have wished it had let him go. By the time of his intended departure Cromwell had inherited a property in Ely from his mother's brother, his uncle Sir Thomas, and he returned to live close to the wide open fens.

In 1640 Charles I called another Parliament, and Cromwell was elected MP for Cambridge. He found himself among fellow dissatisfied landowners led by John Pym. They were all aggrieved at Charles's taxation policy of imposing Ship Money on the likes of John Hampden and disillusioned by the corruption of the clergy. Pym organized a "Grand Remonstrance" in November 1641, challenging the King. The King responded by attempting to arrest five MPs for treason. (Samuel Hartlib was active behind the scenes at this time.)

A late document links Cromwell (via his cousin Oliver St John) with Hartlib and those campaigning between April and October 1640 for a new Parliament: "The true cause of the calling the Long Parliament thus: at the dissolution of the former Short Parliament the members both Lords and Commons had a great opinion that the king's affairs ere long would necessitate him to call them together again, therefore such as resided about London met together frequently and gave intelligence by Mr. Samuel Hartlib...to those in the country of affairs. Ere long, they gave a more general summons to come all up, who not only came themselves but brought up also such country gentlemen as they could confide in, amongst the rest Mr Oliver St John brought with him Mr Oliver Cromwell, the first public meeting this gentleman ever appeared at. They agreed to send down a petition to the King at York, subscribed by twenty Lords and above 40 Commons to pray him to call a parliament, that 2 Lords and 4 Commons of their number should carry it down....The names of the Commons I have forgotten but Cromwell I am sure was the last."[42]

Was Cromwell linked to Hartlib's Rosicrucian circle in 1640? Yes. Cromwell greatly respected Comenius, who arrived in England in 1641 amid considerable publicity, and Parliament welcomed Hartlib, who addressed his *Macaria* to it in 1641. Cromwell knew Hartlib from at least 1640-1, From at least 1641, and possibly from 1628, Hartlib had Cromwell's ear as a Puritan, whose philosophy was actually Rosicrucian. As Christopher Hill observes in *Milton and the English Revolution*, Milton shared his "revolutionary Protestant internationalism" with a number of men, including the poet Andrew Marvell and Oliver Cromwell.[43] Throughout his rise to power, Cromwell was surrounded by an Invisible College of foreign divines and philosophers, all of whom came into contact with Hartlib, whose essentially millenarian vision had a huge influence on the ideals and policies of the Protectorate.

So *was* Cromwell a Socinian? He surrounded himself with Rosicrucians – Rosicrucianism having begun in the 1610s as we have seen, during his formative student days – and Puritanism was clearly as much a spin for Rosicrucianism as for Socinianism, whether Freemasonry was invented by Bacon or Cromwell. Cromwell was strongly linked with Rosicrucian Freemasonry and frequented a Rosicrucian Masonic lodge called "Crown", which he could only have done if he were a Rosicrucian Mason himself. As we are about to see, it seems that Cromwell promised to rebuild Solomon's Temple within Freemasonry in exchange for financial support from Amsterdam Jews.

Menasseh and the Jews of Amsterdam

Menasseh ben Israel,[44] a Jewish rabbi, was also inspired by Bacon and Andreae and the 17th-century surfacing of invisible Rosicrucianism that passed into Puritanism and was taken up by Hartlib's group. Menasseh, alias Manoel Dias Soeiro, was born in Lisbon, a maritime centre for distant voyages, or in Madeira, into a family of Marranos, Spanish-Portuguese Jews who claimed to be Christian but privately practised Judaism. (We must note that the invisibility practised by the

Rosicrucians in their Christian Unions was actually replicating the approach of Marrano Jews who still practised their own religion under a different label.) Menasseh's father appeared at an *auto da fé* held by the Spanish Inquisition, and the family escaped across Europe to Amsterdam, where Jewish settlement was officially permitted.

The Netherlands had revolted against Philip II of Spain's Counter-Reformation religious policies (see ch 3). Protestantism had spread to the northern Netherlands – first Lutheranism, then Calvinism, which was always an international movement (like Catholicism). In 1567 Philip sent the Duke of Alva to restore order, and soon the entire Spanish Netherlands were in revolt. The Duke of Palma arrived and secured the southern Catholic provinces, which remained Spanish until 1713, but the now solidly Calvinist northern Provinces proclaimed their independence in 1581 under the hereditary rule of William of Orange. The northern provinces then became the Republic of the United Provinces and went on to become the greatest maritime nation in Europe, though their independence (as the United Provinces) was not recognized until 1648.

The United Provinces looked askance at Spain across the border, and welcomed as friends all enemies of its Catholic oppressor – including Jewish refugees from the Inquisition such as Menasseh's family. They arrived at a time when internationalist Calvinism was falling apart. The first and last international Calvinist Council, the Synod of Dort, held in 1618-19, assumed that the Calvinist churches of Scotland, England, Switzerland, the Netherlands, the Palatinate and France would help each other against the Catholics.[45] But following James I's refusal to intervene directly to save his Calvinist son-in-law and daughter from their common Spanish Catholic enemy in the Palatinate and the failure of England and the Netherlands to combine against Spain, Richelieu seized the (Calvinist) Huguenot territories in France while James was negotiating with Spain for his son Charles to marry the Infanta. As the Calvinist international spirit declined in the Republic of the United Provinces the Kabbalist tradition of the Jewish refugees came into its own.

In 1622 Menasseh, who had been a brilliant theological student, became the rabbi of a Portuguese Jewish congregation in Amsterdam. He was only 18. In 1626 he founded Amsterdam's first Hebrew printing press – he was only 22 – and during the next three decades published his works in Hebrew, Latin, Spanish and Portuguese. He was a Kabbalist and a Rosicrucian, very much in the tradition of Fludd and Andreae, but brought a Jewish emphasis to Rosicrucianism. Within the Republic of the United Provinces Amsterdam, where he lived, was in the county of Holland; so was The Hague, where Frederick and Elizabeth Stuart settled in exile and perpetuated the Rosicrucian court they had held in Heidelberg, living with Prince Maurice of Orange until he died in 1625.

The Rosicrucians of the county of Holland were linked to the Priory of Sion, whose Grand Master was then the English Rosicrucian Robert Fludd, and they were opposed to the Templars who had captured the English throne through James I. James had been succeeded in 1625 by Charles I, who had married a Catholic, Henrietta-Maria of France, sister of the French King Louis XIII, and who had the image of being a Catholic sympathizer. As we have seen, (p88) the Priory of Sion wanted to overthrow the Templar Stuart dynasty and return England to the Rose of Sion, as had happened when Sion restored Henry Tudor after two Yorkist kings.

After Frederick V's death in 1632 the Priory of Sion (Fludd and Andreae) bypassed Elizabeth Stuart as a contender for the English, Bohemian or Palatinate throne. She remained in exile for 40 years with her three children, Frederick Henry (who died in 1629 three years before her husband); Charles Louis (who was restored to the Palatinate in 1648 and ignored her pleas to return to Heidelberg); and Prince Rupert, who had been born in 1619 and would leave the Continent to fight in the English Civil War for his uncle Charles. (It must not be forgotten that Prince Rupert had come from the Rosicrucian background of the Palatinate. However he was probably too young to have absorbed much, and Elizabeth clearly saw him as an English prince rather than a Palatinate or Bohemian prince.) It seems evident from this that her allegiance reverted to the Templar Stuarts and it was no surprise when Charles II eventually allowed her to return to England in 1661.

From 1632 Menasseh pursued a rabbi's Kabbalist Rosicrucian way of life, ignoring the court of Elizabeth Stuart and publishing his writings, for instance his three-volume *Conciliador* (1632-51), which reconciled contradictory passages in the Bible and won him a reputation among both the Jewish and Christian communities of Amsterdam. He was friendly with the Dutch Hugo Grotius (born 1583), who in 1618 had been arrested by Prince Maurice and sentenced to life imprisonment for opposing his government. (Grotius had in the past called for tough action against the Spanish and Portuguese, and in 1604 had defended the seizure of a Portuguese ship, the *Santa Catarina*, by a Dutch admiral.) He escaped in 1621 to France. He returned when Prince Maurice died but had to flee Holland again. Menasseh was also friendly with Rembrandt, corresponded with Queen Christina of Sweden and taught Spinoza (who was born in 1632).

Menasseh Ben Israel

By 1642 Menasseh ben Israel was already prominent enough to have his portrait painted: it shows a squat and smiling face with wide eyes, hair combed forward and a pointed beard, wearing black garb with a wide white collar, looking for all the world like an English Puritan.

In 1642 Henrietta Maria, Charles I's queen, visited Amsterdam to bring her ten-year-old daughter Mary to her bridegroom William, son of the Prince of Orange. She expressed a desire to see Jews at prayer and on May 22, 1642 visited the synagogue on the Houtgracht. Menasseh delivered the official address of welcome and referred to her as "worthy consort of the Most August Charles, King of Great Britain, France and Ireland."[46] By 1647 Menasseh was known in England as the principal exponent of Jewish science – and of the idea that the Jews should return to England.

To understand how Menasseh came to campaign for the return of the Jews to England, how he might raise funds for Cromwell and how he came to visit Cromwell on behalf of all Jews, we need to understand what his Kabbalistic studies were telling him. The Kabbalah that Menasseh studied was the Kabbalah that had been corrupted by the Pharisees during the Babylonian exile (see Appendices B, Appendix 1). It had ceased to apply to the whole world and had become nationalistic, applying only to Jews.

From his Kabbalist studies Menasseh had come to believe that a Messiah would return to lead the Jews back to the Holy Land when their dispersal had been completed. This idea came from the prophecy of Moses in the book of *Deuteronomy* (28,64): "And the Lord shall scatter thee among all people, from one end of the earth even unto the other." To Jews the "end of the earth" suggested the Jewish term *Kezeh ha-Arez,* "the angle or limit of the earth," which Jews associated with England ("Angle-terre"). The Jews had to return to England for the dispersal to be completed and for their return to Palestine to be possible. The Messiah who would lead the Jews back to the Holy Land via England was the nationalistic Messiah of the Pharisees and the false Kabbalah.

Edward I's expulsion of the Jews in 1290 had been the culmination of a long, slow process in which the English authorities had systematically turned against the Jews. For centuries, there had been an outcry against Jewish moneylenders in England. Feeling against the Jews there was already high in 1190 when Crusaders in debt to Jewish moneylenders (Richard Malebysse and members of the Percy, Faulconbridge and Darrel families) attacked two Jewish households in York, causing Jewish refugees to seize the castle. When the sheriff brought armed forces to evict them 150 Jews, led by Rabbi Yomtob of Joigny, set fire to their possessions and the castle, and killed themselves. Next morning the besiegers hunted Jews and, promising clemency if they embraced Christianity, massacred all they could find.

In 1275 Jews had been forbidden to lend money for interest. Other measures had followed, and in 1278 Jews across the country had been arrested and house-by-house searches were made of their quarters in every city. Some 680 had been imprisoned in the Tower of London and many were hanged the following year. In 1290 English families in debt to Jewish moneylenders raised such an outcry throughout England that Edward I moved against the Jews. Edward I now decided that all his measures had failed and the banishment of the Jews was the only course left. The Jews were not now of primary importance to the Exchequer, and on July 18, 1290, by an act of the king in his Council, all Jews were ordered to leave England before the feast of All Saints (November 1). Any Jews found in England after that date would be put to death. All Jewish synagogues, cemeteries, houses and bonds became the property of the king. The news was greeted with joy by the population. Soon afterwards the Jews were expelled from France as well.

Menasseh campaigned for the return of the Jews to England, and Jewish merchants wanting to live openly in England welcomed his message.

The common agenda of Menasseh and Cromwell is revealed in Capt Ramsay's *The Nameless War*. He writes: "It is left to us to complete the revelation. To do so we must turn to such other works as the Jewish Encyclopaedia, Sombart's work, *The Jews and Modern Capitalism*, and others. From these we learn that Cromwell, the chief figure of the revolution, was in close contact with powerful Jew financiers in Holland; and was in fact paid large sums of money by Menasseh ben Israel; whilst Fernandez Carvajal, 'The Great Jew' as he was called, was the chief contractor of the New Model Army.

"In *The Jews in England* we read: '1643 brought a large contingent of Jews to England, their rallying point was the house of the Portuguese Ambassador de Souza, a *Marrano* (secret Jew). Prominent among them was Fernandez Carvajal, a great financier and army contractor.'"[47]

Carvajal and the New Model Army

Increasing disorder had led to the demand for a new army. Following Charles's attempt to arrest five MPs in January 1642, groups of Calvinist "operatives" roamed London. These were armed revolutionary groups, a militia of workers for insurrection some ten thousand strong, and they issued revolutionary pamphlets which contained the insurrectionary cry, "To your tents, O Israel!"[48] Shortly afterwards the King and his family left the Palace of Whitehall, and the five MPs were given a triumphal return to Westminster.

Cromwell now began to organize resistance and in July 1642 he obtained Commons permission for Cambridge to form companies to defend itself, and he enlisted a troop of cavalry at Huntingdon.

War broke out when the King raised his standard at Nottingham in August 1642. That October Cromwell was a Captain at the battle of Edgehill. In February 1643 he was appointed a Colonel and began to recruit a cavalry regiment. He served in the eastern counties, seeking to block the Yorkshire Royalists from penetrating south. In July 1643 he won the battle of Gainsborough in Lincolnshire. As a reward Cromwell was made Governor of the Isle of Ely and named one of four Colonels under Manchester, Commander in the eastern counties. He fought alongside Sir Thomas Fairfax at Wincely in Lincolnshire and besieged Newark in Nottinghamshire. He then persuaded the Commons to create a new army.

It was against this background that the *Marrano* de Souza, Portuguese Ambassador to England, met Don Antonio Fernandez de Carvajal. A French Jew from Rouen, Carvajal settled in England and gathered political intelligence for Cromwell. It was Carvajal's clerk, Moses Athias, thought to be a rabbi, who owned the secret synagogue visited by *Marranos* in Cree Church Lane, Leadenhall Street, London. Carvajal, a merchant known as "the Great Jew" was believed to import bullion worth £100,000 a year. He rode fine horses and collected armour. He lived in Leadenhall Street near the Royal Exchange as confirmed by a letter to him from Thurloe which has survived, addressed to *Monsieur Ferdinando Carnevall, Marchand Aupres de la Bourse*. "Carnevall" seems to have been an intelligence *nom-de-plume* he used. He lived with his wife Maria Fernandez Carvajal, who when widowed organized a petition to Charles II from her house to claim that Royalist Jews had supported King Charles in Holland.

What is being suggested is that Carvajal, who received bullion worth £100,000 a year, was the contractor of the New Model Army which Cromwell was organizing at the end of 1644 and the beginning of 1645. It is suggested that the money was collected by Menasseh ben Israel, who was acting on behalf of the Jews of Amsterdam. It is known that Carvajal enjoyed the Protector's friendship later on, although it is uncertain whether he had met Cromwell by 1643. Nevertheless it is known that in 1645 an informer denounced him for not attending a Protestant church – perhaps the authorities thought Carvajal was up to something and were trying to arraign him on some pretext. He was defended by leading Jewish merchants and the Lords quashed the proceedings against him. Was this with Cromwell's knowledge or at his instigation even?

Puritan philo-Semitism is well documented. The Christian Kabbalists had focused on the *Old Testament*, and the Bible-literalists were very interested in Israel and God's covenant with the people of New Israel, which they interpreted as the English. "To your tents, O Israel!", the cry of the revolutionary armed groups, reflects this, as does the psalm-singing of the Puritan troops. Cromwell himself was very interested in the way the Christian and Judaic religions overlapped – a Unitarian interest – and in how Kabbalism and Puritanism overlapped and merged in the Rose Croix (the rose representing Rosicrucian Kabbalism, the cross Puritan Christianity). Nevertheless there was more to the funding of the New Model Army than mere philo-Semitism.

The new army was to be under the control of the Earl of Manchester. In 1644 Cromwell was appointed Manchester's second-in-command with the rank of Lieutenant-General on a salary of five pounds a day. He attacked Lincoln, joined the Scots and Yorkshire Parliamentarians at the siege of York, and won the battle of Marston

Moor that gave the north to Parliament. When his army returned to eastern England Cromwell criticized Manchester for sluggishness, and laid his complaints before the Committee of Both Kingdoms. He withdrew his complaints but renewed them before the Commons after the defeat at Newbury. Manchester replied in the Lords, and there was a plan to impeach Cromwell.

In December 1644 Cromwell proposed that no member of the Commons or Lords should hold commands in the armed forces. The Commons accepted the proposal, which excluded Manchester as well as himself. Cromwell put forward Fairfax's name as commander of the new army, which was known as the New Model Army.

The facts about the organization and strength of the New Model Army must be examined. At the end of 1644 Cromwell was placed on two committees. One wrote a letter to the Scots proposing a friendly alliance between the Scottish and English Parliaments; the other committee was a subsidiary of the Committee of Both Kingdoms and was to make decisions regarding the reorganization of the Army. There were to be 10 regiments (some accounts say 11) of cavalry of 600 men each (i.e. 6,000 horse in all); 12 infantry regiments of 1,200 men in each (i.e. 14,400 foot in all); and a regiment of 1,000 dragoons. The bulk of the cavalry came from what had been the Earl of Manchester's army, which had been largely trained by Cromwell. 8,000 men had to be pressed to join the infantry, which was below strength when the campaign began. The total approaching 22,000 men was to be paid for by a levy of £6,000 a month (£72,000 a year) on all the districts under Parliamentary rule. On January 21, 1645 Sir Thomas Fairfax, on Cromwell's recommendation, was chosen Commander-in-Chief. Cromwell and Sir Henry Vane (who had become virtual leader of the Commons following Pym's death in 1643) counted votes for the Yeas, and Fairfax's nomination was supported by 101 votes to 69.

Ostensibly the New Model Army was being funded by a levy. In fact Cromwell was being promised additional funding, as much as he needed, to overthrow the King and permit the Jews to return to England. Parliament did not know about the additional funding, and nor did the King.

Cromwell then planned the new army, to which no second-in-command was appointed. In the summer of 1645, however, when the Civil War reached a climax, Fairfax urged that Cromwell should be his no. 2. Cromwell took the position and he and Fairfax won the battles of Naseby and Langport, destroying the Royalist armies.

The war was over and the army disbanded. The soldiers were disillusioned as they were now unemployed. Cromwell tried to ease their lot and proposed that they should fight in Ireland. In 1645-6, the revolutionary Levellers – called "Levellers" by their opponents because they wanted to "level estates" – emerged with a programme that was strictly political and economic. The Levellers were radical supporters of Parliament who were concerned with helping "the starving poor" and who appealed to owners of small properties. They demanded that sovereignty should be transferred to the Commons (without any remaining with the King or Lords). They demanded regular Parliaments with a redistribution of seats; decentralization of government to local communities; the reopening of enclosed land; and complete freedom of worship.

Boyle's Invisible College

During the brief peace that ensued, a Rosicrucian Invisible College was founded[49] which would become the seat of Sionist power and influence Cromwell. Robert Boyle was the son of the Earl of Cork, who had been one of Bacon's aides and who gave his son the education Bacon had had: Latin, French and European travel. Boyle was brought up as a Baconian, and his Eton Provost, Sir Henry Wotton, was linked with the Rosicrucian circle at Frederick's Palatinate. In 1639, aged twelve, Boyle went on a European tour and spent time among the Medici in Florence, where the descendants of Ficino's circle were still welcome, as was Galileo. He also studied demonology in Geneva. On returning to England in 1645 he immediately made contact with Andreae's friend, Samuel Hartlib. Hartlib seems to have been the "go-between" between Andreae (Grand Master of the Priory of Sion from 1637 to 1654), Cromwell and Boyle, who would himself become

Grand Master of the Priory of Sion from 1654 to 1691.

According to John Willis, the Royal Society grew out of meetings organized in London in 1645 during the Civil War to inquire into natural philosophy, the new experimental philosophy and other parts of human learning.[50.]Those present included Dr Wilkins, who was now chaplain to the Elector Palatine (the eldest son of Frederick V) in London; Theodore Haak, "a German of the Palatinate, and then resident in London, who, I think, gave the first occasion and first suggested these meetings," wrote Wallis; and many others. The Palatinate – and therefore Rosicrucianism – was very heavily involved in the creation of the Royal Society.

Wilkins, Cromwell's brother-in-law, had incredibly proposed the first serious attempts at a manned flight to the moon. He followed his treatise, *The Discovery of a World in the Moone* (1638) by writing a detailed description in 1640 of the machinery needed to fly to the moon, trade with aliens and explore space: a flying chariot (a boat on four wheels) powered by clockwork and springs, with flapping wings made of feathers and gunpowder-firing boosters that would take the "spaceship", with a man in a hat sitting beside the mast, beyond the 20 miles of what he believed was the extent of the earth's magnetic and gravitational pull. It would then float through space. In the 1660s Wilkins' fellow Rosicrucian Boyle and Robert Hooke demonstrated the nature of the vacuum between the earth and the moon – and the impossibility of Wilkins' project.

In letters of 1646 and 1647 Boyle wrote of "the Invisible College," a phrase that echoes the Rosicrucian Manifestos. In 1646 he wrote to his tutor that he was studying natural philosophy according to the principles of "our new philosophical college" and says that his tutor will be "extremely welcome to our Invisible College." In February 1647 Boyle wrote to another friend: "The best on't is, that the cornerstones of the *Invisible* or (as they term themselves) the Philosophical College do now and then honour me with their company…men of so capacious and searching spirits, that school-philosophy is but the lowest region of their knowledge; and yet, though ambitious to lead the way to any generous design, of so humble and teachable a genius, as they disdain not to be directed to the meanest, so he can but plead reason for his opinions; persons that endeavour to put narrow-mindedness out of countenance, by the practice of so extensive a charity that it reaches unto everything called man, and nothing less than an universal good-will can content it. And indeed they are so apprehensive of the want of good employment, that they take the whole body of mankind to their care."[51] In May 1647 Boyle wrote to Hartlib of the "Invisible College" and its public-spirited plan.

The neo-Atlantean Invisible College was to a large extent the creation of Hartlib. Having led a mystical and philanthropic group in Elbing, one of Andreae's Christian Unions or societies which had discarded its Rosicrucian title, he was used to the idea of a Rosicrucian group posing as a Christian group and continuing its Rosicrucian ideals and agenda. The Invisible College imitated the college in Bacon's New Atlantis, in which the brothers were "unseen" by the outside world. (In Boyle's use, "invisible" means "Rosicrucian.") It was run by exiles from the Palatinate as the chief lay patron of Hartlib, Dury and Comenius was still Elizabeth, Queen of Bohemia, who now funded them from her court at The Hague, where the English ambassador was Francis Bacon's executor, Sir William Boswell.[52] A London 1645 group was founded by Theodore Haak, a refugee from the Palatinate and Comenius's agent in London, who was closely involved with Hartlib. There is still some doubt as to who was in the Invisible College, and to what extent Haak's group comprised the whole of it.[53] The College consisted of physicians grouped round Harvey (Glisson, Ent, Scarburgh, Goddard and Merrett) and mathematical scientists grouped round Wilkins (Wallis, Foster and Haak).

Wilkins' *Mathematicall Magik* (1648) was based on Fludd's *Utriusque Cosmi Historia,* and the Invisible College which included Boyle and Christopher Wren met in Wilkins' rooms at Wadham College, Oxford from 1648 to 1659 (the Cromwell years).[54] During this time Thomas Vaughan (brother of the poet Henry) translated the *Fama* and *Confessio* into English. (His patron was Moray, the Mason.)

In 1660 the group combined with the one in London and founded the Royal Society. Boyle's two closest friends were then Isaac Newton and John Locke, the philosopher. Newton had read the Rosicrucian Manifestos, and, dissatisfied with mathematics, copied out great chunks of Michael Maier's works, hoping to find the One (divine Unity) in Rosicrucian alchemy. (He became Grand Master of the Priory of Sion from 1691 to 1727 after Boyle, who was made the Earl of Burlington and gave his name to Burlington House in Piccadilly.)

Hartlib was now overseeing the birth of the College or sacred society devoted to the welfare of mankind which Comenius had called for in *The Way of Light* and had come to England to found – at Harlib's request. Ultimately the College was founded on the Rosicrucian ideals of Bacon and Andreae, and in pressing for science to be part of the general system of education Hartlib was at the very start of what in the 1660s would become the Scientific Revolution (presided over by the Royal Society). Of especial interest to Hartlib were husbandry and agricultural reform, so much so that Webster associated the Age with Hartlib's name: "In view of the high quality and great contemporary popularity of the writings on husbandry associated with Hartlib it is entirely appropriate that Fussell should characterise the period between 1641 and 1660 as 'the Age of Hartlib.'"[55]

The Army Seize the King

Parliament had not been impressed by the Levellers' demands for constitutional change, and the Levellers turned to the people and to the New Model Army. On June 4, 1647 Cromwell left London and threw in his lot with the army, and on the same day a group of soldiers seized the King. According to Isaac D'Israeli's two-volume study of Charles I, whose sources included the records of Melchior de Salom, the French envoy in England during the Puritan revolution, Cornet Joyce, acting on secret orders from Cromwell himself that were unknown even to the Commander-in-Chief Sir Thomas Fairfax, arrived at Holmby House with 500 hand-picked revolutionary troops and seized the King. The plan was devised on May 30, 1647 at a secret meeting held at Cromwell's house while Cromwell was overtly trying to find employment for the disaffected soldiers. He later denied all knowledge of the soldiers' move. Captain Joyce, formerly Cornet Joyce before his rapid promotion, is one of the four men suspected of being Charles I's executioner.[56]

A few days after the seizure of the King, on June 16 1647, Cromwell wrote to the Mulheim Synagogue requesting financial support. He received a reply on July 12, 1647 agreeing once Charles was removed. Both letters were carried by the courier Ebenezer Pratt, who left England for Mulheim and probably waited for a reply, which he then brought back. Details of these now overlooked and forgotten letters, which were known about in Napoleon's time and were lost until they surfaced in an old library in Amsterdam, appear in Capt. Ramsey's *The Nameless War*. Ramsey quotes a letter published in a weekly review edited by Alfred, Lord Douglas. According to the letter published in *Plain English* on September 3, 1921:

"The learned Elders have been in existence for a much longer period than they have perhaps suspected. My friend Mr L. D. van Valckert of Amsterdam, has recently sent me a letter containing two extracts from the Synagogue at Mulheim. The volume in which they are contained was lost at some period during the Napoleonic Wars, and has recently come into Mr van Valckert's possession. It is written in German and contains extracts of letters sent and received by the authorities of the Mulheim Synagogue. The first entry he sends me is of a letter received:

16th June, 1647

From O. C. (i.e. Oliver Cromwell), by Ebenezer Pratt.

In return for financial support will advocate admission of Jews to England: This however impossible while Charles living. Charles cannot be executed without trial, adequate grounds for which do not at present exist. Therefore advise that Charles be assassinated, but will have nothing to do with arrangements for procuring an assassin, though willing to help in his escape.

In reply was despatched the following:

12th July, 1647

To O. C. by E. Pratt.

Will grant financial aid as soon as Charles removed and Jews admitted. Assassination too dangerous. Charles shall be given opportunity to escape: His recapture will make trial and execution possible. The support will be liberal, but useless to discuss terms until trial commences."

This correspondence is remarkable and raises more questions. Where is Mulheim? Was it a district in Amsterdam? Was it the Mulheim south-west of Frankfurt, down towards Zurich and south-west of (and outside) the territory of the Palatinate? In fact it was the small German town on the Ruhr (now with seven bridges) just north of Düsseldorf (south of Essen, two miles below Cologne), not far from the Dutch border. This was where in 1605 Sir Horace Vere had arrived, in charge of the English contingent, with Prince Frederick Henry of the Palatinate (Frederick V's father) and Prince Maurice of Orange and had encountered the Spanish General Spinola. It was then "a small village consisting of one street on a steep slope at right angles with the stream."[57]

Mulheim had originally been part of the Duchy of Berg and became a town in 1508. Duke John III of Cleves, father of Anne of Cleves (who married Henry VIII in 1540), inherited the duchies of Jülich and Berg and the county of Ravensberg. The ducal dynasty became extinct in 1609, when the insane last Duke died. There was a dispute about the succession and in 1614 the territory was partitioned: Jülich and Berg were annexed by the Count Palatine of Neuburg, of the Palatinate-Neuburg line of the Bavarian house of Wittelsbach, who had converted to Catholicism. (Neuburg was on the Danube.) Cleves, Mark and Ravensberg fell to the Elector of Brandenburg. Thus Mulheim in the Duchy of Berg was owned by the Rosicrucian Palatinate Wittelsbachs (the family which provided the Rhenish Palatinate with its rulers) in the

1640s and eventually became part of Germany. An undated picture of Mulheim Synagogue has survived. It is not clear whether this was the 17th-century synagogue or a 20th-century rebuild on the same site: not many synagogues survived the Nazi cleansing period, and the original synagogue may have been destroyed during the Nazi period and later rebuilt.

Mulheim Synagogue

What was the link between the Mulheim Synagogue and Menasseh? There must surely have been a link in view of Menasseh's funding of Carvajal's creation of the New Model Army. Was Menasseh a rabbi under the Mulheim Synagogue? Was there a link with his colleague Rabbi Templo,[58] who designed the coat of arms that was adopted as the symbol of the Grand Lodge Assembly in London?

The link between Menasseh and Mulheim is likely to have been Jewish Rosicrucians. Frederick V was Elector Palatine of the Rhine. He held two of the seven electorates that elected the Holy Roman Emperor (the German king). He was the Count Palatine of the Rhine and King of Bohemia. We have seen that he ruled a Rosicrucian kingdom from the castle at Heidelberg. He and his wife Elizabeth Stuart were in exile at The Hague near Amsterdam. No doubt they were still in touch with the Palatinate, which owned Mulheim where the Mulheim Synagogue was based. The Kabbalistic Menasseh was clearly linked to the Jews of Amsterdam, where he lived and was a well-known rabbi; and perhaps through them to the Jews of the Rosicrucian Palatinate at Mulheim. Menasseh was a Rosicrucian Kabbalist.

In the 1647 exchange of letters, Cromwell promised the admission of Jews to England in return for the assassination of Charles and Jewish financial support. The Mulheim Synagogue advised that Charles should be given an opportunity to escape and that would make possible a trial and his execution. Discussion of the funding would commence at the trial, but would only begin when Charles was removed and the Jews had been admitted.

This exchange of letters – if genuine – explains the subsequent events. In September 1647 Menasseh wrote a letter to an English correspondent. He attributed the deposition of the King to Edward I's expulsion of the Jews from England in 1290. He began: "Sir, I cannot express the joy that I have when I read your letters, full of desires to see your country prosperous, which is heavily afflicted with civil wars, without doubt by the just judgment of God. And it should not be vain to attribute it to the punishment of your predecessor's faults, committed against ours; when ours being deprived of their liberty under deceitfulness, so many men were slain only because they kept close under the tenets of Moses, their legislator."[59]

On November 12, 1647 the King was allowed to escape from Hampton Court Palace. On the Isle of Wight he asked Scottish commissioners to restore him to the throne on terms that would suit the Scots. Several authors[60] consider that Charles's flight was a stratagem of Cromwell's to prepare public opinion for a trial. From the day of his deportation from Holmby to his flight to the Isle of Wight, Charles was a puppet dancing on Cromwell's string.

The Royalists took up arms and a second civil war began. Cromwell had to fight in Wales and then Scotland, and besieged Pontefract in

Yorkshire. Meanwhile he was negotiating with the King, who was still on the Isle of Wight.

On December 5, 1648 the Commons sat all night and voted "That the King's concessions were satisfactory to a settlement." Had this agreement been reached, Cromwell would not have stood to receive large sums of money from the Mulheim Jews. Cromwell, who was travelling back to London at Fairfax's request, on December 6, gave instructions to Colonel Pride (via Ireton, his father-in-law and front) to purge Parliament of 140 Presbyterians proscribed by the Army so that there were only 50 Independent members left – the "communist" rump – who now claimed supreme authority. By the time he arrived all the MPs who favoured continuing negotiations with the King had been purged in what came to be known as Pride's Purge of December 6, 1648.

Cromwell and Ireton had acted as mediators between King and Parliament, and had overtly opposed extreme measures (the abolition of the monarchy that was being proposed in Parliament). Covertly, Cromwell had manipulated the democratic process by means of his purge, which he had instructed Ireton to make, and had stood back and said that it was nothing to do with him.

The Execution of Charles I

Ireton now urged that the King be tried and – the official version goes – Cromwell reluctantly agreed. He was one of 135 commissioners in the High Court of Justice proclaimed on January 9, 1649. Two-thirds of its members were Levellers from the army.

Algernon Sidney, one of the judges, told Cromwell: "First, the King can be tried by no court; secondly no man can be tried by this court." Cromwell replied, "I tell you we will cut off his head with the crown upon it." To which Sidney said, "You may take your own course, I cannot stop you, but I will keep myself clean from having any hand in this business."[61] No English lawyer would consent to draw up the charge and in the end that task was performed by the Jewish Dr Dorislaus, recently Parliament's envoy to the Netherlands and Cromwell's friend. (In May 1649 he was assassinated by Royalists just after being appointed envoy to Holland. He was given a public funeral and buried in Westminster Abbey, which was packed with soldiers who appeared to be guarding the Commonwealth leaders rather than mourning Dorislaus.) Dorislaus would of course have been known to both Menasseh in Holland and Carvajal in London. Charles refused to plead. In spite of Algernon Sidney's statement sentence was passed by 68 votes to 67, a majority of one, and Cromwell signed the death warrant.

The execution of Charles I took place in Whitehall. Charles walked through the Banqueting Room, looked up for the last time at the Rubens painting on the ceiling and stepped out of the second window from the right up some steps at the end of the Hall, onto the scaffold. According to one observer the King "came forwards with the same indifference as 'he would have entered Whitehall on a masque-night.' He looked towards St James's and smiled!" The poet Andrew Marvell summed up the King's demeanour with grudging admiration in his *Horatian Ode*:

"He nothing common did or mean
Upon that memorable Scene."

The King then registered concern that the block, placed in the centre of the scaffold, was so low. It was about eighteen inches long and six inches in height, flat at the bottom and curved at the top. He was anxious that such a low block would not allow him to kneel, forcing him instead to adopt a far more submissive posture of lying on his stomach. He asked if there was a higher one available only to be told that there was not.

According to the contemporary account published in 1650 *King Charles His Trial at the High Court of Justice*,[62] "The King looked out at the people assembled in the area, at the several ranks of footsoldiers ranged immediately around the scaffold, at the troops of horse at one side towards King Street and at the other towards Charing Cross. He saw that the citizens of London were kept beyond the barrier fences, too far away either to hear any of the words of the speech he proposed to make or to see anything that occurred below the level of the draped railings on the scaffold. The only people who might see the King die would be those who thronged the upper windows and roofs of the surrounding buildings. King Charles took a small piece of paper from his pocket and from the notes written earlier he began his last speech to his people as the winter sun came through the clouds. He spoke, addressing his words to those on the scaffold, glancing frequently at Matthew Thomlinson" (a Colonel who commanded the troops guarding him).

Charles began by protesting his "innocency": "All the world knows that I never did begin a war with the two Houses of Parliament....I never did intend for to encroach upon their privileges. They began upon me....I do believe that ill instruments between them and me have been the chief cause of all this bloodshed." He said that he had "forgiven all the world and even those in particular that have been the chief causers of my death. Who they are, God knows; I do not desire to know." He accused his enemies of being conquerors: "Conquest, sirs, in my opinion is never just, except there be a good just cause....But if it be only matter of conquest, then it is a great robbery; as a pirate said to Alexander the Great that he was the great robber, he [the pirate] was but a petty robber." Ill instruments, "invisible" murders, "conquests by forces of world imperialism" (Alexander the Great) – Charles I seemed to understand in his soul that he was the victim of international Rosicrucian Freemasonry.

He must have spoken at least three minutes before he reached the central part: "You will never do right, nor God will never prosper you, until you give God His due, the King his due, that is, my successors, and the people their due. I am as much for them as any of you. You must give God his due by regulating rightly his Church....For the King, indeed I will not – (*then turning to a gentleman that touched the axe said, 'Hurt not the axe that may hurt me', meaning if he did blunt the edge*) – for the King, the laws of the land will clearly instruct you for that. Therefore, because it concerns my own particular, I only give you a touch of it. For the people…I desire their liberty and freedom as much as anybody.…It is not for having a share in government, sirs; that is nothing pertaining to them. A subject and a sovereign are clean different things.…Sirs, it was for this that now I am come here. If I would have given way to an arbitrary way for to have all laws changed according to the power of the sword, I need not have come here.…I am the martyr of the people."

When the King had finished his speech, Bishop Juxon, his friend and chaplain, offered some comforting words, and instructed the King to look on his execution as a voyage to Heaven. Charles then uttered his famous words, "I go from a corruptible to an incorruptible crown, where no disturbance can be, no disturbance in the world." A silent crowd watched from Whitehall as the King took off his doublet and then took off his gold ring, which had a picture of himself set in it, and gave it to Bishop Juxon.[63] He knelt down very low (as the block was so low), and instructed the headsman to strike when he stretched his hands out.

A contemporary account[64] describes Charles's end: "Having said two or three words (as he stood) to himself with hands and eyes lifted up, immediately stooping down laid his neck upon the Block, and then the Executioner again putting his hair under his cap, the King said (thinking he had been going to strike): Stay for the sign! Executioner: Yes I will, an it please Your Majesty. And after a very little pause, the King stretching forth his hands, the Executioner at one blow severed his head from his body."

The execution was an illegal act, and was in no way justified by appeals to Parliamentary authority. But then all revolutions are by definition illegal and the sudden, transformation of revolution can only be effected by violent, unconstitutional means.

On the surface, it looked a straightforward case of an authoritarian King being beheaded by a Parliament that had lost patience. It seemed that Cromwell and the other Puritans pushed the execution through without Fairfax's knowledge purely because the King had become a constitutional liability. But the involvement of Carvajal as a supplier of arms funded from Holland by Menasseh, and the promise of "financial aid" in the letter from Mulheim in return for Charles's execution and the readmission of the Jews into England, suggest that there was a more secret motive for the execution. Isaac D'Israeli was very aware of the need to unearth the "secret history" of the 17th century: "Vast and innumerable are the sources of secret history which, during the last half-century, have accumulated in masses....It was fated that England should be the theatre of the first of a series of Revolutions which is not yet finished."[65]

There have long been suggestions that through intermediaries the Jews were taking revenge for their expulsion from England by Edward I in 1290. It is possible that some believed that Charles I was descended from the 5th century Merovée, father of the Merovingian line and allegedly a descendant of Jesus, and that Charles was a victim of the ages-old war between Jew and Christian. In particular, it has been maintained that the Priory of Sion were outraged that James I, Charles's father, was a Templar, and wanted to return the English throne to their own rule. As we have seen, it has been suggested that the Priory of Sion created Rosicrucianism. Was the Priory of Sion behind the execution of Charles I?

CONSOLIDATION: THE PROTECTORATE

After the execution of the King, Cromwell became the first Chairman of the Council of State, which ran the new republic (named the Commonwealth).

Cromwell prepared for his Protectorate by abolishing the House of Lords in March 1649. Cromwell allegedly wanted to retain it, but the Commons abolished it "as a great inconvenience" on the grounds that peers did not represent the people. He tried to set up a Puritan Church in place of the destroyed Anglican Church which would maintain a spirit of tolerance. Hartlib's plans for social reform were implemented; committees known as Triers and Ejectors set standards for clergymen and schoolmasters. Cromwell took an interest in education and was Chancellor of Oxford. Cromwell's Protectorate was decidedly conservative in nature.

Hartlib's circle focused comprehensively on agriculture, education, industry, medicine, schemes for the poor, poor relief, economic problems, religion, technology and trade, natural history, continental science, chemistry, foreign intelligence, and of course his fraternities or colonies of the Antilia/Macaria model. In short, his circle was a mini-government-in-waiting, a kind of think-tank and policy unit for the new Puritan government. At the same time it implemented Bacon's advancement of learning. In June 1649 Hartlib was appointed State Agent for Universal Learning ("Agent for the Advancement of Universal Learning"). His social reforms included workhouses and led to many projects which involved State assistance for humanitarian goals. He also proposed a labour exchange known as the Bureau of Addresses. It is a measure of Cromwell's regard for the Polish-Prussian refugee that he awarded him an annual pension of £300 for his concern with educational legislation in the Long Parliament (1640-53). (Hartlib's final plan for English education was published in *Considerations Tending to the Happy Accomplishment of England's Reformation in Church and State*, in 1647.) His work was curtailed when the Protectorate ended and a State-funded paradise collapsed. The pension ended with the Restoration of the monarchy in 1660, and Hartlib died two years later.

Hartlib's Baconian Utopianism gave rise to Utopian agricultural experiments. Out of Hartlib's ideas the Puritan revolutionaries threw up political groups with social programmes that had an impact on the Commonwealth. These groups sought to convert the Utopian aspirations of Bacon's *New Atlantis* and Hartlib's *Macaria* into practical programmes of social reform.

In April 1647 the ordinary army soldiers had elected a council of agitators who stood for Leveller ideas. In October 1647 they had discussed the Agreement of the People, a Leveller-inspired document to refound the State after Parliament's victory in the Civil War. The army leadership restored control, and in April 1649 John Lilburne and other

Leveller leaders were imprisoned. On Cromwell's order a mutiny of Leveller troops was suppressed at Burford in May 1649.

The Levellers had tried to take on the army and make the revolution more extreme, but they failed to secure the support of either Parliament or the army. From Cromwell's point of view they had served their purpose for they had helped create a climate in which the King could be tried and executed. Once this had happened they were superfluous and he had no hesitation in suppressing them.

The Diggers were more extreme agrarian revolutionaries who also wanted to help "the starving poor." In a sense they were the first communists and flourished in 1649-50 under their leaders Gerrard Winstanley and William Everard. They began as a group of 20 who seized common land at St George's Hill, Walton-on-Thames, Surrey (near Weybridge, ironically where many rich and famous now have mansions) and began cultivating it. They held that the Civil War had been fought against the King and the major landowners and that land should now be available for the poor. Because of the war, food prices in shops were very high, and it was their contention that waste land should belong to the poor. Winstanley was a natural Baconian, and in his communes workers pursued experimental philosophy as did the citizens of New Atlantis or Macaria. The Diggers called themselves "True levellers" but the Levellers denounced their Communism. Local landowners also wanted the common land the Diggers had occupied, and this gave the Commonwealth cause for concern. Legal actions and skirmishes resulted in the Diggers being dispersed by March 1650.

Thus Hartlib's ideas in agriculture nearly brought about an army-backed agrarian revolution.

Cromwell's military consolidation of the English Revolution began with his infamous Irish campaign, which lasted from August 1649 to the end of May 1650. After the Civil War the now redundant army needed to be gainfully employed; hence the Irish campaign. He reinvigorated the ideals of the revolution by presenting the campaign as a Puritan crusade against the Catholics. He saw the English as Israelites come to expel the idolatrous tribes from Canaan, with himself as Joshua.

The biggest blots on Cromwell's reputation were the massacres at Drogheda in September 1649 (up to 4,000 dead) and at Wexford the following month (where 1,500 civilians were butchered). The most horrific episode at Drogheda was the deliberate holocaust of refugees in the steeple of St Peter's church in the north of the town. Cromwell himself spoke of the "effusion of blood." It is clear that to him the blood-letting of the body natural was a metaphor for a blood-letting in the body politic of the British Isles. The blood-letting purge is an essential element of the revolutionary dynamic.

In December 1649 the Catholic prelates and clergy convened at the ancient monastery of Clonmacnoise, and declared a holy war (*bellum praelaticum et religiosum*) against the English. Cromwell replied the following month with his own "Declaration," his language saturated with fanatical religious fervour: "You are a part of Antichrist, whose Kingdom the Scripture so expressly speaks should be 'laid in blood,'" he thundered, "yea 'in the blood of the Saints.'"[66]

Cromwell's Irish campaign was followed by a no less ruthlessly efficient campaign in Scotland. In May 1650 Cromwell became Captain-General in Scotland in place of Fairfax, who had refused the command. He trounced the future King Charles II's forces under David Leslie at the Battle of Dunbar in September 1650. The English battle-cry at Dunbar was "The Lord of Hosts!" He then defeated the future Charles II at Worcester.

Now Cromwell had suppressed the Levellers and triumphed in campaigns in Ireland and Scotland, he dissolved Parliament on April 20, 1653 and appointed a new assembly to take its place, a "little Parliament" (or Barebones Parliament, so named after the Anabaptist Praisegod Barebones) to establish a Puritan republic, an "Assembly of Saints." In December 1653 the Assembly of Saints surrendered its power to Cromwell following the coup by Major-General Lambert.

Cromwell forcibly dissolved Parliament using Lambert as his intermediary. The understanding was that power would be delivered into Cromwell's hands, but the title he would adopt had not been settled. It was suggested that he should accept the title of King.

Cromwell "reluctantly" accepted that Providence had chosen him, as one of the Elect, to rule. He had a nostalgic respect for the institution of monarchy, and his agonizing suggested that he wanted to be King. However, the Army was full of republicans who might object and Cromwell preferred a title that had less permanent implications than Kingship. On December 13 or 14, Lambert proposed "Lord Governour." Cromwell, protesting that he would rather have a modest shepherd's staff (or crook) as a badge of his office, eventually settled on "Lord Protector." It seems that Cromwell did want the title of King, for four years later he complained that the Army had blocked his acceptance of the title of King: "Time was when they boggled not at the word [King]."[67]

Cromwell's consolidation now became political as well as military. Although he had abolished both the monarchs and the House of Lords and purged the Commons (whom he could never endure for long), satisfactory government eluded him. Even the Protectorship and Council of State failed to secure him the authority he desired. He again dissolved Parliament on January 22, 1655. Republicans, Royalists and Levellers all stirred. So, following the rising of Colonel Penruddock in March 1655, Cromwell divided England and Wales into 11 regions (or "cantons" as his detractors termed them) under the direct rule of 11 Major-Generals.

The Major-Generals, many of whom were former officers of the New Model Army, instituted martial law. They had permanent cavalry troops at their disposal, paid for by a new tax of 10 per cent (the Decimation tax) levied on the income of all those known or thought to have Royalist sympathies. They were there to enforce the Puritan regime, and did not scruple to use force. Even such harmless recreations as horse-racing, cock-fighting and play-acting were all strictly prohibited.

In April 1654 Cromwell had moved into Whitehall palace and about the same time took possession of Hampton Court, where he spent weekends hawking and hunting, using it as the modern British Prime Minister uses Chequers. He was acting as a King just as George

Orwell's pig Napoleon acted as the farmer after the revolution that gave him control of Animal Farm, and he now claimed that his government had *prevented* anarchy and social revolution! He now defended England's long-established institutions against the Levellers, whom he had encouraged, and dissolved his two Parliaments because republicans were agitating for extreme measures. Revolutionaries often find themselves enacting the very measures which led them to usurp power from their predecessors. Cromwell was no exception, and when the legal basis of his government was challenged by George Cony, a merchant who refused to pay customs duties, arguing that they had not been sanctioned by Parliament and should be compared to Charles I's Ship tax, Cromwell was as heavy-handed as Charles I and "imprisoned Cony's lawyers – with all the zest of a Charles I."[68]

MENASSEH AND THE RETURN OF THE JEWS TO ENGLAND

We have seen that Menasseh ben Israel was the most prominent Dutch Jew to campaign for the return of the Jews to England. He had sought to influence the fall of Charles I, and in his letter of September 1647 he had seen the deposition of Charles I (the descendant of the offending Edward I) as just retribution for the expulsion of the Jews from Britain in 1290.

Since those days a number of Jews had unobtrusively crept back into England. Following the expulsion of the Jews from Spain and Portugal in 1492, Jewish "converted" *Marranos*, pretending to be Christians, had entered England. They passed themselves off as Spanish or Portuguese and attended Catholic churches. Parliament had tolerated the situation. Menasseh believed that it had not been

Menasseh ben Israel

responsible for the expulsion. Parliament's insistence on the Old Testament and its attitude to Hebrew history made it seem sympathetic to Menasseh's Jewish people. He saw Parliament as the recipient of divine approval and hoped it would reverse the wrong of 1290 and invite Jews back into England.

In 1650 he published *Spes Israeli* (*The Hope of Israel*, also *Esperança de Israel*), in which he reported that the Lost Ten Jewish Tribes had been found in South America. (In 1640 Menasseh had considered emigrating to Brazil.) He dedicated the Latin edition of this work to the English parliament, in admiration of Oliver Cromwell. The translator said that Menasseh's intention was not "to propagate or commend Judaism" but to make the Jews "real Christians." He had English friends among the converts to Judaism in Amsterdam, and this was overtly the reason that he had approached Cromwell. Menasseh wrote in the dedication to *The Hope of Israel*: "As for me (most renowned Fathers) in my dedicating this Discourse to you, I can truly affirm that I am induced to it upon no other ground then this, that I may gain your favour and goodwill to our Nation, now scattered almost all over the earth; neither think that I do this as if I were ignorant how much you have hitherto favoured our Nation; for it is made known to me, and to others of our Nation, by them who are so happy as near at hand, to observe your apprehensions, that you do vouchsafe to help us, not only by your prayers; yea, this hath compelled me to speak to you publikly, and to give you thanks for that your charitable affection towards us, and not such thanks which come only from the tongue, but as are conceived by a grateful mind. Give me leave therefore (most renowned Fathers) to supplicate you, that you would still favour our good, and farther love us...."[69]

In 1651 Cromwell's cousin Oliver St John went to Amsterdam to negotiate for the Anglo-Dutch alliance, which it was hoped would result in Anglo-Dutch union. (This meant that the Dutch would be incorporated into the British Empire, but they were not interested.) John Thurloe, his secretary, met Menasseh. Christopher Hill observes that the English delegation to the Netherlands in 1651, and especially its secretary John Thurloe, saw a great deal of Menasseh ben Israel.[70]

Thurloe suggested he should apply to the Council in England for the resettlement of the Jews. In October 1651 a committee including Cromwell was set up to consider the proposal. Cromwell decided that the Jews should be readmitted. There appeared to be a number of factors behind his decision: Thurloe had helped make him Protector; Cromwell had a high opinion of Jews as intelligence-gatherers, particularly in connection with Spanish naval manoeuvres that might be a threat; Jews might help advance his dreams of imperial expansion, which he harboured from 1654 – for all revolutions turn imperialist and internationalist; and Jews might be expected to bring money into the country. He also had other, ideological reasons as we shall shortly see.

In 1654 a Jewish *Marrano* merchant, Manuel Martinez Dormido, submitted a petition to Cromwell asking for help with the Jews who were suffering under the Spanish Inquisition. Cromwell received him cordially, but the Council rejected his petition.

Menasseh ben Israel, who was still in Amsterdam, now arranged for himself to be invited so he could speak to Cromwell himself. He arrived in London in September 1655 with three rabbis in attendance and was lodged in the Strand by Cromwell, in a house opposite the New Exchange. Menasseh met the Council first, but did not make the impact he had hoped, possibly because he produced too many books.

He met Cromwell for dinner. It was a meeting of minds. Menasseh kissed Cromwell and pressed his hands and touched his clothes, checking to see if he was the Jewish Messiah. It is not known what Cromwell's reaction was, but he was probably extremely embarrassed. Menasseh handed over a petition "on behalf of the Jewish nation." He also had dinner with Comenius and Hartlib at the house of Katherine Ranelagh, sister of the Sionist Rosicrucian Robert Boyle.[71]

His petition called for resettlement and for the Jewish religion to be reinstated. He quoted the prophecy in *Deuteronomy* that once the dispersion of the Jews was completed they would return to the Holy Land. He said the dispersal *was* now completed as there were Jews in every corner of the globe. He said that the commercial expertise of the Jews made them a profitable nation.

Messiah/Return of the Jews by 1656

Millenarianism had begun in the mid-16th century and was widespread in the 17th century. Its adherents believed that the arrival of the millennium, Christ's thousand-year reign on earth in accordance with *Revelations* 20, 1-5, would herald the ultimate Utopia: heaven on earth or the rule of the saints.

Millenarianist feeling at this time put the coming of the Messiah and related events at around 1656, this very year. Many mathematicians from Napier in the late 16th century to Isaac Newton in the 17th century based their calculations on *Daniel* and *Revelations*, and there was a consensus that the millennium would take place 1260 years after the Antichrist set up his power. Protestants took the Antichrist to be the Pope, whose rise was dated from AD 390 to AD 396, which brought the date of the millennium to 1650-56. Other calculations added 1290 years to Julian the Apostate and the destruction of the Temple of Jerusalem, which gave the same result. (One calculation took the Antichrist to be the usurpation of the Bishop of Rome in AD 400-6, and that gave 1666 as the date of the millennium. Yet another calculation took the Antichrist to be the Turkish infidel, and that set the millennium forward into the future.)[72]

Noah's Flood was held to start in 1656 *anno mundi* (i.e. after the beginning of the earth). *Matthew* had said, "As the days of Noah were, so shall also the coming of the Son of Man be." This was interpreted in terms of dates, and so the millennium – the Last Judgment and the end of the world – was put at AD 1656. This was first argued by Osiander, whose book was translated into English by George Joyce in 1548. Thomas Goodwin, writing in the Netherlands, took up the same idea in 1639. In 1651, none other than Samuel Hartlib published a translation of *Clavis Apocalyptica*, in which the years were given as 1655 *anno mundi* for Noah's Flood and AD 1655 for the Last Judgment and the end of the world.

1656 became the main date for the millennium when the millenarian Peter Sterry preached in Parliament in 1651 and gave the year as AD 1656. The millenarians John Tillinghast, John Rogers,

Henry Jessey, Nathanael Homes, Robert Gell, William Oughtred and the Quakers all opted for 1656.

The approach of the millennium was anticipated by a variety of predictions: the overthrow of the Pope, who was to Protestants the Antichrist and whose fall was predicted to happen immediately before the millennium; opposition to the Antichrist by the poor in England; the gathering of the Gentiles as Christianity spread throughout the world; the conversion of the Jews; the Jews' return to Zion, Palestine; the Second Coming of Christ; the Last Judgment; the thousand-year reign of Christ and his saints; and the end of the world.

Many preachers put the end of the world at 1650-6, including John Archer, Raphael Harford, John Cotton, Stanley Gower, William Reyner, Thomas Shepard, James Toppe and Mary Cary. John Canne thought that Christ would "most eminently appear" in 1655, and that there would be "great revolutions...everywhere in Europe." (A pamphlet of 1648 refers to "all these Cabbalistical Millenarians and Jew-restorers.")

The dispersion of the Jews throughout the world and their conversion to Christianity had to be completed by 1650-6. Many writers referred to the conversion of the Jews: for instance Bensalem in Bacon's *New Atlantis* is peopled by converted Jews. In 1641 Comenius had a plan for the conversion of the Jews. The millenarians' sense of urgency was playfully touched on in Marvell's address "To his Coy Mistress": "And you should, if you please, refuse/Till the conversion of the Jews." Such a timetable had been preached in England since the mid-1550s, notably by the Protestants Martin Bucer and Peter Martyr of Strasbourg. Calvinists like Beza had then urged the conversion of the Jews. So had Wycliffe and Hus.

During this millenarianism a shift had taken place. Whereas at first the conversion of the Jews and their return to Zion, Palestine were important because it made possible the Second Coming and the reign of the saints on earth, now the main thing was to achieve the reign of saints in a commonwealth, and the Jews were a secondary consideration. So Gerrard Winstanley, the communist Digger, equated the English with the Israelites. Indeed Winstanley and Everard told Sir Thomas Fairfax that they were "of the race of the Jews."

The equation of England and Israel had come from *Deuteronomy*. The scattering or dispersion of the Jews would end when they had reached the angle or limit of the earth, England. The English should therefore appear as Israelites so that the dispersal of the Jews would end and the millennium could begin. By dressing as Israelites millenarians could demonstrate that Israelite dress had reached England. This would accelerate the arrival of the millennium, the Second Coming and the reign of saints.

Millenarian Englishmen consciously began to look like Jews to assume the identity of Israelites and take part in the first reign of saints. (They were English Israelites, as it were.) The life-style of the Puritans was therefore based on that of strict Orthodox Jews. They wore a black garb with a wide-brimmed hat, as did the Jews. They fasted and advocated plainness of food and dress, as did the Jews. They observed the Sabbath, as did the Jews. They took the *Old Testament* literally and sang psalms, as did the Jews. They believed in sober living and avoided alcohol (except on religious occasions), as did the Jews. The Puritan Malvolio in *Twelfth Night* dresses in black, lives simply and disapproves of the riotous behaviour of Sir Toby Belch. The Jews also disapproved of revelry and riotous behaviour. The Puritans closed the theatres and objected to Church corruption. Such attitudes could also be found among the Jews.

The millenarian Puritans were well-versed in Judaism and the *Old Testament* scriptures and wore the same dress as Orthodox Jews. The Dutch Familists of Hendrik Niclaes (whom James I saw as the source of Puritanism) may have begun this sartorial trend between 1540 and 1560, when Jews and Christians were living happily together in the Family of Love, or Family of God, but within the body of Christ. Many Puritans proposed the adoption of the Mosaic Law in England and awaited the Jewish Messiah. This process of imitating Israelite dress had started in the mid-16th century. The millenarians Bucer, Peter Martyr and Beza in the 1550s, Sitz's privy church of 1567-8 (which saw

England as the Israel which God favoured), Andrew Willet in 1590 and Perkins and Hooker at the turn of the century had all prepared the way.

The early millenarian Puritans who dressed differently clearly modelled themselves on the Jews. In the Elizabethan time, William Cecil, Walsingham and Bacon all wore black garments instead of doublet and hose, and were dressed in garb similar to that worn (in his picture of 1642) by the Dutch Rabbi Menasseh ben Israel. By wearing it they may have been expressing their sympathy for the internationalist aims of the Family of God, "lovers of truth of all nations." Bacon looked towards Israel's Temple of Solomon in his Freemasonry, as we have seen. William Cecil, almost certainly a *Marrano* Jew and the most powerful person in the land excluding the Queen, did not suppress or discourage the rise of the Puritans and may have privately sympathized with the entry of Jews into England as *Marranos*. To encourage a readmission of the Jews, it is possible that he endorsed the millenarian Jewish dress – which Shakespeare (who seems to have despised Lord Burghley) lampooned through Malvolio. According to some very informed opinion, including G. W. Phillips,[73] Shakespeare later satirized Cecil as Shylock.

Shortly before 1650 Jewish-style skull-caps were worn. The Presbyterian minister who visited Charles I after his trial, the Rev. Edmond Calamy, was etched wearing such a skull-cap, and on the morning of his execution Charles I told Herbert which skull-cap he would wear and asked him to have it ready on the scaffold. Bishop Juxon then took charge of it. This had a practical use; Charles used it to tuck in his long hair to bare his neck. In the 1650s many Puritans were painted wearing a much smaller, black Jewish skull-cap, including Henry Marten (the republican politician), John Owen (Cromwell's chaplain on his expedition to Ireland) and the poet Andrew Marvell (who was painted by an unknown artist c1655-60, several years after he wrote "The Garden").

The Puritans were funded by the Jews, but most were only aware of being neo-Israelites in the sense of awaiting the Second Coming. Each Puritan had to live purely to be ready to be among the congregation of

Puritan dress: Jewish-style skull caps.
Marten (left), Owen (centre), Marvell (right)

saints. Most wanted to strip away the gaudiness of religion, which they associated with the Antichrist. Some Jews, expelled from Spain and elsewhere, who had entered Christian congregations as *Marranos*, would have seized on the opportunity to wear Jewish dress. But Jewish garb was not a *Marrano* plot to split Christendom in revenge for expulsions; it was freely chosen by the English Puritans who liked to think of themselves as neo-Israelite saints-in-waiting.

The gathering of the Gentiles that had to precede the millennium would be advanced by English voyages to the New World and the acquisition of territories there. Catholic Spanish territories in the New World had spread the Antichrist, and it was up to Protestant English voyagers to counteract this evil influence by turning Indians, Creoles and negroes against the Spanish. (The Indians were thought to be descended from the lost ten Jewish tribes.) Voyages to the New World would make the millennium more likely by "gathering" into Christianity the Gentiles in Virginia and elsewhere in the New World. This gathering would in turn advance the time of the conversion of the Jews, which would then make possible the Second Coming of Christ. (The same feeling was present in the Rosicrucian Palatinate.) Major-Gen. Harrison said: "The Dutch must be destroyed and we shall have an heaven on earth." John Rolfe, the husband of Pocahontas, said in 1616 that the English were "a peculiar people marked and chosen by the finger of God" to possess North America.

Many millenarians had spoken of returning to Palestine. The *Zohar* was said to predict a return of the Jews to Israel in 1648. Richard Farnham and John Bull, who died in 1642, had tried to sail to Israel in a boat of bulrushes. John Robins the Ranter was inspired to lead 144,000 men to Palestine (the number of the Elect in *Revelations* 7,4 and 14,1-3, comprising 12,000 from each of the 12 tribes of Israel), and he began to train a few men for this task; his associate Thomas Tany assumed the title "King of the Jews" in April 1650. There were many false reports of the return of the Jews to Palestine.

The millenarians wanted English foreign policy to be directed towards the overthrow of the Antichrist. The commander of the Scottish forces in England wanted to march on Rome and burn the headquarters of the Antichrist, and similar expeditions were considered against the Turks.

But central to all the millenarians' thinking was the coming of a Jewish Messiah. Just as the Kabbalah had undergone a change during the Babylonian exile of the Jews, so had the notion of the Messiah. The Messiah expected in the 1650s was not the spiritual Messiah of the Essenes and the true Kabbalah (see Appendices B, Appendix 3) but the political Messiah of the false Kabbalah and the Pharisees, a Messiah who would lead the Jews to a new kingdom on earth, a new Promised Land: the English Israel in England.

With all this going on we can understand how the Messiah was expected by 1656 to begin returning the Jews to "Angle-land" and thus make it possible for them to return to Israel (as Lord Balfour's letter to Lord Rothschild of 1917 would herald their eventual return in 1948). We can also understand how the two strands behind the Puritan revolution – the Rosicrucian and the Jewish – came together in 1656 in a time Milton called "a Paradise." The dashed hopes and unfulfilled expectations of the millennium were profoundly disillusioning and depressing to millenarians, who now resigned themselves to a time in which English and Jews alike sank back into a life of secular commercialism.

The Jews Return

Extracts from Menasseh's petition catch the tone of his approach to Cromwell: "I am not come to make any disturbance...but only to live with my Nation in the fear of the Lord under the shadow of your protection....In this Nation God hath a People, that is very tender hearted, and well wishing to our sore afflicted Nation....This remains only in my judgment, before the MESSIA come and restore our Nation, that first we must have our seat here likewise....Having banished them from their own Country, yet not from his Protection, he (God) hath given them, as it were, a natural instinct, by which they might not only gain what was necessary for their need, but that they should also thrive in Riches and possessions....They should be invited by others to come and dwell in their lands."[74]

Cromwell forwarded the petition to the Council. The motion was that "the Jews deserving it may be admitted to this nation to trade and traffick and dwell amongst us as providence shall give occasion." A sub-committee was set up. Rumours swept London that Cromwell was about to sell St Paul's to Menasseh for a million pounds, so that it could become a synagogue, and that Cromwell had received a bribe of £200,000. There was a suggestion in the Jewish community that Cromwell was the Messiah, and a Jewish investigator rode to Huntingdon and Cambridge to check his family tree.

On December 4, Cromwell spoke to the Council about the Jews. It was the best speech of his life, according to some observers. He said the 1290 expulsion of the Jews was an act of royal prerogative and applied to only those Jews expelled. He played down fears that Jews would cozen English traders. On December 18 the Council returned to the resettlement of the Jews. Cromwell opposed any compromise such as Jews paying extra customs duties. The Council's reaction was hostile and when it reported adversely, Cromwell returned the report, giving himself freedom to decide.

Jews now believed that they had been readmitted, but there was no legal basis for this belief. Meanwhile they petitioned for a cemetery at Mile End and succeeded.

In April 1656 Menasseh wrote a pamphlet, *Vindiciae Judaeorum* ("Vindication of the Jews"), which defended Jews against charges of ritual murder of Christian children and other allegations. But an Anglo-Spanish war now loomed, and *Marranos* posing as Spanish Catholics could have their property confiscated as enemy aliens. A bailiff seized the goods of a Jew called Robles, who had the confiscated property returned as he was "a Jew born in Portugal." This judgment gave Jews confidence, and the *Marranos* who had settled in England earliest were now more open.

Menasseh died before the official charter of protection to the English Jews was granted in August 1664 by Charles II. He had been in desperate financial straits. In 1656 he applied to Cromwell and was awarded £25 and then a pension of £100 – which was not paid by the Treasury. His only son Samuel died, and he had to beg for money to take his body back to Holland. He then received £200 in lieu of pension rights. He believed that his mission had been unsuccessful and was deeply depressed. He died in November 1657 of a broken heart. His epitaph said in Spanish: "He is not dead; for in heaven he lives in supreme glory, whilst on earth his pen has won him immortal remembrance."[75]

Cromwell dissolved Parliament for a fourth time, on February 4, 1658. He died of malaria in September 1658 a couple of weeks after his favourite daughter Bettie had died of cancer. His body was interred in Westminster Abbey, but it was disinterred in 1661 and hung on the Tyburn gallows. His head was cut off and stuck on a pole in Westminster Hall, where it remained throughout Charles II's reign.

In due course Jews were permitted to land freely in England, even though there were strong protests from the sub-committee of the Council of State, which declared that they were a threat to the State and Christian religion.

SUMMARY: THE REVOLUTIONARY DYNAMIC OF THE ENGLISH REVOLUTION

This account raises many questions about Menasseh, not least of which are: How did a Jewish rabbi in Amsterdam come to visit England? Why did Thurloe meet Menasseh in 1651? Why did Menasseh appear to believe that Cromwell was the Messiah? What were his links with Hartlib and Cromwell? What impact did he have on the Puritan revolution? Why was Cromwell really so eager to champion the return of the Jews? What was going on behind the scenes? All these questions are answerable if both Menasseh and Cromwell were being directed by Rosicrucians within the Priory of Sion.

What was the true basis of Lord Protector Cromwell's connection with Menasseh? Cecil Roth, the author of *A Life of Menasseh ben Israel, Rabbi, Printer and Diplomat*, the first comprehensive account of the career of Menasseh, "the funder of Anglo-Jewry," encountered puzzling resistance when he went to Amsterdam in 1927 to research in the records and archives of the Spanish and Portuguese community there: "This work would inevitably have been more comprehensive had use been made in it of the records of the Spanish and Portuguese community of Amsterdam. In 1927, I went to Holland expressly for the purpose of doing research in the Archives of that famous and ancient body. Like many others before me, I found the doors closed, though the Secretary assured me that he would give me any information which I might require. I explained that I had come to make inquiries into the career of Menasseh ben Israel and his contemporaries. 'We have nothing in our Archives relating to Menasseh ben Israel,' the custodian blandly informed me, intimating at the same time that the interview was closed. It is necessary for me to publish the details of this incredible episode as an anticipation of the obvious criticism, that my work has not been based throughout on rock-bottom material."[76]

What was the custodian hiding in 1927? Why was he reluctant to show Roth the records about Menasseh? Was it to prevent him from seeing the 1647 correspondence? Were there records of Jewish financial help for Cromwell's revolution, which he did not want Roth to see? If so, the custodian was successful, for Roth makes no mention of the Mulheim Synagogue or of funding by the Amsterdam Jews.

To what extent was Menasseh's Amsterdam funding of Cromwell to secure a reversal of the 1290 expulsion, and to what extent was he furthering a policy of the Priory of Sion to overthrow the Stuarts? To what extent was he implementing the oath renewed on October 31, 1617 by the Rosicrucian Convention of Seven at Magdeburg, to destroy the Church of Jesus Christ? Or to what extent was he hoping that a new English leader would oppose the Spanish and liberate the southern Netherlands and the Palatinate in a new phase of fighting in the Thirty Years War? What in fact were Menasseh's motives?

Menasseh was clearly seeking the return of the Jews to England; of that there can be no doubt. As a Kabbalist Rosicrucian he was undoubtedly linked with Fludd and Andreae of the Priory of Sion, and the overthrow of Charles and the Stuarts must have been on his agenda. He must have hoped that following James I's abandonment of the Palatinate, a non-Stuart ruler in England would defeat the Spanish and restore the Rosicrucian kingdom. Indeed, as a Rosicrucian, he must have had it in mind that the aim of the Rosicrucian Convention was, like the aim of some Kabbalistic teaching, to split Christendom as had happened during the Reformation. There may have been an element of Jewish revenge in such thinking, for the Amsterdam Jews had not forgotten their expulsion from Spain. (See Appendices B, Appendix 9.)

The Kabbalist Menasseh had visited Cromwell and reversed the 1290 expulsion of the Jews from England. On the face of it the story is of a Kabbalist with a nationalistic mission to act on behalf of his people. But there was more to it than that. Menasseh was, like Cromwell, an Invisible Rosicrucian. Both had a hidden agenda.

Cromwell was first and foremost a Rosicrucian Mason, and secondly a Puritan – like many so-called Puritans. His revolution seems more Rosicrucian-Masonic than Protestant. What evidence is there that Cromwell's revolution was plotted in Rosicrucian Masonic Lodges and that his rise to power was governed by Rosicrucian guile? Does a

Rosicrucian involvement answer the questions about Cromwell's rise to power?

The facts are all unexceptional on the surface. Questions regarding Cromwell's career must be considered in the light of his Rosicrucian contacts and within the Menasseh-Carvajal-Mulheim context. How did Cromwell first become an MP? Was his decision to become an MP influenced from Holland? Was he in Dutch pay from the outset? Why did he begin to organize military forces in 1642? Why did he criticize Manchester? Why did he exclude members of the Commons or Lords from holding office in the New Model Army? We know now who funded the New Model Army; was the "Self-Denying Ordinance" a ruse to create a space for himself to be second-in-command? Probably. Did anyone influence Fairfax into asking for Cromwell to be his number 2? Why did Cromwell throw in his lot with the soldiers? We know that it was at his bidding that on the same day a group of soldiers seized the King. Was there pressure from the Mulheim Synagogue? Yes. Was Cromwell's mediating role a complete sham? Yes. We know that Cromwell influenced Ireton's purge of Parliament. To what extent did Cromwell influence Ireton's urging that the King should be tried? Was Cromwell's reluctance to try the King a complete sham? Yes. Was his agenda the overthrow of Charles I all along? Yes. We know that Cromwell was in touch with Holland. Who was his mentor? Menasseh? Was it trickery, Providence or a secret organization that dislodged Manchester, engineered Cromwell's stunning rise and secured him as second-in-command and eventually Lord Protector?

As in the case of Menasseh the surface events conceal what was really happening, and there are clues beneath the surface of the generally received account which point to the truth. According to the Venetian Ambassador Cromwell met Menasseh in Flanders while travelling in his youth.[77] There is no corroborating evidence and Cromwell is not reported as ever having travelled abroad. Nevertheless it is interesting that the Venetian Ambassador should have said this.

Again, having been a Calvinist, then a Unitarian and then a Congregationalist, Cromwell at some point became a Rosicrucian.

When? His links with Freemasonry have been asserted by French Templar Freemasons, who claim he used the Masonic system for his own elevation to power. Abbé Larudan in *The Freemasons Crushed* (1746) claimed that Cromwell "established the order (of Freemasonry) for the furtherance of his (own) political designs" and that "Freemasonry was organized, its degrees established, (and) its ceremonies and ritual prescribed" by Cromwell and several of the supporters he initiated. "The Institution (of Freemasonry) was used by Cromwell for the advancement of his projects, for the union of the contending parties in England, for the extirpation of the monarchy, and his own subsequent elevation to supreme power."

In fact Freemasonry was founded earlier than Cromwell, as we have seen. According to *History and Evolution of Freemasonry* Cromwell regularly met others at the Masonic Lodge in the tavern called – appropriately – the Crown.[78] This was a Lodge for the new Rosicrucian landed gentry. The goal of the Rosicrucians meeting at the Crown was of course to abolish the monarchy. Cromwell could not have entered the Crown unless he was a Rosicrucian Mason like the rest. Mackey's *Encyclopaedia of Freemasonry* says that Cromwell was a Rosicrucian and was on the best terms with Rosicrucians.[79]

When during his youth could Cromwell have met the Kabbalist Rosicrucian Menasseh? If the Venetian Ambassador is correct, possibly about 1622, soon after Cromwell was married and Menasseh had taken up his position as rabbi in Amsterdam. Perhaps when Cromwell was on a visit to Anne Hooftman's Palavacino relatives with his mother and sisters? Possibly the visit took place when he was an MP in 1628? It could be that this meeting brought about the psychological crisis which ended in the experience of Light. Perhaps the crisis was a result of the conflict between his youthful Calvinism, his developing Unitarianism and the Kabbalist Rosicrucianism of Menasseh? It is not known whether Cromwell met Fludd (who might have been a link to Menasseh) in London, but Hartlib (another link to Menasseh) was Andreae's friend, and he settled in England in 1628. Hartlib was central to the Rosicrucian mission in London, and round him gathered a circle of people who knew Cromwell and who kept him in touch with the Rosicrucian leadership and the Priory of Sion, both of whom wanted to overthrow the Templar Stuart line which Charles I now represented.

According to Lady Queenborough, "The Rose Croix...had spread rapidly among the Puritans."[80] I suspect that Cromwell was not inducted into Rosicrucianism until 1638, the year of his attempted emigration to the New World and of the Ely inheritance. My guess is that Hartlib introduced him to Rosicrucianism in 1638 rather than 1628, by which time Rosicrucianism had spread among the Puritans; and that Cromwell was meeting Hartlib, Hampden, Milton and others at the Crown, the Rosicrucian tavern, in 1641. It could well be that Menasseh paid visits to London at this time. Just as Andreae's Christian Unions and Hartlib's group made their Rosicrucianism invisible, it could be that Cromwell hid his new creed behind the Puritan label of Congregationalism, as did so many others.

We are now in a position to answer the questions we have asked about Menasseh and Cromwell. Menasseh was visited by Thurloe in 1651 because he had already been in touch with Cromwell since 1643, via Carvajal and probably Hartlib. He appeared to believe that Cromwell was the Messiah because that idea would advance the Jewish perception of England as a promised land where Jews could make a new Israel. He was linked with Hartlib through Andreae. His vision of an England without Charles I and with the Jews returned and ruled by a Rosicrucian Protector like Frederick V gave additional political expression to Bacon's Utopian, Atlantean vision and Andreae's Utopian *Societas*, which together formed the occult vision of the revolution. Quite simply, England would be a new Rosicrucian Palatinate under a new Rosicrucian leader. It would be a paradise for Kabbalist Jewish Rosicrucians.

The fundamental purpose of the Puritan revolution was the overthrow of the Stuart line by the invisible Rosicrucians and Priory of Sion, and as an invisible Rosicrucian Cromwell hid his Rose-Croix allegiance under the Puritan "Church Union." He was eager to champion the return of the Jews because he would receive financial

backing for his agenda of revolution, which included sole power as Lord
Protector. This was not Fairfax's or Parliament's agenda.

We can piece together the underlying pattern of events like an
archaeologist reconstructing a mosaic, and answers to our questions
about Cromwell begin to take shape. Did Cromwell trick Manchester
out of his army command by his Self-Denying Ordinance? Yes. Did he
collude with Fairfax from the outset to have joint control of the New
Model Army? Yes. Was Fairfax a Rosicrucian or Cromwell's dupe? It is
possible that he was a Rosicrucian: he had fought with the Dutch
against the Spaniards in 1629 and 1631, and may have met Menasseh
or his agents in Holland. On the other hand, he fell out with Cromwell
after Cromwell became Protector and would not take command in
Scotland, preferring to remain at Nun Appleton House in Yorkshire
where the poet Andrew Marvell was tutor to his daughter and wrote
"The Garden." This poem is the flower of the English contemplative
tradition, but it has not prevented allegations that Marvell was a spy for
the Dutch while he was at Nun Appleton. (Roy MacGregor-Hastie
states of his later career: "Andrew Marvell, who as 'Mr Thomas' was the
Dutch paymaster in the House, observed wryly that he sometimes
forgot who was spying for whom, but he was convinced that it was only
a matter of time before the King [Charles II] himself was brought to the
Bar of the House and arraigned.") In fact, Marvell seems to have been
an English double agent from 1672 to 1674.[81]

Did Cromwell intend to kill Charles I all along? Certainly since
1647 and perhaps since 1643. Was Cromwell's rise due to trickery? Yes.
To Providence? Perhaps. To a secret organization? Yes. For the secret
organization of the Rosicrucians advanced his cause, using secret
meetings to develop his strategy. Who were Cromwell's political
mentors? Hartlib and Menasseh.

We ask again, when did Cromwell become a Rosicrucian? It must
have been before 1643, when he was apparently actively collaborating
with Carvajal. It seems likely that Andreae (who was running both Sion
and the Rose-Croix) was behind Menasseh and Carvajal, with Hartlib
acting as the "agent" who was in regular contact with Cromwell. As we

have said already, it was likely to have been after 1638. But the question is still pressing: when did Cromwell meet Menasseh in his youth? Menasseh certainly added a Jewish intellectual gloss to the vision of Bacon and Andreae, and communicated it to Cromwell via Hartlib.

We can only speculate, but Menasseh's influence on Cromwell seems to have been decisive. The Puritan revolution was run by Sion (Andreae), which made common cause with the Jews (through Menasseh). Hartlib then gave it a Puritan label. Isaac D'Israeli wrote: "The English Revolution under Charles I was unlike any preceding one....From that time and event we contemplate in our history the phases of revolution."

There were to be many more revolutions on similar lines, notably the French revolution, but Cromwell's set the pattern for the future in disguising the true reasons for the revolution behind smokescreens (in his case, Ship Tax, the divine right of kings and Charles's absolutism and so-called tyranny), in subterfuge, Machiavellian intrigue and in disguising its true inspirer – as an Invisible Rosicrucian was required to do.

We are now in a position to draw some conclusions about the English Revolution:

1.   After Tyndale, the Familists and the British Israelite tradition, Bacon's Utopian vision of reformation and the advancement of learning round the concept of the Temple of Solomon was the main inspiration of the revolution.

2.   Andreae's Sionist, Rosicrucian vision of a *Societas* originated the revolution. Acting from the Palatinate and for Rosicrucians who had been invisible since 1617 in conjunction with Fludd, he planned to kill Charles I to make possible a Utopia. He used Jewish finance to distance the revolution from the Priory of Sion.

3.   Hartlib gave intellectual expression to Andreae's vision by implementing the Utopian *Societas* and communicating with Cromwell.

4.   Menasseh added a Jewish dimension of millenarianism, funding the killing of Charles to make possible the return of the Jews to

England and their conversion. He gave intellectual expression to Andreae's ideas about the Jews.

5. Pym gave political expression to Andreae's vision via Hartlib until 1643.

6. Cromwell gave political expression to Andreae's vision via Hartlib, Carvajal and Menasseh after 1643.

7. Menasseh funded Carvajal to create a New Model Army from 1643, and in 1647 promised money to fund a commonwealth once Charles was overthrown.

8. Cromwell's purge of Parliament (using Ireton as his front) on December 6, 1648 got rid of all MPs who were in favour of negotiating with the King. The rise of the "Levellers" and "Rationalists," whose beliefs were those of the French revolutionaries – regicide and communist – enabled Cromwell to purge Parliament on three more occasions (April 20 1653, January 22 1655 and February 4 1658), all of which cemented his power.

9. Cromwell gave physical expression to the revolution as Lord Protector and rewarded his financial backer and arms supplier by paving the way for the return of the Jews to England.

In this pattern, which has involved a completely new interpretation of 17th-century history, Cromwell was acting for Andreae first through Pym via Hartlib's group and then via Carvajal and Menasseh. Although the Puritans were funded by Jews, there would still have been a Puritan revolution without Menasseh and Carvajal, but it would have been different. Charles I may not have been executed.

Cromwell let the Jews back into England because he was implementing a Jewish agenda that involved Menasseh and Carvajal, in return for funding. This Jewish agenda is likely to have been Andreae's, and therefore the Priory of Sion's as Sion wanted the Templar Stuarts overthrown. The Kabbalistic Rosicrucianism of Fludd and Andreae had a Jewish as well as a Hermetic strand to it. The Puritan revolution thus seems to be an alliance between Puritans (i.e. Rosicrucians) and Jews

(Kabbalists like Menasseh and Carvajal), with the Sionist Rosicrucians manipulating the Jews into funding the Puritans (i.e. English Rosicrucians).

In view of our findings, there needs to be a reassessment of Cromwell. Was Cromwell a saint or a sinner? To the extent that he was genuinely seeking to make things better for England, he was a saint. To the extent that he was seeking a personal take-over of England so that he could implement Andreae's (i.e. the Priory of Sion's) agenda of killing the King with Jewish money and achieving supreme dictatorial power, he was a sinner. Cromwell undoubtedly had many reformist and millenarian ideas for a Utopian England, but the earlier saints from the congregation of reigning saints were seriously compromised by foreign gold, if our findings are correct. On the evidence we have assembled, Cromwell was less a neo-Israelite saint than a manipulative, Machiavellian politician whose revolution shook the stability of England to its foundations. Milton may have grasped this when he based his Satan (who is also called Lucifer) on Cromwell.

Both the occult and intellectual dimensions of the revolution expressed the Utopian dreams of the Rosicrucian Brotherhood, and gave the revolution its idealistic *élan*. When, however, this vital force became enmeshed in the two lower dimensions (the political and physical), its fire began to resemble violence more than inspiration and the Utopian idealism of Bacon gave way to the Republican ideology of Cromwell – albeit with the gloss of an infallible and all-justifying Providence.

We can now sum up in terms of the revolutionary dynamic. The heretical occult vision of the English Revolution was found in the more extreme anti-Papal feeling of the Reformation, notably in the Dutch Familists founded by the Hermeticist Hendrik Niclaes and drew on William Tyndale's earlier Kabbalist belief that the British were neo-Israelites.

The heretical occult interpreter was Francis Bacon, the founder of Freemasonry and developer (perhaps founder) of Rosicrucianism, who believed that God's chosen people, once Israel, would now be the

English and that the Temple of Solomon had to be rebuilt by English Israelites, and who wrote of a millennial Utopia.

The occult revolutionary originator was Andreae, author of Rosicrucian texts whose Utopian vision was of a hidden Rosicrucian *Societas* or society. He was supported by Fludd, who was influenced by the Familists.

The thoughtful interpreter who gave the vision a new slant was the Rosicrucian Hartlib, the Prussian German merchant who attended Cambridge University and settled in England in 1628, who put Andreae's overtly Christian (but in fact Rosicrucian) society into practice in the pre-revolutionary system in England, formed a circle of Rosicrucian revolutionaries and gave intellectual expression to Tyndale's and Bacon's vision. He took up Bacon's belief in universal education, translated the Czech Baconian Comenius and in 1641 published *Macaria,* which presented a Utopia based on the philosophy of Bacon and Comenius, whom he invited to England in 1641 to set up a college of social reform.

The semi-political intellectual interpreter who later became political in England was Pym. He articulated the political organization of the revolutionary vision. When the Long Parliament met in November 1640 Pym headed the middle group which dominated the Commons, and he organized the Parliamentary army and called on Scotland to send help. He was one of the five ringleaders Charles I tried to arrest in 1642.

His counterpart in Holland was the Amsterdam rabbi and Kabbalist Rosicrucian Menasseh. He believed the Messiah would return to lead the Jews back to the Holy Land only after their dispersal throughout the world was achieved, and he appeared before Cromwell in 1655, greeted him as if he was the Messiah and pleaded successfully for the Jews to return to England. He continued Tyndale's and Bacon's vision while keeping in touch with his Dutch friend, Grotius. The Puritan Revolution involved turning England into a nation of British Israelites.

The early revolutionary dynamic of the Puritan Revolution can be stated as follows:

Heretical occult vision	Heretical occult interpreter	Occult revolutionary originator	Thoughtful intellectual interpreter	Semi-political intellectual interpreter
Kabbalist/ Hermeticist: William Tyndale's British Israelites/ Dutch Family Of God of Niclaes	Bacon: British Israelites' rebuilding of Temple of Solomon	Rosicrucianism of Andreae/ Fludd	Hartlib: Rosicrucian *Societas* in Puritan England (became Royal Society)	Pym/ Menasseh, returned Jews to England to live among British Israelites

In 1643, the year Pym died, Cromwell took on the political expression of the revolution as military organizer. From being Colonel in February 1643 and Lord Manchester's second-in-command in 1644, he became second-in-command under Lord Fairfax in the New Model Army, which he had planned and organized. After his rise to sole power as Lord Protector he consolidated the revolution by subduing opposition, particularly by crushing the Levellers and conducting military campaigns in Ireland and Scotland, and through his political activities in abolishing the Lords and appointing Major-Generals to run regions after he had become Lord Protector. He died before the process of consolidation was complete; hence the collapse of the Puritan Revolution.

The full revolutionary dynamic of the English Revolution can be stated as follows:

Heretical occult inspiration	Intellectual expression	Political expression	Physical consolidation
Tyndale/Niclaes/ Bacon	Andreae/Fludd/ Hartlib/Menasseh	Pym/ Cromwell	Cromwell

The revolutionary dynamic of the abortive Rosicrucian Revolution can be stated as follows:

Heretical occult inspiration	Intellectual expression	Political expression	Physical consolidation
Bacon	Fludd/Andreae/ Maier	Frederick V's paradise in the Palatinate	Survivors hidden within the Royal Society

We can now state the revolutionary dynamic of the ideas behind the English Revolution as follows:

Heretical occult inspiration	Intellectual expression	Political expression	Physical consolidation
Pro-Israelitism/ Sionist Rosicrucianism	Anti-Catholic Regicides of Invisible College	Puritanism of Commonwealth	Purges of Protectorate

*

A final word needs to be said on the influence of Holland on the Puritan revolution. This happened in different phases:

1. The Dutch Family of God (Familists) began Puritanism and brought together Christians and Jews.
2. Cromwell's uncle's widow (of the Genoese banking family of Palavicino) was Dutch.
3. Amsterdam Jews through Menasseh funded the Puritan revolution via the Mulheim Synagogue.
4. Elizabeth of Bohemia funded Hartlib (and Dury and Comenius) from The Hague.

Being on the fringe of the Thirty Years War and the country that allowed Frederick V of the Palatinate to live in exile, Holland was a hotbed of revolution and Rosicrucian activity. Sefardic Jews had settled in Holland after their expulsion, and took their revenge on the Catholic Empire of Spain by funding Protestant armies in Europe. Now anti-Templars had taken their revenge on the Templar Stuarts by funding their overthrow. Holland also funded the new scientific vision of the Puritans (as expressed in Hartlib's circle).

Holland was a place where Kabbalist Jews from Spain and Rosicrucians from the Palatinate came together. It continued to play an important role in fomenting unrest in England until in 1689 another Dutch-inspired revolution swept the country: the so-called Glorious Revolution.

CHAPTER THREE

THE GLORIOUS REVOLUTION

Whether Lodges as such or Masons as Masons took part
in the initiative to invite William of Orange and his
consort Mary to become joint sovereigns in 1688 is not
known, but the suggestion is plausible.

Stephen Knight, *The Brotherhood*

The climax of the anti-Catholic Glorious Revolution against James II
took place after the Protestant William III's landing in England on
November 5, 1688. The Dutch Armada were supposed to head for
northern England, which is why the English fleet lay in wait off Essex.
An east wind blew them down the Channel to Torbay, and William
landed near Brixham with nearly 14,000 men and marched on London.
The Catholic James II, Charles II's younger brother, fled like his father
Charles I rather than accept William's terms.

On the face of it, it seemed a coup rather than a revolution, as James
II's son-in-law and daughter deposed him with Dutch troops. There was
much rejoicing as England had been saved from becoming Catholic and
was now Protestant, but there was unease that the English crown had
fallen to the Dutch when there had been three Anglo-Dutch wars since
1652.

What appeared to be a Protestant revolution against the Catholic
James II was in fact more sinister. To understand the forces behind it we

need to go back to the Anglican Protestant Restoration of Charles II, in which the Glorious Revolution had its roots.

COUNTER-REVOLUTION: THE RESTORATION OF CHARLES II

In early December 1659, Charles II was in exile in Brussels; his followers were cold, hungry, poor, depressed and in the grip of a Flemish winter.[1] In 1655 they had left Germany for Spanish Flanders, where Royalists enlisted in the Spanish armies. In the autumn of 1658, news came of the death of Oliver Cromwell: "The Devil is Dead." Oliver Cromwell was succeeded by Richard Cromwell, his eldest surviving son. In May, Parliament had been dissolved and the Rump restored with just 50 MPs. A clandestine group of Royalists, the "Sealed Knot," were planning a coup for August 1, and Charles had gone to Calais in anticipation of its success. The attempt was disorganized and poorly managed and quickly collapsed. One of the Sealed Knot, Sir Richard Willis, had been betraying the Royalists to the government. In fact, there were betrayals in every part of England, and the only Royalists to rise were in Cheshire, where 4,000 men were easily defeated by Col. John Lambert. Charles left Brussels and travelled to Rouen to find a boat that would take him to England, but the call never came. He was philosophical and spoke now of a restoration by Spanish and French aid rather than an uprising in England itself. Returning to Flanders, he put on a cheerful front, but his followers were in despair.

The Protectorate, however, was falling apart. There was anarchy in the country and Richard Cromwell could not impose his authority. In October, the Rump had cashiered Lambert, who retaliated by suspending it. Throughout England men whispered "If a single person, why not the King?" They looked to the King across the Water.

General Monck, one of Cromwell's leading generals, realized that England was in danger of being torn apart under Cromwell's successor. He believed that the military should be under civil government. Having secured Scotland, he assembled his troops and told them he proposed to march into England to assert "the freedom and rights of three kingdoms from arbitrary and tyrannical usurpations." In December he crossed the border to the English town of Berwick, and Lambert marched north to oppose him. There were risings against the army in London, Bristol and Southampton.

On January 1, 1660, Monck began his march on London. There was heavy frost and thick snow but the English people rallied to him. Yorkshire joined him in arms and there were many petitions for a Free Parliament. Monck wrote a letter ordering the Rump to admit excluded members, and printed the letter. On February 11 he marched into London, where people were silent and watchful, wondering if there was a new bout of army rule ahead. Monck then went to the Guildhall and told the Mayor and Aldermen what he had done.

Within half an hour the faces of the people were filled with joy. Bonfires were lit in the streets – thirty-one in one street alone – and all the church bells rang. In every tavern people drank the health of the exiled sovereign. Word spread that Monck had declared for the return of the King and for a free Parliament, although Monck still showed no signs of acknowledging the King across the Water. At the end of March, the excluded MPs voted to bring the Long Parliament to an end, and Monck saw the royal emissary Sir John Grenville, who delivered his message to Charles in Brussels. It advised Charles to leave Spanish territory as England was still at war with Spain. Next morning before dawn, Charles galloped across the frontier with his chief adviser Edward Hyde and reached Breda, where he signed a Declaration securing a bloodless counter-revolution – a restoration without conditions. The King would leave all to the will of a free Parliament and Monck would become Captain-General of the King's forces. In April Monck defeated Lambert, who had escaped from the Tower, at Daventry in the Midlands, and the Cavaliers won the Parliamentary elections.

Monck now asked Mrs Monck to prepare Whitehall for the King's arrival. On May 1 Sir John Grenville brought a letter from the King to Parliament which the Speaker read aloud while MPs took off their hats and listened bare-headed. Monck's cousin, William Morrice then moved that the Constitution of England lay in King, Lords and Commons. The vote was carried unanimously, Grenville was thanked, and the King was voted £50,000 and invited to return at once to rule. The Puritan MP Luke Robinson made a tearful speech, recanting for an hour and a half, but no one listened. Everyone was overjoyed. Bells rang, the King's health was toasted in the taverns and bonfires burned. A Monarchy that had ended with much bloodshed had been restored without a drop being spilt.

On May 14, Charles set out from Breda for The Hague with his brother James, Duke of York, his sister Mary and her son William of Orange (his nephew). On May 22 50,000 people gathered on the sand-dunes near Dover to welcome the Royal Fleet. About 3.00 pm on May 25, Charles was rowed towards packed beaches in the Admiral's barge. From every fort and ship guns fired. Charles II stepped ashore, knelt and gave thanks to God then hugged the waiting Monck, kissing him and calling him "Father." Thousands on the beaches cried out "God Save the King!" and "God Save General Monck!"

Charles spent the week-end in Canterbury and then entered London on the 29th. A crowd of 100,000 roared as his procession passed over London Bridge. Evelyn wrote, "Such a restoration was never mentioned in any history, ancient or modern, since the return of the Jews from the Babylonish captivity." Many who had served in the armies of Cromwell were among the spectators. The King arrived at his Whitehall Palace where the Houses of Parliament and their Speakers were waiting for him. He received the address from the Lords and then went to the Banqueting Hall to hear the oration from the Speaker of the Commons. It was through the Banqueting Hall that Charles I had made his last, long, fateful walk.[2]

Charles had arrived in London on his thirtieth birthday, and he was to have more power than he had expected. He was bound by the concessions his father had made in 1640-1, but he was allowed to maintain a standing army and to purge the boroughs of Puritans. Charles's court was located in the Long Stone Gallery of the old half-mile-long Palace of Whitehall, which was home to Ministers as well as the King. The King stocked St James's Park with ducks and swans (whose offspring are still there today).

Having spent so much time in exile on the Continent and having developed a taste for it, Charles introduced a touch of French style into English life, which influenced the arts and drama (Restoration comedy). There was a conscious reaction against the ex-regime's rule of saints and pleasure-denying Puritan code of manners and morals, and a return to the Cavalier pleasures of the senses: drinking, dancing, love-making, gambling and a delight in clothes. Ladies wore colourful dresses and towering lace head-gear while men grew their hair long as in the days of Charles I. The new King was to have many mistresses – in Dryden's words he "scattered his Maker's image o'er the land" – and from autumn 1668 it was his open love for the ex-orange-seller and actress Nell Gwyn (whom he brought to Court as his mistress) that more than anything else set the tone for the new reign. This move followed the dismissal of his chief Minister, Edward Hyde, Earl of Clarendon, who was blamed for the negligence that led to England's naval defeat in the Anglo-Dutch war that ended in 1667, and who was replaced by a council of five ministers.

The Restoration of the monarchy had gone well. There had been disasters in the 1660s – the Great Plague of 1665, the Great Fire of London in 1666, defeat by the Dutch in 1667 – but there was no anarchy and on the face of it, Charles II was less absolutist than his father and made things work. He understood sovereignty and famously said to Lord Bruce in 1681, "I would have every one live under his own vine and fig-tree." (This was a reference to the Golden Age under Solomon that recurs in the Old Testament, notably in 1 Kings IV. 25: "And Judah and Israel dwelt safely, every man under his vine and under his fig tree.") Charles seemed to be suggesting that Protestants and Catholics could co-exist in his England. (Shakespeare was thinking of the same Golden-Age text when he wrote in *King Henry the Eighth*, V. iv. 33-4: "In her [Elizabeth I's] days every man shall eat in safety/Under his own vine what he plants....") However, he was adroit in circumventing the limitations on the monarchy to which his father had had to agree, and subtly, deftly, won back some of the powers the Puritans thought they had removed from Charles I.

Though married to a Portuguese Catholic wife and though not passionate about Anglicanism, he appeared to stand for the Protestant, Anglican monarchy that recognised a free Parliament. His desire for religious tolerance was well known, if not entirely approved.

SHAFTESBURY'S ATTEMPTED ANTI-CATHOLIC REVOLUTION

Boyle and the Royal Society

One of Charles II's first acts had been to grant a royal charter in August 1660 to the group of scientists who called themselves the Royal Society.

Engraved frontispiece of Thomas Sprat's *History of the Royal Society of London*

Bacon was regarded by John Evelyn as the true inspirer of the Royal Society. The engraved frontispiece of Thomas Sprat's *History of the Royal Society of London*, published in 1667, drawn by Evelyn, shows Bacon sitting beside a bust of Charles II surrounded by scientific equipment. The Rosicrucian Bacon, the founder of the Rosi Crosse and the inspirer of the Royal Society, whose work and occult vision were documented in the previous chapter, was the occult inspirer of the Glorious Revolution.

The Rosicrucian Robert Boyle (son of Richard Boyle who was one of Bacon's aides),[3] who also appears in Evelyn's frontispiece, friend of Andreae, Hartlib and Dury and founder of the Royal Society, also inspired the Glorious Revolution. He was among the first public figures to offer allegiance to Charles II, who became patron of the Royal Society (which was formed in 1662). Boyle was presumably hoping he would be on the side of Sion, and not the Templars like his father. In fact Charles, pleased to have such a prestigious appointment that associated him with brilliant scientific minds, took advice from Rosicrucian Sionists instead of from the Templars who restored him to power. Through Boyle, its Grand Master until 1691, Sion preferred to control Charles and keep him pliable rather than assassinate him. Sion's strategy included manipulating the Opposition.

After the Great Fire of London of 1666, which levelled much of the wooden city, the men charged with reconstructing London in stone, including Sir Christopher Wren, were members of the Royal Society. They believed that England was a new Israel, God's chosen country for a new age of enlightenment. Wren rebuilt London as a Utopian New Jerusalem on advice from the Rosicrucian Royal Society.

The Unscrupulous Shaftesbury

The Whig Opposition to Charles II grew out of the opposition to him of the Dutch Jews.[4] Initially, the Jews of Amsterdam were pleased with Charles. In August 1664, a Jewish petition signed by Manuel Martinez Dormido and two others complained that Jews were daily molested and threatened with the seizure and forfeiture of their estates. Sir Henry Bennet replied on behalf of the King that the Jews would enjoy "the same favour as formerly they had had so long as they demean themselves peaceably and quietly with due obedience and without scandal to his Government." An Amsterdam Jew, Jacob Sasportas, who had been a rabbi in London wrote that, "A written statement was issued from him [Charles II], duly signed, affirming that no untoward measures had been or would be initiated against us, and that 'they should not look towards any protector other than his Majesty: during the continuance of whose lifetime they need feel no trepidation because of any sect that might oppose them, inasmuch as he himself would be their advocate and assist them with all his power.'"[5] The spirit of this undertaking was honoured in 1673/4 when Charles ordered the Attorney General to drop a case against some Jews who had rioted.

Eight years after Menasseh's visit to Cromwell, the Jews had received a formal statement of toleration, and although they were blamed for the Great Fire of London in 1666, they had confidence in the Whitehall Conference admission in December 1655 that "there is no law that forbids the Jews' return into England." Charles II had reinforced Cromwell's policy towards the Jews, not revised it; and there was now a base from which Jews could make inroads into English life before the end of the century.

The shifting international alliances between the major powers saw England ally with Holland at first. After the Dutch defeat of the English navy in 1667, the pro-Dutch Ambassador at The Hague, Sir William Temple, was the architect of the Triple Alliance between England, the United Provinces of the Netherlands and Sweden against France (1668). This was broken when Charles II formed an alliance with France and attacked Holland between 1672 and 1674. To many, Charles now seemed secretly pro-French and therefore pro-Catholic, and the politicians aligned themselves accordingly.

During the 1670s, the King's leading ministers were the pro-Catholic Lord Clifford, Lord Arlington (formerly Henry Bennet), the Puritan Duke of Buckingham, the Protestant Anthony Ashley (the Earl of Shaftesbury) and the Duke of Lauderdale, who ruled Scotland. The first letter of their names spelt "CABAL" but though known for being a group, they were completely disunited and were regularly deceived by

Charles into carrying out policies they thought were his, but which he later disowned.

Of the five, the most unscrupulous and sinister was Anthony Ashley, the Earl of Shaftesbury (1621-83), who had discovered the political views of Bacon in the Bodleian library, Oxford in 1637, an author for whom he had a great admiration throughout his entire life. He had been an MP in the Short Parliament of 1640, then sided with Parliament in 1644. He had been a member of Cromwell's Council of State (1653-4 and 1659) after having persuaded the Royalist majority in Parliament to resign its powers to Cromwell. In 1660, he was one of the 12 commissioners sent to Holland to invite Charles II to return, and, having become a member of the King's Cabinet Council, became Lord Chancellor (1672-3). In his career he had supported Charles I, Cromwell and now Charles II. As Dryden expressed it in characterizing him as "the false Achitophel" in his "Absalom and Achitophel":

> "Stiff in opinions, always in the wrong;
> Was everything by starts and nothing long."

Shaftesbury was linked with Boyle – and therefore with Bacon, Rosicrucianism and the Priory of Sion – through John Locke of the Royal Society, and with Bacon through his (Shaftesbury's) work with the New World.

In 1668 Boyle lived with his sister Lady Ranelagh, at whose house he received many visitors from the Continent, including Cosimo II de' Medici. He corresponded voluminously with the Continent, and his letters to the Frenchman George Pierre speak of Boyle's membership of a secret Hermetic society that also included the Duke of Savoy and du Moulin. This was probably the Priory of Sion. During this time Boyle, one of the founders of modern chemistry, was particularly close to John Locke, who had joined the Royal Society in 1668. Locke's subsequent career may have been directed by Boyle in his capacity as Grand Master of the Priory of Sion. In 1667 Locke had become family physician and adviser to Lord Ashley, later Lord Shaftesbury, at Exeter House in the

Strand, London. (He had studied medicine and experimental science outside his chosen subject at Oxford, and had treated Lord Ashley when he was in need of medical attention while staying at Oxford in 1666.) Ashley/Shaftesbury entrusted Locke with negotiating his son's marriage and made him secretary of a group that sought to increase trade with America. Ashley and the physicians John Mapletoft, Thomas Sydenham and James Tyrrell met in Locke's rooms to discuss human knowledge and the powers of the mind, discussions Locke led and which resulted in his philosophical work, *Essay Concerning Human Understanding*. (It was in these discussions that Locke encountered the Cambridge Platonists.) In 1672 Ashley became Earl of Shaftesbury and Lord High Chancellor, and Locke was secretary of his Council of Trade and Plantations from 1672 to 1674 and helped him write the *Fundamental Constitutions* of Carolina.

A Court party formed round Thomas Osborne, later Earl of Danby, a protégé of Buckingham's. Charles had entered into a French alliance against the Dutch, writing to Louis XIV care of his sister "Minette" (Henrietta), who wanted him to become a Catholic. In the secret Treaty of Dover, May 1670, Charles reached an understanding with Louis XIV that he would declare himself a Catholic when he deemed it opportune and that meanwhile he would help the English Catholics. In return Louis would give him £200,000 for each year of war with the Dutch and a further £140,000 to compel Englishmen to go along with his policy. Within three weeks of the treaty's being signed, Minette was dead of peritonitis (it was rumoured she had been poisoned). Charles was grief-stricken and took Louise de Kéroualle, one of his sister's attendants, back to England to be maid-of-honour to Queen Catherine, after which she became one of his mistresses (and eventually Duchess of Portsmouth). Soon afterwards the Protestant Buckingham, who was unaware of the existence of the secret Treaty of Dover, was sent to France to draw up a public Anglo-French alliance, which was concluded in January 1671. It was in the wake of this alliance that English and French troops attacked the United Provinces. The Court, then, was secretly pro-Catholic and anti-Dutch and Charles's support for the

Declaration of Indulgence in 1672 was intended to help Catholics.

Shaftesbury opposed Danby and the Court Party, the dominant small party of the time. The main issue of the decade was the succession, as Charles's wife Queen Catherine was barren and the King therefore had no legitimate heirs. Shaftesbury, who derived his occult Rosicrucian vision from Bacon, the Dutch and the Palatinate, wanted the succession to be Protestant. He was pro-Protestant and pro-Dutch (i.e. on the side of England's enemy), anti-French, anti-Catholic and therefore anti-Queen. (He opposed James, Duke of York's marriage to Mary of Modena, a Catholic princess, in September 1673 and lambasted the King's Catholic mistress as a whore.) Shaftesbury's support came from London where mobs could be mobilized with "No Popery" placards. His followers met in the coffee-houses and produced pamphlets. He himself presided over the Green Ribbon Club whose members flaunted the colours of their allegiance when they met in the King's Head Tavern. They formed the nucleus of a pro-Protestant Country Party which opposed the pro-Catholic Court Party. Their green ribbons may well have been intended as a reference to the countryside, as is the case with our word "Greens," but the "Green Ribbon Club" was clearly a Masonic Group at a time when – since the 1640s meetings in the Crown – Freemasonry and Rosicrucianism had become intermeshed. As early as 1676, the inference is that the Green Ribbon Club was Masonic and courted invisibility, and its members wore green, the same colour the Levellers wore. Indeed an early Masonic pamphlet of 1676 links the Green Ribbon Club with the Rosicrucians: "To give notice, that the Modern Green-ribbon'd Caball, together with the Ancient Brotherhood of the Rosy Cross; the Hermetick Adepti and the company of Accepted Masons intend all to dine together on the 31 of November next."[6] A comic menu is given with a humorous recommendation that all attending should wear spectacles – "for otherwise 'tis thought the said Societies will (as hitherto) make their Appearance Invisible," a reference to Rosicrucian invisibility.

Shaftesbury had supported the Declaration of Indulgence to help dissenters, but he now supported Parliament's reply, the first Test Act which was designed to exclude Catholics from office. He looked to the Dutch for assistance and, having Dutch connections, obtained bribes from Dutch agents. The Dutch paymaster at this time seems to have been the poet Andrew Marvell, who went under the name of Mr Thomas and acted for a foreign power to defend Puritanism and Protestantism against Popery and the encroachments of Catholic France. In November 1675, Parliament was prorogued for 15 months and in February 1677 Shaftesbury, aided by Buckingham, called fresh elections, urging that the long recess amounted to a dissolution. The Lords sent both men to the Tower for impertinence. (Shaftesbury took his cook with him to make sure his food would not be poisoned.)

Shaftesbury's opposition had led to demands that James, Duke of York should be excluded from the Throne, and there was talk of the unsuitability of Charles's Catholic wife (who was anyway childless as a result of miscarriages, while Charles had 13 illegitimate children). Charles was under pressure from Danby to make a concession to the Protestants, and he ordered James's 15-year-old daughter Mary to marry the Dutch Protestant leader, William of Orange. William arrived in the autumn of 1677 to a hero's welcome from Shaftesbury, and the marriage took place in London on November 4. Mary sobbed at the prospect of marrying the small, serious William, but soon threw in her lot with her Protestant husband.

The Popish Plot

The pro-Dutch Whig Shaftesbury gave intellectual expression to the anti-Catholic aspect of the Glorious Revolution. His was the most significant anti-Catholic voice throughout the 1670s, and he above all profited from the so-called "Popish Plot" which burst into the public arena in 1678.

The English people were suspicious of Charles's intentions regarding Catholicism and Popery. They thought Danby wanted to make Charles absolute, like his father, and they were suspicious of France. It was in such a climate that the plot erupted. Titus Oates, chaplain to the Protestants in the Catholic household of Henry Howard, 6th Duke of Norfolk, was urged to betray Catholics to the government by the fanatical anti-Jesuit Israel Tonge. Oates gathered information, becoming a Catholic in March 1677 and studying in Jesuit seminaries in Spain and the Netherlands, from both of which he was expelled. He and Tonge returned to London and alleged that there was a vast Jesuit conspiracy to assassinate Charles II and place his Catholic brother James, Duke of York (who had become a Catholic in 1668 or 1669) on the English throne. Oates it seems had invented the plot.

Danby brought him before the Privy Council on September 29, 1678, and the King himself questioned both Oates and Tonge. Charles listened in astonishment as the plot unfolded. The Pope, Louis XIV, the Jesuits' General, the Archbishop of Dublin and five Catholic peers (Arundel, Bellassis, Powis, Petre and Stafford) who would encourage thousands of Catholics to burn Protestant homes, were all implicated. Charles caught Oates in a lie, for the reputed ringleader, Bellassis, was bedridden. Meanwhile earlier in the month, Oates had made a sworn deposition of his evidence to a well-known JP, Sir Edmund Berry Godfrey, who was found murdered on Primrose Hill with a sword thrust through his body the following month. Rumour swept the country that he had been murdered by the Jesuits, and there was considerable panic.

Overtly Shaftesbury was not responsible for the fabrication and although Roger North[7] accuses him of being the contriver and inventor of the plot, the fact that Oates cleared James, Duke of York of being party to the plot may seem sufficient evidence that Shaftesbury was not the original contriver. On the other hand, being a very subtle man, Shaftesbury may have worked out that he would not be blamed for the plot if the Catholic James was excluded; it may have seemed to him too obvious to include James. Shaftesbury's public posture was that he had not encouraged Oates to come forward and make the conspiracy public. However, once the plot was out, he exploited the situation to the full and turned it to his advantage. Shaftesbury listened eagerly to Oates's allegations and fanned the flames. He gave Oates money[8] and used him as his mouthpiece. A contemporary engraving shows him holding a bag of money in one hand and a noose in the other, and the caption reads, "Lord Shaftesbury dealing with the Witnesses." As Dryden put it:

"Plots, true or false, are necessary things
To raise up commonwealths and ruin kings."

Shaftesbury took the opportunity to use it to extend the organization of the Country Party. He created a strong Party machine, controlled the elections and improved his standing in Parliament. In the bitter exchanges of the time, the parties called each other derogatory names which meant much the same thing. The Court Party were called "Tories" (a name given to Irish thieves and rebels, suggesting Papist outlaws); and the Country Party were called "Whigs" (i.e. Scottish drinkers, horse-thieves or outlaws).

Shaftesbury's agents spread reports of Popish plots and arranged regular Pope-burning processions to inflame the masses. The Bow Bells rang, and people thronged the streets and windows as a bellman led the procession with cries of, "Remember Justice Godfrey" and "No Popery, no slavery." Behind him a man on a horse carried an effigy of the murdered Godfrey. On a great float there followed the enthroned Pope in wax, accompanied by the Devil – a scene that might have taken place in 20th-century Northern Ireland. Behind the Pope came Dame Olympia, "the Pope's Whore," and four nuns called Courtesans. When the procession reached the Green Ribbon Club's headquarters, the King's Head Tavern on the corner of Fleet Street and the Strand, the effigy of the Pope was burned, its stomach filled with cats that caterwauled as they died in the flames.

A reign of terror gripped London. Oates's evidence identified 35 conspirators, and they were all executed. He himself became a popular hero, credited with saving England from the Catholics, but as the hysteria subsided inconsistencies were found in his story. Now that the mania had run its course, Charles had Oates arrested and compelled him to admit that his story was a fabrication. This threw the Whigs into confusion and some of the leaders went into exile. In 1684, James,

Duke of York was awarded £100,000 damages in a libel suit against Oates, and when he became King as James II, Oates was convicted of perjury, pilloried, flogged and sent to prison.

Was the Popish Plot an attempted revolution? Possibly. That is how Francis Ronalds sees it in *The Attempted Whig Revolution of 1678-1681.* If so, then Shaftesbury, or someone, was running Tonge, who was a Whig or Dutch agent, and was using his fabrication to attempt to exclude James, Duke of York from the succession. (Dryden may have been thinking of Tonge when he wrote of "hireling witnesses" in line 922 of "Absalom and Achitophel.") Was Tonge working for himself or for the Dutch? Was Shaftesbury a reformer or a revolutionary? He certainly sought to reform an excessively pro-Catholic monarchy that (following the secret Treaty of Dover) was prepared for the succession to be Catholic. How revolutionary he was depends on the degree of control he exercised over Oates and Monmouth.

The Exclusion Crisis

Shaftesbury precipitated the Exclusion Crisis which intensified public feeling against James and advanced the Glorious Revolution.

Titus Oates's trumped-up revelations led to growing pressure that James should be excluded from succeeding to the throne on the grounds that he was a Catholic. There had been another Test Act in 1678 to exclude Catholics from holding public office, and Danby was in the Tower (after Ralph Montagu, England's former Ambassador to Paris handed letters to the Commons that revealed his knowledge of the last French subsidy).

Meanwhile Shaftesbury had won the latest elections and now intensified his campaign of agitation. In April 1679, the Commons, without Danby, debated the motion that "The Duke of York being a Papist and the hopes of his coming soon to the Crown have given the greatest countenance and encouragement to the present conspiracies and designs of Papists against the King and the Protestant religion." Charles was willing to put restrictions on a Catholic successor, but he insisted that James would not be excluded. In May Shaftesbury put a resolution to the Commons "that a bill be brought to disable the Duke of York to inherit the Imperial Crown of this realm."[9] This was the Exclusion Bill. Shaftesbury's strategy was to steer it through the Commons and exclude James.

Soon after Parliament began to debate the Bill, Charles dissolved it, saying he could not endure the gentlemen of the Commons any longer. The King was now isolated, and Shaftesbury threatened to take proceedings against Louise de Kéroualle as "a common whore." To save her skin, she threw in her lot with Shaftesbury, promising to use her influence with the King to persuade him to accept the Exclusion Bill. Nell Gwynne, known affectionately throughout London as "the Protestant whore," now had supper with the King's enemies, out of similar motives.

Then Shaftesbury pulled off a masterstroke. He persuaded the Protestant James Scott, Duke of Monmouth,[10] Charles's handsome illegitimate son by Lucy Walter (and Dryden's "Absalom") that he could declare him legitimate and thus make him heir to the throne in place of James. Monmouth had been brought up in France and had returned to England in 1662. He was made Captain of the King's guard in 1668, commanded English troops in the Anglo-Dutch war of 1672-4 and was made Captain General of all the English armed forces in 1678. He was the King's eldest and favourite son and the darling of the people. Even so, Charles would not set aside James's claim in favour of his own fawned-on son, and when, in a pre-revolutionary move that signalled a coming attempt at revolution, Shaftesbury's mobs proclaimed Monmouth – who was now his puppet – as the Protestant heir, Charles sadly turned away from him. In June 1679, Monmouth put down an uprising of Scottish Presbyterian rebels at Bothwell Brig, near Lanark and dealt so leniently with the rebels that the Duke of Lauderdale declared derogatorily that he must be a "whig," which was how the term "Whig" came to be applied to Monmouth's supporters and then to the Country Party as a whole. As his military stock rose with the nation, Monmouth became a genuine threat to Charles, and he was deprived of his commands and sent to Holland. At the same time James was sent to Brussels to get him out of the way for a while.

In November 1679, Shaftesbury's Green Ribbon Club organized a demonstration. A long procession marched through the City with pictures of the Pope, Godfrey (the "martyred" JP) and the Jesuits. Shaftesbury himself, who had been dismissed from the Council, marched his private army of "brisk boys" who carried menacing knives and yelled. Monmouth defiantly returned before the end of the month (much to his father's fury) and received a hero's welcome from the City. Rumours circulated about a black box which contained papers showing that Charles married Monmouth's mother. To quell such rumours Charles now announced that the only person he had ever married was the Queen.

The Exclusion Bill was passed in the Commons and went to the Lords. There was a long debate. Shaftesbury led for the Whigs, Halifax for the Tories. Charles listened without intervening, but when Monmouth spoke for Shaftesbury he was heard to murmur, "The kiss of Judas." Halifax won, and the Exclusion Bill was defeated. Charles was now strong enough to announce that the next Parliament would be held in the Royalist stronghold of Oxford. Opinion was turning in his favour, and pamphlets now argued back against Shaftesbury.

Shaftesbury rode to the next Parliament in Oxford in March 1681 with an armed following. He still hoped he could force through the Exclusion Bill. The roads to Oxford were lined with his supporters wearing green ribbons. In Convocation House (now part of the Bodleian), Shaftesbury demanded that Monmouth be declared legitimate. Charles replied that that would be against divine justice and the law. Shaftesbury said he would take care of the law. Charles said he would never be intimidated.

The King then dissolved Parliament. He rode to the Lords and pretended to listen while a sedan-chair arrived with his robes of State. When he had put these on, he summoned the Commons. Believing that Charles was about to yield over the Exclusion Bill, Shaftesbury led the way confidently into the chamber. He was to be bitterly disappointed. The King's dissolution and his own dismissal came as a complete shock and caused profound dismay among the Whigs.

The Royalists now had the upper hand. On July 2, Shaftesbury was seized while in bed and, having been examined by the Council, was put in the Tower. In November he was tried for treason but acquitted by a London jury. (It was just before this trial that Dryden's satirical and highly influential poem "Absalom and Achitophel" appeared.) Oates was now put in prison, and when Shaftesbury tried to stir up his "brisk boys," his private army, he failed. Without a Parliament he was powerless.

Shaftesbury spent a year plotting a rising against the government. On November 5, 1682 his mobs beheaded some opponents in Bishopsgate but a few days later he fled to Holland, where he died after two months (in January 1683), a broken man.

The Exclusionists had not, however, given up and, urged on by the dying Shaftesbury in early 1683, Monmouth and others (such as the Whig Lords Essex and Russell) laid a plot to ambush the royal party at Rye House on the Newmarket road. Both Charles and James were to be assassinated and Monmouth proclaimed King. Charles altered his movements following a devastating fire at Newmarket and the plot collapsed. Informers soon made arrests possible: Russell and Sydney were executed; Essex committed suicide in his cell; and Monmouth fled with a reward of £500 on his head, which Charles did not attempt to implement.

Locke soon followed Shaftesbury to Holland. Locke suffered from asthma and had moved to Oxford, and from 1675 to 1679 he had visited France, living in Paris and Montpellier. He visited the grave of Nostradamus and René d'Anjou, and went to Toulouse, Carcassonne and Narbonne; and possibly Rennes-le-Château. (See ch 1 and Appendices B, Appendix 7.) He studied Inquisition reports on the Cathars and got to know the Duchess of Guise. (The Rosicrucian Fludd, it will be remembered, worked for the Duke of Guise from 1602 to 1620.) All these activities seem to have been inspired by Boyle and the Priory of Sion. In France Locke met the leader of the Gassendist School of Philosophy, François Bernier. Pierre Gassendi held that knowledge of the external world depends on the senses, a view Locke was to share. Locke had returned to England during the Exclusion crisis. Now that Shaftesbury had been in the Tower, it was not safe to be a friend of his in England – the Templar-run Stuarts were purging Sionists – and Locke was watched. Probably encouraged by Boyle, he too fled to Holland in September 1683. Locke lived in Amsterdam, we must assume as Boyle's Sionist agent, and was doubtless in touch with Shaftesbury's circle of exiles. Significantly, in 1684 Charles II personally stripped him of his studentship at Christ Church.

That autumn Monmouth twice visited Charles at Whitehall and agreed to sign a document admitting his guilt. On November 24 he surrendered and the King joyfully received him at court. But his friends urged him to think again, and Monmouth was rash enough to ask for the return of his confession. Charles told him to "go to Hell or Holland" and Monmouth went into exile.

In 1684 Charles attempted another reconciliation and in November, Monmouth again came to Whitehall. He was invited back to London the following February, the month in which Charles died. On Sunday February 1, Charles had contracted a lame foot and tossed restlessly all night. On Monday about 7 am, he "fell down (and scarce any sign of Life remained in him for the space of four houres)," according to a contemporary broadsheet; he was deemed to have suffered "a Fit of an Apoplexy" (i.e. the rupture of a brain artery, a stroke). He was barely conscious throughout Tuesday and Wednesday, and at one point apologized to those around his bed, "I am sorry, gentlemen, for being such an unconscionable time a'dying." On Thursday, Charles declined the Anglican last sacrament. Louise, in her own apartment, told James that Charles had recently become a Catholic. James then fetched Father Huddlestone, the Catholic priest who had helped the King after Worcester, and who now administered the sacrament of extreme unction. Afterwards Charles's illegitimate sons knelt for a blessing: Barbara Palmer's Southampton, Grafton and Northumberland; Nell Gwynne's St Albans; and Louise de Kéroualle's Richmond. The son he loved most, Monmouth, was not present. Charles said goodbye to James, begging him to look after Louise and his children; "and let not poor Nelly starve," he murmured. Soon he was unconscious and lapsed into a coma. He died at midday on Friday, February 6, aged 54. Had he been poisoned by James or a Jesuit? Had he been given a slow-working poison that first made his foot lame and then brought on a stroke?

Monmouth's Attempted Revolution

Whatever the cause of his death, Charles II had died a Catholic, and now James, Duke of York – a Catholic for 17 years – was King as James II. For Monmouth, now in Amsterdam, the death of Charles was a disaster as he could not expect his Catholic uncle James to look kindly upon his position as champion of the Protestant Exclusionists. There were great numbers of English exiles in Amsterdam, where Shaftesbury had died, at that time – Puritans, Anabaptists, Exclusionists and Whigs, including Locke – and a group of exiles including Lord Grey (a close friend of Shaftesbury) continued Shaftesbury's championing of Monmouth and felt that he should invade England and depose the Catholic King. Flattered, the Duke pawned his family's heirlooms to pay for the chartering of a 32-gun frigate that would carry 82 of his followers to the south coast of England. The Duke of Argyll sailed ahead of him in May to raise a rebellion of Scottish Covenanters, which was planned to coincide with Monmouth's rebellion. The idea was to confront James's army with a force from Scotland and move from the south at the same time in the hope of securing risings in Cheshire and London.

But the Scottish rebellion never happened as the Royal army had learned of Argyll's intentions. They captured him and executed him in Edinburgh on June 30. His supporters were transported to the West Indies.

Monmouth landed at Lyme Regis in June with his 82 followers. By his side, Joseph Tyler read out his revolutionary Declaration against James II (written by the

Monmouth

Rev Robert Ferguson, "the Plotter"), which accused the King of being a usurper and a tyrant. It blamed him for all the disasters in the kingdom, including the Fire of London and the poisoning of Charles II. Monmouth's band was joined by large numbers of West Countrymen armed with muskets and scythes. The Whig gentry, however, did not join him. Monmouth marched his army to Taunton, where he was proclaimed King, while James's army of 8,000 men advanced to meet him. But Monmouth, who had been counting on desertions that never materialized, marched on towards Bristol, allowing the Royal army to re-take Lyme and Taunton in his rear.

Bristol was poorly defended but even so Monmouth retreated. On July 5 he resolved to attack the Royal troops under Lord Faversham and his second-in-command John Churchill (later Duke of Marlborough) who were camped on the plain of Sedgemoor, Somerset, surprising them by night. Lord Grey's cavalry ran into a royal outpost, and his soldiers found it hard to cross the Bussex Rhine, a wide ditch.

At dawn Monmouth's men were revealed lining up along the ditch. The royal red-coated infantry swarmed over the Bussex Rhine and put them to flight. Perhaps 400 of his men were killed in the Sedgemoor corn and another thousand by pikes and bayonets while fleeing. Learning that his cavalry had been routed, Monmouth pulled off his armour, took a purse of 100 guineas from his servant and galloped off with Grey and two others to the Polden Hills. They were discovered a few days later by militiamen and arrested. Monmouth was captured hungry and dishevelled under a tree now known as "Monmouth's Ash" near Woodlands, Blandford Forum, Dorset. When he arrived in London he crossed the Thames by boat and was taken straight to the Tower.

Monmouth pleaded for his life on any terms: he would reveal the names of the other conspirators, he would become the King's most loyal subject (as he had said after the Rye House plot), he would even become a Catholic. James may have been impressed by the last promise. On July 14 he agreed to see Monmouth, who was led into the royal presence with his arms bound behind him with silk cord. He threw himself at

James's feet, sobbing and grovelling and begging for a pardon. James however was still incensed at his Declaration, which had now been published. According to Sir John Bramston, he asked Monmouth how he could expect clemency after making "me a murderer and poisoner of my dear brother, besides all the other villainies you charge me with in your declaration?"[11] The King wrote later that day to William of Orange: "The Duke of Monmouth seemed more concerned and desirous to live, and did not behave himself so well as I expected nor as one ought to have expected from one who had taken upon him to be King. I have signed the warrant for his execution tomorrow."[12] Monmouth was sent back to the Tower to be executed under the Bill of Attainder which made a trial unnecessary in cases of high treason.

On July 15 he was brought to Tower Hill for execution. He had recovered his dignity and while apologizing for the trouble he had caused, especially to his own supporters, and while confirming that Charles II had not married his mother, he nevertheless refused to declare that it was a heinous sin to rebel against the King. On the scaffold Monmouth gave the executioner a sum of money and promised his servant would give him more if he severed his head cleanly. To the indignation of the crowd the headsman, Jack Ketch, barely broke the skin of his neck with the first blow and after four more hacks with his axe the head was still on and Monmouth was still alive. Jack Ketch then threw down his axe and refused to continue. The Sheriff of London however persuaded him to finish the job, and Ketch proceeded to cut his head off with a knife, presumably sawing backwards and forwards. Monmouth's rebel followers were either executed or handed over to Judge Jeffreys' Bloody Assizes. Three hundred were hanged, drawn and quartered, their bodies displayed all over the west country as a warning, and a thousand more were transported to the West Indies. Among those hunted for their involvement in Monmouth's invasion was John Locke, whose name was on a list of 84 traitors wanted by the English government in 1685.

The Amsterdam-planned invasion of England by the Protestant Monmouth had come to grief, and the Catholic James had defeated

Monmouth's attempted revolution to replace him.

It is worth noting that the 16th-century split in Christendom between Protestants and Catholics, and then the 17th-century split between Anglicans and Puritans, weakened English civilization and the new bout of Protestant-Catholic division following the Restoration took a further toll. The split into parties in political life, the Court Party and the Country Party, Tories and Whigs, further undermined the unity of English civilization. There was now both religious and political schism. The schism in religious life meant that religious sects were put before God. The schism in political life meant that political parties were put before the nation.

Who was the beneficiary of these splits? *Cui bono?* In the religious and political splits of the Puritan Revolution the beneficiaries were the Rosicrucians and Amsterdam Jews. Were they also the beneficiaries of the Glorious Revolution?

WILLIAM OF ORANGE'S ROSICRUCIAN REVOLUTION

Shaftesbury Urges Rosicrucian William to Marry Mary

William of Orange's[13] forebears came from the town and principality of Orange on the left bank of the Rhône to the north of Avignon in France. In the 13th century the counts of Orange called themselves princes, and in 1544 a count of the German House of Nassau, whose Lahn river bordered the Palatinate, William the Silent, became Prince of Orange as William I. He had extensive holdings in the Netherlands – estates in Brabant with a seat at Breda – and on the death of his cousin René in 1544 he inherited the combined wealth of the Houses of Nassau-Breda and of Chalon-Orange.

This William led the Netherlands' revolt against Spain from 1568 to his death in 1584, which amounted to a revolution. In 1556 the Netherlands, then a collection of 17 Dutch- and French-speaking provinces including Antwerp, the financial centre of the world where every important loan in Europe was negotiated,[14] was under the Duke of Burgundy, the Habsburg Emperor Charles V. The Netherlands realized they was part of the Spanish Empire when he set sail to inherit the Spanish throne, leaving his son Philip in charge. Inspired by Calvinism, in 1566 Dutch noblemen had presented a petition, known as the *Compromis*, addressed to Philip, who was now King of Spain, to his regent in the Netherlands, Margaret of Parma, demanding religious tolerance. It had been written by Philip Marnix, Count of St. Aldegonde, a fervent Calvinist poet and Dutch Israelite who had translated the Psalms. William now gave the Dutch revolt political expression, raising an army in Germany and returning in 1572 to weaken Spain's grip on the Netherlands. He effected a political alliance of all the states at the Pacification of Ghent. When this collapsed, the seven northern Protestant provinces formed the Union of Utrecht, and in 1581 became the United Provinces. After William's assassination by a Spanish agent, Elizabeth I sent the Earl of Leicester and an expeditionary force that included Sir Philip Sidney and Francis Vere to oppose Philip's Spanish rule in the Netherlands. As a result of this expeditionary force Spain began to mobilize against England, although the Spanish Armada did not appear until 1588. Maurice of Nassau had succeeded William, and he consolidated the Dutch republic, rolling back the boundaries to their present extent.

William had founded the dynasty of stadholders or lieutenants in the Netherlands, and had held the office of stadholder in four of the rebellious provinces. From then on it was a tradition in the Dutch Republic that the seven stadholders were identified exclusively with the princes and counts of Orange-Nassau, and the Orange party consisted of nobles, Calvinist leaders and peasants. It was opposed by "anti-foreign" patriotic Dutch libertarians like Johan de Witt. Every royal House in Europe is directly descended from William I, including Queen Juliana of the Netherlands and the monarchs of Denmark, Norway, Sweden, Greece, Monaco and Luxembourg.

William of Orange was the son of William II, who had died of smallpox a week before he was born in 1650. William II had married

Charles I's daughter Mary (who died in 1660). The young William was thus fourth in line to the English throne in his own right, and was the great-nephew of Elizabeth Stuart of the Palatinate on his mother's side. (William was twelve when Elizabeth Stuart died at The Hague in 1662.) He was also connected to Elizabeth Stuart and the Palatinate on his father's side, for his grandfather Frederick Henry (Stadholder-General 1625-47) had been a womanizer who in 1624 had married a lady-in-waiting (Amalia von Solms) to the exiled Elizabeth Stuart and Frederick V, formerly of the Palatinate and now at The Hague. Frederick Henry had become Rosicrucian.

A contemporary print from after 1688 shows the first four princes of Orange – William I, Maurice, Frederick Henry and William II – grouped round the central figure of William III wearing the English crown, and above them all is a rayed sun with an eye in the centre: the Rosicrucian sun with the Sionist eye. This print (see illustration) demonstrates that the House of Orange was Rosicrucian. It was Frederick Henry who made it so.

Until about 1640 Frederick Henry alone was responsible for the United Provinces' foreign policy, and the crowning glory of his strategy was to marry his son William II to Charles I's daughter in 1641. He hoped that William would establish an Orange monarchy. He had presumably used his connection with Elizabeth Stuart through his wife to effect an introduction to Mary, who hated living in Holland and was an English Stuart before a Dutch mother.

William's father had been stadholder of five of the United Provinces of the Netherlands (which was a federation of seven of the seventeen provinces of the Low Countries under Habsburg rule, ten being Spanish), but he had made enemies within the republican oligarchy that dominated Amsterdam and the province of Holland. On his death this party, the States party, excluded the House of Orange from power. Cromwell's hand was in the decision, for Cromwell was suspicious of the House of Orange's links with the Stuarts and had proposed the union of England and Holland, which the Dutch rejected. He now wanted to make sure William had no power. By the Act of Seclusion

William I, Maurice, Frederick Henry and William II –
grouped round the central figure of William III

(1654) William and his descendants were forbidden to hold office in the State of England.

From the outset, however, William had been brought up to rule. He grew up under the watchful eye of his grandmother Amalia von Solms, who embodied Frederick Henry's Rosicrucian influence, and her secretary Huygens. He had his own court when he was two and made public appearances to cheering crowds from the time he was four. At six he was instructed in Calvinism by the Reverend Cornelius Trigland. He was educated first by Frederick van Nassau Zuylestein, an illegitimate son of his grandfather Frederick Henry and a Rosicrucian, and then by Johan de Witt, the leading figure in the States of Holland. As Councillor-Pensioner of Holland from 1653 to 1672, he was one of the foremost European statesmen of the 17th century. (De Witt was opposed to the House of Orange, and presumably hoped to indoctrinate William into renouncing his claim to power.) In 1670 Charles II invited William to England for four months. Charles saw him as an Englishman and a Stuart, and hoped to make common cause against the States party, their mutual enemy. In 1671 Louis XIV of France and Charles II of England were planning a joint attack on the United Provinces. Louis claimed the Spanish Netherlands in the name of his wife, the infanta Maria Theresa, and Charles was concerned that the Dutch Councillor-Pensioner de Witt and his States party were sidelining the House of Orange. William was made Captain General in 1672 despite opposition from patriots like de Witt and the States party.

Mary had felt that England was about to make war against the Dutch because Charles's relative William had not been given his rightful offices by the regents of Holland. There was popular violence, and William tried to do a deal with Charles that would remove England from the war, but he also sought to turn the violence against such political opponents as the de Witt brothers. Orangist pamphlets charged Johan de Witt with crimes, and he resigned his post as Grand Pensionary, to be replaced by Gaspar Fagel. On August 5, 1672 Charles II sent William a letter saying his sole aim was to secure William's just rights against the States party. William sent the letter to Fagel, who had it read in the States General and States of Holland. Cornelius de Witt was already in prison in The Hague, and Johan was lured there by a fake letter. The mob broke down the prison doors in the presence of Orangists such as Frederick Zuylestein and then murdered them and sold their fingers, toes and eyes as souvenirs. (So William's ex-tutor witnessed the murder of his replacement.)

Now the de Witts were gone and their policy of stifling Orange and scorning England was at an end, William could seize power. Encouraged by Fagel, the States of Holland authorized William to change the town councils, and in so doing he removed all his opponents. With power now concentrated in his hands he was able to attack France. When Louis XIV and Charles declared war and French troops overran three provinces and took many towns in Germany and the Spanish Netherlands, William was proclaimed stadholder in July. His first task was to refuse the ruinous peace terms offered by Louis and Charles.

The Holy Roman Emperor, Leopold I, formed an alliance with the Elector of Brandenberg in the autumn of 1672 and with Spain the following year, and with their help and by rebuilding his Army William recaptured the fortress of Naarden in September 1673 and Bonn in November.

In this campaign against the invading French William was heavily dependent on the Jewish firm of Machado and Pereira, the chief contractors for provisions for the republic's land forces from at least 1679. William wrote to Antonio-Moses Alvarez Machado, "*Vous avez sauvé l'état.*"[15]

The French left the United Provinces' soil and William was called "the Redeemer of the Fatherland." Charles II made peace, but Louis continued the war for the next four years. William commanded the Dutch armies in Flanders and was still at war when he made his visit to England to ask for Mary's hand in marriage.

Was it his own decision to propose to Mary, or did someone put him up to it? The first rumours that William might marry Mary were heard when he visited England in 1670, the year of Charles II's secret

Treaty of Dover which created the alliance with France. Mary was then eight, and William twenty, so the proposal was that there should be a diplomatic marriage between two Protestants. Shaftesbury, then a member of the Cabal, was involved in the idea. Nothing happened for four years because of the Anglo-French war with Holland, during which William tried to undermine Charles by supporting the opposition to the Court (i.e. Shaftesbury), but the idea was revived in 1674 when Shaftesbury was leading the pro-Dutch Country Party. Charles II took to the idea, but William replied, "I cannot leave the battlefield, nor believe that it would be agreeable for a lady to be where the battlefield is." By 1676 it seemed as if the Dutch might lose the war with France. It was then that William asked Sir William Temple, who had negotiated the treaty ending the Anglo-Dutch war in 1674, about Mary's character. And it was Sir William together with the Earl of Danby who ended up arranging the marriage. The advantages of a marital alliance with England were obvious – it might prevent England from returning to help France – and though Charles might not offer much of a dowry and his niece Mary might not be any more popular in Holland than William's mother Mary, nevertheless she was heir to the English throne. Even so William managed to be contemptuous of Mary's mother, Anne Hyde, who had been one of his mother's "servants" (in fact a maid of honour).

Beneath the surface relationships of the monarchs and leading politicians, the Sionist Rosicrucians (probably through Sir William Temple) had been aligning William against the Anglo-French Templars. It is safe to assume that Shaftesbury and probably Fagel were Sionist Rosicrucians, as were the House of Orange, as we have seen. Sionist Rosicrucian forces wanted to detach the Templar Stuart Charles II from his Templar French ally and overthrow him, in a re-run of the fate that befell Charles I.

William married James II's daughter Mary in November 1677, and a contemporary Dutch medal celebrating the marriage shows the 27-year-old groom and 15-year-old bride standing beside a two-pillared Masonic Temple under a sun with long rays that resembles the

Dutch medal showing William marrying James II's daughter Mary in 1677

Rosicrucian sun that shines on the young couple of the Palatinate at their marriage. The sun that shone on William and young Mary in the Dutch medal has roses in its orb; it is very blatantly a Rosicrucian sun. There was a strong Rosicrucian Freemasonic influence round William during 1677.

Married life did not go too well at first. They had a terrible crossing to the Continent. Everyone except Mary was seasick. William was irritated by Mary's ladies-in-waiting and her chaplains, and he was tense because he could not bring peace to Holland. Mary miscarried in 1678, and though she believed she was pregnant again there was no child. But she settled in and came to like the Dutch countryside and the architecture of her homes: the Palace of Honselaersdjik, where they started their married life; their House in the Wood on the outskirts of The Hague; and later the formal gardens of Het Loo, which William built from 1686 onwards.

William's relations with England deteriorated. In 1679 his father-in-law James visited them while staying in Brussels to escape the aftermath of the Popish Plot. He lectured William about the dangers that faced the monarchy. William opposed Charles's plan to limit the powers of a future Catholic King because it would affect the Protestant heirs. He also kept apart from the Whigs' clamour for Monmouth to succeed Charles, but he did visit England in July 1681, hoping that Charles would call on Parliament to raise money for a war with France. He soon realized that this would not happen, and decided to contact the Whigs (i.e. Shaftesbury). They invited him to dine in the City twice, but both times Charles invited him to Windsor at the same time to prevent his attendance. (Was this a case of a Templar blocking Sion's advances?) Back in Holland, William received Monmouth in the winter of 1684-5, when Monmouth was in disgrace, and Mary often danced with her exiled cousin.

Amid the gaiety came news that Charles II had died and that James had succeeded as James II, and Mary was suddenly heiress. Life became more formal. Pages knelt to her. So long as no new successor was born William looked poised to capture English wealth and use it in the struggle with France.

As soon as William heard of Charles II's death he ordered Monmouth to leave his court and at James's request made an overture to France. He had little power in Amsterdam and could not prevent Monmouth from organizing his invasion force there. However, William did not want Monmouth on the English throne, and he sent the English regiments in Dutch service to help James crush the rebellion, which appeased the King. Relations between William and James were strained, nevertheless, as James had refused to give Mary an allowance even though her sister Anne had one, and as James would not give William the title "His Royal Highness." James did write to Louis XIV about William's rights in French Orange, but when Louis refused to listen he did no more and wrote to Mary that there was no more he could do short of declaring war. In spite of this James wrote regularly to William and Mary, aware that Mary was heir presumptive. In November 1686 he sent William Penn to persuade them to support his campaign to repeal anti-Catholic penal laws and the Test Acts, and thus open up English offices to Catholics. William and Mary both opposed repeal. Mary wrote a letter to Fagel on the subject, and this was translated by Bishop Gilbert Burnet, a Scottish clergyman who had had to flee England after an anti-Catholic sermon and had arrived at The Hague in 1686. The letter was published, and copies were distributed in England. Burnet discussed Mary's future role as Queen with her, saying that William would probably be consort. Mary was horrified and went to William and assured him that they would rule equally.

Build-up to William's Invasion

The ferocity with which the Catholic James II put down the Monmouth and Argyll rebellions with Parliamentary money caused great public disquiet. James did not disband his army; in fact, he expanded it, giving new regiments to Catholic officers with military experience in Ireland. This had led to conflict with Parliament, which had been prorogued in November 1685 and not reconvened. In 1686 Catholics were admitted to the Privy Council – judges had found that the King had power to excuse individuals from the Test Act – and later to high offices of State and Church; this led to conflict between the King and the Anglican Tories (formerly the Court Party). As Supreme Governor of the Anglican Church, James suspended the Bishop of London for criticizing royal policy. In 1687 he dismissed his Anglican brothers-in-law Clarendon and Rochester and gave Catholics exclusive use of Magdalen College, Oxford. A papal nuncio was accredited to the London Court of St James. In April, James's Declaration of Indulgence suspended the laws against Catholics and Protestant dissenters; and while some thought he genuinely believed in religious toleration, others insisted that he was seeking to make Catholicism the exclusive religion of the State.

All this the British public accepted, albeit with grave reservations. Nevertheless, forces in both Holland and England had an eye to an invasion soon after the failure of Monmouth's rebellion and began to encourage William. In September 1686 Lord Mordaunt called on

William to invade England immediately, and declared there would be no opposition. William replied that he would invade if James altered the succession or threatened Protestantism. Then in November 1687 it was announced that the Queen was pregnant. Now the public stirred. Until then, James's successor would be one of his Protestant daughters by his first marriage, the elder being Mary, who was married to William of Orange, ruler of Holland, the younger being Anne. If the Queen had a boy, however, he would have precedence over the daughters and would be a Catholic heir to the throne.

William clearly took the idea of invasion seriously now because in February 1687 he sent his friend Dijkvelt to England to urge the leading English politicians to resist James's pro-Catholic measures, which he opposed. John Churchill, later the Duke of Marlborough, wrote to William assuring him that both he and Anne (Mary's sister) were loyal to Protestantism.

There was deep suspicion in the country. In April, Mary had written, "I have received an account of the Queen's pregnancy which gives me good cause to suspect that there is some trickery afoot."[16] The account was probably sent to her by her sister Anne, who kept her informed. Both were convinced that James planned to end the Protestant succession by having a male heir who would be brought up as a Catholic. James had been filling Parliament with his supporters since the previous August, and William was now ready to invade. At the end of April, William was visited – probably at Henry Sidney's instigation – by Arthur Herbert and William and Edward Russell at Het Loo and William told them, according to Bishop Burnet, "that if he was invited by some men of the best interest, and the most valued in their nation, who should both in their own name, and in the name of others who trusted them, invite him to come and rescue the nation and the religion, he believed he could be ready by the end of September to come over."[17]

In May James reissued his Declaration of Indulgence and ordered it to be read in all churches. Seeing this as a pro-Catholic move, the Archbishop of Canterbury, William Sancroft, and six bishops objected in a petition, and James tried to prosecute them for seditious libel, outraging all Protestants. Then on June 20, 1688 the Queen gave birth to a son. At once a Jesuit plot was suspected: it was rumoured and widely believed that Jesuits had smuggled the baby into the Queen's bedchamber in a warming-pan. Just three years after Monmouth's invasion feelings ran high that a Protestant succession had been turned into a Catholic one by skulduggery and foul play. England was in crisis, very few in the country believed the boy was really the King's son and the Anglican Church looked towards Holland for deliverance.

William and Mary had seen this coming. They greeted news of the royal birth by asking for prayers to be said, but these were soon stopped. They did not attend the celebration at James's ambassador's house in The Hague. Both Mary and Anne were convinced that the baby was not their half-brother.

At the end of June the Archbishop and six bishops were acquitted and there was enormous public rejoicing for the Catholic policy of James had suffered a reverse. That same day the letter of invitation to William was written. It was signed by seven leading Englishmen: the Earl of Danby, the Earl of Devonshire, Lord Lumley, Edward Russell (who had visited William in April), Charles Talbot (the Earl of Shrewsbury), Henry Sidney and Doctor Henry Compton (the Bishop of London whom James suspended in 1686). It seems that Sidney organized and drafted the letter of invitation, which said that an invasion would succeed as James would not be supported by either the people or the armed forces. Had William intrigued the invitation, or did he merely accept it? On the evidence of our account, we must conclude that he had intrigued it.

In August William sent the son of his old tutor Frederick Zuylestein to England to set up an intelligence organization that would give him confidential information. James Johnstone, a Scot, wrote secrets in invisible ink. William, the younger Zuylestein, also approached officers of both the Army and the Navy to win them to William's cause. Unless the decision to invade had already been taken, this was a curious thing to do, and it seems that William Zuylestein was finalizing details of the invasion. (His public posture was one of congratulation.) Helping him was Henry Sidney (later Earl of Romney), formerly Charles II's envoy to The Hague, an Exclusionist who had hoped that William would succeed Charles II. He encouraged William to seize the throne.

Events in Europe distracted attention from the invasion, and a year slipped by. The Emperor Leopold had driven the Turks back through Hungary, and in August 1688 took Belgrade. Louis XIV, having secured a defensive frontier in the Spanish Netherlands before 1678, had attacked the Rhineland and persecuted the Huguenots. He saw that Leopold would soon turn his attention back to Western Europe and struck against Philippsburg, Cologne and Avignon. James II had refused a French alliance as France was unpopular, but Louis (who was looking for support) sent details of William's invasion plan, which he had discovered. James refused to believe him and was anyway confident that he could repel an invasion. Once Louis' attack had been mounted, William knew that Louis would not attack Holland while he was preoccupied in the Rhineland, and he resolved to invade England under cover of this wider war. To preserve the element of surprise he told Leopold that he would not depose James or harm the Catholics, and Fagel told the States General much the same: "His highness does not intend to dethrone the King or to conquer England, but only to ensure that by the convocation of a free parliament…the reformed religion will be secure and out of danger."[18]

In September 1688 Charles Talbot (the Earl of Shrewsbury), the Whig leader, now operating in the footsteps of Shaftesbury, took £12,000 to Holland as a contribution to the cost of an invasion, and members of the Bank of Amsterdam (which was begun in 1609) also contributed money.

The Jews of Amsterdam were mobilizing on William's behalf. So great had the Jewish community of Amsterdam become since the first settlement of Jews there in the 1590s that the English Jews seemed to be a branch of an Amsterdam-based international company. Amsterdam was now the headquarters of European Jewry and the Jews contributed massively to Holland's growing economic empire. Antonio Machado and Jacob Pereira were the most prominent of the army contractors, the *providiteurs generals* to the Dutch army in the Low Countries and abroad. They had lined up Solomon Medina (or de Medina)[19] as their London factor, to collect sums of money owing to the partnership from the English Crown, and he later paid commission on contracts to John Churchill, the Duke of Marlborough, of £6,000 a year. There is a well-known tradition that Francisco Lopes Suasso financed the invasion of England, advancing two million guilders without any security: "*Si vous êtes heureux, je sais que vous me les rendrez; si vous êtes malheureux, je consens de les perdre.*"[20] Jeronimo Nuñes da Costar, a prominent Sefardic army contractor, handled all troops sent by the Duke of Württemberg. Prayers for the Glorious Revolution were offered in Dutch synagogues. The funding of the revolution came from England, but was also being organized by Dutch Jews.

The Jews of Amsterdam gave the expedition credit; and in return William took many Jews with him to England. It was said that "a Monarch reigned who was indebted to Hebrew gold for his royal diadem."[21] Were donations freely made or did someone go and ask? And what was the link between the Englishmen encouraging invasion, the Dutch lobbying for invasion and the Jews financing invasion? What did the Jews have their eye on as their reward? Were they all acting separately or were they all part of the same process? Jewish money centred in Amsterdam helped William become King, but who gave the orders on William's behalf? Who co-ordinated this effort?

Shaftesbury may have been planning for William to invade England as far back as 1679 during the Popish Plot, but he soon made Monmouth his candidate. It is unlikely that William was thinking about an invasion that early. Mary would succeed to the English throne anyway so long as nothing intervened, and so he bided his time. Who were the Englishmen round William who made the conquest of England and Ireland happen – Lord Mordaunt, John Churchill, Henry Sidney and Lord Shrewsbury? Were they associates of Shaftesbury's? Was the Earl of Shrewsbury who took William £12,000 and accompanied him on his voyage acting for himself? And Sidney? Were they acting on their own behalf or for an organization? Were they acting for Boyle's Rosicrucian Priory of Sion? Who were the two Dutchmen, Everaard Dijkvelt and William Zuylestein? They were both intelligence-gatherers, but were they acting on their own initiative or had they been put up to gather information? William Zuylestein was the grandson of the Rosicrucian Frederick Henry. Were all these men Rosicrucian Freemasons or acting for themselves? Stephen Knight writes that politically conscious people were united by the need to preserve the main gain of the Civil War of 1642-51, the limiting of the power of the King, and that it is plausible to suppose that either Lodges or Masons, i.e. Rosicrucians linked to the Rosicrucian House of Orange, took part in the initiative to invite William and his consort Mary to become joint sovereigns. (Mary was of course heir presumptive, and it was her wish that William should be joint sovereign.)[22]

William Invades

On September 30, 1688 William made a Declaration to the English people, blaming all their grievances on the King's advisers rather than the King, and referring to "the pretended Prince of Wales." He said, "This our expedition is intended for no other design than to have a free and lawful Parliament assembled as soon as possible."[23] In other words, James would remain on the throne. William knew, however, that he may have to depose James; Mary was also aware of the possibility and she prayed for strength to overthrow her own father. On October 16 William put her in the care of the States General. Realizing that an invasion was imminent, James reversed his plans to Catholicize England and fill Parliament with Catholic supporters.

On October 20, William's fleet of 250 ships set sail from Helleveotsluys. They were driven back by a storm and there was damage to some ships, which had to be repaired. William waited for the wind to blow to the east. On November 1 the

William III of England

necessary "Protestant wind" blew, and the armada set off.

Under cover of the war on the Continent, William's armada under Marshal Schomberg avoided the English fleet off Essex. Blown by an east wind, William (accompanied by Bentinck, Shrewsbury and Lord Polwarth) landed at Torbay, near Brixham, Devon, on November 5 with nearly 14,000 men (getting on for 10,000 infantry and 4,000 horse). The wind changed to the west, and the King's fleet was blown back to Kent. William and Marshal Schomberg marched to Exeter and awaited those who had invited him. Jacob Pereira's relative Isaac Pereira looked after Machado and Pereira's interests in England and kept the army supplied with bread, beef, cheese and beer. Slowly the nobility and gentry (starting with Edward Seymour and the Earl of Bath) turned to William as he marched on London.

James joined his army of 40,000 men near Salisbury, but he had reversed his Catholicizing policies – all he had stood for – and lacked the appetite to fight. Desertions began. There were risings in Cheshire under Lord Delamere, in York under the Earl of Danby and in Nottingham under the Earl of Devonshire. Shrewsbury quickly secured Bristol and Gloucester. As William approached James withdrew. It was at this point that the King's three leading Colonels defected: Churchill, later the Duke of Marlborough, who was already in touch with William and probably the Dutch Jewish army contractors; Grafton; and Kurk. On November 28 a Tory assembly recommended that James should negotiate.

William marched slowly towards London. He received James's commissioners at Hungerford on December 7 and stated his terms: James should dismiss all his Catholic officers and pay William's army, after which both James and William would attend the next session of Parliament. (William hoped to persuade a free Parliament to make war on France and disqualify the new Prince of Wales.) The terms implied that James would remain on the throne but with reduced powers.

James II's Exile

The King, however, would not accept these terms, and, having sent his wife and son to France, he made an unsuccessful attempt to join them on December 11, driving along country roads to avoid capture.

James II boarded a customs boat, which promptly ran aground, was arrested by three boatloads of fishermen looking for fugitives and taken to Faversham before being returned to Whitehall. James resumed his life as King, going to Mass and saying Catholic grace before public meals.

William had been delighted to hear that James had gone. There were anti-Catholic riots in London, and the authorities invited William into the City. Now that James was back, however, William had a problem. He called a council of 12, who advised him to allow James to escape (rather as Cromwell had allowed Charles I to escape from Hampton Court in 1647). Dutch troops went to Whitehall and ordered him to go to Ham, Richmond, but James asked permission to go to Rochester instead.

According to one view, William, delighted that James was thinking of leaving the country, supplied Catholic troops from his own army to escort him to Rochester. According to another view, James arranged for a barge to take him from Whitehall to Rochester.

A contemporary Dutch etching shows the King boarding what looks like a small rowing-boat on December 18. He presents a sad figure in a cape and hat standing in a tiny boat by the Whitehall landing-stage with the Tower of London in the distance, full of grief that his daughter Mary was party to his deposition. He did not want to face the headsman's axe, like his father Charles I. Under orders to allow James to escape, the guards did not watch the back of the house where he was staying in Rochester. The king slipped away with his illegitimate son, the Duke of Berwick, in the *Henrietta*.

Another contemporary print shows James at Rochester on December 23. He is boarding a small fishing-boat with two short masts and a furled sail in a rainstorm, clambering over the side from a smaller boat. He landed in France on Christmas Day 1688, having lost two kingdoms (England and Scotland) but still retaining Ireland.

James arrived at the court of Louis XIV, who gave him the Palace of St Germain-en-Laye for his court in exile. The English King had abandoned his people not once but twice, and in February he was considered to have abdicated.

Did James choose to go, or did William force him out? The Tories, who had been wrongfooted by James's flight, were convinced that William had plotted from the outset and forced James out. William insisted he had not sought to be King; rather he had received an invitation to save the Protestant English nation from a Catholic tyrant. He denied that the invasion was a rebellion, and the Whigs, who saw him as their champion, were happy to believe him.

The Constitutional Revolution

The unease of the nation would have deepened had people realized that William was funded by English Rosicrucian Freemasons and supported by Amsterdam Jews, and that he was invited to England by Rosicrucians. The so-called "Glorious Revolution" was a re-run of Menasseh's funding of Cromwell to let the Jews back into England. Only this time the Rosicrucians and Jews were to make further headway as Sion recaptured the monarchy from the last Templar Stuarts.

Anti-Catholic rioting increased and an assembly of peers asked William to restore order. Troops kept the peace until a convention met on January 22, 1689. This held that James had abdicated as a result of his flight following his attempt at Popish absolutism, and that the crown should be offered jointly to William and Mary. The Tories had proposed that the crown should be offered to Mary alone, and there had been a long debate in the Lords between pro-Mary Tories and pro-William Whigs. The Tories had felt that James's royal illegality should not be solved by an even more illegal rebellion; the Whigs had argued that it was right to resist a tyrant through revolution. At this point Mary had written to Danby saying she would only be Queen if William was King. William agreed, and promised to make Anne his heir.

Mary sailed from Holland in the company of John Locke, who had remained in Amsterdam during William's invasion. On February 11 a tearful Mary arrived in England, feeling disloyal towards her father, yet determined to put on a brave face and appear cheerful. On February 13 William and Mary were offered the crown in the Banqueting Hall after being read a Declaration of Rights. They were then proclaimed King and Queen, and they were crowned in April 1689. They were also offered the crown of Scotland.

The Declaration ended the King's power to suspend Parliament and to dispense with its laws. It recited James's "abdication" and declared that William and Mary were King and Queen. After their deaths the succession would be: Mary's children, then Anne and her heirs, then any children William might have by a later marriage. No Catholic could be monarch, and no monarch would have power to suspend laws. It also forbad the King or Queen to raise an army within the kingdom in time of peace "unless it be with the consent of Parliament." There should, it stated, be frequent Parliaments and free elections.

In due course the convention turned itself into a "free Parliament" and the Declaration of Rights was converted into a Bill of Rights, which was passed in December 1689 (just before William dissolved the convention). The foundations of a modern constitutional monarchy were laid, in accordance with the Whig philosophy of John Locke's *Two Treatises of Government* which had been written in the late 1670s and was not published until 1690. Locke, who had been physician and then secretary to Shaftesbury from 1667, writing after Cromwell's revolution and the beheading of Charles I, argued that government was a social contract between the King and his people represented in Parliament, and that the monarchy was therefore a contractual and not a "divine-right" institution. He quickly became the intellectual leader of the Whigs. He renewed his long association with the Sionist Boyle, but the London air still troubled his asthma and he left for Oates in Essex (the house of Sir Francis Masham and his wife Lady Masham who was the daughter of Ralph Cudworth, the Cambridge Platonist who had earlier influenced him, where Locke died in 1704).

In the course of 1689 William became very unpopular, and many felt that James II could recover his throne if he ceased to be a Catholic. William could not understand English when spoken fast, and lived apart from the crowds at Hampton Court with the Dutch Zuylestein, his cousin Ouwerwerk and Bentinck (now Earl of Portland). The only Englishmen he spoke frequently with were Sidney and Charles Montagu, later Earl of Halifax. (Were they acting for the Rosicrucian

Priory of Sion?) Both he and Mary were homesick for the tranquillity of Holland.

Robert Boyle, the Grand Master of the Priory of Sion, had spent much of his time absorbed in alchemy, which he discussed at length with Isaac Newton and John Locke. From 1675-1677 he had published two alchemical treatises, *Incalescence of Quicksilver with Gold* and *A Historical Account of a Degradation of Gold.* In 1689 he declared he could not receive visitors on certain days as they were set aside for alchemical experimentation. It is likely that this was not really the case, but that he was creating some Rosicrucian "invisibility" for himself within which he could work with Sion's new King, the anti-Templar William III, and cement the Priory of Sion's agenda for England.

Boyle, like Newton, was a millenarian. Evelyn's *Diary* records a visit he and Bishop Lloyd made to "Mr. Boyle and Lady Ranelagh, his sister" on June 18, 1690, when the Bishop explained that Louis XIV was the Antichrist and that the reign of Christ on earth (a view that accorded with the Sionist support for a world king in Jerusalem) was only 30 years away, "that the total Kingdom of Antichrist, would yet not be utterly destroyed til 30 years, when Christ sho[u]ld begin the Milennium, not [as] himselfe person[al]ly reigning in Earth Visibly; but that the true Religion & universal peace, should obtaine thro all the world: …the Apocalyps…as meaning onely the Christian Church."[24] Boyle died on December 30, 1691 and his will provided an annual stipend to support a church lectureship that would defend Christianity "against notorious Infidels, namely, Atheists, Theists, Pagans, Jews and Mahometans…and which would be used to answer such new Objections and Difficulties, as may be started [sic], to which good Answers have not yet been made."[25] He meant that answers should be provided regarding the timing of the imminent reign of Christ and the kingship of Jerusalem, in accordance with his Sionist Rosicrucian Freemasonry.

CONSOLIDATION OF THE ROSICRUCIAN REVOLUTION

The consolidation of William's rule took place in Ireland.

The Bloodless Revolution in England, dubbed "the Glorious Revolution" for propaganda purposes, to make William more acceptable to the English people, was threatened by the return of James and his Jacobites to Ireland, which had been split between Catholics and Protestants. In 1641 Ulster had risen against English rule and there was fighting for ten years, until Cromwell confiscated estates from Catholics and Royalists. The Restoration returned lands to some Catholics, but left the Cromwellians in charge. James II had tried to allow the Catholics more religious freedom – while preserving the Protestant status quo. The Irish Catholics' spokesman was Richard Talbot, a friend of James's, who had become Earl of Tyrconnell in 1685. He had been appointed Lord Deputy to James in 1687 and was in effect running Ireland on the King's behalf. This alarmed the Protestants. Tyrconnell controlled Ireland at the time of William's invasion and refused to lay down Catholic arms. By mid-March the Catholics controlled all Ireland except Londonderry and Enniskillen.

Ireland and the Boyne

James arrived from France to start the recovery of his kingdom in Ireland. In April 1689 he called on the people of Derry to surrender. When they refused, he laid seige to the town, which held thirty thousand hungry, sick people within its walls. Food did not arrive from England until July, when the siege was lifted. Men from Enniskillen then defeated a Jacobite army at Newtown Butler, and the Protestants took control of most of Ulster. Feeling alienated after James held a Parliament in Dublin that threatened to confiscate Protestant lands, they gave William's army a base from which it could reconquer Ireland.

William kept his Dutch troops in England and raised new regiments to send to Ireland. The expeditionary force that arrived under its commander, Marshal Schomberg was inexperienced, but whereas James's army had only a fifth of the £100,000 a month it needed,

Schomberg's troops continued to be financed by Dutch Jewish military contractors. Schomberg drove the Jacobites out of Ulster but declined to fight James's army at Dundalk, wintering at Lisburn, where half the army (over 7,000 men) died of exposure and disease.

Shocked and appalled, William went to Ireland to take charge. He landed on the Irish coast near Carrickfergus on June 11. Mary was dismayed, for now her husband was fighting her father. But William was adamant that the Jacobites must be crushed, and took over an army of 44,000 men that was funded and provisioned by Dutch Jewish army contractors. There were ample supplies, and he had £200,000 in cash, some of which was provided by Solomon Medina, Machado, and Pereira's London factor who provided short-term loans to the Dutch army. Isaac Pereira contributed £36,000 to the Irish campaign, and his 28 bakers baked the army's bread in Waringstown, County Down, in ovens built in the spring of 1690. In April Isaac's brother William arrived to help him. Isaac was assisted by Alfonso Rodriguez, alias Isaac Israel de Sequeira, who was joined by his relative David Machado de Sequeira and his grandson Jacob do Porto. Isaac Pereira had such a supply of food waiting for the army that Schomberg sent 18 of Pereira's ships back to England loaded with surplus beef, cheese and beer for the Dutch troops there.[26]

William marched south with 36,000 men, while James sent his army of 25,000 men north. At Dundalk he heard about William's arrival and fell back to defend the southern flank of the River Boyne, west of Drogheda.[27] William's army reached the northern bank on June 30. It had superior artillery and equipment, and more experienced infantry, whereas James's army had a good defensive position. To prevent William from fording the river, James drew up his army on high ground. On June 30 both armies faced each other across the river. There was artillery fire, and a cannonball grazed William's right shoulder; he fell and reports of his death reached Paris, where there was rejoicing.

William now rejected Marshal Schomberg's pleas for caution and sent his son Meinhard across the river. James sent two-thirds of his army to stop him, but the troops could not engage because of ditches.

William now attacked the remaining third of James's army, which was under Tyrconnell, his infantry wading waist-deep through the water. The Irish infantry fled but William's infantry were repeatedly charged by the Irish cavalry – until his own cavalry crossed the river further down and put them to flight. William did not attempt to capture James, who fled to Dublin that evening and to France the next day. He had lost 400 men, including Marshal Schomberg; the Jacobites had lost a thousand. The only injury William sustained was a graze on his leg where a bullet had hit part of one of his boots.

James had been expelled from Ireland for ever, but his army fell back to Connaught and defended the River Shannon. William was unable to take fortified towns such as Limerick (where he lost 2,300 men) and Athlone in August and September, and his attacks were beaten off by the infantry, which fought with new heart. The war would drag on until 1691, partly because a declaration William issued in early July promised no mercy to the Jacobite leaders, who consequently became more obdurate. William returned to England and rejoined Mary while the Duke of Marlborough (John Churchill) attacked and captured Cork and Kinsale.

In 1691 William's army was commanded by the Dutch Godert van Ginckel. In June and July he besieged Athlone, which eventually fell, and on July 12 he won the battle of Aughrim. Limerick was still under siege, and Ginckel was about to withdraw for the winter, when, in September the siege ended in a negotiated settlement which allowed 12,000 Jacobites to return to France, to swell Louis XIV's army. The war in Ireland was now at an end, but there was great ill feeling between the Irish Protestants and Catholics.

For six years after 1691 William spent each year campaigning in the Netherlands trying to restrict French gains. While he was away Mary ran the English government, presiding over the regency council. Her relationship with her sister deteriorated when Marlborough's friends secured from Parliament an allowance of £50,000 a year for Anne. (Anne's lady of the bedchamber and childhood friend Sarah Churchill was Marlborough's wife.) In 1691 Marlborough demanded the command of the English land forces in the next campaign, saying William had too many foreign generals. Having betrayed James II and crossed over to William's side, Marlborough was back in touch with James's court at Saint Germain-en-Laye. Now regarding him as a double turncoat and having lost all trust in him, William dismissed Marlborough in January 1692 and put him in the Tower for conspiracy to restore James II. A few days later Anne came to court with Sarah Churchill at her side. Mary ordered Anne to dismiss Sarah as lady of her bedchamber, and when Anne refused, they never spoke again. In December 1694 Mary fell dangerously ill. William broke down and cried and had a camp bed moved into her room. A week later the Queen died of smallpox, without great pain, aged 32.

William was beside himself with grief and broke down before Parliament. He also broke off his relationship with Betty Villiers. Now she was heir apparent, William gave Anne St James's Palace, while he himself lived in Kensington Palace. Gloomy, bibulous, and in poor health, he used Anne as his hostess when he needed to entertain.

The Bank of England

William further consolidated his rule by creating a central bank: the Bank of England.

William needed money for the war against France, which had for so long threatened his native Holland; it was his lifelong ambition to defeat France and remove the threat. He also needed to reward the Englishmen and Dutch Jews who had made possible his victories in England and Ireland. The Jews had been readmitted into England informally under Cromwell and formally under Charles II, and they were now looking to control London's financial markets.

Under the Declaration of Rights, which became the Bill of Rights, William had promised he would never claim power to dispense with the law (like James II), and that he would never raise money without the consent of Parliament or keep a standing army in time of peace. In the minds of the Whig writers of the Declaration, who favoured a "contractual" monarchy, there was linkage between a King's power to raise money and to keep a standing army.

Despite this promise in the Bill of Rights, in 1694 William – without consulting Parliament – borrowed £1,200,000 in gold from the Jewish money-changers at 8 per cent interest, which was to be repaid a year later. The Jews agreed to lend him the money on condition that he gave them permission to establish a Bank of England and print for themselves in banknotes a sum equal to the King's indebtedness. He thus agreed to pay them 108 per cent interest (100 per cent in bank notes, plus the 8 per cent). As the Scot William Paterson, the first Bank of England spokesman, explained, "The Bank hath benefit of interest on all money it creates out of nothing." The servicing of the loan of £1.2m was to come from revenue from duty on beer, ale and vinegar, which was set aside under the Tonnage Act of 1694.[28]

It was a stunningly simple idea, that money should be created out of nothing and then lent to a government which should repay it with interest from the revenue received from taxation. Parliament strengthened the procedure by declaring that all debts incurred during the war with France were "debts of the nation," which it would repay out of particular taxes. This gave confidence to investors who were willing to make long-term loans, for their repayment was now underwritten by Parliament. At the time it was envisaged that all debts would be swiftly repaid, but more money had to be borrowed to offset the financial crisis of 1695-6, and the national debt was born (i.e. all the loans not paid back plus accumulated interest since 1694), interest on which is paid by the taxpayer.

Now government borrowing was a fact of life. William and his government had surrendered the English nation's sovereign prerogative to create and control its own money, and had passed on to the English nation a £1.2m debt plus interest which had to be paid out of taxation. If the government created its own money, interest-free and debt-free, there would be no national debt and very little need for taxation as the government would not be short of money for health, education and the armed forces. The English nation has never recovered, and is still paying interest on money borrowed to fight the Napoleonic Wars.

The concept of a central bank that had the power to issue note money had already taken hold in Europe. The Bank of Amsterdam, which had helped fund the 1688 invasion, had been started in 1609; the Bank of Hamburg had been chartered in 1619; the Bank of Sweden had issued notes in 1661. These banks were chartered by financiers whose ancestors had been bankers in Venice and Genoa. But whereas the Banks of Venice, Genoa and Amsterdam were primarily banks of deposit, the Bank of England was the first to turn its own credit into coin money.

The Bank of England was officially founded by William Paterson, who was forced out within a year. The man who thought up the new scheme was Charles Montagu (later Earl of Halifax). He had been elected as a Whig MP in 1689 and had been appointed a lord of the Treasury in 1692; he was one of the two Englishmen William was interested in seeing. It was he who devised a system of guaranteed loans to the government to finance the war against France. Another set of loans established the Bank of England, and soon afterwards he was made Chancellor of the Exchequer. In 1695 he pushed through a scheme for renewing English coinage: the Mint bought in worn coins and replaced them with milled coins of the correct weight.

Under the Bank of England's royal Charter granted by William in 1694 the Crown incorporated the subscribers of the £1.2m as a joint-stock bank, whose first home was Powis House in Lincoln's Inn Fields, London. The bank was allowed to deal in bullion and bills of exchange, not just deposits; and the security of the subscribers was provided by the 1694 Tonnage Act, for the Charter made provision that "rates and duties upon tonnage of ships are made security to such persons as shall voluntarily advance the sum of £1,500,000 towards carrying on the war against France." There were 500 original stockholders who were subscribers, 450 of whom lived in London in what was to become "the City" (now the world's leading financial centre).

The Jews with Dutch connections, many of them originally from Spain and Portugal, who bought stock by 1721, according to Sir John Clapham in his *The Bank of England, A History*, included Solomon Medina, Francis Pereira, two Da Costas, Fonseca, Henriquez, Mendez,

Nuñes, Rodriguez, Salvador Teixera de Mattos, Jacob and Theodore Jacobs, and Moses and Jacob Abrabanel.[29] In other words, those who helped fund William's armies in Holland, England, Ireland and elsewhere were given an excellent investment opportunity as a reward for their past services. Since 1751 there has been little trading in Bank of England stock; excepting the Rothschild-intrigued crash of 1815, it has not come onto the market in quantity for 250 years.

There were about 1,300 shareholders in the Bank of England. The English shareholders included William and Mary (who received shares to the value of £10,000 each), Marlborough and Shrewsbury (who invested £10,000 each), Sidney Godolphin (who wrote to William before the invasion and was made Head of Treasury, who invested £7,000), the Earl of Portland (formerly William Bentinck), the Duke of Devonshire, the Earl of Pembroke, the Earl of Carnavon, Edward, Lord Russell (later the Earl of Orford), William Paterson, Michael Godfrey (nephew of Sir Edmund Godfrey, murdered allegedly by Jesuits), Sir John and James Houblon, Solomon Medina (who later supplied Marlborough in Flanders and paid him £6,000 a year, who was the London factor for Machado and Pereira responsible for collecting sums owing to the firm from the English government, and whom William knighted in 1700), Sir Gilbert Heathcote, Charles Montagu (the deviser of the scheme) and the Whig philosopher John Locke.[30] All of these men were involved in the anti-Catholic movement from 1670 to 1694 in some form or other, and all were given the opportunity to buy shares in a lucrative scheme that benefited from the success of Whig ideas.

As a result of the Bank of England and long-term credit, England emerged from the eight-year-long war (1689-1697) in much better shape than France, but with an escalating national debt. The Jews, who until 1656 were not officially allowed to reside in England and were only formally readmitted in 1664, now owned a large part of the Bank of England and controlled England's finances.

The new Grand Master of the Priory of Sion after Boyle's death in 1691, Isaac Newton, became Warden of the Royal Mint in 1696 and was instrumental in fixing the gold standard.[31] (He had been taught alchemy by Robert Boyle, author in the 1670s of two treatises on gold, and owned copies of the Rosicrucian Manifestos, which he had personally annotated. Boyle had died before he could urge William to put into practice Sion's dream of getting its hands on the Templar wealth and outdoing the Templars as bankers.)[32] Gold replaced land as the standard of wealth, and usury replaced husbandry as its true basis. The land lost its lustre; sovereignty was tarnished and the landed nobility came under renewed pressure.

Again, the question must be asked: were the people who organized the Bank of England working for themselves or for an organization? What were the motives of Charles Montagu? He was one of the two Englishmen William would talk to at Hampton Court (the other being Sidney, the ex-Ambassador to The Hague, who probably drafted the invitation to invade). Did William tell him about the Bank of Amsterdam and give him the idea for a Bank of England? Or was Montagu working for the Priory of Sion, perhaps like the Earl of Shrewsbury? And was the creation of the Bank of England one of the objectives of the Glorious Revolution? (This involved the setting-up of the right to print money and charge interest, and the institutionalization of usury, which had traditionally been the province of the Jews.)

Capt. Ramsay sees the aims – indeed, the real objective – of the Glorious Revolution as the creation of the Bank of England in 1694, the suppression of the Royal Mint in Scotland (achieved by the expansionist union of England with Scotland in 1707) and the institution of the national debt in both England and Scotland. The charter handed over the royal perogative of minting money to an anonymous committee, which required the acquiescence of a tame king; it converted the basis of wealth from land to gold, and enabled international money-lenders to secure their loans on the taxes of the country in place of an undertaking given by the ruler, the previous rather dubious form of security.[33]

Whether or not the creation of the Bank of England was the aim of the 1688 revolution, the Mint was now run by a Rosicrucian alchemist,

Newton, and the Bank itself was owned by Whig supporters of William's invasion who had links with Rosicrucianism. The Bank of England must be seen as a Sionist enterprise, and Montagu must be seen as a Sionist Rosicrucian.

Rosicrucian Succession to the English Throne

The Rosicrucian Priory of Sion, whose Royal Society had helped install William on the throne and found the Bank of England, now intrigued a Rosicrucian succession to the English throne through the Rosicrucian philosopher, Gottfried Wilhelm Leibniz (1646-1716), who had to work for his living.[34]

The story of how Leibniz's documentation came to be accepted as the basis for deciding who should succeed Queen Anne on the English throne is a curious one.

Born into a Lutheran family, Leibniz had discovered Bacon while studying Law at the University of Leipzig in 1661. He moved to Nürnberg (Nuremberg), where he apparently joined a Rosicrucian Society in 1666[35] and became its secretary in 1667. There he met one of the most distinguished German statesmen, Johann Christian, Freiherr von Boyneburg, who introduced him to the court of the Prince Elector of Mainz, who consulted him on questions of law and in 1672 sent him to Paris. In swift succession Boyneburg and the Elector died, and Leibniz now concentrated on his scientific studies. He constructed a proto-type of the modern computer, a calculating machine, and presented it to the Royal Society in London in 1673. Here the young Rosicrucian Leibniz came to the attention of the Rosicrucian Grand Master of the Priory of Sion, Robert Boyle.

Boyle must have introduced Leibniz to the Rosicrucian Sophia, the daughter of Frederick V and Elizabeth Stuart (the Rosicrucian King and Queen of the Palatinate) and mother of George Louis (who would become George I of England). Through her good offices, Leibniz was appointed librarian at Hanover in 1676, and he formed a close friendship with Sophia, who was married to Ernest Augustus. Leibniz's position was with Ernest Augustus's elder brother, John Frederick, the Duke of Braunschweig-Lüneburg who had become Duke of Hanover in

1665. Leibniz became councillor in 1678, and to make himself useful devised all sorts of mechanical devices, from hydraulic presses to water pumps operated by windmills. When John Frederick died in 1680, Sophia's husband Ernest Augustus succeeded him. Louis XIV took Strasbourg in 1681 and, working in an atmosphere of French aggression, Leibniz made useful mechanical and practical suggestions that helped the Duke. Meanwhile he sought a universal cause of all being for his metaphysical system.

In 1685 Leibniz became historian for the House of Brunswick – the Rosicrucian Grand Master of the Priory of Sion Andreae, it will be remembered, worked for the Duke of Brunswick towards the end of his life – and also court adviser. He had to prove from genealogical records that the House of Brunswick originated in the Italian princely House of Este, which would allow Hanover to claim a ninth electorate. Leibniz travelled to Italy in search of documents, passing through South Germany and Austria, where he was received by the Emperor. He continued his scientific and philosophical work as he travelled. When he returned in July 1690, as a result of his researches, and to Sophia's delight, Ernest Augustus was invested Elector of Hanover.

He carried on with his work (and took on another librarianship, at Wolfenbüttel, where Andreae had worked) until 1698, when Ernest Augustus died and his son George Louis became Elector of Hanover. George was uneducated, drunken and boorish, and to escape the situation Leibniz travelled to Berlin, Paris and Vienna, seeking to reunify the Church.

In 1700 Queen Anne's heir William, Duke of Gloucester, died. All Anne's other 17 children died in infancy, and George Louis, James I's great-grandson, was now a possible heir to the throne. Probably not at Newton's personal suggestion (as Leibniz and Newton were by now in bitter dispute) but undoubtedly at the instigation of Sionist Rosicrucianism, Sophia asked Leibniz to act as a jurist and historian and advance the argument for the German House of Braunschweig-Lüneburg's claim to the English succession. As a result of his documentation (*Codex Juris Gentium Diplomaticus Hannoverae*) the

English Act of Settlement, in securing the Crown to Protestants, declared that Anne of the House of Stuart was heir presumptive to William, and that if she lacked issue the crown was to go to Sophia, Electress of Hanover, James I's grand-daughter, and her descendants, bypassing all other children of Charles II and the many Roman Catholics in the normal line of succession – including James Edward Stuart, the Old Pretender, and later Charles Edward, the Young Pretender, who attempted to regain the throne in 1715 and 1745 respectively.

So the Rosicrucian Leibniz delivered the English monarchy into the hands of the descendants of the Rosicrucian Palatinate.[36] This Protestant solution to the problem of the succession was popular with Rosicrucians everywhere.

The succession happened as Leibniz had foreseen. James II died in 1701 of a stroke, having given up hope of his restoration following the 1697 Treaty of Rijswijk between England and France. William died in 1702, unlamented, following a fall from his horse, which had stumbled on a molehill. He had broken his collar-bone and died just over two weeks later; his lungs were found to be shrivelled and rotten. He was succeeded by Queen Anne, who died in August 1714. Two months earlier Sophia had died, and as a result of the Act of Settlement George Louis ascended the English throne as George I. He spoke no English, and made no effort to learn; not surprisingly, he was considered unacceptably foreign by many English people. In September 1714 the Holy Roman Emperor Charles VI made Leibniz "adviser to the empire." When Leibniz returned to Hanover soon afterwards he received his reward from George Louis: he was virtually placed under house arrest. When he died in 1716 the entire Court was invited to attend his funeral, but though George I was at Göhrde near Lüneburg, within easy reach of Hanover, no one from the Court appeared and Leibniz was buried in an unmarked grave.

In 1710 Leibniz wrote in *Theodicée*, "All is for the best in the best of all possible worlds," a statement of optimism by a metaphysical philosopher that was savagely satirized by Voltaire in *Candide*. Certainly a metaphysical philosopher should affirm the Universe he has studied, and certainly it was good to be a philosopher or scientific thinker at that time. Locke, Shaftesbury's secretary for American colonies; Newton, Warden of the Royal Mint; Leibniz, genealogist for the Hanoverian royal family – all were appreciated far more than their modern counterparts and given positions that befitted their talents and worth.

The Rosicrucians had good reason to feel pleased with themselves. Within eighty years of becoming invisible they had perpetrated two revolutions, set up the Bank of England and captured (as they saw it) the English throne. Isaac Newton, Grand Master of the Priory of Sion from 1691, who had annotated all the Rosicrucian Manifestos, would have helped forward the Act of Settlement and would have been delighted that the philosophy of the Palatinate and the alchemical Rosicrucian Manifestos had established a new royal dynasty. He did not think much of his fellow-Rosicrucian Leibniz, however; although both arrived at the calculus independently, Newton was first – and wrote several pamphlets under the names of his disciples accusing Leibniz of plagiarism.

The Rosicrucians' cornering of the Bank of England and the succession to the English throne has proved very successful, for since 1694 there has never been a counter-revolution in England, partly because no political force in England has been able to raise money to fund such a challenge and partly because money raised abroad for revolutionary purposes has been successfully prevented from flowing into the country.

The Tories still hoped for the restoration of the Stuart dynasty through a monarch who would declare himself an Anglican, not a foreigner who spoke no English. Had Leibniz's documentation not been accepted, and had Parliament rejected the Catholic and Rosicrucian lines, then there may have been pressure for the oldest surviving Protestant illegitimate son of Charles II to be King; arguably, the Duke of St. Albans, one of the few illegitimate sons of Charles II whose royal ancestry has not been challenged, might have been identified by a pro-Stuart (as opposed to a pro-Rosicrucian) philosopher as being the rightful next-in-line, first on the grounds of age, and secondly on the grounds that the ring with a picture of himself set in it that Charles I had given to Bishop Juxon on the scaffold was given by Charles II to Nell Gwynne's son, the Duke of St. Albans – a clear sign that despite Monmouth, from whom he was now estranged, St. Albans was his heir. To anti-Catholics and anti-Rosicrucians our contemporary Stuart King over the Water is the Duke of St. Albans.

SUMMARY: THE REVOLUTIONARY DYNAMIC OF THE GLORIOUS REVOLUTION

The Glorious Revolution brought about great constitutional, financial and economic changes. The rapid transformation it effected through the violence of William's invasion accords with our criteria as to what a revolution is. In a sense it completed the revolution Cromwell began by creating a constitutional monarchy with reduced powers and a free Parliament in place of an absolutist monarchy. Because William was invited in by Protestants and because the Catholic King fled, the revolution was less bloody than most, and once Ireland was subdued the physical "consolidation" phase was legalistic rather than brutal. It centred on the Act of Settlement that led to a dynastic revolution against the Catholic line (and created Jacobite unrest during the first half of the eighteenth century). The great social change was the exclusion of Catholics from offices of State.

The Rosicrucian Sionist network spread from the Hermetic Boyle via Locke to Shaftesbury, who disseminated it through the Green Ribbon Club and Monmouth and then via Lord Shrewsbury and other Whigs to the Dutch House of Orange. In short, the Whigs were Sionists, and the pro-Stuart Tories were Templars. And Boyle sat in the centre of the web like a great spider.

Sionist Rosicrucians were therefore behind the Popish Plot, Monmouth's invasion and then (third time lucky) William's Bloodless Revolution. The Popish Plot was to discredit the Catholic opposition, not to depose Charles II; Monmouth's uprising was to dethrone the Catholic King; and the same forces had a second go with William. In the wake of the Popish Plot, there may have been a Catholic counterattack through the Jesuits, and Charles II may have been poisoned, as Monmouth claimed; and a baby may have been smuggled into the Queen's bedchamber to be passed off as a future James III.

Thus Sionist Rosicrucians were strong both in England, from Cromwell's day when Freemasonry and Rosicrucianism were intermeshed; and in Holland, particularly Amsterdam. They were identified both with the Jews of Amsterdam, many of whom were Kabbalist Rosicrucians like Menasseh, and, no doubt, with the various army contractors round Solomon Medina. The figurehead at the London end of the London-Amsterdam Rosicrucian movement was Shaftesbury, who paid Oates, and used his Green Ribbon Club as a secret society. The figurehead at the Amsterdam end was William of Orange. Between Shaftesbury and William were a host of go-betweens including Lord Shrewsbury and Lord Grey, who accompanied Monmouth during his rebellion. Among them must be counted Henry Sidney, Edward Russell and Charles Montagu; also the poet Andrew Marvell, the Dutch paymaster. Shaftesbury used Dutch money to bribe the likes of Oates to advance Rosicrucian designs, and he eventually fled to Holland in 1682 after discussing the possibility of a rising against the English government.

The Glorious (and bloodless) Revolution, then, *was* a revolution, but of the two the Puritan Revolution was more fundamental, with the Glorious Revolution finishing the job, dotting the "i"s and crossing the "t"s in modifying royal powers through the Bill of Rights.

The Glorious Revolution can be seen as the crowning moment of one long revolution that began with the Puritan Revolution. The alchemist Robert Boyle, reflecting at the end of his life, might have seen the history of the 17th century as a literal re-enactment of the four stages or processes of Rosicrucian alchemy: first, the Mortification (the humiliation and execution of Charles I); then the Purification (the Puritan régime); then the Restoration (the return of Charles II); and finally the Gold (Rosicrucians capturing the crown and regulating the gold standard in the Bank of England under Newton's Wardenship of the Royal Mint). In alchemy the philosopher's stone turned base metal into gold (which at the spiritual level was a symbol for the discovery of the divine Light and illumination). Rosicrucian alchemy had turned the base metal of royal absolutism into a prosperous constitutional monarchy that would operate through cabinet government and a free Parliament in the 18th century.

We are now in a position to sum up in terms of the revolutionary dynamic. What appeared to be a Protestant revolution against the Catholic James II was in fact a Rosicrucian Masonic plot with Dutch-Jewish help to set up the Bank of England through the Rosicrucian William. At first sight the vision behind the Glorious Revolution appears to be the Protestant Anglicanism of the Restoration, in which it had its roots. In fact the heretical occult vision can be found in Bacon's Rosi Crosse. The heretical occult interpreter was Andreae's Rosicrucianism which entered the Palatinate (see last chapter) and survived in the Dutch Rosicrucian court of Frederick and Elizabeth Stuart, daughter of James I, in exile in The Hague. The occult revolutionary originator was Boyle, who was Grand Master of the Priory of Sion and founder of the Royal Society. The intellectual interpreter who gave the occult vision a new slant was the Rosicrucian Locke, the Whig constitutionalist who saw the relationship between King and people as a social contract. The semi-political intellectual interpreter who later became political was Shaftesbury, who was behind the Exclusion crisis and the invasion of Monmouth. The early revolutionary dynamic of the Glorious Revolution can be stated as follows:

Heretical occult vision	Heretical occult interpreter	Occult revolutionary originator	Thoughtful intellectual interpreter	Semi-political intellectual interpreter
Bacon	Andreae	Boyle	Locke	Shaftesbury

The intellectual expression was through Shaftesbury, who had discovered Bacon in 1637 and was a great admirer of his ideas, and through the members of the Rosicrucian Royal Society, notably Boyle, Locke and Newton.

Political expression came through the reign of the Rosicrucian William and his bride Mary, and their subsequent constitutional reforms. The Dutch House of Orange had been Rosicrucian Masonic since Frederick Henry, as evidenced by the rose-filled sun William and Mary were married under, the two Masonic pillars that stood nearby and the sun with the eye that dominates the post-1688 engraving. There is much circumstantial evidence that the Rosicrucian William III was invited to England by Rosicrucian Mason Robert Boyle of the Royal Society, who as Grand Master restored the Priory of Sion's hold over the English monarchy, which has lasted to this day. The consolidation of the Glorious Revolution was largely legalistic, and its effect was to deliver the Bank of England to Rosicrucians and the English dynasty to the descendants of the Rosicrucian Palatinate, the House of Hanover.

The revolutionary dynamic of the Glorious Revolution against James II can be expressed as follows:

Heretical occult inspiration	Intellectual expression	Political expression	Physical consolidation
Bacon/ Andreae	Shaftesbury/ Royal Society (Boyle/Locke/ Newton/ Leibniz)	William III (Bill of Rights, 1689)	Ireland (Battle of the Boyne)/ Bank of England, 1694/Act of Settlement, 1701/ Hanoverian Succession

Had Monmouth's attempted revolution succeeded the revolutionary dynamic would have been as follows:

Heretical occult inspiration	Intellectual expression	Political expression	Physical consolidation
Dutch Rosicrucianism/ Palatinate/Boyle	Shaftesbury/ Green Ribbon Club	Monmouth	(Intended purge and exclusion of all Catholics and French from English life)

The revolutionary dynamic of the Dutch Revolution can be expressed as follows:

Heretical occult inspiration	Intellectual expression	Political expression	Physical consolidation
Dutch Sionist Rosicrucianism behind Calvinism	Philip Marnix, Count of St. Aldegonde	William of Orange ("the Silent")	Maurice of Nassau

We can now state the revolutionary dynamic of the ideas behind the Glorious Revolution as follows:

Heretical occult inspiration	Intellectual expression	Political expression	Physical consolidation
Sionist Rosicrucianism	Royal Society	William and Mary's constitutional reform	Terror in Ireland/ Bank of England to fund Rosicrucianism

With George I came Rosicrucian Freemasonry, and in 1717 the Grand Lodge of Freemasonry was formed in England when four London lodges of Rosicrucian Freemasons met at the Apple Tree tavern in Charles Street, Covent Garden and turned themselves into a Grand Lodge. Their coat of arms was designed by a colleague of Menasseh's, the Amsterdam Jew Jacob Jehuda Leon Templo.[37] English Freemasonry was now united, and Templar French Freemasonry was exiled to France. The religion of Reason at the heart of Freemasonry and Whiggery tightened its grip on the country. The Age of Rationalism, evident in the work of John Locke, and soon to throw up the deist outlook of the American revolutionaries, had dawned.

PART TWO

TOWARDS A UNIVERSAL REPUBLIC

CHAPTER FOUR

THE AMERICAN REVOLUTION

It is reported that Benjamin Franklin was a Rosicrucian. Thomas Jefferson, John Adams and George Washington were Masons....Though these men were a part of these orders, George Washington warned the Masonic Lodge in America of the dangers of the Illuminati, while Thomas Jefferson and John Adams later disagreed over the use of the Masonic Lodge by the Illuminati.

J. R. Church, *Guardians of the Grail*

In a sense, the American Revolution began with the Boston Tea Party, though there were other incidents that also created resentment. Disguised as Mohawk Indians under cover of darkness so they could not be identified afterwards, between 120 and 200 men had gathered in taverns, houses and warehouses while the crowds surged round the Old South Meeting House. They carried lamps and torches which made the dark "as light as day." Watched by thousands on the banks, to sounds of splitting wood and Indian-like whooping, they made sure the tea could not be landed and that the tax would therefore not have to be paid. Some of the "Indians" smashed open the tea-chests, others emptied them over the ships' sides and more waded in the water below to make sure no tea-leaves survived in a usable form.

The Tea Party was organized by Freemasons[1] who were members of

St. Andrew's Lodge, Boston. Some like Joseph Warren and Paul Revere had been members since 1760, others like John Hancock since 1762.[2] A Lodge of Templar Freemasons (which is what the "Mohawks" were) precipitated a revolution against the Hanoverian descendants of William III's Sionist English government.

In fact the American Revolution began much earlier. To understand its origins fully, we need to go back to late 16th-century Europe, where America was regarded as a blank slate, an opportunity to establish from scratch a New World. The American Revolution was an attempt to construct a new experimental society based on Scottish Jacobite Templarism and Baconian Masonic Atlantean philosophy. The Rosicrucian thinkers of the early 17th century such as Bacon were acutely aware of the opportunities America offered for implementing their Utopian social vision.

THE EUROPEAN BACKGROUND TO AMERICAN TEMPLARISM

Bacon and English Freemasonry

The English Freemasonry possibly founded by Sir Francis Bacon as far back as 1586 was not Templar. It derived from a secret fraternal order known as the Ancient Free and Accepted Masons.[3] According to early Masonic manuscripts its origins go back to Adam, the first Mason. (His fig-leaf is symbolized in the Mason's apron.) The knowledge Adam received after eating of the forbidden tree was passed on to his son Seth and then to Nimrod, who built the Tower of Babel (which suggested the oneness of all the world's peoples). The oneness of all the religions was taught through a secret word, Jah-bul-on, which suggests the oneness of Yahweh, Baal and the Egyptian On. The secret word therefore unites the Judaic, Babylonian and Egyptian cultures. Hiram Abiff, the Master Mason who built Solomon's Temple, would not reveal this word which he engraved on a gold triangle he wore round his neck; he was killed by three fellow Masons. According to Masons, Solomon found the triangle and placed it in a secret vault under the Temple. We have already seen that Solomon's Temple was the occult inspirer of Freemasonry.

Groups of temple- and stadium-builders similar to the Masons existed in Greece (the Dionysiacs) and in Rome (the *Collegium Muriorum*). They were the forerunners of the stonemasons and carpenters who created the great Cathedrals in the Middle Ages. A Grand Lodge of England met at York in 926 and adopted secret handshakes and passwords by which Masons could identify themselves to each other. In the 13th century they formed an association with headquarters at Cologne and lodges at Zurich, Vienna and Strasbourg. They called themselves "Free Masons" and held initiation ceremonies.

At Bacon's instigation towards the end of the 16th century distinguished people who were not builders were admitted into the fraternity (often to help with funding) and were called "Accepted" Masons. They received the secret universal knowledge of the oneness and brotherhood of mankind and the Secret Doctrine of the Ages that America would become a Utopian New Atlantis and create a better world in which humanity would be deified. In this paradise, men would follow a religion of reason and become gods and work for a universal world republic that would replicate the Utopian conditions in Atlantis throughout the world. Meanwhile the secret knowledge would be passed on from generation to generation in the Freemason's Temple.

Freemasonry is fundamentally an occult and philosophical idea, which Bacon regarded as an existential philosophy. Bacon, regarded as the founder of Freemasonry and the Rosicrucian Order whose members guarded universal knowledge, the secret doctrine of the Ages, during the Middle Ages,[4] created secret societies of intellectuals dedicated to the new liberalism and civil and religious freedom. When the moment was right, he threw his group's weight behind the English plan to colonize America believing there could be a great commonwealth in the New Atlantis.[5]

From this it seems that some of the earliest colonial voyages to America which were encouraged by Dee were emotionally supported by the Rosicrucian Freemason Bacon: Frobisher's (which took place when

Bacon was only fifteen), Sir Humphrey Gilbert's and Sir Walter Raleigh's ill-starred voyage to Roanoke. (The Rosicrucian Raleigh was a member of the Baconian circle.) It may be that Bacon was behind his cousin Bartholomew Gosnold's 1602 voyage, which was ostensibly funded by his Cambridge friend, the 3rd Earl of Southampton, according to William Strachey.[6]

Scottish Templars

Scottish Templar Freemasonry grew out of the flight of the Templars from France in the 14th century. The Templars (the Poor Knights of Christ and the Temple of Solomon), who were founded in 1118 in Jerusalem, eventually ended up in Scotland (see Appendices B, Appendix 7), where their headquarters were at the preceptory at Rosslyn. There they founded the Order of the Knights Templar, an Order of Templar Masons into which the Scottish royal family, the Stuarts, were initiated. They used the symbol of the skull and crossbones (on gravestones to identify Templar Masons). They also used the Templar symbol of the splayed cross in an octagon, and sometimes used an octagonal shape by itself. They put the number 13 on gravestones, referring to the 13th day of October 1307 on which the Templar founder Jacques de Molay died.[7]

James I arrived in England in 1603 with an entourage of Scottish Templar Masons. The Templar James replaced the Sionist Elizabeth I on the invitation of Sir Robert Cecil, who, having controlled Elizabeth I for Sion, seems to have switched to the Scottish Templars in the hope of controlling James. The Templar Masons opened their first Lodge in York soon afterwards.[8] (The octagonally-shaped Globe theatre had just been opened in 1599, suggesting that Templar influence had already reached London by then.) They called their Freemasonry "Jacobite Freemasonry" (Latin Jacobus, James but also suggesting Jacques) in memory of Jacques de Molay, and James and his descendants were members of the Royalist Jacobite Lodges.[9]

A Calvinist besides being a Templar, James believed that the Lord had made him King over Israel, which as "the Lord's Anointed" (as Lady Mar called him) he ruled by divine right. He adopted the Israelite analogies used by his Sionist Protestant ancestors Henry VIII (who saw himself as David and Solomon) and Edward VI (who called himself the new Josiah).[10] On his way to London to be crowned he declared that he was going to the Promised Land, and regarded England as our "Zion" (perhaps punning on "Sion"). He liked to be called "the Scottish Solomon." His Templarism was hidden behind a veneer of Puritan attitudes and language.

Templar Masonry took the philosophical idea of Freemasonry and adapted it into a means of securing political power. Though embraced by James I, Templar Masonry sought to transform the world into a universal republic. The goals of Templar Masonry are essentially political (rather than occult and philosophical).

Utopian Voyages to New Atlantis

Bartholomew Gosnold's Jamestown voyage of 1607 took place amid controversy. Bartholomew Gosnold had spent three years securing the funding of the voyage through his relative Sir Thomas Smythe and recruiting the settlers and crew at Otley Hall, Suffolk. About three weeks before their departure in December 1606 the arrangements for the voyage were taken over by the now Templar Sir Robert Cecil, who nominated Admiral Newport to be in overall charge, a great shock and bitter blow to the organizer and man regarded as the real leader, Gosnold. It is possible that Scottish Templar Freemasons hijacked the control of the voyage and named Jamestown after the new Templar King, whose involvement can be gauged by the presence of the Poet Laureate on the dockside as the three ships departed. Michael Drayton's poem catches the settlers' Utopian view of America as a New Eden: "To get the pearl and gold,/And ours to hold/Virginia,/Earth's only paradise."

The First Virginia Company's Council of Seven which ruled Jamestown may have been based on the Templar Council of Wise Men, and like the Templars they mixed vision, defence of their Eden and commerce. Bartholomew Gosnold himself was probably not a Templar – hence the attempt to wrest control from him – but he would have known about the Scottish Templarism at court from his cousin John

Gosnold, who was gentleman usher to James. (He had held the same position under Elizabeth I, and was probably shocked by the arrival of Scottish Templars at what used to be her court.)

As a result of the Utopian spirit conveyed by Gosnold, America became the new focus for the Utopian dream of the Puritans. The discovery of the New World also proved a strong millenarian stimulus, for the American continent was greeted as the Promised Land where paradise could be regained.

Despite the death of some twenty men, including Bartholomew Gosnold himself, of dysentery and swamp fever in August 1607[11] – in recognition of his leadership Gosnold was given a military funeral at which all the ordnance in the fort was "shot off" – the Jamestown colony was the first English-speaking settlement in the New World to survive. Its success under the joint-stock Virginia Company of London meant that there was a renewed interest in America (the New Atlantis). As the disillusion with England set in Utopians and persecuted Puritans looked to the New World, to which Cromwell himself nearly emigrated in 1638. Maryland, Virginia's northern neighbour, had been granted by the crown to a proprietor, George Calvert, Lord Baltimore, in 1632. The colony at Plymouth, Massachusetts, was also financed through private investment. The English *émigrés*, religious separatists from Leyden, Holland, had set sail in the *Mayflower* in 1620. These Pilgrim founders of Plymouth, led by William Bradford and following Gosnold's example in seeking their fortune in the New World, preferred to separate from the Church of England rather than reform it, and they controlled the government in Plymouth until 1660. Other Puritans who landed in Massachusetts Bay hoped to reform the Church of England by their example, not separate; they wanted the colony to be a Zion in the wilderness, a model of purity. John Winthrop of Groton, Suffolk was the first governor of the Massachusetts Bay Colony. On the voyage to America in 1630 he composed a sermon in which he saw the Massachusetts colonists in covenant with God and each other to build "a City upon a Hill," a Utopian vision.

Some New Englanders found the orthodoxy oppressive and left

Massachusetts Bay and founded Connecticut, Rhode Island, New Hampshire and Maine. New Netherland had been founded in 1624 by the Dutch West India Company. The English captured it in 1664 and renamed it New York after the brother of Charles II, James, Duke of York. It then became a royal colony when he became King of England as James II in 1685.

Pennsylvania grew out of a grant of land Charles II made to William Penn along the Delaware River, while New Jersey was part of territory ceded to James, Duke of York in 1664. The eight English proprietors of the Carolinas began to colonize the new territories in 1663, hoping to grow silk – the English crown had issued grants in 1629 – and the proprietors of Georgia, led by James Oglethorpe, planned to import debtors who would rehabilitate themselves by profitable labour.

In all these places there were Utopian experiments that proprietors undertook for commercial purposes, not all of which were successful. The concept was of self-supporting communities where religious freedom could prevail without the interference of the established English Church or State. Soon what was left of the Utopianism would pass into secret societies, where it would be preserved as Freemasonry.

Jacobite Templars and the Sionist Radclyffe

The principal Masonic secret society formed round the new Jacobites. The presence of James II in Ireland had led to his followers becoming known as Irish Jacobites. On the death of James II in 1701 the French King Louis XIV proclaimed his exiled son Francis Edward Stuart James king of England. James was little more than a boy, just thirteen, living in a court in exile in France, but he was a Catholic and Parliament passed a bill of attainder against him. As a result of the 1701 Act of Succession, the Stuart Catholic line was excluded from the succession to the English throne. James's supporters, also known as Jacobites, planned to make the pretender King in place of Queen Anne, and in 1708 James set sail with French ships to invade Scotland. However he was put to flight by the British before he could land. He then fought with the French Army in the War of Spanish Succession

(1701-14).

Queen Anne died in 1714, and James was approached by Robert Harley and Viscount Bolingbroke, who suggested that he should embrace Anglicanism and become heir to the English throne. James refused to renounce Catholicism. Instead he organized another invasion. John Erskine, the Earl of Mar, led a Jacobite rebellion in Scotland in the summer of 1715. Mar advanced to Perth and fought Argyll at the battle of Sheriffmuir on November 13. On December 22, James landed at Peterhead, Aberdeen, too late to do anything but organize the flight of his main supporters to France. By February 10, 1716 the rebellion had collapsed and James had returned to France. He spent the rest of his life in or near Rome (unaffected by another Jacobite rising in the west Scottish Highlands, aided by Spain, which was swiftly crushed at Glemshiel in 1719).

On January 4, 1717 the Scottish Stuarts were formally sent into permanent exile in France. With them went Jacobite Templar Freemasonry.

To unify English resistance to Jacobite Templarism, Sionist Rosicrucian Freemasonry became a "United Grand Lodge" in June 1717. From now the British monarchy and the Church of England both became subservient to Rosicrucian Freemasonry. Since 1737 every male monarch has been a Mason, while the head of the Anglican Church is a Rosicrucian Freemason. Sionist Rosicrucian Freemasonry has controlled both the Crown and the Church.[12] The political aim of Sionist Masonry is to achieve a one-world Kingdom ruled by the King of Jerusalem, not a universal republic.

Meanwhile exiled Stuart sympathizers living in France (rather than Italy) founded the first French Templar lodge in 1725 and used it to keep alive the Jacobite cause round the Pretender's son, Charles Edward Stuart (1720-1788).

After the death of Isaac Newton, the Priory of Sion had chosen Charles Radclyffe as Grand Master.[13] He seems to have founded the first French Templar Lodge in 1725. In 1727 he was a Knight Templar based in Paris, and it is likely that he was spying for Sion on the

Templars under cover of a proposal that Sion should be linked with the Templars through him. Charles Radclyffe had fought in 1715 with his brother James, who had been executed; he had been imprisoned and had escaped to France, where he was welcomed by Jacobites as a trusted supporter. His mother had been an illegitimate daughter of Charles II and as the King's grandson he was the seven-year-old Charles Edward Stuart's cousin, which further enhanced his credibility as a Jacobite.

As Grand Master of the Priory of Sion, Radclyffe targeted the Merovingian "King of Jerusalem" Nicolas-François de Lorraine, the Duke of Lorraine. In 1729, François visited England for two years and became a member of the Rosicrucian Gentleman's Club in Spalding. Isaac Newton had been a member. The poet Alexander Pope was also a member (hence perhaps the Rosicrucian "sylphs" in *The Rape of the Lock*), as was Dr Desaguliers, one of the founders of the Rosicrucian Grand Lodge and a leader of the Royal Society with Newton.[14] In 1731 Desaguliers visited The Hague and initiated François Duke of Lorraine into Freemasonry, and he was also in touch with a Templar in exile in France, Chevalier Ramsay, who visited England at the same time as François and became a member of the Royal Society. Radclyffe sent both Lorraine and Ramsay to the Continent to undermine the French throne. (In 1737 Ramsay made a famous pro-Templar speech in Paris before the Grand Lodge of France, which was presided over by Radclyffe. In his speech, Ramsay traced Freemasonry from Scotland and England into France – a Sionist attempt to guide the Templar Stuarts away from the Scottish and British thrones.)

Bonnie Prince Charlie's Revolution

By 1742, now his secretary, Radclyffe learned that Charles Edward Stuart was planning to invade Scotland to capture the English throne.[15] As Grand Master of the Priory of Sion he sought to prevent the plot, and he employed a German Protestant called Baron Karl von Hundt or Hund, who had been received into the Knights Templar by someone who appeared to be Charles Edward Stuart. In fact it was Radclyffe in disguise. Impersonating the Prince, he told Hund he planned to reclaim the English crown in London and gave him permission to take the embryonic Scottish Rite Freemasonry to Germany. Radclyffe hoped Hund would alert London. In fact Hund returned to Germany and formed what became the Rite of Strict Observance. He waited for orders for ten years. They never came. Early on during his long wait, he revealed Charles Edward Stuart's plan to reclaim the English crown.

In July 1745 Charles landed in western Scotland with about a dozen men. The Highlands rebelled and he entered Edinburgh on September 17 with 2,000 men. He was admitted into the Order of the Knights Templar on September 24 and probably learned there of the Sionist Rosicrucian attempt to block his advance on the Scottish throne. He defeated Sir John Cope's army at Prestonpans and, master of Scotland, crossed the English border in November with 5,500 men. He advanced to Derby and then, confronted by 30,000 government troops, withdrew to Scotland. On April 16, 1746 the Duke of Cumberland defeated him at Culloden Moor in Invernesshire. Some 80 rebels were executed. For five months Charles was pursued by government search-parties. Eventually he escaped by boat to France, where he again became the "King over the Water."

Though his secretary, Radclyffe had not travelled with Charles. He joined him several months later. It is not known why. (Was he organizing Charles's defeat?) In the end he was captured on a French ship off the Dogger Bank and was beheaded at the Tower of London as a Templar Jacobite, an ally of the invaders.

Scottish Rite Templars and the Sionist Charles de Lorraine

Scottish Rite Jacobite Freemasonry (as opposed to Jacobite Templarism) seems to have been devised by Radclyffe and founded in 1747 by Charles Edward Stuart.[16] Charles wrote in the charter, "our sorrows and misfortunes [came] by that of Rose Croix," and he now turned his attention to the Rosicrucian French throne to avenge Jacques de Molay.

Some Jacobite exiles took these attitudes with them to America, and some American Freemasons began to hear about a development in the Priory of Sion. The new Grand Master in 1746 was Charles de Lorraine, the younger brother of François Duke of Lorraine, the "King of Jerusalem," who had appointed him.[17]

After he was initiated into Rosicrucian Freemasonry in 1731, François had married the Merovingian Maria Theresa von Habsburg of Austria in 1735, uniting the offices of "King of Jerusalem" and Empress of the Holy Roman Empire into one family that owned the Spear of Destiny, a Habsburg possession. (This was the spear of Longinus that pierced the side of Christ on the cross, and there was a legend that whoever owned it would rule the world.) It was expected that the Messiah of Israel would soon be born to them in Vienna, and that he would be the Lost King of the Holy Grail bloodline. Austria would become the greatest Great Power if she took France, and François and Maria married their daughter Marie Antoinette to Louis XVI, the Bourbon King of France. The House of Lorraine had thus acquired the throne of Austria, the Holy Roman Empire and a major influence in France. This connection had been good for Charles de Lorraine, for in 1744 he had married Maria Theresa's sister, Marie Anne, and become commander-in-chief of the Austrian army.[18]

Frederick the Great (II) of Prussia had sensed that Jacobite Templarism was planning to topple the French King, and he was initiated into Templar Freemasonry at Brunswick on August 14, 1738 shortly after Ramsay's speech. When he became King of Prussia in 1740, he initiated two of his brothers into Templarism[19] and summoned Voltaire, who had been an agent of the Priory of Sion since spending two years (1726-1728) in London where Alexander Pope became his mentor,[20] where he met the Rosicrucians of the Royal Society, including Newton, and read Locke, and where (according to Baron von Knigge) he joined Rosicrucian Freemasonry in 1728. Voltaire guided Frederick into regarding Templarism as a Continental Order, in accordance with Ramsay's speech.

As a result of the meeting between Frederick and Voltaire, additional degrees were added to Templar Freemasonry which underwent a revival, and by 1746 Frederick had founded 14 Templar lodges.[21] By now Frederick was the Head of Templar Freemasonry, and he used the Scottish Rite lodges to divide France and Austria, who were allies, with a view to intriguing the French throne. The French King was concerned, and Voltaire returned to Prussia in 1750 and turned Frederick's attention away from the French throne to the Catholic Church. By 1755 American Masonry heard tales from Europe about the Templar Scottish Rite advancing to 32 degrees. Charles de Lorraine, Grand Master of the Priory of Sion and commander-in-chief of Austria's armed forces, then led Austria's armies against Prussia in several battles between Sion and the Templars, the last of which (in 1757) Sion/Austria lost. Charles was dismissed as commander-in-chief by Empress Maria Theresa, his sister-in-law, and returned to the capital of Lorraine, Brussels, where he sought to further the work of Sion.

Weishaupt's Sionist Illuminati and Templarism

The vision of the revolutionary originator can be found in the thinking of Adam Weishaupt, who had been selected by Charles de Lorraine to found a secret society that would penetrate and transform Templarism into French revolutionary cells that would prevent Frederick the Great from taking the French throne.[22] Sion's goal was to overthrow the Bourbon dynasty and create a democratic republic through a coalition with the Templars. Weishaupt's brief was to effect this overthrow and shape the New Atlantis in the New World.

The son of a Jewish rabbi, an ex-Jesuit priest and a young professor of Canon Law at the University of Ingolstadt, Weishaupt was instructed by Charles de Lorraine and by the Jewish Rothschilds (who were Freemasons) to leave the Catholic Church and unite all the occult groups, notably Sionism and Templarism. Weishaupt's influence on the American Revolution was a Templar one.

Adam Weishaupt

Working with Mayer Amschel "Rothschild," a Sionist, he founded the Order of the Perfectibilists (a name that recalls the Cathar Parfaits) on May 1, 1776. (Hence the annual May Day celebrations. Also the use of "May-day" as a distress call in castrophes – for the day of the founding of Weishaupt's Order had been universally deemed to be a catastrophic day.) Originally there were five members: Wessely, Moses Mendelssohn, and the bankers Itzig, Friedlander and Meyer, all of whom were under the direction of the newly formed House of Rothschild. Its name was soon changed to the Order of the Ancient Illuminated Seers of Bavaria, and then to the Order of the Bavarian Illuminati, which soon became "the Order of the Illuminati."[23] It followed reason and was opposed to established religion.

Weishaupt had studied the various Masonic writings after meeting a Protestant Freemason from Hanover. Eventually his Illuminatist vision infiltrated Freemasonry, which had absorbed Bacon's occult interpretation. Weishaupt sought to foment revolution in Europe. He founded the Order of the Golden Dawn, a Hermetic Order which was revived in the 1880s, and came up with the idea of replacing Christianity with a religion of Reason and a Freemasonic one-world government, allegedly "to prevent future wars."

Weishaupt's goals were revolutionary and were summarized for initiates who had reached the second degree (Minerval) as: "(1) Abolition of all ordered government; (2) Abolition of private property; (3) Abolition of inheritance; (4) Abolition of patriotism; (5) Abolition of all Religion; (6) Abolition of the family [via abolition of marriage]; and (7) Creation of a World Government."[24] His Order's members were all Rosicrucians and Templars, who co-operated to bring in the New World Order longed for by Sionists and Templars alike.

Weishaupt took the structure of the Jesuits for his new secret society, but followed the Egyptian rites of Ormus, the rites of the Priory of Sion. (Ormus – from the French "Orme" meaning "elm" and recalling the cutting of the elm at Gisors in 1188 – was another name for the Priory of Sion.)[25] He had started the society unofficially when he was at university in 1771 and students there were his first unofficial initiates. In 1771 he had met a Jutland merchant name Kolmer, who initiated him into the Egyptian Rose-Croix. On his way back from Egypt to Germany, immediately before visiting Weishaupt, Kolmer had stopped at Malta and met Cagliostro. The two men performed a public exhibition of magic and were expelled from the island by the Knights of Malta. Kolmer spent five years initiating Weishaupt into his secret doctrine, finishing in 1776. The only mention of Kolmer in history is on Malta in 1771 and in relation to Weishaupt before 1776; otherwise there is no trace of him, and it seems that Kolmer was an alias for Charles de Lorraine, the Grand Master of Sion.[26]

It also seems that Charles de Lorraine gave Cagliostro a task on Malta: to turn Templar Freemasons into revolutionaries, and to unite Rosicrucian and Templar Freemasonry. To further these ends he was to be Charles de Lorraine's link with Weishaupt. Mackey's *Encyclopedia of Freemasonry*, says that Cagliostro's real name was Joseph Balsamo, who is mentioned in Priory documents as having equal status with the Grand Masters of Sion. In April 1776 he was initiated into Rosicrucian Freemasonry in Esperance Lodge no. 289 at the King's Head Tavern. He was then "subsidized" by several very rich men.[27]

When Weishaupt founded the Illuminati in May 1776 he assumed the Order name Spartacus, and in 1777 he was initiated into French Grand Orient Freemasonry, which was founded in 1772 by the Duke of Orléans, cousin of the Bourbon King of France. One of Weishaupt's earliest initiates, the Duke of Orléans had already been initiated into French Grand Lodge Freemasonry and was elected Grand Master in 1771.[28] A year later he founded the Secret French Grand Orient Lodge. The Grand Orient took its name from a line spoken by Lucifer in the ritual Maximus of Ephesus used when initiating Julian the Apostate: "I am the Orient, I am the Morning Star."[29] Weishaupt hid the three Illuminati degrees in the first three degrees of the Duke of Orléans' Grand Orient Freemasonry.[30]

As a result of all these developments in Continental Europe, Scottish Jacobite Templarism, though weakened by being deported from Britain, had strengthened in France and Prussia, ironically largely

due to the activities of the Sionist intelligence agents Radclyffe and
Voltaire. And would-be American revolutionaries seeking to link
themselves to an organization that could help them oppose the Sionist
English colonialists, would naturally have turned to the, by now, major
Freemasonic alternative: Templarism.

AMERICAN REVOLUTION AGAINST ENGLISH COLONIALISM

American Templarism

If Sionist or Templar Freemasonry did not reach America as early as
1607, it seems to have arrived by 1653 when the sequel to *The New
Atlantis* Bacon is believed to have written, which included a timetable
for fulfilling the Masons' Great Plan for America, was taken to
Jamestown by his descendant Nathaniel Bacon and buried in a vault in
the first brick church in Bruton, Williamsburg. Thomas Jefferson seems
to have been the last to read this work.

The group the Earl of Shaftesbury formed in the 1660s to increase
trade with the southern colonies had introduced a further Rosicrucian
contact. (John Locke, secretary of this group, had drafted a constitution
for the new colony of Carolina.) In 1733 Rosicrucian Freemasonry
entered America more formally, for in that year St John's Lodge was
established in Boston, which now became the Masonic capital of
Britain's American colonies. By 1737 lodges had sprung up in
Massachusetts, New York, Pennsylvania and South Carolina, all
committed to implementing the Secret Doctrine and Great Plan for a
Utopian New Atlantis.[31]

Rosicrucian Freemasonry's monopoly in the colonies was
challenged in 1756 when Scottish Jacobite Templarism came to Boston.
The 17th-century intermeshing of Freemasonry and Rosicrucianism
that had led to Sionist Rosicrucianism (and the Puritan and Glorious
Revolutions) underwent a change in the 18th century. Templarism now
established itself alongside Sionism and was set to be responsible for two

more revolutions. After the defeat of Charles Edward Stuart, the Young Pretender, in 1746 many Irish and Scottish Templar Jacobites had fled to America, and some brought with them the French Scottish Rite founded by Charles Edward Stuart. In place of the "Grand Lodge of England" Templarism offered the "Grand Lodge of Scotland" with higher degrees. St Andrew's Lodge in Boston was the Scottish Rite American Templar headquarters. (We have seen that some of the Tea Party Mohawks had joined St Andrew's as early as 1760.) In 1769 it offered a new degree, the Knights Templar Degree. Soon afterwards another branch of Templarism, the Grand Lodge of York, set up lodges in Virginia. This York Rite offered 13 degrees (remembering the death of de Molay on the 13th day of the month). Irish Grand Lodge Masonry also arrived in the New World.[32]

Franklin

Against this background rose the controlling figure of Benjamin Franklin. Born in Boston, the tenth son of 17 children, he was educated until he was ten, then apprenticed to a printer. In 1721 he founded a weekly newspaper, the *New-England Courant*, which was banned. He then moved to Philadelphia. On his arrival he met his wife-to-be, Deborah Read, while returning from a baker, tired and hungry, munching a puffy roll. He

Benjamin Franklin

roomed with her family and in 1724 was set up in business by the Royal Governor of the crown colony, Sir William Keith, who paid for him to return to England to make contacts with stationers and booksellers. He arrived in London to learn that there were no letters of credit or introduction as Keith had promised; Keith was unreliable and often made promises he had no intention of keeping.

Franklin worked as a printer in London until 1726. A fellow passenger on the voyage to London, Thomas Denham, then offered him the position of clerk in his store in Philadelphia, and he returned there. Denham died and Franklin went back to printing in partnership with a friend. In 1727 he founded the Junto or Leather Apron debating club and the club's need for books led to the organizing of the Library Company of Philadelphia. Deborah had married, but had been deserted. In 1730 Franklin had a son by an unknown woman, and in the same year married Deborah. Franklin had written *A Modest Enquiry into the Nature and Necessity of a Paper Currency* (1729), on the strength of which he was asked to print Pennsylvania's paper currency. He quickly became a well-known printer and printed the *Pennsylvania Gazette*.

In February 1731 Franklin became a Sionist Rosicrucian Mason,[33] and in 1734 he became Provincial Grand Master of Pennsylvania, by which time he had become very prosperous, having invested in real estate and gone into partnership with printers in the Carolinas, the West Indies and New York. He had also become a partner in the printing firm Franklin and Hall from which he drew £500 a year for the next eighteen years.

By 1736 Franklin, who published the proceedings of the Indian treaty councils, had become a keen student of the Iroquois Indian constitution, which was perhaps the oldest in the world – the League began c1000 AD according to some; and in 1390 or 1450 according to others. Before Columbus, the "Savages" of the New World had formed a federation to be envied. The Indians of North-East America had been perpetually at war until Deganwidah, a Huron from east Ontario, proposed the creation of a league of five Indian nations. His spokesman Hiawatha negotiated with the warring Indian nations and the Senecas, Onondagas, Oneidas, Mohawks and Cayugas formed a federal union, and were joined by the Tuscaroras in 1714.

At one such treaty council in 1744 representatives of Maryland,

Virginia and Pennsylvania met the chiefs of the Iroquois League and set up an Anglo-Iroquois alliance to block France's domination of the New World. The colonists would stop Scottish and Irish immigrants occupying Indian land and in return the Indians would support the English against France. On July 4 at this council the Indian spokesman Canassatego recommended that the colonies should unite just as the Indians had done long previously.[34]

Franklin followed the treaty council and he read Cadwallader Coden's *History of the Five Indian Nations Depending on the Province of New York in America.* In 1751 he wrote: "I am of the opinion...that securing the friendship of the Indians is of the greatest consequence for these colonies....The surest means of doing it are to regulate Indian trade, so as to convince them [the Indians] that they may have the best and cheapest goods, and the fairest dealings with the English....The colonists should accept the Iroquois advice to form a union in common defence under a common, federal government....It would be a very strange thing if six nations of ignorant savages should be capable of forming a scheme for such an Union and be able to execute it in such a manner as that it has subsisted ages, and appears indissoluble, and yet a like union should be impracticable for ten or a dozen English colonies."[35] In 1753 Franklin became Deputy Postmaster General for the American colonies. The Postmaster General had access to all letters and communications, and was something of a spymaster. He was one of Pennsylvania's commissioners at a meeting with the six Indian nations in Carlisle, Pennsylvania.

In 1754 the French were encroaching into English colonial territory, and the Albany Congress met to confirm the Anglo-Iroquois Alliance and adopted Franklin's Plan of Union, a plan for the union of the 13 colonies in accordance with Canassatego's proposal. The plan set out a common defence policy against the French and relations with the Indians. Franklin based his Plan of Union on the League of Iroquois Nations, which had thrived for at least four centuries. He proposed that a president-general appointed by the crown should be the leader of the colonies (anticipating the office of President of the United States), and that each state should retain its internal sovereignty and constitution; in the Iroquois League, all states were required to agree an action before implementing it. Franklin proposed a single Grand Council like the Iroquois Great Council, and unlike Britain's two chambers. Each colony's representatives would depend on the size of its population; the six Indian nations had varying numbers of members. Franklin suggested 48 delegates against the Iroquois League's 50. He steered a middle course between the crown and the Iroquois as regards military conscription; the crown allowed pressganging, the Iroquois did not, and Franklin proposed that it should be illegal to impress men in the colonies "without the consent of this legislature." He also regulated trade and barred the settlers from seizing Iroquois land.

Franklin therefore anticipated the union of the 13 colonies and its federal system of government. His Albany Plan was not adopted by the state legislatures, however; and the British, fearing a united America would be hard to control, also rejected Franklin's proposal. (The spiritual life of the American Indians was also to influence the ethos and culture of the United States, and Indian religion – described by D. H. Lawrence in his essay *New Mexico* as "a vast and pure religion, without idols or images, even mental ones" and "a cosmic religion ... not broken up into specific gods and systems" which "precedes the god-concept, and is therefore greater and deeper than any god-religion" — was to influence later Americans such as Emerson, Thoreau, Whitman and Frost in its mystical universalism.)

In 1756 Franklin was admitted to the Rosicrucian Royal Society *in absentia* for discovering that lightning and electricity were the same.[36] In 1757 he went to London to represent Pennsylvania in a dispute over lands held by the family of William Penn, and spent until 1762 in England and France. Franklin was initiated as a Rosicrucian in London during his stay there.[37]

Apparently now working for Boyle's Priory of Sion, Franklin was again in England from 1764 to 1775, when he discovered English Freemasonry's Secret Doctrine to create a New World democracy or Baconian "philosophical Atlantis" in America (which Bacon had concealed in his *New Atlantis*). This was a Masonic blueprint for America. He became friendly with Sir Francis Dashwood, his counterpart in the office of British Deputy Postmaster General, a Jacobite Templar whose friends were supporters of Charles Edward Stuart. He stayed with Dashwood at his house in West Wycombe during the summers of 1772, 1773 and 1774.[38]

Franklin was colonial ambassador to France, and made Paris his work-base. His staff included Silas Deane and Arthur Lee, supporters of the Committee of Congress for Secret Correspondence (America's spy network). During this time Franklin, already a Rosicrucian Mason since 1731, acting as a double agent like Radclyffe, became a Templar Mason through his friends in the postal service. English Templar MPs secretly raised money for anti-British activities in America, and sent it to Franklin in Paris, who sent it on to North America by post or bought arms and military supplies in France. Franklin's sister, who was spying for him, introduced him to the Howe brothers (one a General, one an Admiral) who were in charge of England's forces in America. Both were Templar Masons.[39]

The Templars and the Boston Tea Party

Britain's empire in North America had expanded following the end of the French and Indian war in 1763, and there was a need for increased revenue and troops which English ministries, supported by George III, felt should be shared by the colonies. They imposed a number of taxes — on sugar (1764), the quartering of British soldiers and stamps (1765) and a three-penny tax on tea under the Townshend Act (1767). Patriots resisted.

Templar Freemasonry was now in conflict with Sionist Rosicrucian Freemasonry for control of the New Atlantis in America. This conflict first manifested itself in Boston in 1761 as conflict between the Sionist St. John's and the Templar St. Andrew's lodges. The Templars, who included John Hancock and Paul Revere, had the support of Templars in Virginia, notably Patrick Henry and Richard Henry Lee who in 1769 persuaded the Virginia Assembly to condemn the British government. (They were thinking of how in 1761 James Otis had argued in the

Council Chamber of the State House against the British Crown's policy of using search warrants without specifying charges and maintained that colonists had the right to be represented before being taxed.) In 1770 the Boston Massacre took place in the square next to the State House in which British sentries shot dead five rioters. St. John's was on the side of the sentries, St. Andrew's on the side of the rioters.[40]

From this point there was open conflict between England and the American colonies. The day after the Boston Massacre of 1770 the citizens had gathered at the Old South Meeting House and had demanded the removal of British troops from Boston. The troops were removed to Castle Island and the Stamp and Townshend taxes on everything but tea were repealed. Calm prevailed, and through the Committees of Correspondence Americans agreed to boycott tea, maintaining that Parliament had no right to tax the colonies. George III declared, "I am clear there must always be one tax to keep the right, and as such I approve the Tea Duty." In 1771 thirteen rebels were executed for treason in North Carolina. The following year two Templar Masons John Brown and Abraham Whipple burned a customs ship off Rhode Island.[41]

Nevertheless, there was no unified movement for national resistance until the Tea Act of 1773. This was passed by the English Parliament because the British East India Company, which had a monopoly to supply tea to America, was nearly bankrupt and there were 17 million pounds (in weight) of unsold tea in its London warehouses. Under the Act, the Company received a subsidy from Parliament of one shilling for every pound of tea sold in America, and was granted permission to ship 600 chests of excess tea each to New York, Philadelphia and Boston. The British government increased the tax on tea to prevent the British East India Company from going bankrupt. By using "consignees" (i.e. the Royal Governor Thomas Hutchinson's Tory friends) it was able to undercut local American competition and sell its surplus warehouse stocks at a profit. Their sales would in turn bring in the three-penny tax on tea which so many opposed. Local merchants were outraged at what they saw as a threat to free trade.

The first of the three tea ships entered Boston Harbour on November 27.[42] Five thousand clamouring citizens gathered in and round the Old South Meeting House. The cargo could not be sent back to England by law; unless it was unloaded and the duty paid within 20 days, the Governor could confiscate it. For nearly three weeks huge numbers of people milled round the Old South Meeting House while meetings resolved that "the tea should not be landed." The Governor would not compromise, and on the eve of the deadline, with 7,000 people round the Meeting House, Samuel Adams declared, "Gentlemen, this meeting can do nothing more to save the country!"[43]

The Tea Party began at Boston's Old South Meeting House after dark on December 17, 1773. Everyone made their way to Griffin's Wharf, where the three tea ships were moored. What happened next is described in the Ship's log of the *Dartmouth*: "Between six and seven o'clock came down to the wharf a body of about one thousand people. Among them were a number dressed and whooping like Indians. They came on board the ship, and, after warning myself and the Customs House officer to get out of the way, they unlaid the hatches and went down to the hold, where there were 80 whole and 34 half chests of tea, which they hoisted upon deck, and cut the chests to pieces, and hove the tea off overboard, where it was damaged and lost."[44]

At least 120 and possibly up to 200 Templar Masons from St Andrew's had dressed as Mohawk Indians in a clearly pre-arranged act. They had met in the Long Room of Freemasons' Hall, which was formerly the Green Dragon tavern. Other groups meeting there numbered the Long Room Club (which included the Grand Master of St. Andrew's, Joseph Warren), the Committee of Correspondence (which included Joseph Warren and Paul Revere) and the Sons of Liberty (who included Samuel Adams). They emptied 342 chests of tea[45] each weighing 360 lbs, and destroyed 60 tons of tea-leaves, enough to make 24 million cups of tea. Some patriots shouted out, "Boston Harbour a teapot tonight." John Adams wrote in his diary that night, "Depend upon it, they were no ordinary Mohawks....This is the most magnificent moment of all! There is a dignity, a majesty, a sublimity in this last effort of the patriots that I greatly admire. The people should never rise without doing something to be remembered — something notable and striking. This destruction of the tea is so bold, so daring, so firm, intrepid and inflexible, and it must have so important consequences, and so lasting, that I can't but consider it an epoch in history!"[46]

Later that evening there was no celebrating. The streets were quiet. John Adams wrote, "The town of Boston was never more still and calm on a Saturday night." No-one divulged the names of the perpetrators to Governor Hutchinson's investigators, and there was apprehension at what the British response would be.[47]

The reaction came six months later. In May 1774 a ship arrived with details of King George III's retaliation, the four punitive, so-called Intolerable Acts (also known as the Coercive Acts) passed by the British Parliament. This comprised four punitive measures. The colony of Massachusetts's charter of 1699 was abrogated, and it became a crown colony; the elected local government was abolished and General Thomas Gage was appointed military governor. Under the Boston Port Bill, the port of Boston was closed to all boats including ferries until the townspeople had paid for the tea; Boston's sea-trade was simply shut down. Furthermore, court trials of British officials charged with capital offences during law enforcement could be moved to England. Soldiers could be quartered in people's homes against their will. These Acts renewed local indignation and strengthened the unity and resolve of the resentful citizens of the colony, who were now on the brink of revolt.

On September 5, 1774 the First Continental Congress convened at Carpenter's Hall in Philadelphia to plan action against the British, under the presidency of the Templar Freemason (and Provincial Grand Master of Virginia and well-known lawyer) Peyton Randolph. The Congress's secretary was Charles Thompson. Boston delegates included the Son of Liberty Samuel Adams and the Templar Mason Paul Revere. In February 1775 the Massachusetts Provincial Congress met and announced plans for armed resistance. Parliament declared the state of Massachusetts to be in a state of rebellion. Soon afterwards the Virginia

Provincial Assembly met in St. John's church, Richmond and Patrick Henry made his famous speech, "Give me liberty, or give me death."[48]

On April 18 700 British troops were sent to seize militia arms stored at Concord, outside Boston. Paul Revere made his famous ride to announce "The Redcoats are coming!" and 77 armed colonists met them at Lexington. In the ensuing skirmish eight colonists were killed in what was called "the shot heard round the world," and on their way back to Boston the British troops were attacked by 4,000 colonial Americans and suffered 273 casualties (dead or wounded) against 90 suffered by the colonists.

The Declaration of Independence

Into this situation came Thomas Paine. Benjamin Franklin had met Paine during his second stay in London from 1764 to 1775. Paine was a young British ex-excise officer who had collected taxes on alcohol and tobacco and had been dismissed by the British government for agitating for a pay-rise for all customs officers. Seeing him as a disaffected Englishman who could be of use to the colonists – and to himself, as a spy for Sion on the Templars – Franklin advised him to go to America and seek his fortune, and gave him letters of introduction. In November 1774 Paine arrived in Philadelphia and helped edit Franklin's *Pennsylvania Magazine*. On April 19, 1775 Paine argued that America should not just revolt against British taxation but should demand independence.

Franklin returned to America in March 1775, suspecting that revolution was about to break out. He had been dismissed from the post office in January 1774 for helping to publish the letters of Thomas Hutchinson, Governor of Massachusetts to the British government. On May 10 he was a delegate to the Second Continental Congress which was held under Templar control at the State House, two blocks west of Carpenter's Hall in Philadelphia; the president was again the Templar Peyton Randolph and when he died he was succeeded as president on May 10, 1775 by John Hancock of the Templar St. Andrew's lodge.[49]

This Congress regarded itself as the embodiment of the United Colonies, and authorized the raising of a Continental army. It selected one of its delegates, George Washington, a prominent Virginian Templar whose Grand Master was Randolph, to be appointed commander-in-chief. Practically all Washington's military generals were Templars (Richard Montgomery, David Wooster, Hugh Mercer, Arthur St. Clair, Horatio Gates and Israel Putnam). Another of the Congress's delegates was Thomas Jefferson, a Templar Mason from Virginia.

Franklin's disciple Paine based his pamphlet *Common Sense* on his demand for American independence, and it was printed in January 1776 and sold half a million copies. This anticipated and was a major influence on the Declaration of Independence.[50]

Franklin's printing had enabled him more than anyone else to give intellectual expression to the revolution. Between 1765 and 1775 he published 126 newspaper articles on issues of the day, and was the controlling influence behind voices such as Thomas Paine. As a delegate to the Second Continental Congress in Philadelphia (1775) he had met Thomas Jefferson, and when in June 1776 it seemed that a decision to break with Great Britain was imminent following Congress's call[51] to the colonies to organize their own governments as states, a committee was set up to draft a statement of the reasons for this decision. It included Franklin, Jefferson, John Adams, Roger Sherman and Robert Livingstone. Franklin and Adams acknowledged the 33-year-old Jefferson's talents and allowed him to become the main author of the Declaration of Independence.

This was a state paper, but Jefferson saw it as an expression of the American way of thinking. He drafted the document in two weeks, working in the second-floor parlour of the home of a young German bricklayer, Jacob Graff, a room he rented as his lodging. Franklin and Adams made small alterations, and Congress deleted a condemnation of slavery and the slave trade; but the Declaration was handed to President John Hancock and adopted on July 4, 1776 – in the same Council Chamber where James Otis had argued against the Writs of Assistance, overlooking the square where the Boston massacre had taken place.

On the first reading of the Declaration of Independence from the balcony of the Council Chamber to the citizens of Philadelphia assembled in the square on July 8, 1776, the Liberty Bell was rung. Cast in 1752, cracked, and inscribed with a text from *Leviticus*, "Proclaim Liberty throughout all the Land unto all the Inhabitants thereof," it rang out a declaration of liberty. The Declaration of Independence was signed a month later. It proclaimed the self-evident truths of man's equality, and unalienable right to life, liberty and pursuit of happiness, as well as the people's right to alter their government when "a long train of abuses" reduced them to living "under absolute despotism." Its adoption brought the new American nation into existence.

On July 2 two days before publishing the Declaration, Congress had voted for independence and full war was inevitable. After the fighting in Lexington and Concord when British troops were sent from Boston by the British General Thomas Gage, rebel forces had begun a siege of Boston in April 1775. This ended when the American General Henry Knox arrived with artillery captured from Fort Ticonderoga. (Americans under General Richard Montgomery had invaded Canada in the autumn of 1775. Having captured Montreal and besieged Quebec, they had fallen back to the Fort when British reinforcements arrived in spring 1776.) Knox forced General William Howe, the Templar replacement for Gage, to remove all troops from Boston in March 1776. Howe 'withdrew to New York and sent for help, whereupon the British government sent his brother (Richard, Admiral Lord Howe), also a Templar, to New York with orders to pardon the Americans if they submitted. But the Americans refused to consider submitting – and declared independence.[52]

Now Benjamin Franklin returned to Paris as one of three commissioners sent by Congress to seek military and financial aid for the American colonies. While there he met Weishaupt (or possibly an agent of the Illuminati).[53] Franklin, whose first loyalty was always to the Rosicrucian Priory of Sion, did more than anyone else to make revolution virtuous and acceptable. Before his contribution revolution was a pejorative word, but his wit and lovable fur hat and spectacles and grandfatherly image made it admirable. In Paris in 1776, he was fêted as a hero who had led people to freedom from their feudal past, and he must be considered a significant force in the foremath of the French Revolution. (Mirabeau, for example, credited Franklin with having carried out the American Revolution almost single-handed.) He was without a doubt the Samuel Hartlib of the American Revolution.

In Paris Franklin almost immediately formed a relationship with the widow of Claude-Adrien Helvétius, who had led a group of French *philosophes* that included Voltaire and Rousseau.[54] Madame Helvétius belonged to one of the four great families of Lorraine and was related to Charles de Lorraine, to the imperial family of Austria and to Marie-Antoinette. It is likely that Charles de Lorraine (who was Grand Master of the Priory of Sion until his death in 1780, when he was succeeded by his nephew Maximilian de Lorraine) used Madame Helvétius as a go-between to give Franklin his instructions.

Franklin stayed in France and arranged loans through Charles Gravier, Comte de Vergennes, the French Minister for Foreign Affairs. He received money from Templar supporters in the English Parliament who were friends of Sir Francis Dashwood, and sent it back to America to fund the US war effort.[55]

The War of Independence

At first the ensuing war went Britain's way. General Howe landed on Long Island and defeated General George Washington, the American commander-in-chief. George Washington was a Rosicrucian before he became a Templar, having been initiated as a Rosicrucian Mason in the lodge at Fredericksburg, Virginia in 1752.[56] He had become a Templar Mason by 1768, as he confirmed in a letter of September 25, 1798 to the Rev G. W. Snyder: "[I must] correct an error you have run into, of my Presiding over the English lodges in this Country. The fact is, I preside over none, nor have I been in one more than once or twice, within the last 30 years." By "the English lodges" he meant Rosicrucian lodges. Washington was friendly with General Lafayette, another Templar Freemason who twice presented him with Masonic aprons, once in 1784 when he gave Washington an apron which included the All-Seeing Eye. By the time Washington was elected President in 1789, he was Grand Master of the Templar Alexandria lodge no. 22 in Virginia and John Adams was his Vice-President.[57] Washington took issue over the infiltration of lodges by the Illuminati in 1798 and wrote (earlier in the letter to Snyder of September 25, 1798) regarding Robison's book, *Proofs of a Conspiracy.* "I have heard much of the nefarious, and dangerous plan, and doctrines of the Illuminati, but never saw the Book until you were pleased to send it to me."

Washington as a Freemason. (Library of Congress, Washington DC)

Washington also said that none of the American lodges were "contaminated with the principles ascribed to the society of the Illuminati." In another letter to Snyder, dated October 24, 1798, he wrote: "It was not my intention to doubt that, the Doctrines of the Illuminati and Principles of Jacobinism had not spread in the United States. On the contrary, no one is more truly satisfied of this fact than I am."[58]

All this would suggest that Washington was a deist – in other words, he believed in a God who existed merely to create the Universe – who switched from Rosicrucian (English) Freemasonry to Templarism but never embraced the Illuminati, whose practices he found shocking. He was a rationalist deist who was content with Templar Freemasonry.

After his defeat by Howe, Washington[59] withdrew his army to Manhattan, but Howe lured him to Chatterton Hill, near White Plains, and defeated him again on October 28. He captured Washington's garrison at Manhattan while the British General Charles, Lord Cornwallis captured Washington's other garrison at Fort Lee and drove the American army across New Jersey, before setting up winter quarters on the Delaware river.

A reverse in American fortunes began at Christmas, when Washington crossed the Delaware and overran Cornwallis's garrison at Trenton, and he took 1,000 prisoners. Washington then defeated British reinforcements at Princeton and inspired America. Howe, who had 42,000 men and 30,000 German mercenaries against 20,000 American troops (who were mainly farmers), abandoned New Jersey for Pennsylvania. This was a blunder by a General who was being deliberately slothful, many felt, because as a Templar he sympathized with the cause of the enemy.

In 1777 General John Burgoyne's British army in Canada marched south towards Albany to join another force under Lt.-Col. Barry St. Leger, who had marched through the Mohawk Valley. Burgoyne recaptured Fort Ticonderoga on July 5, but when he sent German mercenaries to collect some horses at Bennington, Vermont, they were mauled by American troops. Meanwhile St. Leger's advance was blocked at Oriskany by General Benedict Arnold. Burgoyne was defeated in two encounters by a force under the American General Horatio Gates, and finally had to surrender his army at Saratoga on October 17.

The British had seemed to be doing well, for in September General Howe had sailed from New York to Chesapeake Bay and defeated Washington's forces at Brandywine Creek. However, instead of pursuing Washington and destroying his army he occupied Philadelphia, the

American capital, and allowed Washington to counter by attacking Germantown on October 4. Howe fought him off but allowed him to regroup instead of attacking. While Washington wintered nearby at Valley Forge, a Prussian officer, Baron von Steuben, trained his troops in weaponry and manoeuvres. Howe officially recognized his mistake in failing to destroy Washington's modest force by resigning before operations began in 1778. He was succeeded by General Henry Clinton. Putting von Steuben's training to good use, Washington defeated the British at Monmouth, New Jersey, in June 1778, and the British forces in the north now remained in the vicinity of New York.

As a result of Franklin's deputation to France and his skilful diplomacy in asking the French monarchy for loans and material aid for American democracy against the English King, George III, the French had secretly been helping the Americans against Britain since 1776. From 1776-1778 they sent supplies and funds to the rebels. In 1778, encouraged by the British defeat at Saratoga the previous year and the failure of Britain to reclaim the north, Louis XVI declared war against the British, hoping to wrest part of the New World from their control and place it under French government. He did not realize the consequences this action might have for his own monarchy – that the blooding of French Templars would soon endanger his own French throne.

After 1778 the French gave military and naval support to the Americans. The man who tipped the balance in favour of extensive French involvement was the Templar Marquis de Lafayette. A courtier at the court of Louis XVI at the age of 17, he went out to join the American Revolution at the age of 20. He arrived in Philadelphia in July 1777 and was immediately appointed a Major-General. He struck up a friendship with George Washington, fought at Brandywine, and led the retreat from Barren Hill in May 1778. He returned to France in early 1779 and helped persuade Louis XVI's government to send an expeditionary army of 6,000 soldiers to aid the colonists, as Franklin had requested. He returned to America in April 1780 and was given command of an army in Virginia.

The French sent a fleet of ships under Count D'Estaing, who tried unsuccessfully to take Newport in Rhode Island. They also besieged the British in Savannah in the south. Then in 1779 Spain entered the war (hoping to recover Gibraltar) and the Netherlands followed suit in 1780. It was now an international war.

General Lord Cornwallis destroyed an army led by Gates at Camden, South Carolina in August 1780, and though he suffered reverses at Kings Mountain in October and Cowpens in January 1781, he won a victory at Guilford Court House, North Carolina in March, and in May joined British forces in Virginia. (He had about 8,000 men.) Soon after, an American army of 4,500 troops (commanded by Lafayette, General Wayne and Baron von Steuben) forced Cornwallis to retreat across Virginia. Cornwallis went willingly for he wanted to maintain his sea link with the British army of General Clinton in New York. He fell back to Richmond, then Williamsburg and finally Yorktown, where he was trapped with his back to the sea in July 1781.

Washington saw the opportunity and ordered Lafayette to block Cornwallis's escape by land. Meanwhile Washington's 2,500 troops at New York were reinforced by 4,000 French troops and while part of the combined armies pinned Clinton in New York, Washington's main Franco-American force marched south and was transported to Williamsburg by part of a French fleet of 24 ships, which was blockading Cornwallis's army from the sea. Washington's army then marched to join Lafayette's troops and besieged the 8,000 British troops. A British fleet was unable to defeat the French at the battle of Virginia Capes, and a British rescue fleet arrived too late.

In early October Washington's 14,000 troops surrounded the British fortified positions at Yorktown and outgunned them. (The British earthworks at Yorktown can be visited near the York River, and the reconstructed French and American lines – Washington ordered the original ones to be levelled – are 400 yards beyond them.) There was cannonfire point blank into the British positions and Cornwallis escaped across the river with a thousand men. Finally on October 19, 1781 he had no choice but to surrender. The defeated British marched to what is now called the Surrender Field and laid down their arms as their band played the song, "The World Turned Upside Down." The entire British force of 8,000 men was taken prisoner and surrendered 240 guns. The seizure of Cornwallis at Yorktown had been a consequence of Washington's vision, and Lafayette was now hailed as a "hero of two worlds" (America and Europe).

The British surrender at Yorktown ended the land action in the American War of Independence, and the British cause in America was now lost. There were recriminations, and it has often been pointed out that Britain lacked an overall strategy and that British armies failed to co-operate. In London (following an open letter by "Cicero") blame was laid at the door of Templar Freemasonry. It seems that Cornwallis, Clinton and the Howe brothers were all Templar Freemasons who practised in field lodges. General Howe had served under Amherst and Wolfe in an army where Freemasonry was widespread. In 1781 General Howe and his brother Admiral Howe were accused in the open letter by "Cicero" of belonging to a "faction" which conspired to facilitate the colonists' struggle for independence. The "faction" was Templar Freemasonry. "Washington's whole conduct," "Cicero" claimed, "...demonstrated a confidence which could arise from nothing short of certain knowledge." He accused Admiral Howe of "having secret intrigues with Doctor Franklin." On the question of the meetings with Franklin, Admiral Howe wrote that, "'Cicero' is perfectly right as to the fact though a little deceived in his inferences." In fact, Franklin's sister had brought Howe and Franklin together, overtly to play chess but in fact to discuss the colonists' grievances. The point "Cicero" was making was that because of their Templar sympathies with the Americans, the British General and Admiral had betrayed their country.[60]

The war continued on the high seas. The American effort was largely through privateers. The actual sea-war was fought between Britain and America's European allies: France, Spain and the Netherlands. By the end of the war 12,000 French soldiers and 32,000 French sailors had left France to support Washington. The French navy was heavily defeated by the British in 1782 and as a result France gained little from her participation in the American war. The privateers did well, and by the end of the war they had captured 1,500 British merchant ships. After 1780 the Spanish and Dutch fleets controlled the waters round the British Isles, confining British naval forces there and making sure they could not sail to America.

Franklin, working with Vergennes, had not wanted peace but John Adams and John Jay had overruled him in late 1782, and the treaty was the outcome of their efforts. Under the treaty Great Britain recognized the independence of the United States and its western boundaries to the Mississippi River, and ceded Florida to Spain. There was to be fair treatment for American colonials who had been loyal to Britain. As a result of the defeat, the North government fell in Britain. With the formal ratification of the Treaty of Paris the American War of Independence ended on September 3, 1783.

AMERICAN TEMPLARISM AND POLITICAL REPUBLICANISM

The Great Seal of America

By then, the US had adopted Weishaupt's Seal as the Great Seal of the United States. It had taken six years to agree. Late in the afternoon of July 4, 1776 (the day the Declaration of Independence was adopted), Congress set up a First Committee of three – Franklin, Jefferson and John Adams – to design the Great Seal of the United States.[61] They were to be assisted by the portrait painter Pierre Eugene Du Simitière.[62] Seals of European royalty were known as far back as the 7th century; and Edward the Confessor's first English royal pendant seal, created during his reign from 1042 to 1066, became the model for all English and American seals. The two-sided seal would effectively be the new America's national coat of arms. Franklin's initial suggestion involved Moses, Pharaoh and a ray from a pillar of fire reaching Moses to show that he acted by command of the Deity. Jefferson proposed showing the children of Israel in the wilderness, led by a cloud during the day and a pillar of fire by night. Adams proposed Hercules between virtue and sloth. Du Simitière suggested a shield divided into six (representing England, Scotland, Ireland, Holland, France and Germany) and the goddess of liberty.

Congress rejected the proposals of the First Committee in January 1777 and set up a Second Committee in 1780. It consulted with Hopkinson, who had designed the American flag, as well as some coins and seals for great departments of state, and Hopkinson had used an unfinished pyramid in a 1778 50-dollar colonial bank note. A Third Committee was formed on May 4, 1782. Charles Thomson and William Barton designed the Great Seal of the United States, using Masonic-Illuminist symbolism for the reverse (an unfinished pyramid surmounted by an eye). Their design now appears on the one-dollar bill with an inscription *Novus Ordo Seculorum*. Charles Thomson drew a Phoenix under a cloud of stars and very soon arrived at the seal as we know it.

Something clearly happened to ease the situation between 1781 and 1782. What seems to have happened is that during his meeting in Paris with Adam Weishaupt or an agent of the Illuminati in September 1776 while he was seeking military and financial aid for the colonies in their coming struggle with England, Benjamin Franklin saw a sketch of the Seal Weishaupt had produced for his Sionist-Rosicrucian Illuminati, which sought to unite Sion and the Templars. Franklin, a Rosicrucian among the Templars like Radclyffe, Voltaire and Ramsay, was being encouraged by Sion's latest protégé to move towards Templarism in the hope of effecting a union with Sion.

Part of US dollar bill

reverse   obverse

The Great Seal of the United States of America

The Illuminati Seal's reverse side showed a Templar 13-layered unfinished 4-sided pyramid with its capstone missing. Above was a triangle in sun-rays, and within it was the All-Seeing Eye of Osiris and Sion (as shown in the picture of the House of Orange grouped round the crowned William III on p187). At one level the eye represented Weishaupt's spying system. On the bottom layer of bricks was the year 1776, the year in which Weishaupt founded the Illuminati, whose Seal represented the Secret Doctrine of the Ages, the plan to build a new Atlantis in the New World. (Carr states that Weishaupt adopted the reverse as the symbol of his new society when he founded the Order of Illuminati on May 1, 1776.)[63]

There was a general belief that the university in the Atlantis that sank, where most of the arts and sciences originated, was housed in a great pyramid, with an observatory at the apex to study stars.[64] The university in the old Atlantis heralded the "Invisible College" of Sionist Rosicrucianism, which worked for the New Atlantis. The triangle may suggest the power of the Merovingian thrones. The 13 layers of bricks in the pyramid symbolized the 13 colonies that would become a New Atlantis under Sion's providential (some claimed spying) eye. The 13 – of the layers or steps and of the letters of *"Annuit Coeptis"* – also had Templar symbolism, suggesting the 13th day of the month when de Molay died and the 13 degrees of Templar initiation.[65]

The Illuminati Seal thus suggested the union of Sion and Templarism within one unfinished building of Freemasonry.[66] The obverse side of the Seal showed a tufted phoenix rather than an eagle. Only one phoenix is said to exist at any one time, and it lives for 500 years and nests in a distant part of Arabia. When it dies its body opens and a new phoenix is born. It is a Freemasonic symbol of Atlantis reborn in America. (The phoenix also represents an initiate. It can be said to be "twice-born" as it may appear to be reborn from its own death. This interpretation blurs the fact that a new phoenix is born from the death of its parent.)[67]

At some point before 1782, Franklin convinced Jefferson and John Adams that they should use the Illuminati Seal as the seal of the United States.[68] He pointed out that the year 1776 in Roman numerals represented the year of American independence and that the 13 layers of brick represented the 13 colonies. In 1781 Franklin seems to have sent back from Paris a copy of the Illuminati's republican doctrine and also a replica of its unfinished pyramid Seal. In the person of Weishaupt or his agent, the Illuminati had taught him the Secret Doctrine of the Ages, the plan for a New World democracy rather than an English oligarchic expansion of empire. He sent back this secret knowledge, and was determined to embody it in the American Seal.

Thomas Paine visited Paris (with one John Laurens) in 1781 to raise funds, clothing and ammunition for the American troops, an initiative that contributed to the final success of the revolution. Paine met Franklin and became a Grand Orient Freemason, and therefore a member of the Illuminati. It is likely that Franklin, who was no longer Deputy Postmaster General, sent back a replica of the Illuminati Seal with Paine, who delivered it in time for it to come to the attention of the Third Committee in 1782. After Congress adopted this Seal, the credit was given to Du Simitère and the three committees, but in fact the adoption of the Seal is a measure of the extent to which both Franklin and Jefferson were receptive to Illuminati Ideas.

In 1778 Franklin had joined the Lodge of St John of Jerusalem as well as the Illuminati Grand Orient Lodge *Neuf Soeurs* (Nine Sisters), of which he became Grand Master in 1782 and into which he initiated his Sionist colleague Voltaire at the end of his life. (This Lodge had been founded in Paris in July 1776 by the Swiss Protestant pastor Antoine Court de Gébelin, who in a 9-volume work tried to create a primordial language that would hasten unity "among nations." After Franklin was received, it printed the constitutions of all 13 American states and became Europe's first school of constitutionalism.) The British Government's espionage service was Sionist Masonic and British agents penetrated Franklin's Illuminati Lodge. Also in 1782, now that Sion and the Templars had drawn together in the Illuminati, Franklin joined a Templar organization, the Royal Lodge of Commanders of the Temple West. He did not return to America until 1785. [69]

The Founding Fathers

Thomas Jefferson was, like Franklin, both a Rosicrucian and a Templar Freemason. (A Rosicrucian code has been discovered among his papers,[70] and twenty-nine Masonic journals contain references to his being a Mason.) He was in France from 1784 along with Franklin and John Adams to negotiate a treaty with France following the end of the War of Independence, and he succeeded Franklin as resident US Minister to the French government. He returned to America in 1789, having reputedly been initiated into a Templar lodge in France and having met Weishaupt. He thought the French Revolution "so beautiful a revolution."

Franklin and he are regarded as the founding fathers most responsible for bringing the Illuminati to America. Franklin, Jefferson and Adams were all Illuminati initiates. Their initiation seems to have taken place after the American Revolution, and so did not

Thomas Jefferson

influence the course of the revolution. Jefferson and John Adams fell out when Adams accused him (in three letters in the Wittenburg Square library in Philadelphia) of using lodges he himself had founded for Illuminati purposes. (There were 15 Illuminati lodges in the 13 colonies by 1785.) It could be that Franklin and Jefferson – and Adams – were manipulated by the Illuminati in Paris until Adams realized what was afoot.[71] Jefferson was certainly naïve about the Order. He criticized Illuminism but excused Weishaupt: "Wishaupt [sic] seems to be an enthusiastic philanthropist. He is among those...who believe in the infinite perfectibility of man. He thinks he may in time be rendered so perfect that he will be able to govern himself in every circumstance, so as to injure none, to do all the good he can, to leave government no occasion to exercise their powers over him, and, of course, to render political government useless."[72] In the same passage, he refers to the "ravings against him of Robison" and others, and charitably believes Weishaupt's secrecy must be attributed to the tyranny of the "despot and priests" under which he lived. Jefferson said he hoped the French Revolution would sweep the world. Jefferson, as much as Franklin, helped start the French Revolution.

Of the founding fathers, both Jefferson and Franklin were rationalists who expressed scepticism about the value of metaphysics as being "unamenable to the test of our senses."[73] They were both influenced by the Illuminati, whose sworn goal was the removal of all heads of Church and State and the establishment of a "Universal Republic" with a "Religion of Reason" to steer it. As we saw earlier (p235), the Grand Orient lodges had been founded by the Duke of Orléans in 1772 and swiftly accommodated the Illuminati. The Sionist Franklin was in London from 1772 to 1775 (and stayed with Sir Francis Dashwood the Templar Mason, during the summers of 1772, 1773, and 1774 as we have seen), and his Sionist controller Charles de Lorraine (alias Kolmer) must have told him about Sion's project to set up the Illuminati. It is quite possible that some Illuminati ideas reached Philadelphia and Boston in 1775/6, before Paine's *Common Sense* pamphlet and the writing of the Declaration of Independence.

It must be stressed that it was far more common to be a Freemason in the 18th century than it is today, and that the secrecy of the lodges was a perfect breeding-ground for revolutionary ideas. Meetings on revolutionary themes could happen behind closed doors without risk of arrest, and it would have been normal for a budding revolutionary to join a lodge in the America of the 1770s and 1780s, where to be a Freemason meant to oppose British rule.

Many of the founders of the American nation were Freemasons; nine, according to some, and fifty-three according to others.[74] Franklin, Jefferson, John Adams, Washington, Charles Thomson and the rest were all deists who believed that religious knowledge can be acquired by reason rather than revelation or the teaching of the Church. Deists believe in a God who created the Universe, a Great Architect who then withdrew. In deism man does not need a God, and certainly not a son of God; deists regard Jesus as merely a wise prophet. In fact, deists believe that through reason and initiation (which leads to secret knowledge) man can become a god.

This belief in divinity through reason was very much in keeping with the Age of Reason which Weishaupt launched, and the insights of Freemasonry and the Illuminati.

Internally changes in post-revolutionary America fell short of being truly radical. There was no transfer of power between classes, and slavery remained in force. Political and economic power were held in the same hands as before the war. Nonetheless the new independent states had written constitutions which guaranteed several rights and there was a separation between Church and State. There was increased popular control, suffrage was extended and the legislature confirmed the rights of individuals. In other words, there was rapid progress in democracy. There had been a sudden revolutionary transformation in American life as America ceased to be a colonial possession and became an independent, anti-monarchical republic, with republican institutions.

The Templar Constitution

In 1781/2 Washington spent the winter with the Continental

Congress in Philadelphia. He insisted that the army should be paid, and in 1782 received a letter from Colonel Lewis Nicola urging him to use the army to make himself King. He rejected the proposal with great indignation. (Cromwell also rejected the title of King.) Washington, it seems, felt that America would eventually become a monarchy; indeed, he admitted the necessity of the principle of monarchy. But it seems he could not reconcile this view with his Templar philosophy, which demanded a republic.

The years from 1783 to 1787 saw little progress towards the political expression of the revolution in a new constitution.[75] It was as though the Americans were exhausted from the war of independence and needed time to recover their breath. In fact the way forward for the new republican government had been tortuous. Soon after Saratoga, in November 1777, the Continental Congress had agreed that the new system should be a federation of states, and that each state should ratify the Articles of Confederation, which took until March 1781. At least 80,000 and possibly as many as 200,000 Americans fled to England or Canada during the Revolutionary War, out of a population of 2 million. The new body was now a loose association of states held together by the Articles of Confederation, with a weak central government. It took six more years before, in May 1787, the Constitutional Convention of 55 delegates met in the State House in Philadelphia "to render the Constitution of the Federal Government adequate to the exigencies of the Union"; in other words, to work out the form of a new national government. They were encouraged in their work by Benjamin Franklin, who was now 81.

George Washington, who had led the American army to victory against the most powerful nation on earth and had written to his friends urging "an indissoluble union" of states, once again answered America's call for leadership. He arrived in Philadelphia the day before the Convention opened, and was unanimously chosen as President but did not speak in the debates which lasted four months. His aide-de-camp, Edmund Randolph, acting as his mouthpiece, proposed that the Convention should set up a new basis for central government rather than tinker with the existing Articles of Confederation. This was accepted and the Convention began the process of trying to turn a loose confederation of former provinces into a nation.

Many delegates had read philosophers such as Locke (who saw government as a social contract between ruler and ruled) and Hume (who called republicanism a "dangerous novelty"), Adam Smith and Montesquieu. In fact, they took their main three principles from Freemasonry: the investment of power in the office, not the man; the adoption of a system of "checks and balances" between the executive, legislative and judicial branches of government; and the adoption of the Masonic federal system of organization. The parallel between the federal American constitution and federal Masonic lodges has been brought out by H. C. Clausen. The Articles of Confederation did not provide a strong national government, common currency or consistent judicial system. For the weak Confederation of American States to become a strong, unified nation there must be a strong organization. As the Masonic federal system was the only pattern for effective organization operating in each of the original Thirteen Colonies, it was natural that patriotic American Masons should use it as a model to strengthen the young nation. Consequently the federalism established in the civil government the Constitution created was identical to the federalism of the Grand Lodge system of Masonic government created in *Anderson's Constitutions* of 1723.[76]

The Convention scrapped the Articles of Confederation and then set out to create a radical new democratic system of government. Almost immediately there were heated exchanges over representation. The larger states supported the so-called "Virginia Plan," Madison's brainchild, proposed by Randolph on May 29, that supported representation by their percentage of the total population (i.e. proportional representation) and sought strong national government through the domination of the larger states. They wanted Congress to be bicameral, the Lower House elected, and the Upper picked by the Lower from candidates named by state Legislatures. The smaller states supported the "New Jersey Plan," offered by William Paterson on June

14, which supported an equal voice for all states and opposed centralization and control by the larger states. The plan recommended a one-house legislature elected by states. The result was a compromise (the Connecticut Compromise) proposed by Roger Sherman. There would be proportional representation in the House of Representatives and equal representation in the Senate. On July 5 the Committee reported in favour of Sherman's plan but with another compromise over slavery. Representation in the Lower House would be based on the total of the white population plus three-fifths of the slave population (not the whole of the slave population as the southern delegates wanted). Committees of style and detail met, and eventually the delegates signed the document of the Constitution, a Charter which formed "a more perfect Union."

Washington presided on a low rostrum in the Assembly Hall (where the Declaration of Independence had been approved) from his "rising sun chair." The top of the chair showed half a sun with two eyes and a nose and thirteen rays like hair. Above it on a stem hung a pyramid-shaped plant. The whole is a Templar image. As the delegates signed the new Constitution, Benjamin Franklin told them that the sun on Washington's chair was rising, not setting on the new nation.

The text of the Constitution was submitted to the 13 states for ratification in September 1787. The Constitution was accepted and signed by 39 of the 42 delegates that month, and by July 1788 it had been ratified by the nine states required to put it into effect, thanks to Washington's quiet authority. Some states wanted a Bill of Rights, for the Constitution did not specifically list the rights of all citizens, and Congress proposed 12 amendments in September 1789, of which 10 were passed in December 1791. These 10 amendments guaranteed personal freedoms and are known as the Bill of Rights.

The Masonic Lay-out of Washington D.C.

The federal capital was in the 10 square miles ceded to Congress by Maryland and Virginia, and there was speculation as to who would be the first President. Only one man commanded the respect of both the Federalists and the Anti-Federalists and would give the office prestige in

Europe but Washington prevaricated, preferring to retire to Mount Vernon "under [his] vine and fig tree" as he often said (echoing Solomon). His reluctance, suggesting the posture of a victorious general humbly returning his sword to the hands that gave it, only added to his appeal. (Washington's gesture recalled the example of Lucius Quinctius Cincinnatus, who left his farm to become dictator at Rome in 458 BC and rescue a consular army surrounded by the Aequi, defeated the enemy in a single day and then returned to his farm.) In early 1789 electors were chosen, and on February 4 George Washington was unanimously elected first President of the United States. He accepted reluctantly, apparently doubting his own abilities. He left Mount Vernon on April 16 and was inaugurated in Wall Street, New York on April 30. He stood on the balcony of Federal Hall above a cheering crowd and swore the oath before Chancellor Robert Livingston. In 1789, the first dollar bill had a 4-sided pyramid based on the Great Seal.

The following year George Washington chose a marshy swamp as the site that would become Washington D.C., and selected Pierre Charles L'Enfant, an engineer in the Continental army and a Templar Mason, to design the new city. Between 1783 and 1790 Congress had considered and been unable to agree a number of proposed sites (including Trenton, New Jersey and Germantown, Pennsylvania). A northern site was chosen as the south was threatening to break away from the union. Jefferson and Hamilton struck a deal. If Hamilton agreed to a site of 10 square miles on either side of the river Potomac (to be ceded by Maryland in the north and Virginia in the south), Jefferson would agree to the Federal government's assumption of state war debts. The new site was christened the "Territory of Columbia."

Between 1791 and 1800 Pierre L'Enfant selected Capitol Hill as the focal point, and proposed broad avenues like the spokes of a wheel from centres within a rectangular pattern of streets. His plan was changed, though his avenues and vistas were retained.

In 1795 the Templar Masonic founding fathers laid out the streets of Washington to form Masonic symbols: a compass, square, rule, pentagram, pentagon and octagon. Edward Decker describes facing the

Masonic map of Washington DC.
Top right: compass and square with Goat of Mendes (Goat's head).
Top left: triangle. Bottom left: Pentagon or five-pointed star between the White House and the House of the Temple (HQ of the Supreme Council of 33rd Degree of Freemasonry)

Capitol from the Mall. If the Capitol is the top of a compass, the left leg is Pennsylvania Avenue and stands on the Jefferson Memorial, and the right leg is Maryland Avenue. The square is formed by the intersection of Canal Street and Louisiana Avenue. Behind the Capitol the circular drive and short streets form the head and ears of what is often called the "Goat of Mendes" or "Goat's Head." On top of the White House (to the north) is an inverted 5-pointed star or pentagram, the point facing south in occult style. It is within the intersections of Connecticut and Vermont Avenues to the north with Rhode Island and Massachusetts to the West and Mount Vernon square to the east. The centre of the pentagram is 16th Street where thirteen blocks north of the centre of the White House is the Masonic House of The Temple. The Washington Monument is in perfect line to the intersection of the Masonic square stretching from the House of the Temple to the Capitol. Within the hypotenuse of the right-angled triangle are many of the headquarters of the most powerful government departments, such as the Justice Dept., US Senate and the Internal Revenue Service. All the main Federal buildings from the White House to the Capitol have had a cornerstone and specific Masonic regalia laid in a Masonic ritual.[77]

In fact, the Capitol and the White House were focal points in a geometry devised by Pierre L'Enfant and modified by Washington and Jefferson that produced octagonal patterns in which the splayed cross used by Masonic Templars could be imagined.[78] The geography (and geometry) of Washington D.C. reinforced the Templar symbolism of the Great Seal and the dollar bill.

(After contributing to Masonic Washington, Jefferson enlarged Monticello, his house on his 5,000-acre plantation in Virginia, between 1794 and 1809. Monticello became the focus for Templar ideas. The parlour, the tea-room adjoining the dining-room and the cabinet off Jefferson's bedroom all have octagonal bays, while the west front beneath the dome has been influenced by the front of the Roman temple at Nîmes, the 1st century Maison Carrée, which served as the basis for his design of the Virginia State Capitol in Richmond in 1785. The ornamental decoration was taken from Roman buildings which Jefferson found in books in his library. The frieze of the Temple of Fortuna Virilis inspired the ornamentation in his bed chamber; the Temple of Jupiter the Thunderer inspired his parlour; and the Baths of Diocletian inspired his Apollo or sun-god frieze in the North Piazza. In the parlour were pictures of "the three greatest men that had ever lived" – the Sionist Rosicrucianists Bacon, Newton and Locke. In the dining-room there was a frieze of rosettes and skulls. The overall effect of the octagonal dome room whose purpose is officially "unknown" and the columned, pedimented temple beneath it, is of a Masonic Templar building with Illuminatist embellishments.)[79]

George Washington as Symbol of Virtue

Washington stood apart from all party divisions. His first Cabinet comprised four men, two from each party: Jefferson, Hamilton, Knox and Randolph. He toured all the states, and established the pattern of his republican court. In New York and Philadelphia he rented the best houses and refused to accept the offer of hospitality from General Clinton. He bowed rather than shook hands and drove a coach with six horses and outriders. He tried to maintain peace between Jefferson and Hamilton, though he favoured Hamilton's policy of neutrality when France and England went to war in 1793, and as a result the pro-French Jefferson resigned.

During the eight years of his two terms he was idealized in images of public virtue. He was hero-worshipped and venerated by the people for his military achievements, but also for his virtuous and patriotic austerity and devotion to republican institutions. He was projected as a symbol of duty, goodness, diffidence, frugality, industry, wisdom, genius and piety. In 1789 he was shown as the hub of union, his head-and-shoulders in the centre of a wheel of badges of the states. He became an icon who was idealized like a statue of a Roman god. When he died he was deified. *The apotheosis of Washington* was painted in 1800, a year after his death, by David Edwin; Washington looks into the distance, sitting god-like on clouds, while a cherub reaches out and puts a laurel garland on his head.

Washington the man had been neither brilliant nor self-confident and his experience had not equipped him to lead large armies; yet at the beginning of the war America transformed him into a unifying legend. He became a hero for democracy who embodied the moral sentiments the public expected of a model republican leader. He had a popular image that attracted national feeling, and was admired for being a model leader who went to great lengths to avoid power and gave it back with enthusiasm.

The saintly image the American people had of Washington was a result of his own saintly acts and posture, but it was also enhanced by the presenters and "spin-doctors" of the time, as can be gleaned in Barry Schwartz's *George Washington, The Making of an American Symbol.* Much was made of his Christian piety, but as we have seen Washington was a Masonic deist rather than a Christian.[80] The personality cult that grew round Washington, similar to the cults that grew round 20th-century leaders such as Stalin and Mao, which embellished the truth with tales of how he never told a lie, was linked to America's need to put its republicanism and the conservative instincts that inspired the revolution on a pedestal. Washington became the object of a national religion to the sacredness of republicanism, what John Adams meant by his "I glory in the character of Washington because I know him to be an exemplification of the American character." Seen like this, Washington is a symbol of the values and tendencies of his society and not their source. Washington was the opposite of the traditional conception of heroic leadership. Unlike Cromwell and Napoleon, who were confident of their abilities and used their power to bring about radical change, Washington was diffident and ill at ease with power and revered tradition. Washington is the symbol of a conservative uprising to restore ancient liberties and rights, not create a new order. The new republic regarded self-sacrifice, disinterestedness, moderation, resolution, self-control and piety as the virtues Americans wished to live up to, and self-indulgence, ambition, excess, licentiousness, and religious indifference as the vices they wished to avoid.[81]

The American Revolution was different from other revolutions in that it did not transfer power from one section of society to another. In fact, the revolution was effected by aristocratic republicans who felt a keen conflict between their aristocratic habits and their republican ideals. A radical levelling programme ensued, and it was perhaps because of their saintly disinterestedness that Jefferson referred to those who framed the Constitution as "demi-gods."

Nevertheless, the expulsion of the British, the most powerful nation in the world, and the embodiment of Bacon's New Atlantis had suddenly transformed society, as we have seen. At heart it was a Masonic transformation, a Masonic revolution, and Washington's Masonic leadership was behind the image of him that was so skilfully projected. At his inauguration ceremony in 1798 (which took place shortly after Benjamin Franklin's public funeral, attended by the majority of Philadelphians) he was surrounded by Freemasons – Robert Livingston administered the oath, Gen. Morton was marshal and Gen. Lewis was escort – and the Bible used came from St. John's Lodge No. 1, New York. (Washington was of course Grand Master of Alexandria Lodge No. 22 in Virginia.)

In September 1793 there was a ceremony to lay the cornerstone of the Capitol. It was presided over by the Grand Lodge of Maryland, and Washington, wearing apron and sash, served as Master. There was a big procession and all members of all lodges wore their regalia. The ceremony, a Freemasonic ritual, included placing corn, wine and oil round the cornerstone. When he died in December 1799, Washington was buried at his home at Mount Vernon with full Masonic honours, and members of Alexandria Lodge No. 22 acted as pallbearers.

At that remove, Americans could reflect that they had been greatly outnumbered during the Revolution. They had won because they received French assistance, because they knew their own terrain better than the English, because of their patriotic spirit, and because the British leadership was ineffective. But what tipped the balance more than anything else was the support of secret organizations – of the Sons of Liberty, but most notably of the Templar Masonic lodges. All such influences had been disbanded by the time of the Constitutional Convention – French aid, the militias, the Sons of Liberty – and the only organization that remained, still operating across state borders, was Freemasonry. Of the guiding spirits behind the Constitution, Washington, Franklin, Randolph and John Adams were all Freemasons and subscribed to Masonic ideals. They all shared a common position during and after the Convention. Jefferson, also a Mason and the writer of the Constitution, was at odds with the other four, but even he towed the Masonic line until his resignation. In its essence, American republicanism was Templar.

JACKSON'S CONSOLIDATION

America was now a Templar-created Masonic State ruled by Templars. Although it was primarily an independence movement conducted by Templar Masons, the American Revolution still conforms to our template for revolutions, and has its own "consolidation" phase.

1812 War Against Britain

The Templar John Adams succeeded Washington as President on his retirement. Adams avoided war despite a perpetual threat from France and her ally Spain, and was succeeded by his Vice-President, Jefferson, who pursued a policy of territorial expansion until Britain and France limited American trade with Europe and confiscated hundreds of American ships. After his second term Jefferson was succeeded in 1809 by James Madison, who tried to force Britain and France to respect American shipping. His attempts failed; Britain (ruler of the waves, having defeated the French and their Spanish allies at Trafalgar in 1805) seized American ships at will and America's relations with Britain and France grew worse. In 1812, its appetite whetted by the capture of Florida from the Spanish, the American people began to demand war, and Madison, handicapped by unsure diplomacy, was edged into declaring war against Britain on June 18, 1812.

The American navy's strategy was to remain in dock to defend the cities; a small army and a hastily assembled militia force of 100,000 was to invade Canada at Detroit, Fort Niagara and Lake Champlain. The British strategy was to blockade the American fleet and keep them in harbour. In fact, the Americans surrendered Detroit to the British, and the militiamen refused to cross into Canada at the other two places. At last Madison was persuaded to allow 12 ships to sail out and take on the British fleet, which numbered more than 600 ships. In the course of several engagements, the USS *Constitution* under Isaac Hull and then William Bainbridge destroyed two British frigates (HMS *Guerrière* and *Java*) and the USS *United States* under Stephen Decatur took HMS *Macedonia*, while USS *Wasp* took HMS *Frolic*, and USS *Hornet* defeated HMS *Peacock* – unthinkable victories, as Britain's supremacy on the seas had always ensured victory in such engagements.

In 1813 the Royal Navy trapped the American ships in port, and the British in Canada invaded North-West America. Both sides built ships to cross the lakes; the Americans defeated a British fleet on Lake Erie, moved 4,500 troops across the lake and defeated the British and their Indian allies at the battle of the Thames. Meanwhile the British made diversionary attacks on coastal cities and invaded Fort Niagara, Lake Champlain and New Orleans. In 1811 the republican administration had destroyed the Bank of the United States (which had been chartered by Congress in Philadelphia in 1791 to redeem the War of Independence debt of $56 million and obtain international credit) because of doubts about its constitutional legality, and now it had no credit and therefore no money.

In 1814 the coastal raids destroyed areas on the Connecticut River, Buzzards Bay and Alexandria, Virginia. On August 24 the British took Washington, which was undefended. Eight thousand American troops had fled before 1,200 British, who attacked the public buildings, setting fire to the Capitol and the President's house. (Dolley, the President's wife, fled to Rokeby, the country house of Richard Love, whose black cook refused to make her coffee, saying, "I done heerd Mr Madison and Mr Armstrong done sold the country to the British.") They torched the Treasury building and the Naval Yard as well, and by the time British troops pulled out at 9 pm the next day there were thousands of American refugees. The British bombarded Baltimore, but were repulsed at Fort Niagara and on Lake Champlain. It looked as though the American Revolution against the British would unravel, and that the British would return as the main power in America. President Madison, now in temporary quarters on 18th Street, accepted the resignation of the Navy and Treasury secretaries, and prayed for a savior.

It was now that the Duke of Wellington urged the British to withdraw. He had fought the Peninsular Campaign, and he believed that in wild frontier country fighting could continue for ever without either side winning. The chief negotiators had been meeting American commissioners at Ghent in Belgium for some months, and on

December 24 they agreed to a peace. Everything would return to how it was before war began. The end of the war made Madison popular again, and the Americans began to believe they had won a victory.

Jackson and the Indians

At this point Andrew Jackson[82] burst on the American scene as the consolidator of the American Revolution. Scarred at 12 by a British officer, who whacked him across the face with a saber for declining to black his boots during the British invasion of the western Carolinas in 1780, he had grown into a penniless, hungry, uneducated, violent orphan who took up the law in Tennessee, where the frontier was expanding. He seized lands and dealt with them, speculated and dueled. He married the daughter of the man in whose house be boarded (like Franklin) and, quick to take offence, fought many duels in defence of his wife, generally shooting to kill. In 1796 he helped create the new state of Tennessee, first as a congressman, then as a senator; he even drafted the new constitution. Settling in Nashville in 1801, he became a judge in Tennessee's Superior Court and, a Templar Mason, founded the first Masonic lodge in Nashville. He acquired the Hermitage, a large estate, and in 1802 was elected Major-General of the Tennessee Militia, which he used as his powerless.

In March 1812 when war with Great Britain seemed inevitable, Jackson had called for 50,000 volunteers to invade Canada, and after war was declared in June he offered his militia to the United States. They were slow to accept but had given him command against the Creek Indians, who were allies of the British.

A tall man with red hair and bruised and scarred by his many violent encounters on the frontier, which included several fights and violent mêlées in Nashville fought with guns, daggers and knuckles, Jackson still had a bullet in his chest from a duel with Charles Dickinson in 1806. Dickinson had bled to death; his bullet broke two of Jackson's ribs and buried itself near a lung, creating an abscess which caused him pain all his life. He had Thomas Benson's bullet in his shoulder from another duel. It could not be removed and gave him osteomyelitis. He also suffered from malaria and dysentery, and he treated his wounds with sugar of lead and calomel (which rotted his teeth).

The new republic was ambivalent about the Indians. The Constitution had ignored them, saying that Congress had powers to "regulate commerce with foreign nations, and among the several states, and with the Indian tribes." In 1786 Henry Knox, war secretary in charge of Indian affairs, had persuaded Congress to cut Indian country in two at the Ohio River. This had not led to the government being able to control them, and twice – in 1790 and 1791 – Indians in Ohio repulsed American forces (led by first Gen. Harmar and then Gen. St Clair, who lost 1,400 regulars and militia killed). The republic endeavoured to consolidate the Revolution, and in 1794 Anthony Wayne won the brief battle of Fallen Timbers and forced the Shawnees and other tribes to sign a treaty. But this solved nothing. The Americans wanted to absorb the Indians or push them west. The Indians' nomadic tribal organization did not fit in a new republic of borders (states, counties, towns and parishes). The Indians pursued game across boundaries. Any Indian family detribalizing was given 640 acres, and although many Indians did settle, many preferred to retain their traditional way of life.

The British had allied with the Indians and implemented their policy of arming all opponents of the United States and liberating black slaves. They armed and trained over 4,000 Creeks and Seminoles, who received thousands of weapons. The Shawnee Chief Tecumseh urged the Indian élite, "Let the white race perish! They seize your land. They corrupt your women. They trample on the bones of your dead! Back whence they came, on a trail of blood, they must be driven!" And after war broke out in 1812 they massacred American settlers on the Ohio. The Chickasaw, fearing retribution, attacked the murderers. In this lawless open frontier country white Americans attempted a massacre of the Red Stick Creeks under High-Head Jim. They were beaten off and retreated to Samuel Mims's stockade which housed several hundred whites, militiamen and black slaves. The Creek Indians attacked and killed all except 15 whites: 553 men, women and children were killed, and the scalps of 250 women were taken away on poles.

The violent Andrew Jackson was ordered to take his Tennessee Militia and avenge this massacre. Southerners such as Henry Clay, Speaker of the Kentucky House, and John Caldwell Calhoun, spokesman for South Carolina, wanted all Indians driven west of the Mississippi, and urged the building of roads so settlers could move in to all territory vacated by Indians. With one arm still in a sling from yet another duel, Jackson assembled Gen. Coffee, the legendary David Crockett, other adventurers and over a thousand men and led them to the village of Tallhushatchee, where the ringleaders of the massacre were deemed to live. On November 3 Coffee and his thousand men destroyed the village and shot all 186 men and many women. Their cabins were torched. Jackson found a ten-month-old Indian boy, adopted him, named him Lyncoya and sent him back to the Hermitage.

A week later Jackson attacked a thousand Red Stick Creeks at Talladega and killed 300. Some of the militiamen now wanted to go home. Jackson threatened to shoot any man who left, and, faced with a mutiny, trained artillery on the mutineers and ordered the gunmen to fire. The militiamen changed their minds. When one eighteen-year-old, John Woods, refused an order, Jackson had him shot by firing-squad, with his entire army watching. He made his troops get up at 3.30 am to prevent Indian dawn raids, and soon had an army of 5,000.

Jackson attacked the Creek Indians' main fortress at Horseshoe Bend (Tohopeka), which was filled with 1,000 men. It was in a hundred acres, nearly surround by deep water; the land side had a high wall with firing holes. Jackson's men breached the wall and killed anyone who did not surrender: 557 were killed in the fort – they were counted by cut-off tips of noses – and 300 drowned.

After that Jackson rampaged through Indian territory, burning crops and villages until, on April 14, 1814, the Creek Indians surrendered through their Chief Red Eagle. Under the Treaty of Fort Jackson they gave up 20 million acres, half their lands (three-fifths of present Alabama and a fifth of Georgia). The independence of the Indians east of the Mississippi had been destroyed.

Jackson and the British

Now the United States had a line of communication from Georgia to Mobile and Fort Bower, which Jackson (without authority from Washington) occupied in August and defended against the British in September. In early November Jackson learned that the British had landed at Pensacola, Florida. He marched to Florida and on November 7 occupied the Spanish base at Pensacola, even though America was not at war with Spain. Jackson's capture prevented Admiral Cochrane, the British commander, from cutting off New Orleans.

On December 1 Jackson arrived at New Orleans and found it undefended. He quickly formed a force of pirates – the British hanged pirates on Royal Navy ships – and blacks and built a defensive line. When on January 8, 1815 14,000 British troops arrived, not having heard about the peace treaty that had been signed at Ghent, New Orleans was defended. The British under General Sir Edward Pakenham, Wellington's brother-in-law, tried to capture the rampart from the rear by a flanking operation, but when the flanking force failed to arrive, attacked from the front. Ladders to scale the rampart did not appear, and with Admiral Codrington watching from HMS *Tonnant* the British were slaughtered: 291 were killed, 484 were missing and more than a thousand wounded. Jackson lost only 13 killed.

The British fought on and on February 11 took Fort Bower and prepared to occupy Mobile. News of the peace treaty then arrived; hostilities ceased and the British went home in March.

Although Jackson's victory at New Orleans had not influenced the peace conference at Ghent, it affected the way the treaty was interpreted and implemented. Castlereagh, the British Foreign Minister, became the first British statesman to accept that the United States had a legitimate right to exist, and the United States likewise accepted the existence of Canada. Britain now allowed the United States to expand south of the 49th parallel at the expense of the Spanish and Indians; the British also accepted the American right to the Louisiana Purchase and to be in New Orleans, Mobile and on the Gulf of Mexico. Had Jackson not won, the British would have returned these places to Spain, and retained Fort Bower. Britain made peace with the United States in return for peace in Canada and the profitable West Indies.

The Treaty of Ghent also ended the Indians' aspirations in the south. America agreed to end the war against the Indians, "and forthwith to restore to such tribes...all possessions...which they have enjoyed...in 1811 previous to such hostilities." This meant that Jackson had to return lands taken from the Indians by the Treaty of Fort Jackson. Jackson ignored the Treaty on this point; and America was permitted to expand to the Pacific. Blooded in the war, Jackson's tough adventurers would expand the United States into Texas and beyond. Their leader was now recognized as a hero by the south and the west. He was the first republican hero since Washington, and his path to the Presidency of the United States was assured.

Jackson had fulfilled the role of consolidator, assimilating Indians or pushing them west while advancing the boundaries of the United States. All revolutions are intolerant towards those who defy them, and Jackson represented the violent, physical consolidation phase of the American Revolution.

SUMMARY: THE REVOLUTIONARY DYNAMIC OF THE AMERICAN REVOLUTION

The American Revolution began with the Scottish Jacobite Templarism of James I, the ethos of which may have been conveyed to the New World by Bartholomew Gosnold's expedition to found the Jamestown Settlement in 1607. The Revolution's heretical occult vision can be found in the London court of the Scottish Templar James, who gave his blessing to the voyage by sending the Poet Laureate Michael Drayton to recite a poem describing the New World as "Earth's only paradise" on Blackwall dock before the departure of the ship. (Christopher Columbus thought he had found the Garden of Eden at the mouth of the Orinoco in Venezuela and Drayton may have been referring to this.) The settlers responded by naming the settlement James's Town. As the colony was the first to survive in the New World, Gosnold can be said to have founded English-speaking America as we know it. Though overtly a British colonialist, Gosnold sought to integrate the Indians and had the vision of a continent populated by Europeans speaking English – the future United States.

The heretical occult interpreter of this Freemasonic vision of the New World was Francis Bacon, Gosnold's cousin, whose Utopian *New Atlantis* appeared in 1624. He may have founded Rosicrucian Freemasonry – as opposed to Scottish Templarism – as early as the 1580s as we have seen, but he was not really interested in America until the 1620s, when he saw his cousin's pioneering settlement as the New Atlantis. Templarism was sufficiently well established in the US by 1760 for Templars to conduct the Boston Tea Party.

The revolutionary originator was Adam Weishaupt, who had been selected by Charles de Lorraine, Grand Master of the Priory of Sion, to penetrate Templarism for Sion. He reflected both Sion and Templarism, proclaimed republicanism and produced the Great Seal for his Illuminati, which was to become the Seal of the United States. It was Weishaupt's ideas that gave Templar Masonry its revolutionary dynamic.

The thoughtful intellectual interpreter who gave the vision a new slant was Benjamin Franklin, who visited France and took delivery of Weishaupt's Seal, which became the American Great Seal. A Sionist and member of the Royal Society and acquaintance of Boyle, he more than anyone else set up the constitutional arrangements for the 13 colonies to become free. The semi-political intellectual interpreter who later became political was Thomas Jefferson, who wrote the Declaration of Independence and, though a Sionist Illuminatus, later became a twice-serving President. The early revolutionary dynamic of the American Revolution can be stated as follows:

Heretical occult vision	Heretical occult interpreter	Occult revolutionary originator	Thoughtful intellectual interpreter	Semi-political intellectual interpreter
Scottish Jacobite Templarism (via Gosnold)	Bacon	Weishaupt	Franklin	Jefferson

Weishaupt influenced the founding fathers who gave intellectual expression to his vision, most notably Benjamin Franklin, the only founding father who was an American, English and French Mason; and Thomas Jefferson, a 33rd-degree Templar Mason and almost certainly a member of the Virginia lodge of the Illuminati and one of the Masons who helped the Illuminati infiltrate the New England Masonic lodges. Jefferson's Declaration of Independence and subsequent thinking (for example his Statute for Establishing Religious Freedom) helped forward the Templar Masonic revolution which grew round lodges in Boston (where John Hancock and Paul Revere were Masons) and in Richmond, Virginia (where Patrick Henry and Richard Henry Lee were Masons) and which wrested power from Sionist Rosicrucian England.

The Templar Mason George Washington, Commander-in-Chief of the American army in 1776-7 and until peace was agreed in 1783, gave political expression to the revolution. He presided over the writing of a Federal Constitution in 1787, and in 1789 while he was Grand Master of the Alexandria Lodge no. 22 in Virginia, he was elected first President of the United States.

The American revolution does not have a brutal, physical phase involving white Americans as it was not a revolt against an existing indigenous system of government but rather an anti-colonial movement against the English. It did however follow the pattern of unifying the country by force, and consolidation can be seen at work in Jackson's Indian massacres, a process directed against the native Indian population which continued for decades after Jackson's time.

The American Revolution involved a change in political authority rather than a transformation in the power structure of society. Therefore it does not conform to the model of other revolutions. Edmund Burke, scourge of the cruelty of the French Revolution, championed the independence of the American colonies as a brutal phase did not seem imminent.

The full revolutionary dynamic of the American Revolution can be stated as follows:

Heretical occult inspiration	Intellectual expression	Political expression	Physical consolidation
Scottish Jacobite Templarism (via Gosnold)/Bacon	Weishaupt/ Franklin/ Jefferson/Paine	Washington	Jackson

English Freemasonry seeks to transform society, and we can state the revolutionary dynamic of Freemasonry as follows:

Heretical occult inspiration	Intellectual expression	Political expression	Physical consolidation
Luciferianism/ Solomon's Temple	Religion of reason/deism	Republicanism	World State (as a metaphor of the rebuilt Temple)

We can state the revolutionary dynamic of Templar Masonry as follows:

Heretical occult inspiration	Intellectual expression	Political expression	Physical consolidation
Luciferianism/ de Molay	Council of Wise Men/Masonic Grand Masters	Global oligarchy/ rule by super-rich men-gods	Universal Republic through genocide.

Sionist Masonry like Templar Masonry, focused on the political transformation that could be brought about by occult Freemasonry. We shall see that both Templar and Sionist Masonry permit genocide (though this has been avoided within the US). Sionist Masonry's revolutionary dynamic for transforming society is more Israelite than that of Templar Freemasonry:

Heretical occult inspiration	Intellectual expression	Political expression	Physical consolidation
Kabbalism/ Rosicrucianism: Solomon's Temple/ Yahweh as Demiurge	Sanhedrin/ Council of Elders/Priory of Sion	False Messiah/King of Jerusalem/King appointed by Sanhedrin*	One-world Kingdom through genocide

(*as Sionist Rosicrucians appointed George I)

The American Revolution brought about a constitutional transformation that ended Britain's colonial rule and created republicanism, the political expression of Templar Masonry. The new Atlantis of America was a Templar-created Masonic State.

The revolutionary dynamic of the ideas behind the American Revolution can be stated as follows:

Heretical occult inspiration	Intellectual expression	Political expression	Physical consolidation
New Atlantis	Illuminism	Republicanism	Conquest/westward expansion

CHAPTER FIVE

THE FRENCH REVOLUTION

The Illuminati had 20,000 lodges throughout Europe and America.

David Rivera, *Final Warning*

By 1794 there were 6,800 Jacobin Clubs, totalling half a million members. All were former Grand Orient Masons,…taught revolution by Sion's Illuminati.

John Daniel, *Scarlet and the Beast*

The climax of the French Revolution was the guillotining of King Louis XVI.

In a letter to his brother written in September 1796, the King's confessor, the Abbé Edgeworth de Firmont, who accompanied Louis to the scaffold, wrote: "As soon as the fateful blow was given, I fell upon my knees and thus remained until the vile wretch [Sanson] who acted the principal part in the horrid tragedy, came with shouts of joy, showing the bleeding head to the mob, and sprinkling me with blood that streamed from it. Then indeed, I thought it time to quit the scaffold; but casting my eyes round about, I saw myself invested by twenty or thirty thousand men at arms;…all eyes were fixed on me, as you may suppose. I was not permitted on this occasion to wear any exterior marks of a priest."[1]

We cannot delve far into the French Revolution without being struck by the nobility of the aims of some of the revolutionaries, who almost without exception wanted the betterment of the lot of their fellow men; but also by the fanatical cruelty and inhumanity of their solution as they endeavoured to move towards a better society. As in the case of the English and American revolutions, the French Revolution was intended to bring in a Utopian state that restored the liberty and equality lost in the Garden of Eden.

WEISHAUPT'S UNION OF SION AND TEMPLARS

At the root of the French Revolution was the occult vision of the Cathars, who rejected European civilization and went back to Nature to live like (organized) noble savages in primitive citadels, like their headquarters at Montségur. Condemned by the Papacy as heretics, they were suppressed following the Albigensian crusade, and many survivors fled and joined the Templars. In due course their descendants became Templar Masons and kept alive the Cathar vision within Freemasonry.

Rousseau and Sion

The occult interpreter of the Cathar "back-to-Nature" vision, Jean-Jacques Rousseau, reacted against the rational Enlightenment. This was a European movement that began in the 17th century, arguably with René Descartes who in writing "I think, therefore I am" established reason as the power by which man understands the universe. No longer would truth be revealed to the perceptive intellect (*intellectus*); the reason had revolted and usurped its place. Descartes seems to have been a Rosicrucian. (His first journal, which he wrote at the age of 23, c.1619, contains thoughts on Rosicrucianism, which had just surfaced in Germany. Dr Nicolaes Wassenar claimed in *Historich Verhal*, 1624, that Descartes was a Rosicrucian. He is likely to have known for his son, Jacob Wassenar was a member of the Rosicrucian Circle in Holland and was a close friend of Descartes, who also had long associations with known Rosicrucians such as Cornelius van Hooghelande, Isaac Beekman and Johann Faulhaber.)[2] In the earlier 1660s, the Rosicrucian Isaac Newton used his reason to capture in a few mathematical equations the laws that govern the motion of planets, and a world view emerged that drew on the humanism of Francis Bacon, Renaissance classicism and the rational Luther's Reformation, and synthesized God, reason, nature and man. Reason applied to religion created deism, the "manifest truth" that one God was the architect of a mechanical universe in which man has a duty to be virtuous and pious. Deists were not Christians – in fact, they were anti-Christian – and in all other respects affirmed scepticism, atheism and materialism. They regarded the goals of rational man as knowledge, freedom and happiness.

Philosophers of the rational Enlightenment such as the Sionist Rosicrucian John Locke and Thomas Hobbes denied that man had innate qualities such as goodness or original sin, and saw him as moved by considerations of his own pleasure or pain. The State's function was not to be a city of God as in earlier times, but to protect the natural rights and self-interest of its citizens. Locke's view that there is a social contract between individuals and society conflicted with the reality of European societies, and the optimistic Enlightenment mind became critical and reformist, as can be seen from such Enlightenment thinkers (who all seem to have been influenced by Sionist Rosicrucians) as Jeremy Bentham, Montesquieu, Voltaire, Jefferson – and Leibniz, who regarded this as "the best of all possible worlds Eventually the abstractions of reason turned Utopian and revolutionary. Those who espoused them, such as Robespierre and Saint-Just, argued that the end justifies the means, and sanctioned the guillotine in the interests of a new and better society. And soon the confident Enlightenment belief that rational man could govern himself in an enlightened way was being challenged by screaming mobs and drum rolls, and was in shreds. Weishaupt tapped into this revolutionary convulsion in the Age of Reason and Enlightenment.

The celebration of abstract reason was rejected by some who turned the critical, iconoclastic spirit of the Enlightenment against itself. The most notable of these in France was Jean-Jacques Rousseau, who reacted against reason to explore sensation and emotion and bring in the cultural movement of Romanticism, thus ending the non-violent Age of Reason. A Calvinist from Geneva who arrived in France in 1742 at the age of 30, he spent a year as secretary to the French ambassador in Venice, and met Denis Diderot, a Mason who was editor of the radical French *Encyclopédie*, round which gathered a group of deist intellectuals called "Philosophes." (They were reforming pamphleteers as much as philosophers.) Rousseau, Diderot and the philosopher Condillac often dined together at the Panier Fleuri in Paris. Diderot's *"Philosophes"* were all Masons[3]: Helvétius and Voltaire (both of whom were primarily Sionists), d'Alembert, Condorcet and Condillac, and Rousseau, the most original of them and soon the most prominent. His works were very influential in the French lodges, and we must conclude that under Diderot's influence Rousseau became a Mason.

While walking to Vincennes to visit Diderot at the age of 37, Rousseau had "an illumination" in "a terrible flash," that modern progress – the god of the optimistic Enlightenment philosophers – had corrupted men rather than improved them. In his *Discours sur les Sciences et les Arts* (*Discourse on the Sciences and the Arts*), 1750, he argued that the history of man on earth has been one of decay, that man is good by nature but corrupted by society, which is to blame for his vices. Vices, Rousseau maintained, are not known in a state of nature. The arts, he claimed, are propaganda for the rich.

In *Discours sur l'origine de l'inégalité* (*Discourse on the Origin of Inequality*), 1755, he saw actual law as protecting the status quo. All men were originally equal, he maintained; inequality arose when men formed society and competed with one another – a Communist doctrine. True law is "just law." Rousseau, a great admirer of Machiavelli and of republican government, had stated the rationale for revolutionaries to replace the existing "unjust law" with a new "just law" under which there was equality (*egalité*). His placing of God in nature, especially in mountains and forests untouched by man, and his insistence on the immortality of the soul would lead to the Romanticism of Goethe and Wordsworth, but his critique of civilization led to the French Revolution, and Weishaupt drew on his thinking.

In 1751 Helvétius, the rich host to the Enlightenment *Philosophes*, married into the House of Lorraine and withdrew to his lands at Voré. In 1758 he caused a storm by publishing *De l'Esprit* ("On the Mind," literally "On the Spirit") which attacked all morality based on religion. The book was burned in public, and Voltaire and Rousseau both disassociated themselves from it. Rousseau's view of civilization caused a further rift between himself and the Philosophes. And although Voltaire's *Candide*, which also came out in 1758, showed from the misfortunes the hero sees and suffers that this is not the best of all possible worlds as Leibniz claimed, he finally broke with Rousseau that same year after Rousseau attacked the rational philosophy of the *Philosophes* in *Lettre à d'Alembert sur les Spectacles* (*Letter to d'Alembert on Theatrical Performances*), which held that drama might be abolished. (Voltaire had remained an unrepentant anti-Christian deist Enlightenment reformer, concerned at injustice and tyranny.)

In 1762 Rousseau brought out *Du Contrat Social* (*The Social Contract*) – the title echoes the Rosicrucian Locke's phrase – in which he says that society sometimes had to "force a man to be free," i.e. the law has to correct an individual to return him to his natural state; and that a man coerced by society for a breach of the law is being brought back to an awareness of his own interests.

The reception of *The Social Contract* was not good. It scandalized the Calvinists in Geneva, who ordered the book to be burned. Paris followed suit, and an order went out for Rousseau's arrest. Rousseau had withdrawn from Paris to a cottage near Montmorency, under the protection of the Maréchal de Luxembourg, a Mason, who helped him flee the country. Rousseau was then a fugitive in Switzerland. David Hume, the Scottish philosopher and Mason, became secretary to the British Embassy in Paris in 1763, and then Chargé d'Affaires in 1765. He met Rousseau and took him back to England in 1766 and gave him refuge from persecution in a country house at Wooton in Staffordshire and obtained a pension for him from George III. However, Rousseau became aware that he was being mocked by English intellectuals, and, now somewhat paranoiac, he accused Hume, his benefactor, of participating in the ridicule and returned to France in 1767.

Rousseau's thinking was hugely mistaken,[4] for the rise of civilizations is a good thing rather than a bad thing. If a civilization is imperfect, the cure requires more civilization. If a social system is defective, more civilization is needed to put it right, not less; just as if a garden has been neglected, more cultivation is needed to put it right, not less. It is good for humans to go back to nature for a while to discover (or rediscover) their harmony with the Universe, but not good for them to remain there indefinitely, sacrificing social living for the law of the jungle in which man becomes a brute struggling for material needs and surviving by being stronger than other brutes, having surrendered all moral life. Dissidents such as the Cathars formed their own communities close to nature, and lived carefully regulated lives in accordance with their alternative beliefs; they did not return to the life of the savage – nor did Rousseau himself while living on his royal pension in the Staffordshire country house. One can understand the laughter Rousseau's ideas aroused in 18th-century England.

The Jewish Adam Weishaupt, who interpreted Rousseau[5] in occultist terms and became the occult revolutionary originator of the French Revolution, did not laugh. Between 1771 and 1776 he put Rousseau's philosophy advocating the destruction of civilization, the overthrow of actual law and the adoption of egalitarianism alongside the revolutionary thinking of the late Age of Reason that favoured sweeping away the old society and replacing it with a new society – and so secured the support of Rosicrucian Masonic lodges in Germany.

Rousseau was not the originator of his doctrines and the primitive Utopia of his philosophy was not his own. Certainly his idea of the Noble Savage, drawn from the French Cathars, owed something to Sir Thomas More's *Utopia*[6] and to the Baconian view of Atlantis. While all the Philosophes were Freemasons, some, like Voltaire, were primarily

Sionist yet sufficiently pro-Templar to be invited to Prussia by Frederick II (an invitation perhaps treated as a spying mission encouraged by Sion). Certainly Helvétius seems to have been in that category. He married a relative of Charles de Lorraine's and was invited to Berlin by Frederick II in 1765 (after which the *Philosophes* were back in favour). Benjamin Franklin, who took up with Mme Helvétius in 1776, was also primarily with Sion although at ease with the Templars. Were the Masons Diderot, d'Alembert, Condorcet and Condillac similarly "ambidextrous?"

And what of Rousseau, who arrived in Paris in 1742, after the Templar Grand Lodge had been founded there but before the founding of Jacobite Scottish Rite Freemasonry? Was he (like Diderot) with the Priory of Sion, too, during the 1740s? He regretted his period as a Catholic convert, and (taking his mistress Thérèse Levasseur, an illiterate laundry maid, with him) he returned in 1754 to Geneva and was readmitted into the Protestant Church as a Calvinist, which puts him on the Sionist side (with the Protestants Cromwell and William III). Did Charles de Lorraine, brother-in-law of the Austrian Empress and until 1757 commander-in-chief of Austria's armed forces, who was in touch with the *Philosophes* through Mme Helvétius after 1751, two years after Rousseau's "terrible flash," teach Rousseau his doctrines? In 1757, relieved of his army command by Maria Theresa after his defeat at Leuthen, Charles de Lorraine retired to his capital at Brussels and in his palace there assembled a court that (like his ancestor René d'Anjou's) became a centre for literature, painting, music and theatre – all the arts that fascinated Rousseau. Was it from Charles de Lorraine (who was after Louis XVI's throne) that Rousseau received the influence of the Sionist Rosicrucian Locke, in time to produce his new *Social Contract* by 1762, to spread revolution in the Rosicrucian Masonic lodges? And was the Maréchal de Luxembourg a Sionist Rosicrucian, and did Charles de Lorraine have a hand in introducing Rousseau to Hume? Was the Scottish Hume a Sionist (in the tradition of the Royal Society) rather than a Jacobite Scottish Rite Freemason? And, finally, was Charles de Lorraine behind the spell Rousseau spent at the end of his life on the estates of the Prince de Conti and the Marquis de Girardin? We have seen (pp233-6) how Weishaupt was recruited by Charles de Lorraine, Grand Master of the Priory of Sion, who gave him instructions in the Egyptian and other mysteries for five years. If Rousseau was a Sionist under the House of Lorraine, there is a symmetry in the influence that led to the Illuminati: it would mean that Charles de Lorraine taught Rousseau, and later taught Rousseau's doctrines to Weishaupt; so that Weishaupt appealed to the Sionists by drawing on what was essentially Sionist thought.

Weishaupt Creates the Illuminati for Sion

Weishaupt also drew on Catharism's Parfaits, who opposed the Church in a revolutionary way and affirmed heretical, Luciferian doctrines. The Prussian Frederick the Great wanted to take the French throne for Templarism, and had demonstrated his pro-Catharism in 1767 by founding the Masonic Order of the Architects of Africa, which was devoted to Manichaeism, and another order, the Knights of Light.[7] It seems that Charles de Lorraine chose a Bavarian German (Weishaupt) to found a new Order in the hope that he would pull in Frederick II's German lodges, divert Frederick's attention from France and prevent him from making an attempt to seize the French throne.

From now on the destinies of Germany and France were inextricably interconnected as occult Bavarian Illuminism shaped the cult of Reason in France, and the intermingling of the two cultures was reflected in the territorial disputes over Alsace and Lorraine, and Strasbourg. Weishaupt planned to carry on the work of the "Synagogue of Satan" and unite it with Rousseau's view that civilization was a mistake, that man should "return to nature" outside the paralyzing influence of civilization and restore his natural Garden of Eden. Weishaupt claimed that the chief obstacle to this Utopia was ordered government: "Princes and nations shall vanish from the Earth." There would be no controlling authority, no laws or civil codes – merely anarchy. (In fact the Illuminati governmental system was to be an absolute dictatorship, with Weishaupt at its head.)

Weishaupt advocated a Utopian one-world state that restored the liberty and equality lost in the Garden of Eden and abolished private property, social authority (degree and hierarchy) nationality and all thrones and religions.

If Rousseau paved the way for revolution, Weishaupt devised the machinery of revolution. His organizational skill came from his experience of the Jesuits and also of Freemasonry. Born in 1748, the son of a Jewish rabbi, he was handed over to the Jesuits at an early age following the death of his father in 1753 by his godfather, the curator of the University of Ingolstadt, Baron Johann Adam Ickstatt, whose library he was allowed to use.[8] Weishaupt was educated as a Catholic and became a Jesuit priest before his reading in his godfather's library convinced him he was an atheist. He studied in France, where he met Robespierre,[9] who later led the French Revolution, and made contacts at the French royal courts (including Charles de Lorraine?) who introduced him to Satanism. He graduated at the Bavarian University of Ingolstadt in 1768 and then served as a tutor for four years, during which he met Charles de Lorraine. There have long been reports that Rothschilds funded Weishaupt from 1770 to 1776, and that Mayer Amschel "Rothschild" was in league with Charles de Lorraine. During his five-year apprenticeship under him from 1771 to 1776,[10] Weishaupt studied Manichaeism and other pagan religions, including the Eleusinian mysteries and Pythagoras, and wrote the constitution for a secret society founded on the pagan mystery schools. He also studied the Kabbalah and the Essenes, and *The Major Key of Solomon* and *The Lesser Key of Solomon*, which taught him how to conjure demons and perform occult rituals. At the same time he taught law and supported Protestantism. After 1771 his rise was spectacular. In 1772 he was made Professor of Civil Law, and in 1773 Professor of Canon Law (a post the Jesuits had held for 90 years). In 1773, the year the Jesuits were suppressed, he married against Ickstatt's wishes. There have been reports that Mayer Amschel "Rothschild" met Weishaupt in 1773 to discuss world revolution.[11] When in 1775 he became Dean of the Faculty of Law, the Jesuits were so worried about his growing influence that they tried to block his appointment.

In founding his own organization, he took over the organizational structure of the Jesuits as we saw on **p155**. In 1774 he had made contact with a Masonic lodge in Munich, and was disappointed, as the members knew little about pagan symbolism. His limited experience of Freemasonry gave him ideas about the nature of his own secret society, which combined Jesuit and Masonic hierarchical structures. Weishaupt's Order was made up of three degrees: Novice, Minerval and Illuminated Minerval (Minerva was the Roman form of Pallas Athena, who featured so prominently in Bacon's first Rosicrucian society.) These three degrees corresponded to those in the structures of the Jesuit hierarchy and of Freemasonry.

In the initiation ceremony into the highest grade of the Order the initiate entered a room which contained a throne and table with a crown, sceptre and sword. He was asked to take them, but told that if he did he would not enter the Order. He was then taken to a room draped in black. A curtain revealed an altar covered in black cloth on which lay a cross and a red Phrygian cap of the kind used in the Mithraic Mysteries. The initiate was handed the cap with the words, "Wear this – it means more than the crown of kings." (This cap was to surface in the French Revolution and is still worn by Liberty on French postage stamps.) Weishaupt based the ritual on the Mithraic mysteries in which the neophyte was handed a crown and sword and refused to accept them, saying, "Mithras alone is my crown."[12] Weishaupt believed that humankind could be restored to the perfection it enjoyed before the Fall if it followed the occult traditions of the pagan Mystery schools, which guarded the Ancient Wisdom including the original teachings of Jesus. He claimed that the Church had lost these, but that they were preserved by the Rosicrucian and Freemasonic traditions.

All members were required to adopt classical names. We have seen that Weishaupt himself was "Spartacus" (the name of the leader of a slave revolt in ancient Rome c73 BC); his right hand man, Xavier von Zwack was "Cato"; Nicolai was "Lucian"; Professor Westenreider was "Pythagoras"; Canon Hertel was "Marius"; Marquis di Constanza was "Diomedes"; Massenhausen was "Ajax"; Baron von Schroeckenstein was

"Mahomed" and Baron von Mengenhofen was "Sulla" (often wrongly written "Sylla"). Their headquarters was in Munich and known as the Grand Lodge of the Illuminati. It was codenamed "Athens." There were also lodges at Ingolstadt ("Ephesus"), Rosicrucian Heidelberg ("Utica"), Bavaria ("Achaia") and Frankfurt ("Thebes"). The calendar was reconstructed and the months were given Hebrew-sounding names (January being Dimeh, February Benmeh).[13] Their letters were dated according to the Persian Era (beginning with the first King of Persia, Jezdegerd, who came to the throne in 632 BC). Their new year began on March 21, which is New Year's Day for witches.

Fatal to Weishaupt's Utopia was ownership, the concept of property which compelled men to give up their nomadic, idyllic Paradise for a fixed residence. To regain one's natural liberty and equality one should renounce ownership of property and surrender one's possessions. Similarly patriotism and love of one's family divide man from the whole human race, Weishaupt claimed. If they are done away with there will be universal love among men and nations, and "the human race [would be] one good and happy family." Then, "Reason will be the only law of Man. When at last Reason becomes the religion of Man, then will the problem be solved." At the end of the Age of Reason, reason was to use violent revolutionary methods to create disorder so that a new order could prevail in which all men were citizens of the world before they were owners, members of a family or nation, or private souls. In his *Discourse on the Origin of Inequality*, Rousseau had maintained: "The first man who bethought himself of saying 'This is mine,' and found people simple enough to believe him was the real founder of civil society. What crimes, what wars, what murders, what miseries and horrors would he have spared the human race who, snatching away the spades and filling in the ditches had cried out to his fellows: 'Beware of listening to this impostor; you are lost if you forget that the fruits of the earth belong to all and the earth to no one.'"[14]

Weishaupt wrote regarding the instruction of initiates: "At the moment when men united themselves into nations they ceased to recognize themselves under a common name. Nationalism or National

Love took the place of Universal Love. With the division of the Globe and its countries benevolence restricted itself behind boundaries that it was never again to transgress. Then it became a virtue to spread out at the expense of those who did not happen to be under our dominion. Then, in order to attain this goal, it became permissible to despise foreigners, and to deceive and to offend them. This virtue was called Patriotism. That man was called a Patriot, who, whilst just towards his own people, was unjust to others, who blinded himself to the merits of foreigners and took for perfections the vices of his own country. So one sees that Patriotism gave birth to Localism, to the family spirit and finally to Egoism. Thus the origin of states or governments of civil society was the seed of discord and Patriotism found its punishment in itself....Diminish, do away with this love of country, and men will once more learn to know and love each other as men, there will be no more partiality, the ties between hearts will unroll and extend."[15]

Both Rousseau and Weishaupt idealized primitive society in maintaining that harmony and universal love preceded property and patriotism. In fact skeletons of palaeolithic men are exhumed with flint weapons in their hands, suggesting that early man lived in a state of fear, if not warfare. (Shakespeare, perhaps reacting to the discovery of "savages" – i.e. Indians – on Martha's Vineyard in the course of Bartholomew Gosnold's 1602 voyage, portrayed the – perhaps Martha's Vineyard – Indian Caliban in less idealized terms, but it must be said that the Indian societies before the coming of the English, though well-armed with bows and arrows against outsiders, did live in considerable harmony among themselves.)

Weishaupt and Rousseau may both have been wrong, but their Utopianism has shaped countless revolutions since 1776, and is enormously influential today. We have already (p234) touched on the main aims of Weishaupt's Illuminati, which are fast being achieved:

1. Abolition of Monarchy and all ordered Government.
2. Abolition of private property.
3. Abolition of inheritance.

4.   Abolition of patriotism.
5.   Abolition of the family (i.e. of marriage and all morality, and the institution of the communal education of children).
6.   Abolition of all religion.[16]

Of these aims, the attack on monarchy derived from Charles de Lorraine, who aimed to be monarch after Louis XVI; the attack on ordered government, private property and inheritance derived from Rousseau; the attack on religion came from the Cathars, whom the Templars admired, and from deist Freemasonry; and the attack on patriotism, nationalism, family life, marriage and morality came from the Utopianism of Sir Thomas More and Bacon, and the Sionist Rosicrucian views of radicals like Hartlib. The whole programme amounted to an early statement of Communism.

It is true that at the noble Universalist, nondualistic spiritual level, all souls are equal and free to know universal brotherhood and love, their liberty unchecked by the constraints and attachments of social life (property, inheritance, nationality and family). Unfortunately, there is a degeneration and stepping-down from this noble level to its occult mirror image of a subjugated, unfree world brotherhood; thence to ever lower levels – the intellectual (the creation of heaven on earth in a paradise), the political (the ideal political State) and finally the physical level (the particular State that is totalitarian, such as the USSR or Communist China). Within the physical terrain of a modern Communist State, a communist programme involves subordinating the individual to a tyranny. The degeneration of the occult vision into a physical Communist State has the effect of denying personal responsibility, incentive and rootedness. Weishaupt's programme had ceased to be occult and had become political-physical.

Weishaupt's programme, unveiled on May 1, 1776, united the traditions the Priory of Sion embodied (the Merovingian Kingship of Jerusalem, Kabbalism, the Egyptian origins of the Rose-Croix, the Rosicrucian invisible college, the values of Boyle's Royal Society, the rationalism of Descartes and Newton, and Rousseau's restatement of the

New Atlantis) with the traditions the Templars embodied (republicanism, preservation of the Manichaeism of the Cathars which was at the root of Templarism, and the desire to avenge Jacques de Molay which led to the incarceration of Louis XVI in the Tower of the Temple). Weishaupt united Sion and the Templars in his new organization by uniting different traditions that appealed to both: the rational Enlightenment (or Age of Reason) and Rousseau's revolt against it, both of which inspired Sion; and Manichaean Catharism, which inspired the Templars. The wide spectrum of sources doubtless made his organization seem more attractive to his backers.

Both the House of Lorraine and the Jacobite Templars wanted to overthrow the Bourbon King. Advised by Charles de Lorraine (Grand Master of the Priory of Sion) and funded by the Sionist House of Rothschild (Mayer Amschel "Rothschild") and four other Jews (Wessely, Moses Mendelssohn, Itzig and Fridlander), Weishaupt with Machiavellian cunning put together a package for a world revolution that would draw the Templar Frederick II away from France and hold out the promise of world government. It would also create enormous revolutionary disorder on the way so that Sion's cause (which was now the Templar cause, for Sion had made common cause with the Templars in Weishaupt's programme) could prevail.

In 1777 Weishaupt became a Freemason. He joined the Eclectic Masonic lodge "Theodore of Good Counsel" in Munich.[17] Towards the end of 1778 he announced the idea of merging the Illuminati and the Masons.[18] Weishaupt wrote of the Order to his members in terms reminiscent of the Rosicrucian Invisible College: "Secrecy gives greater zest to the whole....The slightest observation shows that nothing will so much contribute to increased zeal of the members as secret union. The great strength of our Order lies in its concealment, let it never appear in any place in its own name, but always covered by another name, and another occupation. None is fitter than the three lower degrees of Freemasonry; the public is accustomed to it, expects little from it, and therefore takes little notice of it. Next to this, the form of a learned or literary society is best suited to our purpose, and had Free Masonry not existed, this cover would have been employed; and it may be much more than a cover, it may be a powerful engine in our hands. By establishing reading societies and subscription libraries...we may turn the public mind which way we will. In like manner we must try to obtain an influence in...all offices which have any effect, either in forming, or in managing, or even in directing the mind of man....For the Order wishes to be secret, and to work in silence, for thus it is better secured from the oppression of the ruling powers, and because this secrecy gives a greater zest to the whole."[19] In pursuit of this policy, Zwack, his right-hand man, became a Mason in November; he divulged the secrets of the Order of the Illuminati to the Mason Abbé Marotti, and by mid 1779 the Munich Masonic lodge was under the influence of the Illuminati.[20]

By now 60 active members had been recruited to the Order, and another thousand were indirectly affiliated.[21] Within the lodges was the germ of an anarchist Utopian superstate in which there would be no social authority, nationality or private property – just a universal brotherhood living in harmony with free love. Weishaupt wrote that there would be morals and no religion: "Salvation does not lie where strong thrones are defended by swords, where the smoke of censers ascends to heaven or where thousands of strong men pace the rich fields of harvest. The revolution which is about to break will be sterile if it is not complete." It is clear that Weishaupt's targets were the monarchy, the Church and the rich landowners.

New recruits believed that Weishaupt wanted a one-world government to prevent all future wars. Only those near the top ("Areopagite") knew the true direction of the Order: revolution and anarchy to overthrow civilization and return to nature.[22] Such secrecy was achieved by implementing a structure like a family tree: Weishaupt was at the top; beneath him were two "sons," who each had two "children" branching beneath them, who in turn each had two "children" – and so on. The lower down new recruits were, the less they knew about the inner thoughts at the top.[23]

Fools were encouraged to join. Weishaupt wrote: "These good

people swell our numbers and fill our money box; set yourselves to work; these gentlemen must be made to nibble at the bait....But let us beware of telling them our secrets, this sort of people must always be made to believe that the grade they have reached is the last....One must speak sometimes in one way, sometimes in another, so that our real purpose should remain impenetrable to our inferiors." Weishaupt wrote that the true purpose of the Illuminati was "nothing less than to win power and riches, to undermine secular or religious government, and to obtain the mastery of the world."[24]

Initiates were told that the Order represented the highest ideals of the Church, that Christ was the first advocate of Illuminism, and that his secret mission was to restore to men the liberty and equality they had lost in the Garden of Eden. According to Weishaupt, Christ despised riches to prepare for the abolition of property ownership and the sharing of all possessions. He wrote to Zwack: "The most admirable thing of all is that great Protestant and reformed theologians (Lutherans and Calvinists who belong to our Order) really believe they see in it the true and genuine mind of the Christian religion." However, when an initiate reached the higher degrees, the secret would be revealed: "Behold our secret...in order to destroy all Christianity, all religion, we have pretended to have the sole true religion...to deliver one day the human race from all religion."[25]

Weishaupt's choice of his Order's name, "The Illuminati" must be understood against the background of his intention to deceive Christian members. It drew on the Spanish Alumbrados ("Enlightened" or "Illuminated" ones) and also on a 15th-century German sect known as the Illuminati, which practised Satanism. The divine Light of God that inspired Dante and enlightened the Alumbrados mystics and gave them superior intelligence was very different from the "Light" German magicians received from Satan, dark energy which they manipulated with their wills. Mystics who receive the Light of Glory are opened to the highest experience of bliss whereas magicians who work Satanic energy with their wills do so at their peril for they can easily be taken over by dark powers (see pp473-4). Weishaupt was a magician, not a mystic; but he wanted Christian recruits and initiates to believe that they were joining a mystical Order.[26]

Women were targeted, both those who would give the Order respectability and those who would satisfy members' sexual urges. Monetary and sexual blackmail were used to gain control of men in high places, who were threatened with public exposure, ruin and death unless they co-operated with the Order. Some of the Order's women were used to achieve such ends.[27]

Espionage was actively encouraged. The adepts known as "Insinuating Brothers" were urged to act as observers and report on all members. Weishaupt wrote, "Every person shall be made a spy on another and on all around him;...friends, relations, enemies, those who are indifferent – all without exception shall be the object of his inquiries; he shall attempt to discover their strong side and their weak, their passions, their prejudices, their connections, above all, their actions – in a word, the most detailed information about them."[28] The Insinuant was to write his reports twice a month and send them to his Superiors so that the Order could know which people in each town or village it could trust. This system was symbolized in the eye on the Illuminati Great Seal (see p256), and has been used in all Communist societies to chilling effect.

Weishaupt's merging of Illuminism and Freemasonry was advanced when in July 1780 a new member, Baron Franz Friedrich Knigge was recruited. He had served at the courts of Hesse-Kassel and Weimar, and was a well-known writer. He had joined the Masonic lodge of Strict Observance and the Rosicrucians, and wanted to develop a Freemasonry that would take man back to the perfection he enjoyed before the Fall of Adam and Eve. He arrived in Frankfurt and spoke with the Marquis di Constanza, who had been sent from Bavaria to start an Illuminati colony there. Constanza explained that the Illuminati had already reformed Freemasonry. To lure Knigge, Weishaupt presented the Order as representing "advancement" (Bacon's word) in science and philosophy. Knigge joined the Order, was codenamed "Philo" and was soon head of the Westphalia circle.[29]

Knigge was as brilliant an organizer as Weishaupt. (Weishaupt wrote: "Philo is the master from whom to take lessons; give me six men of his stamp and with them I will change the face of the Universe.") He believed along with other members of the "Areopagite" that Weishaupt's authority should be decentralized and delegated, and the changes were adopted in July 1781, after which the expansion of the Order became rapid. The aim now was to split mankind into opposing ideologies, so that national governments and organized religions fought with each other and weakened themselves – in other words, "divide and rule."[30]

Weishaupt Hides the Illuminati in Orléans' Templar Grand Orient

A brilliant organizer, Weishaupt had had the idea of protecting his new Order by infiltrating Templar lodges and hiding it within them. An important development in Templar Masonry had provided him with an opportunity which he seized.

The survival of Templarism was due to Jacques de Molay, the last Grand Master of the Templar Order. After Philippe IV had discovered that the Templars had been plotting against all the thrones of Europe and the Church and had ordered 50 of them to be sent to the stake, de Molay, who was among those condemned to death, established what came to be called Scottish Templar Masonry in Paris, Naples, Stockholm – and Edinburgh. The night before his execution de Molay sent a trusted aide from the Bastille, where he was held, to a secret crypt in Paris – possibly in the Temple – where the Grand Masters of the Order were entombed. From this crypt were removed the crown of the King of Jerusalem, a seven-branched candlestick from Solomon's temple and statues that reputedly once marked the burial place of Christ. The two pillars that stood on either side of the entrance to the crypt (which replicated the pillars at the gateway to Solomon's temple) were hollow and filled with gold coins and manuscripts, and these were removed – eventually to Edinburgh.[31] The following day, we must suppose, the ashes of de Molay were interred in this same crypt, and it was at his tomb, long after Philippe IV and the Pope he colluded with had died in strange and sudden circumstances, that the regicides vowed to avenge de Molay by killing King Louis XVI. As Albert Pike wrote: "The secret movers of the French Revolution had sworn to overturn the Throne and the Altar upon the tomb of Jacques de Molai (sic). When Louis XVI was executed, half the work was done; and thenceforth the Army of the Temple was to direct all its efforts against the Pope."[32]

We have seen (p225) that after the burning of their last Grand Master, the Templars fled to Scotland and survived there as Freemasons, hiding beneath Masonic secret signs and vowing to take revenge on the Bourbon throne which had wiped them out of France. Following their arrival in England with James I, a group moved to France at the time of the Glorious Revolution in 1689 and founded the Grand Lodge of Paris in 1725. Then in 1747 Charles Edward Stuart (who was later offered the American crown) founded French Scottish Rite Jacobite Freemasonry, with the help of his secretary Charles Radclyffe. This introduced higher degrees, including the Royal Arch degree which was reserved for those initiated into the Kabbalah.[33]

It seems that a number of secret societies were working for the overthrow of the French monarchy. Some (such as the Jacobites and the Priory of Sion) wanted to remove Louis XVI in favour of their own candidate for monarch. (The Jacobites wanted a pro-Jacobite monarch – Frederick II, the Great, of Prussia before he died in 1786 and presumably now his successor – and the Priory of Sion wanted a representative of the House of Lorraine: preferably Maximilian de Lorraine who had succeeded as Grand Master of the Priory of Sion in 1780. The Sionist monarch had to be a Merovingian King reputedly descended from Christ and Mary Magdelene – hence the marriage to Louis XVI of Marie-Antoinette of the House of Lorraine, daughter of the then Grand Master of the Priory of Sion, Charles de Lorraine.) Others wanted to destroy the institution of monarchy itself; these included groups connected with Grand Orient Freemasonry, which had been founded by the Templar Grand Lodge of Paris in 1772.

The Duke of Orléans, cousin to Louis XVI, had already been initiated into Templar Grand-Lodge Freemasonry and had become Grand Master in 1771. He converted Blue or National Freemasonry into Grand Orient Freemasonry in 1773. He was so hostile to the

Sionist Marie-Antoinette, Louis XVI's Queen, that he lived away from the royal court of Versailles. According to Dr George Dillon in *Grand Orient Freemasonry Unmasked*,[34] Orléans founded the Grand Orient because French Masons wanted independence from their Mother Lodge in England.

Grand Orient Freemasonry embraced Utopian socialism and coined the rallying cry "Liberty, Equality, Fraternity,"[35] which Weishaupt adopted for the Illuminati and Illuminism. The "Liberty and Equality" had been current in the lodges of the Grand Orient; "Fraternity" was added from the Martinistes, a secret society founded in 1754 by a Rosicrucian Portuguese Jew Martinez Paschalis. The Martinistes split into two branches, one continued by Paschalis's disciple Saint-Martin, and the other a revolutionary body that founded the lodge of the *Philalèthes* in Paris.[36]

On December 20, 1781 an understanding was reached between the Grand Orient Masons and the Illuminati, and a combined Order was adopted. It had three classes: the Minervals; the Freemasons; and the Mysteries (Lesser and Greater), the top two of which were Magus and Rex (Mage and King). The Illuminati degrees were now all within the first class: Preparation, Novice, Minerval and Illuminatus. All Masons had to go through them to progress to the second (Masonic) class, and consequently all Masons therefore underwent the Illuminati degrees. The alliance between Freemasonry and Illuminism was sealed in July 1782 at the Congrès de Wilhelmsbad, which was attended by Masons, Martinistes and representatives of secret societies in Europe, America and Asia. Those present were sworn to secrecy. Comte de Virieu, a member of a Martiniste lodge at Lyons, questioned on the secrets he had learned at the Congress, replied: "I will not confide them to you. I can only tell you that all this is very much more serious than you think. The conspiracy which is being woven is so well thought out that it will be, so to speak, impossible for the Monarchy and the Church to escape from it."[37]

The Congress also passed a resolution to allow Jews into lodges, following a wave of pro-semitism after Dohm's book, *Upon the Civil*

Amelioration of the Condition of the Jews, which was written under the influence of Moses Mendelssohn (one of the five founder-members of the Illuminati and one of its original funders), and after a similar book Mirabeau published in London. Also in 1781 Clootz, the future author of *La République Universelle*, wrote a pamphlet, *Lettre sur les Juifs*. The Illuminati, hidden within the Grand Orient, now moved their headquarters to Frankfurt, a stronghold of Jewish finance, and the Order spread throughout Germany and Austria, including the German poet Goethe and his philosopher friend von Herder among their converts. As branches appeared in Italy, Hungary, France and Switzerland, money flowed in from the leading Jewish families: the Oppenheimers, Wertheimers, Schusters, Speyers, Sterns – and the Rothschilds.[38]

The Illuminati, having concealed themselves behind the Duke of Orléans' Grand Orient name,[39] were now poised for revolution. The union of Sionist and Templar Freemasonry in a Jewish-funded, pro-Cathar, overtly Templar organization in Germany in 1782 meant that Weishaupt and the Templar Duke of Orléans would now share the same movement. Orléans (who succeeded to his father's title in 1785) would be the figurehead, while Weishaupt would be active behind the scenes, fomenting revolution.

The Duke of Orléans, founder of the Grand Orient, was an extravagant, vain and ambitious libertine. By 1780 his entire income of 800,000 livres (£1 = approx. 25 livres) was mortgaged to moneylenders as a result of his reckless gambling, and in 1781 in return for accommodation he handed over his palace, his estates and his house at the Palais-Royal to his creditors. There at the Palais-Royal they formed a centre for politics, printing and pamphleteering, complete with wine-shops, theatres and brothels, where future Jacobins were installed, such as the political adventurer de Laclos (author of *Les Liaisons Dangereuses*).[40]

1781 was a crucial year for the French economy. Jacques Necker, a Brandenberg lawyer who had been transferred to a bank in Paris, had been (strangely, we may feel) put in charge of the French finances as first director of the royal treasury and then director general of the finances in 1777. His great mistake (or was it deliberate policy?) had been to attempt to finance French participation in the American War of Independence without increasing taxation. (He had put all his trust in the gold standard and ended up representing the interests of the debt system rather than the real wealth of the country.) This error had left France with a deficit of 46 million livres. In 1781, trying to raise loans, Necker published his *Compte rendu au Roi* claiming that France had a surplus of 10 million livres. An alliance of the opposition and the Queen, Marie-Antoinette, forced Necker to resign in 1781. France was now on the verge of bankruptcy.[41]

Who was Necker? Was he just incompetent? Or was he acting under instruction? He came from Germany – was he a Templar agent who was asked to help the American Templars in the War of Independence and at the same time wreak havoc in the French finances to allow Frederick II an opportunity to seize the French throne? Or was he a Sionist creating an opportunity for the House of Lorraine? If he were a Sionist, it is strange that Marie-Antoinette of the House of Lorraine was so opposed to him. It is more likely that if he were a Mason he was a Templar who like the Duke of Orléans had a difficult relationship with the Sionist Marie-Antoinette. Why did Louis XVI allow him to continue to run the country's finances for four years? Was Louis himself in some sort of pact with Charles de Lorraine through his wife Marie-Antoinette? This is hard to credit, but if so then his execution must have seemed to him martyrdom for the cause. Louis, as occupant of the French throne, can be left outside the various alliances to seize it, but his sanctioning of the German Necker's incompetence does seem strange.

Cagliostro

The Illuminati were now operating in a France that was financially unstable. The Jewish Kabbalist Cagliostro, alias Joseph Balsamo, who had met the "Jutland merchant Kolmer," alias Charles de Lorraine, on Malta in 1771 and been expelled with him by the Knights of Malta, was now active in the Illuminist cause.[42] On Malta Charles had appointed him to act on his behalf. In April 1776, the year before the Illuminati were founded, he was in London, being received as a Sionist Rosicrucian Mason in Esperance Lodge no. 289 which met at the King's Head tavern in Fleet Street. In 1777, the year Weishaupt was initiated into Grand Orient Freemasonry, he was subsidized by several rich men, probably including Charles de Lorraine and Mayer Amschel "Rothschild." Cagliostro later claimed (in 1790) that the House of Rothschild had funded his activities.

By 1782 the Rothschilds were controlling the Frankfurt headquarters of the new Order. Mayer Amschel "Rothschild" had been born in Frankfurt, the son of a banker and goldsmith. The name was derived from the red shield (*rotschildt*) that hung over the door of the family shop. It was an emblem for the Jews in Eastern Europe. He worked as a clerk in the Oppenheimers' Hanover bank and then as a junior partner; then left to take over his father's business. He dealt in rare coins and in 1769 became a court agent for Prince William IX, Landgrave of Hesse-Kassel, who was grandson of George II of England, cousin of George III, nephew to the King of Denmark and brother-in-law of the King of Sweden. He now became middleman for the Frankfurt bankers Bethmann Brothers and Rueppell and Harnier and began to amass a fortune.[43]

With ample funds from his backers, Cagliostro travelled round Europe. Almost at once he joined the Illuminati and was initiated into the Templar Strict Observance near Frankfurt in 1777 and became an agent of the combined Order.[44] On his own admission, his mission "was to work so as to turn Freemasonry in the direction of Weishaupt's projects" (i.e. to unite Sionist Rosicrucian and Templar Freemasonry). He founded many Kabbalist Egyptian Masonic lodges in the rite of Mizraim, whose symbol is the 6-pointed star which was created as the coat of arms for Rennes-le-Château by the Merovingian king Dagobert II.[45] (The symbolism of the 6-pointed star on the Great Seal of the Illuminati and America is thus linked with the Sionist Merovingians and Rennes.) He founded more Masonic lodges than any single man before or since.

In 1780 Cagliostro formed a good understanding with Knigge as they had both been members of the Templar Strict Observance lodge at Kassel (Knigge from 1772, Cagliostro from 1777). Knigge ("Philo") had been in correspondence with Cagliostro, and had received orders from him to recruit the best men in the Strict Observance for the Illuminati. Weishaupt recognised Knigge's abilities in 1781 and asked him to join him in Bavaria and help create advanced Illuminati degrees, which would go beyond the three degrees already in existence. The aim was that the Illuminati would penetrate Scottish Rite Masonry in France and turn all the French Templars into revolutionaries. Knigge arrived in Bavaria and then discovered that the Order of the Illuminati was not of ancient origin, as he had been led to believe. At first he was disillusioned; it has even been suggested that he had discovered that Weishaupt was a Satanist. However, realizing Weishaupt's brilliance, he complied and made strenuous efforts in advancing the degrees and corresponding with all the various lodges. It seems that he may have been considering his own advancement, or possibly the advancement of the Templars with whom he was first associated. In 1782 Grand Orient Illuminism saturated the French Grand Lodge, so that future Templar Jacobins were in control of French Freemasonry. Through Knigge's work, The Illuminati were moving into France.[46]

But there were tensions between Weishaupt and Knigge. Worried that his control of the Order was diminishing, Weishaupt argued with Knigge repeatedly. He appeared to interfere in his work, imperiously making alterations and additions to Knigge's advanced ritual. Knigge was disgusted at his treatment and withdrew from the Order. He became a "savage anti-Mason" and opposed Weishaupt. In January 1783 he had written to Zwack ("Cato") complaining at Weishaupt's "Jesuitry," "despotism" and tyranny. He clearly felt the same now. On February 15, 1785 a second Masonic Congress was held in Paris. Weishaupt's plan (made the previous year) for the Illuminati to create the atmosphere for mass uprisings in France against the Monarchy was put before it. Cagliostro was present and received funds from the Illuminati to travel Europe spreading revolutionary politics. However other proposals were not adopted because of the rift between Weishaupt and Knigge, and the Congress failed.

It may be that Knigge's anti-Masonry was a planned strategy. For two weeks after Knigge's resignation, the Elector of Bavaria received information about the Illuminati which led to their suppression. Only Knigge could have had access to the Illuminati documents that could have brought this about. On March 2, 1785 the Illuminati were suppressed.[47]

Illuminatist Plot to Discredit the Monarchy

About this time there was an Illuminatist plot to discredit the French Monarchy and Church in the eyes of the people. It centred round Cagliostro. The plot aimed to "expose" the licentiousness of a Catholic priest with Queen Marie-Antoinette, and thus advance the cause of Frederick II and the Illuminati. Presumably with funds granted to him by the Second Congress, Cagliostro ordered a necklace containing 579 diamonds valued at 1,600,000 livres from the Court jewellers in the Queen's name.[48] In the previous reign the Court jeweller Böhmer had commissioned it in the hope that Louis XV would give it to Mme du Barry, but the King had declined, leaving him with expensive stock on his hands. At the same time Cardinal Prince Louis de Rohan, Cardinal-Archbishop of Strasbourg, was persuaded that the Queen wanted him to buy the necklace on her behalf without telling the King. The Cardinal agreed because he wanted to end the Queen's enmity towards him. He was led to believe he was corresponding with her: he wrote the Queen letters which were intercepted and replied to by Jeanne de Valois, Comtess de la Motte (the penniless descendant of an illegitimate son of Henri II), who signed herself "Marie-Antoinette de France" (a title the Queen would never have given herself). She arranged for a prostitute from the Palais-Royal to impersonate the Queen at a midnight assignation. The Cardinal then handed over the necklace in the gardens of Versailles at midnight. The Comtess broke up the necklace and bought a château while her husband went to London to sell the diamonds. On August 9, 1785 Böhmer presented his bill for the first instalment to the Queen, who naturally denied all knowledge of the necklace and said she would never have had such a luxury when the French economy was in such dire straits (as a result of Necker's mismanagement). The midnight meeting was duly reported by the pamphleteers who operated on the printing presses installed in Orléans' old quarters of the palace. Innuendo and scandal now covered the Monarchy and the Church.

Louis XVI arrested the conspirators, including Cagliostro, who remained in the Bastille for nine and a half months. Foolishly he decided to have the ringleaders tried by Parliament, which was anti-Royalist and contained Illuminati and Masonic agents. Cagliostro was acquitted along with the Cardinal, while the Comtess and her accomplice were found guilty. She was sentenced to be flogged, branded and imprisoned for life, but escaped to England. However, the scandal had severely damaged the reputation of the Royal family and the Church, and the public began to lose confidence in them. Napoleon later said that the plot was in no small part responsible for sparking the revolution of 1789.

In November 1786 Cagliostro returned to London and it seems that he was responsible for placing a mysterious notice in a London newspaper on November 2 in Rose-Croix hireoglyphics, apparently informing a leader of the Priory of Sion that his mission had been completed.[49]

The Illuminati Are Banned

While the impression of financial paralysis in France had been advanced by the "Necker and Necklace" affairs, Cagliostro's own standing in the hidden Illuminati had increased, and he, not Weishaupt, was now the real power in the Illuminati. Since its suppression in March 1785 more damaging evidence had reached the Elector on July 10. A low-grade Illuminati initiate and evangelist Jacob Lang (or Lanze) had been sent by the suppressed Illuminati as an emissary to Silesia. At Ratisbon he was allegedly struck and killed by lightning.[50] The story is confused. Edith Miller states that Weishaupt was accompanying him; Nesta Webster that he was travelling alone. He may have been murdered. Sewn in his clothes were the Order's instructions,

Weishaupt's coded communications, a list of 2,000 members and details of lodges in France, Belgium, Denmark, Sweden, Poland, Hungary and Italy. No low-grade initiate would have access to, let alone carry, such incriminating Illuminati documents, and it could be that the documents were planted. The Elector banned the Illuminati and published the documents (which later appeared in Robison's *Proofs of a Conspiracy*, 1798). Weishaupt took refuge with the Duke of Saxe-Gotha (who was related to the Hanoverian English royal family)[51] and overtly Freemasonry now had a chance to dissociate itself from the Illuminati (as George Washington did in America in 1798).

Weishaupt had long prepared for being banned. He wrote to Zwack ("Cato"), "I have considered everything and so prepared it, that if the Order should this day go to ruin, I shall in a year re-establish it more brilliant than ever." Was Weishaupt deliberately "killing off" the Illuminati so that the organization could continue to flourish, undetected, within Templar Freemasonry (both Grand Order and Scottish Rite)? In this case it died what the Rosicrucians termed a "philosophic death." Or had Knigge turned against Weishaupt and reported him to the authorities, and was he "killing off" the Illuminati so that *he* could continue it as a Templar operation, with himself in charge? Alternatively, had the non-Jewish Gentile Grand Orient Templars absorbed Weishaupt's degrees and "killed off" Weishaupt, so that they now ran the Illuminati activities?[52]

There are no clear answers. What is certain is that the Illuminati's activities continued within the Grand Orient and Scottish Rite Templar lodges, and that Cagliostro was now the most powerful Illuminist figure.[53] It is also certain that Knigge, no. 3 in the Illuminati under Weishaupt and Cagliostro, attempted to revive the Illuminati in the German Union in 1788.[54] (On October 11, 1786 the Bavarian authorities had seized more documents at Zwack's house in Landshut, where a Reading Society masked the beginnings of the German Union set up by Dr Charles Bahrdt at Knigge's instigation.)[55] It could be that the wily plotter of the diamond necklace affair, Cagliostro, worked with his old Templar accomplice Knigge to remove the autocratic Weishaupt from the Illuminati so that they could control his plan for world revolution. After his arrest by the Inquisition in 1789, Cagliostro revealed at his interrogatory before the Holy See at Rome in 1790 that the Illuminati were not dead but were actively working to create a revolution in France and overthrow the Papacy. He claimed (as we have seen) that the House of Rothschild had supplied funds and that large sums had been deposited in banks in Holland, Italy, France and England to fund future revolutions. No evidence for this has been uncovered.[56]

The third and final Congress of the Illuminati took place in secret in Frankfurt in 1786. Weishaupt played no part, but all the proposals he made in Paris the previous year were adopted. Illuminated Freemasonry's ends would be: "(1) Pantheism for the higher degrees, atheism for the lower degrees and the populace; (2) Communism of goods, women and general concerns; (3) the Destruction of the Church, and all forms of Christianity, and the removal of all existing human governments to make way for a universal republic in which the utopian ideas of complete liberty from existing social, moral, and religious restraint, absolute equality and social fraternity, should reign. When these ends should be attained, but not till then, the secret work of the atheistic Freemasons should cease."[57] It was reported by two Frenchmen that the Congress decreed the deaths of Louis XVI and Gustavus III of Sweden.[58]

The Illuminized Grand Orient: Mendelssohn and Mirabeau

In 1786 the Illuminized Grand Orient lodges had an impressive hold on France. This was strengthened when the ideas of the Berlin Illuminati reached Versailles, just outside Paris.

Weishaupt, and later Cagliostro, had already given intellectual expression to the spiritual vision of Rousseau, Weishaupt operating in Bavaria and Frankfurt and Cagliostro with some impact on France. This intellectual expression was reinforced in Berlin through Moses Mendelssohn, a Scottish Rite Templar Freemason who was one of the original five members of the Illuminati in Bavaria. He had translated the Torah, the first five books of the Bible, into German and had been father of the subversive Jewish Enlightenment (*Haskala*) movement which sought to integrate Jews within their European societies and destroy both Christianity and Judaism. A student of Locke and Leibniz, he was a rational Enlightenment figure; as such he admired Menasseh ben Israel. He was extremely interested in any project that helped Jews emancipate themselves and relate their religious tradition to German culture and he would have funded the rational Illuminati with this end in view.[59]

The writer Lessing, founder of modern German literature and a Freemason, introduced Mendelssohn (on whom Lessing based his hero in *Nathan the Wise*) to the many illuminés (or Illuminatists) who met in taverns throughout Germany. In 1786 these taverns would become the *Tugendbund* ("Union of Virtue") lodges which were founded as Illuminati fronts. Mendelssohn joined the *Tugendbund* just before his death. This group met in a brothel in Berlin where two of Mendelssohn's daughters were employed, and came to be known as Frankists. Mendelssohn wrote of this Illuminati group: "Those who regulate their lives according to the precepts of this religion of nature and of reason are called virtuous men...and are the children of eternal salvation."

Another aspect of the intellectual expression of the French revolution surfaced in France soon afterwards. Mendelssohn's successor at the Berlin Union of Virtue was the Jewish Illuminatist Marcus Herz, who ran it with his wife Henrietta. Count Mirabeau, a Grand Orient Freemason, travelling backwards and forwards between Berlin and Paris on secret diplomatic missions, lodged at Henrietta Herz's Union of Virtue.[60]

Mirabeau, an aristocrat, had married an heiress but, imprisoned at the request of his father to put him out of reach of creditors, he escaped and fled to Switzerland where he was joined by the very young wife of an old man. He was sentenced to death for seduction and only survived by agreeing to further imprisonment. When he was released he was rejected by his wife and his father, and had to renounce his aristocratic background. It has been suggested that soon after his release in August

1782 he visited the headquarters of the new combined Order in Frankfurt and brought Illuminism back to France. Whether or not he joined the Illuminati this early, he became a secret agent and worked for Louis XVI's ministers.

In 1786 Mirabeau went to Berlin on a secret mission for Louis XVI and was initiated into Illuminism through Col. Jacob Mauvillon. He took the name "Leonidas" (the leader of the Spartans who resisted the Persians at Thermopylae) and became friendly with Dohm, the author of *Upon the Civil Amelioration of the Condition of the Jews.* It was through him that the Illuminati spread within France in 1786. When he returned to Paris he Illuminized the Masonic lodge of *Amis Reunis* (formerly known as *Philalèthes*) and initiated Abbé Talleyrand. The initiation took place at the Grand Lodge of the French Illuminati 30 miles outside Paris, in the Ermenonville mansion owned by the Marquis de Gerardin, and was presided over by the Rosicrucian Comte de Saint-Germain, Cagliostro's mentor.[61]

Also in 1786 Mirabeau, Talleyrand and the Duke of Orléans founded an Illuminati lodge in Versailles, the Club Breton, which was Illuminized by Bode and Guillaume Baron de Busche in 1788. In that same year, Mirabeau popularized the Illuminist ideal in his book *The Prussian Monarchy under Frederick the Great,* which praised rationalistic Illuminists for improving "governments and legislations." This influenced his two successive personal secretaries Desmoulins and Dumont (the friend and protector of Paine in London, who passed the ideas on to him).[62]

THE FOUR FRENCH REVOLUTIONS

The Orléanist Revolution

There were four separate French revolutions, rather than a single rising of the underprivileged against their rich and powerful oppressors; and each of the four revolutions had different aims and different leaders. The first was the Orléanist revolution of 1789.

By then there were at least 266 Illuminized Grand Orient lodges in France.[63] Two contemporary authors, the Templar French clergyman Abbé Barruel and the Scottish Professor John Robison of the Scottish Rite, agree that there was a conspiracy behind the French Revolution. Robison claimed that the Illuminati were in control; Barruel maintained that the Templars were in command, and traced their allegiance to the Manichaean heresy, which had survived through the Cathars, Templars, Freemasons and revolutionaries. Both were right. The French Revolution was masterminded by one body: the Illuminati-within-the-Templars.[64]

The figurehead of Weishaupt's front, the Duke of Orléans, Grand Master of the Illuminized Grand Orient (otherwise known as Philippe-Egalité), who co-founded the Breton Club, was at the centre of the Orléanist conspiracy. He had been exiled to his estates in 1787 following conflict between Louis XVI and the nobles over financial policy; his crime had been to challenge the King's authority before the *Parlement* of Paris. His aim was to oust the King and establish a popular democratic monarchy with himself as monarch. Lacking intelligence, he was a willing stalking-horse for the most moderate stage of revolution and put himself at the disposal of the Illuminati within his Grand Orient, men such as the shadowy Choderlos de Laclos, who ran the conspiracy. He protected the revolutionary club (the Breton Club) with his name and sponsored a march of "women" (actually men in disguise) to Versailles.[65]

Pre-revolutionary France was in chaos. France had the largest population in Europe, yet could not feed herself. The bourgeoisie were excluded from power, and the peasants had withdrawn their support for the feudal system. The *Philosophes* had advocated social and political reform, and had aroused public expectations. The French participation in the American War of Independence had ruined the State's finances. The economy was in such a parlous state that in February 1787 the controller general of finances, Charles-Alexandre de Calonne, had summoned representatives of the clergy, nobles and bourgeoisie (the three estates) to propose an increase in taxation to reduce the deficit.

This assembly demanded the calling of the Estates-General which had not met since 1614. Calonne's reform programme failed and there was unrest in Paris and several other cities. The King recalled Necker in August 1788 to deal with France's mounting deficit (a staggering decision by Louis XVI in view of France's impending bankruptcy, for which Necker had been responsible), promised to convene the Estates-General, and freed the press.[66]

The disaffection of the intellectuals during this turbulent time can be gleaned from Beaumarchais' *Marriage of Figaro* (1784), which is about the difficulty a man without money had in progressing in a social system built on privilege. The middle and lower classes hated the ruling class because it was perceived as an obstacle to professional success. Figaro begins as a barber-surgeon. He tries playwriting and is censored; he tries writing on State finance and is sent to prison; he tries journalism and is suppressed. He tries to get a government job, and is rejected although fitted for the post. Waiting to catch his bride with his master, he reflects of the latter: "Because you are a great lord, you think you are a great genius!...Nobility, fortune, rank, appointments: all this makes a man so proud! But what have you done to deserve so many good things? You took the trouble to get born!" ("*Vous vous êtes donné la peine de naître.*")[67]

The elections to the Estates-General coincided with more riots as the 1788 harvest had not been good. The winter of 1788-9 was very cold; frozen rivers halted transport and flour-milling, and the price of bread rose from 8 to 14 sous by January 1789, setting off riots at bakers and markets and necessitating a tax on millers and food convoys. Parisians felt that food shortage was now a policy of government, that the people were being starved into submission under the repressive sword of royal troops.

Louis XVI's decision to convene the Estates-General at Versailles on May 5, 1789 was a turning-point in French history. The Duke of Orléans was elected to represent the nobles. Being a populist, Orléans supported the Third Estate (the bourgeoisie or majority of the people) against the nobles and the clergy, whom the King favoured. On June 17 the Third Estate proclaimed itself a National Assembly and vowed to give France a new Constitution; and on June 25 Orléans and other nobles joined it. After tense meetings in which the deputies defied him, the King gave in and invited all three estates to form a National Constituent Assembly. Orléans was a hero. An adulatory mob agitated round his house in the Palais-Royal.[68]

It was from about this time that the influential journalism of the Illuminatist Nicholas Bonneville gave intellectual expression to the growing revolutionary feeling, made an impact on the public and precipitated the French Revolution. Initiated into the Illuminati by Weishaupt's "ambassador," Christian Bode (a friend of Lessing) in Paris in 1787, Bonneville was a Weishauptian. He had developed Weishaupt's idea (in his work *The Jesuits Driven from Free Masonry*, 1788) that Freemasonry needed purging from the corruption of the Jesuits. "*Aux armes, citoyens!*" he thundered in his *Tribun du Peuple*, the first use of the cry (uttered by Camille Desmoulins) that later summoned the mob to the Bastille on July 12, 1789 and is now in *La Marseillaise*. Based in the Palais-Royal, the entertainment complex owned by the Duke of Orléans, he created *La Bouche de Fer (The Iron Mouth)*, the voice of reason and of absolute Truth, and dominated the revolutionary journals for the next five years.[69]

The Orléanist revolution began by exploiting the scarcity of grain that summer. Rumours of threats to food supplies reached towns and provinces. It was rumoured that the King and the two privileged estates – the nobles and clergy – would overthrow the third estate. Troops gathered round Paris, and Necker, after concessions to the National Assembly, was dismissed on July 11. This was interpreted (correctly) as the beginning of a counter-revolution by the King, the nobles and the clergy against the bourgeoisie and the National Assembly, and disturbances preceded open rebellion. The Hôtel des Invalides was taken and thousands of rifles handed out. This was followed by a Templar-led storming of the Bastille (an old fortress commanding the Faubourg Saint-Antoine, and a symbol of royal tyranny for nearly 500 years) on July 14.

The garrison resisted and dozens of Parisians were killed. The main object of the attack by the revolutionaries was not to destroy the prison or free prisoners but to seize arms, ammunition and gunpowder for the coming struggle.[70] Several soldiers were massacred by the angry mob after the operation. The Bastille had been the prison where Jacques de Molay, the last Templar Grand Master, spent his final days in 1314, and there was a symbolic Templar significance, which was not lost on the Orléanist Illuminized Grant Orient, in opening the gates of the prison of Jacques de Molay's final confinement. The King capitulated, wearing a new tricolour cockade in deference to the people's sovereignty (white for the Bourbons, red and blue for Paris). The National Assembly was saved from dissolution and Necker was reinstated.

The Duke of Orléans's plan to usurp the throne of France while he was Grand Master of the now Illuminized Grand Orient was at the centre of the "Orléanist Conspiracy" of 1789 which sought to arm the populace against law and order and effect a social revolution. The Duke himself was a fairly feeble person, but he was surrounded by some very determined plotters who made him their figurehead. It is said that the idea originated with Adrien Dupont, a confidant of Orléans and member of the Illuminized Grand Orient. Certainly the organization of what came to be known as "the Great Fear" was Masonic. The Grand Orient lodges aimed "to make a revolution for the bourgeoisie with the people as instruments." This was engineered agitation. On July 22, 1789 in towns and villages throughout France messengers (sent out from lodges) rode on horseback bearing placards saying "Edict of the King" and announcing that brigands were approaching and that citizens should take up arms. Other placards said "The King orders all *chateaux* to be burnt down." The messengers added, "He only wishes to keep his own," hoping that the newly empowered mob would realize that they could burn the King's *chateaux* down with impunity too. The people duly carried out "the King's wishes," thus eclipsing the power of the nobles throughout France and allowing the bourgeoisie, the Third Estate, to fill the vacuum.[71]

The "Orléanist Conspiracy" was an uprising of the bourgeoisie against the nobles, using popular mobs to do the bourgeoisie's dirty work. And so the anti-popular measures followed: food supplies were held up, the Third Estate blocked reforms in the National Assembly – safeguarding property, limiting suffrage to people with a certain level of income and forbidding trade unions – and organized demonstrations that opposed the wishes of the people. There were attacks on men who had befriended the poor: on a factory owner in Reveillon, and on a baker (François) who was murdered in October. The impression across France was of the unity of the Third Estate against the aristocrats.

On August 4, 1789, at a session in the Assembly, liberal nobles and clergy renounced their ancient feudal privileges. The Assembly then decreed "the abolition of feudalism," which included Church tithes and hunting rights. Seigneurial dues were retained for two more years, unless peasants paid huge amounts of compensation to the lords, but nobles lost their hereditary titles in 1790. However, the end of the *ancien regime* had been signalled, and the Assembly could now construct a new regime. On August 22 a new Constitution was planned on the basis of the doctrine of the Rights of Man. On August 27 its basic principles were stated in a *Declaration of the Rights of Man and Citizen*, which was largely based on Rousseau's principles and which the authors believed to be of universal significance. It proclaimed liberty, equality, the inviolability of property and the right to resist oppression. Its first article was the Rousseauesque statement that "men are born and remain free and equal in rights." Benjamin Franklin made available the Constitution of Pennsylvania which he claimed to have written (though it was probably written by Paine's follower, James Cannon) and which was admired by many. The new Constitution would reshape society according to reason and natural rights, and would reject history and tradition. "In the new hemisphere, the brave inhabitants of Philadelphia have given the example of a people who re-established their liberty," said one deputy, but "France would give that example to the rest of the world."

Louis showed his reluctance to sanction the National Assembly's two August achievements, the *Declaration of the Rights of Man* and the destruction of the feudal *ancien regime*, and was seen to resist popular demands. Orléans hoped that the mob would assassinate the King and Queen and proclaim him a democratic King. The Illuminati within his Grand Orient, on the other hand, wanted to remove the royal family from the protection of the army into Paris, where they could exercise more control. Their opportunity came in October when Lafayette, commander of the Paris National Guard, marched through Versailles with a citizen's militia formed to keep order, but including troops that had stormed the Bastille. The King was ready to flee and carriages were brought. The Assembly insisted on the King's acceptance of the constitutional articles. Waiting, Louis went to his desk, then signed and handed his acceptance to Mournier, President of the Assembly.[72]

In the early hours of October 6 some of the crowd broke into the Palace and killed two of the Queen's bodyguards. She fled to the King along a secret passage. The mob slashed her mattress to ribbons, frustrated that she had escaped. The next day both appeared on the balcony. The crowd beneath bayed, "To Paris, to Paris." The King and Queen and royal family were taken the 12 miles from Versailles to Paris with the heads of the two dead bodyguards being carried in front of them on pikes. The journey took seven hours. They were installed in the Tuileries Palace amid cries of "*Vive notre roi d'Orléans!*" Louis was now outside the protection of the royal army.[73]

In December 1789 the Breton Club, which had been founded as a meeting-place for the deputies to the Estates-General, reconstituted itself as the Society of the Friends of the Constitution. It was commonly called the Jacobin Club because it met in a former convent of the Dominicans, who were known as Jacobins. But if there was an echo of Savonarola in the name, there was a stronger echo of Jacques de Molay, the Templar Grand Master who was burned at the stake in 1314, for the Jacobins were all Illuminized Grand Orient Templars who saw the name as echoing "Jacques": they were Jacques-obins, as it were. The purpose of the Club was to protect the gains of the Revolution against aristocratic reaction, and it admitted non-deputy bourgeois and men of letters. By July 1790 there were 1,200 members in the original Paris

Club and 152 affiliated Jacobin Clubs across France.[74]

Just as significant behind the scenes was Bonneville. In the Palais-Royal's Circus in 1790 he created his Universal Confederation of the Friends of the Truth, which was controlled by the "Social Circle" (*Cercle Social*), an intellectual and journalistic *élite* whose headquarters were in an underground chamber deep in the heart of the Palais-Royal. The inner circle met underground and were an alternative court to Versailles; the outer circle, numbering around 6,000, met in the Circus. (In all, Bonneville had three circles: a communist *élite* in the centre, then a socialist and democratic circle, and then an outer liberal circle.) This *élite* inhabited a "circle of light" and talked of purifying themselves and conquering the light, a view that owed much to the Cathar *parfaits*, although they did not seem to realize this. Their aim was to establish a perfect egalitarian government with Truth (i.e. the press) at its centre.[75]

Bonneville described his circle of writers as "the legislators of the Universe," a phrase Shelley adopted in his "poets are the unacknowledged legislators of the world." Through Bonneville, Saint-Just, Desmoulins and Babeuf, all became members of the Illuminati. At the centre of the inner circle was Maréchal, who referred to himself as HSD, *l'Homme Sans Dieu*, the Man without God, and who had immunity from arrest. Maréchal wrote a 6-volume *Voyages of Pythagoras*, which saw Pythagoras's community as a political brotherhood and Pythagoras as a model for revolutionaries. (It was from Pythagoras that Freemasonry took the symbol of the triangle which is found in the Seal of the Illuminati.) In this work *le monde* refers to the new, perfected world of the Illuminati. Antoine Fabré d'Olivet, translator of Pythagoras's *Golden Verses*, was another contemporary of Bonneville's.[76]

Among Bonneville's circle of writers were Restif de la Bretonne, who wrote a universal dictionary and coined the term "communism," and Louis-Sebastien Mercier, who wrote a Utopian novel: *L'An 2440 (The Year 2440)*. Both were pornographers – as was Mirabeau – and Bonneville himself shared his house and his wife with the English revolutionary and Illuminatist Thomas Paine. (In *An Essay on the Origins of Freemasonry*, published in America in 1802, Paine would reveal the influence of Bonneville's "circle of light" by claiming that Freemasons were descendants of sun-worshipping druids, the Zoroastrian cult of fire and Pythagoras, and provided a cult that was an alternative to Christianity.)[77]

The National Constituent Assembly produced a series of revolutionary measures which benefited the bourgeoisie. It nationalized all the lands of the Roman Catholic Church in France to pay off the public debt – a measure in keeping with Weishaupt's policies – and there was a widescale redistribution of property, much of it to the bourgeoisie. The Assembly then decided to reorganize the Church; the Pope and the French clergy resisted. It swept away the administrative system of the *ancien regime* and replaced it with *départements*, districts, cantons and communes administered by elected assemblies. Justice was adapted to the new system and judges were to be elected. The Assembly tried to create a monarchical regime in which King and Assembly shared power, but the weak Louis, surrounded by his aristocratic advisers, prevaricated and vacillated and made the partnership unworkable. As a result France missed its opportunity to have a constitutional monarchy like the British system created under William III.[78]

In May 1790 the Comte de Mirabeau became secret counsellor to Louis XVI and Marie-Antoinette on the recommendation of his friend Auguste, Prince d'Arenberg, Comte de La Marck and with the approval of the Austrian ambassador in Paris, a confidant of Marie-Antoinette, Florimund, Graf Mercy d'Argenteau. Mirabeau, a member of the Illuminati and co-founder of the Jacobin Club, wrote, "I shall make it my chief business to see that the executive power has its place in the constitution." Mirabeau's appointment was probably at the request of the Sionist House of Lorraine, which hoped that he would influence events. He had supported Necker but precipitated his resignation in September 1790 with a speech on the nation's bankruptcy. And now he defended the King's right to make war and peace, saying it was better that France should have no King than a "powerless, superfluous king." A Jacobin pamphlet accused him of treason. The King and Queen had a secret meeting with him on July 3 but took no notice of his advice.

He found it extremely difficult to appear a popular Jacobin while secretly advising the King amid more accusations of treason. He became President of the Assembly for two weeks. In March he suddenly became ill and took to his bed, and at the beginning of April 1791 died. There were allegations that he had been poisoned. He was given a magnificent funeral in the church of Sainte-Geneviève, which had been converted into the Panthéon specially for him, but when papers proving his involvement with the royal family were discovered his remains were removed from the Panthéon by order of the Convention.[79]

Marie-Antoinette had planned to flee the country with the Dauphin, and now she urged Louis to escape from Paris before the Constitution was finalized so that he would not be forced to accept it in its present form. On June 20/21, 1791, leaving the Tuileries separately to avoid recognition, the entire royal family mounted a two-horse carriage and attempted to escape from Paris – and France – across the eastern frontier. At Varennes they had to change horses, and there was no sign of the fresh horses that had been arranged. The King and Queen knocked on doors seeking fresh horses. On the way to Varennes the King had been recognized by an old enemy, a postmaster called Drouet, who had set off in pursuit. Drouet arrived with a posse and demanded the royal passports. They all stepped into the shop of a grocer called Monsieur Sauce. At first Louis denied being the King but then admitted it. He said he only wanted to go to Mont Médy, and he appealed to Sauce to help him. The Queen appealed to Mme Sauce, who sobbed in tears, "What would you have me do, Madame? Your situation is very unfortunate; but you see that would expose Monsieur Sauce: they would cut off his head."[80]

Louis XVI and Marie-Antoinette returned to Paris; Louis had now lost credibility as a constitutional monarch.

The Girondinist Revolution

The moderate-republican Girondins rose to power with the ensuing rise in moderate republican feeling. In July the more extreme Jacobin Club organized a petition calling for Louis's removal. It caused a split and the moderate deputies left and joined the rival club of the

Feuillants. The deputy Maximilien de Robespierre, whom Weishaupt had met in Paris,[81] now became prominent in the Club.

Louis now pinned his hopes on a war with Austria. There had been a Franco-Austrian alliance since 1756 which had blocked Frederick II's dream both of a united Germany under Prussian domination and of the French throne. Louis's Queen, Marie-Antoinette, being a daughter of Empress Maria Theresa, presided over an "Austrian committee," and she hoped that the Austrian army would invade France and defeat Louis's enemies. Foreign intervention, followed by a French military disaster, would restore royal authority, she felt; and Louis, now completely under her influence, agreed. In the declaration of Pillnitz on August 27, 1791 Austria and Prussia (Leopold II and Frederick William II) called on European leaders to assist Louis XVI in re-establishing himself in power.

Numbers of nobles, clergy and some bourgeois emigrated and many *émigrés* formed armed groups on the north-east frontier and asked for foreign support. The rulers were wary at first, but were alarmed when the National Constituent Assembly declared that all peoples had the right to self-determination and annexed the Papal territory of Avignon in September 1791.[82]

The new Legislative Assembly first met on October 1. It was controlled by the Girondin faction from October 1791 to September 1792. The left of the old National Constituent Assembly now became the right; there was a shift leftwards. The Girondins were moderate republicans, many of them from the *département* of Gironde in the Bordeaux region, young lawyers who attracted support from the bourgeois businessmen, merchants and industrialists. Initially their leader was Jacques-Pierre Brissot, and they were known as Brissotins. Their tone was moderately intolerant and belligerent. At first they were critics of the court and inspired the measures against *émigrés* and anti-revolutionary priests, both of which Louis vetoed. And they supported foreign war as a way of uniting the French people behind the Revolution. "The people who after twelve centuries of slavery have won liberty require a war to consolidate it," Brissot said.[83]

On Marie-Antoinette's advice, Louis rejected the urgings of

moderate constitutionalists led by Antoine Barnave that the 1791 Constitution should be implemented; instead he embarked on a policy of deception. Seeing war coming, he refused Lafayette's offer of help and appealed to the Girondins to designate a new Cabinet. The Constitution did not allow ministers to be chosen from the Assembly. On March 23 he appointed a Ministry that would be identified with the Girondins in the Assembly and throw the responsibility for declaring war on them. He admitted Girondins into his government: Clavière, Gen. Dumouriez (who had always hated Austria) and Jean-Marie Roland, whose wife held a salon that was a meeting-place for Girondins.

Dumouriez decided to go to war with Austria, which was ruled by Francis II (nephew of Marie-Antoinette) following Leopold's recent death. On April 20, on the recommendation of the Girondin Ministry Louis, pale, stammering, with tears in his eyes, declared war against Austria using the formula "against the King of Hungary and Bohemia" to guarantee the neutrality of Prussia. It was a war the Girondins had long urged, and it proved to be the culmination of their revolution. It was generally suspected that the Queen's "Austrian Committee" had intrigued it.

The war "revolutionized the Revolution." Louis's concern with constitutional correctness was not acceptable in this time of national danger and the Queen was suspected of betraying French war plans to the enemy – correctly, for on March 26 she gave Mercy, the Austrian ambassador, a resumé of the French campaigns on June 5 and wrote to Ferson that "Luckner's army has been ordered to attack immediately" and sent him more information on June 23. She was afraid that if Austria lost Belgium she would expand and take an equivalent part of France.[84]

The Illuminist Templars had kept quiet amid the popular tumult, but had their eyes firmly on absolute power, busying themselves in organizing the Jacobin Club. The Illuminized Grand Orient Templars now controlled the Jacobin Clubs, and during 1791 and 1792 their creator, the Duke of Orléans, now known as Philippe-Égalité, resigned as Grand Master of the Grand Orient and all lodges in France were closed to prevent counter-revolutionary activities behind closed doors once they seized power. The Templars in France were now in Jacobin Clubs, not in lodges. Now that Illuminism was being fulfilled there was no need for secrecy. Nine hundred towns had clubs by mid-1791, and most of them were affiliated to the original Jacobin Club; there were 6,800 Jacobin Clubs by 1794 with half a million members.[85]

Now the Girondins vacillated. They had three ministers in Louis's government, but they were on the side of the Revolution and wanted a republic. The Girondins did not behave responsibly. In May and June they deliberately devised decrees that would strip Louis of support and embarrass him: one abolishing his 1,800-strong bodyguard, another setting up a camp for 20,000 National Guards near Paris, another deporting the only truly Catholic priests in France. For 10 days Louis was so depressed that he did not utter a word even to his family. On June 12 he dismissed his three most hardline ministers including Clavière and Roland. The rumour spread that the King was about to seize Paris with the aid of *émigré* troops; it was a re-run of what was said when he dismissed Necker in 1789. On June 16 Dumouriez resigned from the Cabinet and left Paris to command the army in the north.

Louis was asked to withdraw a veto on two decrees. (The deputies of the bourgeoisie, the Third Estate, had proclaimed themselves a National Assembly, which the nobility declared illegal.) He expected to be assassinated and summoned his confessor, M. Hébert, writing: "Come and see me; I have never stood in so great a need of your consolation. I have finished with men; I look to Heaven. Great misfortunes are expected tomorrow." The next day, June 20, a petition was presented. A mob invaded the Tuileries for four hours, during which Louis stood on a window-seat separated from the mob by a table and a few grenadiers. He humoured the mob by wearing the cap of Liberty and toasting France, but he did not withdraw his veto on the decrees. Pétion, the Girondin Mayor of Paris, and Santerre of the National Guard made no attempt to call off the mob. Then Pétion arrived, professing not to have known of the situation. When he tried to justify himself the next day, Louis said "Shut up" and turned his back on him.

Louis's courage brought him renewed popular support, and seeing the Prussian army as his potential saviour, he presented a declaration of war on Prussia to the Assembly on July 6. The Girondins now began a campaign for his dethronement. The Assembly was suddenly inundated with petitions from clubs. On July 31 the Mauconseil section withdrew its support for the King. Louis and Marie-Antoinette lived in a state of constant alert and alarm. On July 25 the Austrian commander, the Duke of Brunswick, threatened to destroy Paris if the safety of the royal family was endangered and if the Tuileries was invaded again. The threat was counter-productive and alienated popular support.

Another rising seemed likely. Louis could either hold on until the Prussians arrived at the end of August, in which case he had to do a deal with the Girondins; or he could trust Lafayette, who, having fired on petitioners demanding the abdication of the King in July 1791, had been appointed commander of the army in December. He was the only man who could give Louis an army. The hero of America and therefore France, Lafayette hoped to rule in the King's name now that France was at war with Austria. He was trusted by the King (although the Queen remained hostile), and on June 28 he went to the Assembly and denounced the invasion of the Tuileries. He also announced his intention of reviewing his royal legion and then marching with it to close down the Jacobin Club. According to Lafayette, the Queen (who still loathed him) told Pétion to cancel orders for the review. Whether or not that was the case – and it was a colossal mistake if it was the case – only a few guards assembled and Lafayette returned to his army without moving against the Jacobins.

Lafayette wanted to move the King out of Paris, but the terms of the Constitution forbade Louis going further than twenty leagues, and the King wanted to stick to this. Moreover, the Queen opposed Lafayette's plan to remove the King to Compiègne, and put her opposition in writing to Fersen. Meekly, Louis acceded to her veto.

It seems that Lafayette had been planning a *coup d'état*. He ordered Dumouriez to march on Paris, but the order was ignored. The Ministry now planned to resign *en masse* on July 10, which would force the King to reconsider his escape plan. But the King remained in Paris and dealt with the Girondins, who were still trying to head off an impending Jacobin insurrection when it broke on August 10.

That morning the Tuileries Palace was defended by 1,000 Swiss Guards, 1,000 mounted police and 2,000 National Guards. There were also 300 armed nobles. The numbers could control a mob, but many of the National Guard were against the King. During that night the municipality had been replaced by a revolutionary Commune that was to control the National Guard. Paris had risen and a revolutionary Commune was installed in the Hôtel de Ville. Dejected, the King reviewed the Guard at 6 am. There were shouts of "*Vive le Roi,*" and then boos from the nearby mob. Roederer of the Département advised that the royal family should take refuge in the Assembly as resistance was impossible. They walked between two lines of soldiers to the Assembly, past piles of leaves the gardeners had raked.

Now the Jacobin mob attacked in what came to be known as "The First Terror." Georges Danton was largely behind it; certainly he later claimed he "had been responsible for" the events of August 10. The Swiss Guards resisted, firing and killing or wounding 300. When Louis ordered them to stop firing at 10 am, the mob turned on them and butchered them all.

The Girondin-dominated Assembly suspended Louis but did not depose him. That decision was to be given to a new assembly, a National Convention. The royal family spent the day in the reporters' box. At 2 am they were moved to the Convent of the Feuillants, where they stayed three days. At 6 pm on August 13 they were taken through a hostile crowd to the Temple, the grim residence of the Knights Templar. Having sought refuge in the Assembly, the King had become its prisoner – a prisoner of the Jacobin faction which was now in the ascendancy through the Jacobin Clubs. The turning-point may have been on August 11 when Louis's attendants were ordered to leave the Convent. He said: "I am then in prison, and less fortunate than Charles I, who was allowed to keep all his friends with him to the scaffold." When his courtiers offered him money Louis said as if intuitively knowing what was ahead for him, "Keep your purses, gentlemen, you will need them more than we shall, as you will have longer to live, I hope."

Now the cry "*Vive notre roi d'Orléans*" was replaced by the Masonic Grand Orient Jacobin slogan "Liberty, Equality, Fraternity!"[86] When they arrived at the Temple they were greeted by Jacobin officials of the Commune who kept their hats on their heads and addressed the King as "Monsieur" and not "Sire."

The monarchy had been overthrown by the Jacobins without the participation of the Girondins. The Girondins were now in decline, and more radical groups – the Jacobin Paris Commune, the Paris Masonic-Jacobin mob and the Jacobins under Robespierre – took over the direction of the revolution. On August 17 Lafayette fled to Liège, where he was imprisoned by the Austrians until 1797.

A provisional executive council was set up which included the dismissed Girondins and the Illuminized Masonic Jacobin Danton. But the real power in Paris was with the Commune, whose Templar Masonic Jacobins from the start demanded that the royal family should be held in the Temple.

On September 20, 1792 the National Convention opened in the Tuileries. It took its name from the Convention of the American Revolution. The Girondins were opposed by the Montagnards, deputies from the left elected from Paris who would become Jacobins, named "Men of the Mountain" because they occupied the highest ("mountainous") benches. Among the Montagnards were Danton, Robespierre, Carnot, Marat (with his hideous skin disease), Saint-Just and Philippe-Égalité. The Girondins were linked to Parisian businessmen and local government officials; the Montagnards to the Parisian working class and artisans. In the struggle between the two, the Girondins appeared the more moderate, and stopped short of complete egalitarianism; they rejected government control of prices and relied on the *départements*. The Montagnards called them "federalists." They were reformed by the Jacobin Club, which in September changed its name to "Society of the Jacobins, Friends of Liberty and Equality." It admitted the Montagnard deputies and appeared democratic and popular.

On September 21 the Convention decreed that the monarchy was abolished. The next day (the autumnal equinox, September 22, 1792) it proclaimed that new public acts would be dated from Year 1 of the Republic. On September 25 (at Robespierre's insistence) it declared that "the French Republic was one and indivisible." Like the American Convention, it set about framing a new Constitution. The Jacobin Revolution had moved France from a monarchy to a republic.

In the Temple the King had access to the library of the Knights of Malta and read 250 of the 1,500 volumes there. One day he pointed at the works of Rousseau and Voltaire and whispered to Hue, the *valet-chambre* of the Dauphin, "Those two men have ruined France." In prison the royal family fell into a daily routine: breakfast at 9, home tuition for the Dauphin and sewing at 10, a family walk at noon (braving insults such as smoke being deliberately blown in their faces from the pipe of the filthy old doorman), lunch at 2 – the King drank half a bottle of champagne and a glass of liqueur – and then piquet or backgammon, a sleep at 4, lessons or games at 6 and supper at 9, after which the King read in his study until midnight.

The royal family's companions were removed a few days after their arrival at the Temple, including Princesse de Lamballe, the Queen's companion and relative who had returned to Paris to minister to her in her time of need. News that the Prussians were about to overrun Verdun, the last fortress before Paris, enraged the mob, who (with considerable organization) broke into several prisons. The Illuminized Jacobin Georges Danton was accused of organizing the operation. Many in the mob were Masonic Jacobins. They made Masonic signs, and if the prisoners knew how to reply they were spared; otherwise they were killed. The massacre of the non-Masonic inmates, ie. non-Jacobins, lasted five days and by the end of that time they had killed 1,200 inmates from the nobility and clergy, most of them political prisoners. The Princesse was among them. She was disembowelled and her private parts were carried through Paris as trophies to the Revolution. There was no limit to the disgusting things the mob allowed itself to do. The mob took her corpse and severed head to the Temple to show the Queen, but found its entry barred by a tricolour sash which was stretched across the entrance. The mob then put the Princess's head on a pike and lifted it so that it was visible from the windows of the Tower. They insisted that one of the guards should compel the King and Queen to appear at the windows to see it. The guard advised them to go to the windows and see the head. The Queen fainted. Louis seems to have gone to the window alone.

The Trial and Execution of Louis XVI

The discovery in the Tuileries (now the seat of the Convention) of an iron chest containing Louis's correspondence with *émigrés* and counter-revolutionary activities made a trial inevitable, especially now that the Jacobins had gained the upper hand in the Convention. The Convention decided to try him itself. On December 11 Louis (addressed wrongly as "Louis Capet" rather than "Louis Bourbon" – the Capetian dynasty ended in 1328 and the Capetians of Bourbon succeeded in 1589) was told he would be tried. He had reflected on Charles I and wanted to avoid a formal trial that would make the French nation culpable. Robespierre shared his view – only he thought that Louis should be executed without trial. Louis was brought to court and was accused of "conspiracy against liberty and an attempt against the safety of the State" (a meaningless charge not capable of being legally proved). He was accused of causing an army to march against the citizens of Paris. Marat observed there were too many charges; some were badly framed, others banal. Louis was then confronted with documents which he professed not to recognize (as they might be forged). At the end of his first appearance he returned to the Temple and ate six cutlets, a chicken and some eggs.

Louis made his second appearance on December 26. At the end of the session he made a short speech protesting his innocence. The Convention did not vote for a fortnight. The Girondins, aware that Louis's death would increase the conflict at home and abroad, tried to save his life, proposing that there should be an appeal to the people and attacking the Duke of Orléans (who was present as Philippe-Égalité).

The Jacobins all called for Louis's execution and branded the Girondins as royalists and moderates. Danton offered to spare the King's life if Pitt would pay 2 million francs; Pitt refused (and later called Louis's execution the most atrocious crime in history, forgetting Charles I). Finally, between January 14 and 20 votes were taken on four motions. On his punishment the vote for death was a majority of 1 (361 out of 721 votes).

At 3 am on Sunday January 20 the Convention rose. Later that morning the executioner, Charles-Henri Sanson, whose family lived outside the city limits, received his orders. The execution of the King would take place the following day in the Place de la Révolution. Sanson wrote to the prosecutor's assistant saying he had alerted the carpenter who would build the scaffold and asking questions. He was told to wait for the King on the scaffold. The King would be brought from his Temple prison in a closed carriage, accompanied by two gendarmes. (Sanson was suspected of being a secret royalist who might allow the King to escape, and the organizers were afraid that the Paris mob might vent its fury on an open tumbril and kill the King before he reached the scaffold.)

At 2 pm the Executive Council entered the King's antechamber, including the Ministers of Justice and Foreign Affairs and Santerre, commander of the National Guard. The King was held in the Great Tower of the Temple, the medieval residence of the former Knights Templar, including Jacques de Molay, the last Grand Master of the Order of the Knights Templar ("from which same Towers," Thomas Carlyle[87] writes, "poor Jacques Molay and his Templars were burnt out, by French Royalty five centuries since"). Its walls were nine feet thick and there were slits for windows. Some dozen to 15 men stood while Joseph Garat, the Minister for Justice, addressed the King and asked the Secretary to the Council Philippe Grouvelle, to read the decrees of the Council. In a weak and trembling voice Grouvelle read a statement that Louis Capet was "guilty of a conspiracy against the liberty of the Nation, and of an attempt against the general safety of the State" and "shall suffer the punishment of death." The King was told he would be executed within twenty-four hours. In response the King handed over a letter demanding a delay of three days.

Jean-Baptiste Cléry, the King's valet-de-chambre in the Prison of the Temple, wrote an account of the King's last hours.[88] That evening the King ate little, but heartily. He ate two wings of a chicken and some vegetables and drank two glasses of wine mixed with water and some Malaga wine. With the King's permission his confessor, the Abbé Edgeworth de Firmont, went to the Council Chamber and asked the Commissioners of the Tower to bring ornaments from the nearest church so that the King could receive Mass. After a while he was told that the religious service must finish by seven the next morning "because at eight o'clock exactly Louis Capet will leave for the place of execution." The confessor returned to the King. "The brief account which I gave him, leaving out any mention of the conditions, seemed to afford him the greatest happiness." In other words, he seems not to have told the King that he would be taken for execution at eight o'clock.

The King spent some time with his confessor. He went to bed at half-past twelve, asking to be woken at five. Cléry writes: "I then undressed the King, and, as I was going to roll his hair, he said: 'It is not worth the trouble.'…He was scarcely in bed before he fell into a profound sleep, which lasted, without interruption, till five." Cléry sat by his bed all night on a chair.

The King was woken at five by the noise of Cléry lighting the fire. Outside in the Place de la Révolution carpenters were erecting the scaffold. The King dressed and spent an hour with his confessor in the cabinet. When they returned to the King's bedroom they found an altar had been erected there. The King heard Mass kneeling on the floor. He told his confessor, "How happy I am…that I have been able to act in accordance with my principles! Without them, where should I be at this moment? But now, how sweet death seems to me, for there exists on high an incorruptible judge who will give me the justice that has been refused to me on earth."

Dawn had broken. Now the sound of troop movements, the beating of drums and rumbling of cannon was heard in the Tower. The

King remarked that it was "probably the National Guard assembling." He had promised to see the Queen now, but his confessor begged him not to, to spare her agony which would be unbearable. The King said, "You are right; it would be unendurable for her. It would be better to deprive myself of the happiness of seeing her once again, and to let her live in hope a little longer." It is evident that by now the King knew that his fate was imminent.

At 8 Charles-Henri Sanson left his house in his high dark green hat and white cravat. He was accompanied by his son; they wore daggers and pistols under their coats, anticipating danger. The assistants awaited them on the scaffold. It was foggy and icy, and the National Guard surrounded the scaffold as Sanson tested the blade of the guillotine. Thousands of French citizens crowded into the Place de la Révolution, packing the streets that led to it.

At 8.30 Santerre arrived with seven or eight municipal officers and ten soldiers, who were lined up. Cléry writes: "At this movement, the King came out of his closet, and said to Santerre: 'You are come for me?' 'Yes,' was the answer. 'A moment,' said the King, and went to his closet, from which he instantly returned, followed by his Confessor. His Majesty had his Will in his hand, and addressing a Municipal Officer (named Jacques Roux, a renegade priest), who happened to stand before the others, said: 'I beg you to give this paper to the Queen – to my wife.' 'It is no business of mine,' replied he, refusing to take it; 'I am come here to conduct you to the scaffold.' His Majesty then turned to Gobeau, another Municipal Officer. 'I beg,' said he, 'that you will give this paper to my wife; you may read it; there are some particulars in it I wish to be made known to the Commune.'

"I was standing behind the King near the fireplace, he turned round to me, and I offered him his greatcoat. 'I don't want it,' said he, 'give me only my hat.' I presented it to him – his hand met mine, which he pressed once more for the last time. 'Gentlemen,' said he, addressing the Municipal Officers, 'I should be glad that Cléry might stay with my son, as he has been accustomed to be attended by him; I trust that the Commune will grant this request.' His Majesty then looked at Santerre, and said: 'Lead on.'"

The King's confessor, the Abbé Edgeworth de Firmont, was allowed to accompany him to the scaffold because he was Irish.[89] His account is the most interesting of the eye-witness accounts:

> "The final knock on the door was Santerre and his men. The King opened the door, and they said (but I do not know what words they used) that it was time to go. 'I am occupied for a moment,' he said to them in an authoritative tone, 'wait for me here; I shall be with you in a minute.' He shut the door, and coming to me, knelt in front of me. 'It is finished,' he said [echoing the last words of Christ on the cross]; 'Give me your last blessing, and pray to God that He will uphold me to the end.'
>
> "In a moment or two he rose, and leaving the cabinet walked towards the group of men who were in the bedroom. Their faces showed the most complete assurance; and they all remained covered. Seeing this, the King asked for his hat. While Cléry, with tears running down his face, hurried to look for it, 'If one of you,' said the King, 'is a member of the Commune, I ask you to take charge of this paper.'
>
> "It was his Will....After a moment, in a firm tone the King said, 'Let us go.'
>
> "At these words, everybody went out. The King crossed the first courtyard (formerly the garden) on foot....At the entrance of the second courtyard was a coach; two gendarmes were standing beside its door. When the King approached, one of them got in and sat down on the little seat with his back to the horses; the King then took his place opposite, placing me beside him, and the other gendarme sat down beside his comrade, and shut the door....
>
> "A large number of persons devoted to the King had determined to snatch him by force from the hands of the executioners or at least to dare all with that intent. Two of the

leaders, young men of a very well-known name, had come to warn me of this the day before, and without being entirely sanguine, I did not give up all hope until we reached the very foot of the scaffold....

"The King, finding himself shut in a coach where he could neither speak to me nor hear me without witnesses to our conversation, kept silence. I handed him my breviary, the only book I had with me. He gratefully accepted it; he seemed to wish me to point out the psalms which were best suited to the situation, and recited them alternately with me. The gendarmes, also remaining silent, seemed amazed at the calmness and piety of a monarch whom they had no doubt never seen so close at hand before.

"The drive lasted nearly two hours. All the streets were lined with citizens, armed, some with pikes and some with muskets. The coach itself was surrounded by a large body of troops, no doubt drawn from the most corrupt and revolutionary in Paris. As an additional precaution, a number of drummers marched in front of the horses, in order to prevent any shouts being heard that might be raised in the King's favour. But there were no shouts; not a soul was to be seen in the doorways or in the windows; no one was in the streets save those armed citizens who, no doubt through fear and weakness, connived at a crime which perhaps many of them detested in their hearts.

"The coach arrived, amid a great silence, at the Place Louis XV, and stopped in the middle of a wide empty space which had been left round the scaffold; this space was edged with cannon; and beyond, as far as the eye could reach, one saw an armed multitude.

"As soon as the King felt the coach coming to a stop, he leaned over to me and said in a whisper, 'We have arrived, if I'm not mistaken.' My silence said yes. One of the executioners came forward to open the door of the coach, but the King stopped him....

"As soon as the King had got out of the coach, three of the executioners surrounded him, and tried to remove his outer clothes. He pushed them away with dignity, and took off his coat himself. He also took off his collar and his shirt, and made himself ready with his own hands. The executioners, disconcerted for a moment by the King's proud bearing, recovered themselves and surrounded him again in order to bind his hands. 'What are you doing?' said the King, quickly drawing his hands back. 'Binding your hands,' answered one of them. 'Binding me!' said the King, in a voice of indignation, 'never! Do what you have been ordered, but you shall never bind me.' The executioners insisted; they spoke more loudly, and seemed almost to call for help to force the King to obey.

"This was the most agonising moment of this terrible morning; one minute more, and the best of Kings would have received an outrage a thousand times worse than death, by the violence that they were going to use towards him. He seemed to fear this himself, and turning his head, seemed to be asking my advice. At first I remained silent, but when he continued to look at me, I said, with tears in my eyes, 'Sire in this new outrage I see one last resemblance between Your Majesty and the God Who is about to be your reward.'

"At these words he raised his eyes to heaven with an expression of unutterable sadness. 'Surely,' he replied, 'it needs nothing less than His example to make me submit to such an insult.' Then, turning to the executioners, 'Do what you will; I will drink the cup, even to the dregs.'"

Louis's hands were tied behind his back. He was stout and found it difficult to mount the steep steps of the scaffold, and the Abbé said, "Son of Saint-Louis, ascend to the sky (*au ciel*)." Louis then bustled to the front of the scaffold and tried to address the crowd. He commanded the drum-rollers to be silent, and they fell silent, as the Abbé describes: "The steps of the scaffold were extremely steep. The King was obliged to lean on my arm, and from the difficulty they caused him, I feared that his courage was beginning to wane: but what was my astonishment when, arrived at the top, he let go of me, crossed the scaffold with a firm step, silenced with a glance the fifteen or twenty drummers who had been placed directly opposite, and in a voice so loud that it could be heard as far away as the Pont-tournant, pronounced these unforgettable words, 'I die innocent of all the crimes with which I am charged. I forgive those who are guilty of my death, and I pray God that the blood which you are about to shed may never be required of France.'"

After the early weeks of bloodshed at the guillotine, Charles-Henri Sanson had supervised the guillotine rather than operated it. But this was different. He had been given the task of beheading the King, and he had to do this himself. Usually he and his aides lined the prisoners in rows with their backs to the scaffold. When their names were called, one-at-a-time they mounted the scaffold, Charles-Henri on one side, his assistants on the other. They forced their victim down onto a wooden plank and put his neck in the wooden collar known as the *lunette*.

Sanson himself tells us what happened next:

"Here, in accordance with my promise, is the exact truth of what happened at the execution of Louis Capet.

"When he got out of the carriage, he was told to take off his coat; he demurred, saying that the execution could perfectly well be executed dressed the way he was. When informed that this was impossible, he himself helped us to divest him of his coat. The same situation was repeated when it became a question of binding his hands, and again when it was explained to him, he co-operated. He then asked if the drums would continue to roll, and we answered that we did not know, which was the truth. He climbed onto the scaffold and stepped forward as if to speak; but we told him that was forbidden. He then permitted himself to be led to the place where we fastened him down, and said in a clear voice: 'My people, I die innocent.' Afterwards he turned back to us and said: 'Messieurs, I am innocent of everything of which they accuse me. I can only hope that my blood will cement the happiness of the French people.'

"These, citizen, were his true and last words....To pay homage to the truth, he sustained all of this with sang-froid and strength that astonished us. I am convinced that he derived this strength from the tenets of his religion, because no one could have been a greater believer than he.

"[Signed:] Sanson, executioner of Criminal Justice."[90]

This statement was made on February 21, a month after the execution. In 1806 Charles-Henri informed Napoleon, "Sire, I executed Louis XVI."

Louis's neck was too fat to fit into the groove of the *lunette*, and when the blade fell the back of his neck and jaw-bone were "mangled horribly." There was a lot of blood, which collected in a trough under the guillotine. After the Revolution Marie-Antoinette, his wife, had said she wanted to wash her hands in the blood of Frenchmen, and now Frenchmen pressed forward to rub their palms and fingers in his blood. Some put their bloodstained fingers to their lips and said the blood tasted good; others said it tasted salty. Sanson said, "Wait, I'll get you a bucket and then you can dip in more easily."

The Abbé continues his account: "The youngest of the executioners (he looked to be under eighteen years old) seized the severed head and made the rounds of the scaffold, showing it to the populace. This monstrous ritual was accompanied by loud shouting and obscene gestures. A hollow silence ensued and shortly afterwards there were a few weak cries of 'Long live the Republic.' But little by little the voices multiplied and in less than ten minutes the cry, repeated a thousand times became the unanimous shout of a multitude."

It was at this point that an elderly French Templar Mason dipped

his hands in the royal blood and shouted, "I baptise thee in the name of
Liberty and Jacques." He was referring to Jacques de Molay, the last
Templar Grand Master. Another cried out, "Jacques de Molay, you are
avenged."[91]

The body of Louis XVI was dumped in a wicker basket and placed
in the executioner's cart. It was taken to the cemetery of La Madeleine
and thrown into a grave twelve feet deep and covered in quicklime.

The Girondins, under pressure from the more extreme Jacobins,
were responsible for the guillotining of Louis. As with the execution of
Charles I, there are questions to be answered. Who was behind this act?
Why did they want Louis dead? And, given the Templar Masonic
involvement in the American Revolution, was there any significance in
the choice of Louis's prison – the Temple – and in the shouts that
Jacques de Molay, the last Grand Master of the Templars, had been
avenged? Why of all places was Louis imprisoned in the medieval
residence of the Knights Templar, including Jacques de Molay, when
there were several other prisons available? The answer seems to be that
the Orléanist Templar Grand Orient, who were now a front for
Weishaupt's Illuminati, were behind the Girondist execution of the
King.

The Jacobin Revolution

From April to September 1792 the war had gone badly for France,
and there had been French defeats. Now the revolutionaries began to
gain the upper hand. On September 20 French forces under Dumouriez
and Kellermann turned back the Prussian-Austrian force at Valmy. By
November the French had occupied all Belgium. They were now
opposed by a coalition of Austria, Prussia, Spain, the United Provinces
and Great Britain, which managed to check their progress. In December
the Jacobin-dominated Convention issued a proclamation calling on
the proletariat of Europe to rise in revolt against all ordered
government. It was a call to World Revolution in accordance with
Weishaupt's doctrine, but primarily aimed at the Coalition. The
proletariat did not rise.

In the spring of 1793 the war brought new French defeats (in the

United Provinces, Belgium and on the Rhine). Dumouriez deserted and defected to Austria. The Jacobin power had increased and the Girondins were held responsible for the French army's losses and for Dumouriez's defection, and they lost popularity by not addressing workers' grievances. (It was at this point that Thomas Jefferson who had spent three years in France and believed that most Frenchmen were Jacobins and that the Revolution in France was "beautiful," wrote to Brissot on May 8, 1793, saying that he was "eternally attached to the principles" of the French Revolution.)

A Masonic Jacobin-led popular rising against the Girondins began in Paris on May 31, 1793.[92] On June 2 the Convention was surrounded by armed Masonic Jacobin insurgents. The mob had been armed by the Jacobin Commune and was led by Hanriot who, at canon point, ordered the arrest of 29 Girondin deputies whose names he dictated. The Jacobin Montagnards were now in charge, and they took emergency measures to defend the Revolution and to address the workers' demands. Many Girondins escaped to the provinces to urge more uprisings against the Convention, but these lacked popular support. The Girondinist Revolution was at an end.

The Montagnards – the Jacobins Danton, Robespierre and Marat – ran the Convention after the fall of the Girondins and gave political expression to the Revolution. They favoured the lower classes at the expense of the bourgeoisie, whom the Girondins championed. The country was in a different position; France had been invaded by the Coalition, and 60 départments had risen against the Convention. There was civil war involving the counter-revolutionary movement (the Vendée) and moves towards federalism in Normandy and Provence. A new Constitution based on the *Declaration of the Rights of Man* and recognizing the popular right of insurrection was approved by the Convention, but it could not be put into effect until the threat from the Coalition ended.

The power of the remaining Girondins was diminished after the death of Marat. Marat, a symbol of the Montagnards, was put before a Revolutionary tribunal in April but acquitted. He was treating his skin infection in a bath when Charlotte Corday, a young Girondin supporter, gained admittance to his room and stabbed him many times.

On October 10, the Convention decreed that the provisional government of France would be revolutionary until the restoration of peace. In other words the Jacobin Convention approved in June which allowed universal suffrage, the right to subsistence and free education was shelved. In its place would be strong, centralized, dictatorial government. The Committee of Public Safety had been first set up in April. (No one was safe under this Committee which claimed to defend the public.) Robespierre replaced Danton on it in July, and took his place alongside Saint-André, Carnot, Barère, Couthon and Saint-Just. The Committee of General Security was the chief organ of the Police, and the Law of Suspects it operated was responsible for detaining at least 300,000 citizens, 10,000 of whom died in prison.

Robespierre's Dictatorship and the Reign of Terror

Towards the end of 1793, with the French economy in shambles, the new Revolutionary Republic was faced with hundreds of thousands of workers for whom there was no employment; this was especially the case with those who worked in luxury trades. The revolutionary leaders under Robespierre (who had met Weishaupt in Paris) embarked on "depopulation" (or "population reduction" as it is called today), which he called "indispensable." Quite simply, a population in France of 25 million was to be reduced to 16 million (according to one source) or even 8 million. As Nesta Webster put it, "the system of the Terror was thus the answer to the problem of unemployment."[93]

Robespierre

Revolutionary committees in charge of extermination worked day and night. They used maps to work out the number of culls in each town or province that would give a death toll of 8 million. The bourgeoisie suffered. In the provinces, anyone suspected of counter-revolutionary tendencies was executed after a hurried trial. Hundreds soon died in this way.

On September 5, the Terror was handed over to a special army of 6,000 revolutionaries. It imprisoned those denounced by the local revolutionaries, while revolutionary tribunals and military commissions passed 17,000 death sentences.[94]

Now there was human butchery, cannibalism, drunkenness and theft. A campaign also began against religion, and in September hundreds of imprisoned priests were massacred following a call by Clootz, the Illuminized Jacobin author of *The Universal Republic*. Any village or street whose name recalled Christianity, royalty or feudalism was renamed – in accordance with Weishaupt's policy. The Illuminatus Chaumette (who with Hébert controlled the Paris Commune) made hoarding of food a capital offence, and, in a de-Christianization programme which forbad religious ceremonies within or outside churches, posted notices proclaiming "Death is an Eternal Sleep" (a motto of the Illuminati) in cemeteries. The Cathedral of Notre-Dame was renamed the Temple of Reason, and a chorus girl was enthroned as Goddess of Reason. Feasts of Reason were celebrated in the churches in accordance with Weishaupt's teaching, "Reason should be the only code of man." Religious vestments and vessels were mocked, and the calendar was reformed: a week was now regarded as being ten days, and there were three ten-day periods to a month.

To revolutionaries, the Goddess of Reason was synonymous with the Goddess of Nature as she promised a new Golden Age. There was a fusion of rationalism and paganism, which reflected Freemasonry's interest in pre-Christian antiquity (particularly in the figure of Pythagoras, after whom Weishaupt entitled the work in which he set out Illuminism as a political philosophy). Pagan symbols abounded. The new Republic had been declared at the autumnal equinox on September 22, 1792, at the moment (important to pagans) when there was complete equality between day and night, each of which consisted of exactly 12 hours. The high altar at Notre-Dame was replaced by a mound of earth. The Bastille (which had been stormed in July 1789) had now been razed to the ground and its site returned to nature. It became an earthen arena for the pagan festivals of the new Republic. At its centre was a colossal statue of Isis, or Nature herself. The festivals here and at the larger Champs de Mars fuelled a new spirit of nationalism.[95]

On December 4 the Convention passed a law centralizing authority in a parliamentary dictatorship, with the Committee for Public Safety in charge. Never had there been more Public Danger. All local administrators, tribunals and revolutionary committees came under its control, and the Jacobin Clubs monitored all officials. The Committee tried to stop ultra-revolutionary behaviour, including that of de-Christianizers who vandalized or closed churches. Robespierre favoured a deist civil religion and pronounced such behaviour counter-revolutionary.

On Christmas Day 1793, Robespierre justified the collective dictatorship of the National Convention and administrative centralization. In the Convention the de-Christianizers under the atheist Hébert opposed the "Indulgents" under Danton, who felt that the Terror should be relaxed. In early 1794 Robespierre made himself supreme by having both leaders guillotined following speeches he made: Hébert in April for his Weishauptian anti-Christian activities of which Robespierre, as a deist, disapproved; and Danton (with Désmoulins) in May, for seeking to end the Terror prematurely.

Robespierre's "dictatorship" was now being blamed for the Terror. He more than any other members of the Committee of Public Safety was in the public eye, as he was its major spokesman in the Convention. Robespierre was not a socialist but a follower of Rousseau, and therefore not a true Illuminatus in the mould of Weishaupt. While Weishaupt revelled in the anarchy of the Revolution, wanting destruction and liquidation in their own right, Robespierre and Saint-Just saw the anarchy of the Revolution as a means to an end as it was for Rousseau, one that would bring in a future Utopia in which there would be State Socialism once the bourgeoisie was eliminated. Robespierre was aware that the Committee demanded a public spirit free from self-interest, which he called "Virtue" (following Rousseau) and which he thought could be stimulated by Terror.

In a report to the National Convention in May, he had affirmed that there is a Supreme Being, a "God," and an immortal soul as they reminded men of justice. "Terror is nothing other than justice," declared Robespierre. His disciple Saint-Just decreed that the possessions of suspects should be distributed to patriots. On June 4, 1794, at the age of 35, Robespierre was elected President of the Convention and he presided over the first Festival, which was dedicated to his cult of the Supreme Being. The Illuminized Weishauptian Atheists who followed the cult of Reason were offended at this. News came through that the French army had won a brilliant victory over the Austrians and, feeling strengthened, Robespierre talked of the need for a new purge. On June 10, the Committee of Public Safety introduced new repressive measures and unleashed "The Great Terror" in which 1,300 were guillotined in June alone. It is estimated that 17,000 "counter-revolutionaries" were guillotined during the Reign of Terror in Paris in 1793-4.[96]

Robespierre showed contempt for the Convention from his position of absolute power. He had made 450 speeches in the Legislative Assembly and Jacobin Club, and had become irritable with tiredness. He stayed away from the National Convention and the Committee of Public Safety, speaking only in the Templar Jacobin Club. Fearing for their own lives, members of the Committee of General Security began to plot against him. Robespierre went to the National Convention on July 26, and Tallien, representing a group who were afraid that it might be their turn for the guillotine next unless they got rid of him, accused him (Robespierre "the Incorruptible") of despotism in the National Convention.

Robespierre tried to obtain a hearing, but was arrested and taken to the Luxembourg Prison. The warden refused to jail him, so the Commune released him and he lived in the City Hall (Hôtel de Ville). The *sansculottes* (his mob of small tradesmen supporters) did not rescue him, and the National Convention declared him an outlaw. He refused to lead an insurrection. On July 27 (9 Thermidor) an armed force entered the Hôtel de Ville, and there was a scuffle as the mob tried to arrest him. Robespierre tried to shoot himself but only succeeded in shattering his jaw. On July 28 he was dragged bleeding to the scaffold in the Place de la Révolution (Place de la Concorde), and died on the guillotine with Saint-Just. The tyrant's supporters in the Assembly and the militants in the Commune followed – 108 in all. On July 27 the guillotine executed 45 anti-Robespierrists and during the next three days, 104 Robespierrists. The social laws and ideal of economic equality were no longer applied.[97]

The Thermidorean Revolution

The Thermidorean Revolution under Carnot (who had taken over military offices in August 1793) was a settling of accounts between extremist leaders rather than a coup by moderates against extremists. However, once Robespierre was dead the Convention relaxed, power shifted from the left to the centre, and then to the right, and the change amounted to a moderate coup. It ended the most extreme political phase of the French Revolution, and created a brief "White Terror" against Jacobins. The Revolution reasserted government by the National Convention and the nation at the expense of the Committee of Public Safety and the Paris Commune. The Committee was disarmed, the prisons were emptied and the Jacobin Clubs were purged and closed in November. The law of June 10 (22 Prairial) which unleashed the bloodiest phase of the Terror was repealed.[98] Executions now happened less frequently but 300,000 had died since the beginning of the Terror.[99]

In the south (in Provence and the Rhône) old scores were settled by lynchings, murders and prison massacres of *sansculottes* (Robespierre's supporters). Price controls imposed by Robespierre were abolished. There was a new economic crisis and a new shortage of grain and flour. The Royalists came back to life.

By 1795, there was a famine. Nevertheless the French won a victory in Flanders and Prussia withdrew from the war in March. Instead of implementing the 1793 democratic Constitution, the Thermidorean Convention established a liberal republic similar to that of 1791 with a two-house legislature and a five-man executive Directory.

Paine

Into this new society came the Illuminatus Thomas Paine, who had left America and returned to England in 1787. A Sionist Rosicrucian like Franklin and a Templar Grand Orient Mason (also like Franklin), in 1789 he had warned Pitt (anonymously) not to get involved in a war with France (as war "has but one thing certain and that is increase of taxes"). Edmund Burke had attacked the French Revolution in *Reflections on the Revolution in France* (1790), in which he spoke of "disasters" by which "the glory of Europe is extinguished forever." Paine replied with *Rights of Man* (1791) and a year later brought out *Rights of Man, Part 2*, which analyzed the social conditions in Europe – poverty, illiteracy, unemployment – that had created the Revolution. Paine's arrest was ordered and his book suppressed; but Paine was then *en route* to France, where he hailed the fall of the monarchy but was aghast at the prospect of the King's being guillotined (he recommended banishment). He lived in Bonneville's house and shared Bonneville's wife in a *ménage à trois*, and like Bonneville had been initiated into the Illuminati by Bode. When Robespierre took over, Paine was put in prison (from December 1793 to November 1794) and wrote *Age of Reason*. (*Part 2* followed after his release in 1796.) In these works he revealed his loyalty to the Illuminati whom he had helped infiltrate various lodges. A deist who believed in a Supreme Being (like Robespierre), though regarded as an atheist, Paine was readmitted to the National Convention and stayed in France until 1802. Then he returned to the United States – to discover he had been forgotten.[100]

Babeuf

The new Directory had to deal with the conspiracy of Babeuf,[101] an Illuminatus and disciple of Weishaupt codenamed Gracchus and the French precursor of Communism. Babeuf had taken issue with Robespierre over "the immense secret" of the Terror, a plan to reduce the population of France by as much as 15 million so that the rest of the population could have bread and work. Though in sympathy with Robespierre and the *Declaration of the Rights of Man*, he thought this too drastic. He had already been put in prison for disagreeing with a plan to drive the people to revolt by spreading news of a fictitious famine and then to kill them as insurgents; now he denounced the depopulators in his pamphlet *Sur la Dépopulation de la France*. After the fall of Robespierre Babeuf criticized the Thermidorean Reaction as a disaster and said that the only hope was to complete Robespierre's work and maintain the Constitution of 1793, which was founded on the *Declaration of the Rights of Man* but had never been implemented.

Babeuf was again thrown in prison, at Plessis, then at Arras, where he met like minds who agreed to work for a Weishauptian social revolution for "the common happiness and true equality." Out of prison the *Babouvistes* (Darthé, Germain, Bodson and Buonarotti) remained united "to make equality triumph" and met out of sight of the police in the gardens of the Abbey of Sainte-Geneviève or in the refectory or crypt. As the Panthéon was nearby they were sometimes known as the Panthéonistes. In due course some 2,000 attended these meetings, and now a small secret committee met in the house of Amar, one of the most feared members of the Committee of General Security during the Terror. Property is theft, Babeuf and the others reasoned, and so "no individual property shall exist." The Marquis d'Antonelle said: "The State of Communism is the only just, the only good one; without this state of things no peaceful and really happy societies can exist."

In 1795-6 the Directory objected to Babeuf's activities and he went into hiding from where he edited his two newspapers. When an article was read aloud at a meeting by Darthé, Napoleon himself arrived, closed the place down and put the key in his pocket.

Babeuf decided on a Weishauptian "Secret Directorate" of 12 men who worked in different districts and would not know each other.[102] In April 1796 his *Manifesto of the Equals* was finished; it proclaimed a "Republic of the Equals" in which there would be "community of goods and of labour," i.e. equal pay for all in return for equal hours regardless of the nature of the work. This was to be achieved by peaceful means, yet the populace was to be incited to violence; and on the "Great Day" the "Republic of Equality" came into being, there would be no opposition – only 17,000 men marching on the Legislative Assembly, the army headquarters and the ministers' houses.

The march was planned for May 11. It was betrayed by a soldier called Grisel, and on the morning of the march a placard from the Directory warned the citizens of Paris of a plot. Police then seized Babeuf and Buonarotti, and soon afterwards 45 other leaders. From February to May 1797 all the leaders of the conspiracy were tried. Babeuf blamed superiors in the Illuminati: "The heads and the leaders needed a director of public opinion, I was in the position to enlist this opinion." On May 27 Babeuf and Darthé were sentenced to death along with 28 others (*Babouvistes*) and despite attempts to stab themselves, both of them died on the scaffold.[103]

So ended the French Revolution's last attempt to bring in Weishaupt's scheme, which had been kept alive in the Illuminized lodges referred to by Paine in *Age of Reason* (1794) and by Robison in *Proofs of a Conspiracy* (1797).

NAPOLEON'S CONSOLIDATION

Europe Becomes a Templar Republic

Napoleon gave physical expression to the Revolution. He was selected by Templar Freemasonry to consolidate the Revolution in his name as there were rumours that the exiled Bourbon Royalists would return.[104] The Templars wanted the unification of Europe under a Masonic republic (and not under a Merovingian Grail King of Jerusalem). Dillon writes: "As a lesser evil therefore, and as a means of forwarding the unification of Europe which they had planned by his conquests, the Freemasons placed supreme power in the hands of Bonaparte, and urged him on in his career."[105]

Napoleon was a Templar Jacobin.[106] He sympathized with the Illuminati until they were exposed in 1785; then he became a Templar and planned to capture the Roman Catholic Church so that he could seize the Templar documents stored in the Vatican (as he did in 1810, bringing over three thousand cases of documents from the Vatican to Paris). *Mackey's Encyclopedia* claims that Napoleon was a Mason who was toasted as such by "the Strassburg Lodge."[107]

The Templars brought Napoleon to power through Charles-Morris de Talleyrand-Perigord,[108] a Catholic Cardinal who had sided with the Sionist Illuminati in 1779 and been initiated into an Illuminized Sionist lodge by Mirabeau in 1786. In that year he was a co-founder of the Breton Club, which was taken over by the Templars and renamed the Jacobin Club. Talleyrand became a Templar. At the time he was a member of a Sionist Rosicrucian secret society, the Philadelphes or

Napoleon I, Emperor of the French

Philadelphians ("the circle of the free brothers"), which had apparently been founded in Narbonne in 1780.[109] Its founder was the man who had been Grand Master of the Priory of Sion from 1801, Charles Nodier, the son of a Jacobin French solicitor and a Templar Master Mason and president of his town's revolutionary tribunal. He was a minor literary figure, who invented the genre of melodrama and was Victor Hugo's mentor. It seems that, like Franklin and Voltaire, Talleyrand was a Priory of Sion double agent and that he was acting as an agent of Sion when he spent time with the Templars.

The Philadelphians saw the whole world as a brotherhood, and revolutionary Paris as the centre of a world republic. The seal of the Philadelphians was a 5-pointed star, which Nodier interpreted as a symbol of universal love. (The Philadelphian seal has passed into the design of the Pentagon of the US military.) In 1797 Nodier was exiled to Besançon and named it Philadelphia, then changed the name to Crotona in honour of Pythagoras. (He was the author of *The Apotheosis of Pythagoras*.) This was the internationalist milieu in which Talleyrand moved.

It was at the Jacobin Club that Talleyrand first met Napoleon.[110] When the four Revolutions had run their course Talleyrand advised the Templars, "Put Napoleon on the throne and open the Grand Orients." If he succeeded in persuading the Templars to put Napoleon on the throne he planned to surround Napoleon with Sionist Illuminati, who had been hidden in the Grand Orient lodges until they were closed down in favour of the Jacobin Clubs (see pp321–2).[111]

Napoleon, a *protégé* of Robespierre, had been spotted by an Illuminist, the Vicomte de Barras, who saw him fight off besieging English and Spanish forces at Toulon in 1793. The next day he was promoted Brigadier-General.[112] As a young artillery officer he had put down a rising against the Directory – shot down a column of rebels marching on the National Convention – in Paris in 1795 with just "a whiff of grapeshot." Rewarded with a command against the Austrians in North Italy, Napoleon[113] had triumphed and set up the Cisalpine and Ligurian republics and forced Austria to give up the Austrian Netherlands to France. He had prepared to invade England (while other French armies were setting up the Roman and Helvetic republics) and then went to Egypt to threaten the British Empire but was defeated by Nelson in the naval battle at Aboukir.

The Directory was unpopular following the failure of its currency reform. Barras, who had plotted against Robespierre, was made commander-in-chief of the French military forces, and was then appointed (along with Carnot) to the five-man Directory which governed France; he had become the most powerful man in the country, and he chose Napoleon to lead France's military forces. The election for the legislature in 1797 saw a Royalist majority, and the Directory of five split. Napoleon gave military backing to the majority of three and nullified the election in September. He also clamped down on Bonneville's journalist Social Circle. Outraged at the stifling of free speech, Bonneville compared him to Cromwell as a dictator who had betrayed the revolution. In 1799 the French were defeated by Austria and Russia in Italy. Napoleon returned to Paris and conspired with one of the Directors, Barras, to overthrow the government. (Napoleon fainted at the crucial moment, which suggests he was worked up.) Napoleon was now the first of three consuls.

Having seized power in November 1799, Napoleon abolished the Directory and, fearing that Barras was about to restore the monarchy, cut his link with him, and became sole consul for life. From being invested in twelve (the Committee of Public Safety), power had contracted to five (the Directory) and then three (the Consuls) and now one (Napoleon).

As soon as Napoleon seized power, the Grand Orient lodges opened everywhere.[114] In 1801, however, they merged with the republican Templar Scottish Rite.[115] A plan supposed to benefit the Sionists was now seized upon by the Templars, who saw their chance to unify Europe into a republic under Napoleon. The Templars, through the police chief Joseph Fouché, now suggested that his life consulate should become a hereditary empire, and in 1804 the Templars reluctantly allowed Napoleon to declare himself Emperor of the French.[116] As in the case of Rome, a republic had given way to Empire, and, with encouragement from the Templar Grand Orient Illuminati, Napoleon, who now saw himself as the universal master of Europe, endeavoured to resemble Augustus.

The Templars then conspired with the Empire to undermine the Austrians and Russians at Austerlitz by making information available to the French commanders and hence to give Napoleon the victory.[117] Napoleon's intelligence service was run by Masons,[118] and until 1810 his progress was dramatic. Napoleon installed his brothers on the conquered thrones of Europe – Joseph as King of Naples in 1806 and then as King of Spain in 1808 (when his brother-in-law Murat became King of Naples), Louis as King of Holland and Jerome as King of

Westphalia – and, swollen with pride, wanted to be King of France and take to wife a Habsburg princess to make his reign more legitimate. In 1809 he divorced Josephine of the House of Bourbon and Metternich, the Austrian Minister of Foreign Affairs arranged for Napoleon to marry the Merovingian princess, Archduchess Marie Louise of the House of Habsburg.[119]

Sion Overthrows Napoleon

The Templars now withdrew support for Napoleon, fearing that a dynasty of Napoleonic kings would prevent their universal republic from coming into being.[120] Napoleon in turn showed coldness towards the Templars and sought to prevent them from propagandizing. In 1810 they excommunicated him[121] and (through intermediaries) urged on his disastrous expedition to Moscow where he lost 500,000 men in temperatures that reached -35^0C.

English Sionists had allowed Napoleon to disrupt Europe as they needed chaos to increase their control. They did little before 1810, leaving Napoleon to cause havoc and devastation, but now they plotted to overthrow him. The Philadelphians were central to the plot. The Sionist Rosicrucian German prince William of Hesse had proposed a joint Anglo-German action against the French, and in 1812 the Sionist Gen. Malet, a Rosicrucian Philadelphian, tried to overthrow the Empire. He acted in conjunction with the Grand Master of the Grand Orient, Gen. Massena. The plot included Charles Nodier (Grand Master of the Priory of Sion), Talleyrand, Moreau and Trochot, all Masons. Before the expedition the assembly of Philadelphians was told that Napoleon "would be the last of the oppressors of Jerusalem," meaning that he would be replaced by a Merovingian King of Jerusalem.[122]

Malet was defeated, and the Priory of Sion then used the press to manipulate public opinion (something that happens today). To this end Charles Nodier used his literary talents. The English Rosicrucian Priory of Sion planned the downfall of Napoleon with leaks, lies, partial truths and misinformation. The Templars had reluctantly permitted Napoleon's despotism to advance its universal republic; now they drew the line at kingship and no longer approved of Napoleon's autocracy. They decided to replace him with a member of the House of Bourbon who would be distant from the Catholic Church. After looking at the Masonic King of Holland they opted for Louis XVIII – in June 1795 the Dauphin Louis XVII, on whose education Louis XVI had lavished so much care, mysteriously disappeared while being held in the Temple, and this was his uncle – whom they could control, thus advancing the Templars and wrecking the Church.[123]

The Sionist Merovingian Grail Kings of Europe had by now realized that Illuminized Freemasonry was a threat to their thrones; and they aligned themselves with the German *Tugendbund* (Union of Virtue) under the English Rosicrucian Masonic lodge at Hanover. This was their base for recovering or protecting their thrones under the leadership of Great Britain, which was fighting to oust Napoleon. (Their funding came from the House of Rothschild.) The British Monarchy, Church and Freemasonry were now in alliance.[124]

The Jewish Mayer Amschel "Rothschild" had died in 1812. His eldest son Amschel and his youngest son Carl were managing his bank in Frankfurt; the English Rosicrucian Nathan was running the London branch (England being the most important commercial power in Europe); Solomon was living in Paris and James at Gravelines, near Calais. Nathan sought support from the European kings in the London lodges, and in 1807 the Royal Navy blockaded French ports. In 1810 Rothschilds had financed a revival of the *Tugendbund* which was directed by the Sionist Rosicrucians who opposed Napoleon – unlike the first *Tugendbund*, which was Grand Orient. This new Tugendbund acted as a resistance movement that undermined Napoleon as he spread revolution throughout Europe. When Napoleon realized what was happening he suppressed the *Tugendbund*, and made anti-Masonic statements, saying that Illuminized Freemasonry was "a state within a state" whose influence should be combated.

England was distracted by the American war from 1812 to 1814, but once the treaty of December 1814 was signed, she was back to full strength and, in alliance with Austria, Russia and Prussia, forced Paris to capitulate. In April Talleyrand announced the deposition of the Emperor in favour of Louis XVIII, who had been in exile in Sicily; and Napoleon was exiled to Elba.

Napoleon escaped during the Congress of Vienna in 1815. England sent the English Freemason, the Duke of Wellington, from Portugal to meet Napoleon at Waterloo. He was funded by Nathan Rothschild (acting in the tradition of the Jewish funders of James II and William III), who sent money to his brother James, who handled financial transactions for the French government, and who sent it on to Wellington via Spain.[125] At one point Napoleon seemed to be winning the battle of Waterloo. In fact, Marshal Soult, his second-in-command deliberately failed to carry out his orders, and so gave the Sionist Rosicrucians their victory. After the battle Napoleon was exiled to St Helena. The Templars had raised him up; Sion had brought him down.

When the first military envoy arrived in London with news of Napoleon's success the London stock market collapsed. Nathan bought the stocks at low prices and when they rose he became the richest man in England, and eventually controlled England's central bank. He achieved this by using modern, aggressive business methods. It seems that he had promised a prize to the boat which supplied news of the outcome of the battle fastest. His agent Roworth waited in Ostend, obtained the first news report of the battle in the Dutch Gazette and caught a boat sailing to England. He arrived in London on June 20, 1815, a day ahead of Wellington's envoy Major Percy.[126]

Why did Napoleon fall? Because he lost the support of the Templars, and because Sionist Rosicrucianism with the help of the Rothschilds outmanoeuvred the weak Grand Orients, who had to accept the permanent exile of Napoleon and the return of the Bourbons. The Grand Orient may have been politically weak but it influenced anti-Napoleonic soldiers, including Russians who took it back to Russia where a Grand Orient lodge was founded in 1816. (Forty more lodges soon sprouted from it in Russia and it was implicated in the attempted Revolution of 1825.)[127]

At the Sionist Congress of Vienna of 1815 (and the Congress of

Verona of 1822) the European monarchs renounced the atheistic Grand Orient and supported England; and the Rothschilds moved their banking headquarters to London, and a long association began between the ex-German Rothschilds from Frankfurt and the ex-German Royal Family from Hanover. Uniting with English Sionist Rosicrucianism was the only hope for monarchs opposed to Templar Republicans who were after their crowns. They realized that the Napoleonic wars were a Templar attempt to usurp their thrones.

With Talleyrand representing France, the Congress of Vienna tried to check Templar Republicans by returning the Catholic Church to its unifying role in Europe – and Sion and Catholicism have been in alliance against Templarism ever since. The Congress tried to establish a monarchical United Federation of Europe against Templarism (Metternich's idea), a confederation of independent kingdoms with a governing body in Vienna – a forerunner of the European Community. This was to involve Sweden, Denmark, Spain, Portugal, the Papacy, Bavaria, Saxony, Wurttemberg and France, but not Russia as Tsar Alexander I was immovably Grand Orient. This plan of Metternich's was a first step to a one-world government.[128]

This plan did not happen because Russia wanted a share of the spoils of victory. Instead, out of the Congress came a Triple Alliance, negotiated by Talleyrand with Metternich and Castlereagh, between France, Austria and Great Britain, with France offering an army of 300,000 to check Russia's ambitions in Poland. Russia suspected that the Illuminati were controlling the Congress through Talleyrand, but Weishaupt was still in exile and Nathan Rothschild was not present. Weishaupt was no longer significant; it was the Priory of Sion who counted, as they gained the advantage in their long struggle with the Templars.

The Congress also tried to win the Jews back from their Templar liberators. It established Switzerland as a neutral state for storing Sionist wealth; the Sionist financial headquarters became Zurich, and Sionist Rosicrucianism systematically began to absorb the Swiss Grand Orient lodges.[129]

Sionist Rosicrucian Freemasonry was deist, which to many Freemasons meant Luciferian. Templar Freemasonry was atheist. The Illuminati had been a merging of the two traditions, and some Illuminati were both deist and atheist at the same time. (Weishaupt had seen the Supreme Being as Lucifer – Satan – and Robespierre's deism was a measure of Weishaupt's influence early on.) As the crowned heads of Europe redrew the European map, it was clear that European deists had now got together to keep the Templar atheists at bay.

SUMMARY: THE REVOLUTIONARY DYNAMIC OF THE FRENCH REVOLUTION

What lingers in the mind after examining the revolutionary dynamic of the French Revolution is the idealism of some of its figures – Robespierre and Saint-Just wanted State Socialism, Virtue and Reason – and yet the feeling that in their case somehow the plan went terribly wrong. Three hundred thousand deaths, the guillotine running non-stop with queues of terrified people waiting their turn after hurried trials (if they were lucky) and a plan to kill as many as 15 million French citizens to make the food and jobs go round cannot be a defensible way of reaching Utopia. (It was aristocratic and professional minds that took these decisions. It was not the Paris mob that created the French Revolution, but the aristocrats and professional bourgeoisie: the well-born Duke d'Orléans and Count Mirabeau, the physician Marat and the lawyer Robespierre.) What comes across is the rational virtue of their aims and the viciousness with which they implemented them. Reason and human compassion became separated, and reason and virtue dictated that a whole class (in Robespierre's case the bourgeoisie) should be wiped out. The logic of Robespierre and Saint-Just marked the twilight of the rational Enlightenment, whose notions of progress perished with the guillotine.

We are also left with an impression of how self-interested and unscrupulous some of the revolutionaries were. Some, like Weishaupt, wanted to create chaos in order to rule the world. Others, like the Duke of Orléans (and later Napoleon), wanted to be King of France. In the intellectual and political expression of the Revolution's occult idea some were positioning themselves and considering their own advancement more than promoting a new Utopian society. The pockmarked Marat seemed to have been behind the massacre of the prisoners and the invasion of the Tuileries Palace. Clootz was behind the massacre of the imprisoned priests. Their motives had more to do with Vice than Virtue, with lies and deception rather than Truth. They were not well-intentioned but opportunistic chancers and self-promoters.

We are also struck by how treacherous some of the revolutionaries were. Like Franklin and Voltaire, Mirabeau and Talleyrand played a double game – and both avoided the guillotine. Cagliostro was a brilliant con-man and treacherous towards Weishaupt, and his malevolence deserved to be punished on the scaffold.

Some of the revolutionaries were just naive: Rousseau in his view of civilization, which Weishaupt twisted to his own nefarious ends and anarchistic advantage; and Moses Mendelssohn, who was prepared to believe that Weishaupt supported the aims of his Haskala or Jewish Enlightenment. Weishaupt took advantage of his good will and readiness to fund the Illuminati in the early stages, before he knew what direction the new organization would take.

We can acknowledge that some of the revolutionaries were well-intentioned: Danton, for example, who died trying to end the Terror.

It has to be said that Louis XVI, surrounded by such a scheming group of men, precipitated the Revolution by clumsy diplomacy (ignoring advice, for example, Mirabeau's), vanity and weakness. A cleverer monarch could have prevented the Revolution, for example by not appointing Necker and not following the wishes of his pro-Austrian wife.

Without a doubt, the French Revolution did advance French society: it gave it a Constitution with human rights it would not otherwise have had, and took it from an absolute monarchy to a constitutional republic. The pain in human suffering was very great, perhaps too great. The depopulation policy involving queues at the guillotine was too high a price to pay for the Revolution's gains.

Revolutions occur when a religious society within a religious civilization suddenly turns secular and has its institutions challenged. All civilizations go through a stage in which one or more of their religious societies are convulsed by anti-religious, secular ideas – such as the enthronement of Reason. A revolution is a sudden, violent transformation in a society when its civilization's religion is challenged by secularizing progress. Societies can progress at the same time that civilizations decay. It is as if secularization has risen behind a dam and suddenly overflows. A society can become more secular and humane while the civilization, removed from its original metaphysical idea, decays. Secularization seems progressive but actually accelerates the decline and decay of a civilization, while bolstering human conditions. Progress through the guillotine can correctly be seen as a regressive move, though there was amelioration of the lot of those citizens who lived to see the return of the Bourbons.

To sum up in terms of the revolutionary dynamic, the heretical occult vision of the French Revolution came from the Utopianism of the Cathars. The heretical occult interpreter was the neo-Cathar Rousseau, who revived the "back-to-Nature" vision of the Cathars and developed Sir Thomas More's and Francis Bacon's ideas of an ideal society in which men loved their neighbour. Rousseau may have been directly influenced by Charles de Lorraine, who certainly influenced Weishaupt.

The revolutionary originator who corrupted the vision of the Cathars and Rousseau was Weishaupt, who developed the Cathars' rejection of the Church and envisaged a Utopia in which Supreme Reason flourished. He wanted civilization to be destroyed so there could be a one-world state that would return men to the Garden of Eden and follow the Serpent's lure, "Ye shall be as gods." Weishaupt was the prophet of the enthronement of man made god through Reason. Such spiritual ideas (if we can use the word "spiritual" of the Satanist Weishaupt) were at the back of the Templars' drive for a universal republic and the Sionists' expansion of the Venetian kingdom of Jerusalem into a world-state.

The thoughtful intellectual interpreter who gave the vision a new slant was Cagliostro. He was aided by Moses Mendelssohn, who was identified with the *Tugendbund* lodges. The semi-political intellectual who later became political was Mirabeau. The intellectual expression of the French Revolution reached the people via the journalist Nicholas Bonneville, whose new journals spread the revolutionary message from July 1789 to 1794. The early revolutionary dynamic of the French Revolution can be stated as follows:

Heretical occult vision	Heretical occult interpreter	Occult revolutionary originator	Thoughtful intellectual interpreter	Semi-political intellectual interpreter
Catharism/ Bacon/Sionist Rosicrucianism (via Charles de Lorraine?)	Neo-Cathar Rousseau	Weishaupt	Cagliostro	Mirabeau

Those who gave intellectual expression to the French heretical occult idea were all members of the Illuminati, which was founded to combine Sionists and Templars into one organization.

The political expression of the revolutionary idea was fourfold as there were four separate French Revolutions – the Orléanist, Girondinist, Jacobin and Thermidorean Revolutions – all of which followed in quick succession and had their own leaders. The one that most made its mark was the Jacobin, under Robespierre. The consolidation of the French Revolution was under Napoleon, who was given power by Templars and driven from power by Sionists.

The full revolutionary dynamic of the French Revolution is as follows:

Heretical occult inspiration	Intellectual expression	Political expression	Physical consolidation
Kabbalistic Cathars/ Bacon/Sionist Rosicrucianism: de Lorraine?/ Rousseau	Weishaupt/ Cagliostro/ Mendelssohn/ Mirabeau/ Bonneville/ Marat	Duke of Orléans/ Brissot/ Robespierre/ Carnot	Napoleon

We can state the revolutionary dynamic of the ideas behind the French Revolution as follows:

Heretical occult inspiration	Intellectual expression	Political expression	Physical consolidation
Luciferianism/ Catharism	Illuminism (e.g. of Social Circle)/ Egalitarianism	Republicanism	Terror and conquest of Europe

CHAPTER SIX

THE IMPERIALIST REVOLUTION IN BRITAIN AND GERMANY

The governments of the present day have to deal not merely with other governments, with emperors, kings and ministers, but also with secret societies which have everywhere their unscrupulous agents, and can at the last moment upset all the governments' plans.

Disraeli, speech in Aylesbury on September 10, 1876

The culmination of the Imperialist Revolution was the confrontation between the two nation-state empires it had created, the British and the German Empires, in the titanic conflict of the First World War. Its aim all along had been the Weishauptian one of levelling mighty nation-states through conflict as a preparation for two more revolutions – the Russian and New World Order revolutions – which would bring in a world government. As the purpose of the Imperialist Revolution was to create two warring empires which might destroy each other to begin this levelling process, we need to see it from both the British and German angles.

Although we are focusing on Great Britain and Germany, we cannot ignore France and Italy as they were the cradle and battleground for imperialist developments in the other two nations, and both the Rothschilds[1] and Mazzini were very active in France and Italy.

ROTHSCHILDS' SIONIST EUROPEAN IMPERIALISM

Rothschilds' Fortune

We have seen (p289) that Adam Weishaupt seems to have been funded from 1770 to 1776 by the newly organized House of Rothschild,[2] and that Mayer Amschel "Rothschild" appears to have met Weishaupt in 1773 to plan world revolution.[3] The Order of the Golden Dawn was Weishaupt's attempt to create a private Order for the Rothschilds,[4] who adopted Weishaupt's ideas and became extremely influential in the Illuminati as their business influence grew. From very early on the House of Rothschild was looking for an opportunity to create a Weishauptian world rule[5] on the back of a Great Power that could be urged to become expansionist – imperialist.

By 1806 Napoleon was master of mainland Europe. He had defeated Austria and punished Russia; only Great Britain stood against him. As he prepared to invade Great Britain the German Rothschilds continued to trade with England and to give clandestine support to Napoleon's enemies.

The House of Rothschild "borrowed" to get started. Mayer Amschel "Rothschild" had been agent for the Elector, Prince William IX, Landgrave of Hesse-Kassel, grandson of George II and cousin of George III, who inherited the largest private fortune in Europe when his father died in 1785: $40 million. The money had been paid by Great Britain for the use of 16,800 Hessian troops during the American Revolution. (William's father never paid the troops, but kept the money for himself.) When Napoleon invaded Germany in 1806, William fled to Denmark, leaving some of this fortune ($3 million or £600,000) with Rothschild,[6] who had just finished burying the treasure in wine casks in his little garden in Frankfurt when Napoleon's republican soldiers arrived. They robbed him of all his own money (40,000 thalers) but did not find William's hoard.

William had given Budrus von Carlhausen a power of attorney; Budrus made Mayer Amschel "Rothschild" his banker and gave him

The Elector of Hesse-Kassel entrusts his treasure to Mayer Amschel
Rothschild, Gutle and their daughter Henrietta

responsibility for collecting interest on royal loans. Soon the
Rothschilds were managing the Elector's investments, and in due course
Budrus persuaded William to allow Mayer Amschel "Rothschild's" son
Nathan, who was based in London, to handle some of his funds. In
1808 Nathan bought £150,000 worth of British government 3 per cent
stock, and in 1809 he received another £150,000. The bonds were in
his own name, and the City was astounded by the scale of transactions
that this investment permitted. Although the Elector received no
certificates for the £300,000, Nathan started dealing in bullion, some of
which was sent to the Continent. Napoleon was trying to block British
trade with Europe, and Nathan Rothschild's ships, putting out from
Folkestone under brave captains, time and again slipped past Napoleon's
blockading fleet.

According to numerous reports, the Rothschilds financed Napoleon
after he declared his wish to be King in 1810,[7] a declaration which lost

him the confidence of the Templars. Napoleon was beholden both to the House of Habsburg, who had supplied his new wife, and to Metternich, who had arranged the match, and Metternich would probably have introduced Napoleon to Nathan's brother James, a fellow Sionist who was based in Paris.[8]

At the same time that James was dealing with Napoleon, Mayer Amschel "Rothschild" sent some of Elector William's money to London so that Nathan could finance the Duke of Wellington. Nathan invested it in 800,000 pounds of gold from the East India Company, which he knew would be needed for Wellington's Peninsular War.[9] He then made a 50 per cent profit on the sale of Wellington's paper money, a profit on the sale of the gold to Wellington, a profit on repurchasing it, and a profit on forwarding it to Portugal for the Duke. We have already seen (p351) that Nathan made a fortune by bringing news of a British defeat at Waterloo to London. The Rothschilds may also have had a hand in Napoleon's defeat. The French Emperor felt unwell on the eve of the battle of Waterloo, and may have suffered arsenic poisoning; and Marshal Soult, his no. 2 who took his orders from the Rothschilds[10] having been a recipient of James Rothschild's funding during the five years of the Peninsular War in Spain when he was in charge of the French forces, may have disobeyed Napoleon at their behest. In other words the Rothschilds backed both sides at the battle of Waterloo, making sure that Napoleon lost while giving out the news that he had won.

By the time of his death Mayer Amschel "Rothschild" had become the richest man the world had ever known.[11] This merchant inspirer of imperialism had founded new Rothschild banks in England, France and Germany before he died in 1812. His will established that all important posts within Rothschilds were to be held by male members of the family[12] and that the oldest son of the oldest son (eventually Nathan) was to be patriarch (in the time-honoured Jewish manner). The will stipulated that male members of the family should only marry their first or second cousins to keep the wealth in the family. It also specified that there was to be no public inventory or publication of the value of Mayer

Amschel "Rothschild's" estates.

Mayer Amschel "Rothschild" had five sons, who were symbolized in the quiver of five arrows, joined at the centre, that forms the family crest. He spread them among different European countries. As we have just seen, during the Napoleonic wars one branch of the family funded Napoleon while others funded Great Britain, Germany and other European nations. The different branches are distinguished by the initials of the five sons: Nathan Mayer Rothschild was head of the new Rothschild bank in London, England, which was known as N. M. Rothschild and Sons; James Mayer Rothschild was in charge of the Rothschild bank in Paris, France, which was known as Messieurs de Rothschild Frères; the Rothschild bank in Frankfurt, Germany was known as M. A. Rothschild & Söhne after Mayer Amschel Rothschild; the Rothschild bank in Austria was known as S. M. von Rothschild after Salomon Mayer; and Carl Mayer Rothschild was head of the Rothschild bank in Naples, C. M. von Rothschild. So influential were the Rothschilds now that Amschel Mayer Rothschild said in 1838, "Permit me to issue and control the money of a nation, and I care not who makes its laws."[13]

At the time of the Congress of Vienna, (1814-15) most of the European nations were in debt to the Rothschilds, who hoped to emancipate the Jews of Europe from police control and to create a League of Nations (an Illuminati aspiration) that would give them political control over the world. Prince Metternich, the Austrian Minister of Foreign Affairs and the most influential statesman in Europe, was regarded by some as a Rothschilds agent.[14] He secured an Alliance with Prussia and Russia, hoping to secure a United Federation of Europe as a stepping-stone to world rule. Russia saw through the plan and it never happened. In dudgeon Nathan Rothschild vowed that one day his family would destroy the Tsar and his family.[15]

The reorganization of Europe after the Congress of Vienna had put republican Templarism on the defensive. Incredibly, though Louis XVI had been beheaded by Templars, his younger brother the Bourbon Louis XVIII, to whom N. M. Rothschild advanced £200,000 to cover the immediate expenses of the return of the Bourbons to Paris in 1814,[16] favoured the republican Templar Grand Orient.[17] He made the Sionist Talleyrand, who had many Templar contacts, a Minister, and gave positions to other Masons of Napoleon's time.

Nathan Mayer Rothschild multiplied his wealth dramatically – some estimates say by 2,500 times, others 6,500 – by speculating on the outcome of the battle of Waterloo in 1815.[18] The story is that the London stock market had plunged in expectation of Napoleon's victory. One of his agents, named Roworth, waited at Ostend and brought the first news of Wellington's victory in the first copy of the Dutch Gazette. He caught a boat sailing for London and gave

Nathan Rothschild

the news to Nathan, who reported it to the British government via Herries. Nathan immediately bought up stock at the low price and when it rose made profits of between £20m and £135m. These enabled him to open the Bank of England. Rothschildian sources[19] vary the story; they allege that it was said that Nathan was present at the battle and rode with Wellington, that he sent a message by carrier-pigeons. They maintain that this story had long been debunked, while acknowledging that some gain was made out of the result at Waterloo.

The House of Rothschilds saw their chance to control France in October 1818. The French government was in debt, having secured loans from a French bank in Ouvrard and from London's Baring Brothers, and Rothschilds now bought up French government bonds and dumped them on the open market, bringing down the price and causing panic. Rothschilds, who had already gained control of the English economy in 1815, thus gained control of France.[20]

Between 1815 and 1820 the financial capital of the English branch of Rothschilds had been increased (on a conservative view) from $3 million to $7,500 million – 2,500 times in the course of five years. The five brothers recognized Nathan as foremost and gave him a bigger share of Rothschilds' profits in the division of capital from the family business. The figures in French francs (£1 = approx. 25 francs) are as follows:

	1818	1825	1828
Amschel	7,776,000	18,943,750	19,963,750
Salomon	7,776,000	18,943,750	19,963,750
Nathan	12,000,000	26,875,000	28,200,000
Carl	17,488,000	18,643,750	19,393,750
James	17,488,000	18,643,750	19,393,750[21]

On his death in 1836 Nathan left £3.5 million. To convert this into today's values, it should be multiplied by 35.5 for inflation and related to the GDP, giving a figure of £1,669 million – getting on for £2billion.[22]

The 1830 Revolution in France

Now the Rothschilds had control of France they allied with the Priory of Sion against the Templar Louis XVIII and sought to overthrow him and replace him with a pro-Sionist.[23] When the old King died, they tried to subvert his younger brother and successor Charles X. The assassination of Charles's son in 1820 by a Bonapartist fanatic, Louval, had hastened the reactionary turn of the government and polarized the political scene between royalist and revolutionary factions. Charles X was opposed by his cousin, Louis-Philippe, Duke d'Orléans, the son of the leader of the Orléanist Revolution in 1789, who had been guillotined, and a friend and client of James Rothschild's bank. In 1830 Charles attempted a royal *coup* and shut down the Chamber of Deputies, which had newly met in March, and ordered new elections in July. This led to three days of protest ("*Les Trois Glorieuses*," July 27-29) when barricades went up on the streets manned by students and members of the petite bourgeoisie. The Templar republicans (acting on the Templar Grand Orient's new word, "socialism") fought the Sionist-Orléanist constitutional monarchists who wanted Louis-Philippe on the throne and who confronted the republicans at the Hôtel de Ville. Lafayette supported Louis-Philippe and appeared on the Hôtel balcony with him, wrapped in the tricolour flag, and embraced him as the crowd cheered. Charles X abdicated two days later, and parliament proclaimed Louis-Philippe "King of the French." James Rothschild immediately donated 15,000 francs for the families of the wounded who had fallen in July, and became Louis-Philippe's unofficial adviser with access to his court. He was even closer to the centre of power than his brother and father-in-law, Salomon Mayer – James had married his niece – in Vienna.[24]

The Priory of Sion, having opposed the Bourbons, settled for a constitutional monarchy on the Merovingian model (in which the King ruled but did not govern), as opposed to the absolute monarchy of Louis XVI.[25] It supported Louis-Philippe, whose wife was Maximilian de Lorraine's niece, and thus an ally of the House of Habsburg-Lorraine. The House of Rothschild was behind the new Sionist rule in France, which had distanced itself from the Grand Orient leanings of Louis XVIII.

The Rothschilds were now incredibly powerful in five countries. Nathan was very close to the Duke of Wellington and British inner circles. Salomon controlled Metternich in Austria. James saw the French King every few days. Carl was close to the masters of Italy from Naples to Sardinia. Amschel controlled the German Confederation. All five brothers acted in unison. When Amschel supported Austria financially against Prussia and Bismarck protested, Amschel became "unwell" and inaccessible, and the other four appeased Bismarck with puzzled, soothing reassurances – without withdrawing support from Austria.

The Industrial Revolution

The House of Rothschild had embraced the Industrial Revolution. This used new raw materials and energy – iron, steel, coal, electricity, the steam engine, petroleum and the internal combustion engine – to increase production in factories with less human energy, and to improve transport and communications. Opposed to it were organized bands of weavers and manual workers known as Luddites, who rioted during the years following 1811, calling for the destruction of the new textile machinery that was making them redundant. (In May 1812, after receiving a letter from a Gen. C. Ludd sentencing him to death, the British Prime Minister Spencer Perceval was assassinated in the House of Commons lobby by John Bellingham, who is thought to have been a northern merchant with Luddite sympathies. He pleaded, "It was a private injury – a denial of justice on the part of the government," and the Luddites in Lancashire, Cheshire and Nottinghamshire applauded his act as a Luddite deed. Bellingham was hanged outside Newgate within a week.)

The Rothschilds' financial empire, carried by the five sons into five European capitals, now built Europe's first railways. The first-ever railway had been built in England in 1829 using George Stephenson's steam-coaches. England, the industrial workshop of the world, had taken the lead. In France James Rothschild opened his Paris-St Germain railroad in 1837 and the Paris-Versailles line in 1839. In Austria, Salomon Rothschild opened the Vienna-Bochnia line, which he financed. In 1846 Baron James Rothschild opened his northern railway in France. As a result of Rothschilds' loans in France James Rothschild owned Louis-Philippe, and France herself, slowed up by the French Revolution, did not become an industrial power until 1848. Germany was not industrialized until 1870.[26]

The most telling picture we have of the Industrial Revolution is in Dickens' *Hard Times*: smoky towns, cold hovels of workers' cottages and Gradgrind's insistence on facts. It seems a far cry from the soaring Romantic imagination, yet just as Romanticism had its roots in revolutionism (as can be seen from the writings of Rousseau, Goethe and Blake, who were infused with the revolutionary spirit), and the two movements – one literary, the other political – shared a passion to exalt individual aspirations above those of society, so there is a startling link between Romanticism and the Industrial Revolution, which also professed a common aim. For technology was perceived as a friend of individual liberty: the machine set one free. Luddites fearful of losing their jobs to machines did not quite see things this way, but the otherwise unemployed Romantic poets were not weavers fearful of losing their jobs. Artistic and aesthetic revolutions often grow out of social and political upheavals, and just as the early Reformation threw up the Renaissance as a pro-classical, pre-Christian reaction against the Church, so the Industrial Revolution had a role in throwing up Romanticism as a reaction against scientific materialism.[27]

MAZZINI'S TEMPLAR EUROPEAN REVOLUTIONS

Mazzini, Marx and the 1848 Revolutions

In 1830 Adam Weishaupt, founder of the Illuminati and, despite his exile, perhaps still in charge of the Order, died at the age of 82. His death came at a time when American Freemasonry was separating itself from the Illuminati. It is alleged that on his death-bed the Luciferian Weishaupt repented (like Dr Faust) and joined the Catholic Church.[28] In 1834, the Italian Guiseppe Mazzini, the son of a Genoese doctor, was appointed head of the Illuminati. Some hold that Weishaupt directly appointed him before he died, having been struck by Mazzini's ruthlessness soon after he became a Grand Orient Mason in 1827 at the age of 22. (The Grand Orient had penetrated the Carbonari, an early form of Italian Freemasonry which aimed to eliminate Christianity, and which Mazzini eventually absorbed.)[29]

Mazzini spent his first three years as a Freemason undergoing revolutionary training. He was exiled from Italy to France in 1831 and founded a new Masonic organization, Young Italy, which soon had 60,000 members and was suppressed by the Italian government. With the help of the Freemason (later British statesman) Henry Palmerston he founded Young Europe in Switzerland, and the "Young" secret societies proceeded to proliferate: Young America, Young England and the Young Turks. The "Young" recruits later became initiates in Templar Grand Orient lodges in the countries concerned. By then they had been trained in terrorism and subversion by Templar Scottish Rite and Grand Orient Freemasons. They were taught how to use dynamite in Paris, where they were protected by the French Constitution. They were also known as Anarchists or Nihilists, and their task was to spread Templar revolution throughout Europe, under Mazzini's leadership. In 1833-4 Mazzini led "Young" uprisings in Savoy and at Genoa (where he first worked with Garibaldi, who fled to France shortly afterwards).[30]

In Italy, "Young Italy" gangs robbed banks and burned businesses that had not paid protection money, and kidnapped for ransom, ostensibly to raise money to fight for the reunification of Italy. It was said that throughout Italy *"Mazzini autorizza furti, incendi, e attentati"* ("Mazzini authorizes theft, arson and kidnapping"), which was shortened to MAFIA.[31]

Mazzini's Freemasonry was identical to Weishaupt's: it offered the same degrees, symbols, passwords and grips; used assassination; sought to destroy the Church and establish a world government. The difference between them was that Weishaupt was primarily a Sionist Rosicrucian (although his Illuminati had united both Sion and the Templars), while Mazzini was primarily a Templar. Whereas the Priory of Sion was patently royalist, right wing, capitalist and anti-trade-union, Mazzini's Templars were republican, left wing, communist and pro-trade-union – and used force rather than financial power.[32]

In France the Templar Grand Orients persevered with "socialism" (a word invented by Robert Owen) which had emerged during the 1830 Revolution, and in 1835 they founded the League of the Just (from the remnants of the Jacobin Clubs) to lead the socialist movement. The radicals (as opposed to the pacifist socialists) formed communes to speed up their revolutionary activity and renamed the League of the Just the Communist League. By 1848 their spokesman was Levi Mordechai, a German Jew and 32nd-degree Grand Orient Mason who changed his name to Karl Marx.[33]

Marx had denied his Jewish birth and declared himself an atheist. He studied at universities in Bonn and Berlin, and read Weishaupt and the Illuminatus Clinton Roosevelt's *The Science of Government Founded on Natural Law*, which he had written in 1841 to destroy the US Constitution and communize the United States along Weishauptian principles. He called his plan the New Deal. (This was later implemented by his descendant Franklin D. Roosevelt, whose family was of Dutch origin. The Blair government in Britain has also adopted this Illuminati term for one of its policies.) In 1847, echoing Weishaupt and Clinton Roosevelt, and using a draft written by Engels and a group of Illuminati, Marx wrote *The Communist Manifesto*, which called on workers to revolt and governments to take possession of all property. This work was commissioned by the Illuminati-inspired Communist League (see p409).[34] According to at least one book, in the 1860s Marx's *Das Kapital* was funded by a Rothschild, who gave Marx two checks for several thousand pounds to finalize socialism.[35] It is alleged that these checks were at one time displayed in the British Museum, and that they were signed by Nathan Rothschild, although he died in 1836. It is possible that they were signed by N. M. Rothschild. The British Museum archivist is not aware of these checks. (Although royalists who supported right-wing regimes, the Rothschilds saw socialism as forwarding Weishaupt's vision of a one-world government.)

In 1848 Templar Grand Orient Freemasonry, inspired by the Templar Marx in Brussels and Cologne, and organized by Mazzini, co-ordinated communist uprisings across Europe[36] – beginning in France and spreading to Germany, Italy and the Austrian Empire. Essentially they were Templar assaults on Sionist-Rothschildian monarchs. These uprisings had been anticipated at the Masonic Congress of 1847, at which all the main revolutionary leaders of Europe were present.

In France the Templar republicans had not forgiven Louis-Philippe for commandeering their revolution in 1830. Socialist thinkers such as Enfantin, Fourier, Blanc, Proudhon (whose book *What is Property?*, published in 1840, declared that "property is theft") and Cabat were all active in the 1840s. In 1846 the country suffered crop failures, famines, and a serious economic crisis. The regime of Louis-Philippe seemed to lack moral standards, and lost the support of many intellectuals, including Lamartine and Victor Hugo, a friend of Charles Nodier who became Grand Master of the Priory of Sion in 1844 and supported Louis-Napoleon. The French opposition sought reforms. In February the government cancelled a political "banquet" in Paris, and the Templars organized a workers' communist revolution: students and workers took to the streets, built barricades and clashed with the police. To avoid bloodshed and to appease the demonstrators, Louis-Philippe dismissed Guizot, his chief minister, but that evening the army unit guarding Guizot's house killed 40 protesters. With civil war looming, Louis-Philippe announced his abdication on March 6, and fled to England.[37]

The Chamber of Deputies was invaded by a mob demanding a republic. The Chamber set up a provisional government, nine of whose 11 members were Grand Orient Masons, and, led by the poet Lamartine, members of the provisional government and a delegation of 300 Templar Grand Orient Masons wearing Masonic scarves and jewels, marched to the Hôtel de Ville where leaders of the republicans were setting up a regime. Four of these republicans were included in the provisional government, which, under pressure from the mob, proclaimed the republic. It was announced that all men would have the right to work – that the State should provide jobs for all – and that all men would have the vote. The electorate was immediately increased from 200,000 to 9 million. There were elections for a constituent assembly and the country voted for moderate candidates who refused to help the unemployed, and despite Lamartine's efforts to maintain republican unity, there was civil war in "the June Days" (June 23-6), during which thousands of jobless workers and students put up barricades.

In response the Assembly called on General Cavagnac to rid the streets of barricades. With experience in suppressing Algerian rebels, the General used artillery, killing 1,500 rebels and arresting 12,000, many of whom were exiled to Algeria. (It is likely that Victor Hugo based *Les*

Misérables, recently made into a successful musical, on this episode of the 1848 Revolution.)

With Cavagnac in executive control, the Assembly spent six months producing a democratic Constitution. Elections were held for a President of the republic (chosen by universal male suffrage), and Louis-Napoleon Bonaparte, nephew of Napoleon I, won a landslide. Although the monarchy of Louis-Philippe had been replaced by a republican President of the Assembly, the monarchists had survived as a force equal to that of the republican extremists, and so the French revolution of 1848 could not really be said to have succeeded. Thwarted, Louis-Napoleon staged a *coup*. Barricades went up on the streets, hundreds of demonstrators were killed and 27,000 arrested. Finally, in 1852 Louis-Napoleon defied the Grand Orient and proclaimed himself Emperor of the Second Empire as Napoleon III.[38] The 1848 French Revolution that overthrew Louis-Philippe was accompanied or followed by a series of Templar-led revolutions in Italy, Germany and Austria: in Palermo (January 9), Baden (March 1) and Vienna (March 12), where violent clashes led to Metternich's resignation. He was the first victim of the 1848 revolutions. There were more revolutions in Berlin (March 13), Milan (March 18), Parma (March 20), Vienna again (March 22), London (the Chartist uprising of April 10) and Naples (April 15). There was also trouble in Spain (May 7) and in Russia, where there were 64 risings of serfs. There were also revolutions in Denmark, Ireland and Schleswig-Holstein. In all these revolutions, the leaders were Templar Freemasons.[39]

The uprisings throughout Sicily caused Ferdinand II to issue a Constitution, an example followed soon afterwards in Italy by Grand Duke Leopold II of Tuscany, Charles Albert of Savoy and Pope Pius IX. The German revolution was masterminded by Heinrich Bernard Oppenheim, a former member of the Grand Orient's League of the Just. Mazzini meanwhile had been in England since 1837, and returned to Italy in 1848 to lead the revolution against the Austrians.

The only rulers who did not yield were the Austrians despite uprisings throughout the Habsburg Empire – in Prague, Lvov and

Cracow. At first Austria reinforced garrisons in Lombardy and Venetia and arrested ringleaders in Milan and Venice. But in March Hungary briefly declared freedom from Austria under Louis Kossuth, with whom Mazzini was in close contact. Under Mazzini's influence, Charles Albert, King of Sardinia-Piedmont, declared war on Austria. When revolution spread to Vienna on March 22 Venice and Milan freed themselves. The Austrian counteroffensive retook Lombardy and Milan.[40]

In the course of the summer of 1848 the Habsburg armies, backed by the Priory of Sion and the Rothschilds, put down the uprisings in Bohemia and Italy. The situation in Hungary encouraged a new revolution in Vienna in October, which led to the abdication of Emperor Ferdinand I in favour of his 18-year-old nephew Francis Joseph. By the end of October the Habsburg armies had reconquered Vienna.[41] In November Mazzini arranged for the constitutional government in Rome to convene a Constituent Assembly and proclaim a republic, which he and Garibaldi led. In Prussia Frederick William IV began to assert the crown; and throughout Europe there was a shift to the right. Although in April 1849 Hungary proclaimed a republic under the presidency of Kossuth, it collapsed in August and Kossuth fled to Turkey and many of his followers were executed. By the summer of 1849 the revolutions of the previous year had all been crushed.[42]

At the Masonic Peace Congress held in Paris that year, the Grand Orient ceased its communist agitation. Victor Hugo, Grand Master of the Priory of Sion, made the opening speech. He suggested Europe should unite under the name "The United States of Europe" – the first use of this term (which was Sionist). There was no support and nothing happened; but a few years later the "United States of Europe" was being promoted by International Socialism.[43]

The 1848 Revolutions marked the second attempt by Illuminized Freemasonry – Weishaupt's French Revolution being the first attempt – to create world disorder by unleashing sudden social transformation in France. Mazzini's Templars had been comprehensively defeated but his struggle continued. Like Weishaupt, Mazzini sought to unite both the

Priory of Sion and the Templars. He did this by developing a Templar network throughout Europe so that the Masonic revolutionaries helped each other. Indeed, he had built up a network of Templar Masonic revolutionaries throughout the world: Garibaldi, leader of the Italian revolutionary army; Kossuth, president of Hungary; Vorcell of Poland; Herzen of Russia; Palmerston of Great Britain; Bismarck of Germany; and Albert Pike of the United States. They helped him financially. In particular he called on Palmerston to fund his Grand Orient insurrection in Italy, which lasted until 1865.[44]

Palmerston

Palmerston was a very important figure in world Freemasonry (according to George Dillon).[45] He took over the leadership of the Alta Vendita, the highest lodge of the Carbonari (an extension of the Illuminati) when the Italian nobleman codenamed "Nubius" died in 1837 (possibly poisoned by Mazzini who sought the position for himself). From 1814 to 1848 the Haute Vente Romaine of this society directed the activities of all the secret societies. As Nubius's successor, Palmerston was Grand Patriarch of the Illuminati and Ruler of all the secret societies in the world – though the world's revolutionaries looked to Mazzini more than Palmerston. As British Foreign Secretary from 1830 Palmerston threw all his energies into causing the British government to side with the Masonic programme for revolutionizing Europe, which meant persuading the British taxpayer to fund revolutionaries such as Mazzini.[46]

Palmerston, who was also Grand Master of the British Brotherhood and leader of English Freemasonry, was given the task by the Priory of Sion of driving a wedge between Austria and Russia, as Sionist-Rosicrucian Freemasonry had little control over Austria, and as Russia threatened India. Palmerston's plan was to attack Russia together with France, his Templar partner, and cause a rupture in the Austro-Russian alliance. The weakening of Austria would enable Napoleon III to liberate Italy from Austrian occupation. This was the plan Palmerston followed in what came to be called the Crimean War[47] (to fight which, Rothschilds advanced $80 million to the British government).[48] When

Mazzini asked for financial aid for his Templar revolt in Italy, Palmerston raised funds from the Sionist-Rosicrucian English Parliament, which did not realise it was supporting Templarism.[49]

Mazzini made progress in Italy when in 1851 King Victor Emmanuel II of the House of Savoy, King of Sardinia-Piedmont, decided to hand over his government to Count Cavour, a Grand Lodge Mason opposed to Mazzini's Grand Orient republicans. Mazzini and Cavour came to an agreement that Italy should be united under a Savoyard constitutional monarchy. In accordance with this agreement, Mazzini ordered General Garibaldi, a Scottish Rite Mason, to invade Naples and Sicily and expel the Bourbons, who had been living there under the protectorship of Great Britain.[50]

As part and parcel of his opposition to the Vatican, Mazzini championed and promoted Darwin's theory of evolution. The Weishauptian onslaught on Christianity owed much to 18th-century French materialism, and the further decline of Christianity in the 19th century was largely due to the influence of Darwin.[51] The 18th-century view that the universe consists of granular atomic matter and that mind is dependent on physical processes and has no immaterial soul was compounded by the appearance in 1859 of Darwin's *On the Origin of Species by Means of Natural Selection*, which claimed to show that man evolved from the ape. The effect of Darwin's theory was to reduce man to the status of an animal and deny his immortality – a view that advanced Weishaupt's work in destroying religion.

Darwin's grandfather, the physician Erasmus Darwin, was linked to the Rosicrucian, pro-Weishauptian William Small, who taught Thomas Jefferson at William and Mary College and as his mentor introduced him to the writings of the Rosicrucians Bacon and Newton, and may have initiated him into Weishaupt's Order of the Illuminati. Erasmus Darwin co-founded the Rosicrucian Lunar Society with Small, and, the author of *Zoonomia, or the Laws of Organic Life*, was one of the first to form a theory of the evolution of species, suggesting that the idea came from the Rosicrucians via Small. The purpose of his grandson's *On the Origin of Species* was to "murder God" (i.e. destroy Christianity) according to Darwin – a Weishauptian, Rosicrucian idea. Darwin's family link with the Rosicrucians may explain why *On the Origin of Species* was elevated by the Rosicrucians, who allegedly bought up the entire first printing on the first day of the book's publication in 1859 – to distribute it and give the theory prominence.

In fact the first printing is thought to have been completely bought up by the post-Weishaupt Illuminati, under Mazzini's "Young" groups and Palmerston, who became British Prime Minister again in 1859. The Illuminati used the book as a means of weakening Christianity in Rome and across Europe and destroying civilization. To what extent was Darwin's theory that man is descended from the ape true, and to what extent was it always Weishauptian propaganda?[52]

Garibaldi

In May 1860 the red-shirted Garibaldi, acting on Mazzini's orders, led his guerrilla army of the Expedition of the Thousand to invade Sicily and twice defeat the superior forces of the Bourbon King of Naples. Cavour offered the King of Naples Piedmontese gold, and southern Italy fell to Garibaldi. The capture of Naples in September 1860 united Italy under Victor Emmanuel II of Sardinia-Piedmont. At the same time British Freemasonry, which had been fighting the Second Opium War in China, began to channel opium to Mazzini's Masonic Mafia, and as protector of Sicily, offered Mazzini's Mafia a home there. It moved in behind Garibaldi and the British navy and established its headquarters on the island.

In 1861 Cavour died and, financed by British intelligence, Mazzini's Templar rebels forced Victor Emmanuel II to abdicate. Mazzini then established the Republic of Italy at Piedmont. Victor Emmanuel II retaliated by setting up the Kingdom of Italy in Turin in March 1861, and began a campaign to recapture Rome (which finally proved successful in 1870).[53]

THE PRUSSIAN AND BRITISH EMPIRES

The Sionist Rothschilds and the American Civil War

The Rothschilds (who had of course been on Victor Emmanuel II's side while indirectly financing Mazzini) now turned their attention to America. The second Bank of the United States, created by James Madison in 1816, had collapsed in 1836. The next year Rothschilds sent an agent of theirs, August Belmont, to run a bank in New York and buy government bonds and establish his credentials by advising the President. The Rothschilds' aim was to create an incident that would establish an American central bank; a war, for instance, would require the American government to borrow from Rothschilds to pay for it. England and France could not be participants as they were too far away; Canada and Mexico were not strong enough; and though the Rothschilds had acted as financial agents for Russia for 20 years before the death of Lionel Rothschild, Nathan's son, Russia was not yet under their control.[54]

The Priory of Sion wanted America back from the Templars, so the Rothschilds planned an American civil war. The north was to be a Sionist British colony, annexed to Canada and controlled by Lionel Rothschild; the Templar south was to be given to Napoleon III of France and controlled by James Rothschild. To persuade the south to secede from the union, Illuminized Sionist-Rosicrucian Freemasons used the Knights of the Golden Circle, which had been formed in 1854 by George Bickley, to spread racial tension. Its military arm was the Ku Klux Klan. Jesse James stole gold from banks and buried it – nearly $7 billion – to fund a civil war. The states who seceded would be united in the Confederate State of America; each would eventually be like an independent country. Abraham Lincoln told the American people that "combinations too powerful to be suppressed by the ordinary machinery of peacetime government had assumed control of various southern states."[55]

The Rothschilds financed the north through Belmont, Jay Cooke, the Seligman brothers and Speyer and Co.; and they financed the south through their agent Judah Benjamin, who became Secretary of State for the Confederacy in 1862. His partner in a firm of Louisiana lawyers, John Slidell, was Confederate envoy to France. His daughter was married to Baron D'Erlanger in Frankfurt, who was a relative and agent of the Rothschilds. On behalf of the south Slidell borrowed money from the D'Erlangers to finance the Confederacy.[56]

In 1861 England sent 8,000 troops to Canada, and next year English, French and Spanish troops landed in Mexico, overtly to collect debts. In 1863 France took over Mexico City with 30,000 troops.[57]

Gen. Albert Pike, a General in the Confederate Army, was a pro-French Templar Scottish Rite Mason and the most powerful Freemason in the world; indeed, most of the political and military leaders of the Confederacy were Masons under Pike's secret command.[58] The Confederates offered Louisiana and Texas to Napoleon III if he would send troops against the north. Lincoln, following Tsar Alexander II's lead in freeing the serfs, issued an order to free all slaves in 1863. (In due course the Tsar sent the Russian fleet to support Lincoln.) Congress approved Lincoln's plan to borrow $450 million in return for bonds of states, or "greenbacks," to pay for the civil war – and thus Lincoln did not need to borrow from International bankers like Rothschilds. Bismarck said, "The foreign financiers…understood at once, that the United States would escape their grip. The death of Lincoln was resolved upon."[59]

Lincoln's National Bank Act of 1863 authorized private banks, under charter from the federal government, to issue national bank notes. The International bankers created panic and 172 state banks and 177 private banks closed. In 1865 Lincoln was shot by John Wilkes Booth, a Confederate patriot and member of the Knights of the Golden Circle (along with Jefferson Davis). Coded messages were found in Booth's trunk, and the key to the code was found in Rothschilds' northern agent Judah Benjamin's possessions. (By then Benjamin had fled to England.) Jay Cooke, a banking channel of Rothschilds', was involved.[60]

Rothschilds' plan to create a central bank of America had gone awry, for the time being at least. Their involvement in the Civil War is a measure of their influence on the foreign policy of the British, French and Russian governments, and it is typical of their way of operating that they should finance both sides. In May 1865 Lincoln's successor Andrew Johnson announced that slavery was abolished and that the south would not be responsible for the debt incurred; and Rothschilds consequently lost a lot of money. (America also owed Russia \$7.2 million for sending its fleet, and, having no authority to make a payment to Russia, bought Alaska in 1867.)[61]

The Rothschilds now regrouped and decided to undermine the American financial system from the bottom – a slow process that would take decades.[62]

Bismarck's Prussian Empire Defeats France

Palmerston died in 1865, and Benjamin Disraeli, a Jewish Freemason, became Prime Minister in 1868. Like his predecessor, Disraeli supported Mazzini, but did not raise funds from parliament to finance him. He went to the two leading Jewish bankers, the Freemason Lionel Rothschild and Moses Montefiore. So Rothschilds now funded Mazzini's activities, and as Mazzini was funding Bismarck, the Rothschilds were now indirectly funding Bismarck. However, Mazzini's revolution had begun to crumble. He wanted world war and looked to Germany, where the Templar Freemason Otto von Bismarck had become Prime Minister.[63]

Prussia had a history of Templar-Illuminati involvement. We have seen (see pp232-3) that in the 18th century Frederick II of Prussia, "the Great" (from whom Hitler drew inspiration) was a Templar Freemason and the European Templar leader. It was during his reign (from 1740 to 1786) that Goethe flourished. Goethe was an Illuminatus whom Adam Weishaupt had named Abaris, and it is likely that his Faust was based on Weishaupt. Seen from this perspective, his Romantic movement was a Gnostic revival.[64] Frederick's nephew and successor Frederick William II was an Illuminatus. Under his son Frederick William III Weishaupt's Illuminati controlled the Masonic lodges in Germany and formed the *Tugendbund* (League of Virtue),[65] an Illuminized Templar group committed to dethroning all the princes of Germany except for the King of Prussia, who would govern the resulting United Germany, in accordance with Bismarck's plans. (The *Tugendbund's* Weishauptian plan was identical to the Rothschild plan for the world: to dethrone all the kings except for the King of Jerusalem.) Hegel was the philosopher of Prussia and therefore German nationalism. He advocated replacing the warring German princes with a new middle-class bureaucratic élite. Karl Marx's revolutionary and messianic socialism worked to the benefit of Prussian militarism as it swept away the old forms of government as well as the new liberalism. The 1830 revolution in Paris had an effect on Germany, stimulating Prussia to tear down and renew old social structures.

Frederick William IV, who reigned from 1840 to 1861, believed in the divine right of kings and rebelled against Masonic power. He refused to grant parliamentary reform. This contributed to the 1848 revolutions in Europe – particularly to the uprising in Berlin – in which the Prussian Marx took part following his influential Illuminati-funded *Communist Manifesto*. When the national assembly in Frankfurt offered Frederick William IV the German crown in the following year, he refused. He did not wish to accept the *Tugendbund's* Illuminized Templar crown. He was declared insane in 1857 – the Illuminized Templars simply set him aside – and it was in the year of his death that Bismarck became Prime Minister.[66]

Bismarck used the Jews to replenish his war chest and employed the Jewish socialist agitator, Ferdinand Lassalle, a Grand Orient Freemason, who was propagandist for the Prussian imperial machine. His purpose, like Marx's, was to sweep away existing social and political structures. Bismarck was soon a hero: he had united Germany under Prussian leadership by defeating Austria in the war of 1866 and excluding her from Germany; he had also fought the Franco-German (or Franco-Prussian) war of 1870-1 in which Prussia defeated France, ended French hegemony in Europe, founded the Prussian-dominated German empire and created a new German unity as the North German Confederation was joined by the southern German states.[67]

Prussia was very strong in Germany, but the southern German states had remained independent. It was Bismarck's aim that they should voluntarily join Prussia – by fighting on Prussia's side against a foreign enemy. France under Napoleon III had declared war on Prussia because Napoleon was told by his advisers that war would boost his declining popularity. As there had been Prussian moves to place a Hohenzollern prince on the throne of Spain, France objected, and by sending a provocative telegram, Bismarck was able to make out that King William had been insulted.[68]

The Frankfurt and Parisian Rothschilds were now committed to opposite sides. The English Rothschilds urged Gladstone to change his non-interventionist policy and lobbied Disraeli, leader of the opposition. While the South German states sided with Prussia, France had no support and had to surrender at the battle of Sedan in early September 1870.[69]

A government of national defence then deposed the French Emperor and established the Third Republic. Behind it was the Grand Orient that had wanted to bring Napoleon III down ever since he declared himself Emperor in 1852. The Papacy's temporal power, which had been maintained by Napoleon III, now collapsed and Italian troops entered Rome in September 1870. The Germans besieged Paris, which surrendered in January 1871, and on March 1 Prussian troops entered Paris. Germany then annexed Alsace, Lorraine and Metz, and King William I of Prussia was crowned German Emperor at Versailles as a way of making it clear that France no longer had influence in the German states, the foremost of which was now Prussia. German troops were to remain in France until a huge indemnity was paid (6,000 million francs). The Paris Rothschilds under Alphonse guaranteed the sum to the French government and organized two state loans, which brought in over 48,000 million francs, giving Rothschilds a huge commission.[70]

The 1871 Revolution in Paris

In March 1871 there was an insurrection in Paris against the republican government, and Templar radicals seized the Hôtel de Ville, drove the government out of Versailles and established the Paris Commune in its place, a government that lasted two months. Marx and Engels tried to direct the revolution from London and Marx issued orders, but the regime under the generals of the Commune, Brunel and Bergeret, was too anarchic.[71] On April 26 a deputation of Freemasons arrived to congratulate the Commune, and it was greeted by cries of "The Universal Republic" – the slogan of Illuminism.[72]

War broke out against established institutions: the Reign of Terror of 1793 was invoked, a Committee of Public Safety was formed; newspapers came into being whose names echoed the newspapers of Babeuf and Hébert; and there was widespread desecration of churches. The disciplined Bakunin lamented the disorder. The Column Vendôme, a monument to French national victories, was overthrown as an insult to Internationalism.

This outraged the army, who unleashed a week of streetfighting, during which the generals of the Commune set the Tuileries Palace on fire. There was now a concerted attempt to burn Paris with paraffin. The Palace of the Tuileries, the Ministry of Finances, the Palace of the Legion of Honour, the Palais de Justice and the Hôtel de Ville were all destroyed.[73] Many houses and granaries went up in flames; hostages were massacred, including the Archbishop of Paris. According to Kropotkin 30,000 died before order was restored.[74]

The carnage was well received among revolutionaries abroad; they did not see the suffering and the pain, but embraced an idealized picture of the struggle. One of them looked forward to the day when "we shall be able to dethrone the Queen of England, turn Buckingham Palace into a workshop and pull down the York column." So ended the third Templar experiment in revolutionary government carried out by Weishaupt's descendants in France. The experiments of 1793, 1848 and now 1871 had all ended in failure.[75]

Grand Orient Mazzini and Pike Plan Two Warring Empires in Europe

Created a Prince and Imperial Chancellor as a reward for his victory over France in 1871, Bismarck was at the height of his influence. Mazzini wanted him to divide Europe into two warring camps through peace treaties. To this end he wrote to Albert Pike, the General who initiated the southern revolt in the American civil war.[76]

Pike, leader of the US Scottish Rite Masonry, a 33rd-degree Freemason and author of a huge Masonic handbook, was fascinated by one-world government, and co-ordinated Illuminati activities in the United States. He was Grand Master of a Luciferian Group known as the Order of the Palladium (or Sovereign Council of Wisdom) which had been founded in Paris in 1737. The rite honoured the Templar Baphomet, the "Palladium" coming from the Hindu *"pala"* ("phallus") and suggesting man's generative forces which enable him to achieve divine status, to become a man-god. This was a Templar, not a Sionist-Rosicrucian symbol.[77]

Pike recreated this rite to unite the hierarchies of English, French and American Masonry, and he, Palmerston, Bismarck and Mazzini all spread the doctrine of the Palladium within Templar Scottish Rite lodges.[78] In January 1870 Mazzini had written to Pike regarding the New and Reformed Palladium Rite: "We must create a super rite, which will remain unknown, to which we will call those Masons of high degree whom we shall select."[79] In a letter of August 15, 1871 Pike wrote to Mazzini: "We shall unleash the Nihilists and the atheists, and we shall provoke a formidable social cataclysm which in all its horror will show clearly to the nations the effect of absolute atheism, origin of savagery, and of the most bloody turmoil. Then everywhere, the citizens, obliged to defend themselves against the world minority of revolutionaries, will exterminate those destroyers of civilization, and the multitude, disillusioned with Christianity, whose deistic spirits will from that moment be without compass, anxious for an ideal, but without knowing where to render its adoration, will receive the pure light ... of Lucifer, brought finally out into public view, a manifestation which will result from the general reactionary movement which will follow the destruction of Christianity and atheism, both conquered and exterminated at the same time."[80]

The full text of this prophetic letter, including an appendage, calls for three world wars and two revolutions. The first world war (the "cataclysm") would enable Communist atheism to destroy the Tsar's government in Russia and establish "atheism." The second world war would follow the rise of "Fascism," which would set Great Britain against Germany; Communist Russia would then destroy governments and religion, and advance Zionism. A third world war would begin out of the conflict between Zionists and the Arabs, who would destroy each other and bring the rest of the world into final conflict. There would be social, political and economic chaos, from which a universal Masonic dictatorship would rise. It was a plan for the next hundred years.[81]

This letter, with its appendage that surfaced in 1949, was on display in the British Museum in London until it mysteriously vanished (like the Rothschild checks in favour of Marx), although it is still catalogued. We may be surprised at the mention of "Fascism," a term which was not coined until 1921, and at the reference to a conflict between the Jews and the Arabs, which was not known in 1871 and only really surfaced after the Balfour Declaration of 1917.[82] It could be that Pike's letter is an Illuminati forgery written after 1921 and backdated to attribute post-1921 Illuminati views to the dead Pike, perhaps for reasons of safety. Equally as well it could be an anti-Illuminati forgery to discredit the Illuminati. This is the view of Salem Kirban in *Satan's Angels Exposed,*[83] who wrote: "It is quite possible that these Illuminati schemes for three World Wars are more recent inventions, pre-dated to give authenticity to those who seek to blame the sin and suffering of today's world on some secret few." The difficulty in corroborating this letter is similar to the difficulty we shall encounter with the *Protocols of the Elders of Zion* (see ch. 7), and we should note that the letter was once on display and suspend judgment.

There is no doubt about a dualistic statement Pike put out in 1889 to 23 Supreme Councils, however, which belittled the Christian God Adonay: "Yes, Lucifer is God, and unfortunately Adonay is also God. For the eternal law is that there is no light without shade, no beauty without ugliness, no white without black, for the absolute can only exist as two Gods: darkness being necessary to light....The true and pure philosophic religion is the belief in Lucifer, the equal of Adonay; but

Lucifer, God of Light and God of Good, is struggling for humanity against Adonay, the God of Darkness and Evil." This view could have come straight from the dualistic Manichaean Cathars of the 13th century.[84]

In 1872 Mazzini died, and was replaced as head of the Italian Masonic Mafia by Adriano Lemmi.[85] Before Mazzini died, Bismarck was in constant communication with both him and Lemmi, his fellow Luciferians; all three hated the atheism of the low-degree initiates in the Templar Grand Orient.[86] Bismarck was set to fulfil the Templar Masonic leadership's plan to divide Europe into two warring camps – the British and the German – through imperial competition: the imperialist revolution.[87]

CONSOLIDATION OF THE BRITISH AND GERMAN EMPIRES

There were already formal French and German "Empires" with crowned Emperors, and Great Britain had been following an imperial strategy. These three nation-states now had local Empires and sought to extend their territory by annexing lands overseas.

Rothschilds and the British Empire

The expansion of Europe into other areas of the world was a search for expanding markets and sources of raw materials. There was a tendency for European nations to take a territory by force if it had raw materials it needed; the flag generally followed trade. There was also competition for national prestige.

Rothschilds were to the fore as can be seen from Great Britain's purchase of the Suez Canal. The Jewish imperialist Benjamin Disraeli gave political expression to the British imperialism that had been evolving. An opponent of Gladstone's for twelve years, throughout which his own finances were shaky, he reaffirmed Rothschilds' role of government banker which they had fulfilled since 1815. The Suez Canal, which had been dug between 1859 and 1869 had been financed by the Suez Canal Company, a joint stock company in which Said Pasha owned 44 per cent of the shares in a 100 year concession. Financial troubles required him to put them on the market in 1875, and with the help of Baron Lionel Rothschild (Nathan's son), who advanced £4 million at 24 hours' notice, Disraeli bought the shares.

The story is a fascinating one. Disraeli was having supper with Lionel Rothschild at 148 Piccadilly when the butler brought in a slip of paper on a silver salver. The Khedive (Said Pasha) had offered his shares to the French government but had rejected the French offer. Disraeli asked, "How much?" Rothschild telegraphed Paris. The reply was brought in on the salver: "£4 million." "We will take this," said Disraeli. "Ah," said Lionel. But the funding was a problem. The law forbade the government to borrow from the Bank of England when the House of Commons was not sitting, and there was no time to wait for directors of boards to approve the purchase. The next day Disraeli's secretary visited Lionel Rothschild who was eating muscatel grapes. "I shall give them to you," he said. Within 48 hours N. M. Rothschilds had credited the Khedive's account with £4 million.

It does seem strange that Disraeli was operating from Rothschild's dinner-table, and that the Khedive's message arrived there. The likely explanation is that the Suez Canal was in fact bought on Rothschild's initiative, *as he controlled Disraeli*. The account that has survived of course does not say this, but through their French branch Rothschilds would have had up-to-date information on the French government's bid for the Khedive's shares. The story is more understandable if Rothschild approached Disraeli, offering to fund the project if Disraeli would buy the Canal for the British government. As if in acknowledgement of the underlying situation, Disraeli wrote to the Queen, "The French Government has been out-generalled .... Four millions sterling! and almost immediately. There was only one firm that could do it – Rothschilds."[88]

The shares climbed steadily until 1900, giving England a say in a waterway that offered a short cut to India and which was vital to the Royal Navy's rule of the seas. Great Britain profited hugely from this imperialist investment, which earned her £2.25 million in 1936-7 alone. Disraeli had been able to observe the Rothschilds at close quarters, and in his novel *Coningsby* wrote: "The world is governed by very different personages from what is imagined by those who are not behind the scenes." Following his father Isaac, author of the two-volume *Life of Charles I*, in revealing knowledge about the world revolutionary movement, he transformed Nathan Rothschild (also in *Coningsby*) into the elder Sidonia as "lord and master of the money-market of the world."[89]

Rothschilds were heavily involved in financing the expansion of world trade. The European powers had opened up China (where Britain fought Opium Wars) and India and various staging-post islands. The Portuguese had assembled slaves in Africa (in Angola and Mozambique) and brought them to European capitals. The French moved into Algeria in 1830. The British had settled Canada, Australia and New Zealand and taken possession of South Africa from the Dutch (having moved east into Natal in 1842 and found gold and diamonds in the Boer territories along the Orange and Vaal rivers in 1867). Rothschilds' agents had foreseen the commercial opportunities these territories now offered. Belgium meanwhile had created an empire in the Congo; the Italians took the Italian Somaliland; and the Germans, having held back, advanced into Africa when Kaiser William II inherited the German throne and won German East Africa (Tanganyika), the Cameroons, Togoland and German South West Africa (Namibia). By 1890 the European powers were parcelling out the globe among themselves.[90]

The French and German Empires were never profitable to their mother-countries, the Italian Empire drained Italy, but the British prospered on their way to a second British Empire under Disraeli during the 1860s and 1870s and in a late wave in the 1880s and 1890s.

The Rothschilds were behind Disraeli's imperialistic expansion of Britain into the African interior. Indeed the various branches of Rothschilds had invested in this imperialist *élan* on behalf of all the major European powers. N. M. Rothschild and Son had invested hugely in Indian mines and financed Cecil Rhodes's diamond operation in South Africa. They had banked and made loans throughout South America. In France, Rothschild Frères went into electrical industries, developed the Mediterranean Railway, delved further into North Africa and controlled the Baku oilfields in Russia. In Austria, S. M. Rothschild and Son extended into Hungary through the 1881 gold loan and supported every area of the Habsburg Empire.[91]

Cecil Rhodes tried to bring all Africa south of the Zambezi under British rule to "paint the map red." When Robert Cecil, the Marquess of Salisbury (a descendant of the Elizabethan Cecils), was Prime Minister, Rhodes was opposed by Kruger in his plan to develop northwards. British miners heading north disturbed the Boers (Dutch for "farmers"), who proclaimed their independence from the British who ruled from Capetown. They organized two republics, Transvaal and the Orange Free State. President Kruger of Transvaal would not permit the British to share in his state's political life.[92] Intent on dominating southern Africa, Cecil Rhodes, Prime Minister of Cape Colony, who owned De Beers Mining Company and was an accomplice of Rothschilds, returned to England in 1887 and approached Natty Rothschild (Lionel's son Nathaniel as opposed to Lionel's father Nathan), who guaranteed De Beers £1 million to improve the company's output. Convinced that Rothschild was exclusively imperialistic Rhodes made a will in 1888 nominating Natty to administer his estate so that it would fund a secret society to promote British power. In 1892 Rothschilds, who by now had made investments in South African mines and railways, floated a loan for the Boer government of the Transvaal. As in the Napoleonic wars and the American Civil War the Rothschilds backed both sides. (Their Hegelian method contrasted thesis and antithesis to make a synthesis.)[93]

The Boer War was fought to protect Anglo-Jewish diamond and gold mining interests. Mercantile imperialism trampled on the principle of sovereignty and the rural interests of the Dutch farmers (Boers). Rhodes provoked the Boers into war through the Jamestown raid. In 1899, prompted by British High Commissioner Viscount Milner's aggressive attitude to the Boers – he inflexibly demanded full citizenship for British residents in the Transvaal and started the Boer War – and, backed by Rothschild money, half a million British troops fought 88,000 Boers, who were also funded by the Rothschilds. At first the Boers did well, besieging the main towns and winning victories, but Lord Kitchener and Earl Roberts soon turned the tide. Eventually the Boer population was rounded up and put in concentration camps where 20,000 died. This was the first use of concentration camps, which came to be associated with Nazi Germany (which in fact copied the idea from the British practice in the Boer War). The Boers sued for peace in 1901, and the British annexed the Boer republics.[94]

The German Empire

Against this background Bismarck, who also gave political expression to the Imperialist Revolution, welded Germany into an imperial power.[95] Now that Wilhelm I had been crowned Emperor of Germany in fulfilment of the Illuminized *Tugendbund's* policy, Bismarck allowed the Jews to gain in power. Many held prominent office in his government – for example, von Bleichröder, Lasker, Bamberger and Oppenheimer – and they led the National Liberal majority in the Reichstag. Their ownership of the banking houses also gave them influence over the appointment of ministers. In 1880 Berlin alone had 45,000 Jewish residents (compared to 46,000 in the whole of England). German industry was now expanding at a phenomenal rate under a German government that was controlled by Illuminized Grand Orient Templars, with Bismarck as their figurehead.

The Second Reich (empire) of 1871 led by the Prussian Hohenzollerns – the First Reich was the Holy Roman Empire which lasted a thousand years (from 800 to 1806) – had at first ignored France's imperialist ventures, hoping they would distract her from the pain of losing Alsace and Lorraine. In the middle of the 1880s, however, Germany, now an ally of Russia and the Habsburg monarchy of Austria-Hungary, began to regard French colonial expansion as intolerable and prepared herself for industrial expansion and foreign empire. Bismarck was aware that France would like another war to undo the consequences of the disastrous Franco-Prussian War of 1870-1. In 1882 he isolated France by signing a treaty, known as the Triple Alliance, between Germany, Austria-Hungary and Italy, who were collectively called the Central Powers. Bismarck then clandestinely constructed an alliance of opposing states – Great Britain, Russia and France, collectively called the Allied Powers – and their Triple Entente was ratified in 1907.

In England Lord Rosebery, twice Gladstone's foreign secretary before he became Prime Minister from 1894 to 1895, continued Salisbury's policy of secret collaboration with the Triple Alliance powers. He was married to Hannah Rothschild, the daughter of Mayer,[96] and thus the Rothschilds were now involved in collaborating with Germany and pursuing Pike's policy of dividing Europe into warring camps, which Bismarck had put together before 1890. As a result of Bismarck's diplomacy between 1871 and 1890, when he was dismissed by the new Kaiser William II, Germany was on its way to being Europe's leading industrial nation, and rapidly overtook Great Britain in the production of steel and chemicals and was soon outproducing her altogether.

The Templar Bismarck, influenced by Mazzini's successor Lemmi, had set Europe up for a world war such as Pike had predicted in his letter. On the side of the Triple Alliance were the Illuminized Templars who had followed Mazzini. On the other side were the Sionist-Rosicrucian monarchs who had suppressed the Templar republican uprisings and were now opposed by the Jacobin revolutionaries: the monarchs of Britain, Russia and Imperial France.[97] In fact, the Rothschilds, with help from Mazzini, had created two imperial dragons who would now fight each other to the death.

The Illuminized Grand Orient Stokes up a War

The Templar Grand Orient effectively took control of public opinion in Great Britain before the First World War. There was a wave of popular feeling against the philandering Prince of Wales, Albert Edward (later Edward VII) who was called Bertie by his mother, Queen Victoria. He paid social calls on young married women who had taken his fancy, and word of this spread. The Grand Orient had infiltrated London when Karl Marx arrived in 1849, and Marx's daughter Eleanor

Marx and Engels had continued to spread his ideas after his death. The Marxist Grand Orient Fabian Society, a far-left group founded in 1883-4 on the writings of the Scottish philosopher Thomas Davidson, was active, and its members incited workers' strikes and riots. In 1887 revolutionary socialism had progressed to such a point in Great Britain that there was a major riot, and Grand Orient communists turned the working man against the royal family. It seemed to aristocratic English Sionist Freemasonry of the British Grand Lodge, still reeling at the policies of Palmerston, that a communist *coup* was imminent, and at the 1889 Masonic Congress in Paris English Freemasonry, predicting the collapse of monarchies and religions in view of unstoppable Grand Orient activity, accepted State socialism in business and finance to head off a revolution – but insisted that English Freemasonry retained control of politics. Hence English Freemasonry persuaded the British Crown to submit to socialist democracy in return for continued status as a figurehead.[98]

Great Britain was now on the side of its Grand Orient revolutionary partner France and Russia, and against the monarchist Central Powers: Germany, Austria-Hungary and Italy. Templar French Grand Orient Freemasonry planned to replace the Tsar with a revolutionary republican government before the beginning of the global conflict envisioned by both Pike and Bismarck.[99]

Following the 1907 Triple Entente there were crises in Bosnia, Agadir, Tripolitania, the Balkans and Albania. The Grand Orient was involved in all of these. In 1910 there were rumours that the Archduke Franz Ferdinand, heir presumptive to the Austro-Hungarian throne, had been sentenced to death by a Serbian lodge committed to freeing Serbia from Austrian influence.[100]

The Ottoman Empire in Europe had been disintegrating since Greece won her independence in 1831. All the newly autonomous states accepted German princes as their kings except for Serbia, which had a strong pan-Slavic voice and looked to the greatest of the Slavic states, Russia. The Austrians, who were supported by the Priory of Sion, objected to Serbia's pan-Slavism, and in 1908 annexed Bosnia and

Herzegovina (which included Sarajevo).

Grand Orient Princip Kills the Archduke

Franz Ferdinand stood in the way of the Grand Orient's revolutionary aims. He was a Merovingian, and therefore in line to be Sion's "King of Jerusalem"; he was also a Catholic, and on the eve of the First World War there was a secret treaty to annex Serbia to the Vatican State and create a new Catholic country. The eight men who were plotting to kill him were members of the Serbian Black Hand Masonic lodge (or Union or Death Brotherhood), the terrorist wing of Narodna Odbrana who used terror against Habsburg or Ottoman rule to achieve the independence of Bosnia-Herzegovina.[101]

The aim of Narodna Odbrana was to unite all the Slav southern states into one federation, which could only be done by killing Archduke Franz Ferdinand. The mastermind was the Grand Orient Mason Radislav Kazimirovitch, who travelled on the Continent and returned with revolvers and bombs. These were supplied via the Grand Orient Major Tankosich to the Grand Orient Mason Gavrilo Princip, a young Bosnian Serb, and seven other assassins. Another Serbian Grand Orient Mason Major Todorovitch kept a diary about the plot; and this was later used as court evidence. Meanwhile Templar Scottish Rite Freemasonry's international branch, which had been founded by Pike and Mazzini, printed propaganda against Germany and Austria, and this led to a Masonic uprising in Serbia under Col. Dimitrijevic, who was head of Serbia's military intelligence and also head of the secret society Union or Death. He was codenamed Apis and had been influenced by the Russian Grand Orient Mason Bakunin.[102]

On June 28, 1914 the Sionist-supported Archduke and his morganatic wife Sophie (a former lady-in-waiting), who was pregnant, returned to Sarajevo from an official tour. They sat in the back of a black limousine with the rear half of the roof folded back, and the Archduke wore a blue uniform and round peaked hat. Eight assassins were waiting in the crowd. When the car reached Cumurja bridge, Cabrinovic threw a bomb which wounded some of the crowd and the occupants of the car behind the Archduke's. The Archduke ordered his car to stop and enquired about the wounded. He and his wife then proceeded to an official reception at the town hall. Afterwards they got into the car and returned towards Cumurja bridge with Count Harrach standing on the step of the car to shield the Archduke and Archduchess on the side from which they had earlier been attacked. Many in the crowd threw flowers at the royal couple.

After the car crossed the bridge (now known as Gavrilo Princip bridge) it stopped on the corner of Francis-Joseph Street. Princip fired several shots from an automatic. Both the Archduke and the Archduchess were hit. Sophie's head fell on the Archduke's shoulder, and a trickle of blood ran down his lips as he murmured, "Sophie, do not die, live for the sake of our children." They were driven to the Governor's palace, where both were pronounced dead.[103]

In October, twenty Grand Orient Freemasons were tried. Eight were the armed assassins, and of them Illic and two others were sentenced to death and hanged. Strangely, the main participants Princip, Cabrinovic and Grabez were sentenced to twenty years' imprisonment. All died in prison before 1918.[104]

The Grand Orient Achieves War

The Grand Orient assassins had advanced Pike's plan, and world war broke out five weeks later[105] as threats and ultimatums led to mobilizations, and treaties set up by the Grand Orient Bismarck and other Grand Orient Freemasons were invoked. In retaliation for the assassination the Austrians (notably, the chief of general staff von Hötzendorf and the Foreign Minister von Berchtold) presented Serbia with an ultimatum it could not accept. This included the demand that Serbian officials should be dismissed and that Austro-Hungarian officials should enter Serbian territory and crush anti-Austro-Hungarian forces. Serbia accepted most of the ultimatum but requested international arbitration on these two demands. Austria-Hungary mobilized, believing that Germany would support her under the terms of the Triple Alliance, which had been confirmed in October 1913. Kaiser Wilhelm II told Austria there was no justification for a war, but officials in the German foreign office had encouraged Berchtold to persuade Emperor Francis Joseph to authorize war against Serbia, and Austria now bombarded Belgrade. Russia, protector of Serbia, mobilized.

Germany had long been preparing to fight a war on two fronts – against both France and Russia. Germany demanded that Russian mobilization should cease and required France to promise neutrality if there was a war with Russia. The Kaiser persuaded the Russian Tsar to withdraw his orders, but he was powerless to reverse the mobilization. Consequently both Russia and France ignored these demands. Germany declared war against Russia and demanded that Belgium should give free passage for German troops into France. Germany declared war against France and invaded Belgium, which Great Britain was committed to defend by treaty obligation.

Great Britain declared war against Germany on August 4. Everyone then declared war on everyone else: Austria-Hungary against Russia; Serbia against Germany; Montenegro against Austria-Hungary and Germany; France and Great Britain against Austria-Hungary; Japan against Germany; Austria-Hungary against Japan and Belgium. Italy confirmed the Triple Alliance in 1912 but was not obliged to support her allies in a war of aggression or against England and (now having a constitutional monarchy) positioned herself on the side of the Entente. On September 5 Great Britain, France and Russia reaffirmed the Triple Entente in the Treaty of London, and each promised not to make a separate peace with the Central Powers.[106]

The Templar Grand-Orient successors of Bismarck and Mazzini had manoeuvred Germany and Austria-Hungary into an aggressive war against the now Templar-influenced (but Sionist-ruled) Great Britain, Templar republican France and Tsarist Russia. Kaiser Wilhelm II (whose war machine was financed by the Grand Orient Max Warburg, who was also Chief of Police in Germany)[107] presided over the German Empire's consolidation in Europe, while George V's Prime Ministers Asquith and later Lloyd George presided over the British Empire's consolidation. For both of them the front line was the trenches on the western front in France. The Sionist Rosicrucian[108] Lord

Kitchener, Secretary for War, shared the British army's low opinion of the politicians.

The Rothschilds, split between five countries, reacted by funding their own governments, particularly those of Great Britain and Austria-Hungary and fighting for their own countries, but they were not in control of events. While the British army under Sir John French blocked the drive for Paris of von Hindenburg's German forces at the River Marne, where there was stalemate for four years, events were being controlled in America, where American Freemasonry (which now represented two million men) had passed a resolution to give Great Britain and her allies all possible support in the war.[109]

The key American figure was a 33rd-degree English Grand Lodge Freemason who had strong links with the Grand Orient, Col. E. M. House, personal adviser to President Woodrow Wilson. Wilson campaigned for re-election on a policy of keeping America out of the war, while House was secretly committing America to war on the English side.[110] America had loaned the Allies $3 billion and another $6 billion for exports, and House was representing those who had made these loans: J. P. Morgan and the new oil giant John D. Rockefeller, both of whom were connected to Templar organizations; and Warburg and Schiff, who were Grand Orient Freemasons.[111] All four wanted to protect their investments in Europe, and it was their influence that took America into the war. While Col. House was in England committing America, Wilson said in 1916: "We have come to be one of the worst-ruled, one of the most completely controlled governments in the civilized world – no longer a government of free opinion, no longer a government by conviction and the vote of the majority, but a government by the opinion and duress of a small group of dominant men."

In April 1917 Congress declared war, presenting the war as "a war to end all wars" and a war "to make the world safe for democracy." America shipped over 2 million men across the Atlantic to France, and this proved decisive.[112]

The International Congress of Freemasonry held at the Grand

Orient headquarters in Rue Cadet, Paris in April 1917, requested that Masonic journalists should write articles calling for Wilhelm II of Germany and Charles I of Austria to be deposed and replaced by republicans with revolutionary socialist principles. Freemasons in Germany now prepared for revolution, and the revolutions which broke out in the Kiel shipyards and in other ports, and eventually spread to Munich, led to the abdication of the Kaiser.[113]

Grand Orient Templars Now Rule Europe

From the Masonic point of view, the main aim of the First World War, in which 8.5 million died,[114] was to overthrow monarchies and damage the Catholic Great Powers in order to institute a universal or world republic. (Other aims had been the capture of the Tsar's wealth, the destruction of the Russian Orthodox Church, the creation of the League of Nations, the imposition of the gold standard world-wide and a promise to transfer Palestine to the Jews.) The Treaty of Versailles was to transfer the wealth of the fallen monarchs to the financially hard-up Grand Orient nations in the form of huge war reparations. This was achieved. The American Freemasons had supported the spread of republican governments against autocracy, although Anglophile Sionist American Freemasons (like Col. House) had ensured that Great Britain's monarch George V survived.

The Templar radicals who controlled Sionist England had defeated monarchist Germany and Sionist Austria. Wilhelm II, surrounded by Grand Orient Templars, must have rued not having managed to ally himself with the Rothschilds. He had pleaded with the Rothschilds to establish a bank in Berlin – first with Mayer Carl (Amschel's nephew) and then in 1908 with Edouard (Alphonse's son), but without success. (Mayer Carl had felt discriminated against when he was awarded the Order of the Red Eagle, Third Class by Wilhelm I and Bismarck. He was given a specially designed Jewish eagle rather than the usual cruciform Prussian emblem, and this slight to the family had resulted in the Rothschild family's boycotting both Kaiser Wilhelm I and Kaiser Wilhelm II.[115] At least, that is the official version. It is more likely that the Sionist Rothschilds would not contemplate opening a bank in

Templar Grand Orient Berlin.) Both Germany and Great Britain had consolidated their Empires against France, which had opposed Great Britain in Napoleon's time and Germany in the Franco-Prussian War.

The consolidation of the British Empire had strengthened the British Imperialist Revolution while weakening the mother-country. On the other hand, the consolidation of the German Empire ended in its collapse in 1918. The same was true of the Austro-Hungarian Empire, which had its own parallel revolutionary dynamic.

The outcome of the First World War was different from the outcome of the Napoleonic wars. The French Revolution of 1789 ended in the republicanization of Europe under Napoleon. This was reversed by the Sionist Congress of Vienna in 1814-15. The First World War of 1914 ended in a new republicanization of Europe into democratic, socialist and communist Masonic republics that replaced four imperial dynasties (Germany, Russia, Austria-Hungary and Turkey), all of whom had been supported by the Priory of Sion and the Sionist Rothschilds. The Imperialist Revolution began as a Sionist-Rothschildian project as the British Empire grew, and became Templar with the rise of the German Empire, although Austria remained Sionist. The First World War ended with the post-war advantage going to the Templars. Europe was in consequence Grand Orient Templar from 1918 to 1930.

SUMMARY: THE REVOLUTIONARY DYNAMIC OF THE 19TH-CENTURY IMPERIALIST REVOLUTION

The rival expansions of the Rothschilds and Bismarck had ended catastrophically. The development of imperialism had led to the disastrous end envisaged by Pike.

The British imperialist record is better than most, and Britain left many of the territories – which contained a quarter of the world's population at the zenith of the British Empire – better off than they would have been had there been no British presence: better developed, more advanced and better educated; more ready for self-rule. Nevertheless, the imperialist dream is one of territorial expansion which, carried to its logical conclusion, ends in expansion throughout the globe or world domination. The capitalist, Rothschildian imperialism of the Second British Empire appeared more of a degeneration from the Universalist spiritual vision of the oneness of mankind than the First British Empire because it emphasized commerce and placed money above the law, whereas the First British Empire was driven by honour: the desire to spread the glory of England and her Queen (and later King) throughout the world.

To sum up in terms of the revolutionary dynamic, Weishaupt's Illuminism as communicated to Mayer Amschel "Rothschild" and then to his (Weishaupt's) successor Mazzini provided the heretical occult vision of the Imperialist Revolution in Great Britain and Germany. This vision was interpreted by the heretical occult interpreters, the Sionist Mayer Amschel "Rothschild" and the Templar Mazzini, in two different ways that would result in two different processes – one that would end in a universal kingdom, the other in a universal republic. The occult revolutionary originator who would give the vision a new slant was Lord Palmerston, who was both Grand Master of English Freemasonry (a Sionist) and Grand Patriarch of the Illuminati and Ruler of all secret societies in the world (and therefore Templar). The intellectual interpreter of this occult vision was Pike, who appears to have forecast the First World War. The semi-political intellectual interpreter who later became political was Disraeli in Great Britain and Lassalle (who was a front for Bismarck) in Germany. Freemasonry – in the persons of Weishaupt, Palmerston and Pike – was common to both the British and German Empires, and helped to precipitate the conflict. The early revolutionary dynamic of the Imperialist Revolution was as follows:

Empire	Heretical occult vision	Heretical occult interpreter	Occult revolutionary originator	Thoughtful intellectual interpreter	Semi-political intellectual interpreter
Gt. Britain (Sion)	Weishaupt	Rothschild	Palmerston	Pike	Disraeli
Prussian/ German (Templar)	Weishaupt	Mazzini (and 1848 revolutions)	Palmerston	Pike	Lassalle (Bismarck)

The intellectual expression of the Imperialist Revolution led to abortive revolutions in France in 1830 (caused by Rothschilds), 1848 (caused by Mazzini) and 1871 (caused by Marx).

The revolutionary dynamic of the 1830 Revolution can be stated as follows:

Heretical occult inspiration	Intellectual expression	Political expression	Physical consolidation
Duke d'Orléans (Philippe-Égalité)/ Mayer Amschel Rothschild	Lafayette	Louis-Philippe	Bourgeois monarchy: crushing of uprisings*

(*by republicans in Lyon, 1831, and pretender Louis-Napoleon, 1836 and 1840)

The revolutionary dynamic of the 1848 Revolution in France was:

Heretical occult inspiration	Intellectual expression	Political expression	Physical consolidation
Marx/Mazzini	Lamartine/ Blanc	Louis-Napoleon Bonaparte (Napoleon III)	Arrests following the *coup*/Second Empire

The revolutionary dynamic of the 1871 Revolution in France was:

Heretical occult inspiration	Intellectual expression	Political expression	Physical consolidation
Marx	Brunel/ Bergeret	Paris Commune	Massacres and burning of Paris; 30,000 dead

The political expression of the Imperialist Revolution is to be found in the creation of the Second British Empire through Salisbury and Rhodes, the Second French Empire through Louis-Napoleon (Napoleon III), the Italian republic through Garibaldi and the Prussian Empire through Bismarck. The consolidation of the British and German Empires took place as their respective armies fought in the Boer War and in German Africa, where German armies put down the 1905 Maji Maji rising in Tanganyika, and crushed the 1905-07 uprising of Nama and Herero peoples in South West Africa, reducing the Herero population from 70,000 to 16,000.[116] The destructive plan was fulfilled in the devastation of Europe's cities and levelling havoc wreaked throughout Europe by the First World War, which made possible new revolutions in Russia and throughout Europe and the world (the New World Order Revolution).

The full revolutionary dynamic of the Imperialist Revolution in the main European countries of the 19th century is as follows:

Great power	Heretical occult inspiration	Intellectual expression	Political expression	Physical consolidation
Gt Britain	Weishaupt/ Rothschilds	Palmerston/ Disraeli	2nd British Empire of Salisbury/ Rhodes	British Army/ George V in Boer War/ First World War
Prussia-Germany	Weishaupt/ Mazzini	Lassalle	Prussian Empire of Bismarck in Africa/First World War	German Army/Kaiser Wilhelm II
France	Marx/ Mazzini	Lamartine/ Blanc	Rule of Louis-Napoleon Bonaparte	Empire of Napoleon III, 1852-71
Italy	Weishaupt/ Mazzini	Cavour	Italian Republic of Garibaldi	Kingdom of Italy of Victor Emmanuel II

What were the ideas that inspired the Imperialist Revolution? Imperialism and revolution have always been inextricably linked as the revolutionary Utopia is imagined for all the world as well as one nation. Since the American and French revolutions, which had both sought to advance the cause of freedom, revolution had become more loftily "spiritual," although actually occult. The Romantic movement of the 1790s, which had its origins in Rousseau and Goethe (both occult Rosicrucians at some time), praised the spiritual aims of revolutionaries in willing a sudden and rapid transformation in society and saw revolution as a spiritual upheaval. Blake wrote a poem about America in which revolution is portrayed as a spiritual (actually, occult) force; his Hell, where "energy is eternal Delight," is home to the successors of Satan's rebels, while Heaven belongs to the old regime. Wordsworth went to France and enthused about the French Revolution before becoming disillusioned by the Reign of Terror and the guillotine. Kant and the Marquis de Condorcet saw revolution as a force that transcended politics. All these writers were briefly captivated by revolution's occult vision.

Around the time of the Congress of Vienna (1814-15) the probably Rosicrucian Hegel, who became a professor in Heidelberg, capital of the former Palatinate, saw human history as a manifestation of a World Spirit (a Rosicrucian idea) that unites contradictions and brings freedom. (Hegel wrote of the "inwardness of the German people" which had burst out into the revolution of the Reformation.) Under the influence of Romanticism in the 19th century the view arose that the political results of revolution were secondary in importance to the "spiritual" (in fact, occult) revolution that gave rise to them.

Revolution became materialistic again decades later when Karl Marx gave Hegelianism a scientific basis, starting at the material end of Hegel's dynamic of spirit-matter. To Marx, control of the means of production and the class that exercized that control gave history a pattern. A new class overthrows an old one, a new social order replaces an old one. History is the story of revolutionaries seizing power.

Nineteenth-century imperialism grew out of the one-world vision that could be brought about by a single nation-state. The Sionist scheme called for a one-world Masonic kingdom, while the Templar scheme called for a one-world Masonic republic (or "universal republic"). Either way, conceptually imperialism was an attempt by a (Sionist- or Templar-encouraged) nation-state to impose world rule through the revolutionary process. On the Sionist side, the interpreter was the Rothschilds, and on the Templar republican side, Mazzini. As the Sionists had secured all the European monarchies following the Congress of Vienna, the Rothschilds worked with monarchs – this was not always the case, for example the Rothschilds funded Marx – whereas Mazzini was more subversive and worked with revolutionaries. The Rothschilds were the imperialists of Sion; Mazzini was the imperialist of the Templars.

Of course, imperialism was more than world rule. In economic terms, the Great Powers used Utopian capitalism: their industrial expansion and production, drawing on new raw materials and energy resources, as well as machines and factories, sought new markets as outlets for goods, investment capital and over-population. (Expanding markets overseas was a more acceptable alternative to depopulation by the guillotine.) In capitalism the means of production are privately owned and production is guided by the markets, which determine income. Adam Smith in *Inquiry into the Nature and Causes of the Wealth of Nations*, which was published in 1776, held that market forces govern economic decisions, and after the Napoleonic wars his policies were put into practice: free trade – under the terms of which a government does not interfere with exports or discriminate against imports – became desirable; there was sound money based on the gold standard, budgets were balanced, and there was minimal poor relief. Critics of capitalism, however, see empires as absorbing over-production and surplus capital. Be that as it may, the empires formed by the imperialists did provide markets for home production and contributed to the health of the home economies. New machines promised a new Utopia at home as well as abroad as steam-ships carried goods to far-away places.

The revolutionary left admired the Industrial Revolution. At the end of the 18th century the German Illuminized Templars sent "missions" into England, where they made several converts, including Thomas Paine, the revolutionary propagandist friend of Blake and Franklin who famously defended the French Revolution against Edmund Burke. Paine established several Illuminized lodges in England which preached social revolution, an idea now firmly linked to industrial revolution. (Industrial revolution was a Puritan idea, commending industry or hard work, and people assumed that greater industrialization would lead to more freedom.) Communist social revolutionary propagandists urged agrarian workers to turn away from the land to factories and place themselves at the disposal of commercial forces. The countryside was mechanized at home as the Empire, which was a potent symbol of Christian civilization in the world despite its foundation in technology, free trade and secular industrial capitalism, expanded abroad.

The British Empire was overtly Christian, the German Empire blatantly pagan. But as we look more carefully, we see that there were two British Empires; behind the Christian one with its missionaries confronting native blacks in darkest Africa, Bible in hand, was a hidden Masonic Empire acting out the Utopian idea of world domination and putting into practice the depopulating principle of "the survival of the fittest" in accordance with the philosophy of Charles Darwin, whose *On the Origin of Species* was published in 1859. This Masonic Empire watched as the Christian British Empire and the pagan German Empire fought to the death. But it was not as simple as that, for there were also two contenders for the Empire of Jewish Freemasonry: the Rothschilds and Sion; and Mazzini and the Templars.

With all this in mind it is possible to state the revolutionary dynamic of imperialism in terms of the ideas that inspired the inspirers:

Heretical occult inspiration	*Intellectual expression*	*Political expression*	*Physical consolidation*
Lucifer/Satan	Capitalism/ materialism/free trade/mercantilism	World government	World war

It is a melancholy reflection that the logic of competing nation-states' imperialism leads to world war. The end of the 18th century saw the collapse of the notion of Enlightenment progress through human reason: progress perished along with 300,000[117] victims in the French Revolution, whose ghastly climax was played out at the guillotine of Robespierre and Saint-Just. In the 19th century a new idea replaced rational progress: nation-state competitive imperialism. The early 20th century saw the collapse of the notion of liberal capitalist imperialist competition among nation-states; for the imperialist idea resulted in the slaughter and carnage in Europe during the First World War, and 8.5 million dead. This lesson was repeated in imperial territories and colonies throughout the globe for much of the rest of the 20th century.

Now two new ideas arose almost simultaneously: revolutionary socialist (nominally anti-imperialist, but in practice imperialistic) communism as a one-world empire; and a world federation of states, a united states of the world replacing all nation-states. Both ideas were essentially one idea, two sides of the same coin. Both ideas were not-so-new: they were variants of Baconian Utopianism and of Freemasonry's "universal republic." Would they also collapse?

CHAPTER SEVEN

THE RUSSIAN REVOLUTION

Lenin was sent to Russia...in the same way that you might send a vial containing a culture of typhoid or of cholera to be poured into the water supply of a great city, and it worked with amazing accuracy....He gathered together the leading spirits of a formidable sect, the most formidable sect in the world.

Winston Churchill, speech to the House of Commons on November 5, 1919

The climax of the Russian Revolution was the execution of Tsar Nicholas II and his family at Ekaterinburg on July 17, 1918 after the Bolsheviks' October Revolution. The climax of the terrorism that created the climate in which the Russian Revolution could happen was the assassination of Tsar Alexander II, who was shot after his coach was ambushed in snow in March 1881. This successful Nihilist operation marked the end of an anarchist process that can be seen as originating with Mazzini, who met Bakunin in London in 1861 and discussed political assassinations, including that of Napoleon III.

The Russian Intelligentsia had come into being between the European revolutions of 1830 and 1848. It had imported the communistic ideas[1] of the Virginian colonists' and Pilgrim Fathers' settlements, where all laboured equally and fed from the common source of food; of the Diggers of Winstanley; and of the 18th-century Shakers, who settled in Watervliet, near New York. It was strongly influenced by the ideas of the French Utopian socialists Saint-Simon, Proudhon, Fourier, Babeuf and Louis Blanc. Of these, Babeuf was the most influential. We have seen (p343–5) how Babeuf, a member of the Illuminati known as Gracchus[2] whose ideas were similar to Weishaupt's, wrote *Manifesto of the Equals*, held meetings for as many as 2,000 members near the Pantheon, and was tried and hanged. Fourier planned model communities or communes but failed to establish one near Versailles in 1832. The ideas of Robert Owen, a Scottish textile factory-owner who like Weishaupt wanted "to make the human race...one good and happy family"[3] and founded the Socialist movement, also reached Russia. He wanted to convert the world into "villages of 300 to 2,000 souls."[4]

All the members of the Russian Intelligentsia shared a common goal: social and political reform. This meant curbing the power of the Tsar and emancipating the serfs. On these matters the Russian Intelligentsia was divided. The Slavophils, who developed in the 1830s and were influenced by the German philosopher Schelling, concluded that Russia should not use Western Europe as a model for her development and modernization, but should follow a course determined by her own character and history. They believed that Peter I, the Great, had corrupted Russia by imitating the West. They were mystic nationalists who believed in Russia's unique destiny based on Russian Orthodoxy and the community principle embodied in the Mir (with its common lands). By contrast, the Westernizers of the 1840s and 1850s saw Russia as part of Western culture and favoured parliamentary democracy, industrialization and modern secular education. This debate was passionate and sincere and concerned national self-interest. Revolution came in from outside.[5]

The new idea of Communism grew out of revolutionary socialism, which came from England and France. It also grew out of the ideological struggles within the Prusso-German Empire. In particular, Weishaupt aside, Hegel, the Prussian philosopher who introduced the dialectical method into history, synthezising the World Spirit and matter, and his fellow Prussian Marx, who with Engels took up his ideas, were the three inspirers of Communism and are the starting-point for our approach to the Russian Revolution.

THE GRAND ORIENT AND COMMUNISTS

Despite the earlier influences (notably, the Diggers we have just mentioned, see pp107, 135), the heretical occult vision that shaped the Russian revolution was Weishaupt's. The Communist programme sought to implement his six-point plan (see p292–3) throughout the world.

Hegel

Hegel's background[6] does not sound promising for an occult interpreter of the heretical vision that was to inspire the Russian Revolution. In his youth he was friendly with Hölderlin, the German pantheist poet, and Schelling, the German Idealist; and he had a profound religious conviction of the reality of the Holy Spirit, which gives unity to all contradictions. In fact, unity behind contradictions is a Rosicrucian idea. In 1801 he joined Schelling at Jena, and would have become acquainted with Weishaupt's one-world views through his philosopher-friend. (He had also learned about Weishaupt while visiting the Weimar house of Goethe, alias "Abaris" in Weishaupt's Order.)[7] He regarded Prussia as a corrupt bureaucracy, and was pleased when Napoleon won a victory at Jena, and would have become acquainted with Weishaupt's one-world views through his philosopher-friend in 1806. His lectures in philosophy, history and religion there and at Heidelberg and later Berlin, given in a thin voice interspersed by frequent coughs to a handful of students, established a philosophy of history centred on the World Spirit (another Rosicrucian idea) and a one-world perspective that became Hegelianism before he died of cholera in 1831.

Marx and Engels

The revolutionary originator who gave the Weishauptian and Hegelian vision a new slant and really inspired the Russian Revolution was Karl Marx,[8] who was born Moses Mordecai Marx Levi, a Prussian German Jew. Marx studied in Bonn and Berlin, where he joined the Young Hegelians and encountered the ideas of Weishaupt and Hegel, and in 1841 took his doctor's degree at the university of Jena, where he was strongly influenced by the works of Hegel. Marx took up Hegel's method of stating two opposites (thesis and antithesis) and then reconciling them in a synthesis, and combined Hegel's dialectic with Feuerbach's materialism. He now counterpoised a new historical Materialism against Hegel's (Rosicrucian) Idealism. He became a journalist on a recently founded newspaper in Cologne, and one of his colleagues (Moses Hess) introduced him to socialist ideas. He became editor, but soon his newspaper was suppressed by the Prussian government.[9] He emigrated to Paris in 1843, met French socialist writers, and became a 32nd-degree Grand Orient Mason – and absorbed more of Weishaupt's ideas.[10]

Marx was a Luciferian, like Weishaupt. Around 1840 he had joined the Satanist church in Berlin run by disciples of Joanna Southcott (died 1814) who was said to be in contact with the demon Shiloh,[11] and called the Christian religion "the most immoral of all religions." He studied economics in Paris, where he learned about French Communism and became a revolutionary and a communist. Though Jewish he wrote *A World Without Jews*[12] in 1844, and began a lifelong friendship with Frederick Engels.

Engels was very important in bringing the Marxist vision to birth; in fact, it can be argued that he rather than Marx implemented Weishaupt's vision. Engels was a Prussian gentile, son of a wealthy textile mill owner in the German Rhineland. He had joined Young Germany, which had been established in Switzerland in 1835 by Mazzini and Palmerston, Great Britain's Foreign Secretary.[13] He was trained in Illuminati ideas in Switzerland, and became a Templar Grand Orient Freemason. From 1838 to 1841 he was in Bremen working as a business apprentice in his father's firm. After hours he joined the left-wing Young Hegelians, and from them he took the Hegelian dialectic, that rational progress and revolutionary historical change result from the conflict of opposing views which end in a new synthesis.[14]

He joined the Prussian military service, serving with an artillery regiment in Berlin, and there became a member of a Young Hegelian circle known as The Free. In 1842 he met Marx's colleague, Moses Hess, who was nicknamed "the communist rabbi," and who converted him to communism by demonstrating that the logical conclusion of the Hegelian philosophy and dialectic was communism. Hess stressed that England would be the battleground for the new philosophy because of its advanced industry, powerful capitalists and expanding proletariat.[15]

Engels went to England to continue his training in a Manchester branch of the family business. He spent most of his time writing articles on communism and meeting radical leaders. In 1844 he wrote two articles in *German-French Yearbooks*,[16] a newspaper which was controlled by Templar Grand Orient Freemasonry and co-edited by Marx and Arnold Ruge, an agent of Palmerston's.[17] They were read by Palmerston, who as we have seen controlled all secret societies. He saw that Engels was developing a doctrine for the communist movement. Palmerston ensured that the Masonic press promoted Engels, and that Engels' fame spread throughout Germany.[18]

Templar Grand Orient Freemasonry was now promoting communism, and wanted a Jew to be the apparent father of the movement. It seems that Jews were to take the blame if the communist conspiracy was exposed.[19] (In 1918, on the other hand, the Illuminati went out of their way to disguise Jewish involvement in the Russian Revolution – a change of policy, as Jews had ceased to be marginal and had by then become central to the Russian Revolution.)

Engels had first met Marx in Cologne, where Marx was a newspaper editor in 1842. Later, on his way home from England, he went to Paris for a 10-day visit with his future collaborator. In 1845 the Prussian government again intervened and arranged for Marx to be expelled from France, whereupon he moved to Brussels and renounced his Prussian nationality. In 1845 Engels joined him in Brussels and then took him back to England.[20]

In 1848, at the age of 30, Marx published his *Communist Manifesto* from a draft (entitled *Confessions of a Communist*) written by Engels. He sought to convert the socialist secret society the League of the Just (which was an extension of the Illuminati) to his, and Marx's, communist views. Engels was successful, for as we have seen (p369) the *Communist Manifesto* was commissioned by the Communist League in London, formerly the League of the Just or the League of the Just Men. This League was an offshoot of the Parisian Outlaws League,[21] which had been founded by Illuminati members (all Grand Orient Masons) after they had fled from Paris to Germany when the Jacobin Clubs were closed down at the end of the Reign of Terror in the French Revolution. The League of the Just or "Bund" changed its name when Marx and Engels (at its request) became members in 1847, and it later became known as the International Communist Party.[22] Marx and Engels persuaded the second Communist Congress in London to adopt their views. The London-based Communists asked Marx and Engels to write the League's programme. They worked on it from December 1847 to the end of January 1848, then sent their manuscript back to London where it was immediately adopted as the League's manifesto: the *Communist Manifesto* of the Communist League. Within days revolutions broke out across Europe, as we have seen.[23]

Marx's vision was one of world war. He wrote in 1848: "The coming world war will cause not only reactionary classes and dynasties, but entire reactionary peoples, to disappear from the face of the earth." His revolutionary plans for socialism included the abolition of all religion and property and echoed the doctrines of Weishaupt. It was a programme for a perfect State. The workers would overthrow the private ownership of industry, and the government would own all property. The dictatorship would wither away and goods would be distributed on the basis of need, leaving a classless Utopia.[24]

Engels was the true father of Marxism, but the Grand Orient did not want him to appear as the founder of communism because he was a gentile. In actual fact, the founder of communism was Templar

Freemasonry, and the Grand Orient fixed on Marx as the ideal "founder."[25]

Marx and Engels co-ordinated the 1848 uprisings from London (where they associated with followers of Robert Owen). As the German states cast aside an authoritarian form of government for a more constitutional and representative one, Marx and Engels were given their first (and only) opportunity to take part in a revolution and devise tactics that would bring about a communist victory. Marx went to Paris on the invitation of the provisional government and then on to the Rhineland, to Cologne, where he again wrote for the newspaper he had once edited (now reopened), urging against proletarian revolution and advocating co-operation with the liberal bourgeoisie. Marx and Engels had made a tactical judgment that the proletariats of Europe stood a better chance of seizing power if they worked with the bourgeoisie rather than confronted them. Prompted by Engels (who was being advised by Palmerston's Masonic network) Marx urged that the *Communist Manifesto* should be shelved and that the Communist League should be disbanded. (No doubt the Grand Orient had seen that the uprisings were proving unsuccessful and were concerned to keep their revolutionary leaders out of prison.)

Marx urged a constitutional democracy and war with Russia, and when the King of Prussia dissolved the Prussian Assembly in Berlin, he took up arms and organized resistance. In due course he was arrested and tried, but was unanimously acquitted and thanked by the jury when he pleaded that the Prussian crown had made an unlawful attempt at counter-revolution. Nevertheless, with uprisings continuing, in May 1849 Marx was banished by the Prussian government, and returned, unfunded and unemployed, to London, which was to be his home for the rest of his life.

In London Marx advocated a bolder revolutionary policy, and with Engels wrote *Address of the Central Committee to the Communist League*.[26] Militants who were impatient for revolution now ridiculed Marx as a revolutionary who merely lectured and did not act. Marx lived in two small rooms in London's Soho in extreme hardship, financially supported by Engels who took a subordinate position in the Manchester family firm of Ermen and Engels and at first could only manage to send £5 notes. Several of Marx's children died. His one source of income was writing for *The New York Tribune*, for which he wrote some 500 articles, many of them written for him in Manchester by Engels. Otherwise he researched into economic and social history in the British Museum Reading Room.[27]

Engels continued to help forward the vision. With Marx as a passive partner he founded the International Working Men's Association in London in 1864, which later became known as the First Socialist International: "The Internationale." Mazzini's personal secretary, Wilhelm Wolff, a friend of Marx, urged the adoption of statutes similar to Mazzini's/Weishaupt's, and Marx later wrote to Engels: "I was present, only as a dumb personage on the platform." Nevertheless, he assumed control of the organization, which received the support of Masonic lodges world-wide. (The International was in fact a secret society with no interest whatever in the fate of working men.) He was a member of the General Council and regularly attended meetings and saw the International grow to 800,000 members by 1869 when, at its 4th Congress, Weishaupt's communist programme was fully adopted. (For instance, the abolition of private property was called for.) By now the International was fast becoming a pan-German Illuminist association.[28]

Marx continued working for his Illuminized Templar Grand Orient (Illuminati) bosses by writing the first volume of *Das Kapital* in 1867. It drew heavily on Weishaupt's ideas, which he found in books in the British Museum Reading Room. We have seen (p369) that a Rothschild (a descendant of Mayer Amschel "Rothschild" who funded Weishaupt) may have written Marx two checks at this time, although the British Museum, which is alleged to have displayed the checks, is not now aware of them. Still proselytizing, Engels rewrote parts of the book in a more accessible language.[29]

Herzen

Another London exile gave intellectual expression to the early communism of the Russian Revolution. Aleksander Herzen,[30] the illegitimate son of a Russian nobleman and a low-born German girl, had lived in his father's house in Moscow and was educated by French, German and Russian tutors. He was greatly influenced by the 1825 uprising against Nicholas I and vowed to continue the Decembrists' struggle for Russian freedom. He attended the University of Moscow from 1829 until 1833, where with his friend Ogaryov he formed a circle that developed an idealistic philosophy of history influenced by Schelling and Saint-Simon, in which the (occult) World Spirit moved towards freedom and justice. His group was arrested in 1834 and he was exiled (in Russia) for six years, during which he married, and read Hegel and Feuerbach. Now more materialistic, he held that the Hegelian dialectic was the "algebra of revolution" and that the disembodied truths of science (German idealism) must be realized in deeds that struggled for justice. In his way he was groping for a revolutionary dialectic that begins with (occult) spirit and ends in a physical deed.

In 1842 Herzen returned to Moscow, where he became a Westernizer, absorbed European rationalism and founded the revolutionary movement in Russia. He was influenced by Proudhon's anarchist socialism, and when his father died in 1846, leaving him a substantial fortune, he went to Paris, where he met Mikhail Bakunin, another disciple of Proudhon, became a Grand Orient Freemason and witnessed the 1848 Revolution. The failure of this revolution and the Italian upheaval convinced Herzen that Europe's social order would never be levelled and that Europe was finished as a historical force. He returned to Russia, convinced that Russia's way forward lay in revolution as its past held nothing worth conserving. He saw the peasant commune as the basis of a new Socialist order (as later did Chairman Mao in China), and he communicated this idea in letters to Mazzini in 1850-1.

In 1852 Herzen moved to London and founded the Free Russian Press, the first-ever uncensored printing operation in the history of Russia. When the reforming Alexander II became Tsar and announced that he intended emancipating the serfs, reformers were allowed more freedom and a new climate of revolt arose in Russia. The new materialist philosophies and revolutionary ideologies of the West (principally Marxism and anarchism) freely entered Russia and turned liberal reformers into radicals. Herzen sent back periodicals created in London in 1855 and 1856, and then in 1857 his influential political newspaper *Kolokol* (*The Bell*), which supported the emancipation of the peasants. In view of the Tsar's reformist posture, he moderated his opposition, knowing that *Kolokol* was read by both the Tsar's Ministers and by the revolutionary opposition. Soon Herzen had fallen between two stools: he was criticized both by moderate intellectuals such as Turgenev for his Utopian recklessness, and also by younger radicals such as Chernyshevsky, who felt he had not gone far enough. Later he himself criticized the 1861 Emancipation Act as insufficiently radical and as betraying the peasants.

Herzen now became more extreme and allied with the anarchist Mikhail Bakunin, and *Kolokol* supported the Polish revolt of 1863. This lost him his moderate readers without winning more support among the revolutionaries. He moved to Geneva to be near Russian exiles, but when *Kolokol* closed in 1867, he took an interest in the First International and Marx's federation of working-class organizations.

It is possible to regard Herzen (who identified the revolutionary implications of Hegel's dialectic in the 1830s) as Marx's co-intellectual-originator as he died nearly 50 years before the Russian Revolution and had a Utopian vision for peasants to complement Marx's Utopian vision for workers. However, Herzen gave Marx's revolutionary outlook intellectual expression through his work in Russia in the 1840s and his periodicals and newspapers in the 1850s and 1860s, and it makes sense to regard him as giving intellectual expression to Marx's revolutionary origination while adding his own peasant gloss rather than to see him as a break-away originator.

INTELLECTUAL NIHILISTS AND ANARCHISTS

Alexander II and the Nihilists

Alexander II came to the throne at the height of the Crimean war, in 1855. The Tsars had proved the last bastion of absolutism in the first half of the 19th century, and although Alexander I and Nicholas I showed interest in reforms and in catching up with the West, neither offered a constitution or agreed to a constitutional monarchy. All revolts had been ruthlessly suppressed: the uprising of the Decembrist reformers in 1825 (following which five ringleaders were hanged in public – twice as the first time was bungled), the Polish uprising in 1830 and the uprisings of the Austrian minorities in 1848, which Nicholas helped Austria crush.

Alexander II did want internal reform, and he must take credit for emancipating the serfs in 1861 and giving local district councils (*Zemstvos*) a measure of self-government (1864). Reformers were granted more freedom to develop their movements. Many took this opportunity to support the new Polish uprising of 1863, and more extreme attitudes bloomed.[31]

The Nihilists ("nothing-ists" from the Latin *nihil,* "nothing")[32] surfaced in the early years of Alexander's reign. It was the materialism of Western revolutionary thought that gave rise to Nihilism, which rejected all moral and social bonds and advocated rational scientific truth as the only standard of judgment. Nihilism therefore was a new incarnation of Weishaupt's "religion of reason." It threatened to destroy the very fabric of society and civilization. At first the Nihilists were negationist sceptics, like Turgenev's Bazarov in *Fathers and Sons,* a novel that was published in 1862. Bazarov's philosophy is one of negation. Against the established social order and all philosophical systems and forms of aestheticism, Bazarov sees evil as deriving from ignorance, which must be combated by scientific truth and utilitarianism. Bazarov approves of what is "useful" and has no time for the "useless" existing social order and culture. He shows contempt for history and tradition, and represents a new revolutionary generation that puts its trust exclusively in rationalism and Darwinism. The materialist Feuerbach and the scientific rationalists Darwin and Herbert Spencer were the early nihilists' heroes.

Freemasonry had been banned in Russia by Alexander I following the 1822 Congress of Verona, where Metternich warned all governments to take action against Freemasonry. ("Absolute monarchies, constitutional monarchies and even republics are all threatened by the Levellers.") Alexander I had been an enthusiastic Grand Orient Mason until then, and his court had been dominated by the female Masons Mme Bouche and Mme de Krudner. As soon as the Tsar banned the Grand Orients and Grand Lodges, Pavel Pestel, the Grand Master of the Grand Orients formed a plan to assassinate him. The revolution was scheduled for 1829 but brought forward by Alexander I's sudden death. After the failure of the Pestel-organized Grand Orient Decembrist uprising and the execution of the Grand Orient rebels, the Russian Grand Orient operated in France and it was from there that the Russian revolutionary movement was organized and manipulated.[33]

The influence of Illuminized Templar Grand Orient Freemasonry can be seen in all the Russian revolutionary movements of the second half of the 19th century. Its presence was verified by the scathing attacks on Freemasonry by Tolstoy, through Pierre in *War and Peace*, and by Dostoevsky, through the Grand Inquisitor in *The Brothers Karamazov*. The emancipation of the serfs in 1861 led to an influx into the cities and the growth of a new urban industrial proletariat which was manipulated by the London International set up in 1864. As capitalism spread banks, factories and railways, it also spread Templar-organized Masonic revolution among the new generation.

But nihilism soon took on a second meaning: negationist revolution. For revolutionaries, Nihilism involved the negation of all conventional morality and moral principles, and acted against tyranny and hypocrisy for the sake of individual freedom. Their belief was the negation of the Church's belief in the soul and the State's authority which derived from divine right (which they denied), and they justified terror and destruction as a way of attaining their goals. Their aims were very close to those of the Illuminati, with whom most were linked.

Bakunin and Anarchism

Mikhail Bakunin gave thoughtful intellectual expression to Marx's occult vision. Because he was so influential among the Nihilists, who also gave intellectual expression to the classless Utopia of Communism, it may be thought that he should be considered as having originated the vision. In fact, he was a prophet of the means, the creation of anarchy through terrorism, by which the end of the Utopian vision could be achieved.

The son of a Russian landowner, Bakunin was sent to the Artillery School in St. Petersburg and then to a military unit on the Polish frontier. He deserted and went home and studied Hegel and the German philosopher Fichte and then moved to Moscow, where he met Herzen. He moved on to Berlin and joined the young Hegelians, then to Dresden, where he published a revolutionary tract that ended, "The passion for destruction is also a creative passion." On reading this, the Tsarist administration ordered him to return to Moscow, and withdrew his passport when he refused. Bakunin went to Switzerland and then Belgium and finally settled in Paris, where he associated with Proudhon and Marx, and met Polish *émigrés* who urged him to help them liberate the Slav peoples.[34]

During this time he became a Grand Orient Freemason and a Russian disciple of Weishaupt. He took up anarchism, adapting Proudhon's version to include the need for violent (and "destructive") revolutionary action through loosely linked, autonomous workers' associations. He became a Satanist – like Marx – and saw Satan as the spiritual head of revolutionaries, as both the supreme rebel and supreme freedom-fighter and liberator of human beings.[35] With Weishaupt he saw Church and State as oppressors, and held: "Satan [is] the eternal rebel, the first freethinker and the emancipator of worlds. He makes man ashamed of his bestial ignorance and obedience; he emancipates him, stamps upon his brow the seal of liberty and humanity, in urging him to disobey and eat of the fruit of knowledge."[36]

In February 1848 Bakunin fought in the Paris streets, and after a few days moved to Germany and then Poland, hoping to spread the revolution. In Prague that June he attended the Slav Congress and later in *An Appeal to the Slavs* he called for the peasants to overthrow the Habsburg Empire and create a free federation of Slav peoples.

Bakunin was involved in the Dresden uprising in May 1849, was arrested by the Saxon authorities and sent back to Russia, where he was put in the Peter-Paul Fortress in St. Petersburg for three years. He was then transferred to another prison for a further three years. He was released in 1857 on condition that he lived in Siberia. The Governor of Eastern Siberia was a cousin of his mother's, and through him, it seems, Bakunin obtained permission to do some local business. He managed to board an American ship bound for Japan and then the United States, whence he made his way to Great Britain, arriving in 1861.

In London Bakunin met Mazzini and, according to one source, they both plotted the assassination of Napoleon III (who had opposed the unification of Italy). He was also reunited with Herzen, whom he had last seen in 1847, but the two men quickly fell out. In 1863 Bakunin sailed with a boatload of Polish volunteers to spread the uprising in Poland, after which he moved to Italy for four years. There he formulated his branch of anarchism, which advocated a violent overthrow of the existing order without any centralized control or authority. This philosophy influenced the Nihilists of the 1860s.

Bakunin had settled in Geneva in 1868. He was more extreme than Marx, who urged non-violent revolution through workers' strikes as opposed to violent and destructive revolution. (Marx's centralized, authoritarian control – the dictatorship of the proletariat – was the opposite way to Bakunin's local groups acting without central authority, as members of a Social Democratic Alliance.)

It was in Geneva in March 1869 that Bakunin met Sergey Nechayev, a former student of St. Petersburg University who had also taught at a St. Petersburg school. Then a student of 21 and a member of St. Petersburg's revolutionary movement, Nechayev announced to

Bakunin that he was a delegate of a (fictitious) "Russian Revolutionary Committee." Bakunin appointed him to an equally fictitious "Russian Section of the World Revolutionary Alliance" and gave him a "fictitious" number, 2771, suggesting that the make-believe organization already had 2,770 members.[37]

On this dubious basis Nechayev began a collaboration with Bakunin and returning to Moscow in September, founded the Peoples' Retribution (also known as the Society of the Axe), whose members had to agree to submit to the will of the leader. When Ivanov, a student member, protested, Nechayev ordered his execution, which was carried out by himself and three other members of his group. They lured Ivanov to the Moscow School of Agriculture, shot him, strangled him – Ivanov bit Nechayev badly on his hand – and dumped the body in a half-frozen pond, where it was found four days later.

The crime was discovered, and it transpired that Nechayev, despite his youth, was a blackmailer, extortioner and confidence trickster as well as a ruthless murderer. He fled to Switzerland while 67 members of his Bakuninist organization were tried. The Satanist Bakunin distanced himself; Nechayev was too unprincipled even for him. The young man was arrested by the Swiss police in 1872 and returned to Russia; he was sentenced to 20 years in the Peter-Paul Fortress, where he died. By then he had become notorious for his ruthless Nihilistic murder of Ivanov, and Dostoevsky based Peter Verhovensky – Stavrogin – on him in *The Possessed.* (Shatov was based on Ivanov.)[38]

Another Nihilist who imported Bakunin's branch of anarchism into Russia was Prince Peter Kropotkin, who likewise gave intellectual expression to the communist vision. Educated at the Corps of Pages in St. Petersburg, he served as an aide to Alexander II and, from 1862 to 1867, as an army officer in Siberia, where he won a reputation for scientific observations. He was asked to be secretary to the Russian Geographical Society, but refused so that he could devote his life to anarchism, and in 1872 joined a revolutionary group in St. Petersburg. He was imprisoned in 1874, but escaped by racing out of the prison yard through the gates, pursued by a sentry and three soldiers. Outside he jumped into a carriage with a fast horse, brought by an accomplice, and with all the cabs engaged by other accomplices he drove to a restaurant and lunched in a private room while soldiers searched the streets for him. He then sailed for England. He lived in Switzerland until he was expelled in 1881 and then moved to France where he was again imprisoned for three years. After his release he settled in England for the next 30 years, until 1917, when he returned to Russia. During his long exile he gave anarchism a scientific basis as "anarchist communism," and condoned violence, referring to it as "propaganda by the deed." Because of his writings he must be regarded as the main founder of both the English and the Russian anarchist movements, who, more than Bakunin, spread anarchist communism into Russia.[39]

Most of the Nihilists are known primarily for their sayings. Bielinsky, lover of Hegel, said: "Negation is my god, as reality formerly was. My heroes are the destroyers of the past." Herzen echoed this in his "the annihilation of the past is the procreation of the future." Pisarev asked himself if he was justified in killing his own mother, and answered his own question (in words that would have found support from Nechayev): "And why not, if I want to do so, and I find it useful?" (Reason turned all the Nihilists away from conventional morality towards rational egoism and self-interest.) Proudhon's declaration that God is Evil ("Come, Satan, victim of the calumnies of kings and of the petty-minded!") was taken up by his follower Bakunin, "Evil is the Satanic rebellion against divine authority, a rebellion in which we, nevertheless, see the fruitful seed of every form of human emancipation." Nechayev took the logic of revolution – "all is permitted" – to its conclusion: homicide.[40]

As they applied negation to morality, the Nihilists found themselves adopting some strange attitudes. Pisarev and Chernyshevsky were both pro-feminist. Pisarev, writing for *Dawn*, a Russian women's magazine and wanting to marry his cousin Raisa, told her that she must be free to take lovers. When she arranged to marry someone else, Pisarev waylaid her husband-to-be at St. Petersburg railway station and fought him with his fists and later challenged him to a duel. Likewise Chernyshevsky explained to the vivacious Olga that after their marriage she would be free to run off and have a child by another man, and he was dismayed when she took him literally and became the mistress of a Polish émigré (among others) in an alcove in the same room in which her husband was writing.[41]

Nihilist Terrorist Acts

But experimental attitudes in negation aside, the Nihilists were primarily known for their deeds. The first student riots outside St. Petersburg University were in 1861. Students protested at the appointment of General Philipson as Curator of the Educational District, and there were clashes with police and troops. Twenty students were beaten with rifle butts, and several hundred were put in the Peter-Paul Fortress. Mysterious fires terrified St. Petersburg in 1862, and the Polish rebellion took place a year later.

There was an attempt on Alexander II's life by Dmitry Karakozov (who had been sent down from two universities). The pale-faced, long-haired Karakozov belonged to a group called *The Organization* which was based in Moscow and had a branch in St. Petersburg. Its leader was Nicholas Ishutin who admired Chernyshevsky. Karakozov announced that he would kill the Tsar, and on April 4, 1866 he shot at the Tsar as he returned home from a walk in St. Petersburg's Summer Garden. He missed, and was tried and hanged before a large crowd on the Smolensk Field in St. Petersburg. Ishutin, who had also been sentenced to hang, was reprieved at the last minute and sent to Siberia. As a result of the incident, police repression intensified, and there was a counter-revolutionary wave of violence in the late 1860s that was known as the White Terror.[42]

Bakunin fell out with his revolutionary originator, Marx, over the 1871 revolution in France.[43] The 1871 Paris Commune made Marx an international figure. We have seen (p381) that he and Engels supported it from London, and after it collapsed Marx hailed it in *Civil War in France*: "History has no comparable example of such greatness....Its martyrs are enshrined forever in the great heart of the working class." Engels called it history's first example of the "dictatorship of the proletariat." However, the International Working Men's Association was divided over Marx's support for the Commune, and split.

Marx's ideas reached Russia through his support for the Paris Commune and through his conflict with his critic, the Russian Mikhail Bakunin, who had never forgotten Marx's accusation in 1848 that he was a Russian Tsarist agent. Bakunin admired the revolutionary direct action of the Commune and felt Marx was an authoritarian German Jew who favoured centralized structures; he felt that Marx should look to peasants and students rather than effete proletariat workers. He set up the International Alliance of Social Democracy, which Marx succeeded in keeping out of the International, citing Bakunin's involvement with the murderer Nechayev.

At the Congress of the International at The Hague in 1872 Marx defeated the Bakuninists. Engels then proposed that the International's General Council should be based in New York, not London. This proposal came from the Grand Orient, and the General Council petered out in Philadelphia four years later.

Marx now hoped for a European war that would overthrow Russian Tsarism, the main force of reaction in Europe, and at the end of his life he admired the Russian terrorists who assassinated Tsar Alexander II in 1881.[44]

In the 1870s hostility towards the Russian government increased, especially after the Russo-Turkish war of 1877-8 which revealed Russian incompetence to the public at home, although Russia won the war. There were more attempts to ferment peasant uprisings[45] in the 1870s. In 1877 Bakuninist revolutionaries stirred up the peasants at Chigirin, near Kiev, by printing a charter purporting to come from the Tsar, urging revolution against the landlords. About 1,000 peasants were recruited in this way, and when the plot was broken up several hundred peasants were arrested and many exiled to Siberia. In October, 193 were tried in St. Petersburg: half were acquitted, but the 14 ringleaders received penal servitude.

The day after the sentences were announced, January 24, 1878, the

Nihilist, Vera Zasulich shot and wounded Gen. Trepov, City Prefect of St. Petersburg. Trepov had been responsible for breaking up a workers' demonstration in December 1876, during which the police seized a Nihilist known as Bogolyubov, who had not taken part but happened to be passing. He was tried and sentenced to 15 years' penal servitude. In July 1877 there was trouble at the Remand Prison in St. Petersburg where he was being held along with the 193, and Gen. Trepov had arrived to look into the matter. Bogolyubov refused to take his cap off to Trepov, who, in a rage, tore it off his head, hit him with his fists and shouted that he was to be flogged. The flogging took place in the prison corridor the next day. It was very severe and brutal, and there was a prison mutiny. As a result some prisoners were beaten unconscious and thrown into punishment cells. News had spread to the outside world, and Vera Zasulich wanted to avenge the treatment meted out to Bogolyubov (whom she had never met).

She joined a crowd of petitioners waiting for Gen. Trepov, and after he fell wounded, calmly waited to be arrested. The authorities allowed her to be tried by jury, thinking that the judge would deliver the sentence they sought. In fact, the jury found her not guilty despite the evidence of many eye-witnesses. It was a popular verdict that was applauded in court. As she left, a free woman, there was a riot as the crowd outside suspected she was about to be re-arrested. In the confusion Vera was whisked away.

Vera Zasulich began a new wave of Nihilist militancy. In January 1878 the Odessa police raided the lodgings of Ivan Kovalsky, who kept a secret printing press. He held them off with a revolver and dagger, shooting at them while friends frantically burned incriminating documents. He was sentenced to death and shot in August. In February revolutionaries killed a police spy; they belonged to Valerian Osinsky's Executive Committee of the Russian Socialist Revolutionary Party. Osinsky then shot at the Public Prosecutor of Kiev. Gregory Popko stabbed a gendarme to death, and two days later three men helped the three Chigirin ringleaders to escape from prison. In August (two days after Kovalsky's execution) Sergey Kravchinsky stabbed Gen.

Mezentsov, Chief of the Gendarmes in a St. Petersburg street in what appeared to be a Nihilist counter-attack.

In February 1879, Governor-General Kropotkin, cousin of the revolutionary Peter Kropotkin, was shot dead in his carriage by Gregory Goldenberg, who was later arrested and confessed all he knew to a sympathetic revolutionary (in fact a police informer) who shared his cell. Realizing he had betrayed his fellow Nihilists, Goldenberg hanged himself in his cell.

On April 2, 1879 another attempt was made on the life of Alexander II. Alexander Solovyov fired five times at the Tsar as he walked in the grounds of the Winter Palace. The Tsar zig-zagged away and escaped with a hole in his greatcoat. Solovyov was arrested, tried by court martial – the court which now tried all cases against the State – and hanged on May 28 before a large crowd. Military Governor-Generals were now imposed on St. Petersburg, Kharkov and Odessa.

During the rest of 1879 16 Nihilists were hanged (14 of them in southern Russia). The offences of these Nihilists included attempted murder of a police spy, armed resistance to arrest, possession of dynamite and involvement in the Chigirin Revolt. One of those hanged, Dmitry Lizogub, merely distributed revolutionary propaganda. The three men who had actually killed – Popko, Kravchinsky and Goldenberg – all escaped the public hangman. (Kravchinsky later taught Russian to Constance Garnett, the famous translator of Russian novels into English.)

The Governor-General of Kharkov, Loris Melikov, who was admired by the Tsar for his firm but moderate leadership, was given dictatorial powers over the whole of Russia in February 1880. Within days of this appointment he was fired at by Mlodetsky, who missed and was hanged two days later.

The Assassination of Alexander II

The Nihilists were still plotting to kill the Tsar. A new group was formed called The People's Will. Its inspiration was the Satanist Bakunin, whose anarchist Party urged terrorism and assassination as a means of overthrowing all forms of existing government. (Bakunin had criticized Herzen for condemning Karakosov's attempt to kill Alexander II in 1866.) At a meeting in a forest on August 26, 1879 The People's Will sentenced Alexander II to execution. Its leader was Alexander Mikhaylov, and after two failed attempts with revolvers it was decided to use buried explosives. The group had no hope of overthrowing the Tsar's government; the best they could expect would be the replacement of Alexander II by Alexander III.

The People's Will made six unsuccessful attempts to blow up the Tsar between late 1879 and early 1880, five of them as he travelled between St. Petersburg and his holiday home at Livadia in the Crimea.

Following Mikhaylov's arrest, when he attempted to collect snapshots of two executed colleagues from a photographer's shop, Andrey Zhelyabov had become leader of The People's Will. He and his girlfriend Sophia Perovsky arranged for Nihilists to stalk the Tsar, and they discovered that late in the morning every Sunday he drove in his carriage from the Winter Palace down Nevsky Prospekt and then up Malaya Sadovaya Street to the Mikhaylov cavalry parade ground (the name echoed that of the group's arrested leader), where he reviewed his troops and then returned. He was escorted by mounted Cossacks followed by sleighs full of police and military officers.

The Nihilists rented business premises on the corner where he would turn, tunnelled under the road and set up a cheese shop under the name Mr. and Mrs. Kovozev. On February 27 Zhelyabov was arrested, so it was decided to proceed on March 1 with Sophia Perovsky in command. Four Nihilists armed with nitroglycerine hand grenades (each weighing 5 lbs) would finish the Tsar off if necessary.

At 12.55 pm on Sunday March 1, ironically after signing a proclamation announcing his intention to grant a Constitution, the Tsar drove out of the Winter Palace, taking a different route to the parade-ground, along Catherine Quay. It was clear that he would return by that same route, as he was visiting his cousin the Grand Duchess Catherine at the Mikhaylov Palace on his way back.

The four Nihilists with their grenades took up new positions. Sophia Perovsky co-ordinated their movements, giving them signals with her handkerchief (for example, by blowing her nose). She crossed the canal, saw the Imperial cavalcade approaching and signalled with her handkerchief.

The Imperial coach was driven by a liveried coachman wearing a red cloak; fur-capped Cossacks in scarlet coats rode on black horses beside it. Two sleighs followed across the snow, one bearing the St. Petersburg Chief of Police. One of the young Nihilists, Nicholas Rysakov, threw a grenade. It hit the back axle of the coach and exploded without penetrating through the floor. The horses bolted, whipped on by the coachman. Unhurt, the Tsar ordered the coach to stop and walked back to the grenade-thrower, who had been seized by the police. An officer asked, "Where's the Tsar?" The Tsar replied, "Thank God I am safe," thus giving himself away.

As he walked back to his coach another Nihilist threw a second nitroglycerine grenade. It landed behind the Tsar, at his feet. There was another explosion, and bodies were hurled through a cloud of snow and smoke. When it cleared the Tsar was sitting by the railing of the Catherine Canal, helmetless, cloakless, his uniform in shreds, his legs and face covered in blood. He called for help, and said he was feeling cold. Twenty people lay injured, the second grenade-thrower (who died that night in hospital) among them.

The Tsar was carried back to the Winter Palace, where he died before 4 pm. He was succeeded by the less reformist Alexander III. Zhelyabov heard the news of the attack in prison and immediately confessed to his role in the killing and demanded to be hanged, saying that it would be unfair to give him a lesser sentence. Arrests followed, and Nicholas Rysakov informed on his comrades, hoping to save himself.

On the morning of April 7 the five condemned assassins were strapped on top of tumbrils with 14-foot-high platforms, their wrists and ankles chained, and with placards saying "Tsaricide" round their necks. The first tumbril carried Zhelyabov and Rysakov. The second carried Sophia Perovsky, with Kibalchich (the explosives expert) and Timothy Mikhaylov (who had not thrown his grenade-bomb) on either side. They rode to Semyonov Square, where 80,000 crowded round a scaffold 20-feet high. The five were chained to pillars and their sentences were read to them. All five kissed the cross as drums rolled. Sophia Perovsky kissed Zhelyabov, who went to his death smiling. Then, hooded, they stood on low stands, which were kicked away, leaving them to writhe as they slowly strangled. Mikhaylov was heavy and three times his noose slipped and began to pull away the metal ring from which the rope hung. He was hanged at the third attempt. Rysakov had to be dragged to the rope and he desperately tried to keep his feet on the footstand after it was kicked away. All the other four met their deaths with great dignity.

So ended the Bakuninist, Grand Orient-sponsored Nihilists who operated in the reign of Alexander II and gave intellectual expression to the Russian Revolution. There were still terrorists in Russia, but from now on they were full-time revolutionaries.

THREE RUSSIAN REVOLUTIONS

Alexander III

Alexander III was a reactionary. He had always opposed his father's reform programme, and had taken the side of the French in the Franco-Prussian war while his father supported the Prussians. He lost no time in cancelling his father's promise of a Constitution and set about reforms that would confirm his autocratic power and dismantle leniency towards the liberals. He wanted one Russian nation with one religion and one language, and had no time for concessions to the Slavs. He again suppressed Freemasonry, but it was now too powerful to be wiped out. His policies played into the hands of Marxist propagandists, and when there was a Bakuninist, Grand Orient-sponsored attempt on his life in 1887 he dealt as severely with it as he had dealt with The People's Will, hanging another five rebels, one of whom, Alexander Ulyanov, was Lenin's older brother. In 1890 Russia's alliance with Germany ended and he aligned Russia with France.[46]

Alexander III and his equally autocratic successor in 1894, his son
Nicholas II, opened up Russia to Western mercantile capitalists. The
key figure was Sergey Witte, who was Russian Minister of Finance from
1892 to 1903. His policy was to encourage the economic development
of Russia following Germany's southern industrial expansion. The State
Bank was remodelled to provide industry with capital; steamship
companies were established, as were savings banks; and company law
was reformed. He also introduced the gold standard and took Russia
into the international credit system. The rouble was made convertible,
and Russian industrialization was financed by loans from investors in
France, Britain, Belgium and Germany – including the Rothschilds.
(Railway-building linked Europe and Asia to Russia.) Witte's policy let
in the capitalist Freemasons, and, drawing on French capital with
reckless abandon, Russia became one of the largest debtor nations.
Witte created the State liquor monopoly, with the result that peasants
and workers now drank their wages.[47]

The Grand Orient and Lenin's Attempted 1905 Revolution

A disastrous war with Japan in 1904-5, partly provoked by Russia's
expansionist policy in Korea and Manchuria, resulted in the destruction
of Russia's Baltic Fleet and created (in Lenin's phrase) "the locomotive
of revolution." Japan's war costs were funded by the Grand Orient,
which saw its opportunity to weaken Russia so that it would not be able
to resist the revolution the Grand Orient had scheduled for 1905. The
war would tie down Russian troops in the east, leaving the western front
relatively unguarded. A loan of $30 million was made to the Japanese
by a Warburg bank in New York, which was run by the Grand Orient
Freemason Jacob Schiff. This was a Rothschild subsidiary, Kuhn Loeb
and Co., which then floated war loans.[48] In 1904, together with the
Grand Orient, Rothschilds had a strategic plan for obtaining the Tsar's
wealth. This plan may eventually have included retaining $1 billion the
Tsar is alleged to have deposited in Rothschild banks in Europe and
New York. (see p461 for deposits of $80m and $400m.)[49]

By now Kuhn, Loeb & Co. were also Rockefellers' bankers,[50] and
Rockefellers were linked with Warburgs. Rockefellers had their eye on

Russia's Baku oilfields in Azerbaijan, on the western shore of the
Caspian Sea. This oilfield had been developed in 1872 and by 1900 it
had become the largest in the world and was under the Rothschilds'
control.[51] It continued to be the largest Soviet oilfield, supplying
Russia up the Volga River, until the 1940s. The situation in early 1905
was that Rockefellers wanted Rothschilds' Baku oilfield, and were
prepared to create a revolution in Russia to seize it.[52] Rothschilds also
had their eye on the Tsar's wealth.[53] And, as we have seen at the
beginning of this paragraph, both Rockefellers and Rothschilds
employed Warburgs and Kuhn, Loeb & Co.[54] The situation was
complex.

Vladimir Ilich Lenin   Lev Davidovich Bronstein (Trotsky)

Against this changed background, the main intellectual expression
of the revolutionary vision of Marx and Engels was provided by its semi-
political interpreter, Trotsky,[55] who was born Lev Davidovich
Bronstein of Jewish parents near Odessa. In 1895 with Lenin and others
he founded the Social Democratic Labour Party, which became the All-
Russia Communist Party in 1918. In 1898 Trotsky, already (at the age
of 19) a member of the Grand Orient (and therefore acquainted with
Weishaupt's ideas), used the Grand Orient lodges to organize a

revolutionary society, the South Russian Workers' Union, in Nikolayev, a Black Sea port near his home.[56] In 1899 he and his Masonic friends were arrested by the Tsar's police and exiled to Siberia. In 1902 he escaped and fled to Western Europe, where in London he met Lenin who had emerged as leader of the majority group ("Bolsheviks," "majority") in the Russian Social Democratic Party. Trotsky declined to join the Bolshevik programme which sought the violent overthrow of the government. (He preferred workers' strikes.) He went to Austria and then Paris and visited the Grand Orient lodges,[57] raising financial support for his revolutions. The Marxist leaders in Paris supported him and when the French Grand Orient sent him back into Russia to foment revolution in the spring of 1905, he founded the "Soviet of Workers" in St Petersburg.[58] (Lenin also returned to Russia in 1905 but took no part in these Soviets.) Trotsky had also founded a daily newspaper, *Nachalo* (*The Beginning*), backed by Dr Herzenstein, a wealthy Jewish publisher. It sold half a million copies a day, far more than Lenin's daily *Novoya Zhizn* (*New Life*), and through it he promulgated the vision.[59]

Both papers reached the House of Warburg in Germany. Max Warburg, a Grand Orient Freemason and head of the Rothschild-affiliated Warburg Bank in Frankfurt, was funding the Japanese war against Russia through Schiff. Warburg financed Trotsky,[60] who reflected his own view of world revolution, but backed Lenin to run a revolutionary government. He secured the co-operation of both men. Trotsky eventually saw that workers' strikes would prove ineffectual and he came to support violent overthrow. The Bolshevik movement was funded by Grand Orient Masons in Berlin, Paris and London.[61]

Lenin was nine years older than Trotsky, and was his rival both as a revolutionary and as a journalist. Born Vladimir Ilich Ulyanov of a Jewish mother and gentile father, he was much affected by the ideals of his revolutionary elder brother, who was hanged for attempting to assassinate Alexander III when Lenin was seventeen. Like his brother, Lenin looked back to the anarchist Bakunin, a Russian Grand Orient Mason. In 1889 he joined Grand Orient Freemasonry, began reading

Marx and became a Marxist while a student at the university of Kazan. He practised law and moved to St Petersburg as a public defender, which brought him into contact with revolutionary Marxists. In 1895 he was arrested as a subversive, jailed for 15 months and exiled to Siberia. On his return, he lived from 1900 in Western Europe and as leader of the Bolsheviks plotted the violent overthrow of the Tsar's government. In 1902 his *What is to be Done?* presented the Social Democratic Party as "the vanguard of the proletariat." In 1905 he travelled to London to raise funds from the Socialist Fabian Society, from such Freemasons as George Bernard Shaw, H. G. Wells and Annie Besant.[62]

In St. Petersburg the discontent following the Russo-Japanese war felt by workers and students was co-ordinated by the Union of Liberation. In January 1905 legal labour unions held a wave of strikes. One of these unions, the Assembly of Russian Workingmen, led by Georgy Gapon, arranged a mass peaceful demonstration before the Winter Palace at which Gapon would present the workers' request for reform to Nicholas II. The workers carried religious icons and pictures of Nicholas towards the square. In the Tsar's absence from the city, his uncle, Chief of the Security Police, Grand Duke Vladimir, tried to stop the march and then ordered his police to fire at the demonstrators. More than 100 were killed and several hundred were wounded in a massacre known as Bloody Sunday.

There were immediate protests: general strikes in St. Petersburg and other cities, peasant uprisings in the countryside and mutinies in the army, collectively known as the Revolution of 1905.[63] Nicholas II responded in February by announcing his intention of establishing an elected assembly to advise the government. The striking workers, peasants and others demanded a constituent assembly. The revolt spread to Poland, Finland, the Baltic and Georgia, and there were clashes as counter-revolutionaries attacked socialists and Jews.[64]

In spring 1905 Lenin returned to St Petersburg to receive additional funds from a Mason, Joseph Stalin, who was known as "the Jesse James of the Urals" as he had been robbing banks to fund the Bolsheviks.

Lenin began his revolution on May 1, 1905 (because it was the anniversary of the founding of the Illuminati).[65] In June, the crew of the battleship *Potemkin* mutinied at Odessa.

In August a decree announced elections for the Tsar's original idea of an advisory assembly. He had not moved at all, and the news was greeted by more protest. In October the railways were on strike, and soon there was a permanent general strike. A workers' council, or soviet, was formed in Ivanovo-Vosnesensk, and another followed in St. Petersburg. This directed the general strike, and as social democrats, particularly Mensheviks (the "minority") joined it, it had the force of revolutionary government, not unlike the Paris Commune of 1871. Soviets were also formed in Moscow, Odessa and elsewhere.

Nicholas was forced to act. Reluctantly, on the advice of Witte, he issued the October Manifesto, which promised a Constitution and an elected legislature (the Duma), and he made Witte president of a new Council of Ministers.[66] Alexander II had promised a Constitution on the day of his assassination in 1881,[67] and this announcement merely conceded what Russia would have obtained 25 years previously had Alexander not been assassinated. It was not enough for the revolutionaries, who wanted a republic with a democratic assembly, but many workers stopped striking and went back to work, which was enough to break the St. Petersburg Soviet.[68] Many of the revolutionary leaders were arrested: Lenin was exiled to Switzerland, Trotsky and Stalin to Siberia. The events of 1905 marked a failure for both Trotsky and Lenin but they transformed the Russian government from an autocracy to a constitutional monarchy.

Terrorist incidents continued. One of the most notable, which Camus focused on in *The Rebel* (and also in his play *Les Justes*) concerned Kaliayev, a member of the Organization for Combat, which had been created in 1903 by the Revolutionary Socialist Party of Savinkov. Kaliayev "the Poet" believed in God. Shortly before an assassination attempt which failed, Savinkov saw him in a street, "by an icon, a bomb in one hand and making the sign of the cross with the other." Called on to kill the Grand Duke Sergey, he saw the necessity of killing to bring about change but did not believe in murder. The first time he refused to carry out his mission as there were children in the Grand Duke's carriage; the second time, however, he succeeded in killing him. He then gave himself up and asked for death. At his execution, dressed in black and wearing a felt hat, "the Poet" turned away from the proffered crucifix, saying, "I already told you that I have finished with life and that I am prepared for death." The conscientious Kaliayev; his colleague Sazanov, killer of Plehva in 1905, who wrote, "our chivalry was permeated with such a degree of feeling that the word 'brother' in no way conveyed, with sufficient clarity, the essence of our relations with one another"; Voinarovsky, who died throwing a bomb at Admiral Dubassov and earlier declared, "if Dubassov is accompanied by his wife, I shall not throw the bomb" – all reveal a nobility within the heart of Nihilism that is highly moral and defies the rejection of conventional morality.[69] What the Nihilists were called on to do by their Grand Orient controllers was shocking and disgusting, but one cannot help admiring their courage and loyalty to each other. Such insights take us close to the network of loyalties that surrounded Trotsky and Lenin.

The Protocols of Zion and Rasputin

It was at this point in 1905 – in November when peace had been agreed with Japan the first communist revolution had come to an end, the Tsar had agreed to a transition to democracy and the faith healer Rasputin had just joined the Tsar's family to heal the young Aleksei – that the *Protocols of the Learned Elders of Zion* (sometimes written *Sion*) were published in Russia. The *Protocols* (which are defined in the work as "minutes") purported to record a Jewish plan to acquire the wealth of all peoples, overthrow all governments and create a Kingdom of the Jews with a Jewish King. They suggested that the revolution of 1905 was inspired by Jews, and Rasputin told the Tsar that the 1905 uprising had been a Jewish conspiracy to destroy the Romanov dynasty. He advised the Tsar to slaughter the Jews, who, as the pogroms of Kiev, Alexandrovsk and Odessa took place, now joined revolutionary groups for protection.[70]

A lot has been written about the authenticity of the *Protocols*. It has been claimed that they were written by none other than Adam Weishaupt, to blame the Jews for the Illuminati's plan to set up a world dictatorship. More plausibly, they seem to have been written for the Zionist Congress of 1897, though the Jews have always denied Jewish authorship. The *Protocols* allegedly fell into the hands of Sergey Nilus, who in 1903 presented them to the Tsar, perhaps to discredit Rasputin's predecessor, Monsieur Philippe.[71]

According to the Russian historian Mikhail Lepekhine, who had access to recently opened archives, the *Protocols* are a forgery, the work of Mathieu Golovinski, whose father was a friend of Dostoevsky. Golovinski worked for the Tsarist secret service and apparently wrote the *Protocols* in 1900 or early 1901 to demonstrate to the Tsar that the rising tide of capitalism and modernizing was really a Jewish conspiracy aimed at overthrowing him and the old order. He modelled his work on a pamphlet written in 1864 by an anti-Bonapartist lawyer who claimed that Napoleon III was ready to usurp the power of the French people.[72]

It has also been claimed that the original version was plagiarized from the French *Dialogues of Geneva* by Maurice Joly, who was a close friend of the Jewish Adolphe Cremieux, a Supreme Commander of the Scottish Rite of Grand Orient Freemasons and a 33rd-degree Freemason of the Supreme Council of the Ancient and Primitive Rite of Mizraim in Paris, a Rosicrucian Masonic lodge founded by the Illuminized Sionist Cagliostro. At that time this lodge was the headquarters of the Priory of Sion, whose aim of establishing a universal throne in Europe occupied by the "King of Jerusalem" was threatened by Zionism. In 1860 the Priory of Sion founded the Alliance Israelite Universelle from the Paris lodge to appeal to Reform Jews such as Jacob Schiff and the Warburgs. In reaction, the pro-Zionist House of Rothschild assumed the leadership of European Zionists and gave huge sums of money to the cause – and found themselves against the Warburgs. Sionism and Zionism were now on opposite sides.[73]

In 1884 the Priory of Sion arranged for the "theft" of the *Protocols* from its own Mizraim lodge (which in 1875 had merged with the

Rosicrucian Orders of Memphis and Martin).[74] The *Protocols* were then carried to Russia to be used as propaganda against Zionist Jews. For twenty years all was quiet, then in November 1905 the *Protocols* appeared.

One view (the anti-Bolshevik view) is that they were published to associate the Jewish Trotsky and Lenin with a Jewish plan for world revolution. Rasputin, who was probably a Sionist agent, encouraged programs against the Jews to destroy Zionism.[75] The Jews sought protection from the two revolutionary groups: the moderate Social Democratic Workers' Party (formerly the Mensheviks or "minority" of Trotsky), who were funded by the pro-Zionist Rothschilds; and the extremist Bolsheviks, a faction that had broken away and become an independent party under Lenin in 1912, who were funded by the anti-Zionist Warburgs.[76]

Another view (the anti-Zionist view) was that as the Rothschilds and Grand Orient Warburgs were now on opposite sides,[77] as were the Rothschilds and the Priory of Sion, the *Protocols* were originally written to discredit Rothschildian Zionism. Their reappearance was designed to discredit Zionism and the policies of the Jewish Trotsky and Lenin.

A third view (the anti-Rothschild view) is that Rockefellers were attempting to undermine Rothschilds' use of the Baku oilfield, and that they arranged for the *Protocols* to be shown to the Tsar to blame Rothschilds for the failed 1905 Revolution, in the hope that the Tsar would remove Baku from Rothschilds' influence. If this view is correct, then Rockefellers were behind the reappearance of the *Protocols*, through their banker-agent Jacob Schiff.

Trotsky escaped from Siberia almost as soon as he arrived and returned to St. Petersburg, where he was hidden by his Grand Orient friends. He then left Russia and toured Europe, speaking in different cities without being caught. In Paris aristocratic Russian intellectuals joined lodges and discussed a new revolution; back in Russia they founded a Grand Orient lodge in St. Petersburg (Polar Star lodge) and another in Moscow. These lodges had virtually no ritual and were in fact revolutionary clubs.[78]

By this time Rasputin, always a holy man in the presence of the Tsar and Tsarina, was using his power to undermine the Tsar's throne in a sinister, destructive way. He had advised incompetent legislators to be placed in the Duma, incompetent ministers in the government and incompetent generals in the army. He had a number of mistresses and tried to seduce many other women. Following a report on him by the Prime Minister, the Tsar dismissed him in 1911, but the Tsarina, Alexandra, secured his return a few months later. When Nicholas II left St. Petersburg to direct the troops at the front, Rasputin virtually ran the government. He turned the Tsarina against the Commander-in-Chief of the army, who was the Tsar's nephew.[79] A feeling grew that the only way of saving the monarchy was to depose Nicholas II, and Prince Lvov and Kerensky, two Grand Orient Freemasons, began plotting a coup.[80]

Rothschilds' and Kerensky's "February 1917" Revolution

In 1914 Trotsky was in Austria, editing the revolutionary paper *Pravda*. The Grand Orient had already assassinated the Archduke and had a following in the police, who did not intern him but advised him to leave Austria. Trotsky then went to Switzerland, leaving his documents in the care of his lodge in Vienna. He joined Lenin and organized the Third International (which was to promote "civil war not civil peace"). After Switzerland he moved to Paris and then to Spain, was arrested and exiled to New York, where in 1916 he was received by Grand Orient Freemason Jacob Schiff, who was agent for the Grand Orient's Felix and Max Warburg.[81] He was installed in an expensive apartment and received a chauffeur-driven limousine. Schiff gave him a job editing the communist paper *Novy Mir* (New World) along with Nikolai Bukharin. For part of his time in America, Trotsky was living in Rockefeller-Standard Oil property on the site of a refinery at Constable Hook, Bayonne, New Jersey.[82] Trotsky was thus a Rockefeller agent.

In Russia protests were rife. Thanks largely to Rasputin's influence the government was increasingly corrupt and inefficient. The Duma too had been dissolved on several occasions, and the World War was going badly. The troops were poorly led and ill-equipped, and the Russian army suffered severe losses: a million men in 1915 and another million in a single battle (the counter-attack against Austria) in 1916. Food was scarce and there were riots in Petrograd (as St. Petersburg was renamed).

English Freemasonry and the House of Rothschild had planned the first revolution of 1917 for some time.[83] It is likely that Rothschilds were bent on recovering the Baku oilfield, which they had surrendered in 1911 in return for shares in Shell.[84] Rockefellers had taken over Rothschilds' oilfields around Mosul in the Ottoman region that came to be Iraq, after the battle of Verdun in 1916,[85] and, mindful of Rockefellers' attempt to seize Baku through the failed 1905 Revolution (since when Rothschilds had got out and into Shell),[86] it is likely that Rothschilds were acting to increase their oil assets – and to seize the Tsar's wealth.

The war was also a factor. In 1916 the Central Powers had seemed to be winning the World War: there was stalemate in France and the war-weary Tsar was ready to negotiate a separate peace. Meanwhile Germany had made a peace offer to Great Britain. If Britain was going to win the war, it was vital that she intrigue United States involvement as well as keep the Russians fighting. That meant replacing the Tsar. In 1916 Alexander Kerensky, a 32nd-degree Scottish Rite Mason and member of the Grand Orient Lodge (Polar Star) in St. Petersburg, who controlled the right wing of the Social Revolutionary Party and supported Russia's participation in the World War, had sent word to London that the government of his republican regime would keep Russia in the war if the British would finance his *coup*.[87] The British government immediately responded and Rothschilds, who had long eyed the Tsar's wealth, seem to have guaranteed the funding.[88] Their close associate (through South Africa, the Round Table and the British government) Lord Milner spent 21 million roubles funding Kerensky's revolution, some $3m – money he did not have personally and which can be presumed to be Rothschilds'.[89] English Freemasons were secretly meeting Kerensky by the autumn of 1916.[90]

In December 1916 – and there must be a link with these secret meetings – Rasputin's influence over the Tsar was eliminated. He was murdered after being lured to the house of Prince Yusupov, who seems to have been a Grand Orient Mason and an ally of Kerensky's, where he was poisoned in the basement and then shot. He ran up the narrow stairs to the courtyard and Yusupov shot him again. Still he would not die. A hole was cut in the ice of the Neva River and Rasputin was pushed in and drowned.[91]

On January 19, 1917 Lord Milner, a member of the War Cabinet in London, a 33rd-degree Mason and head of the Round Table groups, left London and spent three weeks in Petrograd keeping the Russian forces supplied with Western arms. The plot to install Kerensky was finalized in the British Embassy in Moscow.[92]

Lord Milner sent Sydney Reilly of MI6 to secure the Baku oilfields for British investment (Shell) and also for Rockefellers. (Bruce Lockhart of MI6 was Lord Milner's personal representative who controlled Lenin and Trotsky.) Kerensky was supposed to indicate that the real opposition to the Bolsheviks was coming from Britain and the US when the opposite was true; via Somerset Maugham of MI6, Kerensky sent Lloyd George a letter requesting arms. Lloyd George declined to help.[93]

On March 12 there was an uprising in Petrograd. (Under the old dating system the uprising took place on February 27, hence it is known as the February Revolution.) Most of the army garrison joined the revolt. In Petrograd a Soviet of Workers' and Soldiers' Deputies was formed, and because all the main troops were on the Austro-German front, a well-organized *coup* was unlikely to fail.[94]

In a swift *coup* by the Duma, Tsar Nicholas was forced to abdicate three days later by Prince Lvov. Nicholas's brother Grand Duke Michael refused the throne, and 300 years of Romanov rule and 1,000 years of Russian monarchy were at an end. With the approval of the Soviet the Duma committee appointed a provisional government, headed by Lvov, in which Kerensky became Justice Minister.[95]

If Rothschilds did indeed give financial aid to Kerensky – if they were behind and ultimately responsible for Milner's 21m roubles and for the sum of at least $1m given by J. P. Morgan organization at the request on December 2, 1917 of a Federal Reserve Bank of New York director who was a friend of Kerensky's in Petrograd[96] – then their price may have been Lord Balfour's Declaration on November 2, 1917 to Walter, Lord Rothschild agreeing to a Jewish settlement in Palestine that would become a Zionist state of Israel.[97] Lord Balfour was the British Foreign Minister and the British were still desperate to draw the United States into the war. The United States had a strong Jewish population that exercised great influence over the government. The way to secure American entry into the war might be to promise the Jews the restoration of Palestine in return for their persuasion of the American government.[98] Sir Mark Sykes of the War Cabinet approached the German House of Warburg, which controlled American banking, but they (Felix Warburg and Jacob Schiff) were anti-Zionist and not interested. He approached Lord Milner, who via a Jewish Scottish Rite 33rd-degree Mason (Justice Brandeis) put him in touch with Col. House, a 33rd-degree Jewish Grand Lodge Mason, who advised President Woodrow Wilson. He was a Zionist and brought in Dr. Chaim Weizmann, another Jewish English Freemason and Zionist. A compact was agreed: a Jewish Palestine in return for American troops.[99]

On February 7, 1917 Anglo-Zionists including James de Rothschild and Dr. Weizmann gathered to hear Sykes' plan. The Zionists then sent messages round the world, first to Russian Zionist leaders urging them to aid the Kerensky revolution. At the Priory of Sion's headquarters, the anti-Zionist, pro-"Jerusalem King" Alliance Israelite Universelle ridiculed the idea that Jews would want to return and settle in Palestine. Only Baron Edmond de Rothschild was for the idea. The Pope, by contrast, approved. The Arabs were unhappy, but the English Freemason and British intelligence agent T. E. Lawrence was asked to work with them through the Masonic lodges (founded by Mazzini as the Young Turks and known later as the Moslem Brotherhood). Lawrence was thus in contact with Mazzini followers. The Jewish Freemasons Dr. Weizmann and the American Justice Brandeis kept in touch, and Weizmann met Freemason Lord Balfour.[100]

Weizmann drafted the Declaration. It was sent to Brandeis, who passed it to Col. House for President Wilson's agreement. Baron Edmond de Rothschild agreed to it in France, and it was then put to the War Cabinet in London and eventually signed in November 1917. But long before then the Jewish lobby secured American entry in to the war, which happened in April 1917, a month after Kerensky's revolution.[101]

Meanwhile, though officially reacting, Rothschilds had been actively working this network, first to finance and install Kerensky with a view to seizing the Tsar's fortune, and then to secure a Jewish homeland in Palestine.[102] It is fair to assume that the "Jewish Palestine for American Troops" idea originated with the Rothschilds.

The Grand Orient and Lenin's October 1917 Revolution

The Grand Orient Trotsky, Lenin and Warburgs were shocked by Kerensky's revolution, which took them by surprise. As Minister for Justice in the provisional government Kerensky swiftly introduced civil liberties, including freedom of speech. In May he became the dominant figure in the government, and by July he was Prime Minister. As the Duma was elected he was in charge of an elected government.

Warburgs were aghast that their financial rival, Rothschilds, were funding a Kerensky government and preparing (as they saw it) to loot the Tsar's wealth. They were appalled that Kerensky was backed by Zionists. Although his revolution was Grand Orient Masonic – by 1914 there were 42 Grand Orient lodges in Russia, and all Kerensky's government were members[103] – it was too bourgeois and had not introduced urgent social and economic reforms. Furthermore he had kept Russia in the war and the losses were mounting.

Felix Warburg's brother Max was head of the Kaiser's secret service, and the German branch of the family financed the Kaiser's war machine. He immediately planned a counter-revolution, and called a meeting in the Grand Orient lodge in Hamburg.[104]

Word went out to the anti-Zionist Schiff in New York to send Trotsky to Petrograd. Lenin was contacted in Switzerland and told to meet Trotsky there. The two men still led separate revolutionary movements: Trotsky's was more democratic and in line with Kerensky's than Lenin's extremist movement. Max Warburg was at the farewell party for Lenin held at his Swiss lodge.[105]

A trust fund of $20 million had been set up in Trotsky's name in a Warburg bank in Sweden, the Nya Bank of Stockholm.[106] The account was opened by Max Warburg and Co. of Hamburg and the Rhineland Westphalia Syndicate. Col. House informed the British that this funding had occurred, and that Trotsky had sailed for Russia with 300 terrorists.

A British warship impounded Trotsky's ship in Canada and put its occupants in a prison camp. Schiff at once complained to President Woodrow Wilson's close adviser, Col. House, who, as one of Trotsky's fellow Freemasons, persuaded President Wilson to demand that the ship be freed or else the United States would not enter the war. Trotsky was freed by the British as American entry into the war was a matter of Britain's national survival, and he sailed for Russia via Stockholm, where he collected a $20 million bank draft.[107]

Meanwhile Max Warburg, head of the Kaiser's secret police, presented Lenin as a German agent who would undermine the Russian enemy. He loaded Lenin and a band of Bolshevik terrorists into a sealed freight carriage with $5-6 million in gold and conveyed him across Germany to Russia.[108] He met up with Trotsky in Petrograd in May 1917, and they were both joined by bandit and bankrobber Joseph Stalin. Together they launched a propaganda campaign to replace Kerensky's provisional government with a nationwide system of Soviets (or revolutionary Workers' Councils).[109] A series of terrorist attacks was launched on the Rothschilds and the republican government; and on the army and navy (the two forces that might prevent anarchy). A "Former Russian Commissar" wrote that these attacks were "to defeat the more conservative, moderate aims of the Rothschilds."[110]

The Grand Orient, through the Templar funders Warburgs and Schiff, now set about capturing Russia. Money poured in from other sources. In revealing these sources, it is difficult to distinguish between individuals and their commercial firms, conglomerates of companies or corporations, and by placing inverted commas round family names

–"Rockefellers," "J. P. Morgan" or "Rothschilds" – I seek to make clear that I am not referring to particular individuals but to a particular emphasis of a commercial outlook. During the First World War the financial and business structure of the United States was dominated by two conglomerates: Standard Oil, the "Rockefeller" enterprises (covering petroleum, minerals and banks); and the "J. P. Morgan" complex of finance and transportation companies (covering railways and banks such as the Chase National Bank, which was affiliated to "Rockefellers"). Not surprisingly all the financial support came from these two giants.[111] (At the end of the war "J. P. Morgan" had assets of $640 million, "Rockefellers," Carnegie and Ford totalled $2 billion of publicly declared funds – in 1937 "Rockefellers" owned a known fortune of at least $5b – while "Rothschilds" had assets stated, or rather understated, at $500 billion.)[112]

"Rockefellers" had given financial support to the revolutionaries after the Tsar refused their Standard Oil access to the Russian oilfields, which were already being pumped by the "Rothschild-owned" Royal Dutch Co. and Shell (in which, incidentally, John D. Rockefeller possessed $15 million in bonds). "J. P. Morgan" gave at least $1 million, as we have just seen. Sir George Buchanan, the Swedish Olaf Aschberg (of Stockholm's Nya Bank), the Rhine Westphalia Syndicate and a financier Jovotosky (whose daughter later married Trotsky) all contributed funds. William Boyce Thompson (a director of the Rockefeller-affiliated Chase National Bank) gave $1 million, and Albert Wiggin (President of the same Bank) also gave money. All hoped for a considerable return on their investment in Trotsky and Lenin.[113]

Throughout April 1917 Lenin won acceptance for his idea of withholding support for the provisional government and then seizing power (in accordance with his Bakuninist belief that a proletarian revolution must smash the State machinery and introduce a "dictatorship of the proletariat").[114] This policy was endorsed by a national conference of Bolsheviks at the end of April when it elected a new Central Committee. Its 133 delegates represented just 75,000 members, a tiny number in relation to the entire Russian population.

Nevertheless, the Petrograd Soviet, whose 2,500 delegates to the Soviet came from factories and military units, had more authority than the government, which was hated for continuing the war.

On March 14 the Soviet had directed the military to obey the Soviet's orders, not the government's, and the government was powerless to cancel this command. Being reorganized four times between March and October, and being dependent on a coalition, it had little power to cope with the seizure of lands by peasants, independence movements in the "minority" areas and defeatist attitudes in the army.[115] In a general election to the First Constitutional Assembly, the All-Russia Congress of Soviets, Kerensky's Socialist Revolutionary Party had a majority, and Lenin's Bolsheviks were in a minority.[116] (Trotsky meanwhile had taken over the leadership of the Menshevik left-wing "minority" faction.) The Bolsheviks were attacked from all sides and when Kerensky accused him of being a "German agent" (no doubt referring to Max Warburg's backing) Lenin had to go into hiding in Finland.[117] Stalin took over as his deputy.

Trotsky and Lenin needed a proletariat army, and they recruited one from the downtrodden underclass of criminals and the poor. In July 1917 Trotsky's army created an uprising in Petrograd. (This was Trotsky's "July Days" attempt at a *coup*.) The uprising was a protest at the presence of a Romanov, Prince Lvov, in the provisional government. Lvov duly resigned and Kerensky, who appointed only Freemasons to his government, took over.[118]

One of those arrested in Kerensky's clampdown was Trotsky. In August, while he was still in prison, he was admitted to Lenin's Bolsheviks and was elected to their Central Committee. Previously he had condemned Lenin's dictatorship, but now he had decided to subordinate himself to his leadership, thus compromising his own ideals.[119]

At the end of August Kerensky put down a *coup* attempted by the army commander General Lavr Kornilov, whose position he took on himself. His Socialist Revolutionary Party split as the left wing broke away – disillusioned because he would not implement their programme

– and allied with the Bolsheviks, who were still in a minority. By mid-September the Bolsheviks had achieved a number of political victories in the Soviets, and had control of the key Petrograd and Moscow ruling councils.[120]

From Finland Lenin saw that Russia would either be a soviet republic – a dictatorship of the propertyless majority – or a parliamentary republic – a dictatorship of the bourgeoisie or propertied minority. He sent a number of articles to Petrograd urging the Party Central Committee to organize an armed uprising immediately. On October 20 he returned to Petrograd in disguise and spoke to the Bolshevik Central Committee on October 23. After a ten-hour debate they agreed "to place armed insurrection on the agenda." (Only Zinoviev and Kamenev opposed this.) Steps were taken to train soldiers, sailors and Red Guards (the workers' militia) under the guise of self-defence of the Petrograd Soviet. Trotsky, now elected Chairman of the Petrograd Soviet, co-operated, urging that an armed uprising had to take place as soon as possible.[121]

On November 6 Kerensky sent troops to close the Bolshevik newspapers; the Bolsheviks saw this as the beginning of a counter-revolutionary *coup*. Lenin, in hiding in Petrograd, wrote a letter to the Central Committee urging them to arrest members of the provisional government that night.[122] Trotsky meanwhile directed countermeasures from the Petrograd Soviet by surrounding the Congress of Soviets. He assured the public that his Military Revolutionary Committee was merely defending the Congress of Soviets. In fact, he was perpetrating a *coup* for the Bolsheviks.[123]

On November 7 and 8 Bolshevik-led soldiers, sailors and Red Guards besieged and captured the provisional government in the Winter Palace, deposing it in a near-bloodless *coup*, by occupying government buildings and telegraph stations.[124] Trotsky continued to be the military leader of the Revolution, and organized the forces that defeated Kerensky's attempt to retake Petrograd with loyal troops at the Battle of Pulkovo on November 13. He then sided with Lenin in defeating proposals for a coalition government of Bolsheviks,

Mensheviks and Socialist Revolutionaries.[125] Trotsky, who had changed his allegiance since May, was now acting as a Bolshevik rather than a Menshevik. As for Kerensky and the Masons in his government, they fled to France where they established Grand Orient lodges.[126]

The Bolsheviks announced that State power was with the Soviets. The Marxist Bolsheviks and the break-away left wing of the Socialist Revolutionary Party now had a substantial majority in the Second All-Russia Congress of Soviets, which (as it had been arranged) met immediately, accepted full power and ratified the *coup*. They elected Lenin as Chairman of the Council of People's Commissars, the new Soviet government. In one swift move, he had gone from fugitive to head of the (then) world's largest country.[127]

LENIN AS POLITICAL LEADER OF THE SOVIET REVOLUTION

Lenin's Masonic Plan

The Grand Orient Marxist Bolshevik Lenin now gave political expression to the Russian Revolution. His seizure of power was copied in Soviets throughout Russia. In Moscow there was fighting for a week, and there was resistance in Southern Russia, the Ukraine and among the Don Cossacks.

Lenin operated from the Kremlin. A series of decrees abolished private property and distributed land to the peasants who worked it. This ratified seizures of land already made by peasants. Decrees gave workers control in industry and nationalized banks, abolished old courts and police and put revolutionary tribunals and workers' militias in their place. Further decrees abolished class privileges, titles and inheritance, and established equality of the sexes. Calendar reform was instituted to bring Russia into line with Western dating.[128]

There was a debate between those who wanted one party (Lenin and Trotsky) and those who wanted a coalition (Zinoviev and

Kamenev). Lenin suppressed the opposition. At elections for the Constituent Assembly in November, the Bolsheviks won only a quarter of the seats, so he closed it down in January as a counter-revolutionary body.[129]

To achieve his Weishauptian objectives, Lenin immediately began eroding all sense of the Russian nation. From the Grand Orient's point of view, the purpose of the First World War, which Bismarck had set up in accordance with Pike's plan, was to foment revolution in Russia so it could become a platform for world revolution. Freemasonry wanted to destroy the Russian Orthodox Church, and it knew it could not do this without killing the Tsar, who embodied the mystery and authority of the Church and the divine right to rule. (The Eastern Orthodox Church had never suffered a Reformation and had a strong hold on the minds and hearts of the Russian people.) The mainstay of the Church was the bourgeoisie, who were to be eliminated. Russian people had to be stripped of their sense of nationality: the Russian army became the Red army and the Russian flag became the Red flag of international socialism. The State anthem became the Internationale and Russia became the "Union of Soviets" (or revolutionary councils).

The Mensheviks and the right wing Socialist Revolutionary Party refused to accept the Soviet system and were dispersed with the closure of the Constituent Assembly. Soviet government along the lines of the Paris Commune had replaced parliamentary government.[130]

The Soviets wanted peace, but the Allies refused to recognize the new regime. Under Trotsky's direction as Foreign Commissar the Soviet government immediately began to make a separate peace with the Central Powers, and after an armistice in December, Lenin overruled Trotsky (who wanted "no war, no peace") and Bukharin (who called for revolutionary war) and gave up part of Soviet territory to be at peace under the Treaty of Brest-Litovsk in March 1918. Trotsky resigned as Foreign Commissar in protest, and was immediately made War Commissar.[131]

Lenin established a government of Jews. He himself had a Jewish mother, but there were so many Jews in his government that it seemed to many that the Jews had masterminded the Bolshevik *coup.*[132] An American intelligence report sent back to the US Army Staff 2nd bureau by the US Ambassador to France lists the most conspicuous individuals in the Soviets: 31 out of 32 were Jews. They included Lenin, Trotsky, but not Stalin (who was the one exception, though he was a Martinist Rosicrucian, a member of Martinez Paschalis's secret society, see pp300, 452). A table made in April 1918 shows that there were over 300 Jews among the 384 Commissars.[133] Of the 546 members in Lenin's and Trotsky's Bolshevik administration, 447 were Jews, most of whom were Freemasons.[134] The American government was informed that the Bolshevik Revolution was a Jewish uprising; in fact, it was a Grand Orient Masonic uprising planned by Warburgs, using Grand Orient Jews so that *the Jews would be blamed and not the Grand Orient.* As a result, Freemasonry according to Max Warburg's and Lenin's plan was not implicated. In fact, the plan was all along anti-religious and anti-Semitic – a Satanic plot to destroy both Judaism and Christianity on Weishauptian lines.[135]

The gentile Masonic plan was that Trotsky would destroy the Tsar's monarchy and the Russian Orthodox Church. Then Lenin would destroy Trotsky and his followers. When Lenin died prematurely, Stalin inherited the task of destroying Trotsky.[136]

In accordance with the plan, Trotsky, now War Commissar, took over the military forces of the Soviets and began to build a new Red Army – perhaps so-called because of the Rothschilds' "red shield"[137] – out of the old Russian Army to defend the revolutionary government against foreign intervention and civil war. Many revolutionaries (including Stalin) criticized him for abandoning the guerrilla tactics that had effected the Revolution. Trotsky now called his forces "Workers' and Soldiers' Soviets." Many of the military were criminals who had been initiated into the Ordo Templi Orientis,[138] which was housed within the 33rd-degree Grand Orient and combined with the Order of the Golden Dawn. (The Satanist Alistair Crowley would become its most famous member, and, it was alleged, indulged in human sacrifice in its rituals.) The Red Army adopted the five-pointed Masonic star or pentagram as its emblem. Trotsky started a spy system that ruthlessly exterminated all disloyal members; this became the Cheka, which seems to have been formed of OTO Grand Orient Masons, who carried out Satanic ritual murders. Eventually it became the KGB.[139]

Civil War

Civil war broke out in May 1918 between Soviet forces and the Czechoslovak legion, who were being evacuated from Russia. The Soviets' Red Army were opposed by the "Whites" from Belorussia ("White Russia"), who took control from the River Volga to the Pacific. They were headed by former Tsarist generals and admirals, and supported by the Allies.[140] Dismayed at seeing Russia taken from their grasp, English Freemasonry and "Rothschilds" now funded and supported the Whites, hoping for a counter-revolution against the Bolsheviks.[141] This struggle began in early 1919 and developed into civil war, which had been on the agenda of the Third International since Lenin proposed it in 1915. Lenin headed the Whites off by offering minorities the right to self-determination, and by championing the rights of peasants to take land from owners without compensation.[142]

The Allies invaded parts of Russia to stop ammunition and weapons from falling into German hands. The British landed in Murmansk in March, the US in northern Russia, the US and Japan in eastern Siberia. All supported the Whites, who, with foreign backing, launched offensives towards Moscow in 1919 (from Siberia, the Baltic and the Don; and from the Crimea). Each was repelled.[143]

The Soviet Union was encircled by its enemies, and to break out of this confinement, in 1919 Lenin founded a Third Communist International (which he had been planning since 1915), for which Trotsky wrote the manifesto. This International broke with the reformist, socialist Second International, which stood for parliamentary democracy; instead, it held up the Russian Communist Party and Bolshevik Revolution as a model for all communist parties in all countries. All those countries round Russia (including the Eastern European countries) should now go communist and relieve the pressure of encirclement – that was Lenin's plan.[144]

The Red Army drove the foreigners out of the country. By 1920 the Whites were not able to resist the Reds in the Crimea and abandoned Southern Russia. The civil war was as good as over. Bela Kuhn (Cohen), who had organized the Grand Orient slaughter in Hungary, became Trotsky's commander-in-chief in the Crimea. In the autumn of 1922 the Japanese withdrew and the Whites went into exile.[145]

The civil war turned Lenin's communist regime into a terroristic one-party dictatorship. The Constituent Assembly was closed and conservative parties suppressed. The left-wing Socialist Revolutionary faction resigned from the Council of People's Commissars in protest at the Treaty of Brest-Litovsk, leaving a one-party Communist Executive. When in July 1918 they rose against the government, they were suppressed; as were the Mensheviks in 1920. Lenin, giving political expression to the Russian Revolution made one-party rule by the communists a matter of principle. The "dictatorship of the proletariat" had arrived. In it Lenin was no. 1 and Trotsky was his no. 2.[146]

Murder of the Tsar

The Weishauptian Masonic plan demanded the elimination of the royal family as an important part of the overthrow of the old order of Church and State. Trotsky wanted the Tsar and his family dead, as the Romanovs were a danger to the Bolshevik Revolution. His fear was that the people would ask for their return, as had happened with the Bourbons after the French Revolution. On July 17, 1918 a Jew, Yourowsky, acting for the Cheka on Trotsky's orders, shot or bayoneted the Tsar, Tsarina, Tsarevitch, the four Grand Duchesses and their doctor, servant couple, cook and dog in Ekaterinberg. The following night three Grand Dukes and a Grand Duchess were thrown down a well in Siberia. Another Grand Duke was assassinated at Perm.[147] Above the bodies of the Tsar and his family a symbolic message was painted on a wall: three Kabbalistic "L" letters with a line beneath them, suggesting that the assassin was carrying out a command for a superior. It was a Satanic Kabbalistic message suggesting that the assassins were Freemasons before they were Jews: followers of the OTO of the Grand Orient, or possibly of the Satanist Bakunin, who was a student of the

Kabbalah; or they could even have been agents of the Priory of Sion, for whom the Romanovs could not be Kings of Jerusalem because they were not of Merovingian, Holy Grail extraction.[148]

In August 1918, only a month after the murder of the royal family for which he was widely held responsible, Lenin was shot by a Tsarist assassin, who fired two bullets into him as he left a factory after making a speech. He recovered rapidly but carried one of the bullets in his neck, which would eventually contribute to the early breakdown of his health.[149]

The Red Terror

The Social Revolutionaries, who were doctrinally terrorists, assassinated some of the communist leaders, and were blamed for wounding Lenin in August 1918. Lenin responded with the Red Terror, which came into being to terrorize and root out any opposition to the regime. Reds executed White prisoners, who retaliated; 100,000 lost their lives in this tit-for-tat manoeuvring, and two million emigrated. The Communist Party now became more authoritarian.[150]

The Red Terror was launched by Trotsky and the Masonic Grand Orient OTO.[151] The main duty of the Soviets now was to exterminate the bourgeoisie as a class. (Membership of the bourgeois class was a good enough reason for a person to be executed.) All educated people were targets. In Kiev the Cheka used a large garage as an execution hall. Masonic symbols were carved into the flesh of victims' faces, necks and torsos, just as they were during the French Revolution. Like the Grand Orient Jacobins in the French Reign of Terror in 1793, the Grand Orient communists destroyed the old economic and political structure.[152]

During 1918-19 1.7 million people were slaughtered according to the Denikin Commission of Enquiry, and another 1.5 million were killed in the winter of 1920. One list of the killed, published in 1923, which makes chilling reading, includes the figure of 535,250 members of the intellectual and liberal professions. In villages throughout Southern Russia a band of ex-convicts would descend and kill the two or three hundred inhabitants, the men first having to watch while their womenfolk were raped. When ammunition ran short, hundreds were lined up on piers in the Crimea, tied to scrap iron and drowned in the sea. In 1928 Nikolay Bukharin, Trotsky's colleague in New York, boasted in a letter, "There is not...in the whole of Russia a single household in which we have not killed in some manner."[153]

An attempt to create the classless Utopia began in mid-1918 with greater nationalization and centralization. This was War Communism, a new communism designed to win the civil war. It was in 1918 too that the Reds created famines to kill. Under "reorganization of agriculture" all farm equipment was confiscated, and all grain, and a barter system replaced currency and wages. Any hidden machinery or grain resulted in execution. Horses were taken for use in the Red Army, all cattle were slaughtered, and relief organizations had to come in to feed the starving. (In 1945 Stalin told Churchill that 12 million peasants had died through the "reorganization of agriculture.")[154]

By 1921, however, Lenin with the backing of Trotsky had abandoned the experiment as an error. He now rejected "workers' control," and his New Economic Policy enabled the country to return to peace. It was a retreat from ideal communism and satisfied public agitation for a measure of democracy through trade unions. State capitalism, denationalization and decentralization were now in vogue. The effect was similar to that of the Thermidorean reaction in the French revolution: social and intellectual life in the Soviet Union returned to how it was in pre-revolutionary Russia. Lenin therefore launched a purge of the party membership, which fell from 700,000 to 400,000, and in April 1922 Stalin became General Secretary of the Party. The appointment of such a ruthless man was the last thing the poor suffering communist rank and file needed at such a time.[155]

In 1921 the show trials began, to repress opponents of Bolshevism. The penalty was generally death, and these trials, more than any other measure of Lenin's, prepared the way for Stalin's one-man rule. (Lenin himself of course believed in a "dictatorship of the proletariat" and therefore opposed one-man rule.)[156]

Death of Lenin

In the same month that Stalin was appointed, doctors removed one of the August 1918 assassin's two bullets from Lenin's neck. He recovered from the operation, but in May he suffered the first of a series of cerebral haemorrhages or strokes. This may have been caused by the bullets, but it has been surmised that he had syphilis.[157]

The battle for the succession began. Trotsky was the second-ranking figure, but he was opposed by all the Politburo and by most of the Central Committee, who put a *troika* in charge: a triumvirate consisting of Zinoviev, Kamenev and Stalin. In December Lenin was semi-paralyzed by another stroke, and dictated his political testament, which called for Stalin to be removed from his position as Secretary-General. In lucid moments, Lenin attacked the *troika* in letters, particularly Stalin (whose growing power he did not like) for forcing non-Russian soviet republics into formal federation with the USSR. Lenin hoped that Trotsky would attack Stalin's growing power, an indication that he regarded Stalin as the least unsuitable successor.[158]

In March 1923 Lenin finally lost the power of speech due to another stroke. That autumn Trotsky attacked the *troika*, alleging a violation in democracy in a critique submitted to the Central Committee. Stalin mounted a counter-attack, accusing Trotsky of being an opportunist who worked for his own faction's ends. Trotsky then fell ill with a fever (had there been an attempt to poison him?), and in June 1924 the 13th Party Congress confirmed the *troika* and condemned Trotsky's opposition as a factional deviation.[159]

Lenin suffered yet another stroke in January 1924. On his deathbed he said: "I committed a great error. My nightmare is to have the feeling that I'm lost in an ocean of blood from the innumerable victims. It is too late to return."[160] He was not wrong. The cost of Lenin, and of the Illuminized Grand Orient in Russia, was colossal. The civil war between the Reds and the Whites resulted in the deaths of 28 million Russians between 1919 and 1922. Famine caused another 5 million deaths.[161] Lenin was responsible for a staggering number of 33 million deaths. These deathbed words make it clear that Lenin knew that Stalin would be a bloody successor. And though he was a Bakuninist who, like the Nihilists, rejected conventional morality, he felt bad about the Russians he had killed – just as many of the Bakuninist Nihilists felt remorse about what they had done. Lenin's Utopia had killed a hundred times the number killed by the French Revolution.

STALIN'S CONSOLIDATION THROUGH PURGES

Stalin Succeeds Lenin

The Rosicrucian Stalin[162] won a power struggle with the Grand Orient Trotsky and now consolidated the Russian Revolution in a brutal, physical phase. Born Iosif Visarionovich Dzhugashvili, he had smallpox as a child, which left him with a pockmarked face. The son of a poor, drunken cobbler who beat him, he spoke Georgian at home and learned Russian at a church school. Earmarked for the priesthood, he moved to a theological seminary but soon deviated and was expelled for revolutionary activities after secretly reading Karl Marx. He became a clerk and embarked on a revolutionary career fomenting strikes.[163] In 1900 he spent a year living with Gurdjieff, a "Magus" from Georgia and Martinist Rosicrucian Freemason, who initiated Stalin into Martinist Freemasonry.[164] In 1904 he married a Georgian girl who died three years later, leaving a son.

He had been a follower of Lenin and robbed banks to raise funds for the Bolsheviks. He was arrested seven times for revolutionary activity between 1902 and 1913, and was given short terms of imprisonment and exile. (The lenient sentences have led to speculation that he was a police informer.) He took the name Stalin to suggest strength (Russian *stal,* "steel"), and by 1917 he was editor of *Pravda.*[165] He was also by now a 33rd-degree Martinist Rosicrucian Freemason and Sionist.[166] In 1919 he married a Jewess who sought to moderate his actions.

The struggle for the succession to Lenin amounted to a fourth

Russian revolution. It was long and bitter. Stalin had guile. He arranged for Trotsky, who was convalescing on the Black Sea coast from his fever, to be told that Lenin's funeral would take place at a later date. As a result Trotsky did not appear for the funeral, at which Stalin played a leading role, a public indication of the power he had already gathered to himself. In 1923 there had been a Soviet-inspired communist uprising in Germany which had failed. Trotsky blamed Zinoviev and Kamenev, while the *troika* attacked Trotsky, and denounced his theory of permanent revolution as a Menshevik heresy. In June 1925 Trotsky was deprived of the post of War Commissar.[167]

In December 1925 Zinoviev and Kamenev tried to unseat Stalin at the 14th Party Congress, but Stalin survived and removed Zinoviev's supporters from Leningrad. Then early in 1926 Zinoviev and Kamenev joined forces with their old adversary Trotsky in a "United Opposition." They emphasized parliamentary democracy and economic planning, criticized State capitalism and (Lenin's) economic mismanagement, and sought to strengthen the proletarian workers against the peasants. In foreign affairs they advocated a policy of world revolution, which allowed them to suggest that Stalin was deviating in an unsocialist direction because Russia was isolated.[168]

Isolation of a Masonic State

In response Stalin revived his theory (first stated in 1924) of "socialism in one country." Lenin had written in 1915 that the Soviet Union should build socialism by itself without waiting for other countries in the West to have Communist revolutions. The "United Opposition" criticized his theory as little more than a pretext for abandoning world revolution.[169]

In fact the debate went much deeper and concerned Freemasonry. The Soviet Union had swiftly become a Masonic State. In 1922 Freemasonry had set up Russian-speaking Grand Orient lodges in Paris to house "a temporary committee recognized by the Supreme Council of France, which will subsequently become the Supreme Council of the Scottish Rite in Russia."[170] The task was "to restore to Russia a normal government and...ordinary conditions of economic and political life."[171] Once this task was accomplished there would be a new legislative body comprising the people and the republics. This body was called the "Supreme Soviet" ("Soviet," "Council") after the 33rd-degree Supreme Council of Freemasonry. The appellation indicated that the Soviet Union was now a fully Masonic State. The Iron Curtain that would confine socialism to Russia was designed in part to keep the Masonic secret of the Soviet State.[172]

Once the Masonic State had come into being, Freemasonry was banned following a resolution at the 4th Congress of the Communist International. There was no need for it now, and its closed doors could only foment revolution.[173] (When Gorbachev reopened the Grand Orient lodges in 1989, having been initiated into the Grand Orient in Paris in 1984, the reopened lodges swiftly brought about the end of Communism. It is possible that Gorbachev's position was intrigued by the Freemason Philby to achieve this. If so, then Philby, who had no KGB controller but worked under Blunt, was a patriotic British spy all along, and a fantastically successful triple-agent.)[174]

The Supreme Soviet was thus controlled by a Communist Party hierarchy.[175]

Had Lenin lived, he would have restrained the Jews within Russia, a task that Stalin now inherited. Stalin was an anti-Zionist who wanted to keep Zionism contained within his borders, a position in line with the Priory of Sion. Stalin planned to purge Jews (such as Trotsky, Zinoviev and Kamenev) and then close his borders so they could not emigrate. The Zionist Rothschild, on the other hand, wanted the Jews to emigrate to Palestine.[176] Svetlana Stalin has confirmed[177] that Stalin, who was anti-Rothschild, wanted to get rid of all Zionists.

Stalin's Oil Deal with "Rockefellers"

There had been a long tussle between Rockefellers, Russia and the British for the Caucasian oilfields, notably Baku.[178] In 1918 the British had sent an expedition headed by Gen. Dunsterville that combined forces with a White Russian brigade led by Gen. Bitcherakov. They occupied Baku, forcing the Soviet forces to withdraw, but were ousted by Turkish forces led by German officers. In November 1918 the

British returned and seized Baku. *The Financial News* jubilantly spoke of a second India and of British forces spreading to Batum, Tiflis, Asia Minor, Messopotamia and Persia. Rockefellers, however, had encouraged the British Labour movement, which opposed further military occupation of the Caucasus and forced the troops to be withdrawn. Denikin took over with British support in August 1919 and set up two British vassal states: Georgia and Azerbaijan. The Rockefeller-dominated US State Department refused to recognize them and blocked the hand-over of the Caucasian oilfields to Royal Dutch and Shell. In February 1920 the Bolsheviks entered Baku and took Georgia, and Royal Dutch was shut out.[179]

In 1920 Rockefeller Standard Oil bought a half-interest in Nobel and Co.'s production in Baku from the Bolsheviks, thus establishing legal title to the Caucasian fields.[180] Shortly afterwards they bought a 50-year concession to the North Persian oilfields from the Persian government. This brought them into contact with British and Soviet interests: the Russians had sold on to Anglo-Persian Co. a concession they had bought in 1920, and both the Russian and British governments objected to Rockefellers' concession.[181]

Rockefellers played the British Royal-Dutch interests off against Russia. They blocked Royal Dutch's attempt to obtain a monopolistic oil concession from Russia, first by blockading Russian oil and then by using an intermediary, Harry Sinclair, to seek a concession for the Baku and Grozny oilfields. In November 1923 an agreement was reached giving Sinclair and the Russian government equal shares. A Rockefeller proxy, Sen. Burton Wheeler, demanded an investigation into Sinclair on corruption charges, and Sinclair went to jail for contempt of court. Rockefellers then took possession of his companies. Now their plans for world monopoly were threatened by the glut of Russian oil.[182] Therefore in 1925 Standard Oil allied with Royal Dutch and Shell and bought 290,000 tons of kerosene and gasoline from Moscow, thus gaining control of Russian oil.[183]

Also in 1925 on behalf of the *troika* Stalin entered into a compact with the "Rockefellers" under which he sold a half interest in Russia's oilfields, including Baku (previously used by the Zionist Rothschilds) in return for funding for his five-year plans.[184]

From the moment he entered into an agreement with "Rockefellers," Stalin became, in part, something of a "Rockefeller" agent; his link with Rockefellers may have pre-dated the 1917 Bolshevik Revolution, but from now, at least, he had great loyalty to Rockefellers. In March 1926 Rockefellers' Standard Oil of New York and its subsidiary Vacuum Oil Co. entered into an agreement with the Naphtha Syndicate, the Russian government monopoly, to buy 800,000 tons of crude oil and 100,000 tons of kerosene and market Soviet oil throughout Europe.[185] This was the first commercial transaction between Rockefeller Standard Oil and the Soviet government. However, as a Rosicrucian Stalin retained his links with the Priory of Sion, and put a Sionist agenda into practice in the 1930s.[186]

Exile of Trotsky

Trotsky wanted to spread Communism worldwide –"world revolution" – and he wanted open borders. Stalin however wanted "socialism in one country," and when he proposed isolating Russia (lowering the Iron Curtain) Trotsky in a rage shouted, "You have betrayed the Revolution!" Irritated, Stalin moved against him. In autumn 1926 (having allied with rightists Bukharin and Rykov) Stalin stripped Trotsky, Zinoviev, Kamenev and their supporters of their Party and governmental positions (expelling them from the Politburo) and filled them with his own supporters. Then at the 15th Party Congress in December 1927 Stalin organized the expulsion of the "United Opposition" from the Central Committee of the Communist Party. Zinoviev and Kamenev recanted and were readmitted, and although Stalin was not strong enough to kill Trotsky, he exiled him and his supporters to remote parts of the Soviet Union. Trotsky himself was sent to Alma Ata in Central Asia, before being deported from the Soviet Union in January 1929. He had finally been banished.[187]

Trotsky fled to Turkey and then to France and was protected by the French Prime Minister Blum, a Grand Orient Freemason who opposed Stalin's isolationism. Hunted by Stalin's secret service Trotsky fled to

Mexico, where there was a strong Grand Orient community that gave him a good house and provided him with luxuries. Between 1934 and 1938 Stalin's secret police killed many Trotskyites. Trotsky retaliated by founding the Fourth International, which was to mobilize the revolutionary masses against the ruling class everywhere, but particularly against Hitler and also, of course, Stalin; for the Grand Orient Trotsky still hoped to return to Russia and kill the Rosicrucian Stalin. But Stalin's agents eventually caught up with him in 1940. A Spanish Communist who had won his confidence, Ramón Mercader (a NKVD agent), murdered him with an axe. The Soviet government denied all responsibility.[188]

In 1928 Stalin had made himself supreme and imposed one-man rule on the Communist Party – exactly what Lenin had dreaded. He was the unchallenged ruler of the Communist Party, and enforced Communist Party control on every aspect of daily life to achieve economic development. He also distanced himself from all those he had shared leadership with during the discredited New Economic Policy. His shift to the left was opposed by Bukharin (editor of *Pravda*), Rykov (Chairman of the Council of People's Commissars) and Tomsky (Chairman of the trade unions), who were removed from their positions in 1929 and 1930. In 1929 there was a purge of intellectuals in every field of the arts and sciences, and another purge of the Party similar to that of 1921.[189] Stalin's own wife was bitterly opposed to these purges, and she committed suicide in 1932 as an act of defiance.[190]

The Great Purge

Stalin now instigated a new revolution as momentous for Russians as that of 1917, which took the Soviet economy from State capitalism to socialism. He reintroduced the concept of a planned economy with centralized economic controls for forced rapid industrialization. The State Planning Commission drew up a second Five-Year Plan with ambitious targets, which he implemented in early 1933. Under the plan, 25 million Soviet peasant households were forcibly reorganized into collective farms. They underwent compulsory collectivization: private land holding was abolished and production quotas had to be met on pain of penalties. Thus Stalin guaranteed food supplies for the cities. Not surprisingly, there was considerable resistance from the peasants, but this was crushed by the imposition of a totalitarian regime, through troops and the political police (OGPU). Such measures were made possible because under Stalin the Communist Party was strictly centralized.[191]

In 1934 Stalin launched the Great Purge to enforce industrialization, collectivization and totalitarianism, the three planks of his platform. There was unrest among the peasants and intellectuals; there were famines – yet Stalin continued to export grain – and there were misgivings about his brutal policy. Millions were arrested and liquidated, mainly communists and officials in the government and industry. (All opposition to Stalin was deemed counter-revolutionary and punished with death.) The murder in December 1934 of Stalin's no. 2 Kirov, who had protested against collectivization and was assassinated (probably by the secret police on Stalin's instructions, as Krushchev alleged publicly in 1956), precipitated the Purge. It was used as a pretext for mass arrests. Stalin's old opponents Zinoviev and Kamenev were tried for aiding the assassination, and the following year they confessed to conspiring to assassinate the entire Soviet leadership and were shot. Then in 1937 prominent supporters of Trotsky made confessions and were shot. In 1938 the same fate befell Bukharin, Rykov and Yagoda (head of the NKVD who had organized the trial of Zinoviev and Kamenev) – after they confessed to attempting to assassinate Lenin in 1918! Many Zionist Jews were executed, while others were sentenced to decades in labour camps.[192]

In the Great Purge of 1934-8, Stalin virtually eliminated Bolshevism. It is likely that he was acting for the Rosicrucian Priory of Sion against Grand Orient Templarism. In so far as Stalin's purge was eliminating the Bolsheviks who overthrew Kerensky, it is likely that "Rothschilds" were pleased that the Bolsheviks had had their comeuppance. In so far as it involved killing Jews, they would have strongly disapproved and withdrawn their support. It seems that the purge caused "Rockefellers" to go cold on Stalin, temporarily at least, and finance Hitler to take Moscow and overthrow the Soviet leader. (See the companion volume to this book, *The Syndicate*.) It is likely that "Rockefellers" were pursuing the old "Rothschildian" tactic (demonstrated in the American Civil War) of backing both sides in a war.

We know about the network of prison labour camps called the Gulag Archipelago, through the writings of one of its victims, Aleksandr Solzhenitsyn. It is likely that Stalin was responsible for killing at least 40 million people during his one-man dictatorship.[193] (48 million Soviet people were killed in the Second World War, and many of these deaths were due to Stalin.)[194] Lenin's dictatorship of the proletariat had become Stalin's one-man tyrannical dictatorship.

Through such purges and prison camps, continuing Weishaupt's programme, Stalin consolidated the Russian Revolution across the vast tracts of the Soviet Union, the world's largest country, and led it to victory over Hitler in the Second World War and into leadership of the Eastern European Empire in its aftermath.

SUMMARY: THE REVOLUTIONARY DYNAMIC OF THE RUSSIAN REVOLUTION

To sum up in terms of the revolutionary dynamic, the heretical occult vision of the Russian Revolution came from the Sionist Rosicrucian Weishaupt. The heretical occult interpreter was Hegel, who lectured at Heidelberg and took his main idea (the World Spirit) from Rosicrucianism. The occult revolutionary originator who gave the vision a new slant was Marx, who owed much to his mentor Engels (and drew on Winstanley's Diggers and on Saint-Simon, Proudhon, Babeuf and other French socialists). They must be linked in this role. The thoughtful intellectual interpreter was Bakunin, whose anarchism inspired the Nihilists. The semi-political intellectual interpreter who later became political was Trotsky, who attempted the first Russian revolution of 1905. The early revolutionary dynamic of the Russian revolution can be stated as follows:

Heretical occult vision	Heretical occult interpreter	Occult revolutionary originator	Thoughtful intellectual interpreter	Semi-political intellectual interpreter
Weishaupt	Hegel	Marx/Engels	Bakunin	Trotsky

Weishaupt influenced – indeed, inspired – Hegel, Marx/Engels, Bakunin and Trotsky, but the Russian Intelligentsia may not have seen this.

The intellectual expression of the Russian Revolution included Herzen, Kropotkin and Kerensky, who led the second of the four Russian revolutions. The political expression of the Russian Revolution can be found in Lenin, who led the third Russian revolution. The consolidation was done by Stalin, who intrigued the fourth Russian revolution and whose purges clamped down on any form of dissidence. But behind all four Russian revolutions can be found the imperialism of "Rothschilds" – and of the American "Rockefellers," a new force on the international scene. The full revolutionary dynamic of the Russian Revolution can be stated as follows:

Heretical occult inspiration	Intellectual expression	Political expression	Physical consolidation
Weishaupt/Hegel ("Rockefellers"/ "Rothschilds" behind all four stages)	Marx/Engels, Herzen/Bakunin/ Kropotkin/the Nihilists/Trotsky	Lenin	Stalin

Stalin had regained the revolution for the Priory of Sion, but now the system of alliances had been turned on its head. The alliance between the Priory of Sion and the Templars within the Illuminati, having been born of expediency (i.e. to overthrow the Bourbons), had always been uneasy. From 1776 to 1900, the Priory of Sion had supported "Rothschilds" and English Freemasonry, and in effect worked for the "King of Jerusalem." A Jewish homeland in Palestine had changed that. The Priory of Sion were anti-Zionist, wanted Jews to remain in Russia and were therefore anti-Rothschild in Russia. (As "Rothschilds" were close to English Freemasonry, the Priory of Sion had pulled away from England on the Russian issue.) "Rothschilds" on the other hand were pro-Zionist, wanted Jews out of Russia and into a new Palestinian homeland, and had funded English Freemasonry and Kerensky to this end via Milner and J. P. Morgan organization. (It is likely that they never recovered this outlay as Lenin never repaid it. However, they may have been compensated in other ways. It has been alleged that the Tsar deposited $80 million in the Rothschild Bank in Paris after 1905, and $400 million in "Rockefellers'" Chase Bank, National City Bank, Guaranty Trust Bank, the Hanover Trust Bank, and Manufacturers Trust Bank.[195] Did his deposits total $1 billion as has also been alleged? If so, what happened, in the months following his execution, to the Tsar's deposits?) The Gentile Templar Grand Orient was linked with Warburgs and backed both Trotsky and Lenin and the Bolsheviks – the Jacobins in Russian garb – and blamed the Jews for a Grand Orient smash-and-grab.

In this tangled confusion is the truth that the two main players, the Priory of Sion and the Templars, used "Rothschilds," "Warburgs" and the Jews for their own ends, changing the alliances to suit themselves as they sought to keep the Jews within Russia (anti-Zionist Priory of Sion) or to blame the Jews for the Russian Revolution (Templar Grand Orient using "Warburgs") or to let them out (Zionist "Rothschilds" using English Freemasonry)? On this analysis was the Grand Orient using Trotsky to blame the Jews, and were "Rothschilds" using Kerensky to blame the Grand Orient? Arguably the Priory of Sion played a very clever game: applying Hegel's dialectic of thesis-antithesis-synthesis, they waited for English Freemasonry's and "Rothschilds'" candidate Kerensky, and the two Grand Orient Templar candidates (Trotsky and Lenin) to knock each other out and exhaust themselves, before coming through with their candidate, who was already "Rockefellers'" candidate (Stalin). We can state this tangle of alliances as follows:

Contender	Candidate	Funder	Pro/Anti Zionism
English Freemasonry	Kerensky	Milner ($3m)/ J. P. Morgan ($1m) on behalf of "Rothschilds"	Pro-Zionist
Grand Orient Templars	Trotsky/ Lenin	Schiff ($20m) via "Warburgs" on behalf of "Rockefellers"	Anti-Zionist
Priory of Sion	Stalin	"Rockefellers"	Anti-Zionist

"Rockefellers" were a newcomer in the funding of revolutionary movements. They began as "Rothschilds'" agents in America and became rich through "Rothschild" loans. We have also seen that in 1926 they secured the Russian oilfields from "Rothschilds" in a deal to market Soviet oil in Europe. From this time "Rockefellers" were in competition with "Rothschilds," and their alliance with the Priory of Sion began with their funding of Stalin's Five-Year Plans. From the First World War (from which they are alleged to have made $200 million[196]) "Rockefellers" became a major player in the drive towards world revolution and world government.

The Russian Revolution's idea of progress – Utopian communist classlessness – perished in the Red Terror and the Great Purge. The dictatorship of the proletariat degenerated into a tyranny: the dictatorship of one psychopathic man.

George Orwell lampooned such egalitarianism in his satire *Animal Farm*: "All animals are equal, but some are more equal than others." The "new class" of pigs (under a pig called Napoleon) rule the other animals. In *1984* he showed Big Brother, the Party and O'Brien as those who were "more equal" than Winston Smith, who had to be taught (by mind-control) that 2 + 2 = 5; in other words, to believe whatever the Party wanted him to believe. Communist egalitarianism disintegrated into collective brainwashing.

Nevertheless, Russian society did make gains, although the Byzantine-Russian civilization and its Orthodox religion proceeded further towards disintegration. Russian society was industrialized rapidly and achieved at huge cost – 12 million dead in collectivization – what Bismarck achieved less brutally in Germany. It could be claimed that Stalin did bring agrarian Russia into the 20th century.

A conservative death toll makes Lenin responsible for 33 million deaths (see p451) and Stalin for another 40 million[197] (excluding his complicity in the 33 million when he held office under Lenin).

We can now state the revolutionary dynamic of the ideas behind the Russian Revolution as follows:

Heretical occult inspiration	Intellectual expression	Political expression	Physical consolidation
Luciferian rebellion to win classlessness	Anarchism, Nihilistic negation, egalitarianism	Communism	Terror: 73m dead, elimination of bourgeoisie and Zionists
(Weishaupt of Orléanist Grand Orient)	(Marx/Engels & Bakunin of Grand Orient)	(Lenin/Trotsky of Grand Orient)	(Stalin, ally of "Rockefellers" and Priory of Sion)

Hidden agenda:

"Rothschilds"	Anarchism	Zionism	Malthusian depopulation?
		(Kerensky of Grand Orient)	(Stalin, ally of Priory of Sion)

At the end of ch 6 (p403) we asked if revolutionary socialist communism and the linked idea of a world federation of states or united states of the world would collapse in the same way that liberal capitalist imperialist competition had collapsed as a result of the First World War. We have seen the collapse of Soviet communism with the breaching of the Berlin Wall in 1989, although Chinese communism is still a force to be reckoned with. For the prospects of communism and of a united states of the world in our own time, see the companion volume to this book, *The Syndicate: The Story of the Coming World Government.*

CHAPTER EIGHT

CONCLUSION: REVOLUTIONS' COMMON SOURCE

Though few Masons know it, the god of Masonry is Lucifer. What's the difference between Lucifer and Satan? Luciferians think they are doing good. Satanists know they are evil.

William Still, *New World Order: The Ancient Plan of Secret Societies*

Anyone reading the previous seven chapters cannot fail to be surprised, even startled and perhaps impressed, at the impact of secret organizations on Western history at critical times of rapid change in the European, North American and Byzantine-Russian civilizations. In each revolution a secret organization requires us to reassess who the revolutionaries were: the reformers of the Reformation were generally Kabbalists; the Puritans were actually Rosicrucians, as were the Dutch Protestants (and later Hanoverians); the American revolutionaries were actually Templars; the French revolutionaries were Illuminatists, as were the Imperialists and Russian revolutionaries. When history books speak of revolutionaries, they actually mean something else.

If this is true of the story behind the revolutions, what about all the other bits of Western history – the wars and creation of empires not covered in the previous pages? Are they also the story of the workings of a hidden hand? As regards the time span of this book (the Renaissance to the 20th century), that part of the story remains to be told. As regards the time span from 1900 to date, that story can be found in the companion volume to this book, *The Syndicate: The Story Behind the Coming World Government.*

What has our look at secret organizations in this book told us about the pattern of history? Looking back, we can make some tentative generalizations and form a number of conclusions – and in particular, one over-all conclusion.

Revolutions as Destructive Freemasonic Utopias

The European, North American and Byzantine-Russian civilizations have gone through a period of crisis, the response to which is rapid revolution. There is a case to be made for maintaining that all civilizations at some time have a revolution which brings about a rapid change in social conditions. Since 1450 the revolutions have been against oppressors: the oppressive Catholic Church (the Reformation and Glorious Revolutions) and oppressive monarchs (Charles I, George III, Louis XVI and the Russian Tsars). All oppressors have undoubtedly been cartoonized to mobilize popular fury.

Revolutions are launched with extravagant hopes to bring about rapid change to societies by violent means. An old order has to be dismantled so that the new order can come through. In the revolutions we have examined, the old order is a social class – the nobles and bourgeoisie in the French Revolution, the bourgeoisie in the Russian Revolution – and the destruction of this class enables a revolutionary society to advance – progress – through the formation of a new constitution and the bestowal and guarantee of new human rights under the law.

However, the changes are destructive to the civilization in which the revolutionary society functions and while there is progress in individual liberties, the central or essential idea of the civilization which cradles the society undergoes decay. All civilizations begin with a metaphysical idea,[1] and the replacement of religion by the goddess of Reason in France, for example, contributed to the erosion of the European civilization's essentially metaphysical and religious central idea.

In short, revolutions advance individual liberties among certain classes of citizens, but accelerate the decline of their civilization by dismantling institutions that have encouraged its growth. Revolutions make citizens more rather than less secular, and the secularization of civilizations hastens their decay – their decline from the metaphysical central idea which inspired their growth.

All the revolutions we have looked at have been intrigued from abroad by a secret organization with links to the occult. The "outside generator" is always a political as opposed to an occult force, but behind the political force that effects the revolution there is always an occult transnational agency or brotherhood (e.g. Rosicrucians, Freemasons), as we can see by listing our seven main revolutions; the country from which the outside (political) generator operated; and the outside (occult) agency or brotherhood:

Political Revolution	Country of Outside Generator	Occult Outside Agency/ Brotherhood
Reformation	France (Cathars)	Luciferian Kabbalists
English		
Puritan	Holland (Amsterdam Jews)	Rosicrucians
Glorious	Holland	Rosicrucians
American	Germany (Bavaria/France)	Illuminati/Grand Orient Templar Masons
French	Germany (Bavaria/Berlin)	Illuminati/Grand Orient Templar Masons
Imperialist	France (Sion)/Italy (Mazzini)	Illuminati/Grand Orient Templar Masons
Russian	US/Britain/Germany (Warburgs)	Illuminati/Grand Orient Templar Masons

We can see from the "outside agency" column that all the principal revolutions have strong Freemasonic links. They have been inspired by a Secret Brotherhood of Kabbalists, Rosicrucians, Illuminati, and Grand

Orient or Templar Masons; all from the various branches of Freemasonry.

Freemasonry, which seeks to make a better world from its Utopian vision, has been a secularizing influence on the idiosyncrasy and integrity of civilizations, especially of the European and North American civilizations. Freemasonry holds that through Luciferian rebellion man becomes a god. (See the Epilogue of *The Syndicate*.) Freemasons become iconoclastic Bolsheviks and tear down the religious structure that has inspired the growth of a civilization – to make it better for one particular group or social class and, through it, for the fortunes and vested interests of Freemasonry itself.

The Freemasonic ideas that have inspired and guided revolutions have been quick to affect other societies, and in this sense in the Reformation, Puritan, Glorious, American, French, Imperial, Russian Revolutions, revolution has proved a driving-force of modern history, although it has conflicted with the longer-term *élan* within the civilization in which it originated. All the revolutions we have examined have a revolutionary dynamic of four stages. In the 16th and 17th centuries, the three revolutions were against the Catholic religion (Charles I was widely suspected of being a Catholic). In the 18th and 19th centuries the revolutions were against monarchs.

Freemasonry has accumulated centuries of revolutionary experience, and has prepared the ground for the revolutions in our time that have led to our contemporary New World Order whose globalism has been in evidence in the Global Coalition that has made war in Afghanistan. (See *The Syndicate*.)

The roots of the New World Order can be found in the dismantling of Catholic Europe, first by the Protestant Revolution which freed practices such as Freemasonry from the clutches of the Inquisition, and secondly by moves towards republicanism in the anti-monarchist American, French and Russian Revolutions.

On the surface, the revolutions may have seemed to be forward-thinking and anti-imperialistic, and not necessarily socialistic. (Forces for good within them have benefited societies and individual human rights.) The revolutions, however, have a darker side. They were themselves imperialistic and atrociously cruel. We have seen that alongside their idealistic Freemasonic Utopian vision which hopes for good co-exists a murderous vision that achieves its ends by killing. The occult Utopianism of their conception and of their intellectual idea became corrupted as they were entrammelled in political organization and physical consolidation, and so was compromised. An intention to free people ended up enslaving them.

Our study is full of Utopian ideas that have failed: progress through the Protestant Reformation which split Christendom into warring sects; progress through Cromwell's Protectorate (Paradise Lost); progress through Dutch Protestant constitutional reform; progress through Templar deist anti-Britishness; progress through Reason in France; progress through imperialist competition in the 19th century and progress through Communist egalitarianism in Russia.

Utopianism does not have to end in disaster (although all the Utopian revolutions so far have). Just as alchemy was the process of transmuting base metal into gold, so revolution was used – as an alchemical agent – to transform the base metal of society into the gold of Utopia. Can the revolutionaries – Luther, Cromwell, William III, Washington, Robespierre, the "Rothschilds," Lenin and the "Rockefellers" – be vindicated by a new Utopianism which transmutes their failures into new success? See *The Syndicate* for the answer to this question.

Revolutions' Luciferian Inspiration

We have analyzed the principal revolutions of the last 550 years. What are our findings? Do they all have a common source?

We are now in a position to say that they were all created by a hidden hand. The Kabbalists, relatively hidden in their day, shaped the Reformation Revolution and split Christendom; Amsterdam Rosicrucian Freemasons shaped the Puritan and Glorious Revolutions; Illuminati Grand Orient Templar Masons shaped the American, French, Imperialist-Prussian and Russian Revolutions, while Rothschildian Sionist English Freemasonry shaped the British

Imperialist Revolution. All these hidden influences were Freemasonic. Though the Reformation Revolution predated the official founding of Freemasonry, Kabbalism was a hidden influence in its day which had an impact on Catharism from the schools in Languedoc, and the Freemasonic tradition is an offshoot of Kabbalism: both look back to the Temple of Solomon and the Old Testament tradition.

On the evidence of our study of revolutions from the Renaissance to the Russian Revolution, the influences on these upheavals are Freemasonic. Secret societies met behind closed doors and urged sudden and rapid change in their societies. The ringleaders had the confidence to operate in secrecy, in the belief that their fraternity would not betray them. The same principle has been behind the growth of the New World Order in the 20th century, whose roots are Freemasonic.

All our revolutions have been republican. Freemasonry (excluding its Sionist form, which favours monarchy) is essentially republican. All our revolutions have looked to Satan – or Lucifer, to give him his more acceptable name – as a role model. Freemasonry is essentially Luciferian: the secret taught to 32nd and 33rd degree Masons is that Lucifer is the Architect of the Universe.[2] (See the Epilogue of *The Syndicate*.) All our revolutions aspire to bring in the world rule of Lucifer as a metaphor and as an actuality in whose invisible will they believe.

We can see this in the Kabbalistic, Gnostic tradition we have traced. Belief in Lucifer compromised the unity of creation. At the metaphysical level, creation is one, a unity, a nonduality. Over the centuries the pure spiritual vision and its symbolic truths became literalized, and the unity of creation became divided. An occult counterpart to the spiritual vision focused on this division. The original unitary Kabbalah, the received oral Jewish tradition, became corrupted and a divided, false, occult Kabbalah which saw the world in terms of Jews and Gentiles gave rise to dualistic Gnosticism, out of which grew the myth that God's eldest son was Satanail or Satan ("enemy" or "adversary" in Hebrew), or Lucifer, an angel who rebelled and fell. See Appendices B for further details.

Those who held the initial spiritual vision of universal love – the authors of *Genesis* and *Isaiah*, and indeed Milton – were fully aware that their presentation of the unitary vision would be understood in dualistic, literal terms. They were aware of the co-existence of good and evil, of nobility and bestiality, saintly love and despicable cruelty of man to man, and their presentation enfolded all the opposites, which are reconciled in the unity of the spiritual vision. The opposites included man's revolt against God and the natural order of the Universe in the example of the mythical Lucifer.

Over the centuries, as their symbolic truths were literalized, the occult vision ascribed dark powers to Satan/Lucifer, who acquired a metaphysical reality beyond the mythological. As dualism emerged, Satan/Lucifer's dark power opposed God. To many this power had come to have an objective force and the power of darkness challenged the unitary reality and shaped men's lives for ill. Satan/Lucifer could provide his followers with wealth and fame, as Marlowe's Dr Faustus discovered. Satan/Lucifer became the god of money, and had obvious appeal for the richest families in the world. Satan/Lucifer had become the icon of world revolution.

Lucifer was the personification of revolution. The lesson from the story of Lucifer is that attempted revolution involves rebellion against the natural order of things, which is God's order. His rebellion against Heaven is described in *Isaiah*:

"How art thou fallen from heaven, O Lucifer, son of the morning! How art thou cut down to the ground, which didst weaken the nations!

"For thou has said in thine heart, I will ascend into heaven, I will exalt my throne above the stars of God: I will sit also upon the mount of the congregation in the sides of the north:

"I will ascend above the heights of the clouds; I will be like the Most High.

"Yet thou shalt be brought down to hell, to the sides of the pit."
(14,12-15)

His was an attempted revolution. From being a prosecutor of human weakness as in *Job* – like a Persian official who roamed the earth strengthening what is good by reporting individuals and acts of weakness to the King – he sought to replace God as King of Heaven and transform Heaven for his followers. His was an unsuccessful revolution: it ended in his being cast into outer darkness.

According to occult, dualistic legend, Lucifer, the Angel Satanail or Satanael, was the elder son of God (Christ being the second son of God). As Prince of the Angels Lucifer had extensive power but his ambition to be greater than the Father destroyed him. He attempted to overthrow the power of God and become ruler of Heaven and Earth. The archangel Michael flung him into the abyss and as he fell an emerald became detached from his diadem and landed in the Hindu Kush Mountains (near where bin Laden had a mountain hide-out). According to one view this was later fashioned into the Grail Cup.[3]

Lucifer's new attempt to overthrow God's established order was a "revolution" as it sought to transform Heaven. Lucifer/Satanail and Christ, the two brothers according to legend, represent rebellion against the established order (Lucifer/Satanail) and support for it (Christ). These two brothers/sons of God personify the fundamental split in the human psyche and represent the divided self. The conflicting attitudes of the two brothers echo throughout Judaeo-Christian literature, as in the conflict between Edmund and Edgar in Shakespeare's *King Lear*.

Part of the tradition looks to Christ and part to Lucifer/Satanail. In every sense, Lucifer/Satanail is the archetypal revolutionary, and all revolutionaries look back to him as did the pro-revolutionary Blake in his pro-Hell watercolours that picture Satan holding a spear and shield aloft, his eyes filled with energetic purpose. The joyous Satan of *Glad Day* proclaims that "Energy is eternal delight."[4]

After Lucifer was cast into outer darkness, he came to earth to take revenge on God, his Father, by spoiling his creation, man. He made his way to Paradise, we are told in *Genesis*, to Eden, and, disguised as a serpent, now Satan, tempted Eve with an apple, saying, "Ye shall be as gods" (*Genesis* 3.5.), and persuaded her to eat of the Tree of Knowledge of Good and Evil. She lost her innocence, and Adam followed. Now the Fall had happened, a literary device for drawing attention to the fact that mankind has an ever-present choice between following the way of obedience to God's authority or rebellion against it – the Luciferian way. By the time Milton took up the story in *Paradise Lost*, the example of Lucifer had inspired the Puritan Revolution. (Milton's Satan was modelled on Cromwell.)

It has to be said that a number of literary and artistic works which are at the forefront of our traditional culture and are on university syllabuses were produced within the movements we have been studying, and may affirm occult Luciferian values. We have seen that a number of European authors, artists and thinkers need to be treated warily as their attitudes towards the Luciferian theme are ambivalent. Is Grand Master Botticelli (Sandro Filipepi) on the side of Dante's Hell in his sketches, or horrified by it? Do Marlowe, Milton and Blake sympathise with Mephistopheles and Satan, or do they denounce dabbling in the black arts? Is Goethe, the ex-Illuminatus Abaris, on the side of Faust's necromancy, or is he looking back at his misguided youth and delivering a warning? As Rousseau was probably influenced by Charles de Lorraine and Goethe by Weishaupt, was Romanticism a Sionist movement? Does Descartes "think" before he declares his existence because he follows the Rosicrucian view of man? Are Grand Master Newton and Darwin Rosicrucian propagandists rather than objective scientists? Is Grand Master Cocteau presenting Luciferian values in his *Testament d'Orphée*? There is a healthy, "good" mystical line in Western culture, and a tainted, "bad", occult-Luciferian line whose practitioners are linked to secret organizations and revolutions we have been studying. In poetry, it is the difference between Eliot and Yeats, who was a member of the Rosicrucian Order of the Golden Dawn and who drew heavily on the occult. It is the difference between Dostoevsky, who condemned the Satanic Nechayev in his novel *The Possessed* (or *The Devils*), and Aleister Crowley, the Satanist of the Order of the Golden Dawn and OTO so admired by contemporary rock groups. It has to be said that the modern consciousness identifies more with the occult vision of the rebellious

Lucifer than with the mystical vision of the One; hence the prominence of Crowleyan attitudes in the younger generation today. How many of the established writers, artists and thinkers on university courses reflect this polluted tradition and contaminate the young?

The spiritual vision which sees "all is One" implies that everything and everyone are part of a greater whole and that at the spiritual level a certain egalitarianism is therefore part of the natural order of the Universe. Not everything and everyone is equal in degree and hierarchy, however, and the revolutionary, like Lucifer, seeks to usurp the existing degree and hierarchy and replace them with a physically egalitarian outlook: Lucifer's band of Angels hoped to transform Heaven so that they all had a share in its delights once they had seized power.

Those who created the story of Lucifer portray this archetypal revolutionary as arrogating to himself (and to his supporters among the Angels) what was rightfully God's. In Lucifer's case its cause was his own envy and ambition, though to justify his forcible action he would no doubt argue that God's Heaven was imperfect.[5] The effect of Lucifer's attempted revolution was to divide Heaven. Revolution divides the order it seeks to replace.

Revolution cannot be understood without making this connection to the archetypal revolutionary Lucifer for it is his dominance that explains the extremism of its political and physical stages. Robespierre's guillotine and the Rosicrucian Stalin's firing-squads have a ruthlessness about them that can only be understood at the Satanic level. Revolution in its consolidation phase is necessarily destructive.

Yet, within the whole pattern of all civilizations, revolutions have a necessary place. They move their civilizations forward as we have seen, advance individual liberties while they increase secularization and advance the civilization's decay. It is as though civilizations are tussles between two opposing and conflicting principles, one a principle of order, the other of destruction and decay. Revolutions are like the autumn wind that savagely shakes the leaves from a tree – so that they can be renewed the following spring.

Destructive revolutions do the bidding of creative civilizations just as Satan, for all his temptations and his cruelty (perhaps without realising it) does the will of God, the supreme creative and therefore positive Being who could not keep the Whole renewed and dynamic without the help of destruction and negativity.

✳

We have looked long and hard at the secret history of revolutions, probing the secret organizations beneath their surface and rediscovering the true significance of events which stand like rocks on the beach after the sea has receded. We have reconstructed what it was like when the tide was in.

Our narrative contains a mixture of hard facts, circumstantial evidence and speculation. We have not based our theme on suppositions. The events of the revolutions all happened, and by assembling circumstantial material regarding the impact on them of secret organizations we have restored to them a meaning they have lost in the intervening centuries or decades. We have now arrived at an in-depth understanding of the politics of our own time, which includes the globalist roots of the New World Order and the soil from which it has grown.

History is more than a bald statement of events. "Why did they happen?" is what historians need to ask. New answers to this question have presented themselves during the course of this study: because of the hitherto unacknowledged impact of specific secret organizations. The history of the last 550 years is a cautionary tale for our time. Will it be heeded?

In the course of the last 550 years leaders have made statements, but hidden organizations below the surface have influenced their statements and that is what we have been examining. Most of the leaders and organizations we have been considering have been outside the democratic process. Where the leaders have been subject to the democratic process, decisions they have made have often been based on advice from secret organizations which are outside the democratic process, which means that the spirit of the democratic process has been bypassed. People are not fools, and while they demand evidence for conspiracies, they do not rush into agreeing with bland assurances that there never were or never are hidden forces in history working for an ulterior agenda – not any more.

In *The Syndicate: The Story of the Coming World Government* I apply this principle and perspective to the 20th century and our own time, with extremely revealing results. I conclude that 20th- and 21st-century secret organizations are stealing the United States and Britain by constitutional theft – by planning to hold the last American election in 2016 and by imposing the new European constitution. Their goal is to dominate the world by creating a Freemasonic world government through world revolution. I urge you to read the companion volume to this work to follow the story of the hidden hand through from 1900 to our own precarious situation in our troubled time, when the hidden hand looks set to strike with an iron fist and destroy our long tradition and proud history. It must not be allowed to succeed.

APPENDICES

A
THE HIDDEN HAND IN WESTERN HISTORY

APPENDIX I

THE CONCEPT AND DYNAMIC OF REVOLUTION

Secret organizations are dormant much of the time, hidden away like a sleeper agent, unobtrusive and ignored. Then suddenly and dramatically, like terrorists who have blended with their surroundings, their activists manifest at times of revolution. They reveal themselves during revolutions. We have been asking a number of questions. What secret organizations have influenced what revolutions? Are they connected? What hidden hand can be detected behind each of Western history's main revolutions? To answer these questions we have focused on the revolutions the secret organizations intrigued.

But there is a wider question that needs to be addressed. When we speak of a revolution, what do we mean? What is a revolution?

Revolutionaries such as Cromwell, Robespierre and Lenin have one thing in common: they seek to transform society more rapidly than the normal legal processes will allow.

This transformation is a process that begins with an invisible incubatory phase in which a thinker has a hidden, occult vision of transformation that spreads slowly, in the course of years or even decades, until it commands the intellectual assent of a body of followers who belong to a secret organization. The vision and its spreading are occult in the sense that they are hidden from view, concealed, kept secret, heretical in relation to the orthodoxy of the established Church.

The occult vision differs notoriously from the spiritual vision with which it is often confused. In the spiritual vision the self opens to the divine, the One, and channels divine energy. It can reveal itself outside the Church; indeed, as I showed in *The Fire and the Stones*, each of the world's 25 civilizations was inspired by such a spiritual vision of God as Light (see Appendices A, Appendix 2), and the spiritual is found in all the world's religions, whose mystics open to the Light, shut down their egos and channel revelations of the divine energy to the world through contemplation, meditation or prayer – as a force for good, to help others. In the occult vision the self psychically contacts and controls a dark Luciferian energy that it manipulates to advance its worldly power – as a force to promote self-interest, to harm others. Occultists claim to be promoting the good of sections of mankind. Those who have the vision of revolution seek to improve on God's world and turn it into a Utopia by suppressing a social class that holds back another social class. They challenge the spiritual vision of the civilization that has become the status quo, they are opposed to their civilization's religion and seek to rebel against it and replace it, as Lucifer sought to replace God.

Those who have the vision of revolution claim to have their own line to "the Light." Like Weishaupt, they pride themselves on their "Illuminism." In so far as they seek to control "the Light" and use it on God's world which they want to improve, make better, in their own terms, to suit themselves, they are occultists. Like all occultists, they attempt to dominate this same Light, manipulate its energy, turn it to serve their own will. The ego of the occultist or magician is always in charge whereas the mystic's is obliterated by the reception of the Light, the vision of God. In seeking to manipulate the divine Light, occultists convert it into dark, psychic and demonic energy which can be used for self-aggrandizement and self-enrichment, the energy of black magic and witchcraft, of Satan/Lucifer – a force for evil. Those who have the vision of revolution, of rebelling and making God's world better, admire Lucifer and are in rebellion against God.

Some theologians (such as the late Bede Griffiths), quoting one particular tradition of mysticism that goes back to Dionysius the Areopagite, hold that God is known in darkness, and that the vision of Light is from Lucifer. This view is not borne out by my study of the visions of the divine that inspired civilizations. It can be said that the vision of God is a vision of divine Light which mystics receive with submissive joy and which occultists try to control and use for their own ends, seeking to be Lords of Creation, as gods, Olympians.

It is difficult to generalize as a spiritual universalism is to be found in all religions and cultures, and in spiritual/occult matters nothing is simply light or dark, white or black, but rather shades of grey in differing emphases. The occult vision that leads to revolution is heretical (i.e. outside the orthodoxy of the mainstream religion/Church), self-interested (in championing a particular social class) and manipulative (in seeking to control the divine energy). The occult use of divine energy appears psychic, even demonic and dark – Luciferian, or blatantly Satanic – and actively opposes the Church. In short, spiritual energy approaches God, occult energy approaches Lucifer/Satan and challenges the Church.

We have found that the first two gradual stages in the transformation of society (the occult vision and its intellectual spreading) are then followed by political and physical stages: a phase of very rapid political change followed by a period of physical consolidation that may result in brutal purges of "enemies of the Revolution." These two stages may involve overthrowing an obstructive government that has made the revolution necessary – or in the case of world revolution, governments – and radically changing the economic system, social structure and cultural values of the society involved. The revolutionaries have to use force or apply social pressure to effect the change. They generally target a particular social class, on which they declare war.

In all there are four stages – the occult, intellectual, political and physical – as the movement is from an interior conception of transformation to its external realization in the outside world. These stages are part of the natural cycle of intellectual life, although they may later seem to have been planned. They are part of a revolutionary dynamic which is a process from conception to implementation. Those who had the vision of transformation and instigated it in the first two stages were as much part of the hidden hand as those who realized and implemented it in the last two stages.

The original spiritual vision of the mystics is purist and entirely peaceful; in it the visionary perceives the nonduality of the Universe, its Oneness in which humankind can live in harmony with the natural order in universal bliss and grace, opening to the divine will without being persecuted or suppressed by any authority. The vision is of a world better than the existing world, and the visionary dreams of transforming the world to make it a better place, one that is fit to accommodate the vision of beauty.

The occult version of this vision which revolutionaries follow seeks the benefits of this pure vision by the violent overthrow of an established class that stands in its way, just as Lucifer sought the violent overthrow of God's Angels. In the occult vision, Utopia is reached in one sudden bound by eliminating a social class on which war has been declared: the nobility or the bourgeoisie.

The remaining three stages mark the progressive degeneration of this occult vision as it becomes increasingly interpreted in material, physical terms. The intellectual vision is an attempt to translate the occult vision into a blueprint to create (or recreate) heaven on earth for a particular social class. We have a seemingly innate wish to live in a better world of the kind described in Plato's *Republic*, More's *Utopia* and other works, and the intellectual vision focuses on such an ideal world, the Kingdom of Heaven on earth. It describes Paradise, the Promised Land, Nirvana, Shambala and other ideal places which reflect the spiritual vision, where it can dwell in harmony. The occult vision is for a particular segment of a people, whose declaration of war on everyone else in order to achieve their Utopia parodies the spiritual vision of the Good, and the intellectualization of the ideal conditions in which it can thrive has inspired all revolutions.

More fully, we have found that the initial occult vision is interpreted by an occult interpreter, whose book is implemented by a revolutionary originator in terms of a Freemasonic tradition. A thoughtful intellectual interpreter carries the vision forward in action, and a semi-political intellectual interpreter takes over and gives the vision political expression, and prepares the way for a political stage. See Appendices A, Appendix 2, *Civilizations and Revolutions: Two Dynamics* for a fuller explanation.

The political stage always compromises the vision. What seemed so perfect and blissful in the visionary trance is now set in an ideal political state which may be a totalitarian regime, a colonialist empire or a fundamentalist religious rule of clerics. The State is now run by members of a secret organization under a political or military leader. The social class that has to be eliminated is now confronted.

The physical consolidation of the revolution involves the kind of repression associated with revolutionary regimes such as the USSR and Communist China. The hidden hand now strikes with an iron fist. The offending social class is now suppressed, for bloodshed is now a means of bringing in the degenerated occult vision, and at the same time all opposition to the revolution is eliminated.

The intellectual, political and physical stages of the revolutionary dynamic have progressivly separated each revolution from its occult vision. Each revolution is now dominated by a political (and often military) leader who is a member of a secret organization rather than a visionary or thinker. We have seen that the full revolutionary dynamic of the four main revolutions can be stated as follows:

Revolution	Heretical occult inspiration	Intellectual expression	Political expression	Physical consolidation
English	Bacon/Andreae Menasseh	Hartlib/ Cromwell (or Manasseh)	Pym/	Cromwell
American	Bacon/ Weishaupt	Franklin/ Jefferson	Washington	Jackson
French	Weishaupt/ Rousseau	Cagliostro/ Mirabeau	Robespierre	Napoleon
Russian	Weishaupt/ Hegel/Marx/ Engels	Herzen/ Trotsky	Lenin	Stalin

We have also seen that all those named belonged to secret organizations.[1]

Revolution suggests the revolving of a wheel round an axle or axis, a rotation. The circular movement effects a complete change in society, it turns things upside down, it reverses – or rather progresses – conditions. The wheel turns and revolves and is positioned anew, just as the Wheel of Fortune turned, bringing changes. (In *Consolation of Philosophy*, Boethius describes Fortune's "turning" wheel in a passage that was the source for all the medieval allusions to Fortune and her wheel, in *Romance of the Rose*, Dante and Chaucer, for example.) The wheel is turned by the hidden hand of a secret organization.

The turning of a "revolution" suggests rapid stages of transformation, an attempt to overthrow the government or established political system. "Revolution" is also used of economic and social changes that are sudden and dramatic in their effect, as when we speak of "the Industrial Revolution," but which have taken a considerable time to evolve. (Instances of this in our own time include the movements for civil rights, feminism and the colonial liberation movements such as the Indian independence movement that saw Ghandian non-violence.) In either case a revolution involves a four-stage process that culminates in a sudden, radical departure from the previous system; and *all* revolutions are subject to this four-stage dynamic that is described in the next section. A revolution is a revolving of society, a process which begins slowly and surfaces relatively suddenly, transforming the society's system or pattern.

A revolution is quite different from a rebellion, which is organized armed resistance to an established government, though in the case of Cromwell's "Great Rebellion" (1642-51) there was both armed resistance to Charles I *and* a sudden revolutionary transformation in English society. A rebellion's armed resistance is like a mutiny, and if it is successful it can turn revolutionary. A rebel against the established Church openly resists the authority of the Church. Such a rebel was Dostoevsky's Ivan Karamazov when he told his story about the Grand Inquisitor. Camus' *The Rebel*, a translation of *L'Homme Revolté*, focuses on the man who rebels against the "absurd" order of things in the name of justice. Whether it is military or metaphysical, rebellion focuses on the resistance of the rebel rather than on the transformation of society.

A revolt is like a rebellion or a rising. It is a rising against a ruler and a transfer of allegiance to a rival power. As with rebellion it may lead to a revolution, though the Peasants' Revolt of 1381 led by Wat Tyler never became a revolution.

A revolution must also be distinguished from a *coup d'état*, which is a violent and often illegal change in government. This is often a military strike at dawn by one faction in an army or government against the other factions, and may not transform society or change the system. Often as a result of a *coup* a new face rules within the same system. A *coup* is often called a revolution, but it only becomes a revolution if the force used in the take-over rapidly transforms society and brings about a change in its economic, social and cultural system.

The hallmarks of a revolution, then, are:

1. It transforms society (through the revolutionary process, society is transformed);
2. After a slow incubation the transformation is relatively rapid;
3. Force is used (or social pressure);
4. There is a complete change to the economic, social and cultural structure of society.

5.   Above all, behind its workings we can detect the hidden hand of a particular secret organization which has a destructive agenda (to destroy the old order).

If we leave aside archetypal, mythological or literary revolutionaries such as Lucifer and Prometheus (who stole fire from Zeus) and focus on Western civilization rather than the earlier ancient world, Pythagoras, the 6th century Greek philosopher and mathematician, may have been one of the first Western revolutionaries. It is known that he rebelled against Polycrates and was exiled in 532 BC from Samos to Croton in Italy. His religious Orphic sect, which was known as the Pythagorean brotherhood and influenced the thinking of Plato and Aristotle, is believed to have been responsible for his exile, but it is possible that it was also a political Utopian commune and that he was expelled for being a political subversive as well as for religious reasons.

From the earliest times revolution has been seen as a destructive force. The Greeks saw many instances of changes of power between tyrants in city-states. Athens had seen the absolute rule of Peisistratus, who had implemented Solon's reforms, and the oligarchic rule of the Thirty Tyrants following Sparta's victory over Athens in 404 BC. Plato, who defended stable republican government, asks in his *Republic* (book 8, 545-6): "Is this the simple and unvarying rule, that in every form of government revolution takes its start from the ruling class itself when dissension arises in that...innovation is impossible?" Plato sees revolution in terms of destruction. He champions belief in traditional values against the decaying moral and religious tenets of society, and hopes that such belief will prevent revolution. Aristotle also defined the republican ideal and saw that if a society's values are shaky, it will be liable to revolution. The Romans knew dictators such as Sulla and Julius Caesar. They saw the attempted revolution of the Gracchi, who tried to push through land reform without consulting the Senate. Tiberius Sempronius Gracchus was killed by a lynch-mob, and the consensus of opinion was that it was good that the established order had been defended.

The growth of the Church stifled revolutionary feeling. In the

Middle Ages the powerful authority of the Church, which cemented God's rule, prevented revolution. The established beliefs and forms of government held back and even suppressed attempted revolutions such as the Peasants' Revolt, which never became a revolution. It was believed, especially by the Church, that revolutionaries (such as the impostor Perkin Warbeck) sought the desecration of society; consequently they were given short shrift, and revolutionary thinking did not develop.

We have seen that the concept of revolution changed during the Renaissance, when the power of the Church declined. Revolution re-emerged with the emergence of secular values. The advent of secular Humanism focused on the condition of human beings, and also on the nature of the State, which should be able to endure the threat of revolution. The thinking of Nicolò Machiavelli was crucial to this development. In two almost contradictory books written at the same time he championed both hereditary principalities (in *The Prince*, 1513, revised 1516) and republics (in *The Discourses*, 1513-1519), and was an advocate of either according to the circumstances of the case. (Castiglione's *The Book of the Courtier*, 1508-16, though earlier, does not focus so systematically on the State.) *The Discourses* follow Plato in seeing the republic as the best of all worlds. They contain advice as to how to avoid insurrections and maintain internal security. Machiavelli, who held power after the Medici left Florence in 1598, advocated changes in the structure of government, and though he never used the word "revolution" in his writings and was concerned to create a stable State, he placed himself at the very front of modern revolutionary thinking. We have seen that Thomas Cromwell's view of the State in the England of the 1530s was deeply influenced by his time in Italy and his contact with Machiavelli's works. A hidden hand supported Luther.

By the 1630s the concept of revolution had changed fundamentally, and John Milton had come to believe that revolution helped a society achieve its true potential. As we have seen, Milton saw revolution as society's right to stand up to "tyrants" such as Charles I, win liberty and create a new order that reflected people's needs. He believed that an earthly Paradise could be won and lamented the "Paradise lost" of Cromwell's revolution after its collapse. In fact, Cromwell's Utopia was put in place by the hidden hand of a secret organization.

We have seen that by the 1780s the concept of revolution had changed again. Revolutionary thinking had developed as a result of the German philosopher Immanuel Kant, who claimed that revolution advanced mankind and gave society a higher ethical foundation. Revolution was the method by which freedom was seized from oppressive leaders. In the American Revolution (or Revolutionary War), liberty was taken from the colonial system of George III, and in the French Revolution from the monarchy of Louis XVI. In both cases, particular secret organizations were at work.

We have seen that in the 19th century the concept of revolution had changed yet again. Revolutionary thinking developed through another German philosopher, Hegel, who saw revolutions as fulfilling human destiny. Hegel's dialectical method (thesis-antithesis-synthesis) was adopted by the Jewish Moses Mordecai Levi, alias Karl Marx, who saw revolution as a class struggle by which the workers (thesis) eliminated the capitalists (antithesis) and took over a society's economy to create a Paradise on earth (synthesis). Marx held that the proletariat or working class must capture the means of production. His thought led to Communist revolutions by Marxists in Russia, Yugoslavia, China, Vietnam and Cuba in the 20th century, and inspired numerous so-called revolutions in the Middle and Far East, Africa and Latin America, including the Islamic revolution in Iran. Behind Marx, and Marxism, was a secret organization.

In all the revolutions we have mentioned, there is a so-called natural order that is rebelled against. The spiritual vision sees all humankind as belonging to one greater whole and as being equal at a spiritual level. Its occult counterpart wants to apply this vision to a particular group or social class. This occult vision becomes debased in the physical, human world, and in acting out its physical counterpart the revolutionaries have egalitarian principles and seek to pull down degree and hierarchy. Without exception, they are anti-monarchic and anti-constitutional, and seek to destroy pre-existing social systems, national borders and ethnic cultures. Ultimately revolution is anarchic: it overthrows existing rules and laws and replaces them with its own.

In that they look back to a mythical Golden Age, revolutions are Utopian and regressive. The word "Utopia" (from the Greek ou+topos, "not place," i.e. Nowhere, but also eu+topos, "good place") was first used by Sir Thomas More. Sir Thomas More's *Utopia* (1516) described an imaginary place with a perfect social and political system – an ideally perfect place. Bacon looked back to the time of Solomon (Salomon's House in *The New Atlantis* suggests Solomon) and his follower Oliver Cromwell looked back to the people of Israel. Franklin looked back to a Baconian New Atlantis as a New World democracy, a Utopian view of the Atlantis that sank. (Freemasonry planned to raise Atlantis out of the sea philosophically and re-establish democracy as a New World Order. Indeed Freemasonry traced itself back to the "Lost Continent of Atlantis.")[2] Rousseau looked back to the Noble Savage and to a time when there were no aristocrats. Lenin looked back to a Slavophile Mother Russia. All sought to create from their backward look a perfect social and political system.

Why did the revolutionaries rebel? Was it because they spontaneously wanted a better world, a Utopian perfect society? Did they all have an idealistic vision? Or were there other reasons for their action? Were they affiliated to an organization that gave the orders, and to which they swore allegiance? What did the revolutionaries rebel against? The incompetence of regimes? Monarchies? The corruption of their contemporary institutions? Did they have a cartooned image of their opponents as obstructing ciphers, labels to be hooted at as they lay before the guillotine, or did they see them as real people, shivering human beings with feelings?

On the evidence we have studied, the main revolutionaries did have Utopian dreams and did detest the institutions that held the world back. They also had links with international Freemasonic organizations and obeyed their commands (e.g. Trotsky, who was ordered into Russia in 1905). The answer to all the above questions is inevitably mixed, but the revolutionaries would probably recognize most of the motives as theirs.

All those revolutionaries responsible for the political and physical stages of a revolution (such as Cromwell, Lenin and Napoleon) still retain a spark of the occult Freemasonic vision in the Messianic quality of their characters. This spark is clearly identifiable in their behaviour, and its Messianism sets them apart from other political leaders. The "revolutionary profile" of a leader responsible for the phase of rapid transformation includes a fervour that may be considered fanaticism. This can be attributed to the evangelical spirit that sustains the Utopian vision.

Such revolutionaries have shining eyes and speak with the sort of messianic passion and urgency that is more common to the pulpit than the hustings. They seek to convert their audiences to the reality (however corrupt) of their Utopia. They communicate their fervour to their public. "Bliss was it in that dawn to be alive" ("French Revolution, as it Appeared to Enthusiasts") and "Glory and hope to new-born Liberty!" (*Prelude*, bk 6, 442) wrote Wordsworth of the heady early days of the French revolution in terms that recall Blake's joyous *Glad Day* – but after the Reign of Terror he changed his view. The queue at the guillotine was not what he had anticipated. Something had gone badly wrong.

Messianic revolutionary leaders are intolerant towards their opponents, threatening them with execution and imprisonment. When he speaks of his opponents, there is no mistaking a revolutionary leader: Mao, Gaddafi and Khomenei, revolutionaries in our time, were all distinguished by their willingness to call in the firing-squads.

It is instructive to contrast the Utopian ideal and the number of dead in each revolution:

Revolution	Utopian Ideal	Number Dead	Population
English (1642-60)	New Jerusalem	830,725 (incl. Scottish and Irish) 100,000* in civil wars (1 in 50)	5m

American (1775-83)	New Atlantis	25,000* (1 in 100)	2.5m
French (1789-1815)	New Eden of Noble Savage	1.3m* (1 in 20)	26m
Russian (1905-39)	Communist Paradise	1.3m (excl. Stalin's consolidation) 16m* (1905-39)[3] (1 in 10)	160m

It is interesting to compare these figures with three other revolutions:

Revolution	Utopian Ideal	Number Dead	Population
Mexican (1910-34)	New Mexico	2m* (1 in 8.5)	26m
Chinese (1949-76)	Communist Paradise	60m* (1 in 10)	600m
Cambodian (Khmers Rouges, 1975-9)	Communist Paradise	2m*[3] (1 in 3.5)	7m

We have seen that another aspect of revolutions – and of world revolution – is population reduction. The number of dead is not an accidental consequence of revolutions but is actually part of their agenda and may in some cases be their *raison d'être*. It is integral in the occult vision. We have seen that in all revolutions a certain class of people (in the case of the Russian revolution, the bourgeoisie) has to be eliminated so that a Utopian paradise can be brought in (in the case of the Russian revolution, a proletarian paradise).

All the major revolutions we have mentioned sought to bring in a global ideology. They overthrew tyranny and oppression in their own nation-state but then extended the principle of revolution world-wide. Thus did Soviet Communism turn its attention outwards to direct its revolutionary zeal towards other "tyrannies" (which it identified as colonial states). The American Revolution engendered the same missionary spirit, supporting all nations struggling to be free from tyranny and oppression. The French Revolution exported the Statue of Liberty to its American brothers. This universal aspect of revolutions means that they are imperialistic in the sense of seeking to widen their vision to the whole world, and they scorn sovereignty – at first the sovereignty they overthrow but then the sovereignty of other nation-states which are candidates for overthrow in the internationalist "extension" phase of revolutions.

We have seen that all revolutions are ultimately part of a single drive towards the overthrow of national governments through world revolution and the establishment of a single world government. It is for this reason that they are international and march beneath the banner of the brotherhood of man. We have seen that revolutions impose an ideal for all mankind, which means imposing a totalitarian egalitarianism (one that is subservient to the State) where they can.

While such idealism may be valid on an occult level, in the political sphere it inevitably led to oppression as the revolutionary leadership relied on coercion to enforce its Utopian principles. Citizens were compelled, often on pain of death, to accept the "perfect society" that revolutions imposed on them. The same is true of world revolution.

In our time we are seeing the creation of a New World Order. The term was first used in the modern media by New York Governor Nelson Rockefeller, who was quoted in *AP* (July 26, 1968) as saying he would "work toward international creation of 'a new world order.'" It was widely used following the collapse of the Berlin Wall in 1989. President George Bush used the term several times before the Gulf War; for instance, "Out of these troubled times…a New World Order can emerge" (September 11, 1990). And the term has been much-used following the terrorist attacks on New York's Twin Towers and Washington's Pentagon on September 11, 2001, and in association with President George W. Bush's ensuing war in Afghanistan. A new world arrangement is taking place.

The New World Order has frequently been associated with

American world dominance and increasing the powers of the UN. Essentially it is the creation of a world revolution to form a United States of the World. A world revolution cannot happen everywhere simultaneously; it is by its very nature piecemeal, involving component revolutions in specific local places, now here, now there. In the companion volume to this work, *The Syndicate: The Story of the Coming World Government,* I have shown that all the revolutions in the modern time have levelled their societies not merely with the aim of addressing local concerns but rather to prepare for a coming world government.

That work addressed the immediate roots of the New World Order and found that what I called a "Syndicate" of banking and governing families seeking to control the world's oil, in which the European Rothschilds and American Rockefellers were principal influences, have had a dynastic drive for a one-world regime ever since 1900. This drive has been linked with Templar Grand Orient Freemasonry. Is the same principle at work in earlier revolutions? Are all revolutions driven by a desire to create a one-world government?

There are other questions. Are separate revolutions linked? Is there one tide running through all the various revolutions since the Renaissance? Have the individual revolutions cumulatively led to our current globalism? Are the revolutions of the last 550 years the individual waves of a high tide of world revolution that is reaching high-water mark in world government in our time? Are any organizations (such as the Templars) dynastically involved in revolutions in different centuries?

The answers to such questions have taken on a new urgency because we can see a New World Order taking shape in our own time and being used as the justification for wars like the ones waged in Afghanistan against the Taliban, and against Iraq. The war in Afghanistan has created 6 million starving refugees according to most sources, more than the 5 million Jewish refugees who went on to die in Hitler's concentration camps. The 6 million Afghan refugees are justified on the grounds that the New World Order had no alternative but to take the action it took. We need to know more about the New World Order, in whose name appalling humanitarian catastrophes are taking place. It justified making war on the Taliban, bin Laden and Saddam Hussein on the grounds that the West was threatened with nuclear and chemical weapons which have so far not been found.

To answer these questions we have analysed the roots of the New World Order in depth. It is not enough to go back to 1900. We have analyzed the revolutionary history of the last 550 years to see if they all have one dynastic source. Our findings have shown that they do. We are now in a position to make true judgments about the nature of the New World Order and the world revolution it is perpetrating.

The world revolution from nation-statehood to global-villagedom, made possible by 20th-century advances in technology, is a different kind of revolution from the nation-state revolutions against old orders that are found in British, French and Russian history, and from the nation-state revolution against colonial rule that is found in American history. Nevertheless, as the companion volume to this work, *The Syndicate*, has shown, close inspection shows the same forces lie behind it; and that the nation-state revolutions are stepping-stones towards a world revolution.

APPENDIX 2

CIVILIZATIONS AND REVOLUTIONS: TWO DYNAMICS

The revolutionary dynamic is a concentrated version and occult counterpart of the spiritual dynamic which drives the rise and fall of civilizations, as I have shown in *The Fire and the Stones*. Civilizations begin with an inspired spiritual vision that founds a new religion – like Mohammed's vision of Fire that became the first page of the *Koran* – and rise as the vision is spread.[4] They decline as the original vision descends into the intellectual and political realms and, after passing through numerous phases, end during an often brutal phase of physical foreign conquest and military severity. A civilization grows through a metaphysical idea and declines when it loses contact with that idea and turns secular. Just as the metaphysical inspires a civilization's rise, so the secular (in other words, the absence of the metaphysical) is responsible for its decline and fall.

The older civilizations of the West follow this pattern. The European civilization rose round the metaphysical idea of the Christian God. Its art, philosophy and culture was all Church-related during the European civilization's rise. Secularization began its decline, but with it came progress in society and human values. As society progresses, its underlying civilization moves further away from its original idea and declines. In the English and French revolutions, secularization challenged the old Anglican (English) and Catholic (French) religions and took society forward but the underlying civilization moved further towards its end, and therefore into decline. In the Byzantine-Russian civilization, the Russian Revolution challenged the old Orthodox religion and took society forward while the underlying civilization moved further into decline.

In the case of the American civilization, which is much younger than the others (dating arguably from 1607, the English expedition to and settlement of Jamestown), the American Revolution is different: it was a breaking-free from colonialism and imperialism, a discovery of national identity which brought into being the new United States.

A revolution against a civilization's own central idea secularizes; a revolution against an outside oppressor helps define a young civilization's new central idea. In both, revolution is a sudden, violent, transforming process in which a civilization moves from one stage to another – in the case of the European and Byzantine-Russian civilizations, towards secularism; in the case of the American civilization, towards growth and the defining of its central universalist idea: the spreading of a democratic universal republic.

In all pre-revolutionary societies the revolutionary dynamic grows within the civilization's spiritual vision. Revolutions begin with an inspired occult Freemasonic vision which spreads as it is transmitted from person to person like a forest fire. The vision wanes as the original occult dream of Utopia declines first into the intellectual and then into the political realm. Finally there is a physical phase which is often brutal, i.e. consolidation takes place. Interestingly, the four phases of the revolutionary dynamic correspond to the four worlds of the Kabbalah: the divine, the "spiritual" (in fact "occult"), the psychological and the physical.

On the evidence of our four main revolutions – the English, American, French and Russian – revolutions begin under an established spiritual vision of the oneness of mankind living in harmony with the universal order and open to divine will. An occult counterpart forms which inspires a revolution. It reacts against the luxury of the established religion and court, and expresses this reaction puritanically – rejecting luxury and riches. The vision is adapted by an interpreter who reflects the puritanical occult vision. This interpreted vision is opposed to the vision of established religion and is deemed heretical by the religious orthodoxy of the day (Christianity), which has inspired the growth of the civilization. It is important to grasp that the occult vision that inspires revolutions gathers strength outside the mainstream religious tradition.

The adaptation of the vision is then corrupted by a revolutionary originator who interprets the occult vision in terms of an occult or hidden *tradition* that keeps its knowledge secret by seeking invisibility (Rosicrucianism, Freemasonry). This tradition advocates some destruction and runs counter to the spiritual vision of nondualistic creative Light that begins civilizations. We should not be surprised at this. Revolutions within sovereign nation-states are destructive to civilizations and advance their decline and disintegration when a heresy, a new tradition that opposes the religious orthodoxy, dilutes the civilization's orthodox religion. (The American Revolution, as we have seen, does not conform to this pattern as it was essentially an independence movement that created a new American nation at the expense of English colonialism.)

This variation of the original vision in terms of an occult or secret Freemasonic tradition is then itself interpreted and adapted and given intellectual expression by a thoughtful intellectual who follows the secret tradition, whose thinking has a new slant. It is then further interpreted by a semi-political intellectual who later becomes an active participant in the political expression of the revolution and acts as a bridge to the next phase of the revolutionary dynamic, its political expression.

To take our four revolutions one by one and identify the occult and intellectual stages of each, we have seen that in the English revolution the occult Freemasonic Kabbalistic message was interpreted by Sir Francis Bacon, a Rosicrucian message taken up by Johann Valentin Andreae, whose occult or secret tradition was Rosicrucianism. England was to be a new Israel. (We have seen how the Puritan ideal grew out of this idea.)

In the American revolution, which was a political revolution against

British colonialism more than a social transformation, we have seen that the guiding occult Scottish Templar Freemasonic Kabbalistic vision was interpreted by Bacon in terms of a Utopian New Atlantis and that the occult vision of the revolutionary originator was Adam Weishaupt's vision of a world government based on Freemasonic, egalitarian principles, which affected all the founding fathers.

In the French revolution we have seen that the guiding occult Freemasonic Cathar/Templar vision was interpreted by the Freemason Rousseau and mixed with Weishaupt's vision, which originated in the occult Freemasonic or secret tradition of the Order of the Illuminati, a society that looked back to the time of the Noble Savage and which had no degree or hierarchy, no aristocrats.

We have seen that the Russian revolution grew out of Weishaupt's occult vision, which was interpreted by Hegel and corrupted by the revolutionary originators Marx and Engels into the revolutionary philosophy known as Communism.

We have seen that the detailed movement within the occult and intellectual stages of the revolutionary dynamic in the four main revolutions can be summarized as follows:

Revolution	Heretical occult vision	Heretical occult interpreter	Occult revolutionary originator	Thoughtful intellectual interpreter	Semi-political intellectual interpreter
English	Freemasonic Kabbalism: British Israelites' Puritan vision	Bacon's Utopia	Andreae's/ Fludd's Rosicrucianism	Hartlib	Pym (in England)/ Menasseh (in Holland)
American	Freemasonic Kabbalism: Scottish Jacobite Templar Puritan vision	Bacon's Utopia	Weishaupt's Illuminism	Franklin	Jefferson

French	Freemasonic Cathar/ Templar Puritan vision	Rousseau's Paradise	Weishaupt's Illuminism	Cagliostro	Mirabeau
Russian	Weishaupt's Freemasonic Illuminist vision	Hegel's Paradisal synthesis of world and spirit	Marx's/ Engels' Communism	Herzen	Trotsky

For the political and physical stages of the revolutionary dynamic, see page 482.

'B'

THE HIDDEN HAND:
THE KABBALISTIC ROOTS OF
REVOLUTION

APPENDIX I

THE BABYLONIAN CAPTIVITY
OF THE JEWS

In the 10th century BC Solomon, the son and successor of David and the greatest king of Israel, inherited a commercial empire stretching from Egypt to the Euphrates. He founded the Judaean dynasty and set up Israelite colonies. In *1 Kings* we learn of his life-style. He was obviously a great lover: he had 700 wives and 300 concubines. He had various cities (including Megiddo, later Armageddon); 1,400 chariots and 12,000 horses. He was a sage whose aphorisms are found in *The Book of Proverbs* and according to tradition the poet of 1,500 songs, including *The Song of Solomon*, one of the greatest love poems in literature. Solomon had also completed a vast building programme that erected fortresses and garrisons across his kingdom – and in Jerusalem his royal palace and famous Temple.

The original Jewish Temple had been built on Mount Moriah (Mount Zion), where God tested Abraham's faith by commanding him to sacrifice his son Isaac. Solomon's Temple was built on land, bought by David, which had been Araunah the Jebusite's threshing-floor. Begun in 964 BC and designed by Hiram Abiff, it took 200,000 men seven years to construct and was erected to house the Ark of the Covenant, Israel's most sacred treasure. It was finished in 957 BC.

When Solomon dedicated the Temple or "house" ("a place for the ark") he prayed to the one and only God of the Universe (*1 Kings 8*): "And Solomon stood before the altar of the Lord in the presence of all the congregation of Israel, and spread forth his hands towards Heaven: And he said, Lord God of Israel, there is no God like thee, in Heaven above or on Earth beneath." (22-3)

He invoked blessings on God's people Israel, but being a natural Universalist who believed that all mankind worshipped the same one God he also built shrines for foreigners to worship at. In his prayer he asked God to heed the prayers of "strangers" (foreigners or aliens) who had come to Jerusalem from the ends of the earth. He reminded God that helping these foreigners would enhance the reputation of both God and his Temple in every land, for the foreigners would take back good reports when they returned home: "Moreover concerning a stranger that is not of thy people Israel, but cometh out of a far country for thy name's sake; (For they shall hear of thy great name and of thy strong hand, and of thy stretched out arm;) when he shall come and pray toward this house: Hear thou in heaven thy dwelling place, and do according to all that the stranger calleth to thee for: that all people of the earth may know thy name to fear thee, as do thy people Israel." (41-3)

Solomon was involved in international trade and therefore understood the need for peace. His outlook was one of spiritual and intellectual Universalism. He was far ahead of his time, and it took centuries for the universality of his age to be reflected in the words of Israel's prophets.

In the 10th century BC under Solomon the Israelite God belonged to everyone, Jew and Gentile alike. All humankind was catered for in Solomon's Jerusalem. This attitude Solomon had acquired from the Oral tradition which went back to the time of Abraham (19th or 18th/17th centuries BC) and of Moses (13th century BC), when God reigned over all nations and was the father of all men, Israelites and foreigners alike. This was the pure unadulterated (Oral) tradition of old Israel, the unwritten Torah or divine revelation communicated by God to Moses and handed down by word of mouth.

The Temple of Solomon was destroyed in 586 BC when the Babylonians invaded Jerusalem. The Jews were deported from the southern kingdom of Judah until the conqueror of Babylonia, the Persian Cyrus the Great, gave them permission to return in 539.

The modern spirit of world revolution can be traced back to the Babylonian captivity of the Jews (587/6-538 BC). Many exiled Jewish priests came into contact with Chaldean science and the sect of the Pharisees was formed. Unlike the Sadducees, the party of the high priesthood that based its teaching on the Torah or Written Law, under the influence of the Chaldeans the Pharisees went back to the Oral Law that God communicated to Moses and tradition has it, to the legendary Adam: the teachings of the prophets and the oral tradition of the Jewish people. This often secret oral approach became the early Kabbalah, the Tradition of the Pharisees that went back to Moses. It challenged the authority of the Sadducees, which eventually collapsed with the destruction of the Temple by the Roman Emperor Titus in AD 70. The Kabbalah was then supreme.

The Kabbalah was originally spiritual and revealed the God of Moses who reigned over all nations and was the father of all men, and a Messiah who would redeem the sin of all men in the world, gentiles as well as Jews. They were echoed later in the God and Messiah of the Essenes, the sect who guarded the Dead Sea Scrolls in the caves of Qumran.

The Judaistic outlook underwent a great change as a result of the exile of the Jews to Babylon. Part of the population of Judah had been deported into slavery, and exiled Jewish priests came into contact with Chaldean Magi. The Magi were originally Persian Fire-worshippers who taught the divine Fire or Light in Chaldean mystery schools; the Chaldeans ruled Mesopotamia in the 8th and 7th centuries BC until the Persian Cyrus the Great conquered Babylon in 539 BC, and they brought the Magi there. The Magi passed on the Iranian tradition, in particular the beliefs of the Zoroastrians as found in the *Zend Avesta*.

As a result, the Jews opened themselves to Iranian dualism in which Light battled Darkness, Ahura Mazda battling the Iranian Satan, Ahriman. They absorbed the Iranian monotheism of Ahura Mazda and a hierarchy of Babylonian angels and demons, and they took on board the role of Ahriman/Satan as the being responsible for all that was dark or evil in the world. Ahriman came to be called The Lie, "Who, independent, opposed the One Light,/Ahura, though sharing in creation."[5] During the Babylonian captivity the unitary tradition of the Kabbalah and of Solomon's universalism was corrupted and degenerated into dualism.

Over the centuries the Tradition of the Kabbalah became corrupted and offered a magical God who would allow material domination of the Universe by Jews, and the Messiah became a temporal King of the Jews who would make Israel master of the world. The Pharisees came to teach a pro-Jewish, vengeful God and a Messiah who acted for Jews alone and would help them seize political power.

This change-over happened as Jews created Gnosticism. (Evidence for Jewish Kabbalism's role in creating Gnosticism was found in the library at Naj-Hammadi or Chenoboskion in Upper Egypt in 1945.) Jewish Gnosticism was dualistic, and saw the world of matter as being created by an anti-God or Platonic Demiurge, who was Satan. God, the Heavenly Father of the *New Testament* opposed the world of matter, which was the realm of Satan. The divine realm of Light was opposed to the cosmos, which was a realm of darkness. The spiritual Kabbalah revealed the God of Light; the magical, occult Kabbalah revealed Satan, ruler of the material world and darkness, and this Gnostic Kabbalah turned into a theosophical revolt against Christianity which challenged the Church. In the Middle Ages the spiritual Kabbalah was adopted into the teachings of the Church; the idea of Gnosticism on the other hand was one of world revolution and sought to replace Christianity with an alternative that saw the world as the province of Satan.

Out of the magical, occult Gnostic Kabbalah came the medieval sects deemed heretical by the Church – the Cathars and Templars – which perpetuated the Gnostic challenge to Christianity that was to surface in the Reformation (including the theology of Luther). The dualistic Cathars came out of the 8th-century Jewish-run officially Visigothic kingdom of Septimania (see Appendix 6) and surfaced in the first half of the 11th century in the Kabbalistic schools of Languedoc, notably Narbonne. The Templars came out of the Kingdom of Jerusalem; they were founded in 1119 to guard pilgrims to Jerusalem during the reign of Baldwin II and lived in the site of the Old Temple of Solomon. They too inherited the Kabbalistic tradition. Both sects preserved the revolutionary attitude that was to surface dramatically in modern revolutionary history.

APPENDIX 2

THE TWO KABBALAHS

In Babylon during the 6th century BC (see Appendix 1) the original Kabbalah, the Oral tradition of Solomon, became corrupted. In secret meetings of a few hundred adepts, a sect that surfaced for the first time in these harsh conditions, the Pharisees, kept up morale by reviving orthodox faith – and national pride. In this difficult time, the original Kabbalah ceased to be interpreted universally and came to have a racist, Hebrew application. The Pharisees applied it to what would benefit and advance the Jews. A new false (magical) tradition denied the universality of God and interpreted the "God of Israel" as being, literally, the God of the Jews. Solomon's building of shrines for foreigners was forgotten. Now God was anti-Gentile. Instead of referring to an enlightened state of consciousness achievable by people of every race, the appellation "Children of Israel" now became limited to the Hebrew nation alone. The philosophy of the early patriarchs – Adam, Noah, Enoch and Abraham – lost its symbolic force and became literal, and now Hebrew Children of Israel awaited a Messiah who was no longer the World's Redeemer but the Saviour of the Jews, a temporal king who would establish the Jewish Kingdom on earth and bring universal dominion to the Jews. Similarly the Promised Land, which in the true universalist Kabbalah represented the reality of the soul, became the divinely sanctioned State of Israel.

Lt Gen Netchvolodow wrote of how the Pharisees corrupted the false Kabbalah. The sect of the Pharisees came into being during the Babylonian captivity and is first mentioned in the Old Testament and in the writings of the Jewish historians after the captivity. Their Kaballah, or "Tradition of the Pharisees," was at first transmitted orally. Eventually their precepts formed the Talmud and received their final form in the *Sepher ha Zohar*. Although they embraced pantheistic Chaldeism, the Pharisees preserved their ethnic pride during the captivity. Literalizing the religion of man divinised which they had absorbed in Babylon, they saw it as applying solely to Jews. They interpreted the reign of the universalist God of Moses over the nations as the exclusive God of the Jews who would permit material domination by the Jews. The Messiah they awaited was no longer a spiritual Redeemer but a temporal king, who would serve the interests of Jewish Israel.[6]

This literalization of symbolic truths had the effect of dividing the unity of Creation into Jews and Gentiles, and grew dualistic Gnosticism out of the false Kabbalah's division, for example the occult system of the Jewish Simon Magus, "the Magician" (1st century AD), a false Kabbalist who "bewitched" Samaria into believing he possessed the "great power of God" – which he attempted to buy from the apostles (hence our word "simony"). The dualism of Gnosticism further divided the unity of Creation and gave rise to the literalized figure of Lucifer, who sought to formalize such a division with his rebellion, and the false Kabbalah can therefore be seen as being dualistically Luciferian.

Nesta Webster writes perceptively on the true and false Kabbalahs. The speculative side of the Jewish Kabbalah taken from the Persian Magi, the Neo-Platonists and the Neo-Pythagoreans was not of purely Jewish origin.[7] Gougenot des Mousseaux asserted that there were therefore two Kabbalahs: the ancient sacred tradition handed down from the first patriarchs and an evil, occult Kabbalah, in which this sacred tradition was mingled by the Rabbis with barbaric superstitions.[8] Drach refers to the ancient and true Kabbalah based on revelation to the first patriarchs, which should be distinguished from the modern false Kabbalah, the work of the Rabbis who perverted the Talmudic tradition. Sixtus of Sienna held that there was a Kabbalah which elucidates the Torah by analogy, and a false Kabbalah which is full of (literalized) falsehoods.[9]

The false Kabbalah was concerned with theoretical theosophical speculations (on the sephiroths or the ten power-centres in the Kabbalistic psyche and Tree of Life, good and bad angels, demons and the appearance of God, the "Ancient of Ancients," and claims that Adam cohabited with female devils and Eve with male devils and the serpent) and practical magical practices which reduce the Kabbalah to a magical, occult system.

Bacon also maintained the distinction between the true and false Kabbalah in his *New Atlantis,* in which he reports a meeting with a Jewish merchant called Joabin who maintained that "Moses by a secret cabala ordained the laws of Bensalem" and that "when the Messiah should come, and sit in His throne at Jerusalem, the King of Bensalem should sit at His feet, whereas other kings should keep a great distance."

APPENDIX 3

THE ESSENE MESSIAH

It seems it was during the difficult time of the Babylonian captivity that the Essenes were formed as a strict Order that would keep alive the old teachings of Solomon. When the Jews returned to Jerusalem after the Maccabean victories the Essenes were shocked at what exile had done to their beliefs and disillusioned by their lack of strictness. It seems they withdrew to the desert at Qumran to preserve the Oral tradition of Abraham, Moses and Solomon.

In the Qumran desert in the 1st century BC the Essenes awaited the Jewish Messiah. They were versed in the true Kabbalah – the Oral tradition of Abraham, Moses and Solomon – and they anticipated the Messiah as Redeemer of his chosen people, the children of Abraham, "the children of Israel." To the Essenes the "Children of Israel" were the enlightened children of Solomon's God; those who had reached an enlightened state of consciousness regardless of race, under God, the father of all humanity. Shimon Halevi writes in *The Way of the Kabbalah* that the name "Children of Israel" is a precise Kabbalistic term that applies to everyone on earth, not merely to people of Hebrew extraction.[10]

The Essenes had existed a very long time before they became known as "Essenes" in the 2nd century BC, reputedly because they claimed descent from Esnoch (or Enoch), "The founder of our Brotherhood" and subject of an Essene text, *The Vision of Enoch*; but perhaps because they were descended from Esrael (or Israel), the elect of the people, the 70 elders to whom Moses gave the Communions at

Mount Sinai in the 13th century BC. They were strict followers of the Law or Torah Moses taught, and there is an Essene *Book of Moses*. The Essene tradition expected two Messiahs, a spiritual one and a political one: a priest Messiah (of the House of Moses' brother Aaron) and a King Messiah (of the royal blood of David). The spiritual one would be "the Son of Man" (the Judge of the world of *Daniel* and *1 Enoch*) whose kingdom was Heaven and the political one would be "the Son of God," the royal Messiah who would be King of Free Israel, whom the Zealots, the anti-Roman liberation movement, awaited. There are references to the "Son of Man", the spiritual Messiah, in *1 Enoch*, which is thought by many to be a Jewish work dating from the 3rd century BC. The Messianic passages may have been written in between 165 and 161 BC.

The Essenes had preserved the traditional universal God and the spiritual Messiah who would judge the world. The advent of this spiritual Messiah was generally expected among the Jews of the Holy Land before the birth of Christ. But while the 1st century BC Essenes kept alive the true tradition of the Oral Kabbalah, their compatriots in Jerusalem were continuing a corrupted version of the tradition.

The Essenes retained the true Kabbalah though they absorbed the Zoroastrian angels of Heaven and Earth. Of their unadulterated tradition Nesta Webster writes that the Essenes' Kabbalah descended to them from pre-Christian times and had remained uncontaminated by the anti-Christian strain introduced into it by the Rabbis after the death of Christ.[11] And though a Second Temple was built – the foundation-stone was laid by Zerubbabel in 537 BC, under the direction of King Cyrus of Persia, and was dedicated in 515 BC – and the Pharisees followed the Kabbalah in Jerusalem, the Essenes stayed apart.

On their return from exile in Babylon, the Jews' hopes, traditions, philosophy and religion were all focused on a Messiah who would be *their* Redeemer. It is therefore easy to understand the Jews' reaction to Jesus, whom they regarded as a "false" Messiah as he did not speak of the Jews as the promised race but came to redeem the whole of mankind in accordance with the true Kabbalah the Essenes followed.

The Pharisees' Oral Tradition was by now corrupted, and they would have led the condemnation against Jesus. Jesus was an itinerant preacher with twelve disciples who proclaimed a message that owed much to John the Baptist, that the Kingdom of Heaven (experience of the divine Light) could be known here and now, and that since God was Heavenly Father (or "Abba," meaning "Daddy") then he, Jesus, like all "Sons of Men" and Children of Light was a "Son of God." To Jesus the title "Son of God" expressed an intimate relationship with God; it did not claim that he was a royal Messiah who would be King of the Jews.

Jesus does not appear to have thought of himself as the spiritual Messiah until his meeting with Caiaphas, the Sadducean High Priest. Caiaphas asks him if he is the "Son of God" (*Matthew*), "Son of the Blessed" (*Mark*) and "the Christ" (*Luke*). In all three Gospels he says Caiaphas will see "the Son of Man" sitting "on the right hand of power." In *John* Caiaphas asks if he is the "King of the Jews." All references to the "Son of Man" (or spiritual Messiah) before he meets Caiaphas are corrupt texts added by the Church. And the references in the Essene *Gospel of Peace*, where "Son of Man" appears on virtually every page, mean "man" rather than the Messiah.

The Essene Gospels show Jesus as an Essene Master, and the Jews – expecting a political Messiah who was "King of the Jews" (as Caiaphas expected in *John*) and the "Son of God" (the three other Gospels), a nationalistic leader – would not have taken kindly to Jesus's tolerance (when he preached "love thine enemy") and his teaching of the Spiritual Way of the Kabbalah ("I am the true vine"). In parable after parable Jesus had preached that all men are capable of enlightenment, that being enlightened was more important than going to a synagogue or cheering the Roman eagle. To Jews expecting a political Messiah Jesus's message undermined the Jewish Orthodoxy of Caiaphas and the maintenance of order in the Roman Empire of Pilate. Jesus declared that his Kingdom was not of this world. The Promised Land was a spiritual reality, not an Israel winning independence from Rome. To the Jews he was a false Messiah, and though Pilate found no fault with him the crowd wanted Barabbas freed and pressured Pilate to crucify Jesus under the mocking title, "King of the Jews."

APPENDIX 4

GNOSTICISM

The Gnostics were a number of different sects with a similar outlook, which emerged in Syria and Egypt in the 1st and 2nd centuries AD. Our knowledge of Gnosticism has increased greatly since the discovery of a Gnostic library at Naj-Hammadi (in Upper Egypt), which confirmed that the elements blended in the syncretistic Gnostic religion descend from Jewish Kabbalism: Iranian dualism, Babylonian and Indian thought, Greek Platonism, Helenistic paganism and of course Judaism.

The first leader of a Gnostic sect was Simon Magus, who operated in Sumeria (1st century AD). An adept of the Kabbalah who referred to himself as "Faustus" in Latin countries, he had found a prostitute called Helena in a brothel in Tyre, who in his mind symbolized Thought (Ennoia). She travelled everywhere with him to be a ready visual aid. According to Hippolytus he held that the world was created by Babylonian-Iranian angels (a clear Kabbalistic influence). In the 2nd century the Alexandrian Basilides drew on the Buddhist concept of Nirvana (extinction of desire). Another Alexandrian, Valentinus, who lived in Rome and later Palestine, held that there are two Absolutes. Marcion of Sinope taught that there is an Alien Father and Demiurge. There were several shadowy sects. The Barbelo-gnosis produced the *Apocryphon of John*, which taught that the psychical Adam was the First Man. This echoes Adam Kadmon in the Kabbalah. The Ophites cursed the physical Jesus as they worshipped the Serpent. The Naassenes (*nahash*, Hebrew for "serpent") claimed that the *Gospel of Thomas* contained Jesus's secret sayings. The Mandaeans came from Syria-Palestine and revered John the Baptist.

All taught of a *pneuma* or spark which comes into man's soul as he lives in the world of Darkness and makes him yearn for vanished Light. All held there are many emanations between man and the Most High (an echo of the *sephiroth*, the emanations of Jewish Kabbalism). All denied the divinity of Christ, who was transformed into a mere initiate. Each was dualistic (more often than not, multi-emanational), and either professed two Absolutes or an Absolute and a Demiurge who created the Dark Universe, and who could be approached through magic. Each dispensed with the idea of the authority of God and the Church, and grace, the doctrine by which God chooses who is enlightened by the divine Light. As a result, each regarded man as deified by the Light and thus insubordinate to God. The Gnostics taught this deification of humanity – like Lucifer immediately after his rebellion, each man was his own master, and had not the Serpent told Adam and Eve "Ye shall be as gods?" – and as man was now a god they looked forward to Heaven on Earth. With Goethe's Faust they could ask, "Am I a god? I feel the Light." These heretics were revolutionaries against the early Church and they formed themselves into secret societies – sects – and slowly revealed or "rolled back" (*revolutum* in Latin suggesting the rolling of a wheel) the secret that they guarded: that man is god, that like Lucifer man has taken the place of God. (Dostoevsky was alert to this in his creation of the revolutionary Kirilov who proclaimed the man-god in his novel *The Possessed*.)

These early Gnostic sects all had different doctrines and different emanations and aeons – the Ennoia (Thought), Sophia (Wisdom), the Pleroma, the Archons and so on – but we can speak of a Gnostic (syncretistic) heresy for they all had their own rites and places of assembly and emphasized divine revelation and salvation, just as different Christian sects have their own rites and varying churches within the Christian religion. A Kabbalist would have been able to go to any Gnostic group and immediately understand what was happening in the 1st and 2nd centuries AD.

In the 3rd century the Gnostic vision was Christianized by the Alexandrian School (which was centred on the Christian Catechetical School, the first Christian institution of higher learning), notably Clement of Alexandria who put forward a Christian Gnosticism with *pistis* (faith) the basis of *gnosis* (knowledge). The Gnostic vision in turn developed into the Hellenistic pagan Hermetic thought of Hermes Trismegistos, who also taught at the Alexandrian School and is sometimes regarded as the writer of the *Corpus Hermeticum*; and into the Neoplatonism of Plotinus (c205-270), who studied under Ammonius Saccas at the Alexandrian School. Both described emanations that recall the 10 sephiroth of the Kabbalah – Hermes' Mind, Life, Light in his dialogue *Poimandres*, and Plotinus's Mind, Soul and a descending hierarchical order of spheres of being which are expressed in the maze floor of Chartres Cathedral as concentric circles widening from a point until they merge into the One. Plotinus refused to regard the Demiurge as evil and focused on the soul's "flight to the One."[12]

APPENDIX 5

THE DIASPORA

The Diaspora was a process that began with the Babylonian Exile in 586 BC, when part of the Jewish population of Judah was deported into slavery. Although Cyrus gave the Jews permission to return in 538 BC many chose to remain in Babylon. In the 1st century BC there were many Jews in Alexandria; in fact, nearly half the population of Alexandria was Jewish. By the 1st century AD five million Jews lived outside Palestine, outnumbering those in Palestine. The Claudian census of AD 48 found there were nearly 7 million Jews within the Roman Empire, of whom nearly 2.5 million lived in Palestine. There were probably another million living outside the Roman Empire.

A new dispersal took place under Titus. The co-operation between the Sadducee Caiaphas and Pilate that condemned Jesus did not last. Following a rebellion at the Roman garrison at Masada, when Jewish rebels put Romans to the sword, and following a similar incident at the Roman fortress of Antonia, the Romans decided to take Jerusalem. They asked the city to surrender but three Jewish factions in the city were at each others' throats and the Roman emissaries were killed. In AD 70 the Romans under Titus sacked Jerusalem and razed to the ground the Second Temple (which had undergone a major restoration beginning with King Herod and lasting 46 years), leaving only a portion of the Western Wall standing (now called the Wailing Wall). Almost a million Jews died or were sold into slavery. The power of the Sadducees, the High Priests, was now at an end, leaving the Pharisees in command as guardians of the true and false Kabbalahs. The rebuilding of the

Temple would become the central aim of Freemasonry.

The whole of Palestine was now under Roman control except for the fortress of Masada, which (like the Cathar stronghold of Montségur nearly 1,200 years later) held out for three more years before finally yielding in AD 73. Then, unable to resist the Romans any longer, 950 men, women and children committed suicide rather than be captured.

The height of the Diaspora, the dispersion of the Jews throughout Europe, came after the Jews had lived at peace with the Romans for 50 prosperous years. When Hadrian came to the throne he alienated the Jews with two clumsy edicts. He ordered a new city to be built on the ruins of Jerusalem – it was to be called *Aelia Capitolina* – and he banned circumcision as a barbaric practice ("mutilation"). The Jews rebelled under the leadership of Simeon Bar Kokhba, whom many thought to be the Messiah. By then the expectation of an earthly Messiah and the foundation of a Jewish kingdom had become the strongest impulse for Jewish political revolution against the Roman Empire. The rebels were convinced that Bar Kokhba would establish God's kingdom on earth as King of the Jews. At first they routed the Roman legions and cleared Judah of Romans. Hadrian recalled Severus from Britain, put down the revolt and executed Bar Kokhba. Half a million Jews were killed, those who escaped death were sold into slavery or sent to Roman gladiatorial arenas. A temple to Jupiter Capitolina was built on the site of the sanctuary, and the name Judah was abolished. The province was now called Syria Palestine. Jews were forbidden to enter Jerusalem,[13] and the Emperor Hadrian expelled all living Jews from Palestine.

All the Diaspora Jews looked towards Palestine – their homeland, the Land of Israel – as the centre of their religion and cultural life. After the destruction of Jerusalem in AD 70, the Jewish centres moved from Babylonia to Persia, Spain, France, Germany, Poland, Russia and eventually England and the United States. Among the Diaspora Jews there were two attitudes. Some, the Zionists, wanted to return to Palestine; others saw dispersal as Providential as it spread monotheism throughout the world.

Following their persecution by the Romans, the Christians were also scattered and began to spread their message across the world. Jewish Diaspora exiles came into rivalry and conflict with dispersed Christians from the Roman Empire. As a result the Kabbalistic teachings, already false from the time of the Babylonian captivity, became anti-Christian. The *Babylonian Talmud*, written down in the 6th century AD, was subject to the same bias.

From this time a Jewish ambition evolved to undermine Christianity and split its unity through the formation of heretical sects. This anti-Christianity had already been expressed by Kabbalistic Jewish Gnostics claiming to possess true versions of the Christian Gospels. Both the false, occult Jewish Kabbalah and Gnostic Manichaeism represented Adam and Eve as the offspring of devils so that Christians might believe that humanity was of Satanic (Luciferian) origin. Adam and Eve were held to co-habit with devils, as we have seen. There were apocryphal Gnostic books of Thomas and Judas. The Ebionites had a corrupted Gospel of St Matthew, the Marcosians a corrupted Gospel of St Luke, and the Valentinians a corrupted Gospel of St John. All claimed these were true versions of the Christian Gospels. Ophite texts described serpent worship. The false, occult Jewish Kabbalah drew strength from the anti-Christian attitudes in the Gnostics and Manichaeans whose sects it had spawned.

There is nothing anti-Semitic[14] in drawing attention to this early anti-Christian strand within the false Kabbalistic tradition, which conflicts with Solomon's inclusive policy on foreigners. Nor are we suggesting that there is now a Jewish conspiracy whose aim is world domination. (As you can read in the companion volume to this work, Jews are represented on the Syndicate, but in no sense has the Syndicate been a Jewish operation.) The early Rabbinical texts are full of this post-Diaspora anti-Christian rivalry. The basis of Rabbinical Judaism was the idea that the Jews were the Chosen People. The *Zohar* explains that the Feast of Tabernacles celebrates the time when Israel triumphs over the other peoples of the world; carrying the Loulab (branches of trees tied together) as a trophy demonstrates this. According to several passages in the Kabbalah, all the *Goyim* (Gentiles) are to be swept off the face of the earth when Israel comes into its own. The *Zohar* relates that the Messiah will declare war on the whole world. "At the moment when the Holy One…will exterminate all the *Goyim* of the world, Israel alone will subsist."[15]

Passages from the Talmud give clear instructions on how Jews should behave towards Christians. In the *Zohar* alone, Jews are told that "idolatrous people (Christians) befoul the world" (I, 131a); that "Christians are to be destroyed as idolators" (I, 25a); that "the Christian birth rate must be diminished materially" (II, 64b); and that Jews must always try to deceive Christians (I, 160c). Or, as Shakespeare's Shylock put it, "I hate him for he is a Christian." (I.iii.37)

As the Church grew in power sects arose that challenged Christianity, which deemed them heretical. The attitudes of these sects, which were transmitted to the modern revolutionary movement, are to be found in the false, occult Kabbalah which from the 6th century BC focused on the advancement of the Hebrews and eventually recommended hostility to Christianity. This pattern continued in the centuries following the fall of Jerusalem and the collapse of Judah. The sects were influenced by the new false Jewish Kabbalism, and the effect of their existence was to divide and weaken Christianity.

APPENDIX 6

SEPTIMANIA

In the 8th century there were so many Jews in Languedoc that a Jewish principality was created in Septimania in 768. This is not widely known. The received view is that during the reign of the Roman Emperor Augustus, Septimania was settled by veterans of the Seventh Legion or Septimani. It was the last region in Gaul to be held by the Spanish Visigoths who made Narbonne their capital after they sacked Rome and included seven cities or dioceses: Narbonne, Nîmes, Béziers, Magulonne, Lodêve, Agde and Uzès (afterwards Elne and Carcassonne). The Moors, or Saracens, invaded southern France at the beginning of the 8th century, and from 720 to 759 Septimania was in Islamic hands. Charles Martel led the Frankish resistance and drove the Moors back to Narbonne and unsuccessfully besieged the city, which was defended by both Moors and Jews. Charles Martel's son Pépin the Short took up the challenge, and after a seven-year-long siege he made a pact with the Jewish population of the city. The official view in the local Narbonne guide-book of what happened next is as follows: "In 759, the Frankish king, Pépin the Short, Charlemagne's father, entered the city, with help from the local people. Narbonne became, and remained for many years, a frontier post facing Spain, a bulwark of Christendom against Islam." Another local guide book says simply: "In 759 after a long siege Pépin the Short recaptured Narbonne."

What actually happened next is described by the authors of *The Holy Blood and the Holy Grail.* Their theme – that Jesus survived the Crucifixion and married Mary Magdelene and had a family that created the Merovingian dynasty, which is therefore Jewish – may be speculative and unproved (they are scrupulous in calling it a "hypothesis") but on the question of Septimania their research is excellent. Pépin made a pact with Narbonne's Jewish population in 759 under which the Jews would endorse him as David's descendant and he would receive Jewish aid against the Moors. In return he would grant the Jews of Septimania a principality, and a king, of their own.

In that same year the Jews of Narbonne killed the city's Moslem defenders, opened the gates of the fortress to the besieging Franks and acknowledged Pépin as their nominal overlord. In 768 Pépin created a Jewish principality in Septimania which paid nominal allegiance to Pépin but was essentially independent. A ruler was installed as king of the Jews. He is referred to as Aymery in romances. He was received into the Frankish nobility and took the name Theodoric or Thierry. He was recognized by both Pépin and the caliph of Baghdad, as the "seed of the royal house of David." In later centuries attempts were made to eliminate from the records all trace of the Jewish Kingdom of Septimania, and the confusion of Goths and Jews can be attributed to these attempts.[16] The Jewish principality of Septimania became part of the Kingdom of Aquitaine – Guillem de Gellone died in 812 and his bloodline culminated in the first Dukes of Aquitaine – and in 817 Charlemagne created the separate duchy of Gothie with Narbonne as the capital. There were several seigneurial estates: the city belonged to the archbishop, the town to the Viscount and the New Town to the Jews, who remained there until the 14th century. In 877 Gothie passed to the Counts of Toulouse. The name lasted into the Middle Ages.

During the time of Jewish rule under a King of the Jews after 768, Septimania was a magnet for Diaspora Jews who brought with them the Kabbalistic-Gnostic and Manichaean outlooks and settled throughout Languedoc. The Kabbalah (by now meaning "received" and therefore "tradition") was thus well established in southern France in the 12th century. After 1148 as a result of the Second Crusade there was a new influx of Jews from Italy who brought the Kabbalah into the Talmudic academies of Languedoc, Provence and Roussillon, and Spanish-Arab Jewish refugees from the Berber Muslim invasion of Spain c1147-8 brought a fresh influx of Babylonian tradition and more Persian knowledge of Manichaeism. There was a mixture of the Sefardic tradition of the Jews of Arab-Muslim Spain (Arabic prose and Hebrew poetry) and the Ashkenazic tradition of the Jews of Latin-Christian France and Germany (writing in Hebrew). At this time it was said that the Kabbalah was received by Abraham from Melchizedek, King of Salem or Jerusalem, or at least by Moses when God communicated with him on Mount Sinai.

All the occult developments of the previous two millennia were found in the Kabbalah in southern France in the 12th century: Zoroastrianism – there was a tradition that Zoroaster himself had taught the exiled Jews in Chaldean Babylon; Gnosticism; Neoplatonism; the *Hermetica*; and the *Merkava* (Hebrew for "chariot") mysticism of Jews who contemplated Ezekiel's vision of the divine throne (*Ezekiel*, chs 1 and 10). Most of these developments can be found in the 10th century *Sefer Yetzira*. In 12th-century France there were two schools: the first – a *Merkava* school – produced the *Sefer ha-Bahir* (or *Book of Brightness*, 1150-75); the second was Neoplatonic and produced a commentary on the *Sefer Yetzira* and moved to Spain. The classic Kabbalah work, the *Sefer ha-Zohar*, (or *Book of Splendour*) reputed to be a 2nd-century work, was written in Spain c1275 by Moses de Léon and circulated in Castile in the 1280s.[17]

Septimania, the cradle of the Jewish Golden Age in France and Spain (9th-13th centuries) out of which flourished the early Renaissance of the Grail literature (c1190-1215) that inspired Dante, had preserved Manichaeism, which influenced the revolutionary Cathars who emerged from Septimania-Languedoc. The authors of *The Holy Blood and the Holy Grail* state that the most recent research suggests that the Cathars arose from Kabbalistic-Manichaean schools long established in France rather than from the Bulgarian Bogomils.[18]

APPENDIX 7

SION AND THE TEMPLARS

Ostensibly, the founding of the Templars was linked with St Bernard of Clairvaux, a Cistercian monk (1091-1153). The Cistercians had been founded in 1098 and had spread rapidly due to crusading fervour. Bernard, who renounced his career as a knight in 1122, became the spiritual leader of Europe when he established Innocent II as Pope, advocated mysticism as opposed to the rationalism of the Scholiast Abelard, and promoted the Second Crusade. St Bernard wrote the Templars' Rule and encouraged them to protect the newly established Kingdom of Jerusalem, which was continually harassed by Moslem armies. The founding of the Templars grew out of a decision to protect the Kingdom taken in 1113-5.

The first nine Templars (who included Bernard's uncle, André de Montbard) arrived in Jerusalem in 1119, and Baldwin II, King of Jerusalem, gave them the site of the Temple of Solomon. Their headquarters were in the royal palace of Solomon, in the area of Solomon's Temple on Mount Zion or Sion which had housed the Ark that disappeared c586 BC. This contained the tablets of the Ten Commandments brought to Jerusalem by David. The early Templars lived in the oblong palace that was supported by internal columns above Solomon's stables, which once housed ten thousand horses. An eye-witness reported that they were building a new cloister and laying the foundations of a new church. The excavations suggest that the Templars were searching for treasure on the site of the Temple of Solomon.

In fact the Templars were founded by the Order of Sion. One of the nine was the actual founder, Hugues de Payens, who became Grand Master of the Knights Templar. The Order of Sion, later the Prieuré

Notre-Dame de Sion, was virtually unknown until the authors of *The Holy Blood and the Holy Grail* discovered papers relating to it. It was founded in 1090 by Godfroi de Bouillon, whom Catholic Crusaders put on the throne of Jerusalem. Claiming to be of the lineage of David, while tutored by Peter the Hermit Godfroi organized a secret society which would prepare him to be King of Jerusalem. In 1095 Pope Urban II called for a crusade, a holy war that would take the tomb of Christ from the Moslem infidel, and in 1099 Godfroi took Jerusalem. He was offered the throne by a secret conclave that included Peter the Hermit, who was already in Jerusalem. The Order of Sion now worked to rule the world from the throne of David in Jerusalem through the Merovingian bloodline. Godfroi ordered an abbey to be built on Mount Zion to house the Order of Sion. Godfroi died the following year in 1100, and was succeeded by his younger brother, Baudouin, who became King of Jerusalem. It was then that the Order of Sion urged Hugues de Payens to found the Knights Templar. J. R. Church gives the reason: "The secret purpose for the Knights Templar was to preserve the Merovingian bloodline in hopes of one day establishing a world government and putting their king upon the throne – a king who could claim to be the offspring of Jesus Christ and Mary Magdalene."[19] In March 1117 Baudouin I took the constitution of the Knights Templar to the Order of Sion, which gave its approval in 1118.

The excavations in Solomon's palace seem to have been for a reason, for as early as 1104 Hugues de Payens reported a find there to his vassal lord in France, Hugues, Count of Champagne. The Count immediately left for the Holy Land and did not return until 1108. He went to Jerusalem again in 1114, intending to be initiated into the Knights Templar, and returned the following year. During his time in Jerusalem c1114-5 he and his nine fellow Knights Templar found treasure. The Count went back to France and began to prepare a vault as a storehouse. By 1115 money was flowing back to Europe and to the Cistercians, who, through St Bernard, endorsed the Order of the Temple. Bernard's sermons were increasingly about Solomon, and from 1130 to 1150 he commissioned several Cistercian Gothic cathedrals (whose height was an Islamic feature), which were built by a guild called "the Children of Solomon." During the next ten years the Templars became very wealthy – officially by being paid for protecting tens of thousands of Crusaders. However, there were still only nine Templars, and protection of so many on such a scale by so few in return for a fortune is not conceivable. When pressed by officialdom, the Templars said they had discovered the alchemistic secret of transmuting metal into gold.

In 1146 the Templars adopted the Merovingian splayed red cross, and they accompanied Louis VII of France on the Second Crusade. In 1153, they had a new Grand Master, Bertrand de Blanchefort, a nobleman from a Cathar family whose ancestral home was on a mountain peak a few miles from Rennes-le-Château, which lies about half-way along the main route between Carcassonne and Montségur, and which was reputedly home to the post-crucified Jesus. According to one view, the Templar treasure was buried at Rennes-le-Château. Soon afterwards the Templars descended into pagan practices; nevertheless Blanchefort transformed them into a disciplined, well-organized society. In 1156 he brought German-speaking miners to Rennes-le-Château to work the gold mines on Mount Blanchefort which were exhausted by the Romans. In fact the miners were not mining but creating a crypt or storehouse with underground vaults in which to store 24 hoards of treasure from Solomon's Temple which they had smelted.

Almost at once the Templars became bankers to every throne in Europe. They lent money to hard-up monarchs at low interest rates and transferred money for merchant traders. Through a system of promissory notes they allowed money deposited in one city to be drawn in another. They became money-changers and powerful capitalists who conducted diplomacy between monarchs. In England the Master of the Temple was soon given precedence over all other priors and abbots.

As a result of these banking activities in Europe the Templars neglected their role as guardians of the Order of Sion's Merovingian King of Jerusalem in the Holy Land. After the death of Baudouin IV, King of Jerusalem, in 1185 the Templar Grand Master Gerard de Ridefort aggravated the battle to succeed him by breaking an oath made to Baudouin IV before he died and brought the Crusaders close to civil war, while his supercilious and offhand treatment of the Saracens caused them to break a long-standing truce. He made the mistake of fighting at Hattin in July 1187, and was defeated. Having taken Solomon's treasure the Templars had had enough of Jerusalem and began to resent the Order of Sion, which they now regarded as a rival. Indeed, they planned to destroy the Order of Sion and to leave the Holy Land. When two months later Saladin took Jerusalem, the Order of Sion blamed de Ridefort for the loss and bitterly accused him of treason, causing a rift between the Templars and Sion. The Order of Sion's *Dossiers Secrets* record the break, which involved a "cutting of the elm" at Gisors in northern France in 1188. Following a battle there between Henry II of England and Philippe II of France, there was a truce, and an elm was cut down as an emblem of the schism. The truce between the Templars and Sion allowed each body to operate independently.

From 1188 the Order of Sion's protector became the King of England. It was now called the Priory of Sion. The Templar headquarters remained at Rennes-le-Château, where Solomon's wealth was supposedly hidden.

The Sion/Templar struggle continued throughout the next 800 years and was behind the British, American, French and Russian revolutions, as we have seen. It also prefigures the schism in the world government today between Rockefellers and Rothschilds.[20] Soon after 1891 the Priory of Sion succeeded in wresting the church of Rennes-le-Château from the Templars, when Abbé Bérenger Saunière, a young penniless priest sent in 1885 to a poverty-stricken parish which had always had fewer than 200 parishioners, suddenly embarked on an extravagant building programme to refurbish his church. (According to letters the restoration work alone cost 350 million centimes, some £700,000 in today's values.) This followed reports from others in the village that he had discovered treasure in a tomb in the church crypt. The church had been consecrated to Mary Magdelene (the bride of Christ according to Sionist Merovingians) in 1059. According to some, he discovered ancient documents proving that Jesus survived the crucifixion, married Mary Magdelene, and died in France, and the Vatican bought his silence. Between 1891 and his death in 1917 he spent a fortune and left cryptograms and codes that may indicate the source of his sudden wealth.

In 1892 Saunière went to Paris and met the Freemason Emile Hoffet and the singer Emma Calvé who was linked with Joseph Péladan. In 1891 Péladan had co-founded (with the Count of Larochefoucauld) the Kabbalistic Rosicrucian Order of the Rose Cross of the Temple and the Grail. All three were frequent guests at Rennes-le-Château, and the effect of the building work done by Saunière in the church was to transform it from a Templar headquarters into a Sion headquarters either out of the treasure he seems to have found locally or out of Vatican hush-money. The Templars may have co-operated in permitting this change of emphasis.

The Order of Sion was, and is, committed to establishing a Kingdom of the World with Jerusalem as its capital and the rightful descendant of David on its throne. Over the entrance porch of the village church of Rennes-le-Château deep in Cathar country are carved the words *Regnum Mundi* or "Kingdom of the World." (The Cathars called the Demiurge or – as they saw it – the evil God of material creation, *Rex Mundi,* "King of the World.") The full lettering over the porch reads:

"REGNUM MUNDI ET OMNEM ORNATUM SOECULI CONTEMPSI
PROPTER ANOREM DOMINI MEI JESU CHRISTTI QUEM VIDI
QUEN (sic) AMAVI IN QUEM CREMINI QUEM DILEXI."

As there are "mistakes" in the Latin and the inscription does not appear to make sense, and as Saunière never made mistakes but did everything deliberately, it has been suggested that this inscription too is a code (22 words, 114 letters long) waiting to be deciphered. Speculative attempts at deciphering have been made.[21]

In the course of his renovations Saunière claimed to have found four parchments inside a hollow 8th-century Carolingian altar support.

Two of them allegedly contained genealogies dating from 1244 and 1644. These parchments contained a list of Grand Masters of both the Knights Templar and the Priory of Sion as well as a history of the Merovingian bloodline. These ancient documents could have been placed in the hollow cavity by Saunière himself, acting on behalf of the two Kabbalist Rosicrucians who were so often his guests.[22]

Following the separation between the Templars and Sion at Gisors, Sion took on the name Ormus ("orme," French for "elm") and followed the religion of the Egyptian Ormus, an Alexandrian Gnostic who was converted to Christianity in AD 46. Ormus's symbol was a red cross, and Merovée (the ruler from 448 to 458 from whom the Merovingian kings of the Franks derived their name) was born with a red-cross birth mark over his heart. At the request of Sion's Grand Master Jean de Gisors (1188-1220) the Priory of Sion took the red cross of Ormus as its emblem and called itself "L'Ordre de la Rose-Croix Veritas" (Order of the True Red Cross). Sionists now claim that Jean de Gisors founded the Rose-Croix or Rosicrucianism. At the same time Sion adopted the All-seeing Eye of Osiris, which the Templars had also adopted. Such similarities allowed Sionists to penetrate Templar meetings.

The Count of Champagne, Hugues de Champagne, who had been party to finding the Templar treasure, had a relative, Marie Countess of Champagne, who was the daughter of Eleanor of Aquitaine (the wife of Louis VII of France and Henry II of England). Chrétien de Troyes, first teller of the Grail story, lived at her court. Philippe d'Alsace, Count of Flanders, had tried to marry Marie in 1182; Chrétien's poem *Perceval* or *Le Conte du Graal* is dedicated to him. Did Chrétien hear about the Grail cup from Marie – or Philippe – who had in turn heard the story from its finder, Hugues de Champagne?

Following the schism the Templars became Satanists. They had encountered eastern mysteries in the Holy Land, particularly the false, magical, occult Kabbalah, and their contact with the Cathars had reinforced their Gnosticism. They took hashish and practised black magic and witchcraft. They saw Jesus and the Catholic Church as their enemy. They spat on the cross. They went back to the Gnostic dualism of God having two sons, Satanail/Lucifer (the elder), and Jesus (the younger), and held that the elder son alone had the right to homage. They worshipped Lucifer, the god of evil, and bowed down before the Baphomet, Satan as a goat's head within an upside-down star, and adopted the Satanic skull and crossbones.

In 1291 Acre, the last bastion of the Crusaders in the Holy Land was taken by the Saracens and the Kingdom of Jerusalem which began with Godfroi was no more. The Templars had lost their place of operation and therefore their *raison d'être*. For the next 15 years they were in deep decline.

Sion had no funds and was having to borrow from the Templars they had created, whose treason had removed the treasure of Solomon that was rightfully theirs. Philippe IV of France was a financially insecure monarch who envied the Templar wealth and determined to destroy the Order with the clandestine aid of both Sion, which knew their passwords, and the Vatican. When Philippe's ally Clement V became Pope, the French King made sure that he called for the suppression of the Knights Templar. He wanted their wealth, and Sion wanted the return of the treasure of Solomon, including the Holy Grail which the Templars allegedly had. (One tradition said that Mary Magdalene took it with her to France in AD 70.) An infiltrator (possibly Sionist, certainly the French King's) obtained a confession from a Templar which enabled Philippe to act. At dawn on Friday October 13, 1307 all Templars in France were to be seized and their goods confiscated.

Philippe never found the Templars' gold. It had been in Paris, where the Templars were bankers for all Europe, and local report had it that following a tip-off it was taken to the Templar naval base at La Rochelle and loaded into 18 galleys and never seen again. It is not impossible that the Priory of Sion took possession of the gold either at La Rochelle or later, perhaps via the English-controlled Knights Hospitaller of St John, and took it to England, which rapidly became the dominant world power and over the next 400 years the most powerful and wealthy nation on earth. Today the City of London is still the world's financial centre. Was Templar gold later at the heart of the British Empire? If the gold went to England, it would explain why suppressed Templars fled to Scotland and fought with Robert the Bruce at Bannockburn against England in 1314. Their Scottish headquarters was at their preceptory at Rosslyn. No Templars were arrested at Rennes-le-Château, and it is unclear what happened to the treasure of Solomon. In 1981 Pierre Plantard, the Grand Master of the Priory of Sion, claimed to throw light on the treasure of Solomon: "The Order actually possesses the lost treasure of the Temple of Jerusalem. It will be returned to Israel when the time is right."[23] The right time may be when a Merovingian ascends the throne of David and becomes King of Jerusalem.

Jacques de Molay, last Grand Master of the Templars, was not captured until 1314. He was tried and roasted over a slow fire on Paris's Île de la Cité in the Seine. With him was Geoffroi de Charnay, who owned the Turin Shroud that was stolen from Constantinople. As he choked and suffocated to death from the smoke of the slow fire, de Molay cursed the Pope and the King and cried out that Clement and Philippe should appear before God to answer for their act within a year. The Pope died of dysentery within a month, and the King died of mysterious symptoms (Templar or Sion poison?) by the end of the year. The curse on the monarchy echoed through pre-revolutionary France, and the Jacobins were named after de Molay's first name, Jacques. The Bourbons were linked by marriage to Philippe IV, and the Jacobins' execution of the Bourbon Louis XVI and termination of the monarchy were in fulfilment of de Molay's curse. (After Louis' head had fallen a French Templar Freemason is reputed to have leapt on to the scaffold and cried out, "Jacques de Molay, you are avenged!")

With de Molay's death the Temple officially ceased to exist. Having been welcomed in Scotland by Robert Bruce, the Templars used the ritual murder of Hiram Abiff to symbolize the death of Jacques de Molay, and introduced it into their "3rd degree," the initiation rite for Master Masons. They spent 400 years in Scotland and controlled the Stuart dynasty, including James VI of Scotland who became James I of England. James I was an initiate of the Scottish Templars and brought them to London. Charles I continued the Stuart Templar tradition. Eventually the Templars would be exiled to France with the Stuarts in 1689.

The Templars, then, were a heretical sect whose impact was out of all proportion to its numbers. They influenced the Church of St Bernard's day, banked for the kings of Europe and challenged Christianity. Like the Cathars, the Templars possessed a genuine mysticism and spirituality, but their ideas and religion were corrupted by eastern magical practices that echoed magical Kabbalism, which was slowly melding disparate heretical groups into modern Freemasonry for an agenda of world rule.

Sion wanted to wrest England back from the Templars. England had been Sionist from 1188 until 1603, and if the Templars had taken Solomon's treasure to England, Sion had a double reason for wanting England back – and there is evidence that Sion was involved in the Puritan Revolution.

APPENDIX 8

THE SPANISH INQUISITION

The Sefardic Jews had been persecuted on and off since June 1391 when urban mobs rioted in Seville and murdered hundreds of Jews. Jews had been ordered to convert from Judaism to Christianity, and there were mass "conversions" in 1391. Their descendants (also called *conversos*) were in due course felt to be unreliable Christians and suitable for the attention of the Inquisition. Regional expulsions of Jews by the Inquisition had taken place since 1481, the year before Torquemada's appointment. The first *auto-da-fé* and the proposal to expel all Jews who did not convert was an extension of this policy. In an edict issued in Aragon King Ferdinand made it clear that the proposal came from the Inquisition. Jews had been expelled from Provence and the Italian duchies of Palma and Milan in 1488 and 1490, though many converted. One estimate reckons that some 170,000 families – 800,000 souls – may have left Castile and Aragon in 1492. Another estimate believes 300,000 Jews left "all the provinces of the King."[24] Their suffering was very great. Before they left they tried to sell their houses: often a house changed hands for an ass, a vineyard for linen. No gold or silver could be removed. The ships waiting at the ports were overcrowded and badly maintained, and storms drove many back to Spain. The Jews on board had no option but to land in Spain and convert. Many who reached Africa were robbed and murdered. Many Jews expelled from Spain emigrated to Poland and Italy, and later Holland. Those who remained in Spain espoused the Catholic faith and were known as *Marranos*.

The reason for the expulsion seems to be that the conversos were not good Christians; the crown did not profit and actually lost revenue. The Sultan of Turkey marvelled at the expulsion "since it was to expel wealth." After 1492 the practice of Judaism was forbidden in Spain and its colonies, though it was still allowed in Milan (which was under Spanish control from the mid-16th century) until the 1590s.

The Spanish Inquisition's severe treatment of the Jews undoubtedly created a great deal of opposition to the Catholic Church in which the Inquisitors held office, and accelerated the demand for reform.

1492 was also the year in which first mention was made of the "Alumbrados" ("enlightened ones," also translated "illuminists"). These were Franciscan mystics who emphasized passive union of the soul with God as Light, and one group, patronized by the Mendoza Duke of Infantado in his palace at Guadalajara, was formed round Isabel de la Cruz and Pedro Ruiz de Alcaraz. The Inquisition was alarmed that the Illuminists' activities might be heretical, and after a long, slow, patient inquiry lasting several years, the Illuminist leaders were detained. Isabel and Alcaraz were arrested in 1524. In 1525 the Inquisitor General issued an "edict on the Alumbrados" which declared them heretical. Isabel and Alcaraz were eventually sentenced to appear in an *auto-da-fé* at Toledo in 1529.

APPENDIX 9

THE JEWS IN SPAIN

There is some evidence that Jews had tried to undermine the Spanish Church before 1492. The Jews of Europe, alarmed at the expulsions and persecutions, had appealed to the Sanhedrin in Constantinople. The letter was signed by Chemor Rabbi of Arles, Provence. In November 1489 the reply had come back over the signature "V.S.S. V.F.F., Prince of the Jews." It advised the Jews of Europe to adopt the tactics of the Trojan Horse: to become Christian priests, lawyers and doctors and work to destroy the Christian structure from within. There is a view that *Marrano* Jews were secretly working to destroy the Church in Spain, and that the Spanish Inquisition was set up to cleanse the country of the underminers. After the expulsion of the Jews from Spain Jews had travelled across Europe to Holland. They needed a powerful seafaring nation to which they could attach themselves and undertake international commerce to all corners of the globe. Holland was a rising naval power, but following the defeat of the Spanish Armada and her voyages to America, England had a better international naval structure within which mercantile shipping could work. Moreover it was already divided between Protestant and Catholic, and now between Protestant and Puritan. Jews could exploit these divisions in Christendom, take revenge for the 1290 expulsion (and the *autos-da-fé* of the Inquisition that had, for example, persecuted Menasseh's father) and expand Jewish commerce through British fleets. The Jewish financiers of Amsterdam probably had mixed motives for backing Cromwell to overthrow the King.

APPENDIX 10

BRITISH ISRAEL IN THE REFORMATION AND PURITAN REVOLUTIONS

The idea that the Celtic-Anglo-Saxon peoples that inhabit the British Isles and its English-speaking dominions (the US, Canada, South Africa, Australia and New Zealand), as well as parts of Protestant Holland, are the "lost" Israelites of Biblical prophecy is, together with the accounts of Christ's visit to the West of England, rooted in the folk consciousness of Britain. To what extent such traditions flourished in the Dark and Middle Ages is not known, but at the time of the Reformation in England (1500-1650) the idea of God's covenant with Abraham passing to the British people expressed itself in the literature and politics of the nation-state. The Common Law too, as entrenched by King Alfred, was clearly based on the Ten Commandments given by God to Moses.

Evidence for "the British Israel theory," as it has come to be known, can be found in the three great books of literature/prophecy in the English language: *The Book of Common Prayer* (1549), the *King James Bible* (1611) – the theory is also found in earlier English versions of the Bible such as Tyndale's – and Shakespeare's *First Folio* (1623). Throughout the *Prayer Book*, the English are identified with the people of Israel and termed the sheep of God's pasture. In the responses when the Priest says "Endue thy ministers with righteousness," the congregation respond, "And make thy chosen people joyful." In her book *My Past Atheism* the theosophist Annie Besant attacked the *Prayer Book*, saying that in it the English make claims that have nothing to with their race, "unless those people are right who say that the English nation is descended from the lost Ten Tribes."

Archbishop Cranmer compiled the 1549 *Prayer Book*, and in the preface he offered to prove that its contents had been in use in the British Church for over 1,500 years. Both he and William Tyndale, the "Apostle of England," believed in British Israel and the Apostolic origin of the Church in Britain. With the spread of the Scriptures in English, for which Tyndale was largely responsible, an awareness dawned among the British that they were indeed Israelites. The belief too that the English monarch was of the royal line of David and was crowned sitting on the Stone of Destiny (Jacob's pillow) confirmed the British Israelite view. Much of the force of Elizabethan culture was drawn from this understanding. Elizabeth herself was known as "The Light of Israel," and Francis Drake in a letter to John Foxe (author of *The Book of Martyrs*) urged him to pray that "God may be glorified, his Church, our Queen and country preserved, the enemies of truth vanquished and that we might have continual peace in Israel."

British Israel, whether consciously understood or held subliminally spurred Tudor nationalism, especially under Elizabeth I. James I was famed as a British Israelite, but his outlook may have been an intellectual fantasy rather than a deeply held belief. Though he was famous for saying that the Lord had made him "King over Israel" and was dubbed the "Scottish Solomon," it must be remembered that James was reared not on English Common Law, but on the Civil Law of the Scots, which effectively placed the King above the law. Hence he may not have acquired an understanding of the Mosaic foundations of English law, and his sympathy for the British-Israel belief may only have been skin-deep. Cromwell, a radical British Israelite, played on this new patriotism in his open reverence for the lost golden age of Elizabeth. (He held national celebrations every year on the anniversary of her accession.)

C

VENETIAN FOREIGN POLICY AND ROSICRUCIAN FREEMASONRY

There is a view that Venice is behind the secret organizations we have been describing. By the 15th century, military and economic conquest had taken the power of the Venetian republic along the north Adriatic, north-east and south-west Greece and Crete. Having warded off threats from Norman Sicily, Genoa and Pisa, Venice was now faced with the advancing armies of Islam.

Venice's impact on Western Europe goes back to the University of Padua, which was run by Venice to train the Venetian *élite*. Galileo taught there from 1590 to 1610. At the University Aristotle replaced Plato; the focus was on man remote from the Creator and subject to ethics, not morality, as there is no right or wrong and no knowable truth.

After the League of Cambrai (an alliance of Pope, Holy Roman Emperor and the Kings of France and Aragon against Venice) almost destroyed Venice between 1509 and 1513, the Venetian Humanist and Cardinal Gasparo Contarini, a pupil of Pietro Pomponazi, the leading Aristotelian at the University of Padua, founded *Il Spirituali* to counter Venetian hedonism and create protestant reformers within the Catholic Church. Fearing that Spain would threaten Venice by land, Contarini and his associates sought to ally with Luther to undermine Spain in her Habsburg lands. Having disputed with Luther, they became reconciled with the Lutherans and formulated a theology of salvation acceptible to them. Luther was then called to account by the Spanish Habsburg Emperor Charles V as Contarini had hoped, and Luther's standing rose throughout Europe.

Venice now turned its attention to England, where Henry VIII was married to Charles V's aunt, Catherine of Aragon, and had taken Spain's side against France. When the Spanish Holy Roman Emperor Charles V defeated France at the battle of Pavia (in 1525) and sacked Rome (in 1527), Venice panicked and tried to drive a wedge between Spain and England. The plan was for Henry VIII to be induced to divorce Catherine, and Thomas Cromwell, a Venetian agent trained in Venice, became one of Henry's chief advisers. (He had gone abroad at an early age and had spent some time in Italy.)

In 1529 Francesco Zorzi (or Georgi), a close friend and relative of Contarini, a Christian Kabbalist, came to England and advised Thomas Cranmer, Archbishop of Canterbury, on the original Old Testament Hebrew. His task was to discern whether Henry's marriage to Catherine had ever been valid, bearing in mind that Catherine had previously been married to Henry's elder brother, Arthur for a few months before he died. Catherine said that this marriage was unconsummated. In the Old Testament there are conflicting passages, one saying that a man is obliged to marry his deceased brother's wife and one forbidding this. Zorzi told Henry that the "forbidding" passage was authoritative, and that the other one (which was supported by the Pope) was not applicable. He argued that Henry had never been legally married to Catherine.

Zorzi's main work, *De Harmonia Mundi* (1525), advocated following the Neoplatonist One, which (he claimed) is directly knowable, and attacked Nicholas of Cusa (1401?-1461), who championed the "*Docta ignorantia*" of Plato's *Parmenides* (i.e., proving that any attempt to resolve the paradox of the One and the many leads to contradiction). Zorzi's debunking of Plato in favour of Aristotle was a Venetian attempt to destroy Christianity. In 1536 he wrote *Scripturam Sacram Problemata*, a manual of magic. Zorzi was a source for Dee, who was a source – Yates, in *The Occult Philosophy in the Elizabethan Age*, says "the source" – of the Rosicrucian Manifestos. Contarini's relative Zorzi may therefore have been the Venetian originator of Rosicrucianism.

Venetian ambassadors' reports to the Venetian Senate, which are now public, make it clear that as Flanders and the Netherlands were Spanish, English control of the Channel was the key to destroying Spain. Henry VIII's setting up of the Anglican Church divided Renaissance men. Erasmus dedicated his *Enchiridion of the Militant Christian* to Henry VIII, and his *Education of a Christian Prince* to Charles V, the Spanish King and Holy Roman Emperor.

There is a view that the Renaissance did not only come from an occult return to pre-Christian religions and a revival of Neoplatonism, as Ficino's work suggests and as Frances Yates' books have outlined. Erasmus, for example, came out of a teaching movement called the Brethren of the Common Life. The Renaissance attack on the Aristotelian Schoolmen created groupings around Erasmus and Sir Thomas More which, on this view, created a flowering of real Christianity and culture that led to Shakespeare. However, Shakespeare's works are full of occult and Neoplatonist references. The introduction of Plato, who had been translated by Ficino (who was funded by Cosimo de Medici), came as a relief to men like Erasmus and More, but alongside Plato's works came the translation of *Poimandres* which was attributed to Hermes Trismegistus, who was supposed to have lived around 1500 BC but who in reality lived in the 2nd century AD. His alleged antiquity was the result of a new Platonist fraud. Ficino, who wrote a preface to the translation, did not know this. He translated Hermetic and Neoplatonist works in which the soul was midway between spirit and matter, the Renaissance belief being that man could coax spirit into matter through the magical use of the soul. Pico denied the individual soul and held that man is a receptacle of the world soul; he held that the Kabbalah is the fount of ancient wisdom.

Padua-trained Aristotelians in the Church attacked the Renaissance as pagan and humanistic, hoping to destroy Nicholas of Cusa's outlook and Christianity. Occult Neoplatonists and Kabbalists poured into England and influenced the poets Sir Philip Sidney, a follower of Zorzi, and Spenser (who hinted at England's imperial destiny and British Israel). On the other hand Marlowe attacked – or reflected – the Aristotelian Schoolmen ("live and die in Aristotle's works") and necromancy at the court of Elizabeth I in his play *Dr Faustus*, whose hero makes a pact with the Devil. Marlowe's Faustus actually refers to Zorzi when he tells Mephistophilis (i.e. Mephistopheles), "Go, and return an old Franciscan friar;/That holy shape becomes a devil best." (This play was written soon after 1587; Marlowe was reported to have been assassinated in 1593.) Shakespeare may have been attacking – or reflecting – Zorzi's influence in *Othello, the Moor of Venice* – and in *The Tempest*, where Prospero's magic and Ariel, a spirit of the air, suggest the slightly later Rosicrucian world-view.

In the 1580s, following the English defeat of the Spanish Armada, a Venetian grouping round Fra Paolo Sarpi took on Pope Paul VI. The Pope had demanded that Venice repeal a law restricting church building and hand over two priests. Venice refused and the Senate and Doge (Venetian head of state) were excommunicated, as was Sarpi. Sarpi opposed the Pope in his pamphlets, claiming that princes derive their authority from God, not from the Pope. He refused to appear before the Roman Inquisition, and (Venice having successfully defied the Pope) in 1607 was stabbed in the street. James I was extremely interested in the Venetian stand against Rome as it was similar to the Anglican stand under Henry VIII. Sarpi had many admirers in England, including Henry Wotton (English ambassador in Venice on and off from 1604 to 1623, who hoped to persuade Venice to adopt a reform similar to the Anglican reform);[25] Donne (who had invoked Elizabeth Stuart as "a new star" and who had a portrait of Sarpi hanging in his study in later years); and Bacon, who became his friend.

From the point of view of Venice, the marriage of Frederick V, Elector of Palatine and James I's daughter Elizabeth Stuart ("the marriage of Thames and Rhine") in 1613 was a Protestant-Anglican marriage that outwardly counterbalanced the Catholic Spanish Habsburgs.

The appearance in 1614 of the first two Rosicrucian tracts, the *Fama* (which called for the formation of a Brotherhood of the Rosy Cross – it was subtitled "*Or a Discovery of the Fraternity of The Most Noble Order of The Rosy Cross*") and *Confessio* (which called the Pope an anti-Christ) were Neoplatonist-Kabbalist works. The grave of Christian Rosenkreutz consisted of a number of vaults in which shone different suns, a Neoplatonist image. These two works were followed by Fludd's solving of the relationship between the microcosm and macrocosm in his work. Venice hoped that Frederick V would form a Protestant League, take the Bohemian crown and defeat the Catholic Habsburgs. Frederick V's adviser, Christian Anhalt, was a friend of Sarpi – and of Henry Wotton (who called at Heidelberg on his journeys to and from Venice). In fact, Frederick V was defeated because James I, the English King and his father-in-law did not support him. As a result Venetians wanted to expel the Stuarts and bring a more radical English government to power. Venice supported Oliver Cromwell, and we should be looking for a link between Venice and the Mulheim Synagogue, which financed the New Model Army.

Sarpi was in close contact with Bacon, whose inductive method was taken from Sarpi's *"Arte di ben Pensare"* and other writings, and with Hobbes – sometimes directly and sometimes with William Cavendish, Earl of Devonshire. Hobbes translated Italian letters, including 77 from Micanzo to Cavendish ("Candiscio"). Cavendish and Hobbes visited Venice in September 1614 and presumably met Sarpi and Micanzo.

Out of the meetings of this group, which included Bacon, Fludd and Descartes, came Rosicrucian Freemasonry. It founded the Royal Society, which really began in 1640 (the first year of the Long Parliament). With the defeat of the Palatinate Hartlib and the Bohemian Comenius arrived in England. Hartlib wrote *Macaria*, Comenius *The Way of Light*. Both called in Rosicrucian code for an "Invisible College." In 1645 Theodore Haak from the Palatinate met Dr John Wilkins, chaplain to the Elector of Palatine, who, in *Mathematical Magic* (1648) mentioned the Rosi Cross, Fludd and Dee. Wilkins and Boyle (who in letters of 1646 referred to an "Invisible College") were behind the Oxford meetings that led in 1660 to the founding of the English Royal Society. In 1654 Elias Ashmole wrote a letter to ask "the Rosicrucians to allow him to join their fraternity." Newton was a co-founder of the Royal Society; he possessed copies of the *Fama* and

Confessio, and was a Rosicrucian. Yates, quoting De Quincey, says, "Freemasonry is neither more nor less than Rosicrucianism as modified by those who transplanted it in England, whence it was re-exported to the other countries of Europe."

Milton was also an admirer of Sarpi. He was a pro-Venetian Puritan; he held that the Son of God was inferior to the Father and not necessary to Christianity. He was a contempory of Sabbatai Zevi, the false messiah from Smyrna, Turkey, whose father was an agent for English Puritan merchants. Milton's *Paradise Regained* may be based on Sabbatai Zevi's life.

Venice, which may have been behind Rosicrucian Freemasonry and the Royal Society, may also have been at the bottom of the "Glorious Revolution" (perhaps a phrase of Venetian spin) by manipulating the Dutch Rosicrucians into supporting William III, John Locke and the architect of the Bank of England, Charles Montagu, who later became British ambassador to Venice. There is a view that the Bank of England was a gigantic Venetian "recoinage" swindle – circulating English coinage was halved and new taxes were loaded into the collapsing English economy – and that Newton, who oversaw the Bank of England and allowed his niece to be Montagu's mistress, served the new Rosicrucian English State as did Locke, who defended usury and whose concept of social contract justified William's usurpation of the English throne; James II, he said, had broken the contract. By 1697 Venice arguably controlled the British purse-strings. In 1701 Locke advocated revoking all the American colonies' independent charters and placing all their economic activity under William in a further attempt to control English finances.

Leibniz is something of an enigma. At the philosophical level he opposed the Aristotelian empiricism of Bacon, Hobbes, Descartes, Newton and Locke. Swift took up his refutation in "A Digression on Madness" in *A Tale of a Tub* (1696), claiming that "the great introducers of new schemes in philosophy" were "persons crazed, or out of their wits." However, as we have seen (pp212-4), Leibniz, though opposed by Newton, had joined a Rosicrucian Society and was employed by

Rosicrucians and his report influenced the 1701 Act of Settlement that made Sophie, head of the House of Hanover, successor to Queen Anne and let the German-speaking Rosicrucian Hanoverians in to occupy the British throne – as Venice would have wanted. Leibniz was an anti-Aristotelian Rosicrucian fellow-traveller.

Though her international position had dwindled, Venice supported key oligarchic families such as the Spencers and the Churchills. Venetians sought to destroy France, the biggest economic power in Europe, and in 1701 England launched a war in which John Churchill, later the first Duke of Marlborough, shone. Queen Anne was most influenced at court by the Duke and Duchess of Marlborough, whom Swift opposed. Swift allied with Leibniz, adviser to Sophia of Hanover, and together they brought the composer Handel from Hanover to London in 1710.

There is a view that Queen Anne died of poison at the age of 49. Was she poisoned on Venetian instructions so that the Rosicrucian Hanoverians would succeed her? The exiled Duke of Marlborough landed the same day and George of Hanover was proclaimed king. Queen Anne was buried secretly at night in Westminster Abbey; beneath the tomb of Mary, Queen of Scots. No stone or tablet marks her grave. Swift, appointed Dean of St Patrick's Cathedral in Dublin by Queen Anne, in effect became the leader of all Ireland during the 1720s with such pamphlets as *A Modest Proposal*, and extended Leibniz's concept of the pursuit of happiness through liberty and sovereignty. In England, Venetian-influenced Hell-Fire Clubs spread. Sir Francis Dashwood, Benjamin Franklin's superior, was head of the Hell-Fire Club.

There is a case for seeing Venice as being at the bottom of the creation of the Reformation, the Rosicrucian movement and Freemasonry that dominate England. It may also have been behind the Cromwellian Revolution. Rosicrucian Freemasonry created the English Royal Society, which used Aristotelian empiricism to attack Nicholas of Cusa's Platonist influence on Kepler and Leibniz. Freemasonry is dedicated to the destruction of monotheistic religion, including

Christianity, and a return to paganism. It created the Illuminati which, in England, through Jeremy Bentham and Lord Shelburne (William Petty Fitzmaurice, 1st Marquis of Lansdowne, who as English Prime Minister from July 1782 to February 1783 renegotiated the Treaty of Paris which ended the American Revolution), created the Jacobins and, through the British Foreign Office of Palmerston and his collaboration with Mazzini, both Communism and Fascism. Freemasonry also created the New Age in England, which seeks the return of paganism and the destruction of monotheistic religion, including Christianity. Out of the rational empiricism of Rosicrucian Freemasonry have come Bacon, Hobbes, Locke and Hume in philosophy, and in our time the occult rationalism of Bertrand Russell, Aldous Huxley and Aleister Crowley.

At the very least, Venice may have played an important part in spreading occult beliefs which found their way into revolutionary movements. Venetian foreign policy is a part of the European picture which should not be completely neglected.

On the basis of the above, there may now have to be a detailed, evidential study of the impact of Venice on the secret Freemasonic organizations behind the early revolutions.[26]

NOTE TO THE READER ON THE NOTES/SOURCES

In this work I am presenting the impact of secret organizations on Western history, in particular on the Western revolutions whose patterns they have shaped. It is therefore more important to give sources for the impact of secret organizations and for the patterns of revolutions than for the numerous historical events on which the secret organizations impact and which provide much of the detail of the patterns.

The sources for the secret organizations and patterns can be found in numerous books. To simplify things for the reader, I have narrowed the references to particular books so that facts can be readily checked. It would be possible to give references to half a dozen works for each reference to a historical event, but that would add to the complexity, reduce accessibility and, quite simply, put the reader off. I have therefore included references to the *Encyclopaedia Britannica*, which is in the public domain and where the ingredients of the patterns (dates, people, deeds) can be swiftly verified and their accuracy agreed. The reader will bear in mind that each reference to the *Encyclopaedia Britannica* could be replaced by a clutch of references – which would not achieve my aim of corroborating evidence succinctly.

This work interprets history to arrive at a new way of seeing familiar historical events. My main sources are therefore interpretative works by authors who have reflected deeply on secret history for decades: Frances Yates, Christopher Hill, Nesta Webster; Michael Baigent, Richard Leigh and Henry Lincoln; Antony Sutton, Emanuel Josephson; and most recently Gary Allen, Des Griffin, David Rivera, William Still and John Daniel. Through their probings and determination to smoke out the truth, I have been able to show how secret organizations have been at the root of familiar events. I am indebted to my sources for helping me to offer a portrait of a Western culture that is disturbing. I hope it will act as a warning, and that a new generation will purify our culture of its more dubious influences.

I have chosen these works because I have demanded that my interpretative sources should have done decades of research and that they should have an impressive grasp of their approach. All their approaches are partial; this is the first book to cover the whole field of secret organizations and revolutions. Although partial, these main sources all see the distant mountain peak of the whole. For example, although Baigent, Leigh and Lincoln do not even mention Weishaupt and Nesta Webster barely mentions Cromwell, they are all clear that secret organizations are promoting a "King of Jerusalem". None of my chosen sources refers to the revolutionary dynamic in detailing how the secret organizations impact on history. The revolutionary dynamic is my work alone.

All websites were active when these notes were compiled.

NOTES/SOURCES

PART ONE: THE PROTESTANT REVOLUTION

Chapter One: The Reformation Revolution

1. For Manichaeism and Mani, Marcion, Bardesanes and the "Ship of Light", see Hans Jonas, *The Gnostic Religion*. Also Hagger, *The Fire and the Stones*, pp134-6.

2. The Cathar sources can be found in Arthur Gurdham, *The Great Heresy, The History and Beliefs of the Cathars*. I derived much information from books I bought locally while visiting the Languedoc region of France: Bély, *The* Cathars: Aubarbaier, Binet and Bouchard, *Wonderful Cathar Country*: and Aué, *Discover Cathar Country*. See The Grail section in Hagger, *The Fire and the Stones, op. cit.*, pp188-197.

3. Aubarbaier, Binet and Bouchard, *op. cit.*, p80: "The enemies of Catharism had nicknamed Montségur the 'Vatican of Heresy', the 'Dragon's Head' and 'Satan's Synagogue'." Reference to "Satan's Synagogue" was also made in 1243 (see three paragraphs below): "At a Catholic conclave held in Béziers in the spring of 1243, a call to bring down the 'synagogue of Satan' at Montségur was issued." See
    http://www.russianbooks.org/montsegur/montsegur3.htm.

4. See The Grail section in Hagger, *The Fire and the Stones, op. cit.*, pp188-197.

5. J. M. Church, *Guardians of the Grail*, p25.

6. For the story of Rennes-le-Château, see Appendices B, Appendix 7, pp353-355. The story can be found in Fanthorpe, *Rennes-le-Château, Its Mysteries and Secrets* and James, *The Treasure Maps of Rennes-le-Château*.

7. Laurence Gardner, *Bloodline of the Holy Grail*, p340.

8. For Wycliffe and Hus, see Stewart Easton, *A Brief History of the Western World*, pp210-211; and many books on the Reformation.

9. My view of the Rennaisance is based on my many books about the Medici family and on material acquired in Florence, where I visited the villa at Careggi. For Ficino, see *Selected Letters of Marsilio Ficino* and also *The Letters of Marsilio Ficino* vols 1-7. For Pico see Yates, *The Occult Philosophy in the Elizabethan Age*, pp17-22.

10. See John Daniel, *Scarlet and the Beast* vol 1, pp78-80.

11. Compare note 6. Genealogies relating to the Priory of Sion compiled by Henri Lobenau (an alias, according to some, for Leo Schidlof) and reflected in the secret records of the Priory of Sion were allegedly discovered by Father Sauniére at Rennes-le-Château. It has been claimed that the *Dossiers Secrets* are a forgery. The discovery of the *Dossiers* was thoroughly investigated by the authors of *The Holy Blood and the Holy Grail*, and the claim that they are a forgery itself needs to be treated with some scepticism. If the Priory of Sion exists, and there is much evidence to suggest that it does, then it would claim that the *Dossiers Secrets* are a forgery to restore the secrecy blown by *The Holy Blood and the Holy Grail*.

12. For Savonarola, see Villari, *Life and Times of Girolamo Savonarola*.

13. For a bird's-eye view of the Protestant Reformation, see Easton, *op. cit.*, pp209-220.

14. Kim Dowley (ed), *The History of Christianity*, p360.

15. Daniel, *Scarlet and the Beast*, vol 1, p398.

16. Nesta H, Webster, *Secret Societies and Subversive Movements*, p21.

17. The Anabaptists were a radical, left-wing movement whose communes in Transylvania and Hungary had been known for their passivism, hard work and brotherly love. In Zurich they were more extreme than followers of Zwingli. They favoured adult baptism, arguing that child baptism was invalid as children did not know what they were promising; only adult baptism was meaningful. They were anti-State – the State punished sinners, and the Church should be separate from the State – and would not swear civil oaths. The Anabaptist Thomas Müntzer asserted that the Inner Light, not the Bible, was the true spiritual authority on earth, and declared that he was living near the end of the world. He led the Thuringian peasants in revolt in 1525 and was executed. Thousands of Anabaptists were killed but the sect became strong in the Netherlands and North Germany.

18. Referred to in Captain A. H. M. Ramsay, *The Nameless War*, p11. A report in the Catholic Gazette of February 1936 also claimed that Calvin was of Jewish extraction.

19. Isaac D'Israeli, *Life of Charles the First*, two volumes. Much of his information is obtained from the records of Melchior de Salom, French envoy in England during the time of Charles I.

20. Matthew Brook, Master of Trinity College, Cambridge, to Archbishop Abbott, December 12, 1630, quoted by P. Heylyn, *Historical and Miscellaneous Tracts*, p539.

21. For Henry VIII, Thomas Cromwell and Sir Thomas More, see any general history of the time, such as the Book Club Associates' *Henry VIII*. For Holbein's painting, see John North, *The Ambassadors' Secret*.

22. For a bird's-eye view of the Counter-Reformation, see Easton, *op. cit.*, pp220-3.

23. These two poems, *Non So Se S'è* and *Vorrei, Voler, Signore* can be found in *Michelangelo, a Self-Portrait*, ed Clements, pp93, 69.

24. Ignatius of Loyola, *Testament*, ch 3.

25. Referred to in Nesta Webster, *Secret Societies and Subversive Movements, op. cit.*, p125, quoting manuscripts of the Prince of Hesse published by Lecouteulx de Canteleu.

26. For Elizabeth I and Cecil, see Neville Williams, *Elizabeth I*. For Dee, see note 37.

27. Alan Gordon Smith, *William Cecil, the Power behind Elizabeth*, p3.

28. Michael Howard, *The Occult Conspiracy, Secret Societies – Their Influence and Power in World History*, p52.

29. See Michael Baigent, Richard Leigh and Henry Lincoln, *The Holy Blood and the Holy Grail*, p452.

30. Baigent, Leigh and Lincoln, *The Holy Blood and the Holy Grail, op. cit.*, pp39-41. I have brought out the pun of Arques/Arcadia. Also, see note 6.

31. Based on my own research. I have visited the study.

32. Robert Lacey, *Sir Walter Raleigh*, p341.

33. Lacey, *op. cit.*, pp340, 344-5.

34. I researched the European and English voyages during my tenure of Otley Hall.

35. Everett Hale's book, *Prospero's Island*, gives chapter and verse on the link between Gosnold's 1602 voyage and the geography of Shakespeare's *Tempest*. See also Gookin and Barbour, *Bartholomew Gosnold*.

36. Comyns Beaumont, *The Private Life of the Virgin Queen*, p115.

37. From Frederick the Great's *Collected Works*.

38. Peter French, *John Dee, The World of an Elizabethan Magus*, pp31, 195-7.

Chapter Two: The Puritan Revolution

1. For the idea that Britain actually *was* Israel, because the British were descended from the Israelites, and that London was the New Jerusalem, see Adrian Gilbert, *The New Jerusalem*, pp4-5, 45-6 and ch 13 ('The Rise and Fall of British Israel'). Reference to Jewish-style clothes is made in many books.

2. For Tyndale as "arch-heretic", see A. W. Reed, "William Tindale" (sic) in Garvin, *The Great Tudors*, pp119-130. For Niclaes (next paragraph), see *Encyclopaedia Britannica*, "Familists".

3. Diarmaid MacCulloch, *Tudor Church Militant, Edward VI and the Protestant Reformation*, pp14-15, 18. For the rise of Puritanism, see *Encyclopaedia Britannica*, "Protestantism, The Rise of Puritanism".

4. See for example Francis Edwards S. J., *Guy Fawkes: The Real Story of the Gunpowder Plot?*.

5. Quoted in Brinton, *The Anatomy of Revolution*, p61.

6. There are numerous sources for Bacon's belief that the English were Israelites, for example Gilbert, *op. cit.*, pp142-4. In *The New Atlantis* Bacon describes the allegorical island of Bensalem, which means "Son of (Jeru)Salem". Britain, the gathering place of the lost tribes of Israel, was believed to be the son of Jerusalem. The utopia of Bensalem was heavily influenced by the castle at Heidelberg (pp48, 54-5).

7. For all the points in this paragraph, see Howard, *op. cit.*, p48.

8. For all the points in this paragraph see George V. Tudhope, *Bacon Masonry*, pp26, 30-1.

9. Alfred Dodd, *Francis Bacon's Personal Life-Story*, pp140-2.

10. All the points about Frederick V and the rise and decline of Rosicrucianism, Andreae and Fludd, can be found in Frances A. Yates, *The Rosicrucian Enlightenment*.

11. Yates, *The Rosicrucian Enlightenment, op. cit.*, p90.

12. Daniel, *op. cit.*, p683.

13. Wittemans, *Histoire des Rose Croix*, p71, quoted in Lady

Queenborough, *Occult Theocrasy,* p153. For the events in Luther's life, see *Encyclopaedia Britannica,* "Luther".

14. Yates, *The Rosicrucian Enlightenment, op. cit.,* p119.

15. Yates, *The Rosicrucian Enlightenment, op. cit.,* p125.

16. Yates, *The Rosicrucian Enlightenment, op. cit.,* p125.

17. Manly Hall, *The Secret Teachings of All Ages,* ppCXL111-CXL1V.

18. Yates, *The Rosicrucian Enlightenment, op. cit.,* pp103-4.

19. Charlotte Stopes, *The Third Earl of Southampton,* pp361-2.

20. Yates, *The Rosicrucian Enlightenment, op. cit.,* p127.

21. Manly Hall, *The Secret Teachings of All Ages, op. cit.,* p143.

22. Tudhope, *op. cit.,* p32.

23. R. Warwick Bond, *The Complete Works of John Lyly,* p34.

24. Bond, *op. cit.,* pp46, 62.

25. Kate H. Prescott, *Reminiscences of a Baconian,* pp60-61.

26. Tudhope, *op. cit.,* p38.

27. Manly Hall, *The Secret Teachings of All Ages, op. cit.,* p168. Also Tudhope, *op. cit.,* p120.

28. Lady Queenborough, *op. cit.,* pp152-3.

29. Frances Yates, *The Occult Philosophy in the Elizabethan Age,* p181.

30. Christopher Hill, *Milton and the English Revolution,* p146. For the displaced Rosicrucians mentioned in the previous paragraph, see Baigent, Leigh and Lincoln, *The Holy Blood and the Holy Grail, op. cit.,* p147.

31. G. H. Turnbull, *Hartlib, Dury and Comenius,* p74ff. The Latin texts of the two works together with the English translation of them by Hall are printed in G. H. Turnbull's article, "Johann Valentin Andreae's Societas Christiana," Zeitschrift für Deutsch Philologie, 73, 1954, pp407-32; 74, 1955, pp151-85. See also Baigent, Leigh and Lincoln, *The Holy Blood and The Holy Grail, op. cit.,* pp146-7.

32. Margery Purver, *The Royal Society: Concept and Creation,* pp222-3.

33. Keith Feiling, *A History of England,* p454.

34. Charles Webster, *The Great Instauration: Science, Medicine and*

Reform, 1626-1660, p42, referring to *Letters from Pym to Hartlib, 1636-1642*, HP XXXI 3: HDC, p270.

35. H. R. Trevor-Roper, *Religion, the Reformation and Social Change*, p256.

36. G. H. Turnbull, *op. cit.*, pp127ff; Trevor-Roper, *op. cit.* pp251ff.

37. Yates, *The Rosicrucian Enlightenment, op. cit.*, p155.

38. Yates, *The Rosicrucian Enlightenment, op. cit.*, pp169-70.

39. Hill, *Milton and the English Revolution, op. cit.*, pp298-304.

40. For tales of Cromwell's life, see Firth, *Oliver Cromwell and the Rule of the Puritans in England*, and Antonia Fraser *Cromwell, Our Chief of Men*. For details of Charles I's life, see Derek Wilson, *The King and the Gentleman*. For Cromwell's link with Socinianism, see Dillon, *Grand Orient Freemasonry Unmasked*, pp11-13.

41. See Firth, *op. cit.*, pp39 (Cromwell's conversion) and 470-2.

42. J. S. Morrill, *The Nature of the English Revolution*, 1993, pp141-2; quoted in Wilson, *The King and the Gentleman, op. cit.*, p280.

43. Hill, *Milton and the English Revolution, op. cit.*, p283. For Cromwell's membership of the Crown, see Daniel, *op. cit.*, p820, quoting Darrah, *History and Evolution of Freemasonry*, p174.

44. For details of Menasseh's life, see Cecil Roth, *Menasseh ben Israel*, and Hill, *Religion and Politics in 17th-century England*.

45. Hill, *Religion and Politics in 17th-century England, op. cit.*, pp30-33.

46. Roth, *op. cit.*, p66.

47. Ramsay, *op. cit.*, pp13-14.

48. Isaac D'Israeli, *op. cit.*

49. For the Royal Society springing from the Invisible College, see Tudhope, *op. cit.*. p116.

50. Purver, *op. cit.* (The concept recalls Bacon's advancement of learning.)

51. Quoted in Yates, *The Rosicrucian Enlightenment, op. cit.*, p183. For Wilkins' space mission, see the London *Independent on Sunday*, October 10, 2004: "Cromwell's moon shot: how one

Jacobean scientist tried to kick off the space race".

52. Yates, *The Rosicrucian Enlightenment, op.cit.*, p175.

53. H. R. Trevor-Roper, p256.

54. Charles Webster, *op. cit.*, pp57-63.

55. Charles Webster, *op. cit.*, p473.

56. Graham Edwards, *The Last Days of Charles I*, p174. The other three men suspected of being executioners were: Richard Brandon, expert headsman; Hugh Peters, Independent minister of religion; and sergeant William Hulet. John Alured and Phineas Payne boasted of executing Charles in later life but were found to have fabricated the claim.

57. Clements R Markham, *The Fighting Veres*, pp370-5. In the next paragraph for Mulheim's being in the Duchy of Berg, see http://38.1911encyclopedia.org/M/MU/MULHEIM_AN_DE R_RUHR.htm. For Mulheim's being owned by the Palatinate, see http://www.fact-index.com/b/be/berg_german_region_html; also http://www.infoplease.com/ce6/history/A0812557.html.

58. Nesta Webster, *Secret Societies and Subversive Movements, op. cit.*, p126.

59. Roth, *op. cit.*, p188.

60. For example Hollis and Ludlow.

61. R. W. Blencowe (ed), *Sidney Papers*, 1825, p237. Quoted in Fraser, *op. cit.*, p282.

62. *King Charles his Trial at the High Court of Justice,* 2nd edition, London 1650, printed in Dee Lagomarsino and C. T. Wood, *A Documentary History of the Trial of Charles I,* pp138-44.

63. Bishop Juxon was made Archbishop of Canterbury by Charles II and returned the ring. Charles II gave it to his son by Nell Gwyn. It is now in the possession of the Duke of St Albans, who is descended from Nell Gwyn's son.

64. *King Charles his Trial at the High Court of Justice, op. cit.*, pp138-44.

65. Isaac D'Israeli, *op. cit.*, vol. 1, pp vi, 4, vol. 2, pp568-73.

66. From *A Declaration of the Lord Lieutenant of Ireland…in answer*

to certain late Declarations and Acts, framed by the Irish Popish Prelates and Clergy, in a Conventicle at Clonmacnoise, reprinted in *Oliver Cromwell's Letters and Speeches,* edited by Thomas Carlyle, p108.

67. Ludlow, I, p370; C. S. P. Domestic, 1653-4, p297; Abbott, IV, p417. Quoted in Fraser, *op. cit.,* pp448-9.

68. Fraser, *op. cit.,* p558.

69. Roth,, *op. cit.,* p189.

70. Hill, *Religion and Politics in 17th Century England, op. cit.,* p284.

71. For an account of Menasseh's mission to England, see Roth, *op. cit.,* especially p251; and Lucian Wolf (ed), *Menasseh ben Israel's mission to Oliver Cromwell,* 1901, especially pXLVII. For Millenarianism in Cromwell's time, see Hill, *Religion and Politics in 17th Century England, op. cit.,* pp269-292.

72. A fuller account of information in this paragraph and in much of this section can be found in Hill, *Religion and Politics in 17th Century England, op. cit.*

73. G. W. Phillips, *Lord Burghley in Shakespeare,* pp190-5.

74. Menasseh ben Israel, *Humble Addresses,* p75.

75. For a fuller version of the events in this section, see Fraser, *op. cit.,* pp561-6.

76. Roth, *op. cit.,* pxi.

77. C. S. P. Venetian 1655-6, p160. Reported sceptically in a footnote in Fraser, *op. cit.,* p563.

78. Darrah, *History and Evolution of Freemasonry, op. cit.,* p174.

79. Albert G. Mackey, *Mackey's Encyclopedia of Freemasonry,* 5th ed. 3 vols, *op. cit.,* "Cromwell."

80. Lady Queenborough, *op. cit.,* p157.

81. Roy MacGregor-Hastie, *Nell Gwyn,* p121. Marvell/"Mr Thomas" was active in a Dutch-based, anti-French, anti-Catholic fifth column during the war with France from 1672 to 1674. He was in fact a double-agent, as he worked for John Thurloe, then Head of the British Secret Service. The Dutch were a British ally in the war against France. He promoted Dutch interests in

England, and was in touch with Dutch secret agents. He was mentioned by government spies as a member of a Dutch fifth column in England. See http://www.cichw.net/pmarvel.html.

Chapter Three: The Glorious Revolution

1. For details of the return of Charles II, see Arthur Bryant, *King Charles II*, ch 3.
2. Bryant, *op. cit.*, p77.
3. Tudhope, *op. cit.*, p117.
4. For details of the life of Charles II and Shaftesbury, see Christopher Falkus, *The Life and Times of Charles II*. For the events in Shaftesbury's life, see *Encyclopaedia Britannica*, "Shaftesbury, 1st earl of".
5. Quoted in David S. Katz *The Jews in the History of England, 1485-1850*, p143.
6. Kanoop, Jones and Hammer, *Early Masonic Pamphlets*, Manchester 1945, p31; quoted in Yates, *The Rosicrucian Enlightenment, op. cit.*, p211.
7. North, *Examen*, p95; quoted in Francis S. Ronalds, *The Attempted Whig Revolution of 1678-1681*, p75.
8. Howell, *State Trials* Vol IX, p490; Ralph, *History of England*, vol I, p539; quoted in Ronalds, *op. cit.*, p75.
9. The two quotations in this paragraph are quoted in Falkus, *op. cit.*, p180.
10. For details of Monmouth's life, see David G. Chandler, *Sedgemoor 1685*.
11. Sloane Manuscripts. 4194, f.404 (British Library). Quoted on p81 of Chandler, *op. cit.*, which gives a full account of Monmouth's end.
12. W. Turner, *James II*, London, p279; quoted in Chandler, *op. cit.*, p81.

13.   For the events of William III's life, see *Enclyclopaedia Britannica*, "William III" and John Miller, *The Life and Times of William and Mary*. Also see *Enclyclopaedia Britannica*, "William I the Silent, Prince of Orange".

14.   C. V. Wedgewood, *William the Silent*.

15.   Katz, *op. cit.*, p157. For de Witt, see *Enclyclopaedia Britannica*, "Witt, Johan de".

16.   Quoted in Miller, *op. cit.*, p85.

17.   Miller, *op. cit.*, p85.

18.   Quoted in Miller, *op. cit.*, p95.

19.   For Solomon Medina, Machado and Pereira, see the entry in *The Jewish Encyclopaedia* under "Medina."

20.   Quoted in Katz, *op. cit.*, p157.

21.   Nesta Webster, *Secret Societies and Subversive Movements, op. cit.*, pp179-80.

22.   Stephen Knight, *The Brotherhood*, pp21-2.

23.   Quoted in Miller, *op. cit.*, p95.

24.   Evelyn, *Diary*, v.25/6 (June 18, 1690); quoted in Katz, *op. cit.*, pp173-4. For the two treatises in the previous paragraph, see Baigent, Leigh and Lincoln, *The Holy Blood and the Holy Grail, op. cit.*, pp453-5.

25.   Eustace Budgell, *Memoirs of the Lives and Characters of the Illustrious Family of the Boyles*, London, 1737, p25; quoted in Katz, *op. cit.*, p174.

26.   Katz, *op. cit.*, pp158-161. See also Mullins, *The World Order, Our Secret Rulers*, p28.

27.   For a full account of the Battle of the Boyne, see John Kinross, *The Boyne and Aughrim*.

28.   Des Griffin, *Fourth Reich of the Rich*, p177, which quotes Christopher Hollis, *The Breakdown of Money* on the £1.2m offered by a group of men under the leadership of William Paterson. See Gerry Rough,
       http://www.floodlight.org/theory/bofe3.html for the view that only £720,000 was actually invested. Also see Mullins, *op. cit.*,

pp28-31, which explains that William's granting of the Charter of the Bank of England in 1694 was presented as part of the Tonnage Act. The shareholders of the Bank of England were "a Society of about 1,300 persons," and Mullins details the Spanish and Portuguese Jews who bought stock: Medina, two Da Costas, Fonseca, Henriquz, Mendez, Nunes, Roderiquez, Salvador Teixera de Mattos, Jacob and Theodore Jacobs, Moses and Jacob Abrabanel, and Francis Pereira.

29. Mullins, *op. cit.*, pp28, 31.

30. Mullins, *op. cit.*, pp29-31. For the events of Locke's life in this chapter, see *Enclyclopaedia Britannica*, "Locke".

31. Baigent, Leigh and Lincoln, *The Holy Blood and the Holy Grail, op. cit.*, p456.

32. Baigent, Leigh and Lincoln, *The Holy Blood and the Holy Grail, op. cit.*, p457.

33. Ramsay, *op. cit.*, pp18-19.

34. For Leibniz's role in the succession of the Hanoverians to the English throne, see Mullins, *op. cit.*, p27; and H. Graham Lowry, "How the Venetian Virus Infected and Took Over England," Executive Intelligence Review, April 15, 1994, which can be found   in http://members.tripod.com/~american_almanac/venlowry.htm. See Appendices C. For the events in Leibniz's life, see *Enclyclopaedia Britannica*, "Leibniz". For a full account of the connection between Leibniz and the House of Brunswick, see "The House of Brunswick, The Leibniz Connection", http://www.hfac.uh.edu/gbrown/philosophers/leibniz/Brunswic k/LeibnizConnection.h...

35. L. Couturat, *La Logique de Leibniz*, Hildesheim, 1961; quoted in Yates, *The Rosicrucian Enlightenment, op. cit.*, ch 11; Mullins, *op. cit.*, p27: "Her (Sophie's) son, now Elector of Hanover, was able to overcome the other claimants because of Leibniz's carefully documented reports. Leibniz not only brought the Hanovers to England, but also Freemasonry. His Rosicrucian

connections...placed a Freemason on the throne of England. Taking the name of George I, Hanover spoke no English, and indignantly refused to learn the language of his new domain."

36.   See Mullins, *op. cit.*, p27, for Leibniz's role in the Act of Settlement of 1701 and the Hanoverian succession (previous two paragraphs). Also *Encyclopaedia Britannica*, macropaedia entry for "Leibniz", which says coyly: "It fell to Leibniz, jurist and historian, to develop his arguments concerning the rights of the House of Braunschweig-Lüneburg with respect to this succession." The truth was, Leibniz spent twenty years in documenting the claim of the Brunswick family, which befriended him in 1676 – the first contact was actually in 1669 – and employed him from 1685. It was a German *coup* – as George I spoke no English. Having put George I on the throne, Leibniz petitioned him through Caroline and the Hanoverian Prime Minister, seeking to become historiographer of England on the grounds that his history of the House of Brunswick required him to take account of the history of England. George I refused to invite Leibniz to England.

37.   Nesta Webster, *Secret Societies and Subversive Movements, op. cit.*, p123.

PART TWO:
TOWARDS A UNIVERSAL REPUBLIC

Chapter Four: The American Revolution

1.   For the link between Freemasons and the Boston Tea Party see Michael Baigent and Richard Leigh, *The Temple and the Lodge*, pp221-5 and Daniel, *op. cit.*, pp688-9.

2.   See Baigent and Leigh, *The Temple and the Lodge, op. cit.*, p287 for a list of participants in the Tea Party who were also members of St. Andrew's Lodge.

3.   Tudhope, *op. cit.*, p26.

4.   Manly Hall, *The Secret Teachings of All Ages*, p10.

5.   Manly Hall, *The Adepts in the Western Esoteric Tradition*, pp59-60.

6.   William Strachey, *The Historie of Travel into Virginia Britania*, ed. L.B. Wright and Virginia Freund, Hakluyt Society, pp150-1.

7.   Daniel, *op. cit.*, pp32-3, 89-90.

8.   Daniel, *op. cit.*, pp32, 90.

9.   Daniel, *op. cit.*, p90.

10.   MacCulloch, *op. cit.*, p14.

11.   It has been suggested that the twenty men, and another 500 during the next few years, died as a result of poisoning by arsenic, which was used in small quantities to purify water. It is possible that the Templar faction wiped out the non-Templars.

12.   Daniel, *op. cit.*, p136.

13.   For details of the life of Charles Radclyffe, see Baigent, Leigh and Lincoln, *The Holy Blood and the Holy Grail, op. cit.*, pp148-154; also Daniel, *op. cit.*, pp135-42, and Baigent and Leigh, *The Temple and the Lodge, op. cit.*, chs 12 and 13. For Radclyffe's blood link with Charles II (end of paragraph), see Baigent, Leigh and Lincoln, *The Holy Blood and the Holy Grail, op. cit.*, p148.

14. Daniel, *op. cit.*, p137.

15. See Baigent, Leigh and Lincoln, *The Holy Blood and the Holy Grail, op. cit.*, pp149-154. For details of Radclyffe and Hund, see Daniel, *op. cit.*, pp138-9.

16. Baigent, Leigh and Lincoln, *The Holy Blood and the Holy Grail, op. cit.*, p149.

17. Daniel, *op. cit.*, p142.

18. Daniel, *op. cit.*, p142.

19. Daniel, *op. cit.*, p143.

20. Baigent, Leigh and Lincoln, *The Holy Blood and the Holy Grail, op. cit.*, p150.

21. Daniel, *op. cit.*, p144 for all the points in this paragraph.

22. Daniel, *op. cit.*, p149. For details of Weishaupt's work, see Daniel, *op. cit.*, pp145-52; David Allen Rivera, *Final Warning, A History of the New World Order*, ch 1; Nesta Webster, *World Revolution*, ch 1; Howard, *op. cit.*, pp61-4.

23. Rivera, *op. cit.*, p6. For the origin of May-day, see Daniel, *op. cit.*, p161.

24. Salem Kirban, *Satan's Angels Exposed*. Also Nesta Webster, *World Revolution, op. cit.*, p22.

25. Daniel, *op. cit.*, p146, pp79-80.

26. Daniel, *op. cit.*, p149.

27. Daniel, *op. cit.*, pp149-151.

28. Daniel, *op. cit.*, pp146-147.

29. Daniel, *op. cit.*, pp162-3.

30. Daniel, *op. cit.*, p162.

31. Daniel, *op. cit.*, p684.

32. Daniel, *op. cit.*, p684.

33. Baigent and Leigh, *The Temple and the Lodge, op. cit.*, pp202, 233; and Daniel, *op. cit.*, p686.

34. For more information on the Anglo-Iroquois Alliance and Franklin's Plan of Union, see Robert Hieronimus, *America's Secret Destiny*, pp7-13.

35. A. Kennedy, *The Importance of Gaining and Preserving the*

Friendship of the Indians to the British Interest Considered, New York, 1751; quoted in Hieronimus, *op. cit.,* p11.

36. Daniel, *op. cit.,* p167.
37. Daniel, *op. cit.,* p167.
38. Daniel, *op. cit.,* pp686-7.
39. Daniel, *op. cit.,* pp687-8.
40. Daniel, *op. cit.,* p688.
41. Baigent and Leigh, *The Temple and the Lodge, op. cit.,* p233 and Daniel, *op. cit.,* pp688-9.
42. For details of the Tea Party, see Baigent and Leigh, *The Temple and the Lodge, op. cit.,* pp223-5; and Charles Bahne, *The Complete Guide to Boston's Freedom Trail.*
43. Barros, *Discover-It-Yourself Guide to Boston's Freedom Trail,* p31.
44. Quoted in Bahne, *op. cit.,* p24.
45. Baigent and Leigh, *The Temple and the Lodge, op. cit.,* pp224.
46. Bahne, *op. cit.,* p25.
47. Bahne, *op. cit.,* p25.
48. *The History of the American Revolution,* p3; and Daniel, *op. cit.,* p689.
49. Daniel, *op. cit.,* p689.
50. Daniel, *op. cit.,* p689.
51. John Adams spoke in the Assembly Room of the State House.
52. *The History of the American Revolution, op. cit.,* pp4-5.
53. Daniel, *op. cit.,* pp686 and 166.
54. Kinbrough, *Four Americans in Paris.*
55. Daniel, *op. cit.,* p688.
56. Still, *New World Order: The Ancient Plan of Secret Societies,* p60; also see Roberts, *G. Washington – Master Mason.*
57. Daniel, *op. cit.,* p692.
58. All three extracts from Washington's letters to Snyder are quoted in Still, *op. cit.,* pp60-1.
59. See *The History of the American Revolution* for a summary of Washington's military campaigns and also Baigent and Leigh, *The Temple and the Lodge, op. cit.,* ch 15.

60. See *A Letter from Cicero to the Right Hon. Lord Viscount Howe*, London, 1781; quoted in Baigent and Leigh, *The Temple and the Lodge, op. cit.*, p236.

61. Raymond E. Capt, *Our Great Seal: The Symbols of our Heritage and our Destiny*, p11; quoted in Daniel, *op. cit.*, p708.

62. For details regarding the choosing and creation of the Great Seal in this paragraph and in the ensuing four paragraphs, see Capt, *op. cit.*; Hieronimus, *op. cit.*, pp48-56 and 63-92; Daniel, *op. cit.*, p709 and Still, *op. cit.*, pp65-8.

63. William Guy Carr, *The Conspiracy to Destroy all Existing Governments and Religions*, pXIII.

64. Still, *op. cit.*, p41; Daniel, *op. cit.*, p679.

65. Daniel, *op. cit.*, pp167-8, 684-5.

66. Daniel, *op. cit.*, p708.

67. Still, *op. cit.*, p65; Daniel, *op. cit.*, p713.

68. Hieronimus, *op. cit.*, pp48-56; Daniel, *op. cit.*, p709.

69. Daniel, *op. cit.*, pp166, 688.

70. Hieronimus, *op. cit.*, p39. See fig 6 in Hieronimus for an illustration of this Rosicrucian code.

71. Daniel, *op. cit.*, pp165-6.

72. V. Stauffer, *New England and the Bavarian Illuminati*, p312.

73. Quoted in Hieronimus, *op. cit.*, p38.

74. Paul Bessel maintains that only nine of the 56 who signed the Declaration of Independence were Freemasons, and that only 13 of the 39 who signed the US Constitution were Freemasons. See: http://bessel.org/declmas.htm. Bessel is a Masonic source, but Baigent and Leigh in *The Temple and the Lodge, op. cit.*, p219, support this view. Still, *op. cit.*, p61, states that 53 of the 56 who signed the Declaration of Independence were Freemasons according to the 1951 Masonic edition of the *Holy Bible*. For fuller details, see ch 4, note 2 in Hagger, *The Syndicate*.

75. For Washington and the Constitutional Convention, see Baigent and Leigh, *The Temple and the Lodge, op. cit.*, p256-8; and Morris, *The Framing of the Federal Constitution*, p6ff.

76. H. C. Clausen, *Masons Who Helped Shape Our Nation*.

77. Edward Decker, *Freemasonry: Satan's Door to America*; quoted in Daniel, *op. cit.*, p707.

78. Baigent and Leigh, *The Temple and the Lodge, op. cit.*, p262.

79. This paragraph is based on books on Monticello on sale at the house.

80. Barry Schwartz, *George Washington, The Making of an American Symbol*, pp172-3; which draws on Mason L. Weems, *A History of the Life and Death, Virtues and Exploits of General George Washington*, pp14, 15, 60, 61, 66.

81. Schwartz, *op. cit.*, pp79-80.

82. For a full account of Andrew Jackson see, Kierner, *Revolutionary America 1750-1815*, pp273-285. For a fuller account of Andrew Jackson's activities, see Paul Johnson, *A History of the American People*, pp273-285.

Chapter Five: The French Revolution

1. The Abbé Edgeworth de Firmont, *The Last Hours of Louis XVI, King of France*, published in Cléry, *A Journal of the Terror*.

2. See Henri Gaston Gouhier *Les Premières Pensées de* Descartes, 1958, for the material on Descartes' journal, or notebook. Gouhier does not reveal where he acquired the journal, or its present location. See Gary L. Stewart, *Awakened Attitude*, on Rosicrucian Library website, http://www.crcsite.org/affiliation.htm, paragraphs 8-12, which cites Nicolaes Wassenar and Charles Adam, the French historian, as believing that Descartes was a Rosicrucian, but holds that although Descartes was preoccupied with Rosicrucianism at an early age and was surrounded by many Rosicrucians, there is no final evidence for his Rosicrucian allegiance.

3. See *Encyclopaedia Britannica*, "Diderot", for the Panier Fleuri.

Nesta Webster, *Secret Societies and Subversive Movements, op. cit.*, p162.

4. For the events in Rousseau's life, see *Encyclopaedia* Britannica, "Rousseau". Compare Nesta Webster, *World Revolution, op. cit.* pp1-2.

5. Still, *op. cit.*, p69: "Weishaupt adopted the teachings of radical French philosophers such as Jean-Jacques Rousseau."

6. Nesta Webster, *World Revolution, op. cit.* p1.

7. Howard, *op. cit.*, p61.

8. For details of Weishaupt's life, see Daniel, *op. cit.*, pp145-151; Rivera, *op. cit.*, pp5-9; Nesta Webster, *World Revolution, op. cit.*, p8ff; Still, *op. cit.*, pp69-82; Howard, *op. cit.*, pp61-4.

9. Rivera, *op. cit.*, p5.

10. Carr, *The Conspiracy to Destroy all Existing Governments and Religions, op. cit.*, p1.

11. Neal Wilgus, *The Illuminoids*, p154.

12. Howard, *op. cit.*, p63.

13. Nesta Webster, *World Revolution, op. cit.*, p11. For the Persian calendar, see Nesta Webster, *Secret Societies and Subversive Movements, op. cit.*, p201.

14. Nesta Webster, *World Revolution, op. cit.*, pp1-2.

15. Weishaupt, *Nachtrag…Originalschriften (des Illuminaten Ordens)*, Zweit Abtheilung, p65; quoted in Nesta Webster, *World Revolution op. cit.*, p10.

16. See Nesta Webster, *World Revolution, op. cit.*, p22.

17. Nesta Webster, *World Revolution, op. cit.*, p17; Daniel, *op. cit.*, p148.

18. Nesta Webster, *World Revolution, op. cit.*, p17; Rivera, *op. cit.*, p7.

19. John Robison, *Proofs of a Conspiracy*, p112.

20. Rivera, *op. cit.*, p7.

21. Rivera, *op. cit.*, p8.

22. Rivera, *op. cit.*, p8.

23. Nesta Webster, *World Revolution, op. cit.*, p16.

24. Rivera, *op. cit.*, p8.

25.   Rivera, *op. cit.*, p8.

26.   Rivera, *op. cit.*, pp6-7.

27.   Nesta Webster, *World Revolution, op. cit.*, p15.

28.   Nesta Webster, *World Revolution, op. cit.*, p16.

29.   Rivera, *op. cit.*, pp8-9.

30.   Rivera, *op. cit.*, p9.

31.   Baigent, Leigh and Lincoln, *The Holy Blood and the Holy Grail,*
      op. cit., p72: "The Templar treasure may have been loaded into
      eighteen galleys at the Templar naval base at La Rochelle, whence
      it reached Scotland." Also Sinclair, *The Sword and the Grail,* p42.
      For the Templar treasure being put aboard ship at La Rochelle, see
      http://home.gwi.net/ages/Main%20Body/History/Templar%20
      Origins.html; and
      http://www.electricscotland.com/history/kt12.htm.

32.   Albert Pike, *Morals and Dogma, of the Ancient and Accepted*
      Scottish Rite of Freemasonry, pp821, 823-4.

33.   Nesta Webster, *Secret Societies and Subversive Movements, op.cit.*,
      pp132-3.

34.   Dillon, *op. cit.,* p19. For the conversion of French Freemasonry
      into Grand Orient Freemasonry, see Ramsay, *op. cit,* p26.

35.   Saint-Martin, *Des Erreurs et de la Vérité,* 1775, *op. cit.*

36.   Nesta Webster, *World Revolution, op.cit.*, p7.

37.   Rivera, *op. cit.*, p9; Nesta Webster, *World Revolution, op. cit.*, p18-
      19.

38.   Rivera, *op. cit.*, p9.

39.   Daniel, *op. cit.*, pp147, 162.

40.   Nesta Webster, *World Revolution, op. cit.*, p31; also Ramsay, *op.*
      cit., p27.

41.   For Necker's dismissal, see Brinton, *op. cit.*, pp77, 85, 87.
      Encylopedia Britannica, "History of France".

42.   Daniel, *op. cit.*, p150.

43.   Rivera, *op. cit.*, p10.

44.   Nesta Webster, *Secret Societies and Subversive Movements, op.cit.*,
      p233.

45.   Daniel, *op. cit.*, pp151, 187-8.

46.   Daniel, *op. cit.*, pp262-3, 264-5.

47.   Daniel, *op. cit.*, p263.

48.   For the episode of the necklace, see Nesta Webster, *Secret Societies and Subversive Movements, op.cit.*, pp234-5; Howard, *op. cit.*, pp65-6; Daniel, *op. cit.*, p265; and Ramsay, *op. cit.*, p29.

49.   Nesta Webster, *Secret Societies and Subversive Movements, op.cit.*, p235; Daniel, *op. cit.*, pp265-6.

50.   Nesta Webster, *Secret Societies and Subversive Movements, op.cit.*, p235; Daniel, *op. cit.*, pp263-4.

51.   Rivera, *op. cit.*, pp20-1.

52.   Daniel, *op. cit.*, p264.

53.   Daniel, *op. cit.*, p266.

54.   Daniel, *op. cit.*, pp266, 269.

55.   Rivera, *op. cit.*, p22.

56.   Howard, *op. cit.*, p69.

57.   Dillon, *op. cit.*, p46.

58.   Nesta Webster, *World Revolution, op. cit.*, p20.

59.   Daniel, *op. cit.*, p190.

60.   Daniel, *op. cit.*, pp190-1, 195.

61.   *Encyclopaedia Britannica*, "Mirabeau"; Nesta Webster, *World Revolution, op. cit.*, pp27-8; Nesta Webster, *Secret Societies and Subversive Movements, op.cit.*, pp236-7; and Rivera, *op. cit.*, pp23-4.

62.   Daniel, *op. cit.*, pp195-6; Billington *Fire in the Minds of Men: Origins of the Revolutionary Faith*, p96.

63.   Barruel, quoted in Frost, *Secret Societies of the European Revolution*; quoted in Nesta Webster, *World Revolution, op. cit.*, p28.

64.   Daniel, *op. cit.*, pp260-1.

65.   Nesta Webster, *World Revolution, op. cit.*, pp30-2; *Encyclopaedia Britannica*, "Orléans".

66.   *Encyclopaedia Britannica*, "History of France".

67.   Brinton, *op. cit.*, pp70-1.

68. *Encyclopaedia Britannica*, "France"; *Encyclopaedia Britannica*, "History of France".

69. Billington, *op. cit.*, pp26, 42, 96-7.

70. *Encyclopaedia Britannica*, "History of France"; *Encyclopaedia Britannica*, "France".

71. Nesta Webster, *World Revolution, op. cit.*, pp31-2.

72. Nesta Webster, *World Revolution, op. cit.*, p32; *Encyclopaedia Britannica*, "History of France".

73. For the conflicting accounts regarding the beheading of the two guardsmen, see Steven Blakemore and Fred Hembree, *Historian*, spring 2001, http://www.findarticles.com/p/articles/mi_m2082/is_3_63/ai_75162013/pg_2. Guidebook to Versailles; Levy, *Legacy of Death*.

74. *Encyclopaedia Britannica*, "Jacobin Club"; Rivera, *op. cit.*, p24; Daniel, op. cit., p292.

75. Billington, op. cit., p35.

76. Billington, op. cit., p35, 104, 116.

77. Billington, op. cit., p79, 85, 103.

78. *Encyclopaedia Britannica*, "History of France".

79. *Encyclopaedia Britannica*, "Mirabeau". For the alleged poisoning of Mirabeau, see Ramsay, *op. cit.*, p31.

80. *Encyclopaedia Britannica*, "History of France"; Levy, *op. cit.*

81. Rivera, *op. cit.*, p5 and p24: "Robespierre…was made head of the Revolution by Weishaupt."

82. Easton, *op. cit.*, pp282-3; *Encyclopaedia Britannica*, "History of France".

83. *Encyclopaedia Britannica*, "History of France".

84. See John Hardman, *Louis XVI*, for more details about Louis and Marie-Antoinette during the Girondist time and for the events that culminated in the overthrow of the monarchy on August 10 and the months leading up to Louis XVI's trial. Also see Levy, *op. cit.*

85. Nesta Webster, *World Revolution, op. cit.*, p34; Daniel, *op. cit.*, p292.

86. Nesta Webster, *World Revolution, op. cit.*, p35.

87. Thomas Carlyle, *The French Revolution*, vol II, p118.

88. Jean-Baptiste Cléry, *A Journal of the Terror*.

89. The Abbé Edgeworth de Firmont, *op. cit.*

90. Levy, *op. cit.*, pp115-6. The remaining quotations in this section come from this work.

91. Baigent, Leigh and Lincoln, *The Holy Bood and the Holy Grail*, *op. cit.*, p77; Daniel, *op. cit.*, p292.

92. See *Encyclopaedia Britannica*, "Robespierre" for the third, Jacobin revolution.

93. See Nesta Webster, *World Revolution*, *op. cit.*, pp45-6 for the depopulation figures. According to Webster, serious consideration was given by Dubois Crancé to reducing the French population to 14m.

94. *Encyclopaedia Britannica*, "French Revolution, war, regicide, and the Reign of Terror".

95. Nesta Webster, *World Revolution*, *op. cit.*, p35; *Encyclopaedia Britannica*, "History of France". For the Feasts of Reason, see Still, *op. cit.*, p87.

96. *Encyclopaedia Britannica*, "History of France". For the figure of 17,000, see *Encyclopaedia Britannica*, "French Revolution, war, regicide, and the Reign of Terror".

97. *Encyclopaedia Britannica*, "Robespierre".

98. *Encyclopaedia Britannica*, "History of France".

99. Nesta Webster, *World Revolution*, *op. cit.*, p47, quoting Prudhomme, *Crimes de la Révolution*, vol. vi, Table VI.

100. *Encyclopaedia Britannica*, "Paine".

101. For the story of Babeuf's "Conspiracy of the Equals", see Nesta Webster, *World Revolution*, *op. cit.*, pp52-72.

102. For Babeuf's Weishauptian link, see Nesta Webster, *World Revolution*, *op. cit.*, pp55-6.

103. For the march and executions, see Nesta Webster, *World Revolution*, *op. cit.*, pp67-72.

104. Daniel, *op. cit.*, p304.

105. Dillon, *op. cit.*, pp34-5.

106. Daniel, *op. cit.*, p305.

107. Daniel, *op. cit.*, p305.

108. For this paragraph and the next two paragraphs see Daniel, *op. cit.*, pp306-10.

109. See Baigent, Leigh and Lincoln, *The Holy Blood and the Holy Grail, op. cit.*, p157: there were at least three groups called Philadelphes – one which may have been founded in Narbonne in 1780; another Nodier created in 1793; and a third one founded in 1797.

110. Daniel, *op. cit.*, pp306-7.

111. Daniel, *op. cit.*, p307.

112. Rivera, *op. cit.*, p25.

113. Easton, *op. cit.*, pp284-5; and events in this paragraph and in the next two paragraphs can be found in *Encyclopaedia Britannica*, "Napoleon".

114. Daniel, *op. cit.*, p307, quoting Dillon, *op. cit.*, pp35, 38.

115. Daniel, *op. cit.*, p307.

116. Daniel, *op. cit.*, p307.

117. Daniel, *op. cit.*, p307.

118. Daniel, *op. cit.*, p307.

119. Easton, *op. cit.*, pp289-90.

120. Daniel, *op. cit.*, p308. For the figure of 500,000, see *Encyclopaedia Britannica*, "French revolutionary and Napoleonic wars".

121. Daniel, *op. cit.*, p308.

122. Daniel, *op. cit.*, p308. See *Encyclopaedia Britannica*, "French revolutionary and Napoleonic wars" for Napoleon's 500,000 men in -35° Centigrade.

123. Daniel, *op. cit.*, pp308, 311.

124. For the events in this paragraph and in the next two paragraphs, see Daniel, *op. cit.*, pp311-2. Also see Hagger, *The Syndicate*, pp7-10.

125. Daniel, *op. cit.*, p312.

126. Daniel, *op. cit.*, p313.

127. Daniel, *op. cit.*, pp315-7, 322-3.

128. Daniel, *op. cit.*, pp317, 321, 324-5. See also, for the Congress of Vienna, Easton, *op. cit.*, pp305-7 and 310-1.
See Daniel, *op. cit.*, p317 for the countries involved in Metternich's plan (Sweden, Denmark etc.), which were all monarchies.

129. Daniel, *op. cit.*, p325.

Chapter Six: The Imperialist Revolution in Britain and Germany

1. For the origins of the Rothschilds, see Derek Wilson, *Rothschild, A Story of Wealth and Power*, pp9-33; Frederick Morton, *The Rothschilds*, pp17-36; Count Egon Caesar Corti, *The Rise of the House of Rothschild*, pp1-26; George Armstrong, *The Rothschild Money Trust*, pp21-2; and Niall Ferguson, *The World's Banker, The History of the House of Rothschild*.

2. Carr, *op. cit.*, p1. See also Hagger, *The Syndicate, op. cit.*, ch 2.

3. Wilgus, *op. cit.*, p154. See also Hagger, *The Syndicate, op. cit.*, ch 2.

4. Many sources, for example Rivera, *op. cit.*, p6.

5. Many sources, for example Daniel, *op. cit.*, p198.

6. Armstrong, *op. cit.*, p21; Wilson, *Rothschild, A Story of Wealth and Power, op. cit.*, p32.

7. Daniel, *op. cit.*, p198. Napoleon insisted on applying to the Jews of Frankfurt the full freedom guaranteed by the Code of Napoleon, and this goodwill towards Jews was because "history reveals that Rothschild loaned money to both sides" (Daniel). Daniel says that Napoleon made the first advance and that Rothschild responded to save Jewish lives in Frankfurt.

8. Nathan Mayer Rothschild was initiated into Freemasonry in Emulation Lodge, No. 12, London, on October 24, 1802 – see

Daniel, *op. cit.*, p199. James was a 33rd degree Mason – see Daniel, *op. cit.*, p312. Napoleon was a Templar Jacobin in the Strassburg Lodge by March 1807, when he was toasted as "brother" – see Daniel, *op. cit.*, p305. The Templars had brought Napoleon to power – see Daniel, *op. cit.*, p306. Freemasonry was on Napoleon's side until 1810 – see Daniel, *op. cit.*, p307. All these connections would have made it relatively simple for Metternich, a Freemason, to introduce James Rothschild to Napoleon.

9.   *The Jewish Encyclopedia.*

10.   Soult was Napoleon's chief of staff at Waterloo. In 1808 he was put in charge of all French armies involved in the Peninsular War (1808-14) in Spain, where he opposed the English under Arthur Wellesley (later Duke of Wellington). Wellesley defeated him at Toulouse in April 1814. Napoleon made two major blunders at Waterloo. He delayed his opening attack on Wellington from morning until midday to allow the ground to dry. This delay gave Blücher's Prussian troops time to reach Waterloo in support of Wellington. Around 6 p.m. Marshal Ney requested reinforcements. The request was refused because Napoleon was preoccupied with the Prussian flank attack. Napoleon released reinforcements after 7 p.m., by which time Wellington had reorganized his defences. Both Sion and the English Rothschilds had opposed Napoleon, and Charles Nodier was involved in two separate plots against him in 1804 and again in 1812. Sion wanted to depose Napoleon from around 1810. That did not stop James Rothschild from funding Napoleon and James Rothschild's links with Marshal Soult – Soult took orders from Rothschild in the sense that James Rothschild was Napoleon's funder and presumably had a say in how his money was spent – may have contributed to the perpetrating of deliberate blunders at the battle of Waterloo. With the stock market crashing in London, and a fortune to be made, it would make sense from the Rothschilds' point of view to fix the result of Waterloo in

advance, by fixing Soult.

11. Armstrong, *op. cit.*, p24.

12. Ferguson, *op. cit.*, pp78-9.

13. Rivera, *op. cit.*, p11.

14. For Metternich as a Rothschilds agent, see Rivera, *op. cit.*, p31 and Daniel, *op. cit.*, pp322-3. Metternich was regarded as the organizer of Napoleon's expulsion to Corsica by putting together an alliance of Russia, Prussia, Austria and Great Britain. His plan for a United Federation of Europe anticipated the European Union, a long-held Rothschild aspiration. It is possible that Metternich's plan implemented a Rothschild idea. Nathan Rothschild did not attend the Congress of Vienna, which led Corti to write (pp149-150): "There is no proof that Rothschild had any particular influence with the minister (i.e. Metternich) at that time." Many have thought otherwise – both the Rothschilds and Metternich were Sionists, and the S. M. von Rothschild bank in Austria funded Metternich. Salomon was known as the "Emperor of Austria". See Wilson, *Rothschild, A Story of Wealth and Power, op. cit.*, p77 for the close bond between Salomon and Metternich, the most powerful man in Europe.

15. Rivera, *op. cit.*, p31. See Daniel, *op. cit.*, p474 for Sionists wanting revenge against Russia, and in particular the unco-operative Romanovs (who were not of Merovingian blood) for torpedoing the Metternich Plan for a monarchical United Federation of Europe at the Congress of Vienna.

16. Wilson, *Rothschild, A Story of Wealth and Power, op. cit.*, p55.

17. Daniel, *op. cit.*, p327.

18. Armstrong, *op. cit.*, p35. Also see Hagger, *The Syndicate, op. cit..* ch 2.

19. See Ferguson, *op. cit.,* p103.

20. Rivera, *op. cit.*, p11.

21. Quoted in Wilson, *Rothschild, A Story of Wealth and Power,* citing E. Corti, *The Rise of the House of Rothschild,* trans. Brian and Beatrix Lunn, I, 1928, p458.

22. Ferguson, *op. cit.*, p1035.

23. Daniel, *op. cit.*, pp308-14 (on Rothschilds' alliance with Sion) and 327 (on Louis XVIII's alliance with the Templar Grand Orient).

24. *Encyclopaedia Britannica*, "France, The Revolution of 1830"; and Wilson, *Rothschild, A Story of Wealth and Power, op. cit.*, pp97-8. For the Industrial Revolution, see Easton, *op. cit.*, pp295-302.

25. Daniel, *op. cit.*, pp328-9. For the links between the five brothers in the next paragraph, see Morton, *op. cit.*, pp104-5.

26. Wilson, *Rothschild, A Story of Wealth and Power, op. cit.*, pp128-132.

27. See A. N. Whitehead, *Science and the Modern World*, ch 5, "The Romantic Reaction," for the link between Wordsworth and Shelley and scientific materialism.

28. Rivera, *op. cit.*, p33.

29. Daniel, *op. cit.*, pp329-330, 331-2.

30. Daniel, *op. cit.*, pp330-1.

31. Daniel, *op. cit.*, p331.

32. Daniel, *op. cit.*, p32.

33. Daniel, *op. cit.*, p336.

34. Rivera, *op. cit.*, p33.

35. Rivera, *op. cit.*, p34. Internet version: http://user.pa.net/~drivera/fw7.htm. Rivera speaks of "Nathan" – obviously not the Nathan who died in 1836, but possibly a Nathaniel (Nathan for short). The checks may have been signed by N. M. Rothschild, i.e. by the firm. However, the British Museum archivist Gary Thorn was not aware of their existence in 2004. Compare ch 3, note 11 in Hagger, *The Syndicate*.

36. Daniel, *op. cit.*, p336.

37. *Encyclopaedia Britannica*, "France, The Revolution of 1848".

38. *Encyclopaedia Britannica*, "France, The Second Republic, 1848-52".

39. Nesta Webster, *World Revolution, op. cit.*, p155; Daniel, *op. cit.*, p336.

40. *Encyclopaedia Britannica,* "Italy and Sicily, History of" and "Austria".

41. *Encyclopaedia Britannica,* "Germany" and "Austria".

42. *Encyclopaedia Britannica,* "Italy and Sicily" and "Austria".

43. Daniel, *op. cit.,* p337.

44. Daniel, *op. cit.,* pp332-3.

45. Dillon, *op. cit.,* pp71-88.

46. See Nesta Webster, *World Revolution, op. cit.,* pp86-7 for Alta Vendita and Nubius and the facts in this paragraph. Also, Still, *op. cit.,* pp120-121.

47. Dillon, *op. cit.,* p84; Daniel, *op. cit.,* pp447-8.

48. Jewish Encyclopedia, quoted in Armstrong, *op. cit.,* p28. For Rothschilds' "near monopoly" over British war finance, see Ferguson, *op. cit.,* pp582-3.

49. Daniel, *op. cit.,* p334.

50. Daniel, *op. cit.,* p448.

51. See W. R. Thompson, Introduction to *On the Origin of the Species,* 6th edition.

52. *Encyclopaedia Britannica,* "Darwin": "The first edition sold out immediately." For the selling out of Charles Darwin's book on the first day of publication, see http://www.amazon.com/exec/obidos/tg/detail/-/0517123207/103-2030278-8347854?v=glance. The alleged purchase by the Illuminati/"Young" groups is referred to in several sources encountered by the author in the course of his research. For the link between Small and Erasmus Darwin, see http://www.tribwatch.com/utopia.htm.

53. Daniel, *op. cit.,* p448.

54. Rivera, *op. cit.,* pp39-40.

55. Rivera, *op. cit.,* p40.

56. Rivera, *op. cit.,* p41.

57. Rivera, *op. cit.,* p41.

58. Daniel, *op. cit.,* p387.

59. Rivera, *op. cit.,* p41.

60.   Rivera, *op. cit.*, pp41-2.

61.   Rivera, *op. cit.*, p43.

62.   See Hagger, *The Syndicate, op. cit.*

63.   Daniel, *op. cit.*, pp449, 448.

64.   Author's research for *Overlord*, bk 3, lines 16-20: "…Weishaupt named you Abaris/After the Hyperborean Druid-priest/Apollo sent to seek Pythagoras." See Paul Nettl, *Mozart and Masonry*, p10 for Goethe as Abaris. For Abaris as a British Druid astronomer, see Strabo's account, quoted in Isabel Hill Elder, *Celt, Druid and Culdee*, pp58-9. The Hebrew for Abaris is Rabbi. Also see Rivera, *op. cit.*, p19.

65.   Nesta Webster, *World Revolution, op. cit.*, p159.

66.   Nesta Webster, *World Revolution, op. cit.*, pp159, 167.

67.   Nesta Webster, *World Revolution, op. cit.*, p166.

68.   Easton, *op. cit.*, pp319-20.

69.   Wilson, *Rothschild, A Story of Wealth and Power, op. cit.*, p215.

70.   Wilson, *Rothschild, A Story of Wealth and Power, op. cit.*, pp212-3.

71.   Nesta Webster, *World Revolution, op. cit.*, p211.

72.   Nesta Webster, *World Revolution, op. cit.*, p207.

73.   Nesta Webster, *World Revolution, op. cit.*, pp205-6, 214.

74.   Nesta Webster, *World Revolution, op. cit.*, p213.

75.   Nesta Webster, *World Revolution, op. cit.*, pp214 and 213.

76.   Daniel, *op. cit.*, pp448-9.

77.   Rivera, *op. cit.*, pp34-5; Daniel, *op. cit.*, pp391-4, 400-1.

78.   Daniel, *op. cit.*, pp400-1, 449.

79.   Rivera, *op. cit.*, p35.

80.   Myron Fagan, *The Illuminati*, audio cassette, rec 1967 (transcribed from two audio cassettes by Sons of Liberty, 1985), 8; quoted in Daniel, *op. cit.*, p445 and Rivera, *op. cit.*, p35. This letter used to be on display in the British Museum Library in London, and is catalogued.

81.   Daniel, *op. cit.*, pp445-6; Rivera, *op. cit.*, p35-6.

82.   Daniel, *op. cit.*, pp446-7.

83.   Kirban, *op. cit.*

84. Daniel, *op. cit.*, pp387, 393-4; Rivera, *op. cit.*, p36.

85. Rivera, *op. cit.*, p36.

86. Daniel, *op. cit.*, p449.

87. Daniel, *op. cit.*, pp448-9.

88. For the story of the purchase of the Suez Canal, see Frederic Morton, *The Rothschilds, A Family Portrait*, pp150-2.

89. Wilson, *Rothschild, A Story of Wealth and Power, op. cit.*, p102.

90. Easton, *op. cit.*, pp338-341.

91. Based on Wilson, *Rothschild, A Story of Wealth and Power, op. cit., passim*; also *Encyclopaedia Britannica*. See Hagger, *The Syndicate, op. cit.*, pp8-9.

92. *Encyclopaedia Britannica*, "Rhodes".

93. Wilson, *Rothschild, A Story of Wealth and Power, op. cit.*, pp304-5.

94. *Encyclopaedia Britannica*, "UK, Imperialism and British politics".

95. For facts relating to the German Empire, see *Encyclopaedia Britannica*, "Germany" and "Bismarck".

96. Wilson, *Rothschild, A Story of Wealth and Power, op. cit.*, p263.

97. Daniel, *op. cit.*, pp449-50.

98. Daniel, *op. cit.*, pp450-2.

99. Daniel, *op. cit.*, p450.

100. Daniel, *op. cit.*, pp453-4.

101. Daniel, *op. cit.*, pp455-6.

102. Daniel, *op. cit.*, pp456-7.

103. Daniel, *op. cit.*, pp457-8.

104. Daniel, *op. cit.*, pp460-1.

105. For the events leading to the outbreak of the First World War, see *Encyclopaedia Britannica*.

106. Daniel, *op. cit.*, p461.

107. Daniel, *op. cit.*, p499.

108. Daniel, *op. cit.*, pp571-2.

109. Daniel, *op. cit.*, p461.

110. Daniel, *op. cit.*, p462.

111. Josephson, *Rockefeller "Internationalist"*, p4; Allen, *None Dare Call It Conspiracy*, p83. Also see Hagger, *The Syndicate, op. cit.*,

p18.

112. For Wilson's words, see Rivera, *op. cit.*, p78. For the 2m men, see *Encyclopaedia Britannica*, "Wilson, Woodrow"; Allen, *op. cit.*, p64.

113. Daniel, *op. cit.*, p462.

114. *Encyclopaedia Britannica*, "World Wars", Table 4.

115. Morton, *op. cit.*, p159; Ferguson, *op. cit.*, pp634-5.

116. *Encyclopaedia Britannica*, "Southern Africa".

117. Nesta Webster, *World Revolution, op. cit.*, p47, quoting Prudhomme, *Crimes de la Révolution*, vol. vi, Table VI.

Chapter Seven: The Russian Revolution

1. For the origins of communism in this paragraph, see Rivera, *op. cit.*, p119.

2. Rivera, *op. cit.*, p119.

3. For Weishaupt's words, see Rivera, *op. cit.*, p120.

4. Rivera, *op. cit.*, p120.

5. For Slavophils (or Slavophiles) and Westernizers, see *Encyclopaedia Britannica*, "Union of Soviet Socialist Republics, Education and intellectual life".

6. For the events in Hegel's life, see *Encyclopaedia Britannica*, "Hegel's Life and Thought".

7. See ch 6, note 64. Hegel's philosophy has an occult, Weishauptian, Gnostic basis.

8. *Encyclopaedia Britannica*, "Marx".

9. *Encyclopaedia Britannica*, "Marxism".

10. Daniel, *op. cit.*, p236.

11. Wurmbrand, *Was Karl Marx A Satanist?*, p7; quoted in Ralph Epperson, *The Unseen Hand*, p91. Also Rivera, *op. cit.*, p123.

12. Rivera, *op. cit.*, p123-4; Daniel, *op. cit.*, p236.

13. Daniel, *op. cit.*, p238.

14. *Encyclopaedia Britannica*, "Engels".

15.   *Encyclopaedia Britannica*, "Engels".

16.   *Encyclopaedia Britannica*, "Engels".

17.   Daniel, *op. cit.*, p239.

18.   Daniel, *op. cit.*, p238.

19.   Daniel, *op. cit.*, p239.

20.   *Encyclopaedia Britannica*, "Engels".

21.   Rivera, *op. cit.*, p124.

22.   Daniel, *op. cit.*, p236.

23.   *Encyclopaedia Britannica*, "Engels" and "Marxism".

24.   Rivera, *op. cit.*, p124.

25.   Daniel, *op. cit.*, p239.

26.   For this *Address* and many points in the two previous paragraphs, see *Encyclopaedia Britannica*, "Marxism".

27.   *Encyclopaedia Britannica*, "Engels" and "Marxism". Also Rivera, *op. cit.*, p124.

28.   Rivera, *op. cit.*, p125.

29.   Rivera, *op. cit.*, p125; *Encyclopaedia Britannica*, "Engels".

30.   For the events in Herzen's life in this section, see *Encyclopaedia Britannica*, "Herzen".

31.   *Encyclopaedia Britannica*, "Alexander II".

32.   For the events of the Nihilists, and Anarchists in the coming pages, and for further details on the Nihilists, see Ronald Hingley, *Nihilists.* Also *Encyclopaedia Britannica*, "Nihilism".

33.   Daniel, *op. cit.*, pp479-81.

34.   *Encyclopaedia Britannica*, "Bakunin".

35.   Daniel, *op. cit.*, pp481-2, quoting Baigent, Leigh and Lincoln, *The Messianic Legacy,* pp186-7: "Bakunin was a self-proclaimed Satanist."

36.   Epperson, *The New World Order*, p67; quoted in Daniel, *op. cit.*, p482.

37.   For points in this and the previous four paragraphs, see *Encyclopaedia Britannica*, "Bakunin".

38.   See *Encyclopaedia Britannica*, "Nechayev"; also see Hingley, *op. cit.*

39. *Encyclopaedia Britannica*, "Kropotkin, Peter".

40. For these sayings, see Camus, *The Rebel*. Also, Hingley, *op. cit.*

41. Camus, *op. cit.*; Hingley, *op. cit.*

42. Hingley, *op. cit.*

43. Daniel, *op. cit.*, p482.

44. For points in this and the previous three paragraphs, see *Encyclopaedia Britannica*, "Marxism".

45. For the events in this paragraph and the next 17 paragraphs, see Hingley, *op. cit.*

46. *Encyclopaedia Britannica*, "Alexander III"; Hingley, *op. cit.*

47. *Encyclopaedia Britannica*, "Witte, Sergey Yulyevich".

48. Daniel, *op. cit.*, pp484-5.

49. Rivera, *op. cit.*, p127.

50. Josephson, *Rockefeller "Internationalist"*, *op. cit.*, p204.

51. Hagger, *The Syndicate*, *op. cit.*, p14: Josephson, *Rockefeller "Internationalist"*, *op. cit.*, p187; F. William Engdahl, *A Century of War, Anglo-American Oil Politics and the New World Order*, p29.

52. Josephson, *Rockefeller "Internationalist"*, *op. cit.*, pp204-5; Daniel, *op. cit.*, pp493-4, 497-8.

53. Rivera, *op. cit.*, p127.

54. Josephson, *Rockefeller "Internationalist"*, *op. cit.*, p204.

55. For many of the points in this paragraph, see *Encyclopaedia Britannica*, "Trotsky".

56. Daniel, *op. cit.*, p487.

57. Daniel, *op. cit.*, p487.

58. Daniel, *op. cit.*, p487.

59. Daniel, *op. cit.*, p487; *Encyclopaedia Britannica*, "Trotsky".

60. Trotsky in 1905 was financed by Rockefellers via Kuhn, Loeb. Hagger, *The Syndicate*, *op. cit.*, p20: Josephson, *The Truth About Rockefeller, Public Enemy No. 1*, p19; Josephson, *Rockefeller "Internationalist"*, *op. cit.*, p204. For a hint that Trotsky was also financed by Warburg, see Daniel, *op. cit.*, p487.

61. Daniel, *op. cit.*, pp487-8.

62. Daniel, *op. cit.*, pp483-4 (with two corrections: Lenin's brother attempted to assassinate Alexander III, not Alexander II, when Lenin was seventeen, not eleven.) See *Encyclopaedia Britannica*, "Lenin". For *What is to be Done?*, see *Encyclopaedia Britannica*, "Lenin".

63. *Encyclopaedia Britannica*, "Bloody Sunday".

64. *Encyclopaedia Britannica*, "Russian Revolution of 1905".

65. Daniel, *op. cit.*, p485.

66. *Encyclopaedia Britannica*, "Russian Revolution of 1905".

67. *Encyclopaedia Britannica*, "Alexander II".

68. *Encyclopaedia Britannica*, "Russian Revolution of 1905".

69. Camus, *op. cit.*

70. Daniel, *op. cit.*, p491.

71. Daniel, *op. cit.*, pp352, 379-81. Also Introduction to *The Protocols of the Elders of Zion*.

72. For Golovinski, see *Daily Telegraph*, November 19, 1999 (http://www.telegraph.co.uk), quoting Lepekhine's findings published in the French magazine *L'Express* on November 18, 1999. For Napoleon III as target, see Daniel, *op. cit.*, p366.

73. Daniel, *op. cit.*, pp353-6, 362-8, 490-3.

74. Daniel, *op. cit.*, p359.

75. Daniel, *op. cit.*, p491.

76. Daniel, *op. cit.*, pp351, 484, 487, 494.

77. Daniel, *op. cit.*, pp351, 489.

78. Daniel, *op. cit.*, pp487-9.

79. Daniel, *op. cit.*, pp491-2; *Encyclopaedia Britannica*, "Rasputin".

80. Daniel, *op. cit.*, p493.

81. *Encyclopaedia Britannica*, "Trotsky"; Daniel, *op. cit.*, pp487, 492-3.

82. Hagger, *The Syndicate*, *op. cit.*, p21/ch 2, note 77: http://jerusalem.indymedia.org/news/2004/02/130046.php.

83. Daniel, *op. cit.*, pp493-4.

84. Ferguson, *op. cit.*, p881; Hagger, *The Syndicate*, *op. cit.*, p16.

85. Hagger, *The Syndicate*, *op. cit.*, pp18-19; Josephson, *The "Federal" Reserve Conspiracy and Rockefeller*, *op. cit.*, p75;

Josephson, *The Strange Death of Franklin D. Roosevelt*, *op. cit.*, p71. Also Engdahl, *op. cit.*, ch 4, "Oil Becomes the Weapon, the Near East the Battleground."

86.   Hagger, *The Syndicate*, *op. cit.*, p16; Ferguson, *op. cit.*, p881.

87.   Daniel, *op. cit.*, pp493-4.

88.   Daniel, *op. cit.*, p494; Rivera, *op. cit.*, p127.

89.   Josephson, *The Truth About Rockefeller, Public Enemy No. 1*, *op. cit.*, p44. Also Hagger, *The Syndicate*, *op. cit.*, p20. Also see Daniel, *op. cit.*, pp498-9; Rivera, *op. cit.*, p127.

90.   Daniel, *op. cit.*, p494.

91.   *Encyclopaedia Britannica*, "Rasputin"; author's investigation at the murder scene in St Petersburg. A story in the London *Sunday Telegraph* (September 19, 2004) claims that Oswald Rayner, a British member of the Secret Intelligence Bureau who was working at the Russian court in St Petersburg, was one of three gunmen who killed Rasputin; the other two being Vladimir Purishkevich and Prince Yusupov. Rayner is alleged to have fired the fatal third shot into Rasputin's forehead. Rayner may be a link between Rothschilds/Milner and Yusupov/Kerensky.

92.   Daniel, *op. cit.*, p494, quoting *Macmillan's History of the Times*, 1912-1920, vol IV, p244.

93.   Author's research; and Coleman, *Diplomacy by Deception*, p128.

94.   *Encyclopaedia Britannica*, "Russian Revolution of 1917".

95.   *Encyclopaedia Britannica*, "Union of Soviet Socialist Republics"; Daniel, *op. cit.*, p497.

96.   Documents show that J. P. Morgan organization gave at least $1m. See Sutton, *Wall Street and the Bolshevik Revolution*, pp18, 91, 97-8, 111 for the request (dated December 2, 1917 in a telegram from Petrograd) by William Boyce Thompson, a director of the Federal Reserve Bank of New York to Thomas W. Lamont, a partner in the Morgan organization who was in Paris with Col. House. Lamont influenced Lloyd George and the British War Cabinet to effect a change in British policy towards Kerensky. Thompson also supported Kerensky with $1m of his

own money, which went into the Russian Liberty Loan to keep Russia in the First World War so that Germany would not invade Russia and commercially capture the post-war Russian market to the detriment of the Rothschild-allied Federal Reserve Bank of New York and Federal Reserve System. The Morgan $1m support for Kerensky was no doubt justified on the same grounds.

97. Daniel, *op. cit.*, p497.

98. Daniel, *op. cit.*, pp495-6.

99. Daniel, *op. cit.*, p496.

100. Daniel, *op. cit.*, pp496-7.

101. Daniel, *op. cit.*, p497.

102. Daniel, *op. cit.*, pp497-8.

103. Daniel, *op. cit.*, p502.

104. Daniel, *op. cit.*, p498.

105. Daniel, *op. cit.*, p498.

106. Daniel, *op. cit.*, p499; Rivera, *op. cit.*, p127. Also, "Today it is estimated by Jacob's grandson John Schiff, that the old man sank about $20,000,000 for the final triumph of Bolshevism in Russia," *New York Journal-American*, February 3, 1949; quoted in Réne Wormser, *Foundations, Their Power and Influence*.

107. Daniel, *op. cit.*, p499.

108. Allen, *op. cit.*, p68; Rivera, *op. cit.*, p128. Also Hagger, *The Syndicate, op. cit.*, p21 and *Bankers and the Russian Revolution*: http://wsi.matriots.com/Bankers/RusRev.html.

109. Daniel, *op. cit.*, p501.

110. Former Russian Commissar, Trotsky and the Jews Behind the Russian Revolution, 1937, pp30-1.

111. Antony C. Sutton, *Wall Street and the Bolshevik Revolution*, p49.

112. Of Morgans' assets, $400m came from British interest on arms loans by 1917 (2% of $20b worth of arms). See Hagger, *The Syndicate, op. cit.*, p18. For Rockefellers' $5b, see Hagger, *The Syndicate, op. cit.*, p15, quoting Josephson, *Rockefeller "Internationalist"*, *op. cit.*, p24 and Kutz, *Rockefeller Power*, p87

note. For Rothschilds' $500b, see Armstrong, *op. cit.*, p36 and Hagger, *The Syndicate, op. cit.*, p8.

113. See Sutton, *op. cit.*, ch 4 and elsewhere for further details on points made in this paragraph.

114. *Encyclopaedia Britannica*, "Union of Soviet Socialist Republics".

115. *Encyclopaedia Britannica*, "Russian Revolution of 1917".

116. *Encyclopaedia Britannica*, "Trotsky".

117. *Encyclopaedia Britannica*, "Lenin".

118. Daniel, *op. cit.*, pp501-2.

119. *Encyclopaedia Britannica*, "Trotsky".

120. *Encyclopaedia Britannica*, "Russian Revolution of 1917".

121. *Encyclopaedia Britannica*, "Lenin" and "Union of Soviet Socialist Republics".

122. *Encyclopaedia Britannica*, "Lenin".

123. *Encyclopaedia Britannica*, "Trotsky".

124. *Encyclopaedia Britannica*, "Lenin".

125. *Encyclopaedia Britannica*, "Trotsky".

126. Daniel, *op. cit.*, p502.

127. *Encyclopaedia Britannica*, "Lenin".

128. *Encyclopaedia Britannica*, "Union of Soviet Socialist Republics".

129. *Encyclopaedia Britannica*, "Union of Soviet Socialist Republics".

130. *Encyclopaedia Britannica*, "Lenin".

131. *Encyclopaedia Britannica*, "Union of Soviet Socialist Republics".

132. Daniel, *op. cit.*, p506.

133. Daniel, *op. cit.*, p504.

134. Daniel, *op. cit.*, p506.

135. Daniel, *op. cit.*, pp498, 503.

136. Daniel, *op. cit.*, p506.

137. Rivera, *op. cit.*, p129.

138. Daniel, *op. cit.*, p506.

139. Daniel, *op. cit.*, pp506-7.

140. *Encyclopaedia Britannica*, "Union of Soviet Socialist Republics".

141. Daniel, *op. cit.*, pp352, 516.

142. *Encyclopaedia Britannica*, "Lenin".

143. *Encyclopaedia Britannica*, "Union of Soviet Socialist Republics".
144. *Encyclopaedia Britannica*, "Lenin".
145. *Encyclopaedia Britannica*, "Union of Soviet Socialist Republics"; Daniel, *op. cit.*, p510.
146. *Encyclopaedia Britannica*, "Union of Soviet Socialist Republics" and "Trotsky".
147. Daniel, *op. cit.*, p521.
148. Daniel, *op. cit.*, pp526-7.
149. *Encyclopaedia Britannica*, "Lenin".
150. *Encyclopaedia Britannica*, "Union of Soviet Socialist Republics".
151. Daniel, *op. cit.*, p506.
152. Daniel, *op. cit.*, p509.
153. Daniel, *op. cit.*, pp509-11.
154. Daniel, *op. cit.*, pp510-11.
155. *Encyclopaedia Britannica*, "Union of Soviet Socialist Republics".
156. *Encyclopaedia Britannica*, "Lenin".
157. *Encyclopaedia Britannica*, "Lenin".
158. *Encyclopaedia Britannica*, "Union of Soviet Socialist Republics".
159. *Encyclopaedia Britannica*, "Union of Soviet Socialist Republics", "Lenin" and "Trotsky".
160. Still, *op. cit*, p142.
161. Daniel, *op. cit.*, p512.
162. Daniel, *op. cit.*, pp512, 515.
163. *Encyclopaedia Britannica*, "Stalin".
164. Baigent, Leigh and Lincoln, *The Messianic Legacy, op. cit.*, p187; Daniel, *op. cit.*, pp572-3.
165. *Encyclopaedia Britannica*, "Stalin".
166. Daniel, *op. cit.*, pp512, 573.
167. *Encyclopaedia Britannica*, "Stalin" and "Trotsky".
168. *Encyclopaedia Britannica*, "Trotsky".
169. *Encyclopaedia Britannica*, "Stalin".
170. Daniel, *op. cit.*, p513.
171. Masonic Periodical *Builder*, June and August 1927.
172. Daniel, *op. cit.*, p513.

173. Daniel, *op. cit.*, pp513-4.

174. Daniel, *op. cit.*, pp516-7.

175. Daniel, *op. cit.*, p514.

176. Daniel, *op. cit.*, pp515-6.

177. In conversation with Nicholas Hagger.

178. Hagger, *The Syndicate, op. cit.*, pp14-15.

179. Josephson, *Rockefeller "Internationalist", op. cit.*, pp204-5; Hagger, *The Syndicate, op. cit.*, p20.

180. Hagger, *The Syndicate, op. cit.*, p20; Josephson, *The "Federal" Reserve Conspiracy and Rockefeller, op. cit.*, pp74-5; Josephson, *The Strange Death of Franklin D. Roosevelt, op. cit.*, pp70-1; Josephson, *Rockefeller "Internationalist", op. cit.*, p205.

181. Josephson, *Rockefeller "Internationalist", op. cit.*, pp205-6.

182. Josephson, *Rockefeller "Internationalist", op. cit.*, pp206, 209, 211-2.

183. Josephson, *Rockefeller "Internationalist", op. cit.*, p212.

184. Hagger, *The Syndicate, op. cit.*, p22; Josephson, *Rockefeller "Internationalist", op. cit.*, pp204-31, particularly p212; Josephson, *The Truth About Rockefeller, Public Enemy No. 1, op. cit.*, pp44, 133.

185. Hagger, *The Syndicate, op. cit.*, p22; Josephson, *Rockefeller "Internationalist", op. cit.*, p212.

186. Daniel, *op. cit.*, p515.

187. *Encyclopaedia Britannica*, "Union of Soviet Socialist Republics" and "Trotsky"; and Daniel, *op. cit.*, p515.

188. *Encyclopaedia Britannica*, "Trotsky".

189. *Encyclopaedia Britannica*, "Union of Soviet Socialist Republics".

190. Svetlana Stalin, Stalin's daughter, in conversation with Nicholas Hagger, to whom she passed papers showing that her mother committed suicide as an act of defiance.

191. *Encyclopaedia Britannica*, "Stalin".

192. *Encyclopaedia Britannica*, "Stalin" and "Union of Soviet Socialist Republics".

193. Daniel, *op. cit.*, p512.

194. John Erickson and David Dilks, eds, *Barbarossa, The Axis and The Allies*, pp256-8.

195. Rivera, *op. cit.*, p127.

196. Rivera, *op. cit.*, p78.

197. Daniel, *op. cit.*, p512.

Chapter Eight: Conclusion

1. Hagger, *The Fire and the Stones, op.cit.*

2. Still, *op. cit.*, pp26-7, 30-31, 33-4; Daniel, *op. cit.*, p393 and *Passim*.

3. J. M. Church, *op. cit.*, p25.

4. Blake, *Marriage of Heaven and Hell.*

5. Compare Nicholas Hagger's Satan in *Overlord*. He too argues that God's Heaven is imperfect.

Appendices

A

The Hidden Hand in Western History

1. Although it fails to grasp the fundamental point about the inspiration and dynamic of revolutions, Crane Brinton's *The Anatomy of Revolution* offers an excellent analysis of the societies that preceded the English, American, French and Russian revolutions, of the social and political tensions that led to a fracture in political authority and the governing body's relying on force to remain in power.

    In all four societies the government was in financial difficulties, not the societies themselves, which were in fact prosperous and on their way upward. As a result of such tensions, the governments of these four societies favoured one set of economic interests (existing feudal arrangements that benefited the aristocratic ruling class) against another (the interests of the middle-class merchants and capitalists), with the result that certain groups (the middle and lower classes) felt that their opportunities for getting on were limited by government policies. (See Brinton, *The Anatomy of Revolution*, pp 34-7.) The governments were inefficient, and there was administrative confusion, even chaos – for example, the inadequate tax-collection system of James I. Consequently, there were attempts to reform the machinery of government. (Contrary to the usual idea, old regimes are seldom out-and-out tyrannies. They are inefficient and corrupt, and their attempts at reform are ineffectual.)

    Reformers then emerged who emphasized the corruption of the political authority. There was a feeling among the intellectuals (the writers, artists and teachers) that things were not right. The intellectuals criticized the government and withdrew their support, and the idea grew that the upperdogs did not deserve their positions. Class distinctions ceased to be regarded as barriers that only the clever or ambitious could cross; they came to be seen as unnatural and unjust privileges that wicked men had acquired by accident or by treachery, against the will of God. Whereas before the poor dreamt of joining the ruling class, they now dreamt of dislodging it. As a result, the ruling class (the politicians, the key civil servants, the bankers, the landowners, the officers, the "priesthood" and leading intellectuals) lost confidence in itself. Members of the ruling class were converted to the belief that their privileges were unjust or harmful to society, and some of the upperdogs sided with the underdogs, which made them even more unfit to rule.

Confronted with this pre-revolutionary malaise, the political order began to lose its grip on authority. In all four societies the momentum gathered and the different opposition splinter groups banded together to topple the authority. After the revolution there was a period of optimistic idealism. This receded before the practical difficulties of running a post-revolutionary country. Factions struggled for power, and civil war was likely. To win, a faction had to use force against the other factions. The first goals of the revolution faded and in each of the four societies a totalitarian regime took charge. It incorporated some, but not all of the tenets of the original revolutionary movement.

What Brinton failed to grasp, however, is that each of the four major revolutions was inspired by a secret organization's occult vision which set in motion what I call the "revolutionary dynamic". In each there was a strong occult message.

2. George H. Steinmetz, *Freemasonry: Its Hidden Meaning*, p33.
3. Asterisked figures taken from Mark Almond, *Revolution*.
4. See Nicholas Hagger, *The Fire and the Stones: A Grand Unified Theory of World History and Religion*, in which I stated the dynamic that governs civilizations and showed that the spiritual vision that drives civilizations is a vision of the pure divine Light.

B

The Hidden Hand: The Kabbalistic
Roots of Revolution

Events referred to in these Appendices can be verified from the *Encyclopaedia Britannica*; Nesta Webster's *Secret Societies and Subversive Movements*, chs 1, 2, 3 and 8; Lady Queenborough's *Occult Theocrasy*, ch 7; and Daniel's *Scarlet and the Beast*, vol 1.

5.　Hagger, *Overlord*, *op. cit.*, bk 1, 201-2.

6.　Lt Gen Netchvolodow, *Nicolas II et les Juifs*, 1924, p139 et seq; quoted in Lady Queenborough, *Occult Theocrasy*, ch 7, "Judaism, The Pharisees", p76. See this work for the Pharisees.

7.　Nesta Webster, *Secret Societies and Subversive Movements*, *op. cit.*, p11.

8.　Nesta Webster, *Secret Societies and Subversive Movements*, *op. cit.*, p11.

9.　Nesta Webster, *Secret Societies and Subversive Movements*, *op. cit.*, pp11-12; P. L. B. Drach, *De l'Harmonie entre l'Église et la Synagogue*, 1844, vol I pXIII and vol II pXIX.

10.　Shimon Halevi, *Way of the Kabbalah*, *op. cit.*, p70.

11.　Nesta Webster, *Secret Societies and Subversive Movements*, *op. cit.*, p27.

12.　For a fuller account of Gnosticism, see Hagger, *The Fire and the Stones*, *op. cit.*, pp119-124.

13.　See Andrew J. Hurley, *Israel and the New World Order*, ch 2 for points in this paragraph.

14.　Anyone who thinks I am the slightest anti-Semitic should read bk 5 of my *Overlord*. This is about a heroic revolt of the Jews against the Nazi SS in Auschwitz, which shocked Himmler into suspending the Holocaust.

15.　Nesta Webster, *Secret Societies and Subversive Movements*, op. cit., ch 15, pp370, 371, 374, 378.

16.　Baigent, Leigh and Lincoln, *The Holy Blood and the Holy Grail*, *op. cit.*, pp415, 419.

17.　For a fuller account of the books of the Classical Kabbalah, see Hagger, *The Fire and the Stones*, *op. cit.*, pp197-204.

18. Baigent, Leigh and Lincoln, *The Holy Blood and The Holy Grail,* *op. cit.*, p407.

19. Church, *op. cit.*, p25.

20. See Hagger, *The Syndicate, op. cit.*

21. For example, Lionel and Patricia Fanthorpe, *Rennes-le-Château, Its Mysteries and Secrets,* and Stanley James, *The Treasure Maps of Rennes-le-Château.*

22. See ch 1, the subheading "Sidney and Raleigh's Circle," for a less sceptical explanation.

23. Baigent, Leigh and Lincoln, *The Messianic Legacy, op. cit.* pxvi.

24. Henry Kamen, *The Spanish Inquisition,* p23.

C

Venetian Foreign Policy and Rosicrucian Freemasonry

25. Yates, *The Rosicrucian Enlightenment, op. cit.*, ch 10.

26. See Gerry Rose, address on September 5, 1993, http://members,tripod.com/~american_almanac/venfreem.htm. Also H. Graham Lowry, *Executive Intelligence Review,* April 15, 1994, http://members,tripod.com/~almanac/venlowry.htm. Yates in *The Rosicrucian Enlightenment, op. cit.*, ch 10, writes: "No historian seems to have examined the connections of this (Venetian) movement with the movements around the Elector Palatine." She notes they are not mentioned in W. J. Bouwsma, *Venice and the Defence of Republican Liberty.*

BIBLIOGRAPHY

Allen, Gary, *None Dare Call It Conspiracy*, Concord Press, 1972.

Almond, Mark, *Revolution*, De Agostini Editions, 1996.

Armstrong, George, *The Rothschild Money Trust*, Omni Publications, California, 1940.

Aubarbaier, Jean-Luc; Binet, Michel; and Bouchard, Jean-Pierre, *Wonderful Cathar Country*, Ouest-France, 1994.

Aué, Michèle, *Discover Cathar Country*, MSM, 1999.

Bahne, Charles *The Complete Guide to Boston's Freedom Trail*, Newtowne Publishing, Massachusetts, 1990.

Baigent, Michael; Leigh, Richard; and Lincoln, Henry, *The Holy Blood and the Holy Grail*, Corgi Books, 1982.

Baigent, Michael; Leigh, Richard; and Lincoln, Henry, *The Messianic Legacy*, Corgi Books, 1987.

Baigent, Michael and Leigh, Richard, *The Temple and the Lodge*, Arcade Publishing, New York, 1989.

Barros, Barbara L., *Discover-It-Yourself Guide to Boston's Freedom Trail*, Beacon Guides, 1987.

Beaumont, Comyns, *The Private Life of the Virgin Queen*, Comyns (Publishers).

Bély, Lucien, *The Cathars*, Sud Ouest, 1995.

Billington, James H., *Fire in the Minds of Men: Origins of the Revolutionary Faith*, Transaction, USA, 1999.

Blake, William, "Marriage of Heaven and Hell," in *Collected Poems*, Dover Pubns, 1994.

Bond, R. Warwick, *The Complete Works of John Lyly*, Oxford University Press, 1902.

Bouwsma, W. J., *Venice and the Defence of Republican Liberty*, University of California Press, 1968.

Brinton, Crane, *The Anatomy of Revolution*, Vintage Books, New York, 1957.

Bryant, Arthur, *King Charles II*, Longmans Green and Co, 1946.

Builder, Masonic periodical, June and August 1927.

Camus, Albert, *The Rebel*, Vintage Books, 1956.

Capt, Raymond E., *Our Great Seal: The Symbols of our Heritage and our Destiny*, Thousand Oaks, CA: Artisan Sales, 1979.

Carlyle, Thomas, (ed), *Oliver Cromwell's Letters and Speeches*, Chapman and Hall, London, 1888.

Carlyle, Thomas, *The French Revolution*, OUP, The World's Classics, 1989 edition, vol II.

Carr, William Guy, *The Conspiracy to Destroy all Existing Governments and Religions*, Canada, 1959.

Catholic Gazette, February 1936.

Chandler, David G., *Sedgemoor 1685*, Anthony Mott, London, 1985.

Church, J. M., *Guardians of the Grail*, Oklahoma City, OK: Prophecy Publications,

1989.

Clausen, H. C., *Masons Who Helped Shape Our Nation*, Washington, 1976.

Clements, Robert J., ed., *Michelangelo, a Self-Portrait*, Prentice Hall, USA, 1963.

Cléry, Jean-Baptiste, *A Journal of the Terror*, J. M. Dent, 1974.

Coleman, Dr John, *Diplomacy by Deception*, Joseph Publishing Co., 1993.

Corti, Count Egon Caesar, *The Rise of the House of Rothschild*, Western Islands, USA, 1928, 1972.

Daniel, John, *Scarlet and the Beast*, vol 1, John Kregel, Texas, 1995.

Darrah, *History and Evolution of Freemasonry*, 1954, Chicago, Powner, 1979.

Dillon, George E., *Grand Orient Freemasonry Unmasked as the Secret Power Behind Communism*, Metairie: Sons of Liberty, 1885.

D'Israeli, Isaac, *Life of Charles the First*, two volumes, Henry Colburn, New Burlington Street, London, 1828 and 1851.

Dodd, Alfred, *Francis Bacon's Personal Life-Story*, Rider, 1986.

Dowley, Kim, (ed), *The History of Christianity*, Lion Publishing, 1977.

Drach, P. L. B., *De l'Harmonie entre l'Église et la Synagogue*, 1844, vol I pXIII and vol II pXIX.

Easton, Stewart C., *A Brief History of the Western World*, Barnes and Noble, 1962.

Edwards, Francis, *Guy Fawkes: The Real Story of the Gunpowder Plot?*, Rupert Hart-Davis, London, 1969.

Edwards, Graham, *The Last Days of Charles I*, Sutton Publishing, 1999.

Elder, Isabel Hill, *Celt, Druid and Culdee*, Covenant, London, 1973.

Epperson, Ralph, *The New World Order*, Publius Press, 1990.

Epperson, Ralph, *The Unseen Hand*, Publius Press, 1985.

Erickson, John and Dilks, David, eds, *Barbarossa, The Axis and The Allies*, Edinburgh University Press, 1994.

Fagan, Myron, *The Illuminati*, audio cassette, rec 1967 (transcribed from two audio cassettes by Sons of Liberty, 1985).

Falkus, Christopher, *The Life and Times of Charles II*, Weidenfeld and Nicolson, 1972.

Fanthorpe, Lionel and Patricia, *Rennes-le-Château, Its Mysteries and Secrets*, Bellevue Books, UK, 1991.

Feiling, Keith, *A History of England*, Book Club Associates, 1970.

Ferguson, Niall, *The World's Banker, The History of the House of Rothschild*, Weidenfeld and Nicolson, 1998.

Ficino, Marsilio, *Selected Letters of: Meditations on the Soul*, Shepheard-Walwyn, 2002.

Ficino, Marsilio, *The Letters of*, vols 1-7, Shepheard-Walwyn, 1975-2003.

Firth, Sir Charles, *Oliver Cromwell and the Rule of the Puritans in England*, The World's Classics, 1900 and 1961/University Press of the Pacific, 2003.

Former Russian Commissar, *Trotsky and the Jews Behind the Russian Revolution*, 1937, Metairie, LA: Sons of Liberty, 1980.

Fraser, Antonia, *Cromwell, Our Chief of Men*, Mandarin Paperbacks, UK, 1993.

Frederick II of Prussia (Frederick the Great), *Collected Works*, 31 vols, 1846-57.

French, Peter, *John Dee, The World of an Elizabethan Magus*, Dorset Press, 1972.

Gardner, Laurence, *Bloodline of the Holy Grail*, paperback, Element, 1996.

Garvin, Katharine, *The Great Tudors*, Fulcroft Library Editions, 1974.

Gilbert, Adrian, *The New Jerusalem*, Bantam Press, 2002.

Gookin, Warner F., and Barbour, Philip L., *Bartholomew Gosnold*, Archon Books, 1963.

Gouhier, Henri Gaston, *Les Premières Pensées de Descartes*, Paris, 1958.

Gurdham, Arthur, *The Great Heresy, The History and Beliefs of the Cathars*, Neville Spearman, UK, 1977.

Hagger, Nicholas, *Overlord*, Element, 1995-7.

Hagger, Nicholas, *The Fire and the Stones: A Grand Unified Theory of World History and Religion*, Element, 1991.

Hagger, Nicholas, *The Syndicate*, John Hunt, 2004. (www.thesyndicate.biz).

Halevi, Shimon, *Way of the Kabbalah*, Red Wheel/Weiser, 1991.

Hall, Manly, *The Adepts in the Western Esoteric Tradition*, The Philosophical Research Society, LA, 1949.

Hall, Manly, *The Secret Teachings of All Ages, An Encyclopedic Outline of Masonic, Hermetic, Qabbalistic and Rosicrucian Symbolic Philosophy*, The Philosophical Research Society Inc, California, 1988.

Hardman, John, *Louis XVI*, Yale University Press, 1993.

Heylyn, P., *Historical and Miscellaneous Tracts*, 1681.

Hieronimus, Robert, *America's Secret Destiny*, Destiny Books, 1989.

Hill, Christopher, *Milton and the English Revolution*, Faber, 1977.

Hill, Christopher, *Religion and Politics in 17th-century England*, Harvester Press, 1986.

Hingley, Ronald, *Nihilists*, Weidenfeld and Nicolson, 1967.

Howard, Michael, *The Occult Conspiracy, Secret Societies – Their Influence and Power in World History*, Destiny Books, 1989.

Hurley, Andrew J., *Israel and the New World Order*, Fithian Press/Foundation for a New World Order, 1991.

James, Stanley *The Treasure Maps of Rennes-le-Château*, Seven Lights, 1984.

Johnson, Paul, *A History of the American People*, Phoenix Giant, 1998.

Jonas, Hans, *The Gnostic Religion*, Beacon, USA, 1963.

Josephson, Emanuel M., *Rockefeller 'Internationalist', The Man who Misrules the World*, Chedney Press, New York, 1952.

Josephson, Emanuel M., *The 'Federal' Reserve Conspiracy and Rockefeller*, Chedney Press, New York, 1948.

Josephson, Emanuel M., *The Strange Death of Franklin D. Roosevelt*, Chedney Press, New York, 1948.

Josephson, Emanuel M., *The Truth About Rockefeller, Public Enemy no. 1*, Chedney Press, 1964.

Kamen, Henry, *The Spanish Inquisition*, Weidenfeld and Nicolson, 1965.

Katz, David S., *The Jews in the History of England, 1485-1850*, Clarendon Press, Oxford, 1994.

Kierner, Cynthia A., *Revolutionary America 1750-1815*, Prentice Hall, 2002.

Kinbrough, Sara Dodge, *Four Americans in Paris*, University Press of Mississippi, 1976.

Kinross, John, *The Boyne and Aughrim, The War of the Two Kings*, Windrush Press, 1997.

Kirban, Salem, *Satan's Angels Exposed*, Rossville, GA: Grapevine Book Distributors, 1980.

Knight, Stephen, *The Brotherhood*, Panther Books, 1985.

Kutz, Myer, *Rockefeller Power*, Pinnacle Books, New York, 1974.

Lacey, Robert, *Sir Walter Raleigh*, New York, 1973.

Lagomarsino, Dee and Wood, C. T., *A Documentary History of the Trial of Charles I*, University Press of New England, Dartmouth College, 1989.

Levy, Barbara, *Legacy of Death*, Saxon House, 1973.

MacCulloch, Diarmaid, *Tudor Church Militant, Edward VI and the Protestant Reformation*, Allen Lane, 1999.

MacGregor-Hastie, Roy, *Nell Gwyn*, Robert Hale, London, 1987.

Mackey, Albert G., *Mackey's Encyclopedia of Freemasonry*, 5th ed. 3 vols, Chicago: The Masonic History Company, 1950, "Cromwell."

Markham, Clements R., *The Fighting Veres*, Houghton Mifflin, Boston and New York, 1888.

Menasseh ben Israel, *Humble Addresses to the Lord Protector*, 1655.

Miller, John, *The Life and Times of William and Mary*, Weidenfeld and Nicolson, 1974.

Morris, Richard B., *The Framing of the Federal Constitution*, Division of Publications, National Parks Service, 1986.

Morton, Frederic, *The Rothschilds, A Family Portrait*, Atheneum, New York, 1962.

Mullins, Eustace, *The World Order, Our Secret Rulers*, Ezra Pound Institute of Civilization, 1992.

Netchvolodow, Lt Gen, *Nicolas II et les Juifs*, 1924.

Nettl, Paul, *Mozart and Masonry*, The Philosophical Library, New York, 1957.

North, John, *The Ambassadors' Secret, Holbein and the World of the Renaissance*, Hambledon and London, 2002.

Phillips, G. W., *Lord Burghley in Shakespeare*, London, 1936.

Pike, Albert, *Morals and Dogma, of the Ancient and Accepted Scottish Rite of Freemasonry*, Richmond, L. H. Jenkins, 1871/1921.

Prescott, Kate H., *Reminiscences of a Baconian*, Haven Press, New York, 1949.

Protocols of the Learned Elders of Zion: World Conquest through World Government, trans. by Victor E. Marsden, Eyre and Spottiswoode, 1968.

Purver, Margery, *The Royal Society: Concept and Creation*, London, 1967.

Queenborough, Lady, *Occult Theocrasy*, Emissary Publications, USA, 1981.

Ramsay, Captain A. H. M., *The Nameless War*, Britons Publishing Company, Devon, UK, 1968.

Reed, A. W., *The Great Tudors*, Ivor Nicholson and Watson, London, 1935.

Rivera, David Allen, *Final Warning, A History of the New World Order*, Rivera Enterprises, 1984, 1994.

Roberts, Allen E., *G. Washington: Master Mason*, Macoy Pub. and Masonic Supply Co., 1976.

Robison, John, *Proofs of a Conspiracy*, Americanist Classics, 1798/1967.

Ronalds, Francis S., *The Attempted Whig Revolution of 1678-1681*, Rowman and Littlefield, New Jersey and The Boydell Press, Ipswich, 1937.

Roth, Cecil, *Menasseh ben Israel*, Jewish Publication Society of America, Philadelphia 1934.

Saint-Martin, *Des Erreurs et de la Vérité*, 1775.

Schwartz, Barry, *George Washington, The Making of an American Symbol*, The Free Press, 1987.

Sinclair, Andrew, *The Sword and the Grail*, Crown Publishers, New York, 1992.

Smith, Alan Gordon, *William Cecil, the Power behind Elizabeth*, London, 1934.

Stauffer, V., *New England and the Bavarian Illuminati*, Columbia University Press, New York, 1918.

Steinmetz, George H., *Freemasonry: Its Hidden Meaning*, Richmond: Macoy, 1948, reprinted in 1976.

Still, William T., *New World Order: The Ancient Plan of Secret Societies*, Huntingdon

House, 1990.

Stopes, Charlotte, *The Third Earl of Southampton*, Cambridge University Press, 1922.

Strachey, William, *The Historie of Travel into Virginia Britania*, written 1612, ed. L. B. Wright and Virginia Freund, Hakluyt Society, 1953.

Sutton, Antony C., *Wall Street and the Bolshevik Revolution*, Veritas, 1981.

The History of the American Revolution, Highlights of the Important Battles and Documents of Freedom, Historical Documents Co., 1993.

The Jewish Encyclopaedia.

Thompson, W. R., Introduction to *On the Origin of the Species*, 6th edition, E. P. Dutton & Co, New York, 1956.

Trevor-Roper, H. R., *Religion, the Reformation, and Social Change*, London, 1967.

Tudhope, George V., *Bacon Masonry*, 1954, reprinted by Health Research, 1989.

Turnbull, G. H., *Hartlib, Dury and Comenius*, Liverpool, 1947.

Villari, Pasquale, *Life and Times of Girolamo Savonarola*, trans by Linda Villari, T. Fisher Unwin, London, 1888, reprinted.

Webster, Charles, *The Great Instauration: Science, Medicine and Reform*, 1626-1660 Duckworth, 1975.

Webster, Nesta H., *Secret Societies and Subversive Movements*, Christian Book Club of America, 1925.

Webster, Nesta H., *World Revolution*, Constable, 1921.

Wedgewood, C. V., *William the Silent*, Jonathan Cape, 1944.

Weems, Mason L., *A History of the Life and Death, Virtues and Exploits of General George Washington*, Georgetown, D. C., Green and English, 1800.

Whitehead, A. N., *Science and the Modern World*, Free Press, reissue edition, 1997.

Wilgus, Neal, *The Illuminoids*, New York: Pocket Books, 1979.

Williams, Neville, *Elizabeth I*, Book Club Associates, 1972.

Wilson, Derek, *Rothschild, A Story of Wealth and Power*, Mandarin, 1988.

Wilson, Derek *The King and the Gentleman*, Hutchinson, London, 1999.

Wolf, Lucian, (ed) *Menasseh ben Israel's mission to Oliver Cromwell*, 1901.

Wurmbrand, Richard, *Was Karl Marx A Satanist?*, Diane Books, Glendale Ca, 1976,

Yates, Frances A., *The Occult Philosophy in the Elizabethan Age*, Routledge, London, 1979.

Yates, Frances A., *The Rosicrucian Enlightenment*, Routledge and Kegan Paul, 1972, reprinted 1998.

O

is a symbol of the world,
of oneness and unity. O Books
explores the many paths of wholeness
and spiritual understanding which
different traditions have developed down
the ages. It aims to bring this knowledge
in accessible form, to a general readership,
providing practical spirituality to today's seekers.
For the full list of over 200 titles covering:

- CHILDREN'S PRAYER, NOVELTY AND GIFT BOOKS
  - CHILDREN'S CHRISTIAN AND SPIRITUALITY
    - CHRISTMAS AND EASTER
      - RELIGION/PHILOSOPHY
        - SCHOOL TITLES
      - ANGELS/CHANNELLING
      - HEALING/MEDITATION
    - SELF-HELP/RELATIONSHIPS
    - ASTROLOGY/NUMEROLOGY
      - SPIRITUAL ENQUIRY
  - CHRISTIANITY, EVANGELICAL
    AND LIBERAL/RADICAL
      - CURRENT AFFAIRS
      - HISTORY/BIOGRAPHY
  - INSPIRATIONAL/DEVOTIONAL
- WORLD RELIGIONS/INTERFAITH
    - BIOGRAPHY AND FICTION
      - BIBLE AND REFERENCE
      - SCIENCE/PSYCHOLOGY

Please visit our website,
www.O-books.net

SOME RECENT O BOOKS

THE CENSORED MESSIAH
Peter Cresswell

Peter Cresswell has a revolutionary new theory about the life of Jesus
and the origins of Christianity. It is a thrilling story, based on modern
scholarship, of how a Jewish man tried to change the direction of the
religious leadership of his people. It describes a breathtaking piece of
brinkmanship carried out against the Roman occupiers of Israel, a
journey into the mouth of death and beyond which appeared to
succeed.

Peter Cresswell is a freelance writer with degrees from Cambridge and
York Universities in Social Anthropology.

1 903816 67 X
£9.99 $14.95

THE INVISIBLE DISEASE
*The Dangers of Environmental Illnesses caused by Electromagnetic Fields
and Chemical Emissions*
Gunni Nordstrom

Millions of people today, particularly in the West, know they are ill
even though their doctors can't make a proper diagnosis.
Environmental illnesses are known under a number of names, like
Multiple Chemical Sensitivity, Chronic Fatigue Syndrome (ME),
Immune Dysfunction Syndrome, Fibromyalgia, Electro-
Hypersensitivity, Sick Building Syndrome.

This is the first book to make the connections between the range of
illnesses and chemicals used in the manufacture of modern appliances
that we mistakenly consider safe. They're not.

Gunni Nordstrom is an investigative journalist in Sweden, the world-

wide centre of the mobile phone industry, where much of the research
on Environmental Illness has been carried out.

1-903816-71-8
£9.99 $14.95

PATRICK AND THE CAT WHO SAW BEYOND TIME
Zoe d'Ay

A story of a moon cat, the Mother of all cats, the Pharoah's daughter
and the Buddha's plaything, who takes the boy Patrick on a series of
interior journeys through the DreamDoors.
In understanding the creation stories of the land and inhabitants, and
of people around the world, the meaning of birth and resurrection,
Bethlehem and Calvary, Patrick finds the Sacred Mountain of his
inner self, his own myth come true.

"A magical story, truly inspired. It is itself a myth." Bede Griffiths

Zoe d'Ay is an Oblate of the Benedictine Saccidananda Ashram in
Shantivanam, India, currently living in Glastonbury, England.

1-903816-72-6
£6.99 $9.95

THE WISDOM OF MARCUS AURELIUS
Alan Jacobs

The Meditations of Marcus Aurelius have been described as the best
book of practical philosophy ever written. The message is simple but
powerful; we have a short time on earth, we don't know what is going
to happen, and it doesn't matter. It is the best defence available against
the problems and stresses of our time. Most translations are literal and
arid, but here Alan Jacobs, a distinguished poet, uses contemporary
free verse and added metaphors to convey the essential emotional
meaning of the text.

Alan Jacobs is Chair of the Ramana Maharshi Foundation UK. He is author of *Poetry for the Spirit, The Bhagavad Gita (O Books), The Principal Upanishads (O Books)*.

1-903816-74-2
£9.99 $14.95

GOOD AS NEW
A radical re-telling of the Christian Scriptures
John Henson

This radical new translation conveys the early Christian scriptures in the idiom of today. It is "inclusive," following the principles which Jesus adopted in relation to his culture. It is women, gay and sinner friendly. It follows principles of cultural and contextual translation, and returns to the selection of books that the early Church held in highest esteem. It drops Revelation and includes the Gospel of Thomas,

"a presentation of extraordinary power." Rowan Williams, Archbishop of Canterbury
"I can't rate this version of the Christian scriptures highly enough. It is amazingly fresh, imaginative, engaging and bold." Adrian Thatcher, Professor of Applied Theology, College of St Mark and St John, Plymouth

"I found this a literally shocking read. It made me think, it made me laugh, it made me cry, it made me angry and it made me joyful. It made me feel like an early Christian hearing these texts for the first time." Elizabeth Stuart, Professor of Christian Theology, King Alfred's College, Winchester

John Henson, a retired Baptist minister, has co-ordinated this translation over the last 12 years on behalf of *ONE for Christian Exploration*, a network of radical Christians and over twenty organisations in the UK

1-903816-74-2
£19.99 $29.95 hb

THE THOUGHTFUL GUIDE TO THE BIBLE
Roy Robinson

Most Christians are unaware of the revolution in how the Bible may be understood that has taken place over the last two hundred years. This book seeks to share the fruits of the Biblical revolution in an easily accessible manner. It seeks to inform you of its main features and to encourage you to do your own thinking and come to your own conclusions.

Roy Robinson is a United Reformed Church minister, now retired and living in England. A former missionary in Zaire this work arises from a lifetime of study and Bible teaching at the Oxted Christian Centre, which he founded.

1-903816-75-0
£14.99 $19.95

LET THE STANDING STONES SPEAK
Messages from the Archangels revealed
Natasha Hoffman with Hamilton Hill

The messages encoded in the standing stones of Carnac in Brittany, France, combine and transcend spiritual truths from many disciplines and traditions, even though their builders lived thousands of years before Buddha, Christ and MuhammAd. The revelations received by the authors as they read the stones make up a New Age Bible for today.

"an evergreen..a permanent point of reference for the serious seeker."
Ian Graham, author of *God is Never Late*

Natasha Hoffman is a practising artist, healer and intuitive, and lives with her partner Hamilton in Rouziers, France.

1-903816-79-3
£9.99 $14.95

BRINGING GOD BACK TO EARTH
John Hunt

Religion is an essential part of our humanity. We all follow some form of religion, in the original meaning of the word. But organised religion establishes definitions, boundaries and hierarchies which the founders would be amazed by. If we could recover the original teachings and live by them, we could change ourselves and the world for the better. We could bring God back to earth.

"The best modern religious book I have read. A masterwork." Robert Van de Weyer, author of *A World Religions Bible*

"Answers all the questions you ever wanted to ask about God and some you never even thought of." Richard Holloway, former Primus Episcopus and author of *Doubts and Loves*

John Hunt runs a publishing company of which O Books is an imprint.

1-903816-81-5
£9.99 $14.95

ZEN ECONOMICS
Robert Van de Weyer

Just as Zen sages taught that attitudes and behaviour can suddenly alter, Van de Weyer combines economic analysis with social and philosophical insight to reveal how the entire world is on the verge of an economic and social transformation. The thrift practised by the Japanese, which has caused their economy to stagnate, will soon spread to all affluent countries, because it is the rational response to the economic, social and spiritual challenges that affluent people are now facing.

But thrift on a global scale, far from causing stagnation, will enable many of the world's most intractable problems to be solved. Van de Weyer offers practical financial and personal advice on how to participate in and cope with this global change. This book carries several messages of hope, which are linked by the theme of saving and investing. It's single most important message is that in the western world most of us have reached a point of prosperity where the investment with the highest rate of return is investing in the self.

Robert Van de Weyer lectured in Economics for twenty years at Cambridge University, England. He has written and edited over fifty books on a variety of themes, including economics, religion and history.

1-903816-78-5
£9.99 $12.95

TORN CLOUDS
Judy Hall

Drawing on thirty years experience as a regression therapist and her own memories and experiences in Egypt, ancient and modern, *Torn Clouds* is a remarkable first novel by an internationally-acclaimed MBS author, one of Britain's leading experts on reincarnation. It features time-traveller Megan McKennar, whose past life memories thrust themselves into the present day as she traces a love affair that transcends time. Haunted by her dreams, she is driven by forces she cannot understand to take a trip to Egypt in a quest to understand the cause of her unhappy current life circumstances. Once there, swooning into a previous existence in Pharaonic Egypt, she lives again as Meck'an'ar, priestess of the Goddess Sekhmet, the fearful lion headed deity who was simultaneously the Goddess of Terror, Magic and Healing.

Caught up in the dark historical secrets of Egypt, Megan is forced to fight for her soul. She succeeds in breaking the curse that had been cast upon her in two incarnations.

Judy Hall is a modern seer who manages the difficult task of evoking the present world, plus the realm of Ancient Egypt, and making them seem real. There is an energy behind the prose, and a power in her imagery which hints that this is more than just a story of character and plot, but an outpouring from another age, a genuine glimpse into beyond-time Mysteries which affect us all today. Alan Richardson, author of *Inner Guide to Egypt*.

Judy Hall has been a karmic counsellor for thirty years. Her books have been translated into over fourteen languages.
1 903816 80 7
£9.99/$14.95

THE QUEST
Joycelin Dawes

What is your sense of soul? Although we may each understand the word differently, we treasure a sense of who we are, what it is to be alive and awareness of an inner experience and connection with "something more." In *The Quest* you explore this sense of soul through a regular practice based on skills of spiritual reflection and be reviewing the story of your life journey, your encounter with spiritual experience and your efforts to live in a sacred way.

Here you become the teller and explorer of your own story. You can find your own answers. You can deepen your spiritual life through the wisdom and insight of the world's religious traditions. You can revisit the building blocks of your beliefs and face the changes in your life. You can look more deeply at wholeness and connection and make your contribution to finding a new and better way.
So well written, constructed and presented, by a small independent group of individuals with many years experience in personal and spiritual growth, education and community, that it is a joy to work with. It is a life-long companion on the spiritual path and an outstanding achievement; it is a labour of love, created with love to bring more love into our world. Susanna Michaelis, *Caduceus*

1 903816 93 9
£9.99/$16.95